SPORT PSYCHOLOGY

Daniel L. Wann
Murray State University

PRENTICE HALL
Upper Saddle River, New Jersey 07458

Library of Congress Cataloging-in-Publication Data

Wann, Daniel L.
    Sport Psychology / Daniel L. Wann.
       p.   cm.
    Includes bibliographical references and index.
    ISBN 0–02–424512–7
    1. Sports—Psychological aspects.   I. Title.
    GV706.4.W36   1997
    796'.01—dc20   96–38684
                                        CIP

This book was set in 10/12 ITC Garamond by The Composing Room of Michigan, Inc.
and was printed and bound by RR Donnelley & Sons Company.
The cover was printed by The Lehigh Press, Inc.

Editor-in-chief: Pete Janzow
Acquisition editor: Heidi Freund
Director of production and manufacturing: Barbara Kittle
Managing editor: Bonnie Biller
Project manager: Fran Russello
Editorial/production supervision and interior design: Mary McDonald/P.M. Gordon
Manufacturing manager: Nick Sklitsis
Prepress and manufacturing buyer: Tricia Kenny
Cover design: Bruce Kenselaar
Electronic art creation: Asterisk Group Inc.
Marketing manager: Michael Alread
Copy editor: Ann Donahue
Director, Image Resource Center: Lori Morris-Nantz
Photo research supervisor: Melinda Lee Reo
Image permission supervisor: Kay Dellosa
Photo researcher: Kim Moss

© 1997 by Prentice-Hall, Inc.
Simon & Schuster/A Viacom Company
Upper Saddle River, New Jersey 07458

Printed in the United States of America
10 9 8 7 6 5 4 3 2 1

ISBN 0-02-424512-7

Prentice-Hall International (UK) Limited, *London*
Prentice-Hall of Australia Pty. Limited, *Sydney*
Prentice-Hall Canada Inc., *Toronto*
Prentice-Hall Hispanoamericana, S.A., *Mexico*
Prentice-Hall of India Private Limited, *New Delhi*
Prentice-Hall of Japan, Inc., *Tokyo*
Simon & Schuster Asia Pte. Ltd., *Singapore*
Editora Prentice-Hall do Brasil, Ltda., *Rio de Janeiro*

To Jennifer

CONTENTS

PART II   PARTICIPATION IN SPORT: WHY AND BY WHOM?

**3   Sport Socialization and the Motivation to Participate
in Sport   42**

PART VI   SPORT FANS AND SPORT SPECTATORS

15   The Psychology of Sport Fans and Sport Spectators   325

16   The Emotional and Aggressive Reactions of Sport Spectators   348

PREFACE

Because sport psychology encompasses a number of topics and a diverse array of professionals, writing a comprehensive sport psychology textbook is a difficult undertaking. In attempting this task, I have chosen to cover a wide spectrum of sport psychology subject matter rather than to examine only a limited number of topics. This means the reader is presented with a general overview of the application of psychology to sport settings.

To facilitate the reader's understanding of the topical areas of sport psychology, I have divided this textbook into six sections. The first section (Chapters 1 and 2) covers the foundations of sport psychology. Chapter 1 introduces the reader to the different types of sport psychologists as well as to the activities of these individuals and includes a brief history of the field of sport psychology. Chapter 2 involves experimentation and testing issues relevant to sport psychology.

Chapters 3 and 4 constitute the second section and examine participation in sport. Chapter 3 focuses on the socialization process as well as several participation motives, such as the desires to have fun and to be with other people. Chapter 4 examines the personalities of sport participants, comparing the personalities of athletes and nonathletes, athletes of different skill levels, and athletes of different sports. This chapter also examines several different sport populations including female athletes and black athletes.

The third section (Chapters 5–9) covers topics related directly or indirectly to athletic performance. Chapter 5 examines the types of learning relevant to sport psychology and includes suggestions for enhancing learning in sport. Chapter 6 focuses on attentional processes in sport including memory and different attentional styles. Chapter 7 covers arousal and anxiety in sport, particularly the relationships among arousal, anxiety, and athletic performance. Chapter 8 focuses on motivational processes and examines the application of several theories of motivation to sport settings. Chapter 9 examines sport-based attributions and errors in the attribution process.

The fourth section includes Chapters 10 and 11 and focuses on sport psychology intervention strategies. Chapter 10 reviews a number of methods for regulating the anxiety and arousal of athletes. This chapter also examines several intervention strategies used to assist injured athletes. Chapter 11 examines interventions designed to increase self-confidence, imagery skills, and attention control, as well as comprehensive programs designed to enhance a number of psychological skills.

The fifth section (Chapters 12–14) examines the social psychology of sport. Chapter 12 deals with player aggression in sport and includes an analysis of the origin of aggression and situational factors that facilitate player aggression. This chapter also includes a list of suggestions for curbing player aggression. Chapter 13 focuses on leadership, with particular attention placed on issues of power, the types of behaviors of successful leaders, and the application of several leadership theories to sport settings. Chapter 14 examines the social nature of sport by focusing on three topics: team cohesion, audience effects (social facilitation and the home field advantage), and self-presentation.

The final section (Chapters 15 and 16) examines sport fans and spectators. Chapter 15 focuses on the psychology of the sport fan addressing fan/spectator demographics, team identification, and biased evaluations of team performance. Chapter 16 focuses on the emotional and aggressive reactions of fans and spectators.

Each chapter in this textbook contains items designed to enhance the reader's interest in and understanding of the material. First, each chapter contains a boxed section titled "A Closer Look" in which a peripherally related or special topic is examined in greater detail. In addition, several examples, tables, figures, and illustrations have been included to enhance the reader's visualization of the material. At the end of each chapter, the reader will find several learning aids. First, a chapter summary has been included as a quick reference to specific topics. This is followed by a glossary of all key terms used in the textbook. The terms included in the glossary are printed in bold italics in the body of the text. Third, several application and review questions have been included to help facilitate and enhance the reader's comprehension of the material. Finally, several suggested readings are provided for students wanting to learn more about specific topics.

ACKNOWLEDGMENTS

Because writing a textbook is a long and involved process, a number of people contribute to the finished project. A few of the individuals who assisted in the completion of this work warrant special attention.

First, a note of thanks must be given to the staff at Prentice Hall, particularly to managing editor Heidi A. Freund and editorial assistant Jeffrey Arkin, without whose efforts this project would never have been completed.

Second, a special note of thanks is given to the following individuals who were kind enough to review earlier versions of this manuscript: Michael Sachs, Temple University; Eric Cooley, Western Oregon State College; Rick Albrecht, Michigan State University; Diane Gill, University of North Carolina—Greensboro; Elizabeth Gardner, Pine Manor College; and Britton W. Brewer, Springfield College. Their suggestions and comments improved and strengthened the final product.

Third, I am grateful to Dean Joseph Cartwright, Department Chair Thomas B. Posey, and the Murray State University department of psychology for allowing me the release time and support needed to complete this project.

Fourth, I would like to thank the Murray State University library staff for their assistance. In particular, I am grateful to the interlibrary loan staff for their efforts in acquiring the books and articles discussed throughout this text.

Fifth, I wish to thank the following former professors and mentors: Dr. Rand Ziegler, Dr. Stephen F. Davis, Dr. Kenneth A. Weaver, and Dr. Nyla R. Branscombe. Each had a unique and important impact on my development as a psychologist. My gratitude for your assistance throughout my career cannot be measured.

Finally, the tireless efforts of Michael P. Schrader and Linda Metcalf deserve a special note of thanks. Your work as my graduate assistants during the past few years was vital to the completion of this manuscript. I thank you for your energy, your suggestions, your diligence, and your ability to put up with all of my "lists."

Daniel L. Wann

Chapter 1

AN INTRODUCTION TO SPORT PSYCHOLOGY

Consider the following scenarios:

1. Two well-known and successful professional athletes (one a basketball player and the other a baseball player) retire during the prime of their careers because they no longer feel motivated to compete in their respective sports.
2. A college basketball national championship is decided in part because of a single lapse of attention and breakdown in communication.
3. A top-ranked tennis player is brutally assaulted by a spectator, causing her to miss 2 years of playing time.
4. A successful professional golfer struggles to regain his past glory, lost due to a substance abuse problem.
5. A top-ranked professional boxer is convicted of rape.
6. To motivate his players, a successful college football coach has his players watch the castration of a bull.
7. A successful pitcher performs poorly during one World Series and is unable to regain his previous form.
8. A tennis star receives so much abuse from her father that he is no longer allowed to watch her play.

What do each of these incidents have in common? First, they are all recent real-life events from the sport world. Second, they are all examples of the impact of psychology in sport settings. In this book, we will examine how psychological factors played a role in these and other sport-related behaviors. In this first chapter, we will begin our examination of sport psychology by defining several key terms. We will then examine the different types of sport psychologists and sport consultants and discuss the activities of these individuals (the terms "sport psychologist" and "sport consultant" will be used interchangeably throughout this text). We will conclude this chapter by examining the history of sport psychology.

SETTING THE BOUNDARIES OF SPORT PSYCHOLOGY

First and foremost, this is a textbook written from the perspective of a psychologist, one who happens to be interested in the psychological variables impacting the world of professional and amateur sport. As such, it is important that we begin our discussion of sport psychology with a definition of psychology. While several acceptable definitions for psychology have been offered, many are too broad and, therefore, fail to set the appropriate boundaries for the science of psychology. For example, in the original general psychology textbook, *Principles of Psychology,* James (1890) defined psychology as the study of consciousness. While this is no doubt true, such a broad definition lacks the precision needed when defining abstract constructs. Other more recent definitions of psychology, while scoring well on precision, appear to have a rather limited vision of psychology and, as such, exclude many important areas of psychological research. For example, Ornstein (1988, p. 37) referred to psychology as "the complete science of human experience" while Myers (1989, p. 4) defined psychology as "the science of behavior and mental processes." While more precise than James' definition, these two examples appear to be somewhat narrow in focus. That is, these definitions either exclude work on animals (research that has been vital in the area of learning), nonscientific endeavors (such as a large portion of Sigmund Freud's work), or emotional responses (an area of psychology with special importance to sport competitions).

In an attempt to rectify these shortcomings, I prefer to define **psychology** as the primarily scientific study of human and animal behavior, affect, and cognition. This definition has several advantages. First, it allows for the inclusion of information gained using both scientific and nonscientific means. Certainly, one should interpret data collected through nonscientific methods cautiously, but to reject the data outright results in the loss of valuable information. Second, this definition explicitly includes research testing both human and animal subjects. This seems appropriate because most textbooks devoted to psychological study (including this one) review research involving a variety of subject types. Finally, our working definition of psychology includes a variety of experiences: behaviors (actions such as running, jumping, and throwing), affect (emotions and feelings such as anger, excitement, and discouragement), and cognition (mental processes such as thoughts, memories, and imagery).

Sport Defined

As with the term psychology, there are many different definitions for sport. However, many definitions of sport are too narrow because they limit the scope of sport to situations involving elite and highly trained athletes. These perspectives ignore the weekend athlete, a breed of sport participant greatly outnumbering those at the professional and Olympic levels. For example, sport has been defined as "competitive activity that is guided by established rules" (Eitzen & Sage, 1986, p. 16). This and similar definitions seem to argue that participating in golf as a professional would be an example of sport, while a noncompetitive round of golf with friends would not be. Further, recreational activities such as hunting, jogging, hiking, and mountain climbing would not be considered sporting activities, although most persons would argue that these activities are sporting in nature.

A more inclusive definition of sport was presented by Spears and Swanson (1983, p. 3). These authors view sport as "activities involving physical prowess and skill, competition, strategy, and/or chance, and engaged in for the enjoyment and satisfaction of the participant and/or others." They further state that their definition "includes both organized sport and sport for recreational purposes" and "sport as entertainment." As discussed by LeUnes and Nation (1989, p. 11) in their examination of the various definitions of sport, the description of sport offered by Spears and Swanson allows for a "sport for all" perspective on athletics. Such a perspective will also be subscribed to here. That is, as depicted in Figure 1.1, a variety of activities appear to be appropriately defined as sport, although some activities are more formal than others.

Because a large portion of the population is involved with sport as a fan and/or spectator (one study estimated that approximately 70% of the population is involved with spectatorship activities on a daily basis [Thomas, 1986]), we would be remiss if we did not also include these activities in our definition. Although not explicitly stated, it appears that Spears and Swanson's (1983) definition accounts for spectators by including activities by persons other than athletes. However, to encompass fully all that is a part of sport, a bit needs to be added to the Spears and Swanson (1983) definition. Some athletes state that they are involved with sport simply to gain rewards (such as money and fame). In fact, these persons often report that they dislike sport altogether, unless they themselves are participating. Certainly, these athletes are not primarily motivated to participate in sport by "enjoyment and satisfaction" (Spears & Swanson, 1983, p. 3). Thus, I will use the definition of sport offered by Spears and Swanson, with two additions. Specifically, ***sport*** is defined as activities involving powers and skills, competition, strategy, and/or chance, and engaged in for the enjoyment, satisfaction, and/or personal gain (such as income) of the participant and/or others (e.g., spectators), including organized and recreational sports, as well as sport as entertainment.

FIGURE 1.1 Using our definition of sport, activities that are less than formal and/or competitive could be defined as a sport. (Source: Universal Press Syndicate.)

Sport Psychology Defined

Although sport psychology is still a young discipline, there has been a surprisingly large number of definitions offered for the subject, with most definitions reflecting the background of the authors (Dishman, 1983; Salmela, 1981). In fact, the definitions to date have been so inconsistent that Martens (1980) argued that sport psychology should simply be defined as what sport psychologists do. That is, he believed that research conducted by sport psychologists should be used to define sport psychology. Although Martens' suggestion was well-intended, it appears vital for a young discipline to identify its boundaries. Without boundaries, we are left without a grasp of what sport psychology is and without a clear understanding of what it means to be a sport psychologist (LeUnes & Nation, 1989).

Although generally diverse, most definitions of sport psychology share a common theme: the study of psychology and behavior in sport settings. This appears to be a good starting point toward a definition of sport psychology. However, by borrowing from the previously reviewed definitions of both psychology and sport, the parameters of sport psychology can be better articulated. That is, it appears that a more appropriate definition of *sport psychology* would read, "the primarily scientific study of the behavioral, affective, and cognitive reactions to sport settings, including the reactions of both participants and fans." Such a definition does not limit itself to knowledge gained scientifically (anecdotal evidence in sport settings is often quite valuable); explicitly states that we are interested in actions, emotions, and thoughts; and states that the focus of interest can be on the playing field or in the stands.

The Relationship between Sport Psychology and Sport Sociology

Before proceeding further, the relationship between sport psychology and sport sociology should be mentioned. In a general sense, psychological topics tend to be at the micro- or individual level (for example, motivation, performance, and learning), while sociological perspectives are usually macro-level in scope (for example, socioeconomic status and political and racial issues). Yet, the demarcations separating the two disciplines are far from clear and the two areas share many common themes. In fact, some authors have called for an increase in the integration between sport psychology and sport sociology (e.g., Konzak, 1980). Two recent books on the sociology of sport (Leonard, 1993; Vogler & Schwartz, 1993) contain several chapters that overlap the areas covered in this book. Topics such as gender and racial issues in sport, sport socialization, and aggression in sport are a part of both sport psychology and sport sociology.

The overlap between sport psychology and sport sociology can also be found in the journals devoted to sport research. While certain journals have narrowed their focus to one topic or the other, others publish work in both areas. For example, the *Journal of Sport and Social Issues* publishes work from both psychological and sociological perspectives, while the *Journal of Sport Behavior* alternates its publications between psychological and sociological themes. The major sport psychology journals, as well as their publishers and original publication dates, are listed in Table 1.1. It should be noted that journals devoted solely to the history of sport or to motor behavior are generally beyond the scope of this textbook and, as such, have not been included in the list.

TYPES AND ACTIVITIES OF SPORT PSYCHOLOGISTS

In 1983, the United States Olympic Committee (USOC) published an article describing the different types and activities of sport psychologists interested in the behaviors of athletes. According to the USOC, these sport psychologists can be described in one of two ways: as an applied sport psychologist (called practicing sport psychologists by Martens, 1987a) or as a research (i.e., experimental) sport psychologist (Singer, 1984). The USOC further divides applied sport psychologists into two categories: clinical and educational (see Figure 1.2).

Applied Sport Psychologists

Applied sport psychologists apply sport-specific and general psychological theories and research to sport settings in an attempt to increase the psychological well-being, health, and performance of athletic participants. The major organization for applied sport psychologists is the Association for the Advancement of Applied Sport Psychology (AAASP), while the major journals for this group are *The Sport Psychologist* and the *Journal of Applied Sport Psychology*. As noted by Cox (1990), applied sport psychologists are not simply interested in helping professional and Olympic level athletes. Rather, these persons are also interested in increasing the performance and psychological well-being of weekend athletes (Whelan, Meyers, & Donovan, 1995).

Orlick and Partington (1987) examined athletes' perceptions of applied sport

TABLE 1.1 Major Journals in Sport Psychology

Journal	*Organization Represented*	*First Published*
Research Quarterly for Exercise and Sport	American Alliance for Health, Physical Education, Recreation and Dance	1930
International Journal of Sport Psychology	International Society of Sport Psychology	1970
Journal of Sport & Social Issues	Center for the Study of Sport in Society	1976
Journal of Sport Behavior	United States Sports Academy	1978
Journal of Sport & Exercise Psychology	North American Society for Psychology of Sport and Physical Activity	1979
The Sport Psychologist	International Society of Sport Psychology	1987
Journal of Applied Sport Psychology	Association for the Advancement of Applied Sport Psychology	1989

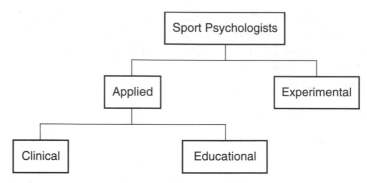

FIGURE 1.2   An overview of the various types of sport psychologists.

psychologists. The subjects were 75 Canadian Olympians who competed in the 1984 summer or winter games. Subjects reported that the best sport psychologists exhibited a number of positive qualities. Specifically, these psychologists (1) maintained numerous contacts, (2) conducted follow-up sessions with the athletes, and (3) appeared to be both available and caring. However, not all psychologists were liked or perceived to have only positive qualities. The athletes also stated that (1) many suggestions did not relate to sport, (2) the consultants did not solicit feedback on success/failure of their suggestions, and (3) the psychologists often demonstrated poor timing by distributing questionnaires immediately prior to a competition. Although the athletes listed several negative qualities, approximately 98% of the athletes believed that the availability of sport psychologists should be increased.

Although the Orlick and Partington (1987) research indicates that working with a sport psychologist is typically viewed as a beneficial activity, some athletes remain skeptical about working with a consultant. Perhaps the best example of this skepticism was offered by Goran Ivanisevic, a professional tennis player. When asked about his view of sport psychologists, Ivanisevic stated "You lie on a couch, they take your money, and you walk out more bananas then when you walk in" (Lidz & Kennedy, 1995, p. 14). As gold medal and champion athletes continue to speak highly of the assistance they received from sport psychologists, negative viewpoints such as this will subside.

Clinical Sport Psychologists.   Some applied sport psychologists can be classified as clinical sport psychologists. ***Clinical sport psychologists*** are specifically trained to deal with the various emotional problems and personality disorders experienced by athletes (e.g., depression and eating disorders). These persons are usually trained in clinical psychology and have received a doctorate degree from a graduate program approved by the American Psychological Association (APA). As a result of this training, these persons are qualified to assist athletes experiencing psychological problems.

Educational Sport Psychologists.   Other applied sport psychologists can be classified as educational sport psychologists. ***Educational sport psychologists*** are individuals with an understanding of the principles of sport psychology who attempt to transmit this information to athletes and coaches. That is, they attempt to educate interested parties on the fundamentals of sport psychology. The USOC (1983, p. 5) described these individuals as persons interested in helping athletes gain "the psychological skills necessary for optimal participation in the sport." Educational sport psychologists inform athletes and coaches about topics such as relaxation training and concentration improvement.

As stated, the main goal of educational sport psychologists is the enhanced performance of athletes (although they are also interested in enhancing the athletes' psychological well-being). However, because educational sport psychologists usually have not received a clinical graduate degree from an APA-accredited institution, these individuals are not qualified to counsel athletes on emotional and personality problems, problems that should remain the responsibility of clinical sport psychologists. Attempts by educational sport psychologists to assist athletes with their psychological problems constitute unethical behavior on the part of the psychologist and may lead to some form of legal action (Brown, 1982; Harrison & Feltz, 1979; Taylor, 1994). When an educational sport psychologist finds that a client is suffering from a psychological disturbance, he or she should refer this individual to someone trained to deal with the problem (Andersen, Denson, Brewer, & Van Raalte, 1994).

To articulate the differences between groups of athletes who work with clinical and educational sport psychologists better, Martens (1987b) presented an informative illustration. As depicted in Figure 1.3, Martens notes that the domain of clinical sport psychologists encompasses athletes displaying behaviors left of normal (i.e., abnormal), while educational sport psychologists focus on moving athletes right of normal to supernormal. By using the term supernormal, Martens refers to attempts by educational sport psychologists to increase the psychological skills of normal athletes, thereby enabling them to perform at peak levels.

Educational sport psychologists can become certified through the Association for the Advancement of Applied Sport Psychology (AAASP). The title of such individuals is "Certified Consultant: Association for the Advancement of Applied Sport Psychology." The preamble of the AAASP application for certification explicitly states that "AAASP certification is intended to indicate that each certified individual has demonstrated that he or she has obtained adequate training and experience to serve as a Certified Consultant" (p. 3). In addition, AAASP is careful in stating that certain

FIGURE 1.3 The distinction between clinical sport psychologists and educational sport psychologists. (Note: From *Coaches Guide to Sport Psychology* [p. 69], Rainer Martens. Champaign IL: Human Kinetics Publishers. Copyright 1987 by Rainer Martens. Reprinted by permission.)

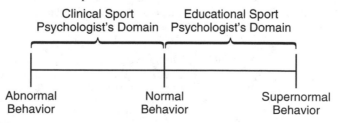

"activities are outside of the scope of services associated with the title Certified Consultant" (p. 2). These activities, which are to remain the responsibility of clinical sport psychologists, include diagnosis and treatment of pathology, treatment of disorders such as substance abuse/chemical dependencies, and therapy. A summary of the criteria for certification with AAASP is presented in Table 1.2.

Becoming an Applied Sport Psychologist.   In 1991, Jim Taylor published an article describing the options and procedures for becoming an applied sport psychologist (see also Simons & Andersen, 1995). Such a discussion is valuable because the educational training of future sport psychologists will influence the direction of the discipline (Alderman, 1980). Taylor's presentation focuses on the formal education required for such a vocation, examining issues relevant for both the level and direction of one's academic experiences. In general, however, he notes that there is no obvious answer to the question of how one is to become a sport psychologist and, as Ogilvie (1979) noted, many sport psychologists are self-taught.

With regard to educational level, Taylor (1991) notes that, as of the early 1990s, there were no undergraduate sport psychology programs available in the United States (although this may change in the coming years). As a result, a graduate degree is required for specialization. Ideally, the graduate curriculum would lead to a doctoral degree. In fact, the Ph.D. is a requirement for registration as a sport psychologist with the USOC as well as for AAASP certification. Taylor states that almost 90% of AAASP members have obtained a doctoral degree (this figure does not include student members). As for the direction of one's education, Taylor (1991) notes that there are two options, psychology or physical education (i.e., sport science), and that AAASP membership for the two directions is about equal. Recent investigations have found that sport psychology courses are far more likely to be offered in sport

---

TABLE 1.2   A Summary of the Criteria for Title of Certified Consultant: Association for the Advancement of Applied Sport Psychology

1. Completion of a doctoral degree from an accredited institution
2. Knowledge of scientific and professional ethics
3. Knowledge of sport psychology subdisciplines (such as exercise and social psychology)
4. Knowledge of the physiological bases of sport
5. Knowledge of the historical, philosophical, social, or motor behavior bases of sport
6. Knowledge of psychopathology
7. Training in the area of counseling psychology*
8. A supervised experience (e.g., internship) with a qualified individual*
9. Knowledge of the skills and techniques of sport (e.g., coaching or playing experience)
10. Knowledge of research design, statistics, and psychological testing*
11. Knowledge of the biological bases of behavior
12. Knowledge of the cognitive and affective bases of behavior
13. Knowledge of the social bases of behavior
14. Knowledge of individual behavior (e.g., personality and/or developmental psychology)

*Indicates that the criterion must be met at the graduate level. Only two of criteria 11 through 14 are required.

science departments than in psychology departments, and sport science faculty and graduate students are more likely than psychology faculty and graduate students to have an interest in the topic (LeUnes & Hayward, 1990; Petrie & Watkins, 1994).

When individuals direct their education toward psychology, the degree of choice is usually the clinical or counseling psychology degree, although other subareas of psychology are viable options. Anshel (1994) lists a number of other subareas of psychology that have relevance to sport psychology, including cognitive, health, physiological, social, developmental, personality, and educational psychology. Singer (1980) adds the areas of learning and psychometrics (i.e., psychological testing) to this list. It should be remembered that, if the student's goal is to become a clinical sport psychologist, the individual should attempt to receive a clinical or counseling degree. Degrees acquired in the other psychological disciplines are more applicable when the student's goal is to become an educational sport psychologist.

Taylor (1991) argues that the sport science degree is the correct choice for persons interested in dealing with issues such as health, motor learning, and exercise. Persons acquiring such a degree should not perform psychopathologic intervention as they are not trained to deal with such matters. Although this is a disadvantage of the sport science degree, Taylor suggests that this shortcoming is at least partially offset by advantages such as shorter graduate programs and greater opportunities for academic employment. Students confronted with the decision of whether to attend a graduate program in psychology or sport science should consult the *Directory of Graduate Programs in Applied Sport Psychology* published by AAASP (Sachs, Burke, & Butcher, 1995). This guide lists more than 100 graduate-level applied sport psychology programs in either psychology or sport science departments. In addition, this guide provides information concerning contact persons, requirements, and a description of each program.

Experimental Sport Psychologists

Experimental sport psychologists are primarily interested in conducting research to further the knowledge and understanding of the psychology of sport. Such individuals were referred to as academic sport psychologists by Martens (1987a), while Singer (1984) referred to them as scientists and scholars. The research attention of experimental sport psychologists is directed toward two populations: (1) athletes and other individuals involved with the competition (such as coaches and officials) or (2) sport fans and spectators. A few experimental sport psychologists divide their attention between both populations.

The major organization for experimental sport psychologists is the North American Society for Psychology of Sport and Physical Activity (NASPSPA) and the major journals include the *Journal of Sport & Exercise Psychology,* the *International Journal of Sport Psychology,* and *Research Quarterly for Exercise and Sport.* Experimental sport psychologists often conduct the research used by applied sport psychologists in their clinical and educational settings. For example, a university professor may test several theories of athletic motivation, the findings of which are used by coaches and applied sport psychologists throughout the athletic community.

Although many sport psychologists spend time in both applied and experimental endeavors (Feltz, 1992), there has often been a lack of communication between individuals devoting their efforts only to applied or experimental work. This lack of communication has been problematic for the development of sport psychology (Danish & Hale, 1981). For the discipline to develop at an effective rate, the areas of applied and experimental sport psychology need a cooperative effort.

ETHICS IN SPORT PSYCHOLOGY

In 1982, NASPSPA published a set of ethical guidelines for research and clinical work in sport psychology. This document describes several requirements of sport psychologists. First, sport psychologists must act responsibly and maintain the highest level of competence. That is, psychologists should only participate in activities for which they are specifically trained (e.g., only clinical sport psychologists should conduct counseling sessions). Also, the NASPSPA ethics document directs sport psychologists to maintain the highest level of legal and moral standards and to be honest in their public statements concerning their qualifications and affiliations. In addition, psychologists must maintain absolute confidentiality, use the appropriate assessment techniques, and protect the welfare of their clients. Further, sport psychologists are instructed to maintain the appropriate relationships with other professionals, that is, to maintain the proper contact and communication with coaches, the media, and others in the sport world. Finally, researchers are instructed to maintain ethical standards in their research.

Also involved in the promotion of ethics among sport psychologists, AAASP published a set of ethical guidelines in 1995 (Meyers, 1995). The AAASP guidelines, which are similar to those adopted by NASPSPA, are based on the ethical standards of a number of organizations including the APA. The AAASP statement presents six principles of ethical behavior. First, AAASP members are expected to maintain competence and understand the limitations of their area of expertise. Second, AAASP members must maintain integrity in their professional activities (e.g., teaching, research, work with athletes). That is, they must be honest when describing their qualifications. Third, AAASP members are to act responsibly in their professional and scientific behavior by serving the interests of their clients and subjects. This responsibility involves correcting or reporting the unethical conduct of a colleague. Fourth, members must respect an individual's rights to privacy, confidentiality, and autonomy, and must be sensitive to cultural, religious, ethical, and other individual differences. Fifth, AAASP members must attempt to enhance the welfare and well-being of others. And, finally, AAASP members must be aware of their social responsibility to their communities.

Recently, Petitpas, Brewer, Rivera, and Van Raalte (1994) asked a large portion of the AAASP membership to complete a survey measuring the members' background and education in ethical principles. Approximately one third of the respondents stated that they had completed a course in ethics, while about 40% of the respondents reported that they had completed a course in which ethics were discussed. Both of these percentages are alarmingly low. Members of AAASP and sport psychologists in general should feel obligated to seek out education on ethical issues, and sport psychology programs should routinely offer courses in ethical conduct.

A BRIEF HISTORY OF SPORT PSYCHOLOGY

To understand fully the direction in which sport psychology is headed, it is necessary to have an understanding of where the discipline has been. Therefore, a brief review of the history of sport psychology is warranted. It should be noted that this presentation of sport psychology's history is brief because an in-depth analysis of the history of the field is beyond the scope of this book. Students interested in a more detailed discussion of the topic should read *The World Sport Psychology Sourcebook* (2nd ed.) by John Salmela (1992). This book describes the current state of sport psychology in over 40 countries, includes a list of over 1,600 prominent sport psychologists, and examines the progress of the discipline. A summary of Salmela's conclusions concerning the progress and state of sport psychology is presented in this chapter's "A Closer Look."

Our discussion of sport psychology's history is divided into two sections: sport psychology prior to and since 1950. Table 1.3 highlights the most important dates in sport psychology for both time frames.

The Early Years: Sport Psychology Prior to 1950

During a conversation on the history of sport psychology, Robert McGowan stated that "Sport psychology is as old as sport" (personal communication, November 7, 1994). McGowan's statement refers to the idea that the first athletes probably had a basic understanding of the importance of an athlete's mental state. That is, even Olympians competing in the first games most likely realized that confidence, self-control, and other psychology factors were related to athletic success. However, it

TABLE 1.3   Important Dates in Sport Psychology

Date	*Event*
1898	First sport psychology study conducted by Triplett.
1925	First sport psychology laboratory established by Griffith.
1965	International Society of Sport Psychology (ISSP) is formed.
1967	North American Society for the Psychology of Sport and Physical Activity (NASPSPA) is formed.
1969	Canadian Society for Psychomotor Learning and Sport Psychology (CSPLSP) is formed.
1985	Association for the Advancement of Applied Sport Psychology (AAASP) is formed.
1987	Division 47 of the American Psychological Association (Exercise and Sport Psychology) is formed.

A CLOSER LOOK:
IS SPORT PSYCHOLOGY AN INDEPENDENT PROFESSION?

In Chapter 1 of *The World Sport Psychology Sourcebook* (2nd ed.), Salmela (1992) examines the current state of sport psychology from the perspective of Wilensky's (1964) criteria for the establishment of an independent profession. Wilensky argued that before a discipline can be considered as an independent profession, it must contain the following five components: (1) a large number of persons engaging in a worthwhile activity on a full-time basis, (2) the establishment of academic training programs, (3) the development of professional organizations, (4) be politically active, and (5) the establishment of a set of ethical principles and guidelines governing the profession. Overall, Salmela reports that sport psychology fared well when examined using Wilensky's standard.

With regard to the first criterion, Salmela (1992) states that there has been a substantial amount of research activity in sport psychology. This research has been conducted by many persons from an impressive diversity of countries. In fact, Salmela reports that the number of sport psychologists worldwide jumped from 1,300 in 1981 to 2,700 in 1989 (these figures are estimates). The number of countries represented by the sport psychologists rose from 39 to 61. However, Salmela notes that, "To assume that most existing professionals in the industrialized world are involved with sport psychology on a full-time basis would be erroneous" (p. 3).

As for the second benchmark, the existence of training programs, Salmela comments that, although a large number of graduate programs in sport psychology have emerged, they are mainly found in North America. The third criterion on Wilensky's list, the establishment of professional organizations, is also a strong point in sport psychology's professional growth. Several national and international organizations have been formed. The major professional sport psychology organizations and their founding dates are listed in Table 1.3. The fourth (political action) and fifth (establishment of ethical guidelines) of Wilensky's criteria have also been met within the field of sport psychology. Salmela lists several past and present topics which have required political activity from sport psychologists, such as licensing and territorial issues. Ethical guidelines for the activities of sport psychologists have also been established. The NASPSPA and AAASP guidelines were reviewed earlier in the current chapter.

Thus, it appears that sport psychology has reached the point at which it can be viewed as a distinct and independent profession. While sport psychology has not completed its growth and evolution as a science, Salmela (1992) concluded that, . . . "sport psychology has now nearly completed its first cycle of full professional development" (p. 6).

Coleman Roberts Griffith is considered by many to be the father of American sport psychology. (Photo courtesy of the University of Illinois Archives.)

was not until the end of the 19th century that researchers began to examine empirically the relationship between psychology and sport behaviors.

The first study in sport psychology was conducted by Norman Triplett in 1898 (see Davis, Huss, & Becker, 1995). For his master's thesis, Triplett examined the records of professional bicycle races and found that paced races (i.e., competitive races) resulted in faster times than unpaced (i.e., solo) races. Triplett also examined the phenomenon in the laboratory. He instructed children to wind reels as fast as they were able. Subjects completed the task either alone or in competition. Consistent with the data from the bicycle races, the results indicated that subjects wound faster in the presence of competition than when they were alone. A short time after Triplett's groundbreaking work, two other articles focusing on sport were published (Howard, 1912; Patrick, 1903). Unlike Triplett's research, however, the focus of these papers was on sport spectating.

The next major event in the evolution of the discipline, occurring in 1925, was the establishment of the first sport psychology research laboratory in the United States. Directed by Coleman Roberts Griffith and located at the University of Illinois, the laboratory was titled the Athletic Research Laboratory. Griffith had been interested in sport psychological phenomena since the 1910s and is often referred to as the father of American sport psychology (for detailed discussions of the contributions of Griffith, see Gould & Pick, 1995; Kroll & Lewis, 1980). In Griffith's laboratory, research tended to focus on three aspects of sporting behavior: psychomotor skills, performance, and personality. He used both laboratory data collection methods and field research. In addition, he interviewed a number of athletes including "Red" Grange, a famous professional football player. Griffith presented his work and ideas in two classic sport psychology books, *The Psychology of Coaching* and *The Psychology of Athletics,* both published in the 1920s. His work continued until 1932 when the laboratory closed. Griffith followed his work at the laboratory by going into administration, with most of his efforts focusing on educational psychology. However, he did maintain an interest in sport psychology and at one point was hired to do a psychological evaluation of the members of the Chicago Cubs professional baseball team. Thus, Griffith was, in a sense, the first sport psychology consultant (Kroll & Lewis, 1980).

The Development of an Independent Discipline: Sport Psychology since 1950

Following the closing of Griffith's laboratory in 1932, relatively little happened in sport psychology until the 1950s. At this time, sport psychology began to separate itself from the study of motor behavior, a time that Landers (1995) refers to as "the formative years" in sport psychology (p. 406). Yet it was not until the 1960s that the discipline of sport psychology began to flourish with the establishment of several sport psychology organizations. In 1965, the International Society of Sport Psychology (ISSP) was formed at the first annual meeting of the International Congress of Sport Psychology. Shortly thereafter, in 1967, NASPSPA was established to serve the needs of experimental sport psychologists. Since its establishment NASPSPA has become an important and productive organization and has been referred to as the world's most influential sport psychology group (Salmela, 1981). In 1969, the Canadian Society for Psychomotor Learning and Sport Psychology (CSPLSP) was founded. In 1985 AAASP was founded to encourage informational exchanges between sport psychology practitioners (i.e., educational and clinical sport psychologists) and may have replaced NASPSPA as the most influential sport psychology organization. Finally, sport psychology was formally recognized by APA in 1987 with the creation of Division 47 of the APA, Exercise and Sport Psychology. Division 47 published a brochure describing sport psychology. Consistent with our previous discussion, this brochure lists three general types of sport psychologists: experimental, educational, and clinical. Also consistent with the previous discussion, the APA brochure indicates that a clinical psychology Ph.D. is required for employment as a clinical sport psychologist.

SUMMARY

To identify the criteria that comprise the discipline of sport psychology, several definitions were presented. First, psychology was defined as the primarily scientific study of human and animal behavior, affect, and cognition. Sport was defined as activities involving powers and skills, competition, strategy, and/or chance, and engaged in for the enjoyment, satisfaction, and/or personal gain (such as income) of the participant and/or others (e.g., spectators), including organized and recreational sports, as well as sport as entertainment. Sport psychology was defined as the primarily scientific study of the behavioral, affective, and cognitive reactions to sport settings, including the reactions of both participants and spectators. It was further noted that research in sport psychology and sport sociology often overlap.

Sport psychologists can be classified as applied sport psychologists and experimental sport psychologists. Applied sport psychologists are further divided into clinical sport psychologists (persons qualified to counsel athletes on personal and emotional problems) and educational sport psychologists (individuals whose primary responsibility is the transmission of sport psychological information to athletes and coaches). The recommended educational level for applied sport psychologists is the doctoral degree, while the educational direction will vary depending on the individual's career goals. Experimental sport psychologists conduct research and test theories of sport behavior. Sport psychologists should follow the ethical standards set by the NASPSPA and the AAASP.

Historically, the first sport psychology experiment was conducted by Triplett in 1898. Triplett's work focused on the influence of competition on performance. The first laboratory devoted to sport psychology research was established in 1925 by Coleman Roberts Griffith. However, sport psychology did not begin to blossom until the 1960s when organizations such as the ISSP (1965) and the NASPSPA (1967) became active. Sport psychology continues to prosper today as indicated by the recent establishment of the AAASP (1985) and the creation of Division 47 (Exercise and Sport Psychology) of the APA (1987).

GLOSSARY

Applied Sport Psychologists   Sport psychologists who apply sport-specific and general psychological theories and research to sport settings in an attempt to increase the psychological well-being, health, and performance of athletic participants.

Clinical Sport Psychologists   Sport psychologists specifically trained to deal with the various emotional problems and personality disorders experienced by athletes.

Educational Sport Psychologists   Sport psychologists with an understanding of the principles of sport psychology who attempt to transmit this information to athletes and coaches.

Experimental Sport Psychologists   Sport psychologists primarily interested in conducting research to further the knowledge and understanding of sport.

Psychology   The primarily scientific study of human and animal behavior, affect, and cognition.

Sport   Activities involving powers and skills, competition, strategy, and/or chance, that are engaged in for the enjoyment, satisfaction, and/or personal gain (such as income) of the participant and/or others (e.g., spectators). Included are organized and recreational sports, as well as sport as entertainment.

Sport Psychology   The primarily scientific study of the behavioral, affective, and cognitive reactions to sport settings, including the reactions of both participants and spectators.

APPLICATION AND REVIEW QUESTIONS

1. Compare and contrast what is meant by psychology, sport, and sport psychology.
2. Compare and contrast the goals and activities of clinical and educational sport psychologists.
3. With regard to education, how does an individual become an applied sport psychologist?
4. Describe the major events in the history of sport psychology.
5. Describe the major organizations in the field of sport psychology.

SUGGESTED READINGS

ANSHEL, M. H., FREEDSON, P., HAMILL, J., HAYWOOD, K., HORVAT, M., & PLOWMAN, S. A. (1991). *Dictionary of the sport and exercise sciences.* Champaign, IL: Human Kinetics. This volume contains the definitions/explanations of approximately 3,000 common and uncommon sport psychology terms. It is a valuable resource for students in the sport psychology and sport science disciplines.

GRANITO, V. J., & WENZ, B. J. (1995). Reading list for professional issues in applied sport psychology. *The Sport Psychologist, 9,* 96–103. This article provides the reader with more than 100 journal articles, books, and chapters relevant to applied sport psychology. The readings are subdivided into eight areas of interest: ethics, special ethical issues, education and training, scope of practice (clinical/educational debate), professional identity (credibility), certification and registry, diversity, and practice issues.

McCULLAGH, P. (Ed.). (1995). Sport psychology: A historical perspective [Special issue]. *The Sport Psychologist, 9*(4). This special issue of *The Sport Psychologist* examines the history of sport psychology. A number of topics are discussed including the works of Triplett and Griffith, women in sport psychology, and current developments.

SACHS, M. L., BURKE, K. L., & BUTCHER, L. A. (1995). *Directory of graduate programs in applied sport psychology* (4th ed.). Morgantown, WV: Fitness Information Technology. This book is a valuable resource for those persons considering graduate work in sport psychology.

SALMELA, J. H. (1992). *The world sport psychology sourcebook* (2nd ed.). Champaign, IL: Human Kinetics. This book contains two major sections. Section 1 describes the state of sport psychology on a global level. Section 2 contains a list of leading authors, researchers, and clinicians in sport psychology, a list in excess of 1,600 names.

TAYLOR, J. (1991). Career direction, development, and opportunities in applied sport psychology. *The Sport Psychologist, 5,* 226–280. This article describes the educational paths leading toward a career as a clinical or educational sport psychologist.

UNITED STATES OLYMPIC COMMITTEE. (1983). U. S. Olympic Committee established guidelines for sport psychology services. *Journal of Sport Psychology, 5,* 4–7. This article describes the various activities, differences, and similarities among clinical, educational, and experimental sport psychologists.

Chapter 2

RESEARCH METHODS AND TESTING IN SPORT PSYCHOLOGY

Quality research is the life blood of any scientific discipline. Without it, disciplines would stagnate, failing to advance past their current limits and understanding. Thankfully, a great number of sport psychologists have dedicated themselves to a career of researching sport psychological phenomena. The current chapter investigates the techniques used by these individuals in their quest for a better understanding of sport. First, we will examine two criteria important to all aspects of research in sport psychology: the research hypothesis and the types of variables involved in sport research. Then, experimental and nonexperimental methods of research will be reviewed. Finally, we will examine psychological testing in sport.

THE RESEARCH HYPOTHESIS

The first thing needed in research is a hypothesis. A **hypothesis** is a statement of causation. That is, the experimenter develops a statement about what she or he believes to be a series of events. Most researchers represent the hypothesis as an **X** causes **Y** relationship. For example, an experimenter may form the hypothesis that specific goals result in better motor performance than nonspecific goals. For this hypothesis, **X** would represent goal type and **Y** would represent performance. This pattern of effects is depicted graphically in Figure 2.1.

Students in scientific disciplines such as sport psychology often wonder how researchers develop their hypotheses. Usually, hypotheses are generated from theories (referred to here as **theory-based hypotheses**). A **theory** is a statement about

X ─────────────────────────────────────► Y
(Goal Type)   (Performance)

FIGURE 2.1   An illustration of a hypothesis.

the relationships involved in a specific phenomenon. The accuracy of a theory is tested through research. After testing a theory, researchers adapt and modify the theory. For example, an investigator may have a theory of sport motivation. Included in this theory would be variables believed to increase motivation, those thought to decrease motivation, and behaviors that are influenced by different levels of motivation. The researcher may also believe that educational level is an important predictor of sport motivation and include this variable in the theory. However, if research indicated that the relationship between education and motivation was trivial or nonexistent, the researcher would need to rework the theory to represent this fact.

In addition to being theory-based, hypotheses are also developed from existing research (called ***research-based hypotheses***). That is, psychologists often read or hear about another researcher's work and begin to develop their own hypotheses about the phenomenon. To demonstrate how this operates, we return to the researcher investigating the relationship between educational level and sport motivation. Although this particular study was theory-based, the results may, in turn, spark new research endeavors. That is, on hearing about the lack of a relationship between educational level and sport motivation, another researcher may generate a different hypothesis, one that is related to these variables. The second researcher may predict that one's desired educational level (as opposed to actual level attained) may be an important predictor of sport motivation.

There are several sources investigators use to develop research-based hypotheses including scholarly journals, conferences, textbooks, and classroom lectures. With advances in computer networks, investigators are able to develop research-based hypotheses targeting new research. Separate networks have been established for sport psychology and sport sociology. Both networks are used by a large number of individuals. Membership in the sport psychology network topped 800 in 1995 and membership in the sport sociology network was approaching 300 by 1996 (for more information on sport networks, see Malec, 1995). Investigators engage in a continuing discussion of sport-related phenomena, presenting new data from their own research. Others, after reading the discussions, are able to develop their own research-based hypotheses from data that have yet to be published!

TYPES OF VARIABLES IN SPORT PSYCHOLOGICAL RESEARCH

A ***variable*** is a construct that varies in magnitude or type. In psychological research, there are four types of variables. The ***independent variable,*** or what is often referred to as the treatment, is the variable that is manipulated by the experimenter. It is also the variable that causes a change in some behavior. In our diagram of a research hypothesis (see Figure 2.1), the independent variable is indicated by the **X.** In our example, the independent variable is the type of goal given to the subjects. The experimenter has determined the various levels of the goal variable and has, in essence, manipulated it. Further, goal level is expected to influence the subjects' performance at the motor task. Thus, the independent variable of goal type was expected to cause the performance level. Performance level, or the outcome of the study, is referred to as the dependent variable and is represented by the letter **Y.** The ***dependent variable*** is the variable that is measured. It is dependent or based on the independent variable. For example, motor performance is dependent on the type of goal present. While the independent variable is perceived as the cause, the dependent variable constitutes the effect.

The third type of variable found in psychological research is a subject variable. Subject variables are sometimes referred to as selection, grouping, trait, and/or causal variables. ***Subject variables*** are traits and characteristics of the subjects. Common subject variables in psychological research include gender, age, height, weight, and race. For example, an investigator may believe that male and female athletes differ in levels of competitiveness. Similarly, another researcher may wish to investigate how motivation levels differ by age. A common mistake made by students is to confuse subject variables and independent variables. Remember, independent variables are manipulated by the researcher while subject variables are attributes subjects bring with them to the experiment.

The final variables found in research are external variables. ***External variables*** (also referred to as control and extraneous variables) are those variables lying outside the **X → Y** relationship that the experimenter attempts to control. External variables represent all remaining potential influences in the study. All variables that are not independent, dependent, or subject variables are classified as external variables. To depict the **X → Y** relationship accurately, we must add the external variables to the figure. This has been accomplished in Figure 2.2 in which external variables are represented by the **Z**'s in the diagram.

When conducting research, investigators attempt to control the external variables. Control of external variables is achieved by insuring that these variables are held constant throughout the research, that is, that all groups and conditions expe-

FIGURE 2.2   The causal relationship between the independent variable (**X**), the dependent variable (**Y**), and several external variables (**Z**).

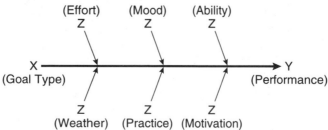

rience the same levels of these variables. Sticking with our earlier example of goal type (the independent variable) and motor performance (the dependent variable), let us assume that the hypothesis was supported in that specific goals resulted in better performance than nonspecific goals. However, there are many other factors that could influence performance. For example, the environment in the testing session, time of day, weather, and the subjects' motivation and ability levels all may influence their performance at the task. The researcher must insure that these external variables (i.e., external to the $X \rightarrow Y$ relationship) remain constant from group to group. If the specific goal condition had been conducted in a comfortable room (in terms of space, temperature, lighting, etc.), while the nonspecific goal subjects were tested in an uncomfortable environment, this would present a problem for interpreting the results of the study. The researcher would be unable to determine if the increased motor performance was due to the specific goal or the comfortable room. Thus, the results of the study would be confounded. ***Confounding*** occurs when an independent variable varies systematically with an external variable. Certainly, not all external variables influence the outcome of a study. However, because it is impossible to determine which confounded variables will have an impact, it is better to be safe than sorry and attempt to control as many external variables as possible.

THE EXPERIMENTAL METHOD

The ***experimental method*** is a method of research in which the experimenter randomly assigns subjects to groups, manipulates an independent variable and measures its influence on a dependent variable, and simultaneously controls several external variables. The experimental method allows the researcher to determine cause and effect relationships. As a result, this is the method of choice for investigators. Whenever the parameters of research allow it, investigators should use the experimental method.

Studies investigating the effects of subject variables on certain behaviors are not true experiments because researchers are unable to manipulate subject variables. As a result, the inference of causation from these studies is not possible. Researchers and students alike often erroneously assume that since differences in the dependent variable were found among the various levels or types of a subject variable, the subject variable caused the behavioral change. As an example, let us return to the study investigating gender differences in levels of competitiveness. Suppose that the researcher had found support for the hypothesized differences in competitiveness between males and females, with males reporting higher levels of competitiveness. Although she or he may be tempted to do so, the investigator is unable to determine cause and effect relationships. Rather than gender causing differential levels of competitiveness, it may have been increases in muscle mass that resulted in higher levels of competitiveness. Since males tend to have larger muscles, it appeared that gender was causing competitiveness. However, males and females of equal muscle mass may have been equal in competitiveness and, therefore, gender and competitiveness may have been unrelated.

Random Selection of Subjects

To draw accurate conclusions from their research, investigators must randomly select their subjects. The ***random selection*** of subjects means that all individuals in a population have an equal chance of being selected for inclusion in the study. Before discussing the parameters of random selection, I would like to describe two important terms: sample and population. A ***population*** is defined as all the potential subjects from which a sample is drawn while a ***sample*** is a group of subjects selected from a population. For example, in a study on the relationship between practice time and performance among college athletes, one's population might be the 500 student-athletes at a university. From this population, the researcher could then draw her or his sample of 100 subjects for the study.

Returning to our discussion of the random selection of subjects, it is vital that sport psychologists select their subjects from the population in a random fashion. Using the example above, the researcher must acquire the 100-subject sample randomly from the 500-person population. This can be achieved in a number of ways. For example, the researcher could simply select every fifth player on a list or she could select those persons whose social security numbers end in a 0 or 1. What happens if researchers do not randomly select their subjects? Let us continue with the practice time and performance study as an illustration. Let us say that the researcher, in order to save time, simply selected members of the football team to serve as participants. Because this sample is not representative of the general population of college athletes, the experimenter is limited in the generalizability of the sample. Because the data were taken solely from a sample of football players, the results of this research are only representative of football players and not college athletes in general. Although the study was intended to be an investigation of all college athletes, the lack of a random sample limited the scope of the research.

Before we conclude our discussion of random selection, I would like to add that there are experimental situations in which the random selection of subjects is unnecessary. For instance, if an investigator wishes to examine a golf team containing 10 members, there is no need to take a sample from this population. Rather, the researcher would be best advised to use the entire team in her or his study.

Random Assignment

Once subjects have been randomly selected from a population, they must be randomly assigned to the various levels of the independent variable. Thus, ***random assignment*** is defined as a process in which all subjects in a sample have an equal and unbiased opportunity to be placed into any one of the research groups. Like random selection of subjects, there are several methods of randomly assigning subjects to groups. When there are only two levels of the independent variable (for example, a study in which one group receives relaxation training while the other group does not), a simple and effective method of randomly assigning subjects is using a coin toss. Those subjects tossing a "heads" would be placed in the relaxation training group, while those who toss a "tails" would be assigned to the no relaxation training condition. When there are more than two groups in the research, two methods of randomly assigning subjects to the levels of the independent variable are most common. First, experimenters can place the names (or identification numbers) of the subjects into a pile and select one name at a time, placing that person into one of the groups. Second, researchers can use a random numbers table. Random numbers tables include randomly (and often computer) generated lists of five digit numbers. These tables can be found in many experimental psychology and statistics textbooks and are a feature on many calculators. Researchers often randomly assign subjects based on the last digit in each number. For example, if there are three levels of the independent variable such as with a study involving relaxation, self-hypnosis, and no training conditions, subjects assigned a number ending with a 1, 2, or 3 would be placed in one group; those assigned a number ending in 4 through 6 would be placed into the second group; and those given a number ending in 7 through 9 would be assigned to the last condition.

Why is the random assignment of subjects important? To best answer this question, let us examine a hypothetical experiment testing the relationship between practice time and motivation. Let us assume that the researcher has predicted that subjects asked to practice 2 hours per day will become more motivated than persons practicing only 1 hour per day. Let us also assume that, to save time and effort, the researcher decided not to randomly assign the 20 subjects to the two groups. Instead, he or she simply placed the first 10 subjects arriving at the testing session into the 2-hour group and the last 10 subjects into the 1-hour group. After conducting the experiment, the researcher examined the data and, as expected, the 2-hour group reported higher levels of motivation relative to the 1-hour group. However, because the subjects were not randomly assigned to the groups, we do not know if the results were due to the treatment (i.e., the amount of practice) or to the differential motivational levels of the two groups. It is possible that the two groups were not equal in motivation when the study began. Rather, the subjects arriving early, who may have been more motivated than those arriving late, were all assigned to the 2-hour group. As a consequence, this group may have been naturally higher in motivation than the 1-hour group. Thus, the random assignment of subjects to the levels of the independent variable controls for subject variables such as age, gender, motivation, and effort by attempting to balance these variables between the groups.

However, random assignment does not guarantee that the composition of the groups will be equal. As a result, researchers sometimes become concerned that subjects in the groups will differ even after random assignment. That is, the investigators believe that, although the participants were randomly assigned to their groups, the personalities and traits of subjects in one condition do not match the personalities and traits of subjects in the other conditions. To deal with this "random assignment paranoia," researchers use a technique called matching. ***Matching*** is a process used to equate subjects in the various experimental conditions. This process involves testing subjects on an important trait and, using scores from the testing, placing subjects into the experimental conditions in an equal fashion. For example, consider a hypothetical experiment testing the relationship between practice time and free throw shooting accuracy. Let us assume that the researcher has predicted that subjects asked to practice 2 hours per day will become better shooters than persons practicing only 1 hour per day. Obviously, the participants' basketball ability will have a huge impact on their performance. Although the researcher had initially planned to use random assignment to help equate the two groups, she is concerned that one group may still possess a higher level of basketball skill. As a result, she has decided to match the subjects based on their self-reported basketball skill level. The top two players could then be placed in separate groups, followed by the next two best players, and so on. Thus, by using the subjects' self-reported ability, the researcher can place an equal number of skilled and unskilled players into each condition, thereby equating the groups.

A final note concerning random assignment must be mentioned. Experimenters cannot randomly assign subjects to the various types and levels of subject variables. For example, if a researcher were interested in the relationship between age and adherence to an exercise program, she or he could not randomly assign the subjects to the various age groups. Similarly, a researcher interested in the relationship between type of sport (e.g., volleyball versus basketball) and motivation could not randomly assign the subjects to the various sports of interest. This researcher would have to take the subjects as they are (i.e., either a member of the volleyball team or the basketball team).

Experimental versus Control Groups

The groups examined in experimental research are categorized as either an experimental group or a control group. ***Experimental groups*** are groups that receive the treatment while ***control groups*** are those that do not receive the treatment. The control group is used as a comparison group. For example, consider an experiment examining the effects of alcohol consumption on spectator aggression. In this two-group study, the group randomly assigned to consume alcohol would be the experimental group, while the group not receiving alcohol would be the control group. I would like to reiterate that researchers should try to equate the groups in their research. That is, the only variable that should differ between the experimental and control groups is the independent variable. Researchers must control the various external variables in the research (e.g., test the experimental and control groups in the same environment) and equate the subject variables between the groups by using random assignment.

Operational Definitions

Consider again our hypothetical experiment involving alcohol consumption and spectator aggression. Prior to watching their team in competition, subjects were to be randomly assigned to groups either receiving or not receiving alcohol. After the competition, the subjects' aggression levels were to be assessed. However, the researcher must consider an important question before beginning the experiment: How is aggression to be measured? Obviously, there are many ways to assess aggression. For example, the researcher could measure aggression by (1) using a pencil and paper questionnaire, (2) assessing the subjects' physiological arousal (e.g., heart rate, blood pressure), (3) recording the subjects' facial expressions, or (4) examining the subjects' verbal responses. These are all acceptable methods of acquiring information concerning one's aggression level and, in fact, all have been used in past research. The researcher's dilemma is to choose what he or she considers to be the best indicator of aggression for that particular study. This problem illustrates the need for operational definitions. ***Operational definitions*** are ways of defining constructs in a manner that describes how they are to be produced and/or measured. Because most constructs can be operationally defined in multiple ways, researchers must determine the most proper method of defining the constructs in their study. The experimenter in the previous example must decide how aggression is to be measured in his or her study. For example, she or he may choose to measure aggression through facial expressions. This operational definition of aggression is really no better or worse than the others listed above; rather, it is just different. This is not to say that wrong operational definitions do not exist. For instance, it would be inappropriate to operationally define aggression as the color of the respondents' hair.

Usually, researchers are interested in operationally defining three types of variables in their research: the independent, dependent, and subject variables. With regard to independent variables, if one were interested in the effects of alcohol consumption, he or she must operationally define what is meant by alcohol consumption (e.g., one ounce, two ounces). Further, as with aggression in the example above, researchers must also define how they are going to measure the dependent variable. And, finally, researchers should operationally define important subject variables. While certain subject variables are self-defining (such as gender), others such as age and skill level require precise operational definitions. For instance, experimenters must operationally define what is meant by "older" athletes and "elite" athletes.

Tying It All Together: An Example of the Experimental Method

Let us examine a hypothetical research study that depicts the major components of the experimental method. The reader should find Figure 2.3 helpful in comprehending this example.

In this experiment, the investigator believed that little league soccer players receiving verbal praise during practice would demonstrate better performance than players not receiving praise. This belief was the researcher's hypothesis. The researcher randomly selected a sample of 50 subjects from a population of 500 players. This was accomplished by acquiring a directory of all little league soccer players and selecting every 10th name from the list. The subjects were randomly assigned, on the basis of a coin toss, to either the praise group or the no praise group (there were 25 subjects assigned to each condition). The group receiving the praise was the experimental group, while the no praise group was the control group. The independent variable was whether or not praise was given to the athletes and the dependent variable was performance. Praise was operationally defined as between 5 and 10 verbal praises per hour of practice. Performance was operationally defined as the number of successful goals scored out of ten 15-yard attempts. Several external variables were held constant in this research. Subject variables such as skill level

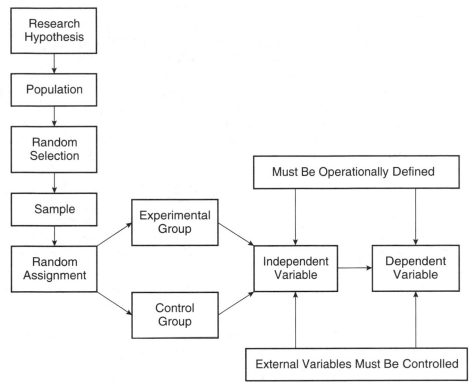

FIGURE 2.3   The major components of the experimental method.

and gender were equated using random assignment to groups. Weather, wind direction, ball size, and goal size were held constant by testing all subjects on the same day using the same equipment.

NONEXPERIMENTAL RESEARCH

In *nonexperimental research* investigators are unable to manipulate the independent variable or cannot randomly assign subjects to the various conditions of the research. As a result, the experimenter is unable to determine cause-effect relationships. With this shortcoming, the reader may be wondering why researchers conduct nonexperimental research? Actually, there are several benefits to nonexperimental methodologies. A comparison of the pros and cons of experimental and nonexperimental work appears in this chapter's "A Closer Look."

Often, nonexperimental research is classified into one of three categories: naturalistic observation, participant observation, and questionnaire/interview research. We will now examine these research strategies in detail. This discussion will be followed by a review of correlational statistics.

A CLOSER LOOK:
THE PROS AND CONS OF EXPERIMENTAL
AND NONEXPERIMENTAL RESEARCH

Many topics of interest to sport psychologists can be examined through both experimental and nonexperimental techniques. The major advantage of experimental research, as noted earlier, is the ability to control the variables and establish causation. This is not possible with nonexperimental techniques. Why then, if they will be unable to establish causal relationships, do experimenters choose to employ nonexperimental strategies in their research? Actually, there are several benefits to nonexperimental research that are often absent from experimental methodologies.

Aronson, Ellsworth, Carlsmith, and Gonzales (1990) list several reasons that justify the use of nonexperimental research methodologies. First, there are situations in which the experimenter is not interested in determining cause and effect relationships. For example, a sport psychologist may simply wish to document the relationship between two variables without concern for which variable causes the other. Second, it may be unethical (e.g., illegal drug use among athletes) or impossible (outcome of a professional contest) to manipulate one or more of the variables of interest. Finally, the researcher may wish to augment or elaborate on her or his experimental research with new and different nonexperimental techniques.

There may be other advantages to using nonexperimental approaches as well. Often, when choosing to conduct nonexperimental research, an investigator has decided to conduct a field research study. *Field research* is research conducted in naturalistic settings with little or no control. Conversely, *laboratory research* consists of work conducted in a controlled environment. Many researchers believe that field research is more realistic (Aronson, Brewer, & Carlsmith, 1985). In fact, because of this increased realism, some sport psychologists have called for an increase in field research on sport phenomena (Dewar & Horn, 1992; Martens, 1987a). Another benefit of field research is that this type of research is often nonreactive and unobtrusive (Elmes, Kantowitz, & Roediger, 1992; Webb, Campbell, Schwartz, Sechrest, & Grove, 1981). Nonreactive/unobtrusive investigations are studies conducted in a manner that does not change or alter the subject's behavior. Observing the subject's behavior from a distance may result in a more natural reaction from the subject compared with a laboratory study in which the subject is well aware that he or she is being observed. Subjects tested in hypothetical laboratory settings may underestimate certain situational cues found only in actual settings and subsequently act in an artificial manner (Wann & Weaver, 1993; Wann, Weaver, & Davis, 1992). Field research is not without drawbacks, however. First and foremost is the lack of control in these settings. Also, the investigator is often unable to gain the informed consent of the subjects (Aronson et al., 1985). If subjects are observed without their knowledge, one cannot gain their approval beforehand.

So, which methodology should researchers employ? Aronson et al. (1985) argue that the best research programs are those employing multiple methodologies. The phenomenon of interest should be examined in controlled laboratory environments using the experimental method, as well as in natural settings using nonexperimental methods. This enables one to apply the findings of laboratory research to real world settings better. Webb et al. (1981) concur, stating that researchers should not be concerned with the single best method but rather with "which set of methods will be best" (p. 315).

Naturalistic Observation

Often, when social scientists wish to further their understanding of a certain behavior, they simply observe individuals who are performing the behavior of interest. On some occasions, the researcher will observe the individual without making the subject aware of his or her presence. This type of investigation is referred to as naturalistic observation. Specifically, ***naturalistic observation*** is defined as the observation of a subject or group of subjects in natural settings and without interference. For example, a researcher may unobtrusively sit in the stands at a baseball game and observe the behaviors of the players as they wait in the on-deck circle. One type of naturalistic observation is a case study (Elmes et al., 1992; Tenenbaum & Bar-Eli, 1992). ***Case studies*** are descriptive investigations in which the researcher examines a single subject in great detail. Often, such research is ***longitudinal,*** that is, a topic is examined over a long period. An example of a case study project in sport psychology would be to examine a specific athlete throughout a series of competitions. Because case studies lack control, generalizing the findings of this form of research should be done with caution (Campbell & Stanley, 1963).

Participant Observation

In contrast to naturalistic participation, ***participant observations*** occur when a researcher becomes actively involved while observing the subject or group of subjects. For example, an experimenter may be interested in the behaviors of amateur golfers. To investigate this phenomenon better, the researcher may caddie for several golfers or join a club and begin to compete with other golfers. An advantage of participant observation, in comparison to naturalistic, is that a great deal of information can be acquired. If the researcher wanted to know why golfers take practice swings, she or he could simply ask the other golfers. This information would be unavailable to naturalistic observers unless the subjects began to discuss the topic on their own. On the other hand, there is a disadvantage to using participant observation strategies, one that is not present with naturalistic techniques. When a researcher participates in the setting, this inevitably changes the natural order of events. It is difficult to determine how the participation alters the behaviors of the subjects and, as a result, one cannot always be certain that the data are truly representative.

Questionnaire/Interview Research

Often, sport psychologists gather data through the use of questionnaires, interviews, or both. These techniques allow the investigator to collect a great deal of information from a large sample. When using questionnaires, researchers distribute forms to subjects who then complete the items on their own. On some occasions the questionnaires are distributed through the mail, while at other times they are given to subjects in person. During an interview, the researcher asks questions directly to subjects and then records the subjects' responses. This oral exchange usually takes place in person, but phone interviews are also common.

Thus, questionnaires and interviews are simply different means of acquiring the same information. So which method is preferable? The answer to this question depends on several factors. First, when the questions are straightforward (i.e., the investigator does not expect subjects to have difficulty understanding the items), the questionnaire method works well. However, if the items are difficult, then one should probably choose the interview method. In this way, if a subject does not understand a question she or he can simply ask the interviewer for an explanation. In questionnaire studies, this option is often unavailable to subjects, especially when questionnaires are mailed to the respondents. If the questions deal with a sensitive topic (such as drug use or homosexuality in sport), one should probably use the questionnaire method because subjects may respond in a more honest fashion. When asked a controversial question in a face-to-face interview, a subject may be hesitant to give a sincere answer. However, on occasion subjects can be less than honest when answering questionnaire items as well because they are attempting to respond in a socially desirable manner (Williams & Krane, 1989). Finally, the amount of time and money available to the researcher should also play a role in his or her decision concerning which data collection technique to employ (Schultz & Schultz, 1994). Usually, interview studies take longer to conduct than questionnaire work. With regard to cost, when the study is conducted in person, the questionnaire method is relatively inexpensive. However, when mailing questionnaires, the researcher must pay postage. Interviews can be expensive if the investigator must pay the interviewers for their assistance.

Correlations: Examining the Relationships between Variables

In nonexperimental research, investigators often employ one of the methods just described to explore the relationship between two variables. For example, a researcher may be interested in the relationship between aggression and performance or between weight and running speed. In studies such as these, the researcher is attempting to document the correlation between the two variables. A ***correlation*** is a statistic used to demonstrate the direction (i.e., type) and magnitude (i.e., strength) of the relationship between two variables. The direction of a relationship may take one of two forms: positive or negative. Positive correlations are relationships in which the amounts of the variables move together. Higher scores on one variable correspond with higher scores on the other. For example, consider effort and performance. Persons who put forth large amounts of effort tend to show higher levels of performance, while those with lower levels of effort perform at lower levels. Scores that move in the opposite direction are said to be negatively correlated. For these relationships, higher amounts on one variable correspond with lower amounts on the other. An example of a negative correlation in sport would involve cognitive anxiety and performance. Individuals with higher levels of cognitive anxiety usually have lower levels of performance, while those with lower levels of anxiety tend to exhibit higher levels of performance. Of course, many variables (such as hair color and performance) are not correlated. Scores on one variable (e.g., hair color) do not systematically correspond to any particular level or amount of the other variable (performance).

The magnitude of a relationship between two variables is indicated by a correlation coefficient. This is a number ranging from -1.00 (a perfect negative correlation) to $+1.00$ (a perfect positive correlation). Variables that are not correlated have coefficients at or near 0.00. Higher numbers indicate stronger relationships, regardless of the direction of the relationship. That is, $-.79$ indicates a stronger correlation than either $-.34$ or $+.57$. The number of subjects in the sample is important for interpreting the magnitude of a correlation. Our confidence in correlations grows as a sample size increases. Let us assume that a psychologist has found a $+.80$ correlation between leaping ability and playing time among volleyball players. We would be more confident in the stability of the correlation if the sample contained 250 players than if the sample contained only 5 players. Adding more subjects to the smaller sample may drastically change the correlation coefficient. With the larger sample of 250 players, the correlation is much more stable.

Correlations and Causation.   The greatest drawback accompanying the use of correlations is the researcher's inability to determine cause and effect relationships (remember, statements concerning causation may only be offered when the experimental method is used). For example, let us return to our earlier illustration of the possible relationship between effort and performance. Let us assume that the researcher did indeed find a strong positive correlation between these variables. There are three possibilities regarding the causal pattern involving the variables, each of which is depicted in Figure 2.4. One possibility is that effort causes performance (written generically as **X** causes **Y**). As athletes put forth more effort, their performance increases. However, the opposite relationship (i.e., **Y,** performance, causes **X,** effort) may also be correct. One could argue that, as a player's performance increases, he or she would subsequently put out more effort to maintain that level of performance. And, finally, a third variable (**W**) may be responsible for the high scores on both **X** and **Y** (i.e., effort and performance). In our example, it is quite likely that higher levels of motivation lead to both higher levels of effort and successful performance.

Although researchers are unable to determine causation from correlations, they are able to acquire suggestions about causal relationships by using a correlational procedure called a cross-lagged panel design. A ***cross-lagged panel design*** involves collecting correlational data on two variables at two separate times. By com-

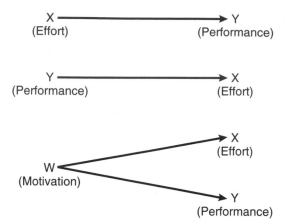

X ——————————→ Y
(Effort)   (Performance)

Y ——————————→ X
(Performance)   (Effort)

W (Motivation) → X (Effort), Y (Performance)

FIGURE 2.4   The three possible causal patterns
between two correlated variables.

Does an athlete's effort lead to a successful
performance or does success lead to higher levels of
effort? Or is there a third variable, such as motivation,
that leads to higher levels of effort and performance?
With correlations, determining the actual causal pattern
is not possible. (Photographer: Al Tielemans. Source:
Duomo Photography.)

paring the cross-lagged correlations (i.e., correlating Variable 1 at Time 1 with Variable 2 at Time 2 and Variable 2 at Time 1 with Variable 1 at Time 2), the researcher receives a hint about the causal relationship between the two variables.

A hypothetical example of a cross-lagged panel design is presented in Figure 2.5. This example involves the relationship between athletic performance and personal satisfaction. Let us assume that performance and satisfaction are positively correlated. That is, athletes with successful performances tend to be the most satisfied athletes. However, the causal relationship between the variables is unclear. Does better performance lead to higher levels of satisfaction or does satisfaction lead to better performance? By using a cross-lagged panel design, the researcher can probe the relationship further, resulting in an indication of the causal pattern. In this study, let us assume that performance and satisfaction at both Time 1 and Time 2 were positively correlated at .40. Performance at Time 1 and 2 and satisfaction at Time 1 and 2 were correlated at .30. What is most important, however, is a comparison between the cross-lagged correlations, that is, the relationship between performance at Time 1 and satisfaction at Time 2 and the relationship between satisfaction at Time 1 and performance at Time 2. As seen in Figure 2.5, the relationship of performance to satisfaction (.50) is much stronger than the relationship of satisfaction to performance (.10). As a result, it appears that performance causes satisfaction to a greater extent than satisfaction causes performance. Thus, the researcher has acquired an indication of the causal relationship.

PSYCHOLOGICAL TESTING IN SPORT

In sport psychology research, experimenters are sometimes interested in qualitative data. The goal of this type of research is simply to demonstrate categorical differences between groups. For example, an investigator may wish to test the prediction that male athletes, as a group, exhibit more competitiveness than do female athletes. However, many researchers wish to move beyond qualitative differences to quantitative differences. As for the competitiveness example, the researcher would not only be interested in the qualitative differences between males and females, but also in

FIGURE 2.5   An example of a cross-lagged panel design correlating athletic performance and personal satisfaction at two different times.

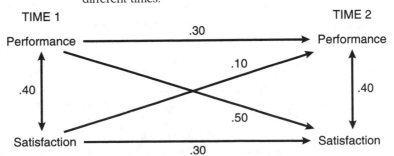

the degree to which males score higher in competitiveness than females. At this point in the research process, the psychometric qualities of tests, questionnaires, and other measurement tools become extremely important. ***Psychometric psychology*** is the area of psychology concerned with the measurement and testing of emotions, cognitions, behaviors, and traits.

Data collected by sport researchers are only as good as the tests and questionnaires used to acquire the data. Therefore, it is imperative that sport psychologists develop high quality instruments for use in research. This is especially true because sport psychologists spend a great number of hours in psychological testing and such activities are considered one of their primary functions (Fogarty, 1995; Nideffer, DuFresne, Nesvig, & Selder, 1980). In this section, we will examine the methods researchers use to demonstrate the quality of their inventories. In addition, we will examine the development of sport-specific and culturally appropriate measures. We will conclude this section with a review of ethical guidelines for sport psychological testing.

DEMONSTRATING THE QUALITY OF PSYCHOLOGICAL INVENTORIES

To demonstrate the psychometric properties of their testing instruments, sport psychologists must demonstrate that the test is reliable and valid. In addition, researchers must report on the standardization and norms for the instrument.

Reliability

When discussing the characteristics of psychological assessment tools, ***reliability*** means consistency among test scores. A subject's score the first time he or she completes a test must correspond with his or her score from a second administration. For example, if the members of a volleyball team were asked to complete a measure assessing levels of assertiveness during the first week of the season and again during the fourth week, we would expect the scores to remain relatively consistent. Players scoring high on assertiveness during the first administration should score high during the second session, while those scoring low should do so during both testing sessions. If there was no relationship between the scores for the two time periods, one would have little confidence in the data. If a subject scored high on one administration but low on the other, should this person be classified as high or low in assertiveness? Without a reliable measure it is impossible to say. Generally, reliability is a greater concern for tests measuring ***trait levels*** of a behavior or characteristic (chronic, stable, and long lasting) than those designed to assess ***state levels*** (acute or temporary). Trait level tests, because they are designed to measure enduring qualities in athletes (for example, chronic levels of anxiety), must be highly consistent. State level tests, because they are designed to measure fluctuations in the behavior of interest (for example, precompetition changes in anxiety), are likely to have lower levels of reliability.

The reliability of a test is usually demonstrated through a correlation coefficient (Anastasi, 1988; Webb et al., 1981). Recall that correlations range from -1.00 to

+1.00. Scores that are positively correlated move together, that is, higher numbers on one measure correspond with higher numbers on the other. Similarly, lower scores on one variable match up with lower scores on the other. To demonstrate the reliability of their measures, psychologists seek very high positive correlations between the two administrations of their inventory.

Types of Reliability.   There are three common methods used to demonstrate the reliability of psychological instruments: test-retest, alternate-form, and split-half. As its name implies, ***test-retest reliability*** involves two administrations of the same test, separated by a predetermined interval. This form of reliability is the most straightforward and obvious (Anastasi, 1988). The length of time separating the testing sessions is crucial to this type of reliability and should always be revealed by the researcher. Usually, a test-retest interval of less than 6 months is viewed as appropriate. The separation should be shorter when testing children because these subjects may change during longer intervals (Anastasi, 1988).

Although the straightforward nature of test-retest reliability enhances its attractiveness to researchers, there is a drawback to this method. Often, subjects become familiarized with the test during the first administration (referred to as ***practice effects***). This familiarity may drastically alter the subjects' responses during the second session. For example, if the test was designed to measure a football teams' knowledge of a playbook, the players' scores would be artificially inflated during the second test due to the knowledge gained from the first testing session. Most college students would be more than happy to have professors use test-retest reliability if the students were to be allowed to use their scores from the second testing date!

Similar to test-retest reliability in that there are two testing sessions, ***alternate-form reliability*** involves the distribution of different forms of the same test. Here, subjects are tested with different test forms believed to measure the same construct. For example, there are several forms of the American College Testing Program (ACT) and the College Board Scholastic Aptitude Test (SAT), tests used as guidelines for admission to college. Although the forms are different, the scores of individuals retaking the test remain consistent. As a result, we may conclude that these tests are reliable. As with test-retest reliability, researchers should pay close attention to the interval separating the administration of the two forms (Anastasi, 1988).

Although alternate-form reliability may relieve a portion of the researcher's concern about practice effects, it does not necessarily eliminate the problem (Anastasi, 1988). If the test forms are designed to measure one's knowledge of a certain domain, information gained from the first test form (such as the types of questions asked, the difficulty level, and the focus of the test) will have an impact on the scores on the second form. In addition, there is a second concern when using alternate-form reliability. The researcher must insure that the two forms are equal in difficulty level and focus (Anastasi, 1988). For example, let us say a researcher designed two forms of a test expected to measure postcompetition anxiety. If only one form measured this construct while the other form assessed something different (for example, aggression), then the reliability would obviously be reduced.

The third common reliability procedure is split-half reliability. When using ***split-half reliability,*** researchers are required to schedule only one administration date during which subjects complete a single inventory that has been divided into two comparable halves. This form of reliability greatly reduces the influence of practice effects. However, equating the two portions of the test in terms of content and difficulty level is still a necessity (Anastasi, 1988). The method used to split a test can assist the researcher in securing two equal halves. Many tests become increasingly difficult as the test progresses. When dealing with these tests, the experimenter should not simply divide the test based on the first and second halves because the halves will differ in difficulty level. In these situations, the researcher should use every other item to develop the two forms (Anastasi, 1988).

Validity

While reliability deals with consistency among scores, the ***validity*** of a measure concerns whether or not the test is measuring what it purports to measure. Anastasi (1988) warns against accepting a measure based on name only—it may or may not actually assess the construct of interest.

Types of Validity.   Researchers routinely demonstrate the validity of their instruments through one of two techniques: content and criterion validity. An inventory is considered to possess ***content validity*** to the degree that it covers a wide representation of the domain of interest. For example, a test designed to assess college student-athletes' satisfaction with their university should include items that focus on the many different aspects of satisfaction. This test would need to incorporate items on academics, coaching, facilities, housing and food service, the faculty, and tuition prices, to name but a few. Had this test only included items on housing and food service, it would not have been considered content valid.

Criterion validity concerns the degree to which a test is correlated with another measure of the construct of interest. There are two common types of criterion validity: concurrent and predictive (Monette, Sullivan, & DeJong, 1994). ***Concurrent validity*** involves testing the relationship between the instrument in question and an already established criterion. For example, sport enjoyment measures should be positively correlated with attendance at practice, a measure that is currently available. Similarly, a test measuring baseball skills should be correlated with current statistics such as batting average and playing time. ***Predictive validity,*** on the other hand, involves using the instrument to predict future events and behaviors. With regard to entrance tests for college (such as the ACT and SAT), if these tests are indeed measuring what they are supposed to measure (namely, intellectual ability), then researchers should be able to use these tests to predict future behaviors such as success in college. Within the world of sport psychology, inventories measuring traits such as aggression and anxiety that are completed during practice must be able to predict the responses of athletes in future competitive settings before they can be considered valid.

Standardization

To be considered an acceptable psychological assessment tool, a test must be standardized. ***Standardization*** refers to the consistent procedures used for administering and scoring the test. Answers to questions such as how long subjects are given to complete the test, what should be done concerning the testing environment, and what instructions should be given to the subjects are all examples of information concerning the standardization of an instrument. Information concerning the standardized procedures for the administration of sport psychological inventories should be included in publications describing the instrument.

An important part of the standardization process is the establishment and presentation of norms. ***Norms*** are normal, average, or typical responses or performances on a test and are established by testing hundreds or even thousands of subjects. Norms are important for the interpretation of scores. For example, let us say a college football player scored a 25 on a test of pregame anxiety (the test ranged from 5 to 50, with higher scores reflecting greater levels of anxiety). Without information on a comparison group, we do not know how to interpret this score. Is a score of 25 representative of a high, low, or moderate level of anxiety? If the test had published norms indicating that the average score was 35, we would then know that this athlete was relatively low in precompetition anxiety.

CRITICAL ISSUES IN SPORT PSYCHOLOGICAL TESTING

When selecting a test for use in a sport setting, there are often a number of instruments from which the researcher or clinician may choose. As such, he or she must take care to select the most appropriate and sound test for that particular situation. The discussion that follows highlights several characteristics of the testing environment that must be considered by psychologists prior to test selection (this is by no means an exhaustive list—other topics such as cost to the researcher and age of the subjects may also be important).

Should the Test Be Objective or Subjective

When selecting between objective and subjective tests, a psychologist is considering the types of responses required of the subjects (Schultz & Schultz, 1994). ***Objective tests*** (or fixed-alternate tests) provide the test-taker with the possible responses to each item. Common examples include multiple choice, true-false, and Likert-scale tests. Conversely, ***subjective tests*** (or open-ended tests) require subjects to respond to the items in their own words. Essay tests would be classified as subjective tests. Each of these test types has benefits and drawbacks. An advantage of objective tests is that more questions can be asked in a given period of time. Further, test scoring and data entry tend to be quicker and easier with objective tests. However, subjective tests have the advantage of assessing information that may have been missed had an objective item format been employed because objective tests are restricted by the possible responses given for each item.

When developing or using subjective tests, the researcher must demonstrate high levels of inter-rater reliability (Anastasi, 1988; Aronson et al., 1990). While the reliability concerns described earlier dealt with the consistency among test scores, ***inter-rater reliability*** (also referred to as inter-observer reliability) concerns the consistency among two or more observers scoring a test. Suppose a researcher asked athletes to write essay descriptions of their precompetition experiences to assess their level of anxiety. To be certain that others would agree with the scoring of the essays, the researcher should have at least two independent raters judge the essays. If a high level of consistency is found between the judges' ratings (i.e., a high level of inter-rater reliability), then we would be confident in the scoring procedures for this test.

Should the Test Be General or Sport-Specific

A second issue to consider when selecting a test is whether to select a general psychological inventory (a test designed for use in a variety of settings) or one that is sport-specific (a test specifically designed for use in sport settings). Gauvin and Russell (1993) argue that this dilemma is a major concern for sport psychologists. They suggest that research designed to investigate a phenomenon unique to sport settings should employ sport-specific measures, while investigations designed to apply a general psychological principle to sport should employ general psychological inventories.

Gauvin and Russell (1993) also state that there has been "a proliferation of context-specific, sport-specific, and even league-specific measures" (p. 893). The increase in sport-specific inventories prompted Anshel (1987) to publish a list of commonly used questionnaires in the sport and exercise sciences. A few years later, the growth of sport-specific measures was large enough to warrant the publication of the *Directory of Psychological Tests in the Sport and Exercise Sciences,* edited by Andrew Ostrow (1990). Ostrow's data paralleled the arguments of Gauvin and Russell as a consistent increase in the development of sport-specific tests was found between 1970 and 1989. Ostrow's text, which describes almost 200 different sport-specific inventories (including information on references, test construction, availability, reliability, validity, and norms), is divided into several chapters, each devoted to a specific type of test (e.g., tests dealing with anxiety, aggression, and motivation). The most common topics and sports examined by the inventories contained in Ostrow's book are listed in Table 2.1.

Cultural Issues in Sport Psychological Testing

When choosing a psychological test for use in sport settings, be it sport-specific or general in nature, Gauvin and Russell (1993) state that investigators should pay particular attention to the cultural considerations of their research. These authors argue that researchers need to be sensitive to language differences and take care when translating a test. In general, they note that researchers should try to identify "Factors that are likely to be affected by culture and socialization," such as, "values, norms, attitudes, beliefs, child-rearing practices, gender stereotypes, or power relations between teammates" (p. 896).

GUIDELINES FOR PSYCHOLOGICAL TESTING IN SPORT

In 1982, NASPSPA published a set of guidelines for testing in sport psychology. These guidelines are quite consistent with the topics discussed in this chapter. The purpose of the guidelines was to "provide guidelines for maintaining quality control of test-

TABLE 2.1   The Number of Tests Focusing on the Most Popular Topics and Sports*

Focus	Number of Tests
Topic	
Motivation	33
Attitudes	21
Confidence	19
Anxiety	17
Body Image	14
Aggression	13
Sport	
Basketball	20
Gymnastics	11
Swimming	11
Wrestling	8
Football	7
Soccer	7
Track and Field	7

*From Ostrow, 1990.

ing instruments used in sport and other physical activity settings" (p. vi). The guidelines were to apply to "instruments and practices dealing with psychological scales, motor learning/control tests, motor development assessment procedures, and social psychological measures" (p. vi). The guidelines were based on two publications by the APA: *Ethical standards for psychologists* (1979) and *Standards for educational and psychological tests* (1974). The document offers six specific guidelines and addresses involvement in test development and use.

First, the test developer must describe the appropriate uses of the test as well as its limitations, and the user must use the instrument in the proper settings. Second, information concerning the proper administration of the test should be provided and followed by the user. Third, the test developer should specify any limitations to administering the test in terms of special qualifications (such as licensing or training). As such, only users who are qualified should administer the test. Fourth, information concerning validity, and, fifth, information on reliability, should be provided. Sixth, normative data should be provided.

SUMMARY

Researchers begin their work with a hypothesis based on a theory or from previous research. Before beginning their research, investigators must identify the variables in the study. There are four types of variables: independent (those manipulated by the researcher), dependent (what is measured), subject (traits and characteristics of the subjects), and external (variables lying outside the $\mathbf{X} \rightarrow \mathbf{Y}$ relationship). Researchers must also operationally define the independent and dependent variables.

Whenever possible, researchers should use the experimental method. This method allows the researcher to determine cause and effect relationships. When using the experimental method, researchers must randomly select their sample from a population, and they must randomly assign the subjects to the research groups. Subjects randomly assigned to receive the independent variable comprise the experimental group, while subjects not receiving the independent variable make up the control group.

Often, researchers are unable to use the experimental method and must, therefore, rely on nonexperimental techniques. These methods differ from the experimental method in that the investigator is unable to manipulate the independent variable and/or cannot randomly assign subjects to the various conditions of the research. Nonexperimental research includes naturalistic and participant observation as well as the use of questionnaires and interviews. In many cases, experimenters use nonexperimental methods to demonstrate the correlation between two variables. The major drawback to this type of work is the inability to establish patterns of cause and effect, although suggestions about causal relationships can be acquired through the cross-lagged panel design.

To increase the effectiveness of data assessment techniques, sport psychologists are concerned with establishing and increasing the quality of their tests, questionnaires, and other measurement tools. This is accomplished by providing information concerning the reliability, validity, and standardization procedures for the assessment tool. Reliability concerns the consistency of scores and is demonstrated in one of three ways: test-retest, alternate-form, and/or split-half. Validity concerns the degree to which a test measures what it is supposed to measure and is demonstrated through content validity, criterion validity, or both. Criterion validity is further divided into concurrent validity and predictive validity. Tests should also be standardized.

When selecting a test, sport psychologists must consider several critical issues. First, they must decide if the test should be objective or subjective. Also, researchers must determine if the test should be a general psychological inventory or a sport-specific inventory. Research testing a general psychological phenomenon in a sport setting is better suited for a general test, while research specifically designed to test a sport psychological phenomenon should use a sport-specific test. Numerous sport-specific tests have been developed, and the number of tests available to researchers and clinicians continues to expand. Finally, researchers should consider the impact of cultural influences when selecting a test.

In 1982, NASPSPA published a document outlining six guidelines for psychological testing in sport settings. These guidelines, directed toward both those developing and those using the tests, cover the following areas: test limitations and appropriate uses, the proper administration of the test, limitations to administering the test in terms of special qualifications of the test-giver (such as liscensure or training), information concerning validity and reliability, and normative data.

GLOSSARY

Alternate-Form Reliability   Reliability involving the two separate distributions of different but comparable forms of a test, each measuring the same construct.

Case Study   Descriptive investigations in which the researcher examines a single subject in great detail.

Concurrent Validity   Involves testing the relationship between an instrument in question and an already established criterion.

Confounding   Occurs when an independent variable varies systematically with an external variable.

Content Validity   The degree to which a test covers a wide representation of the domain of interest.

Control Group   The group that does not receive the treatment.

Correlation   A statistic used to demonstrate the direction and magnitude of the relationship between two variables.

Criterion Validity   The degree to which a test is correlated with another measure of the construct of interest.

Cross-Lagged Panel Design   A design used to acquire a suggestion about the causal relationship between two variables involving the collection of correlational data on the variables at two separate times.

Dependent Variable   The variable that is measured.

Experimental Group   The group that receives the treatment.

Experimental Method   A method of research in which the experimenter randomly assigns subjects to groups, manipulates an independent variable and measures its influence on a dependent variable, and simultaneously controls several external variables.

External Variable   Those variables lying outside the $X \rightarrow Y$ relationship.

Field Research   Research conducted in naturalistic settings with little or no control.

Hypothesis   A statement of causation.

Independent Variable   The variable that is manipulated by the experimenter.

Inter-Rater Reliability   The consistency with which two or more observers score a single test.

Laboratory Research   Research conducted in a controlled environment.

Longitudinal Research   A study in which a topic is examined over a long time.

Matching   A process used to equate subjects in the various experimental conditions.

Naturalistic Observation   The observation of a subject or group of subjects in natural settings and without interference.

Nonexperimental Research   Research in which the investigator is unable to manipulate the independent variable, cannot randomly assign subjects to the various conditions of the research, or both.

Norms   Normal, average, or typical responses or performances on a test established by testing many subjects.

Objective Tests   Tests providing the test-taker with the possible responses to each item.

Operational Definition   A way of defining constructs in a manner that describes how they are to be produced and/or measured.

Participant Observation   Research in which a researcher becomes actively involved in the setting while observing the subject or group of subjects.

Population   All potential subjects from which a sample is drawn.

Practice Effects   A situation in which subjects have become familiarized with a test during previous administrations, causing possible changes in the subjects' responses.

Predictive Validity   Using an instrument to predict future events and behaviors.

Psychometric Psychology   The area of psychology concerned with the measurement and testing of emotions, cognitions, behaviors, and traits.

Random Assignment   A process in which all subjects in a sample have an equal and unbiased opportunity to be placed into any one of the research groups.

Random Selection   A means of acquiring subjects such that all individuals in a population have an equal chance of being selected for inclusion in the study.

Reliability   Consistency among test scores.

Research-Based Hypothesis   A hypothesis developed from existing research.

Sample   A group of subjects selected from a population.

Split-Half Reliability   Reliability involving only one administration date during which subjects complete a single inventory that has been divided into two comparable halves.

Standardization   The consistent procedures for administering and scoring a test.

State Level Tests   Inventories designed to measure acute or temporary behaviors, characteristics, or both.

Subject Variable   Traits and characteristics of subjects.

Subjective Tests   Tests in which subjects are asked to respond to the items in their own words.

Test-Retest Reliability   A measure of reliability involving two administrations of the same test, separated by a predetermined interval.

Theory   A statement about the relationships involved in a specific phenomenon.

Theory-Based Hypothesis   A hypothesis generated from an existing theory or theories.

Trait Level Tests   Inventories designed to measure chronic, stable, and long-lasting behaviors, characteristics, or both.

Validity   The degree to which a test measures what it purports to measure.

Variable   A construct that varies in magnitude or type.

APPLICATION AND REVIEW QUESTIONS

1. Describe the relationship between theories and hypotheses.
2. Describe the four types of variables found in sport psychology research.
3. Describe the key advantage to using the experimental method.
4. Discuss the differences between random selection and random assignment.
5. Develop a sample experiment and identify the major components of the experimental method.
6. Describe how data may be gathered in nonexperimental means.
7. Describe the possible casual patterns between two correlated variables.
8. Describe the term reliability as used in psychological testing and describe three common methods of assessing reliability.
9. Describe validity as it relates to testing, including both content and criterion validity.
10. Why are standardization and norms important to psychological testing?
11. Compare and contrast objective and subjective tests.
12. When should one use a general test and when is one advised to use a sport-specific measure?

SUGGESTED READINGS

ANASTASI, A. (1988). *Psychological testing* (6th ed.). New York: Macmillan. This popular textbook provides the reader with an in-depth review of psychological testing.

ARONSON, E., ELLSWORTH, P. C., CARLSMITH, J. M., & GONZALES, M. H. (1990). *Methods of research in social psychology* (2nd. ed.). New York: McGraw-Hill. This volume describes the research process in great detail. It covers areas such as deception and ethics in research that are beyond the scope of the present textbook but may be of interest to advanced students.

ELMES, D. G., KANTOWITZ, B. H., & ROEDIGER, H. L. (1992). *Research methods in psychology* (4th ed.). New York: West. This textbook describes the basic aspects of research in psychological settings and is a good starting point for those readers interested in a more complex presentation of research methods.

GAUVIN, L., & RUSSELL, S. J. (1993). Sport-specific and culturally adapted measures in sport and exercise psychology research: Issues and strategies.

In R. N. Singer, M. Murphy, & L. K. Tennant (Eds.), *Handbook of research on sport psychology* (pp. 891–900). New York: Macmillan. This article addresses several contemporary issues in sport testing, including a lengthy discussion of the pros and cons of both general and sport-specific tests.

OSTROW, A. C. (1990). *Directory of psychological tests in the sport and exercise sciences*. Morgantown, WV: Fitness Information Technology. This text is a valuable resource for persons interested in sport psychology. It lists more than 100 sport-specific tests as well as information on test construction, reliability, validity, and availability.

WEBB, E. J., CAMPBELL, D. T., SCHWARTZ, R. D., SECHREST, L., & GROVE, J. B. (1981). *Nonreactive measures in the social sciences* (2nd ed.). Dallas: Houghton Mifflin. This book describes numerous nonexperimental methodologies. As such, it is a valuable source for those persons interested in observation and case study research. Further, it has a separate section on nonreactive measures in sport settings.

Chapter 3

SPORT SOCIALIZATION AND THE MOTIVATION TO PARTICIPATE IN SPORT

Imagine for a moment that you are walking by an elementary school during the early afternoon hours in April. As you stroll by the school, you see approximately 100 children playing on the playground. As you watch the children, one thing becomes readily apparent to you: The youngsters are involved in many different activities. Some of the children are participating in organized sporting activities such as kickball and dodgeball, while others are participating in unorganized sports such as running races or playing on the jungle gym and climbing bars. Although many of the children seem to be enjoying themselves, others appear to be unsure of themselves and are happy to let other children take charge of the athletic activities. Other children seem to be completely uninterested in sporting experiences and prefer to sit alone or in small groups, reading or conversing with other children. Why have some children chosen to participate in athletic endeavors while others have avoided them? And of those children who are involved in the sporting games, why do some appear to be self-confident and in control of the situation while others seem uncertain of their abilities and appear to be content to let the other children call the shots? These and similar questions are the focus of social scientists interested in the motives underlying a child's decision to participate in sport. In this chapter, we will examine the research on sport involvement, identifying the factors and motives influencing the participation of young athletes.

Before beginning this examination, however, a note on the term motivation is warranted. When discussing the behaviors of athletes, motivation is used to describe two different phenomena. First, researchers have investigated the motivation to participate originally in sport. As will be discussed in the current chapter, several motives have been identified. Second, for persons who have chosen to participate in athletics, researchers have examined the motivation levels of athletes before, during, and after competition and the relationships among motivation, effort, and performance. These relationships will be reviewed later in a separate chapter.

A MODEL OF THE DECISION TO PARTICIPATE IN SPORT

An individual's decision to participate in sport is not based on a single incident or individual. Rather, a person's decision to play sport consists of a process involving a variety of factors. To facilitate the reader's understanding of this process, a model of sport participation is presented here. This model, depicted in Figure 3.1, contains several components, each of which will be reviewed in this chapter. The reader is advised to reexamine Figure 3.1 periodically while reading this chapter.

THE INDIVIDUAL'S GENETIC PREDISPOSITION

Although psychological factors play a major role in a child's decision to participate in athletics, one cannot deny the impact of physiology. Simply put, some children are born with better physical skills than others (Bouchard & Malina, 1983, 1984; Régnier, Salmela, & Russell, 1993). Thomas, Thomas, and Gallagher (1993) correctly state that "Hereditary advantages/disadvantages obviously are important in skillful performance. The old adage 'If you want to be a good athlete, choose your parents wisely' applies" (p. 73). Early work by Cratty (1959, 1960) indicated that the relationship between one's physical abilities and one's parents' abilities was quite strong.

FIGURE 3.1 A model of sport participation.

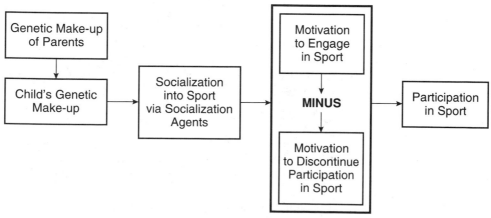

Cratty tested two generations of college freshmen on such tasks as the 100-yard dash and the broad jump. The correlations between the generations was consistently above .6, indicating a strong link between the parents' and child's physical abilities.

The importance of the child's genetic make-up is reflected in the sport participation model seen in Figure 3.1. According to this model, a child's decision to engage in athletics is originally influenced by the genetics of his or her parents. Parents with a high degree of physical prowess and athletic ability will quite likely transfer these traits to their children. Children born with natural athletic talent are more likely to begin and continue to participate in sport (Fries & Wolff, 1953; Scarr, 1966). Please note that this does not mean that all children born with athletic ability will participate in sport, nor does this imply that children born with lesser physical abilities will never participate. Rather, the child's genetic make-up simply sets the stage for athletic participation. Those born with superior physical abilities have a greater likelihood of participating in sport than those not endowed with physical skills.

SOCIALIZATION INTO SPORT

As noted, some children born with superior physical skills choose not to participate in sport, while others with less than adequate athletic abilities do become involved. Thus, there must be other important influences on a child's decision to play sport, influences that are the result of the child's environment and learning. The first of these additional influences is the socialization of the child. ***Socialization*** is the process of learning to live in and understand a culture or subculture by internalizing its values, beliefs, attitudes, and accepted rules of behavior (called ***norms***). For socialization into sport, we can simply add the word "sport" to the definition. Therefore, ***sport socialization*** is the process of learning to live in and understand a sport culture or subculture by internalizing its values, beliefs, attitudes, and norms.

A number of different individuals and institutions can combine to socialize individuals into sport. These ***socialization agents*** include parents, siblings, schools, the community, peers, and the media. Children learn the values, beliefs, attitudes, and norms of the sport culture through interactions with these groups. Below, research examining the impact of these socialization agents is reviewed. In some instances, data suggesting the relative importance of specific socialization agents are mentioned. However, because the importance of socialization agents can differ for various groups of athletes and nonathletes (such as gender, socioeconomic status, and cultural groups), precise statements about the relative importance of each agent are difficult (Coakley, 1993).

Parents

Probably the first socialization agents are the child's parents (Vogler & Schwartz, 1993). Because children spend such a large portion of their time with their parents, it seems logical that parental encouragement would be a major factor in the sport socialization process. Indeed, this line of thinking has been supported by numerous research endeavors (Colley, Eglinton, & Elliott, 1992; Greendorfer, 1993; Hellstedt, 1995; Leonard, 1993; Ommundsen & Vaglum, 1991; Snyder & Spreitzer, 1976; Spreitzer & Snyder, 1976). For example, Sage (1980) questioned several hundred intercollegiate athletes concerning their perceptions of the importance of various socialization agents in their decision to participate in athletics. Sage's results strongly supported the notion that parents are a major sport socialization agent as over 90% of the respondents reported that their parents were either somewhat or very important in their sport involvement. In addition, as summarized in Table 3.1, a large portion of the players' parents were active in sport as either a participant or a spectator.

The influence of one's father may be especially important (Greendorfer, 1992). Several studies found that the past sporting experiences of fathers were a primary socialization factor (Clark, 1980; Greendorfer & Lewko, 1978; Overman & Rao, 1981). Relative to mothers, fathers are more likely to have participated in sport as a child and/or adolescent, and are also more likely to participate in recreational sports as an adult (Iso-Ahola & Hatfield, 1986). Thus, they present the child with many more opportunities to model their behavior than do mothers. As a result, they exert an especially powerful force on the child's sport participation decisions.

Siblings

For readers who have older brothers or sisters, it will most likely come as no surprise that siblings also play a role in the sport socialization process. However, research has indicated that siblings are less important than parents (Eitzen & Sage, 1986; Greendorfer, 1992; Snyder & Spreitzer, 1976).

Schools

Most schools require physical education classes and most elementary schools have recess periods, times when many young children engage in athletic activities. As a result, these institutions can serve as a sport socialization agent. This is particularly true if the school's enrollment is small because children are more likely to partici-

TABLE 3.1   Parental Involvement in Sport during Male and Female Intercollegiate Athletes' Youth

	Males (%)	*Females (%)*
Father Active in Sport (Often, Frequently)	24	21
Mother Active in Sport (Often, Frequently)	7	15.5
Father Watched Sport on TV (1 to 4 times per week)	79	71.6
Mother Watched Sport on TV (1 to 4 times per week)	42.5	35.6
Family Subscribed to Sport Magazine (At least 1)	59.1	44.7
Parents Discussed Sports (Often, Frequently)	71	65.3
Family Conversation Devoted to Sport at Meals (Daily)	36	41.5
Parents Attended Sports Contests (More than once per month)	60	61.9

(Source: Sage, G. H. [1980]. Parental influence and socialization into sport for male and female intercollegiate athletes. *Journal of Sport and Social Issues,* 4: 1–13.)

pate in sport in smaller schools (Grabe, 1981). Because schools have historically reinforced the sport participation of males more than females, schools may be particularly powerful socialization agents for boys (Greendorfer, 1983; Vogler & Schwartz, 1993). However, as participation numbers increase for female interscholastic sports, schools may become equally powerful in the sport socialization of young women (Greendorfer, 1993).

Although some research has indicated that schools and teachers are important components in the sport socialization process (Greendorfer & Ewing, 1981; Greendorfer & Lewko, 1978; Leonard, 1993), Iso-Ahola and Hatfield (1986) note that the impact of schools may not be as great as once believed. Citing the work of several researchers, Iso-Ahola and Hatfield argue that schools tend to be a rather insignificant initiator of sport involvement. However, these authors state that schools may "play a role in advancing and refining the already learned sports skills" of the students (p. 62).

The Community

Because many communities sponsor organized sport programs, Leonard (1993) and Vogler and Schwartz (1993) argue that these institutions should be considered agents of sport socialization. Most schools and communities offer sport programs because they believe that athletic participation helps build the character of participants. However, as discussed in this chapter's "A Closer Look," authors have recently begun to challenge the "sport builds character" ideology.

Peers

The desire to be accepted by one's friends is a powerful force. Because children and adolescents often place a high priority on athletic ability (Evans & Roberts, 1987; Roberts & Treasure, 1992), peers serve as powerful socialization agents for sport participants (Coleman, 1970; Greendorfer, 1977; Vogler & Schwartz, 1993; Weiss & Duncan, 1992; Weiss & Knoppers, 1982). As Iso-Ahola and Hatfield (1986) so succinctly put it, "sports and friends . . . go hand in hand" (p. 63). Eitzen and Sage (1986) argue that the impact of one's peers is especially prominent during adolescence when children begin spending less time with their parents and more time with friends.

Media

The media are also an important factor in sport socialization. Children are bombarded with sport through several forms of media including television, newspapers, and magazines. The information presented by the media has a large impact in shaping the sport perceptions of individuals. Many youngsters view athletes as heros (Russell, 1993a), and parents are generally happy to have their children model the behavior of athletes (Leonard, 1993). As a result, the actions of athletes portrayed in the media help determine the sport attitudes and knowledge of children while the descriptions of commentators can introduce children to the values of sport (Bailey & Sage, 1988).

A CLOSER LOOK:
DOES PARTICIPATION IN ORGANIZED SPORT BUILD CHARACTER?

Many individuals in our society believe that participation in organized sport is a character-building pastime. For example, participation is believed to teach youngsters to strive to do their best, to learn about competition and what it takes to be successful, to motivate students toward academic achievement, to teach sportsmanship and citizenship, to enhance moral development, to build self-esteem, to reduce delinquency and respect authority, and to bring families and communities together (Kamal, Blais, Kelly, & Ekstrand, 1995; Leonard, 1993; Miracle & Rees, 1994; Murray & Matheson, 1993; Seidel & Reppucci, 1993; Shields & Bredemeier, 1995; Tutko, 1989). That is, sport participation is thought to teach the children about life in general and to help them learn skills that will be useful in their adult lives. For instance, Thompson (1993) recently published a book titled *Positive coaching: Building character and self-esteem through sports.* In this text, Thompson states that "Every child can learn important lessons about life by making great efforts, enjoying the taste of victory, and returning to try again after a loss" (pp. 18–19). He then presents suggestions for using sport participation to build the character of young athletes (character traits such as mental toughness, courage, sportsmanship, and commitment). Similarly, in his book *Good sports,* Wolff (1993) argues that athletic participation can build self-esteem, increase self-confidence, and teach good sportsmanship. Like Thompson, Wolff offers suggestions to coaches and parents on how to facilitate the development of these characteristics.

Are these authors correct—does athletic participation build character? Or, on the contrary, does athletic participation inhibit character building by condoning negative behaviors such as cheating and violence (Cullen, 1974; Jones & Pooley, 1986; Shields, Bredemeier, Gardner, & Bostrom, 1995; Shields & Bredemeier, 1995)? Authors Miracle and Rees (1994; see also Leonard, 1993) argue that the idea that sport builds character is a myth. Rather than relying on hearsay and anecdotal evidence, these authors conducted an extensive review of the research literature on the relationship between athletic involvement and character building. They concluded that "there is no evidence to support the claim that sport builds character in high school or anywhere else" (p. 96). Further, their examination found that sport involvement does not promote academic or sociological advancements, nor does it reduce delinquency or prejudice. These authors concluded that there were no long-term benefits of athletic participation and no apparent negative effects. Thus, the sport builds character belief was not substantiated. Yet, because so many persons (including sport psychologists) hold this belief, future research on possible character benefits of sport participation seems likely. As a result, the jury may still be out about the relationship between character building and sport participation.

Perceptions of Influence of the Various Socialization Agents

Before concluding our discussion of the influence of socialization agents, it should be noted that child athletes seem to enjoy sport to a greater degree when they believe that they made the decision to participate independent of others. Children with this belief also report that they are better players than persons who feel that others influenced their sport involvement decision. These relationships between perceptions of socialization agent influence and sport enjoyment and perceived ability were highlighted by the research of McGuire and Cook (1983). These investigators interviewed 93 youth sports participants concerning the extent to which they believed that others had influenced their sport participation decisions. The athletes were also asked the degree to which they had thoughts of quitting and their perceptions of their ability. Subjects believing that they were solely responsible for their decision to participate in athletics were far less likely to have considered quitting than persons who believed that someone else had influenced their decision. In addition, those children who believed that they decided independently were more likely to classify themselves as either "better than average" or as "one of the best players."

MOTIVATION TO CONTINUE OR DISCONTINUE PARTICIPATION IN SPORT

The genetic and socialization backgrounds set the stage for a child's sport involvement. However, there are children who have genetic ability and have been taught the values, beliefs, attitudes, and norms of the sport culture who choose not to participate in athletics. Further, some children who have participated in the past choose to drop out of organized sport. Thus, while genetics and sport socialization are key factors in a youngster's decision concerning sport participation, these factors do not guarantee involvement. As shown in Figure 3.1, an understanding of a child's final decision concerning participation is not complete until one considers various motivations to continue and discontinue participation. If the motives to participate outweigh the reasons to discontinue participation, then the child will most likely become and remain active in athletics. However, if the motives to stop participating are greater than those for continuing participation, the child will most likely not begin or will discontinue his or her sport involvement. Past research has highlighted a number of such motives, several of which may be operating within any given child at a single time. That is, these motives are not mutually exclusive. For example, a child motivated by a desire to achieve success in sport may also be motivated by the self-esteem gains resulting from the achievement.

We will first examine the reasons underlying participation and then review the motives behind the decision to discontinue participation (some of which are simply the inverse of a motive to continue involvement). Before beginning these discussions, it warrants mentioning that, similar to the socialization agents, the relative strength of the motives is hard to determine. Cratty (1989) notes that differences in the strength of the motives may vary with such factors as age and culture (see also Weiss & Chaumeton, 1992). Most likely, differences could be found for groups varying in gender and socioeconomic status as well. While some suggestions concerning the importance of the various motives are presented below, the research has been somewhat inconsistent. Therefore, final conclusions about the relative importance of the specific motives are not yet possible.

Motivations to Continue Participation

Numerous motives for continuing one's participation in athletics have been identified, and several methods for assessing these motives have been developed. However, as noted in Chapter 2, authors should use sound instruments in their research, that is, instruments with proven reliability and validity. Further, if different researchers use the same (or highly similar) scales, then cross-study comparisons are much easier. Alas, this has not generally been the case in participation motivation research. As opposed to other areas of sport psychology in which one or a few sound scales are consistently selected for use, there has been little consistency in the assessment of participation motives. It is hoped that future investigators of sport participation will see the advantages of using the same scale and adopt this procedure. Certainly, high quality scales are readily available. One such scale, the Participation Motivation Inventory (PMI, Gill, Gross, & Huddleston, 1983) would be a good choice for researchers, and, indeed, several persons used this scale in their laboratory (e.g., Flood & Hellstedt, 1991; Gould, Feltz, & Weiss, 1985; Ryckman & Hamel, 1993). The PMI contains 30 items that are combined to form eight different motivational factors (skill development, team affiliation, fun, achievement/status, friendship, energy release, fitness, and situational factors). Below, we will examine many of these factors in detail. In addition, a few motives not directly assessed by this scale will be reviewed. It should also be mentioned that the motives described below are not intended to be an exhaustive list. Rather, the motives covered in the following sections represent a sample of motives chosen for inclusion because they have received a great deal of interest from researchers and theorists.

Having Fun. Children, like adults, choose leisure activities they find enjoyable. Thus, it is not surprising to learn that the desire to have fun is one of the primary motives underlying the sport participation of children. In fact, one of the earliest research endeavors focusing on the motives of young athletes identified the desire to have fun as a major factor (Skubic, 1956). Subsequent work has substantiated the importance of this motive (Crocker, Bouffard, & Gessaroli, 1995; Gill et al, 1983; Scanlan & Simons, 1992; Spink & Longhurst, 1990; Wankel & Berger, 1990), and several studies found that this motive was the primary factor in the child's decision to participate (e.g., Buonamano, Cei, & Mussino, 1995; Gould, Feltz, Weiss, & Petlichkoff, 1982; Reis & Jelsma, 1980).

What do children find enjoyable about sport participation? This was the question asked by Wankel and Sefton (1989) in their investigation of 122 young athletes. These researchers found that the greatest predictor of fun was postgame affective state. Happier players tended to have more fun. The second greatest predictor of fun involved self-perceptions of how well the player believed he or she had played during the game. Increases in perceptions of a well-played game corresponded with perceptions of having fun. A final significant predictor of fun was the perception that the contest was challenging. More recent work by Bakker, de Koning, Schenau, and de Groot (1993) on young Dutch speed skaters found that the act of the sport itself was the primary reason for enjoyment (i.e., "the sensation, perceptions, and/or self-expressiveness associated with the act of skating itself," p. 433). Thus, it appears that there may be cultural, sport, and/or ability differences in perceptions of enjoyment. Because the subjects in these two studies differed in so many ways (e.g., culture and sport), we cannot form any conclusions about the causes of the differences in perceptions of enjoyment. Future research is needed in this area before generalizations from culture to culture and sport to sport are available.

Fitness Benefits. Individual fitness is another motive for children to participate in sport. Citing the research of Sapp and Haubenstricker (1978), LeUnes and Nation (1989) note that approximately 50% of a large adolescent sample believed that fitness was important in their involvement decisions. In their research on young cricket players, Spink and Longhurst (1990) found that fitness was listed in the top half of possible motives. The importance of the fitness motive has been found in other research as well (Buonamano, Cei, & Mussino, 1995; Clough, Shepherd, & Maughan, 1989; Flood & Hellstedt, 1991; Gill et al., 1983; Gould et al., 1982; Leonard, 1991; Ogles, Masters, & Richardson, 1995) and may be a particularly powerful reason for participation among female athletes (Reis & Jelsma, 1980).

Affiliation Needs. The need for affiliation is also a common participation motive (Buonamano, Cei, & Mussino, 1995; Ryckman & Hamel, 1992). As social beings, humans usually have a desire to be with others and to function as members of groups. This desire to fit in can be especially important to youngsters as they try to become associated with the most popular cliques and peer groups, many of which are sport-oriented (Miracle & Rees, 1994; Williams & White, 1983). Group memberships acquired through activities such as athletics allow children to be accepted by their peers, extend their social networks, and give them a sense of belonging. In fact, researchers (Alderman, 1978; Alderman & Wood, 1976) found that the affiliation motive was the most important reason for youth sports participation. Other research has found that children are especially motivated to play with those of similar abilities (Duquin, 1980).

Skill Improvement and the Need for Achievement. Many children remain active in athletics because they have a desire to improve their skills and eventually excel at a particular sport. This ***need for achievement,*** defined as the motivation to strive for success at certain (usually difficult) tasks, is a primary motive for many youngsters (Alderman & Wood, 1976; Ommundsen & Vaglum, 1991; Spink & Longhurst, 1990; Wankel & Kreisel, 1985). Skill development is an especially important motive for children who believe that they are high in physical ability (Ryckman & Hamel, 1993). This topic will be explored in the motivation chapter as well.

Harter's competence motivation theory (1981a, 1981b) has been called the most productive theory regarding the importance of need for achievement in one's decision to participate in athletics (Weiss & Chaumeton, 1992). The ***competence motivation theory*** argues that people are motivated to become competent in a certain area and that competence and success in the chosen activity result in a perception of control, positive emotional reactions, and an enhanced feeling of self-worth. Subsequently, the individual continues to participate in the activity to continue to receive the esteem benefits. Several studies have tested this theory in sport settings (e.g., Feltz & Petlichkoff, 1983; Klint & Weiss, 1987; Roberts, Kleiber, & Duda, 1981; see Weiss, 1987, for a review). In general, this work has supported Harter's contentions in that athletic participants were found to be higher than nonparticipants in perceptions of competence and self-esteem.

Gill and Deeter (1988) developed a sport-specific measure of achievement orientation, the Sport Orientation Questionnaire (SOQ). The SOQ contains 25 Likert-scale items that are combined to form three subscales: competitiveness (e.g., "I look forward to competing."), the desire to win (e.g., "The only time I am satisfied is when I win."), and the desire to reach personal goals (e.g., "I set goals for myself when I compete."). Gill and Deeter's research documented the strong internal consistency, reliability, and validity of the SOQ. Subsequent research efforts have substantiated the sound psychometric properties of the SOQ (e.g., Gill, 1993; Gill, Dzewaltowski, & Deeter, 1988).

Self-Esteem.   As the preceding discussion indicated, many children participate in athletics because sport involvement improves their self-esteem (Branscombe & Wann, 1994a). As a result, sport psychologists and sport sociologists have given special attention to this participation motive. Most individuals have a desire to maintain a positive self-image (Tajfel, 1981), and one of the best strategies for accomplishing this is to participate in activities in which the person is competent. Those children who find success in athletics, be it recreational sports such as those played while at recess or organized sports in school and community leagues, will begin to prefer these activities over other recreational or intellectual pastimes. Children who are not particularly adept at sport will likely choose another activity, one which they are competent at and, thus, will enhance their self-images. These children may come to devalue athletic participation because it is not central to their self-concept (Harter, 1986, 1993).

Eustress.   For many children, the desire to participate in exciting and arousing activities influences their decision to become and remain involved in athletics (Alderman & Wood, 1976; Leonard, 1991; Wankel & Kreisel, 1985). That is, some children are motivated to engage in sport because it provides the stress they seek. This stress, referred to as ***eustress*** (i.e., euphoric stress), is a positive form of stress that stimulates and energizes the individual (this type of stress will be discussed in greater detail in the anxiety chapter). Tendencies to gravitate toward positively stressful situations are often assessed using Zuckerman's (1984) Sensation Seeking Scale. ***Sensation seeking*** is a psychological trait in which the individual seeks out and enjoys thrilling, dangerous, or new experiences. Research has found that higher scores on sensation seeking correspond with participation in a variety of sports (Rowland, Franken, & Harrison, 1986).

Motivations to Discontinue Participation

Before proceeding into a discussion of the possible motives underlying a child's decision to end his or her participation in athletics, I would like to underscore the writing of Weiss and Chaumeton (1992), who state that the assumption that a child's withdrawal from sport is a negative phenomenon is often unwarranted. Rather, as these authors indicate, there are many situations in which the discontinuation of sport involvement is a natural consequence of life as a child, such as conflicts with other activities and sports. Many children reenter the sport world later in childhood or as an adult (Klint & Weiss, 1986). Thus, before concluding that a child's discontinuation from sport was due to a problem such as a negative experience with a coach or parent, one must examine the specifics of that individual case.

It should also be noted that most of the motives for discontinuation involve at least a moderate degree of negative stress and anxiety. Hostile parents and coaches, perceptions of a lack of abilities, and similar discontinuation factors all lead to a highly stressful environment for the young athlete. As a result, the individual may become burnt out and quit. Anxiety and negative stress are reviewed in an upcoming chapter.

No Longer Having Fun. Research has found that, when athletic involvement is no longer viewed as fun, the child or adolescent will often discontinue his or her participation (Burton, 1992a; Cohn, 1990; Reeve, 1992; Scanlan & Lewthwaite, 1986). In fact, Henschen (1993) states that the best method to prevent dropouts from sport may be to insure that the activity is viewed as enjoyable. Numerous factors contribute to perceptions that sport participation is no longer enjoyable. The belief that there is too great an emphasis on winning, not receiving enough playing time, and too much pressure from one's parents can all turn an enjoyable pastime into a nightmare for children (LeUnes & Nation, 1989) and coaches (Strean, 1995).

The negative impact of some parents warrants special attention. Wolff (1993) argues that the most important question a parent can ask himself or herself when their child becomes involved in sport is "What is my goal for my child?" It seems that a much better question would be "What is my child's goal?" One should consider the youngster's goals first because, as Greendorfer (1993) notes, many of the negative experiences of child athletes stem from parents imposing their value system on the sport, values that are often at odds with the goal of having fun. This value system, referred to as the ***professional model of youth sports,*** reflects the belief that the primary and often only goal is winning (Leonard, 1993). This viewpoint can be seen in the comments of Craig Kilborn, a sportscaster for ESPN. During a program in 1995, Kilborn stated the following . . .

> When it's all said and done, all that matters is winning. Oh sure, some say that participating, putting forth an effort is important, but that's not how it works. In all walks of life, from *little league* to the business world, you've got to win. Otherwise, *you're a loser.*

One has to wonder what effect statements such as this have on young athletes.

As a sad but true example of this philosophy, let me share with you an experience I had while umpiring a youth tee-ball league. The league was designed to be a noncompetitive recreational league, and umpires were told to emphasize fun and skill improvement while deemphasizing the importance of winning. We were told to let the children swing until they made solid contact and to allow as many children as possible to score (scoring appeared to be the most enjoyable aspect of the game for most players). We were also told not to keep score, thereby reinforcing the notion that winning was not important. The children rarely asked who was winning until parents, against our wishes, began bringing scorebooks. During a game, after a parents' meeting in which we banned the scorebooks, I found a parent picking up rocks and placing them into his pockets (one pocket per team) so he could keep track of the score, relaying the information to other parents! Clearly, there was nothing I could do to convince this parent that the most important aspects of tee-ball were fun and skill improvement rather than winning.

Certainly, this discussion is not intended to suggest that all parents have a negative impact on youth sports. Quite the contrary, it is obvious that parental support (financial, social, and otherwise) is a necessary part of youth sports programs. However, parents who become overly concerned with their child's abilities, or lack thereof, should think about the enormous pressure they are putting on their child and ask themselves if they would like to operate under such pressure.

Failure to Fulfill Needs for Achievement. Another reason underlying discontinuation concerns the individual's abilities. It was noted earlier that some children participate in sport to fulfill their need for achievement. However, Robinson and Carron (1982) argue that, if a child believes that his or her ability is inadequate, instead of being motivated to achieve excellence the youngster might decide to end his or her involvement. Subsequent research confirmed the importance of this motive for the cessation of sport participation (Burton & Martens, 1986; Feltz & Petlichkoff, 1983).

Failure to Gain Self-Esteem Benefits. A third discontinuation motive concerns the self-esteem of the individual. If children are not succeeding in athletics and thus not receiving self-esteem benefits from participation, they will quite likely seek out another activity to occupy their leisure time. If youngsters find success in the new activity they will probably spend more time participating in that activity and less time in sport.

Conflict from Other Activities. Many young athletes end or curtail their involvement because they have other commitments or develop other interests (Schmidt & Stein, 1991). LeUnes and Nation (1989) reviewed several studies and found this motive to be a major factor in discontinuation decisions. Research has indicated that as many as 84% of young athletes cite conflict from other interests as a reason underlying their discontinuation from sport (Gould et al., 1982). As discussed by Weiss and Chaumeton (1992), the perception that these children "dropped out" of sport can often be premature because the conflicting activity can be a different sport or the same sport at a different level of competition (Gould, Feltz, Horn, & Weiss, 1982; Klint & Weiss, 1986).

Poor Coaching. Because young athletes respond more favorably to certain types of coaches (Black & Weiss, 1992), children also drop out of athletics because of poor coaching. Poor coaches can exhibit a number of inappropriate behaviors including aggressive and abusive actions and behaviors leading to perceptions that the coach is not competent to run the team (e.g., skipping practice or demonstrating a lack of understanding for the sport). As noted by LeUnes and Nation (1989), many well-intended coaches want to offer their players a positive experience but, because of their poor interpersonal or coaching skills, they are ineffective as coaches. Other coaches, either because they possess a "win at all cost" attitude or because they are attempting to relive their youths, are too aggressive or overbearing for the youngsters.

Simply put, not all parents are suited to be coaches. Those who do wish to coach youth sports should receive formal training in coaching skills. Parents may want to enroll in coaching clinics and sport psychology courses at a local college or university. Further, there are programs specifically designed to assist persons wanting to better their coaching skills. One such program, called the American Coaching Effectiveness Program, was developed by Rainer Martens. This program offers work books and study guides in several coaching areas including sport psychology, sport law, sport injuries, and sport physiology. Those who successfully complete the courses are awarded certification through the program. On a more general level, Smoll and Smith (1993) outlined the development and implementation of a universal program for training coaches.

I urge those who plan on becoming a youth coach to participate in one or more of these programs because those who do learn to exhibit positive behaviors such as verbal reinforcements and instructions. Young athletes respond quite favorably to these behaviors (Smith, Smoll, & Curtis, 1978). For example, Smoll, Smith, Barnett, and Everett (1993) presented several baseball coaches with a workshop designed to increase their supportiveness and instructional effectiveness while a control group did

Children often discontinue their sport participation because of poor coaching. (Photographer: Junebug Clark. Source: Photo Researchers, Inc.)

not receive the coaching effectiveness training session. These authors found that coaches in the training group performed better and received better evaluations from players than coaches in the control group, even though the two groups did not differ in won–loss records. In a related study, Smith, Smoll, and Barnett (1995) presented a group of youth baseball coaches with guidelines for reducing player anxiety. A control group of coaches did not receive the training. Smith and his colleagues found that players on teams coached by individuals receiving the training reported having more fun, better evaluations for their coach, and lower levels of anxiety than players on the control teams. Similar to Smoll et al. (1993), these results were found even though the experimental and control teams did not differ in winning percentage.

TYING IT ALL TOGETHER: A FINAL EXAMPLE

Before concluding this chapter, it may be helpful to review an example that encompasses each of the steps proposed in Figure 3.1. The reader may find it useful to consult this illustration while considering the example.

Our example focuses on a 7-year-old girl, Michelle. Michelle is the youngest of three children (she has two older brothers). As depicted in Figure 3.1, to understand Michelle's participation in sport we must first consider the athletic talent of her parents. If Michelle's parents were athletically gifted, chances are that some of this ability would have been passed on to Michelle. On the other hand, if her parents were not athletically skilled, Michelle quite likely would be starting with a disadvantage in comparison to some other children. Remember, however, Michelle's decision concerning participation would not be based solely on her physical talents. For our example, let us assume that Michelle's parents were not athletically inclined and, therefore, Michelle was rather uncoordinated.

Even though her parents were not gifted athletes, they still enjoyed sport and played (albeit poorly) in several recreational leagues. As a result, they were major sport socialization agents for Michelle. Similarly, her older brothers enjoyed sport and, although they did not participate in organized sport, they still spent a great deal of their leisure time playing various sports in the backyard and at the playground. Thus, they too served as primary socialization agents for Michelle. As a result, Michelle was exposed to sport on a daily basis and, even though she was not a good athlete, she held positive beliefs about sport. When the time came to enroll in a youth soccer league, Michelle was more than willing and was actually quite excited about playing in the semistructured and semicompetitive league. It is important to note that, had Michelle not been socialized by her parents and siblings, she might not have chosen to become involved in the soccer league.

After participating in the league for about 1 month and with the first game only 1 week away, Michelle appeared to be enjoying herself. One day on the way home from practice, her mother asked her what it was about playing soccer that she liked most. Michelle stated that she enjoyed being with her friends and getting better at the activity. Thus, she was motivated to continue her participation by affiliation and skill-improvement needs.

Michelle's coach did not play her in the first game. Following the game,

Michelle's attitude toward playing on the team seemed to change. Her parents noticed that she talked less about playing soccer and, in fact, rarely played on her own. Further, she no longer seemed excited about upcoming games and practices. When her father asked about the change, Michelle told him that her coach was abusive to the children and tended to play only certain players, namely, her own child and her child's friends. As a result, Michelle did not seem to be enjoying herself as much as she once did. Will Michelle sign up to play in the soccer league next year? According to Figure 3.1, this decision will depend on the ratio of Michelle's attraction to playing (affiliation and skill improvement) to the relevant motives to discontinue participation (no longer having fun and poor coaching).

SUMMARY

In this chapter, a model of sport participation was presented. The first step in this model involved the genetic make-up of one's parents. The natural physical abilities of parents are transferred to children and, as a result, some youngsters have a physical advantage. However, because some children with a genetic advantage do not participate in sport while others with lesser natural abilities do, there is obviously something more than heredity involved in a decision to participate.

Socialization is the process of learning to live in and understand a culture or subculture by internalizing its values, beliefs, attitudes, and norms. Sport socialization occurs through contact with socialization agents. Parents can be a major sport socialization agent, possibly the primary agent. The influence of one's father can be especially important. Other important socialization agents include siblings, schools, the community, peers, and the media.

The decision to participate in athletics is also influenced by motivational forces. Some factors motivate youngsters to continue their involvement, while other motives lead children to discontinue their participation. As for the motives to continue participation, perhaps the primary reason listed by young athletes is the desire to have fun. Other common motives are fitness benefits, affiliation needs, skill improvement and the need for achievement, self-esteem, and eustress. Regarding the motives to discontinue involvement, no longer having fun, failure to fulfill achievement needs, failure to gain self-esteem, conflict from other activities, and poor coaching are commonly cited factors.

GLOSSARY

Competence Motivation Theory   The theory that people are motivated to become competent in a certain area and that competence and success in the chosen activity result in a perception of control as well as positive emotional reactions and an enhanced feeling of self-worth.

Eustress   A positive form of stress that stimulates and energizes the individual.

Need for Achievement   The motivation to strive for success at certain (usually difficult) tasks.

Norms   Societally prescribed rules for behavior.

Professional Model of Youth Sports   A belief held by many parents that the primary and often only goal of sport is winning.

Sensation Seeking   A psychological trait in which the individual seeks out and enjoys thrilling, dangerous, or new experiences.

Socialization   The process of learning to live in and understand a culture or subculture by internalizing its values, beliefs, attitudes, and norms.

Socialization Agents   Individuals and institutions, such as parents, siblings, and peers, combining to socialize individuals into sport.

Sport Socialization   The process of learning to live in and understand a sport culture or subculture by internalizing its values, beliefs, attitudes, and norms.

APPLICATION AND REVIEW QUESTIONS

1. What are the major socialization agents for sport socialization?
2. What are the major motives for continuation and discontinuation of sport involvement?
3. Develop an example of the sport participation of a hypothetical child and apply the model of sport participation presented in Figure 3.1 to this example.
4. Apply the model of sport participation presented in Figure 3.1 to your own childhood sport experiences.

SUGGESTED READINGS

LEONARD, W. M. (1993). *A sociological perspective of sport* (2nd ed., ch. 5). New York: Macmillan. Chapter 5 of this text examines the sport socialization process in detail, including a discussion of specific socialization agents.

MIRACLE, A. W. JR., & REES, C. R. (1994). *Lessons of the locker room: The myth of school sports*. New York: Prometheus. This book examines the belief that participation in school sports leads to character development. Several interesting and controversial topics are examined including character building, delinquency, and academic progress.

Chapter 4

PERSONALITY RESEARCH IN SPORT PSYCHOLOGY AND RESEARCH TARGETING SPECIFIC SPORT POPULATIONS

In the previous chapter, we examined reasons underlying the decision to participate in athletics. In the current chapter, we will take an in-depth look at the personalities of those individuals who have chosen to participate in sport. **Personality,** defined as "that pattern of characteristic thoughts, feelings, and behaviors that distinguishes one person from another and that persists over time and situations" (Phares, 1991, p. 4), has long been a phenomenon of interest to psychologists. In fact, notable early psychologists such as Sigmund Freud, Carl Jung, and Abram Maslow were interested in this topic. Similarly, one of the first topics investigated in sport psychology was the extent to which athletes and nonathletes possessed different personality characteristics (Vanden Auweele, De Cuyper, Van Mele, & Rzewnicki, 1993). Currently, most sport psychologists view personality from an *interactional approach* (Carron, 1975; Cox, Qiu, & Liu, 1993; Cratty, 1989; Martens, 1975; Vanden Auweele et al., 1993; Vealey, 1992). This perspective is a situational approach to explaining the relationship between personality traits and the environment. The interactional approach argues that individuals bring their personality with them to a given situation. Therefore, to fully understand an athlete's behavior, one must consider the individual (i.e., their personality), the situation, and the interaction between the individual and the situation. For example, let us consider a softball player, Dave, who by nature has an aggressive personality. In most situations, Dave will react aggressively when threatened or frustrated. In fact, his friends can recall many instances when Dave was ejected from his high school baseball games for aggressively and vulgarly attacking the umpires. However, because Dave's softball league is a recreational church league and has rules against such behavior, Dave tends to react mildly when a call goes against him. Thus, to understand Dave's behavior, we must consider the individual trait (aggressiveness) as well as the situation (a recreational church league).

In sport psychology, personality research has been conducted along one of two lines. The original line of research examined the relationship between personality and performance. A more recent trend has been to examine the behaviors of selected sport populations such as female athletes and black athletes. In this chapter, we will examine both lines of research. However, the reader is advised that the research on sport personality has been plagued by several methodological shortcomings (Martens, 1975, 1981; Morgan, 1980a; Silva, 1984). First, and possibly foremost, personality research in sport psychology has tended to be atheoretical as opposed to theoretical. That is, researchers often lack direction and simply assess a variety of traits and attempt to correlate these traits with athletic performance. These investigations are problematic because significant relationships found in this "hunting" method of research are often not replicated. A more appropriate line of research would be to predict a relationship prior to testing and allow the data to support or refute the prediction (i.e., researchers should develop and test theory-based and/or research-based hypotheses).

Other problems found in sport personality research include poorly defined variables (i.e., poor operational definitions), inadequate data sampling techniques, a failure to incorporate the importance of the environment into the research, the use of inappropriate statistical tests for data analysis, the inappropriate use of certain personality inventories (this will be discussed in greater detail below), and, finally, the assumption that correlation equals causation. The unwarranted conclusion that correlation equals causation warrants special mention. Research finding a positive relationship between a personality trait and athletic performance does not justify the conclusion that the trait led to athletic success. When presented with a positive relationship between a personality trait and athletic performance, the researcher is limited to the conclusion that such a relationship exists. Additional research of a longitudinal and/or experimental nature is needed to justify statements of causation.

PERSONALITY TRAITS AND SPORT PSYCHOLOGY

In this section, we will examine research designed to investigate the personality traits of athletes. We will begin by reviewing the most commonly used measurement tools in personality research. We will then compare the personalities of athletes and nonathletes and examine the extent to which athletic participation can alter an athlete's personality. We will also compare the personalities of athletes participating in different sports and compare elite and less skilled athletes. This section will conclude with an examination of the relationship between personality and sport injuries.

Measuring Personality

A number of techniques have been developed to measure various aspects of an individual's personality. These tests are generally divided into two groups: objective personality tests and projective personality tests. As discussed in Chapter 2, objective tests present the test-taker with several options. For example, true-false and multiple choice tests are considered objective because the taker is presented with several choices when answering the items. Several objective personality inventories have been employed in sport settings. One such test is the Minnesota Multiphasic Personality Inventory (MMPI, Hathaway & McKinley, 1943). The MMPI contains more than 500 items measuring several different aspects of one's personality including depression, masculinity-femininity, paranoia, and hysteria. The Cattell 16 Personality Factor Questionnaire (16PF, Cattell, Erber, & Tatsuoka, 1970) has also been used in sport research. This 187-item instrument assesses 16 different personality trait dichotomies such as humble-assertive, trusting-suspicious, and relaxed-tense.

Another test used extensively in sport personality research is the Profile of Mood States (POMS, McNair, Lorr, & Droppleman, 1971; see also Albrecht & Ewing, 1989; LeUnes, Hayward, & Daiss, 1988). As its name implies, the POMS is more a measure of mood and affect than a measure of personality per se. However, because of its popularity among sport psychologists interested in athlete personality, its description here is warranted. The POMS contains 65 Likert-scale items and measures six different mood states: tension, depression, anger, vigor, fatigue, and confusion. Further, a total mood disturbance score can be computed by summing the tension, depression, anger, fatigue, and confusion scores and then subtracting the vigor score. For applied situations with less time to administer the entire scale, Grove and Prapavessis (1992) developed a shorter version of the POMS containing only 40 items.

The second type of personality test is similar to a subjective test. Called ***projective personality tests,*** these instruments are unstructured, opened-ended tests (i.e., no response options are given) in which the inner feelings and motives of the subject are revealed (Anastasi, 1988). While other projective tests have been developed, the most commonly used techniques are the Thematic Apperception Test (TAT) and the Rorschach Inkblot Test. The TAT (Murray, 1971) presents the test-taker with a series of ambiguous pictures from which the taker is asked to develop a story (i.e., describe what is happening, what the characters are thinking). When taking the Rorschach Inkblot Test (Rorschach, 1921/1942), individuals are shown a series of inkblot cards and asked to describe what they see. When administering the TAT and Rorschach tests, psychologists are searching for both unusual responses and the emergence of consistent symbols and themes.

Although each of the aforementioned tests has been used in sport settings, researchers are advised to proceed cautiously when using these instruments. As mentioned by several authors, (e.g., Kroll, 1976; LeUnes & Nation, 1989), because these instruments were designed for use in clinical settings, the reliability and validity of these instruments may be less than optimal when used with nonclinical populations. As a result, researchers should rethink their decision to incorporate these tests into their work.

Instead, it may be more appropriate to design and validate a sport-specific measure of personality. This was the goal of Tutko and his associates (Hammer & Tutko, 1974; Tutko, Lyon, & Ogilvie, 1971) when they constructed the Athletic Motivation Inventory (AMI). The AMI consists of 190 items measuring several personality traits relevant to sport settings including aggressiveness, leadership, and mental toughness. The traits are combined to form three categories: desire to succeed in athletics, ability to withstand the stress of competition, and dedication to the coach. Unfortunately, although early work with the AMI was encouraging and the test was quite popular among sport psychologists, the AMI has also suffered in terms of its psychometric qualities. In fact, several authors have challenged the instrument's reliability and validity (Corbin, 1977; Martens, 1975; Rushall, 1973; Vealey, 1992). As a result, the use of this test has decreased substantially.

Comparing the Personalities of Athletes and Nonathletes

A common research theme in sport personality concerns the extent to which athletes and nonathletes differ in their personality profiles. Morgan (1980b) conducted a review of the research comparing athletes and nonathletes and concluded that athletes were more stable and extroverted, while Cooper's (1969) review indicated that athletes were more competitive, dominant, self-confident, and achievement-oriented (see also Butt & Cox, 1992). Athletes have also been found to be more psychologically well-adjusted (Cooper, 1969; LeUnes & Nation, 1982; Snyder & Kivlin, 1975) and often report higher levels of self-esteem than nonathletes (Kamal et al., 1995; Mahoney, 1989; Marsh, Perry, Horsely, & Roche, 1995; Trujillo, 1983). Research has also indicated that, compared with nonathletes, athletes often hold slightly more conservative political views (Rehberg & Schafer, 1968), are more authoritarian (LeUnes & Nation, 1982), and demonstrate higher levels of persistence (Lufi & Tenenbaum, 1991).

Although differences between athletes and nonathletes such as these have been documented, Vealey (1992) notes that a clear pattern of differences has yet to emerge. Again, this is due at least in part to the methodological shortcomings of sport personality research. Much of the work focusing on differences between athletes and nonathletes has been atheoretical, resulting in what Vealey (1992) referred to as "insignificant significant findings" (p. 44). In fact, she summarizes that, "There are no consistent research findings showing that athletes possess a general personality type distinct from the personality of nonathletes" (p. 50). Thus, it seems we are left to conclude that, although athletes may be more likely than nonathletes to possess certain personality characteristics, a composite personality pattern indicative of athletes has yet to be identified. In fact, this was the conclusion of one of the most methodologically sound studies on personality differences between athletes and nonathletes. In this study, Schurr, Ashley, and Joy (1977) tested more than 1,500 subjects. Participants were grouped as athletes or nonathletes and asked to complete the Cattell 16PF. Several differences between sport participants and nonparticipants were found. However, because of the lack of consistency in the differences, Schurr et al. concluded that their research supported "the contention that there is no single personality profile which distinguishes Athletes from Non-Athletes" (p. 63).

The Influence of Athletic Participation on Personality Development

Because athletes and nonathletes differ in certain personality traits (even if the differences are inconsistent), the reader may wonder whether or not athletic involvement influences or alters an athlete's personality. That is, if the personalities of athletes and nonathletes differ even on a few traits, is it because the athletes and nonathletes were different to begin with or did the athletic participation change the athletes' personalities in some way?

Cratty (1989) presents three possibilities concerning the apparent change in personality due to athletic participation. First, he discusses the ***attrition model*** (called athletic Darwinism by Cox, 1990). Proponents of this approach argue that children not possessing the traits indicative of athletic success eventually drop out of sport. Because it appears as though there are differences between those in and out of athletics, individuals assume that the participation itself influenced the athletes when in reality no personality change took place. For example, let us assume that two youngsters, Cindy and Chris, enroll in a martial arts course. Because she tends to be quite low in self-confidence, Cindy drops out of the course after 4 weeks. Chris, however, possesses a high level of self-assurance and completes the program. Subsequently, individuals who meet these two children may erroneously assume that the martial arts program increased Chris' self-confidence because she is high in this trait and had participated in the program, while Cindy is low in this trait and had not.

A second possibility concerning athletic participation and personality change is the ***selection model***. Supporters of this model argue that only those with certain characteristics choose to participate in athletics. Because it appears as though there are differences between those participating and not participating in sports, individuals again incorrectly infer that participation has altered the athletes' personalities. In the example described above, it is possible that Cindy would never have enrolled in the martial arts class due to her low level of self-confidence. Persons may assume that the martial arts program increased Chris' self-confidence because she possesses this characteristic while Cindy does not.

A final possibility is termed the ***change model***. This perspective is championed by persons believing that sport participation changes the personalities of participants in some meaningful way. As noted by Cratty (1989), support for this model must come from longitudinal research in which the personality traits of participants are monitored over a long period. Should the traits of the participants change relative to a control group comprised of nonathletes, then one may safely conclude that the participation changed the participants' personalities.

So, which of the three models is correct? Actually, research has indicated that all three have merit. As for the attrition and selection models, research has found that persons possessing certain traits are more likely to begin and maintain participation in athletics (e.g., Dubois, 1986; Stevenson, 1975). For example, as noted in the previous chapter, one's genetic predisposition appears to be a major reason behind an individual's decision to begin participating in sport. Other research supporting the change model has found that sport participation can influence one's personality, although the changes in personality can be negative (e.g., increased aggressiveness) as well as positive (Coakley, 1993; Dubois, 1986; Estrada, Gelfand, & Hartmann, 1988; Seidel & Reppucci, 1993; Stevenson, 1975; Trulson, 1986; Vealey, 1992; Werner & Gottheil, 1966).

Comparing the Personalities of Athletes Participating in Different Sports

Cox et al. (1993) are correct in stating that "the question of whether a relationship exists between personality and the types of sports and activities individuals select has not yet been adequately addressed" (p. 6). While certain differences have been found (Cox et al., 1993; Geron, Furst, & Rotstein, 1986; Sadalla, Linder, & Jenkins, 1988; Singer, 1969), Cratty (1989) notes that only a few consistencies have emerged, consistencies that are far from surprising. First, it appears that participants in individual sports, as compared with athletes in team sports, tend to be less anxious and emotional and more introverted. Second, participants in aggressive sports tend to be more aggressive than athletes in nonaggressive sports. However, because research has contradicted these two conclusions (e.g., Colley, Roberts, & Chipps, 1985), or found no differences between different sports (Andre & Holland, 1995; Lakie, 1962; Wann & Lingle, 1994), it is apparent that more work must be done before we can arrive at an understanding of the differences between participants in various sports.

Comparing the Personalities of Athletes of Different Skill Levels

Research comparing the personalities of highly successful and less than successful athletes is often designed to allow sport psychologists to predict athletic success. However, predicting athletic success based on personality testing has proven to be a difficult task. In fact, some individuals have argued that personality testing for athletic success is useless, while others have espoused the belief that such testing is quite beneficial. This argument was best articulated by William Morgan (1980a) in his presentation of the credulous-skeptical argument. Morgan noted that sport psychologists had formed two camps regarding the ability of personality traits to predict athletic success. Individuals belonging to the ***credulous*** group (e.g., Ogilvie & Tutko, 1966) believed that personality profiles could be useful in predicting athletic success while those in the ***skeptical*** camp (e.g., Kroll, 1976; Martens, 1975) felt that personality data had little or no value in predicting performance. Morgan's (1980a) position was that neither viewpoint was correct. Rather, he believed that athletic success was due in part to personality traits (and other psychological variables), but that the situation was important as well. Morgan's position that both personality variables and situational forces are important ingredients in athletic success is consistent with the interactional perspective described earlier.

While some research has supported the skeptical argument and failed to find a relationship between personality and success (e.g., Craighead, Privette, Vallianos, & Byrkit, 1986; Davis & Mogk, 1994; Schurr et al., 1977), other work has supported the credulous argument. For example, research has indicated that the traits of self-confidence (Gould, Weiss, & Weinberg, 1981; Highlen & Bennett, 1980, 1983; Mahoney & Avener, 1977; Meyers, Cooke, Cullen, & Liles, 1979; Vanden Auweele et al., 1993), personality hardiness (Maddi & Hess, 1992), competitiveness (Gill & Deeter, 1988; Gill et al., 1988), sport knowledge (French & Thomas, 1987; Williams & Davids, 1995), emotional stability (Ogilvie, 1976), lower levels of and the ability to cope with anxiety (Highlen & Bennett, 1983; Vanden Auweele et al., 1993), tough mindedness (i.e., being independent, assertive, and self-assured, see Wittig & Schurr, 1994), and having more as well as more successful sport-related dreams (Mahoney & Avener, 1977; Meyers et al., 1979) are all related to athletic success. In addition, successful athletes are more likely to view their sport anxiety as beneficial to performance (Jones & Swain, 1995) and are better able to imagine successfully performing their sport (Barr & Hall, 1992). Further, several authors have argued that extroversion is related to performance (e.g., Kane, 1980; Ogilvie, 1976), although an extensive review of the literature led Vanden Auweele et al. (1993) to conclude that there are no differences between top level and lesser skilled athletes on this trait.

One of the most successful lines of research examining athletes of different skill levels involves the athletes' mood profiles. Using the POMS, Morgan and his colleagues have consistently found differences in the mood profiles of successful and unsuccessful athletes (LeUnes & Nation, 1982; Morgan, 1979, 1980a, 1985; Morgan & Johnson, 1977, 1978; Morgan, O'Connor, Ellickson, & Bradley, 1988; Morgan, O'Connor, Sparling, & Pate, 1987; Morgan & Pollock, 1977). Recall that the POMS measures six mood states: tension, depression, anger, vigor, fatigue, and confusion. As depicted in Figure 4.1, Morgan has found that successful athletes often report a more positive mood profile than unsuccessful athletes by scoring lower on tension, depression, anger, fatigue, and confusion, but higher in vigor. Morgan refers to this mood pattern as the ***iceberg profile***.

However, a few studies have failed to support the notion of an iceberg profile (e.g., Craighead et al., 1986; Daiss, LeUnes, & Nation, 1986; Miller & Miller, 1985), and some authors have recently challenged the notion that successful athletes possess an exceptionally positive mood profile (e.g., Renger, 1993; Terry, 1995). For example, consider the work of Rowley, Landers, Kyllo, and Etnier (1995). These researchers conducted a meta-analysis on 33 studies using the POMS to compare successful and unsuccessful athletes (a meta-analysis is a research technique examining the combined effects of a number of separate studies). They found that, although successful athletes did possess a significantly more positive mood profile than unsuccessful athletes (i.e., they found support for Morgan's iceberg profile), the difference between the groups was very small. In fact, the authors found that mood accounted for less than 1% of the athletes' performances.

So, what conclusions can we draw regarding the mood profiles of successful

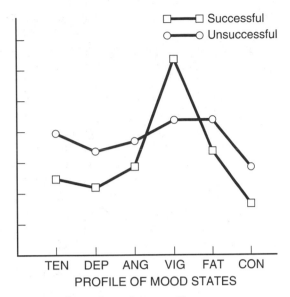

FIGURE 4.1 The iceberg profile.

and unsuccessful athletes? First, it appears that the iceberg profile is a real and statistically significant phenomenon highlighting the positive mood profiles of successful athletes. Second, the profile differences between the groups may not be as great as once believed. That is, although successful athletes tend to possess a more positive mood profile than unsuccessful athletes, the differences between the groups are quite small. Third, situational factors such as sport type and event duration may influence the magnitude of the relationship between mood profiles and athletic performance (Terry, 1995). As for sport type, in some sports higher anger and tension scores can actually facilitate performance, a mood pattern that lies in opposition to the iceberg profile. As for the duration of a sporting event, shorter duration events may result in greater differences because there is less opportunity for individual changes in mood during the competition. That is, the precompetition mood profile of athletes competing in long duration events will be less predictive of success because the athletes' moods will most likely fluctuate during the competition. Conversely, the precompetition mood profiles of athletes participating in short duration events will be better predictors of performance because these shorter events allow for less fluctuation in mood.

The Relationship between Personality and Sport Injury Susceptibility

Sport injuries are a major concern for athletes, coaches, athletic directors, and sport psychologists. The prevalence of major and minor sport injuries, including those at the scholastic and collegiate levels, is alarming. In fact, Kraus and Conroy (1984) stated that as many as 5 million sport injuries occur each year in the United States alone. Sport psychologists have become involved with sport injuries in two ways. First, as will be discussed here, sport psychologists have attempted to identify traits associated with susceptibility to injury, thereby allowing for the prediction of such injuries. Second, educational and clinical sport psychologists have become active in the psychological rehabilitation of injured athletes, a topic that will be examined in Chapter 10.

Research has identified several personality variables correlated with the occurrence of athletic injuries. The personality traits of vigor (an inverse relationship, see Meyers, LeUnes, Elledge, Tolson, & Sterling, 1992), tender-mindedness (Jackson et al., 1978), and being reserved (Jackson et al., 1978) have each been found to correlate with the occurrence of injuries. However, the strongest relationship with injury prevalence appears to involve stress, especially in contact sports (Andersen & Williams, 1988; Hanson, McCullagh, & Tonymon, 1992; Nideffer, 1989; Rotella & Heyman, 1993; Williams & Roepke, 1993). Athletes experiencing high levels of stress are especially likely to report injuries. We will examine the relationship between stress and athletic injuries in Chapter 10.

With the exception of the connection between anxiety and injury, the relationships reported above are far from unequivocal in that some researchers have failed to replicate past research (Pargman, 1993). For example, Wittig and Schurr (1994) failed to find a relationship between tough-mindedness and injury occurrence (in fact, they found that the tough-minded players tended to have more injuries, a finding in direct opposition to past work). Further, Lamb (1986) found no correlation between self-concept and injury proneness. Such inconsistencies led Nideffer (1989) to argue that more research is needed before conclusions can be drawn concerning the relationship between personality and injury.

RESEARCH INVESTIGATING SPECIFIC SPORT POPULATIONS

In this section, we will examine several sport populations: female athletes, black athletes, athletes participating in high risk sports, and wilderness users. The discussion of these populations will include the personality traits and athletic behaviors common to the members of these groups. Further, for female and black athletes we will review how stereotyping and discrimination impact their sport experiences.

Female Athletes

> I hear they're even letting w-o-m-e-n in their sport programs now. That's your Women's Liberation, boy—bunch of goddamn lesbians . . . You can bet your ass that if you have women around . . . you aren't going to be worth a damn . . . the best way to treat a woman . . . is to knock her up and hide her shoes (Vare, 1974, p. 36).

This quote of Woody Hayes (a successful former college football coach), presented by LeUnes and Nation (1989), shows the problem facing female athletes. Female athletes, coaches, fans, and sport reporters all tend to be treated as second-class citizens. For example, female athletes (Cohen, 1993a) and coaches (Williams & Parkhouse, 1988) are perceived in a stereotypical manner by males and females and athletes and nonathletes. Female sport fans are assumed to be less knowledgeable than their male counterparts. For example, when a female caller correctly answered a sport quiz question on a mid-1990s radio show, the male announcer stated "How did you know that—did you ask a guy?" Female sport reporters are also not immune to the influences of stereotyping. In a recent investigation by Ordman and Zillmann (1994), subjects were asked to read a sport commentary written by either a male or female reporter. Regardless of whether the story covered a men's or women's sport or was presented as a print or radio transcript, both male and female subjects believed that the female reporter was less competent, less informed about sport generally, and less informed about the specific sport in question than the male reporter.

These inequities and obstacles are in place today despite the passage of Title IX in 1972. *Title IX* is a law prohibiting sexual discrimination in institutions receiving federal funds. This law, which has its greatest impact on high school and college athletics, directs schools to (1) provide scholarships equal to participation; (2) have equivalent travel, equipment, and medical benefits; and (3) provide equal recruitment and publicity money. Basically, Title IX requires that schools provide equal opportunity to women athletes.

One difficulty regarding Title IX involves accurately and adequately defining terms such as equity and equality (Coakley, 1982; Staurowsky, 1995). For example, some people argue that allocations should be based on student enrollment figures. That is, if 55% of the student body is female, then 55% of athletic money should go to female athletics. Others feel that allocations should be based on the number of female and male varsity athletes competing at the school. Still others believe that equity is best achieved by equating the number of sports available for each gender (e.g., if there are five male sports then there should also be five female sports). Yet another line of reasoning suggests that the sport of football should not be included in calculations of equity because the monetary and participation requirements for this sport are so much larger than other sports (Lederman, 1993). Indeed, the issue of funding for football will remain a heated topic in the coming years as athletic directors attempt to balance their ever-tightening budgets while establishing or maintaining a fair and equitable climate (Shaw, 1995). In 1993, a National Collegiate Athletic Association (NCAA) gender-equity panel came to the ambiguous and confusing conclusion that a sport program should be considered equitable if the male and female programs would be willing to accept the other program as its own (Lederman, 1993). Thus, the NCAA was still struggling to define equity more than 20 years after the adoption of Title IX!

One positive result of the passage of Title IX has been the increase in participation of female athletes, both at the high school and collegiate levels (Oglesby, 1989). Snyder (1993) states that, prior to the passage of the law, there were slightly more than 300,000 female athletes participating in high school and college sports. Today there are approximately 2 million female participants. Greendorfer (1993) notes that in the early 1970s only 15% of intercollegiate athletes were female, but today the percentage is closer to 33%. Herwig (1993) found that, although only 6% of NCAA Division I schools offered female soccer in 1981, 35% offered the sport in 1993. In addition, collegiate conferences such as the Big Ten (Blum, 1992), and institutions such as Washington State University (Livengood, 1992) have taken innovative steps toward gender equity. At an individual level, women have broken the gender barrier in a number of sports. For example, in 1993, Dallas Malloy and Heather Poyner competed in the first sanctioned female boxing match in the United States. One year later, Ila Borders of Southern California College became the first women to pitch on a men's college baseball team.

On a less positive note, although participation rates have increased dramatically since the adoption of Title IX, career opportunities for female professional athletes are still quite limited (Snyder, 1993). In addition, women coaches have yet to receive equal salaries (Knoppers, Meyer, Ewing, & Forrest, 1989). In fact, a 1993–1994 survey conducted by the Women's Basketball Coaches Association (Becker, 1994; Herwig, 1994) found that the average base salary of female coaches ($44,961) was only 59% of that of male coaches ($76,566). Data gathered from other sources also indicate that male athletes get a much larger share of the economic pie than do their female counterparts. Citing an NCAA report on gender equity, Lederman (1992a) states that male athletes receive 70% of athletic scholarship money, 77% of the operating money, and 83% of the recruiting money. Researchers at *The Chronicle of Higher Education* conducted their own study and found similar inequities (Lederman, 1992b). Approximately 67% of the nearly 300 institutions responded to the *Chronicle's* survey, with those not responding citing the sensitivity of the data as the reason behind their failure to participate. The survey revealed that the vast majority of the colleges had a larger female than male enrollment, yet most of the schools had more than twice as many male athletes as female athletes.

There has actually been a decrease in the number of female coaches and administrators since the inception of Title IX (Lopiano, 1993; Oglesby, 1989; Pastore, 1994). Acosta and Carpenter (1992, cited in Snyder, 1993) state that, in 1972, 90% of female athletic programs were run by women but that the percentage had fallen to just 16% in 1990. Similar declines in coaching positions have been found by Birrell (1987) and Hart, Hasbrook, and Mathes (1986). Lydon (1993) reports that the number of females in decision-making positions in academic settings is quite low, resulting in the inequitable hiring practices. The findings of a project conducted by Stangl and Kane (1991) appear to support Lydon's argument. These authors examined the athletic hiring practices of several hundred Ohio high schools. Consistent with past research, fewer sports were offered to female athletes in the early years of Title IX (3.84 sports per school) than in the late 1980s (5.71). Also consistent with past work, the percentage of female sports coached by women at these schools declined over the same time (from 92.7% in 1974–1975 to 33.2% in 1988–1989). Female athletic directors were more likely to hire women head coaches (63.4%) than were male athletic directors (56.2%). However, as depicted in Figure 4.2, an interesting pattern involving the time frame and hiring practices emerged. During the early stages of Title IX, the overwhelming majority of coaches hired by both male and female athletic directors were women. However, over time, the tendency for male athletic directors to hire male coaches increased. That is, while male and female athletic directors differed very little in their hiring practices in the mid-1970s, the differential hiring practices became more and more pronounced as time passed.

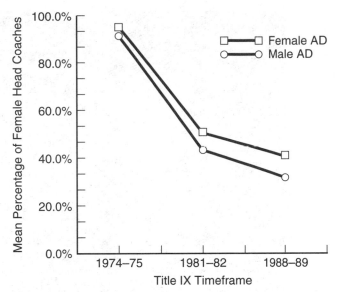

FIGURE 4.2 Percentages of male and female head coaches employed by female and male athletic directors. (Note: From "Structural Variables That Offer Explanatory Power for the Underrepresentation of Women Coaches since Title IX: The Case of Homologous Reproduction," by J. M. Stangl & M. J. Kane. *Sociology of Sport,* 8: 47–60. Copyright 1991 by Human Kinetics Publishers. Reprinted by permission.)

Psychological Phenomena Relevant to Female Athletes. In this section, we will examine psychological research focusing on female participants. Three psychological phenomena will be examined: fear of success, psychological androgyny, and the personality traits of female athletes. It should be noted that these three topics are by no means an exhaustive list of the psychological factors impacting female athletes. In fact, gender differences in a number of sport-relevant behaviors will be examined in future chapters in this text. However, instead of presenting these topics here and then reiterating them in a later chapter, the current discussion has been limited to those topics not covered elsewhere in this text.

FEAR OF SUCCESS. In the early 1970s, Horner (1972) developed a theory concerning the fear of success. ***Fear of success*** occurs when an individual fears or avoids success in a given situation because the success would be inconsistent with his or her sex role. Because our society generally assigns success to the male role, fear of success was expected to be more common among women than men. Success may cause women to feel that they will be rejected socially. Before discussing fear of success further, it may be helpful to define what is meant by a role. ***Roles*** are social positions governed by many norms. Thus, ***sex roles*** (or gender roles) are social expectations based on gender.

Although some females fear success because success violates their gender role expectations, female athletes are less likely to display this trait because they view success as consistent with their athletic role. (Photographer: Jeremiah Brooks. Source: Gamma-Liaison, Inc.)

Although Horner's (1972) theory was supported by research with general populations, investigations involving female athletes found that these persons tend not to exhibit a fear of success (Cox et al., 1993; McElroy & Willis, 1979). McElroy and Willis concluded that the lack of fear of success among female athletes probably indicates that sport is an area in which female success is accepted. In addition, female athletes may not fear success because they have acquired new sex roles through athletic participation, that is, sex roles stressing achievement and success. However, while it appears that female athletes do not fear success, they may shy away from activities that they perceive as inappropriate to their sex role (Cox et al., 1993). That is, although female athletes may feel comfortable playing sports such as tennis and volleyball (sex role consistent sports), they may feel threatened by sports such as boxing and football that violate their sex role stereotypes (Peplau, 1976).

PSYCHOLOGICAL ANDROGYNY.   Another psychological principle that has relevance for female athletes is psychological androgyny. **Psychological androgyny** is a personality trait in which an individual possesses nearly equal levels of both masculine and feminine qualities. Research on psychological androgyny was stimulated by the development of the Bem Sex Role Inventory (BSRI, Bem, 1974). The BSRI contains 60 Likert-scale items, 20 each measuring feminine, masculine, and neutral items. Based on their responses to these items, subjects are classified as masculine, feminine, androgynous, or undifferentiated. Another measure of androgyny, the Personal Attributes Questionnaire (PAQ, Spence, Helmreich, & Stapp, 1975), is also quite popular. The 15-item PAQ is also used to classify individuals as masculine, feminine, androgynous, or undifferentiated.

Although some authors have challenged the quality of these instruments (Locksley & Colten, 1979; Pedhazur & Tetenbaum, 1979), many sport psychology studies have employed these measures. For example, Swain and Jones (1991) used the BSRI to examine the relationship between masculine/feminine sex role orientation and anxiety among male and female track and field athletes. Subjects were asked to complete the BSRI and a trait anxiety inventory prior to a competition. The authors found that masculine males reported lower levels of trait anxiety than the other three groups (i.e., feminine males, masculine females, and feminine females).

LeUnes and Nation (1989) examined a wide body of research on the sex role orientations of athletes and came to several conclusions. First, it is apparent that female athletes tend not to express a feminine sex role orientation. Most of the studies reviewed by LeUnes and Nation reported that fewer than 20% of female athletes express a feminine orientation. The second conclusion drawn by LeUnes and Nation was that masculine sex role orientations are quite common among female athletes. Finally, the authors concluded that the sex role orientation of female athletes was more often masculine or androgynous than it was feminine or undifferentiated. Gill's (1992) review of the sex role orientation literature led her to similar conclusions.

The conclusion that female athletes often possess a masculine sex role orientation parallels research by Martin and Martin (1995) indicating that female athletes are often perceived as masculine. These authors asked introductory psychology students to use the BSRI to rate one of six target persons: ideal male, ideal male athlete, ideal female, ideal female athlete, ideal person, or ideal athlete. In general, the athlete targets were perceived as more masculine than the nonathlete targets. In addition, the female athlete was rated as more masculine than the female nonathlete. However, BSRI ratings for the female athlete and the male athlete did not differ, supporting the notion that individuals believe that female athletes possess a masculine sex role orientation.

PERSONALITY RESEARCH ON FEMALE ATHLETES.   Before reviewing research on the personalities of female athletes, it should be noted that the personality data on this population is limited by two factors. First, as noted previously, research on personality in sport has been plagued by methodological problems. Second, there has been little interest in the personality testing of female athletes. Instead, most work has examined male participants (Cox, 1990; Cratty, 1989; Wann & Hamlet, 1995; Wittig & Schurr, 1994).

Similar to the literature on male athletes, personality research that has been conducted on female athletes suggests that they may possess traits distinguishing them from female nonathletes, although a comprehensive personality profile has yet to be established. Many of the findings indicate that female athletes possess a stable personality profile. For example, compared with nonathlete females, female participants tend to be less angry, confused, depressed, and neurotic (Freedson, Mihevic, Loucks, & Girandola, 1983). Based on her research with female United States Olympians, Balazs (1975) concluded that elite female athletes can best be described as high in the need for achievement and autonomy. In addition, Williams (1980) notes that female athletes often display assertiveness, aggression, and dominance. Williams concluded that female athletes tend to exhibit traits that are more similar to male athletes and nonathletes than to female nonathletes. Although differences such as those listed above do exist, it must be reiterated that the personality picture of female athletes remains incomplete because of the lack of research on this population. It is hoped that, as the acceptance of female athletics grows, so too will our understanding of their personalities.

The Differential Media Coverage of Female Athletics.   In this section, we will examine the differential media coverage of female sports. Researchers have documented the unequal and inequitable coverage of women's athletics in several media sources including newspapers, magazines, television, and even in sport psychology and sport sociology journals. This lack of coverage is unfortunate because it may lead women to believe that sport should remain a male-dominated activity and that their participation is not wanted (Blinde, Greendorfer, & Sankner, 1991; Wann & Hamlet, 1995). Further, because research has found that media coverage of female sports can influence young female athletes' identification with professional athletes (Marovelli & Crawford, 1987), a lack of coverage is problematic because it decreases the young players' opportunities to identify with female professionals.

NEWSPAPER COVERAGE.   Several investigations have documented the lack of newspaper coverage of women's athletics. For example, Theberge (1991) conducted an analysis of four Canadian daily newspapers over a 6-month period and found that only 8.9% of the sports articles were devoted solely to female subjects. In a similar analysis of U.S. newspapers, Sage and Furst (1994) found that female coverage ranged from a high of 22.4% to a low of 3.6%.

One of the more surprising examples of the inequitable newspaper coverage of female athletes was uncovered by Shifflett and Revelle (1994a; see also Malec, 1994; Shifflett & Revelle, 1994b). These authors examined the coverage of female sports in the *NCAA News,* a publication given as a service to members of the NCAA. Because this paper covers collegiate athletics and because colleges are expected to offer similar numbers of male and female sports, Shifflett and Revelle thought that the gender biases found in other papers might not be evident. Instead, their results revealed several inequities. They found that male athletes received over twice the written coverage and almost twice the pictorial coverage of female athletes. Women's sports received an exceptionally low level of coverage during the fall season.

MAGAZINE COVERAGE.   Limited and biased coverage of women's sports has been noted in sport magazines as well. Lumpkin and Williams (1991) examined the feature articles published in *Sports Illustrated* between 1954 and 1987, noting the gender of the authors and subjects. They found that 91.8% of the articles were authored by males, leaving only 8.2% for female writers. Further, 90.8% of the articles covered male athletes, while only 9.2% focused on female athletes. An examination of articles featuring ten same-sport activities (i.e., sports such as basketball, volleyball, and diving that have both male and female participants) revealed that the articles covering male athletes were longer (65.6 column inches) than articles covering female athletes (54.8 inches). Salwen and Wood (1994) examined the cover photographs of *Sports Illustrated*. Consistent with Lumpkin and William's (1991) work on *Sports Illustrated* articles, Salwen and Wood found that less than 7% of the cover photographs depicted female athletes.

Leath and Lumpkin (1992) examined the cover photographs of the magazine *Women's Sports and Fitness* between the years 1975 and 1989. They found that the covers originally portrayed athletes participating in competitive sports but that the emphasis had shifted dramatically to the portrayal of personal fitness and fun. Leath and Lumpkin argue that the change was most likely fueled by the editors' beliefs that such a change increased the marketability of the magazine. The authors concluded that, "with this change, the aspirations of girls and women may be thwarted as they miss the message that being a competitive athlete and female are compatible" (p. 125).

Rintala and Birrell (1984) also studied the photographs appearing in a sport magazine. These authors analyzed the photos appearing in *Young Athlete* between 1975 and 1982. The gender content of more than 3,000 photographs was reviewed. As depicted in Table 4.1, male athletes received a substantially larger amount of coverage. In a supplemental analysis conducted on the photographs, Rintala and Birrell found that only 17% of the photographs of coaches and leaders depicted females. Thus, the magazine was not only biased in terms of the number of photographs of females but also in the content of the photos.

TELEVISION COVERAGE.   Compared with their male counterparts, female athletes have received relatively little television coverage. Although slightly more than half of the U.S. population is female, only 5% of television sport programing is dedicated to female sports (Duncan, Messner, Williams, & Jensen, 1990). Such a lack of coverage intensifies the perception that sport is a male domain.

Higgs and Weiller (1994) conducted an extensive examination of the coverage

TABLE 4.1   Percentage of Photographs of Females and Males, by Prominence of Photograph, in *Young Athlete,* 1975–1982

Prominence of Photograph	*Females*	*Males*	*Both*	*N*
	Percentage by Sex*			
Cover—primary figure	19	72	9	43
Cover—secondary figure	22	78	0	9
Centerfold	13	84	3	38
Full-page color	24	71	5	99
Other photographs	31	63	6	3014

*Excluding those whose sex could not be determined from the photographs.

(Note: From "Fair Treatment for the Active Female: A Content Analysis of Young Athlete Magazine, by J. Rintala & S. Birrell. *Sociology of Sport,* 8: 47–60. Copyright 1991 by Human Kinetics Publishers. Reprinted by permission.)

of the 1992 Summer Olympics. Their analysis reviewed more than 40 hours of televised coverage of same-sport activities. They found that 56% of the coverage was devoted to male athletes, while 44% of the time was devoted to female athletes. Women athletes received an especially poor amount of coverage for team sports. For example, male athletes received 74% of the basketball coverage and 75% of the volleyball air time. In addition to the time differences, Higgs and Weiller also found that men's games had more slow motion replays (16/game versus 9/game) and more verbal and on screen statistics (55/game versus 32/game).

SEXIST COVERAGE.   Perhaps the greatest media obstacle facing female athletes is that the media attention they do receive is often presented in a sexist fashion and often contains homophobic overtones (Burroughs, Ashburn, & Seebohm, 1995). Sport magazine pictures of female athletes are often sexually suggestive (Duncan, 1990), so much so that Cohen (1993b) coined the phrase "The Magazine Industry: Center Court or Centerfold?" (p. 177). The suggestive advertising poses of several athletes have been controversial as well (Hogshead, 1992; Lois, 1992; Nelson, 1992).

Similar to magazine coverage, the portrayal of female athletes on television has also been plagued by sexist overtones. Duncan and Hasbrook (1988) found that the coverage of women's basketball, surfing, and marathon running emphasized the athletes' appearances rather than their performances. Blinde and her colleagues (1991) examined the televised reporting of 16 college basketball games and found that male players were used as a comparison point for female players, female contests were consistently qualified as "women's basketball," and sexist language was quite common. As for less popular sports, the lack of clothing worn by professional beach volleyball players (a sport that has recently begun to receive television coverage) has also been questioned (Lister, 1994a).

Finally, although not technically a form of the media, the portrayal of female athletes on the covers of collegiate media guides can also be quite sexist and provocative (Cohen, 1993b). In fact, one university dressed its female players in Playboy Bunny attire, while another had its female basketball team pose in biker outfits (Lister, 1994b).

SPORT PSYCHOLOGY AND SPORT SOCIOLOGY RESEARCH.   I would like to conclude this section by noting that female athletes have received relatively little attention from sport psychologists and sport sociologists as well, a surprising finding in that female sport psychologists have had a major impact on the development of the field (Gill, 1995). A colleague and I recently conducted a study examining the author and subject gender of research articles published in eight sport psychology and sport sociology journals from 1987 to 1991 (Wann & Hamlet, 1995). A total of 593 articles authored by 1085 persons was reviewed. With regard to author gender, three analyses were conducted: the percentage of female total authors, first authors, and sole authors. The results showed that only 30% of all authors, 28% of first authors, and 22% of the sole authors were female. However, the total author and first author percentages increased significantly over the 5-year period, *indicating a brighter future for female sport researchers.* Table 4.2 depicts the yearly percentages. The lack of female authorship does not necessarily indicate a gender bias on the part of the

TABLE 4.2   Authorship Percentages by Year for Selected Sport Journals

Variable	*1987*	*1988*	*1989*	*1990*	*1991*
Total Authors					
Female	22.3	28.2	29.4	32.1	38.1
Male	77.7	71.8	70.6	67.9	61.9
First Author					
Female	22.0	26.1	26.5	29.6	34.5
Male	78.0	73.9	73.5	70.4	65.5
Sole Author					
Female	20.0	23.1	23.7	21.2	20.3
Male	80.0	76.9	76.3	78.8	79.7

(Adapted from: Wann, D. L. & Hamlet, M. A. [1995]. "Author and Subject Gender in Sports Research." *International Journal of Sport Psychology*, 26: 225–232.)

journal editors. Rather, it probably represents the fact that there are more male sport researchers than female researchers (Wann & Hamlet, 1995).

We believed that the relatively low percentages of female authors may have resulted in fewer studies examining female athletes. Indeed, the data supported our premise. Only 5% of the articles examined female subjects exclusively, while 12% of the studies were comprised entirely of male subjects (most studies included both genders, did not disclose the subjects' gender, or did not include human subjects). However, the data also mirrored the previously reviewed work of Stangl and Kane (1991) concerning the hiring practices of male and female athletic directors. Recall that Stangl and Kane found that female athletic directors were more likely to hire women head coaches than were male athletic directors. Similarly, we found that female first authors were more likely to test female subjects than were male first authors.

Black Athletes

This section focuses on black athletes who, like female participants, face discrimination and stereotyping on a daily basis. Our examination of how these stereotypes impact black athletes will focus on two issues. First, we will examine the overrepresentation of black athletes in U.S. professional sports as well as reasons for the over-representation. We will then examine how stereotypes have resulted in the positioning of players based on race and not talent, a process known as stacking.

The Overrepresentation of Black Athletes.   In the early years of this century, the participation of African-American athletes was limited to two professional sports—boxing and horse racing (Sage, 1993). It was not until the 1940s and 1950s that blacks were allowed in the major sports leagues. While African-Americans represent only about 12% of the population, they reached that percentage of representation in major sports leagues several decades ago (baseball in 1957, basketball in 1958, and football in 1960; Eitzen & Sage, 1986). Currently, they are vastly overrepresented in these sports. Eitzen and Sage, using 1985 data, reported that about 80% of professional basketball, 52% of professional football, and 22% of major league baseball players were black. A more recent study conducted by the Center for the Study of Sport in Society at Northwestern University found similar results (Lapchick & Benedict, 1993). According to this study, as of the early 1990s, 77% of professional basketball, 68% of professional football, and 16% of major league baseball players were black.

Social scientists have attempted to ascertain the causes of the overrepresentation. In general, two possibilities have been offered. Some individuals have adopted the belief that the overrepresentation is due to the genetic superiority of black athletes. Research and theory examining the effects of genetic differences on athletic performance have cast serious doubt on the accuracy of this explanation (Eitzen & Sage, 1986; LeUnes & Nation, 1989). One problem is that the overrepresentation is found in very few sports: those that happen to gain the most media attention (LeUnes & Nation, 1989). For example, there are relatively few elite black participants in golf and swimming. Because of the problems and inaccuracies inherent in the genetic explanation, a more accurate approach is one that examines social and cultural factors accounting for the overrepresentation.

Social/cultural explanations for the dominance of blacks in professional sports have been adopted by many authors (e.g., Eitzen & Sage, 1986; LeUnes & Nation, 1989; Wiggins, 1993). One social/cultural explanation is that African-American children have few role models who are not athletes (Eitzen & Sage, 1986). Children see athletic success as a way to escape poverty. However, the likelihood of the child attaining the status of a professional athlete is extremely small. LeUnes and Nation cite estimates of between 1 in 12,000 and 1 in 25,000 for African-American males and approximately 1 in 250,000 for females. As a result, many athletes have urged black youth to pursue education interests over athletic ones. Social and cultural influences have also been used to explain the lack of participation by black athletes in certain sports. Blacks tend to be underrepresented in skiing, figure skating, and golf because learning and becoming exceptional at these sports require a great deal of money and because minorities are often excluded from country clubs where these activities take place (Eitzen & Sage, 1986).

Stacking.   Another area of concern for sport psychologists and sport sociologists is a phenomenon known as stacking. **Stacking** is defined as the selection of a position for an individual based on his or her race. This practice is one of the most blatant examples of discrimination and prejudice in the sport world. Research has consistently found that blacks are relegated to certain positions in professional sports, especially football and baseball. Stacking in basketball has been less apparent (Edwards, 1973; Leonard, 1987). For example, consider the data presented by Eitzen and Sage (1986). In 1983, only 1% of the quarterbacks and 3% of the centers in the National Football League were black, yet 88% of the running backs and 92% of the cornerbacks were black. In baseball, less than 10% of the pitchers and catchers but more than 45% of the outfielders were black. Similar numbers were evident in the late 1980s and early 1990s (Bivens & Leonard, 1994; Leonard, 1993). The reader may have noticed that the positions assigned to blacks tend to be noncentral. Central positions, such as pitchers and quarterbacks, tend to be given to white players.

Research has indicated that black athletes are often excluded from central positions such as quarterback and catcher. (Photographer: Bryan Yablonsky. Source: Duomo Photography.)

Several suggestions for the causes of stacking in sport have been offered, with each suggestion having research support (Eitzen & Sage, 1986; Johnson & Johnson, 1995; Leonard, 1993; Vogler & Schwartz, 1993). One theory, termed the **modeling hypothesis,** posits that early African-American athletes played certain positions (i.e., outfielder in baseball, cornerback in football) and, therefore, young African-Americans tended to prefer these positions. Subsequently, a large portion of black athletes became skilled at these positions and, as a result, these are the positions they played. A second hypothesis, the **differential opportunity hypothesis,** suggests that black athletes select a certain position based on the number of opportunities to play that position. For example, in baseball there are three outfielders playing at once but only one catcher. Because an athlete is more likely to receive playing time as an outfielder than a catcher, he or she may wish to be an outfielder.

A third possibility is the **stereotype hypothesis.** Proponents of this approach argue that coaches possess stereotypes about white and black players and that these stereotypes suggest to them that members of certain races are better suited for certain positions. For example, coaches may feel that white players are better prepared for the central positions because they are believed to have an intellectual advantage. On the other hand, coaches may believe that black athletes should be placed in positions such as wide receiver and outfielder because they are expected to possess better speed and jumping abilities.

Stereotypes held by coaches and players may have another impact as well. For example, consider the statement made in 1994 by a South African professional golfer: "Blacks like active sports. Golf's too still for them. There are games that they play and games that we play" (O'Brien, 1994, p. 14). Of particular importance in this ridiculous statement is the notion of us (i.e., the ingroup) versus them (the outgroup). Categorization of individuals into ingroups and outgroups can have many effects, including increases in stereotyping. For an interesting perspective on how stereotypes of ingroups and outgroups can influence the evaluation of athletes, please refer to this chapter's "A Closer Look."

A CLOSER LOOK:
EVALUATIONS OF INGROUP AND OUTGROUP
PERFORMANCE: THE IMPORTANCE OF IDENTIFICATION

Recent work by Branscombe, Wann, Noel, and Coleman (1993) suggests that the evaluations of management, coaches, and fans may be biased against minority athletes simply because of the athletes' race. The Branscombe et al. research examined two social psychological phenomena: the outgroup extremity effect and the ingroup extremity effect. The ***outgroup extremity effect*** involves a situation in which individuals' evaluations of outgroup members are more extreme than their evaluations of ingroup persons, both positively and negatively (Linville & Jones, 1980). That is, the highest (i.e., best) evaluation is given to a talented outgroup member while the lowest (i.e., worst) evaluation is given to an untalented outgroup person. The evaluations of ingroup persons are moderate compared with those of the outgroup. For example, if a white individual evaluated whites and blacks, the black individuals would receive both the best and worst evaluations. The outgroup extremity effect can be diagramed as follows:

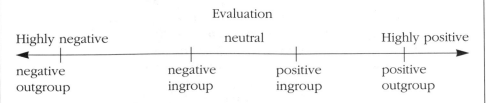

Based in part on the work of Marques, Yzerbyt, and Leyens (1988), Branscombe et al. (1993) proposed an ***ingroup extremity effect.*** Branscombe and her colleagues argued that when individuals are highly identified with an ingroup (e.g., they are highly allegiant, care deeply about the team), they will evaluate members of their own group more extremely than those in the out-group. The most positive and negative evaluations will be given to ingroup members. The ingroup extremity effect can be diagramed as follows:

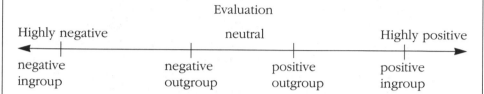

Branscombe et al. (1993) were able to document their hypothesis using sport fans as subjects. Highly identified spectators displayed the ingroup extremity effect rather than the outgroup extremity effect.

How does this research relate to the topic of racism in sport? Simply put, it is likely that the ingroup extremity effect found by Branscombe et al. (1993) is common in sport. Ingroup extremity seems more likely than outgroup extremity because most individuals associated with a sport team are highly identified with the team (a criterion for ingroup extremity). For example, coaches of sport teams tend to be highly involved and invested in the team, two components of identification (Wann & Branscombe, 1993). To best illustrate these processes, a concrete example seems appropriate. Let us assume that a high school baseball team, coached by a white manager, has four players competing for the starting shortstop position. Two of the players are white and two are black. In addition, two of the players, one of each race, are highly qualified for the starting spot. Both have played the same number of years, have similar physical builds, and appear to be equal in talent. The other two players are equally lacking in talent. According to the ingroup extremity effect, which player would be given the starting job (a glance at the figure above may help)? If you stated that it would be the talented white player, you were correct because this is the talented ingroup individual. It should be noted that a threat (such as a loss) appears to intensify the ingroup extremity effect (Branscombe et al., 1993). Thus, coaches of unsuccessful teams or teams being challenged for first place would be especially likely to give a member of their own group the highest rating (and subsequently the most playing time).

The Hiring Practices of Professional Sport Organizations.

An example of the stereotyping of black athletes (and other minorities as well) can also be found in the few professional coaching, management, and administrative positions given to these individuals (Brooks & Althouse, 1993). A report prepared by the Center for the Study of Sport in Society graded the National Football League, the National Basketball Association, and Major League Baseball on their minority hiring practices (Lapchick & Benedict, 1993). Several areas of hiring were evaluated including: head coach or manager, assistant coaches, top management, and front office staff. For these four areas, basketball received the best grades; A, A, B−, and B, respectively. Football (C+, B+, C, C+) and baseball (B+, B+, F, C−) fared much worse. The numbers offered by Lapchick and Benedict paint a sad picture with regard to racial equality in sport. General managers (basketball = 68%, football = 94%, baseball = 100%) and owners (basketball = 97%, football = 100%, baseball = 98%) are almost exclusively white.

Thus, as with female athletes, although black athletes have made strides in gaining equity and equality in sport, racism, prejudice, and discrimination are still harsh realities. Knowing this, it must be especially difficult to be both female and a minority athlete (Acosta, 1993; Corbett & Johnson, 1993; Green, 1993). As research increases on both minorities and women, it is hoped these groups of athletes will be given an equal share of the field, court, and arena.

Athletes Participating in High Risk Sports

Another sport population receiving research attention consists of individuals participating in high risk sports (also called risk recreation and adventure recreation). **High risk sports** involve a high level of danger and the possibility of serious injury or death. Examples include SCUBA diving, sky diving, race car driving, mountain/rock climbing, whitewater boating, and hang gliding. Participation in these activities has been increasing (Ewert & Hollenhorst, 1989). Based on their examination of research targeting high risk participants, LeUnes and Nation (1989) concluded that there were two factors consistently related to participation in these activities. First, individuals who participate in high risk sports tend to score high on sensation seeking, indicating their interest in new and exciting experiences (e.g., Freixanet, 1991). Obviously, the danger of high risk activities helps meet the excitement needs of these persons. The second factor cited by LeUnes and Nation is birth order. Research has found that firstborn children are underrepresented in dangerous sports (Nisbett, 1968; Yiannakis, 1976). As an explanation of this effect, LeUnes and Nation write that "Firstborns may have their needs met in more conventional ways whereas later-born children are forced to resort to nontraditional activities in order to achieve a measure of success and parental and peer approval" (p. 257).

Recently, two models have been presented to account for participation in high risk sports. One model, developed by Ewert and Hollenhorst (1989), is termed the adventure recreation model. The **adventure recreation model** is a model of risk participation incorporating participant characteristics and patterns of use in an attempt to predict one's level of engagement (these authors defined engagement as self-reported skill and experience). This model is depicted graphically in Figure 4.3. Consistent with the interactional perspective described earlier, this model "presents the adventure recreation experience as a merging of the individual with a particular environment; a merging of personal attributes with certain activity/setting attributes" (Ewert & Hollenhorst, 1989, p. 127). Three individual attributes are incorporated into this model: frequency of participation (low to high), skill/experience level (low to high), and locus of control (either a group leader or the individual is in control). Similarly, this model includes three environmental factors: level of risk (low to high), social orientation (alone or with a guide), and environmental orientation (developed or natural).

The interaction of the three personal attributes and the three environmental/set-

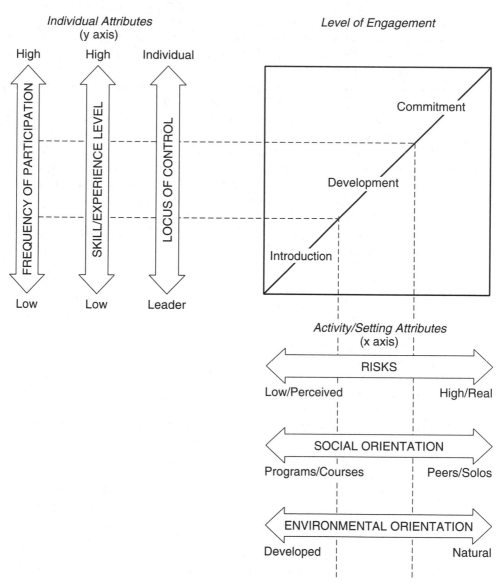

FIGURE 4.3   The adventure recreation model. (From: Ewert, A. & Hollenhorst, S. [1989]. Testing the adventure model: Empirical support for a model of risk recreation participation. *Journal of Leisure Research*, 21: 124–139.)

ting characteristics result in the placement of participants into one of three phases: introduction, developmental, or commitment. Introduction phase participants are individuals with little or no risk recreation experience. According to the model, these persons have low participation and skill levels, tend to rely on a leader or guide for task completion, and usually participate in developed courses with low risk levels (although their perception of risk may be quite high). Ewert and Hollenhorst (1989) define developmental phase participants as individuals with some experience who wish to further their skill at the particular activity. During this phase of engagement, a leader may still be present to help perfect the person's skills. The risk involved is more a reality and the setting is more natural and unpredictable than with introductory phase individuals. Last, persons in the commitment phase have a high level of participation and experience and usually perform the task without guidance. For these individuals, the setting tends to be highly dangerous, natural, and unstructured.

To test the adventure recreation model, Ewert and Hollenhorst (1989) surveyed 106 participants in an Ohio outdoor program. Course activities included rock climbing, caving, backcountry camping, and wilderness canoeing. Based on a questionnaire consisting of 9-point Likert-scale items, subjects were placed into one of the three engagement classifications (1–3, introductory; 4–6, developmental; 7–9, commitment). By computing correlations between level of engagement and the components of the model (i.e., participant attributes of skill, frequency of participation, and locus of control, and setting attributes of risk level, social orientation, and environmental orientation), the authors were able to document support for their model. Increases in levels of engagement corresponded with increases in skill and experience; tendencies toward an internal locus of control; and a preference for risky, natural, and self-oriented environments. Thus, initial work testing the adventure recreation model has been encouraging. Future research testing the model, particularly endeavors with increasingly sound measurement tools (McIntyre, 1992), should further the model's generalizability and usefulness.

A different model of risky sport participation, the ***risk recreation model,*** was advanced by Robinson (1992). This model, depicted in Figure 4.4, describes risk recreation involvement through a five-phase, transactional cycle. Phase one, attraction, involves seeking out and coping with the risk environment. This phase includes two personality attributes: sensation seeking and autonomy. According to the model and consistent with a wide body of literature, individuals high in sensation seeking and autonomy will often be interested in risky activities. In addition to the personality attributes, the attraction phase also includes the social environment surrounding the task. That is, to what extent does the social setting and/or structure facilitate or impede participation?

Phase two, the cognitive appraisal, involves the perceptions of risk. In appraising the risk involved in an activity, Robinson (1992) argues that the individual considers both the probability of failure (outcome uncertainty) and the nature of the failure (from harmless to fatal). Also important here is the competence level of the individual, that is, his or her ability to handle the risks involved. According to the author, one's perceived ratio of competence and risk lead to an anticipated outcome. When perceptions of risk outweigh perceptions of competence, a failure outcome is anticipated and the person most likely will not attempt or discontinue the task. Conversely, if beliefs concerning competence exceed perceptions of risk, then a successful outcome would be expected and the individual most likely would attempt the task. Cognitions about the ratio of risk to competence influence phase three, the decision making of the participant. Persons decide which tasks are appropriate for them (i.e., those at which they can succeed).

Phase four involves the individual's performances and experiences. Successful

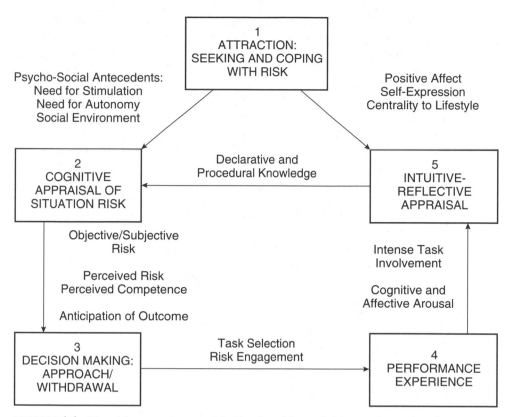

FIGURE 4.4 The risk recreation model. (Reprinted from: Robinson, D. W. [1992]. A descriptive model of enduring risk recreation involvement. *Journal of Leisure Research*, 24: 52–63.)

performances/experiences will lead to increases in task involvement. One's level of involvement is further deepened through perceptions of the ability to control one's cognitive and affective arousal generated by the activity. Because humans are information seekers, a fifth phase, intuitive and reflective appraisal, is included in the model. This phase involves the person's search for the factors responsible for her or his success or failure at the task. When the individual has succeeded at the task, a strong positive emotion will result. By perceiving that the success was an indication of one's ability and self-expression, one experiences enduring positive emotions such as pride and confidence. And, finally, after experiencing positive affect and self-expression, the individual will begin to identify with the activity, viewing the activity as a central component of her or his personality. Perceptions resulting from the intuitive/reflective appraisal stage then influence the attraction and risk appraisal stages for the next outing.

While the risk recreation model appears to be valid, Robinson (1992) did not provide data to support his contentions. Thus, the jury is still out concerning the validity of this model. When comparing the adventure recreation model and the risk recreation model, several similarities are apparent. For example, both models incorporate personality and situational variables, thus adopting an interactional perspective. In addition, both involve perceptions of risk and the importance of the social setting. Subsequent research is needed to identify the most appropriate model. It is quite possible that both models have their merits and are accurate in understanding the behaviors of individuals interested in risky sports.

Wilderness Users

The final population of sport participants that we will examine consists of wilderness users. **Wilderness users** are individuals who prefer and enjoy outdoor recreational and sporting activities such as hunting, fishing, hiking, and camping. Stankey (1972) identified two types of wilderness users: purists and nonpurists. Purists are individuals who want solitude (they want to "get away from it all") and tend to get upset by signs of other humans. Nonpurists are less concerned about others being present. Cicchetti (1972) found that men were more likely than women to classify themselves as purists.

Much of the research on wilderness users has come from environmental psychology. **Environmental psychology** is defined as concern and interest in the interactions and relationships between persons and their environments (McAndrew, 1993). By combining the work of environmental psychologists with the efforts of persons working in related fields (e.g., forestry, geography, and sociology), a profile of wilderness users has been established (McAndrew, 1993). Wilderness users, compared with persons who do not participate in these sports, tend to have higher incomes and often work in professional or technical occupations. In addition, a high percentage of wilderness users come from urban areas, and many of these individuals are college graduates. McAndrew (1993) states that these differences may be attributed to the high cost of many wilderness activities and to wilderness users, especially those from urban surroundings, often wanting to get away from their daily routines and environments.

Citing the work of Knopf (1987), as well as several other researchers, McAndrew (1993) lists several motivating forces underlying the activities of wilderness users. One motive is that the peace and serenity of the wilderness experience serves an energizing and restorative function. Many people seek out wilderness experiences because these experiences help to relieve tension or serve as a diversion from the rest of their lives. Another common motive is that wilderness experiences can foster feelings of competence. Users gain self-confidence and feelings of self-reliance through these activities. Yet another motivation of wilderness users is positive experiences resulting from these activities. Specifically, wilderness use often promotes feelings of happiness and well-being. The final motive discussed by McAndrew involves social pressure. Citing the research of Cheek and Burch (1976), McAndrew notes that the vast majority of wilderness users participate in these activities as a member of a group. This finding, coupled with the fact that approximately half of the wilderness users sampled by Cheek and Burch stated that they were there at the request of someone else, indicates that many people participate in wilderness activities because of pressures to conform to the group's wishes. Because they are less likely to participate in wilderness adventures as members of a group, the motivating forces of social pressures are probably less prominent among purists.

SUMMARY

The personalities of athletes have been a major research focus of sport psychologists. For many sport psychologists, the relationship between personality and behavior is best understood through the interactional approach. This perspective argues that to understand behavior fully one must consider the person, the situation, and the interaction between the person and the situation.

Although many differences between the personalities of athletes and nonathletes have been revealed, as yet a complete athlete personality profile has not been identified. Research examining if and to what extent sport participation alters athletes' personalities has also been a main focus of sport personality researchers. Three theories have been offered to account for the effects of athletic participation on personality development: the attrition model, the selection model, and the change model.

Some sport psychologists believe that personality data can be predictive of athletic success, while others believe that personality profiles cannot be used to predict athletic success. The most successful work on personality differences between successful and unsuccessful athletes has been conducted by Morgan. Based on a large body of research studying elite athletes, Morgan identified the Iceberg Profile, a personality profile of successful athletes marked by low levels of tension, depression, anger, fatigue, and confusion, but high levels of vigor.

A final area of personality research gaining considerable attention among sport psychologists concerns the relationship between personality and injury susceptibility. Numerous personality factors are associated with athletic injury including tendencies toward apprehension and anxiety.

The female sport experience was greatly influenced by a 1972 law, Title IX, prohibiting federally funded institutions from discriminatory practices. Many psychological phenomena relevant to women participants have been investigated. The fear of success is not found among female sport participants. Research on psychological androgyny has found that female athletes tend not to express a feminine sex role orientation. Rather, the sex role orientation of female participants is more likely to be masculine or androgynous. Finally, by examining the personality profiles of female athletes, it has been concluded that female athletes possess several characteristics that distinguish them from nonathletes, many of which indicate psychological stability.

Female athletes have often received differential and biased media coverage. Biased coverage has been found in newspaper, magazine, and television reporting. Sport researchers have also tended to be biased in their coverage of female athletes, choosing to conduct research on male participants rather than both males and females. Unfortunately, when female athletes do receive media coverage, it is often done in a sexist manner.

Black athletes constantly face discrimination and stereotyping in sport. Their overrepresentation in major sport leagues has gained the attention of both sport psychologists and sport sociologists. Two theories have been presented to account for the overrepresentation: genetic differences and social/cultural explanations. The social/cultural viewpoints have received the greatest research support. Stacking is one of the more overt examples of racism in sport. Three hypotheses have been generated in an attempt to account for the stacking phenomenon: the modeling hypothesis, the differential opportunity hypothesis, and the stereotype hypothesis.

Research investigating athletes who prefer high risk sports has found that two factors are consistently correlated with preferences for these activities. First, high risk participants tend to be sensation seekers and, therefore, enjoy new and exciting experiences. Second, high risk athletes tend not to be firstborn children. Two models have been proposed to account for participation in dangerous sports. The adventure recreation model is a model of risk participation that incorporates participant characteristics and patterns of use in an attempt to predict level of engagement, while the risk recreation model describes risk recreation through a five-phase, transactional cycle.

Wilderness users prefer and enjoy outdoor recreational activities such as hunting, fishing, hiking, and camping. Research has found that these persons tend to be motivated by a variety of factors including the peace and serenity of the wilderness experience, the ability to gain self-confidence and self-reliance, and social conformity issues.

GLOSSARY

Adventure Recreation Model   A model of risk participation that incorporates participant characteristics and patterns of use in an attempt to predict level of engagement.

Attrition Model   The belief that children not possessing the traits indicative of athletic success eventually drop out of sport.

Change Model   The belief that sport participation changes the personalities of the participants in some meaningful way.

Credulous Argument   The belief that personality profiles can be useful in predicting athletic performance.

Differential Opportunity Hypothesis   The hypothesis that black athletes select certain positions based on the number of opportunities to play those positions.

Environmental Psychology   Concern and interest in the interactions and relationships between persons and their environments.

Fear of Success   A situation in which individuals, usually female, fear or avoid success in a given situation because the success would be inconsistent with a given sex role.

High Risk Sports   Sports involving a high level of danger and the possibility of serious injury or death.

Iceberg Profile   The psychological profile of successful athletes marked by low levels of tension, depression, anger, fatigue, and confusion, and high levels of vigor.

Ingroup Extremity Effect   A situation in which individuals high in identification with a group evaluate members of their own group more extremely than those in the outgroup.

Interactional Approach   A situational approach to personality arguing that to understand behavior fully one must consider the person, the situation, and the interaction between the person and the situation.

Modeling Hypothesis   The hypothesis that early African-American athletes played certain positions and, therefore, young blacks tended to prefer these positions.

Outgroup Extremity Effect   A situation in which persons' evaluations of outgroup members are more extreme than their evaluations of ingroup persons.

Personality   The pattern of characteristic thoughts, feelings, and behaviors that distinguishes one person from another and that persists over time and situations.

Projective Personality Tests   Unstructured, open-ended tests in which the inner feelings and motives of the subject are revealed.

Psychological Androgyny   A personality trait in which an individual possesses nearly equal levels of both masculine and feminine qualities.

Risk Recreation Model   A model that describes risk recreation through a five-phase, transactional cycle.

Roles   Social positions governed by many norms.

Selection Model   The belief that only those with certain characteristics will choose to participate in athletics.

Sex Roles   Social expectations for individuals based on gender.

Skeptical Argument   The belief that personality data have little or no value in predicting athletic performance.

Stacking   The selection of a position for an individual based on his or her race.

Stereotype Hypothesis   The hypothesis that coaches possess stereotypes about white and black players and that these stereotypes suggest to the coaches that members of certain races are better suited for certain positions.

Title IX   A law prohibiting sexual discrimination in institutions receiving federal funds.

Wilderness Users   Individuals who prefer and enjoy outdoor recreational activities such as hunting, fishing, hiking, and camping.

APPLICATION AND REVIEW QUESTIONS

1. What are some of the methodological problems of past research on sport personality?
2. What are the differences between objective and projective methods of measuring personality?
3. Describe three models proposed to account for the possible personality influences of sport participation on athletes.

4. Describe the Iceberg Profile.
5. How has Title IX influenced women's sports?
6. In what ways has the coverage of female athletics been biased?
7. Which theory best accounts for the overrepresentation of black athletes in football, basketball, and baseball?
8. What is stacking and why does it occur?
9. Compare and contrast the adventure recreation model and the risk recreation model.

SUGGESTED READINGS

BROOK, D., & ALTHOUSE, R. (1993). *Racism in college athletics: The African-American athlete's experience*. Morgantown, WV: Fitness Information Technology. This book does an exceptional job in presenting the issues faced by black college athletes. The two chapters focusing on the concerns of female minority collegiate players are especially noteworthy.

MORGAN, W. P. (1980). The trait psychology controversy. *Research Quarterly for Exercise and Sport, 51,* 50–76. This article presents the topics of interest concerning the personality traits of elite athletes. In addition, Morgan's discussion of the credulous-skeptical argument is extremely enlightening.

OGLESBY, C. A. (1989). Women and sport. In J. H. Goldstein (ed.), *Sports, games, and play: Social and psychological viewpoints* (2nd ed., pp. 129–145). Hillsdale, NJ: Erlbaum. This chapter discusses the current status of women's athletics. Topics reviewed include the passage of Title IX, participation rates, and opportunities for females in coaching and administrative positions.

PHARES, E. J. (1991). *Introduction to personality* (3rd ed.). New York: HarperCollins. This textbook provides an excellent introduction to the topic of personality. In addition to examining the theories of such noted psychologists as Freud, Jung, Rogers, and Bandura, the author also offers an excellent presentation of methods of measuring personality traits.

SHIELDS, D. L., & BREDEMEIER, B. J. (1995). *Character development and physical activity*. Champaign, IL: Human Kinetics. This work examines the relationship between sport participation and character development. A number of topics are addressed including classic and contemporary approaches to moral development. The authors also offer several suggestions for enhancing character development through sport.

Chapter 5

LEARNING IN SPORT

One of the primary responsibilities of coaches and managers is to teach new behaviors to their players. This is especially true for persons coaching younger athletes. For example, a new grip in tennis, the execution of a bunt in baseball, and the proper way to spike a volleyball are all skills that must be learned, and, if the player is to perform at maximum levels, learned properly. An understanding of the psychology of learning and skill acquisition is essential if one is to train and teach players at an optimal level. As Anshel (1994) writes, "Effective coaches are educators. How else could participants learn and improve their skills?" (p. 164). Questions such as how often and how long should the team practice, how effective is verbal praise, and should punishments and reprimands be employed are all important for coaches. It is the psychology of learning that provides the answers to these and other questions concerning athletic training.

The psychology of learning (***learning*** is defined as any relatively permanent change in behavior due to experience) has enjoyed a long and rich tradition in psychology. Originating with the work of influential psychologists such as Ivan Pavlov, E. L. Thorndike, and John Watson, and continuing with the work of B. F. Skinner, a new subdiscipline of psychology emerged during the early years of the 20th century. Termed ***behaviorism,*** this subdiscipline reflected the belief that psychology should be the science of observable behavior and, as such, nonobservable phenomena such as consciousness and the mind were beyond the bounds of the science (see Schwartz, 1989, for a review of behaviorism). Behaviorism led to a large body of research on the most effective methods of learning. A large portion of this work is important for sport psychology and contributes valuable insights into the training of athletes. Three types of learning and their applications to sport psychology are presented in this chapter: classical conditioning, operant conditioning, and observational learning (modeling).

CLASSICAL CONDITIONING

At the turn of the 20th century, Ivan Pavlov established his place in psychology forever. As a Russian physiologist, Pavlov was busy with his research on the digestive system, for which he won a Noble Prize in 1904. His research employed an apparatus in which a dog was strapped in a harness and the animal's salivation gland was surgically moved to the outside of the body (near the cheek). After this minor surgery, a tube was attached to the gland such that saliva entering the tube could be measured (Kimble, 1961). At this point, a research assistant would present food to the animal and record the animal's salivation. However, as the research progressed, something interesting began to happen. The dog began to salivate prematurely, that is, before being presented with food. In fact, the dog began salivating as the research assistant approached and even to the sound of his footsteps (Schultz, 1981).

Why was the animal salivating before the presentation of food? Pavlov (1927) certainly pondered the answer to this question and began to investigate this event diligently. His research subsequently led to the development of the psychological phenomenon referred to as classical conditioning. ***Classical conditioning*** is a form of learning involving involuntary, reflexive responses. Classical conditioning (see Figure 5.1) begins with a stimulus (referred to as the ***unconditioned stimulus*** or US), which automatically elicits a reflexive response (termed the ***unconditioned response*** or UR). The UR is involuntary; it occurs naturally in response to the US. In Pavlov's research, the US was the dog's food, while the UR was the animal's salivation. At this point, a neutral stimulus (referred to as the ***conditioned stimulus*** or CS) is presented immediately prior to the US. After several pairings between the CS and the US, the CS begins to elicit the response (now referred to as the ***conditioned response*** or CR). This is precisely what was occurring in Pavlov's lab. Each day the research assistant fed the dog the food (US) to elicit the salivation (UR). The sights and sounds of the researcher always preceded the presentation of food. As a result, the dog began to salivate at these sights and sounds in anticipation of the food. Therefore, the research assistant became the CS, while salvation was the CR.

Pavlov began to test this serendipitous occurrence scientifically. He completed the surgery on a new dog and placed the animal in the harness. A tone (CS) was presented to the animal followed within a few seconds by the presentation of food (US). During the first few trials, the dog exhibited no salivatory responses to the tone but, when presented with the food, naturally displayed the automatic response of salivation (UR). However, after several trials (10–20) of first presenting the tone and then the food, the dog began to salivate to the sound of the tone, prior to the presentation of the food. At this point, the salivatory response was referred to as the CR

FIGURE 5.1   The classical conditioning paradigm.

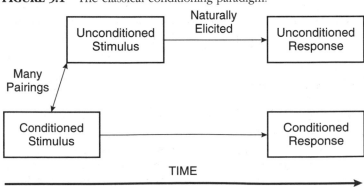

because it was elicited by the CS. It is important to remember that the temporal relationship between the CS and the US is vital: the CS (tone) must be presented prior to the US (food). If the food had been presented first, the animal would have already been salivating when the tone was sounded. As a result, the tone itself would not have elicited the response.

With this basic understanding of classical conditioning, we may now examine how this type of learning operates in sport settings. Remember, classical conditioning involves a stimulus (US) that automatically elicits a reflexive response (UR). For our example, let us examine a tee-ball player, Billy, who is a shy and introverted 4-year-old boy. Billy does not like to leave the safety and security of his own house and, as a result, has few friends and struggles in social settings. In an attempt to increase his social skills, Billy's parents have placed him on the local tee-ball team. All of the coaches and players are strangers to Billy. As a result, going to practice elicits a reflexive response of anxiety. Billy cannot help how he feels; his anxiety is automatic. Before each practice, Billy's mother gives him his baseball glove and hat. At the beginning of the season, Billy's glove and hat did not evoke a response. However, by the middle of the season, just seeing the glove or hat made Billy feel anxious, even on days without practice. Using Figure 5.1 as a guide, we can determine why Billy is anxious at the sight of the baseball equipment. The US (the stimulus that naturally elicits a response) is going to practice. The UR resulting from this stimulus is Billy's anxiety. The presentation of the CS (the glove and hat) just prior to the US ultimately elicited the CR of anxiety.

Principles of Classical Conditioning

A number of classical conditioning principles have been established. Three of these principles will be examined here: extinction, generalization, and discrimination.

Extinction. Let us return to Pavlov's study involving the food (US), tone (CS), and salivation (UR and CR). Recall that, after several pairings of the tone and food, the animal began to salivate to the sound of the tone. We can imagine that Pavlov and his assistants were both excited and fascinated by this finding. As a result, they may have continued to show off their dog to their friends and colleagues. That is, they may have continued to present the tone to the animal and marveled at the animal's salivatory response. But would this behavior continue indefinitely? Based on the title of this section, you probably can guess that it would not. After a short time of presenting the tone without providing food, the animal would no longer salivate to the sound (Schwartz, 1989). This phenomenon is referred to as ***extinction,*** which is defined as the elimination of a response through the removal of the unconditioned stimulus or reward.

To illustrate how extinction operates within the sport world, a return to the introverted tee-ball player may be helpful. Remember that Billy, due to the pairing of the CS (baseball equipment) and the US (practice), became anxious (the CR) at the sight of the baseball glove and hat. If, however, future presentations of the equipment were not followed by the anxiety-provoking practice sessions, Billy's conditioned response to the equipment would be extinguished.

Generalization and Discrimination.   Returning again to Pavlov's experiment with the tone, let us assume that he first trained the dog to salivate to the sound of a tuning fork. The tuning fork (CS) preceded the food presentation (US) on numerous occasions and ultimately the sound alone elicited the salivatory response. What would have happened if Pavlov had then switched the original tuning fork for one with a slightly different pitch? Would the animal have continued to salivate to this somewhat different sound? In reality, the answer to this question is maybe. If the new sound were quite similar to the original tone, there is a strong likelihood that the animal would have continued to display the CR. This phenomenon is termed ***generalization,*** which may be defined as the eliciting of a conditioned response through the presentation of a new conditioned stimulus that is similar to the original conditioned stimulus. If, however, the new CS were quite different from the original CS (for example, if a light were substituted for the tuning fork), the chances of the new CS eliciting the CR would be significantly reduced. This process is referred to as discrimination. ***Discrimination*** is defined as the application of a new conditioned stimulus that is quite dissimilar from the original conditioned stimulus and, as a result, fails to elicit the conditioned response.

As applied to the example involving Billy and his anxious response to the equipment, had Billy's anxiety been triggered by other equipment, for example, a basketball, his response would be representative of generalization. On the other hand, if he did not become anxious at the sight of the basketball, he would be demonstrating discrimination. As this sport-specific example illustrates, it is important to remember that it is the original CS that is either generalized or discriminated.

OPERANT CONDITIONING

While classical conditioning involves involuntary behaviors, voluntary behaviors (behaviors within the control of the individual) are learned through operant conditioning (Mazur, 1994). ***Operant conditioning*** (also referred to as instrumental conditioning) can be defined as the strategic presentation of reinforcements and punishments in an attempt to increase desired voluntary behaviors while decreasing undesired voluntary behaviors.

Thorndike and the Law of Effect

Around 1900, E. L. Thorndike began investigating the voluntary behaviors of animals. His research involved a cage with a door secured by a simple latch and a piece of fish placed near the cage (Klein, 1987). When a hungry cat was placed into the cage, it tried in vain to reach through the bars to get the food. The cat would then try numerous other behaviors in an attempt to escape, such as scratching the cage floor and biting the bars. These behaviors, which basically amounted to trial-and-error efforts, eventually resulted in the cat's movement of a pedal that opened the latch on the cage's door. The cat was rewarded with the piece of fish. The cat was then placed back in the cage with a new piece of fish placed just beyond the animal's reach. Again, the cat would display a variety of behaviors, ending with the accidental pressing of the pedal and the opening of the cage door. This procedure was repeated several times. After the first few trials, the animal began to spend less time with unsuccessful behaviors (such as scratching the floor) and more time with the pedal itself. After approximately 25 trials, the cat would move directly to the pedal, opening the door within seconds of being placed in the cage (Thorndike, 1898).

Based on results such as those described above, Thorndike (1905) proposed a law of effect. The ***law of effect*** states that any behavior followed by a positive consequence will have an increased likelihood of being displayed in the future. Conversely, any behavior followed by a negative consequence will have a decreased likelihood of being displayed in the future. Please note that the law of effect implies that the chances of the behavior being displayed are merely increased or decreased, not that the behavior absolutely will or will not occur again. As applied to Thorndike's cat, the behaviors involved with opening the latch resulted in the positive consequence of food, while the other behaviors did not. Hence, the cat became increasingly likely to manipulate the pedal in order to attain the reward.

The basics of the law of effect are depicted in Figure 5.2. The process begins with a voluntary response (i.e., behavior), depicted graphically as R^V. For example, imagine a volleyball player who has made a slight adjustment of the positioning of her wrist on her serve. This response could lead to one of three possible consequences. One consequence is positive (denoted as C+), that is, something beneficial or enjoyable resulted from the response. To continue with the volleyball example, the player may have served an ace. If so, she would quite likely continue this behavior in an attempt to continue serving aces. A second consequence, a neutral consequence (shown as C?), is one that may either increase the likelihood of repeating the response, decrease the likelihood, or have no impact. If the new grip resulted in an average serve, one indistinguishable from serves with other grips, it is difficult to predict if the player would continue with the new grip. She may try it again, she may replace the grip with her old form, or she may attempt another new style of serve. Finally, the consequence may be negative (illustrated as C−). Negative consequences decrease the likelihood of the behavior. If she had hit a very poor serve, she most likely would not try this grip again.

Operant Conditioning: Advancing the Understanding of Voluntary Behaviors

From the 1930s until the 1980s, the research of B. F. Skinner advanced our understanding of voluntary behaviors and the law of effect (Mazur, 1994). Skinner maintained an active research laboratory at Harvard University and authored a number of books on the topic of operant conditioning. With Skinner leading the charge, he and several other behaviorally oriented psychologists produced volumes of research dur-

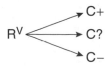

FIGURE 5.2   The law of effect including the three types of consequences (C) resulting from a voluntary response (R^V).

ing this time. An exhaustive review of this literature is beyond the scope of this book. Thus, we will review those research areas having the greatest impact on and relevance for sport psychology.

Figure 5.3 displays a 2 × 2 matrix that includes the fundamental components of operant conditioning. To understand this illustration best, the reader is advised to focus on two sets of information. The first set concerns the valence of the stimulus, that is, whether the stimulus is positive or negative. The second set of information revolves around the presentation of the stimulus, namely, is the stimulus applied or is the stimulus removed? The different combinations of these two sets of information result in the possibilities of operant conditioning. It should be noted that the concept of consequence reviewed above has now been replaced with the term stimulus. This change has been incorporated to remain consistent with other authors.

Applying a positive stimulus, referred to as ***positive reinforcement,*** will most likely lead to an increase in the behavior being reinforced. Within the sport world there are many examples of positive reinforcement. Praise, trophies, self-fulfillment, self-esteem, and ribbons for amateur athletes and increases in salary, playing time, and contract length for professional athletes are all positive reinforcements designed to increase the positive behavior of athletes.

When one applies a negative stimulus to an individual they are attempting ***punishment,*** the goal of which is to decrease behavior. As with positive reinforcement, examples of punishment can readily be found in the sport world. Verbal reprimands, benchings, and suspensions are all methods coaches employ to eliminate negative or problematic athlete behaviors.

Response cost is the removal of a positive stimulus (response cost is also referred to as negative punishment [Mazur, 1994] and omission [Schwartz & Reisberg,

FIGURE 5.3   The 2 × 2 matrix depicting the four strategies used to teach or alter behavior in operant conditioning.

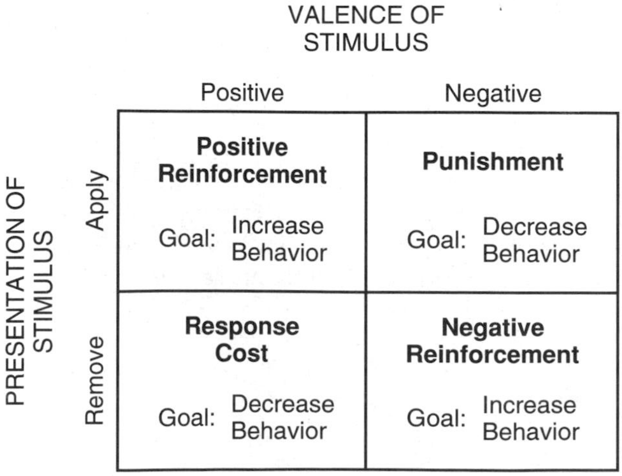

VALENCE OF
STIMULUS

		Positive	Negative
PRESENTATION OF STIMULUS	Apply	**Positive Reinforcement** Goal: Increase Behavior	**Punishment** Goal: Decrease Behavior
	Remove	**Response Cost** Goal: Decrease Behavior	**Negative Reinforcement** Goal: Increase Behavior

1991]). This procedure has the effect of decreasing the target behavior. For example, imagine that a high caliber professional athlete were given the special privilege of being allowed to room by himself on road trips. However, this athlete has been displaying a variety of negative behaviors that are becoming detrimental to his team's spirit and unity. For example, this athlete has been sparring with the media, insulting teammates, and displaying an apathetic attitude. In an attempt to stop these negative behaviors, the coach has decided to remove the player's privilege of rooming alone. Thus, the coach has removed a positive stimulus (rooming alone) in an attempt to decrease the occurrence of undesired behaviors. A real-life example of response cost was described by Warren (1983). The coach of a high school boy's basketball team wanted his players to stop missing free throws. In an innovative (and unethical) attempt to decrease this behavior, the coach removed a positive stimulus from the players each time they missed a shot during practice—he took a piece of their clothing!

Finally, a coach may attempt to increase a desirable behavior by removing a negative stimulus, a process called ***negative reinforcement.*** Continuing with our example from above, let us now assume that, because of his problem behavior, the player was placed on probation (an example of punishment). The probation had the desired effect in that the athlete stopped his negative behaviors. However, the athlete also began to display positive behaviors such as reporting to the field early, helping out younger teammates, and displaying a greater level of effort on the field. The coaches wanted to see a continuation of these positive behaviors so they removed the probation, with the understanding that it would remain removed so long as the positive behaviors were displayed. Thus, the coaches were removing a negative stimulus (probation) to achieve an increase in the desired behaviors.

Principles of Operant Conditioning

With this understanding of the basics of operant conditioning, it is now appropriate to review several principles of this type of learning and their application to sport settings.

Apparatus.   Most psychology students have seen the apparatus commonly used in operant research. This piece of equipment, often called a Skinner box, is a rectangular cage measuring approximately 15 inches by 10 inches. Each Skinner box (also called an operant chamber) contains a dish attached by a tube to a food chamber located on the outside of the apparatus. The box also contains a metal bar attached to a wall. When this bar is pressed, a piece of food is automatically released down the tube into the food dish. The food serves as a reward for exhibiting the desired bar press behavior and, thus, is used in research on reinforcement. The food may also be released into the dish by pressing a button on a hand-held control box. The floor of the cage is often comprised of small metal bars used to apply low levels of shock to the animal. The shock is used for research examining the effects of punishment. While punishment research is quite common, each of the examples in the sections to follow involves reinforcement. A separate section on punishment is presented below. While most operant research employs a Skinner box designed for use with rats, other research has used a box designed for pigeons. These boxes have a key that the pigeon is to peck for reinforcement.

Shaping.   If a researcher placed a naive rat into a Skinner box, how long do you believe it would take for the rat to begin displaying the target behavior of bar pressing? Thinking back to Thorndike's (1905) law of effect, you may estimate that, while it will take a significant amount of time, the rat will eventually press the bar much in the same manner that the cat eventually opened the cage. However, in reality this is unlikely. The rat will most likely never press the bar. How then is one to train the animal to display the behavior? The answer is to use shaping. ***Shaping*** involves reinforcing successive approximations toward a goal behavior (Mazur, 1994; Schwartz, 1989; Warren, 1983). In this procedure, the investigator reinforces the organism for behaviors that are closer and closer approximations of the target behavior. Thus, if the researcher wanted to train the rat to press the bar, she should start by reinforcing the animal for simply looking at the bar. However, if this is the only behavior rewarded, then the researcher would have simply trained the rat to look at the bar. Remember, the target behavior is the bar press. As such, although looking at the bar should be reinforced for a few trials, the researcher should then wait until the animal makes a move toward the bar. This should be followed by reinforcing the rat for walking toward the bar, then for standing next to the bar, for touching it, and finally for actually pressing the bar. Once the animal has pressed the bar and received the reward, the animal is shaped and will continue to press the bar to receive the reward.

The following scenario is an example of shaping in sport settings. Barbara, coach of a tee-ball team, has a player (Curt) who is extremely afraid of the ball. Barbara would like to teach Curt the proper techniques of catching a fly ball and has decided to use the reward of verbal praise to assist in this endeavor. Barbara realizes that if she only rewards Curt for the target behavior of catching the ball she will have a difficult time. That is, because Curt is afraid of the ball to begin with, he most likely will never exhibit the target behavior. As such, this behavior cannot be reinforced. Thus, the coach has decided to use shaping to reach the target goal. At first, Barbara reinforces Curt for getting near a ground ball and then for catching a ground ball. Next, she reinforces him for getting near a thrown ball, catching a thrown ball, getting near a batted ball, touching (with his glove) a batted ball, and, finally, for catching the batted ball. In this way, Curt will slowly but steadily move closer to the target behavior.

Extinction.   Returning for a moment to the operant chamber, imagine a rat who has been successfully shaped to press the bar. What would happen if the researcher ran out of food and, as a result, the rat pressed the bar but did not receive the reward? Most likely, the rat would press the bar a few more times and then stop. That is, the animal would cease to exhibit the target behavior once this behavior was no longer rewarded. This is another type of extinction. Remember that extinction was defined as the elimination of a response through the removal of the unconditioned stimulus or reward. To maintain the behavior, coaches must, on occasion, follow the target response with a reward. Applying this phenomenon to the baseball example mentioned earlier, if the coach ceased to reinforce the player when he caught a fly ball, the player would stop catching the ball.

Schedules of Reinforcement.   Research on schedules of reinforcement has examined the timing and frequency of presentations of reinforcements. A number of schedules of reinforcement have been identified, several of which are examined here.

IMMEDIATE VERSUS DELAYED REINFORCEMENT.   A large body of literature (see Schwartz, 1989) indicates that ***immediate reinforcement*** (reinforcement that immediately follows the target behavior) is much more effective in teaching or changing behavior than ***delayed reinforcement*** (reinforcement in which a substantial amount of time separates the target behavior and the reward). In Skinner's operant chamber, if a 30-second delay period separated the target behavior and the reward, the animal would not be expected to perform the behavior as often. Similarly, had the coach delayed her verbal reinforcement of the young baseball player in the example above, the athlete would have been far less likely to display the desired behavior.

CONTINUOUS VERSUS PARTIAL REINFORCEMENT.   Other researchers have examined the consequences of continuous and partial reinforcement. A ***continuous reinforcement*** schedule involves rewarding a behavior each time it is exhibited. For example, the rat being rewarded with a food pellet each time it pressed the bar and the young baseball player receiving verbal support each time he caught the ball would each be examples of continuous reinforcement. A ***partial reinforcement*** schedule (also called an intermittent schedule) involves rewarding a behavior on only a subset of trials. Rewarding the child every third time he exhibited the behavior would be an example of partial reinforcement.

Research has found that partial schedules are harder to extinguish than continuous schedules (Mazur, 1994; Warren, 1983). To highlight this fact, consider two young football players, each of whom has been taught to perform the correct passing technique using verbal reinforcement. One child has been trained using continuous reinforcement, while the other is on a partial reinforcement schedule in which he is reinforced every fifth time he correctly performs the behavior. If the coach responsible for presenting the children with the reinforcements were absent and the youngsters did not receive the verbal praise when demonstrating the target behavior, the child used to being reinforced each time would probably not wait long before ceasing to show the correct passing form. The child accustomed to being reinforced every fifth time he executes the behavior will most likely continue to exhibit the target response. This child realizes that he does not get reinforced each time and consequently does not expect constant reinforcement.

RATIO SCHEDULES OF REINFORCEMENT.   Ratio reinforcement schedules specify the number of responses necessary for a reward to be presented. ***Fixed ratio*** (FR) schedules are found when a reward is presented each time a specified number of responses has occurred. For example, in a fixed ratio 5 (FR5) schedule of reinforcement, a rat would be given a food pellet every fifth time he pressed the bar; the young athlete would be verbally rewarded every fifth time he caught the ball.

Variable ratio (VR) schedules of reinforcement are similar to FR schedules in that they require the organism to display a certain number of responses prior to reinforcement, but with VR schedules the number of responses required is an average of some number. For example, a VR5 schedule would have a subject rewarded after an average of five responses. Thus, the individual might be reinforced after the third response, then after the seventh, then sixth, then fourth, and so on. As for a rat in the operant chamber, to receive the food pellet he would have to press the bar an average of five times, while the young baseball player would have to catch the ball an average of five times to receive the praise.

Superstition.   It was noted earlier that Thorndike's (1905) law of effect states that behaviors followed by a positive consequence have an increased likelihood of being repeated. Note that this proposition states that the positive consequence simply follows the behavior. The consequence does not have to be based on the behavior. That is, so long as the positive consequence follows the behavior, the behavior should increase, even if the behavior did not directly cause the positive consequence. This fact plays a vital role in superstitious behavior, a common occurrence in sport.

What do you suppose would happen if a pigeon were placed in a Skinner box and a pellet of pigeon food was placed in the food cup every 15 seconds. That is, regardless of what behaviors the pigeon exhibited, every 15 seconds the bird was presented with a reward. This type of reinforcement is termed ***noncontingent reinforcement,*** indicating that the reward is not based on any particular behavior. In contrast, ***contingent reinforcement*** is found when the reward is based on a specific behavior, for example, the rat described earlier who was only reinforced when pressing the bar. This question puzzled Skinner, who attempted this very experiment (Skinner, 1948). When Skinner returned to the box a short time later, he found that most of the pigeons were performing specific behaviors prior to the food presentation. One pigeon was pecking the ground, another spinning in a circle, and so on. Why were these birds displaying these strange behaviors? As you may have guessed, these were the behaviors they were performing just prior to the presentation of the food pellet. As a result, the animals developed the belief that the reinforcement was based (i.e., contingent) on the behavior. Actually, the reward was not related to the behavior, that is, it was noncontingent.

Within the sport world, examples of superstitious behavior abound. Athletes, coaches, and spectators receiving a positive consequence after performing a certain behavior are quite likely to continue the behavior (Neil, 1982), and increases in superstitious beliefs appear to correspond with increases in sport involvement (Neil, Anderson, & Sheppard, 1981). Many superstitious behaviors are exhibited across a variety of sports. Players in a variety of team (e.g., basketball and hockey) and individual (e.g., swimming and track and field) sports report superstitions concerning uniforms and uniform numbers (Gregory & Petrie, 1975). Rickey Henderson's (a professional baseball player) uniform number superstition proved to be quite expensive. Henderson believed that he could only perform well when wearing number 24. However, when Henderson was traded to a new team, he found that his "lucky" number was already taken. Henderson tried to play with a different number (14), but, after a few games, complained that he could not play well without his old number 24. Henderson's superstition was so great that he paid his teammate $25,000 for the use of number 24 (*The National Sports Review,* 1993). Other superstitions found

Most players would avoid wearing uniform number 13 because of their superstition. (Photographer: UPI. Source: Corbis-Bettmann.)

in a variety of sports include a desire to remain alone during pregame periods and carrying lucky charms such as coins (Buhrmann & Zaugg, 1981; Neil, 1982).

Other superstitions are primarily sport-specific. In basketball, behaviors such as making one's last warm-up shot (Gregory & Petrie, 1975), preshot free throw behaviors (Lobmeyer & Wasserman, 1986), and even gum-chewing rituals (Buhrmann

& Zaugg, 1981) are all quite common. Hockey players often feel the need to touch their goalie's pads or helmet, be the last person on the ice, or touch the goal post. Golfers tend to select a ball that has been hit successfully on a previous attempt. Van Raalte, Brewer, Nemeroff, and Linder (1991) found that athletes who express the belief that they hold some control over chance situations are especially likely to select the same colored ball used in a previously successful shot. Gregory and Petrie (1975) report that superstitions found in other sports include suit colors (swimming), lane numbers (track), and lucky brands of balls (tennis).

Certain superstitions are athlete specific, that is, they tend to be demonstrated by only one or a handful of players. Becker (1975) lists several such behaviors including a football player who felt the need to wear the opposing team's colors in his socks and a track athlete who changed his spikes before each meet. While playing professional hockey for the Boston Briuns and New York Rangers, Phil Esposito would drive through the same toll booth he had passed through before his last successful contest (Zimmer, 1984). Recent examples include the behaviors of Wade Boggs and Len Dykstra (major league baseball players). Boggs would eat chicken prior to every game, while Dykstra, if he made an out, felt compelled to throw away his current bag of chewing tobacco and open a new one.

The relationship between an athlete's superstition and his or her actual performance should be mentioned. Certainly, if Boggs were asked if he received special powers from eating chicken he would answer no. Does this mean, then, that his superstition has no impact on his performance? That is, if he were to resist eating chicken prior to a game, would his performance suffer? As a matter of fact, the answer to this question is most likely yes. Even though the superstition has no true direct physical effect on the player's performance, it does have a psychological effect. So, even though Boggs would probably acknowledge that chicken does not cause him to perform better, failing to eat chicken before a game may hurt his performance. The superstitions and pregame rituals tend to lower the athlete's anxiety and, if they are removed, his or her performance may suffer.

An investigation by Lobmeyer and Wasserman (1986) supports these contentions. These researchers had male and female varsity high school and college basketball players attempt a total of 50 free throws. The first 10 free throws were warm-up shots and were not included in the analyses. The participants then attempted 20 free throws in which they were allowed to use their preshot behaviors (e.g., bouncing the ball for a set number of times, hugging the ball) and 20 in which they were not allowed to perform these rituals. The results indicated that, for both the high school and college players, more shots were made when they were allowed to use their preshot rituals. Since free throw shooting percentages are down nation-wide (Anderson, 1994a), coaches may want to try providing players with superstitious preshot rituals!

OBSERVATIONAL LEARNING

Perhaps Mazur (1994) put it most succinctly when he wrote, "Let there be no mistake about it: A large portion of human learning occurs, not through classical con-

Athletes can successfully learn a number of behaviors through observational learning. (Photographer: Ron Rovtar. Source: FPG International.)

ditioning or as a result of reinforcement or punishment, but through observation" (p. 294). ***Observational learning*** is the vicarious learning of behaviors through imitation and modeling. Although most research has examined the impact of other persons as models, some researchers have reviewed the importance of self-modeling (modeling one's own behaviors). This line of research is discussed in this chapter's "A Closer Look."

Bandura's Model of Observational Learning

The leading author and researcher of this third type of learning is Albert Bandura. Bandura has written extensively on the topic since the 1960s (Bandura, 1969) and has continued to refine his theory during the past several decades (Bandura, 1986). Bandura (1986) argues that a four-step process is required for observational learning to occur (see Figure 5.4). The initial step is attention. That is, the individual's attention must be directed toward the model. For example, if a high school basketball player wanted to model the dunking style of Michael Jordan, yet his attention was diverted when Jordan executed the maneuver, the athlete would not be able to repeat Jordan's behavior. Because they are often the focus of players' attention, coaches must be careful that they are modeling the appropriate behaviors (Anshel, 1994).

While this first step of attentional focus may seem rather obvious, several in-

A CLOSER LOOK:
THE USE OF SELF-MODELING IN SPORT PSYCHOLOGY

A number of researchers have demonstrated that self-modeling can be an effective technique for teaching new behaviors and altering established behaviors (Creer & Miklich, 1970; Dowrick, 1991). **Self-modeling** is a procedure in which individuals view themselves correctly performing a task. Usually, the individual is asked to view a videotape, although a still photograph may be sufficient in situations involving the acquisition or alteration of a simple behavior. Because it is vital that the individual observe the correct execution of the behavior, some editing of the videotape is usually required. For instance, a volleyball coach may video an athlete attempting a series of overhand serves. Most likely, some of these serves will be successful while others will be unsuccessful. The coach must edit the tape such that the player views only the successful serves. Allowing the player to view the unsuccessful attempts may result in the modeling of unwanted and incorrect behaviors.

Self-modeling has been used to enhance the skill acquisition of athletes (Franks & Maile, 1991). For example, Dowrick and Dove (1980) used self-modeling to enhance the skills of three youth swimmers with spina bifida. The swimmers were filmed while being encouraged to perform their best. The authors then developed separate 2-minute self-modeling films for each child. Unsuccessful behaviors and signs of the child's distress (e.g., crying and refusal to participate) were deleted from the film. The children were shown the film during a 9-week period. The swimmers' performances were also recorded during this period. The results indicated that the swimmers' performances improved after viewing the self-modeling films.

A more recent investigation of the usefulness of self-modeling in sport was conducted by Templin and Vernacchia (1995). These researchers examined the impact of self-modeling videotapes on the performance of five male college basketball players. In addition, they added inspirational music to the videos, resulting in more motivating and enjoyable videos. Templin and Vernacchia began the study by videotaping the players during home games. The tapes were used to develop individualized self-modeling tapes for each athlete. Research assistants and the athletes collaborated in selecting material for the tapes. The length of the tapes ranged from 3 to 5 minutes. The athletes were then asked to select inspirational music to be added to the tape. The athletes were asked to view the videos prior to predetermined games over the course of a basketball season. The researchers then compared the players' shooting accuracy prior to and after viewing the self-modeling tapes. The results were encouraging as three of the five players exhibited an increase in performance after viewing the video.

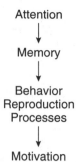

Attention

↓

Memory

↓

Behavior
Reproduction
Processes

↓

Motivation   **FIGURE 5.4**   Bandura's four-step model of observational learning.

teresting and important studies have focused on the characteristics of the model that result in the greatest amount of attention being directed toward that person. The results of this work have found that certain characteristics of the model do result in increased attentional focus. Nurturing (Bandura & Hutson, 1961), affectionate (Zimmerman & Koussa, 1979), prestigious (Mausner, 1953), competent (Baron, 1970), sincere (Klass, 1979), and high status (Landers & Landers, 1973) models have been found to receive a large portion of attention. Thus, these types of models increase the effectiveness of the modeling process.

However, recent work in motor learning has challenged the assumption that these characteristics increase the attentional focus given to targets. McCullagh (1986) asked subjects to view a model performing a motor task and manipulated the status of the model (high or low status). In addition, she manipulated the presentation of information about the model's status. Some subjects received information concerning the model's status during the attentional phase, while others were given status information after the attentional phase. Although McCullagh did find that high status models resulted in better performances than low status models, a timing of status information effect was not found. That is, it did not matter if subjects were presented the information concerning the model's status during or after the attentional phase. McCullagh concluded that, although model status is important for observational learning, the status effects may not be due to increased attentional focus. McCullagh (1987) was able to replicate this finding using similar/dissimilar models.

The second stage in the four-step process of observational learning is memory (Bandura, 1986). Even if an individual had his or her attention directed toward the model as this person exhibited the behavior, without the ability to store the information in memory, there is little likelihood that the behavior would be imitated. This is because the opportunity to model the behavior often comes at a later date. As an example, let us return to the high school student who wanted to imitate Michael Jordan's dunking style. Since this person was most likely observing Jordan's behavior on television or in person, the opportunity to attempt Jordan's behavior was not immediately available. Rather, this individual must go to a basketball court or perhaps his driveway before attempting the dunk. If he has forgotten the behavior when he is finally ready to attempt the task, modeling cannot occur. McCullagh (1993) described four encoding and rehearsal strategies that influence the memory of the target's behavior. Verbalization (verbal rehearsal or guidance), imagery (rehearsing through the use of a cognitive image), organizational strategies (the frequency and type of demonstrations), and physical practice may all increase memory for the behavior.

The third step in the modeling process involves motor reproduction. While the first two steps in the process are primarily cognitive in nature, at some point in the process of observational learning actual motor movements become important. Such is the case with the motor reproduction phase. As Mazur (1994) noted, "the individual must be able to translate some general knowledge . . . into a coordinated pattern of muscle movements" (p. 292). If the individual does not have the physical, intellectual, or developmental abilities to reproduce the behavior, modeling cannot occur. For example, even if the high school basketball player had attended to Jordan and, when he is at the gym, remembers what Jordan did, if he lacks leaping ability or coordination he will not be able to mimic the behavior.

Finally, even if the athlete had his or her attention directed toward Jordan, remembers Jordan's behavior, and possesses the physical, intellectual, and developmental abilities to display the behavior, Jordan's behavior may still not be reproduced. This is because the first three steps simply provide the person with the capacity to model the behavior (Mazur, 1994). The final step, motivation, may override the initial three steps. As a result, the greatest research attention has been devoted to this stage in the observational learning process (McCullagh, 1993). Simply put, the individual must be motivated for the behavior to be exhibited. This is one of many reasons why motivation is so vitally important in sport settings, so much so that an entire chapter in this volume has been devoted to the subject and it is reviewed in several other chapters as well.

Other Factors in Observational Learning

Research on observational learning has identified additional factors that influence the modeling process. Mazur (1994) describes these factors as characteristics of the learner and characteristics of the situation. Regarding characteristics of the learner, individuals who are uncertain or lack confidence in their own abilities are especially likely to imitate a model's behavior (Kanareff & Lanzetta, 1960; Thelen, Dollinger, & Kirkland, 1979). Thus, athletes with lesser abilities and those who doubt their abilities are more likely to imitate other athletes and coaches.

As for characteristics of the situation, Mazur (1994) lists settings that are ambiguous (Jakubczak & Walters, 1959) or involve a difficult task (Harnick, 1978) as situational factors influencing the modeling of behaviors. Athletes who are unclear about what is required of them and athletes asked to perform behaviors that are moderately difficult are especially likely to rely on modeling to facilitate their learning. McCullagh (1993) states that another situational factor, verbal presentations, may also increase learning through observation. Providing verbal cues to athletes along with a visual model should be quite effective in teaching new behaviors.

THE APPLICATION OF THE PSYCHOLOGY
OF LEARNING TO SPORT SETTINGS

Within sport settings, the principles of the psychology of learning are applied through ***effective behavioral coaching*** (EBC, also referred to as applied behavioral analysis). Effective behavioral coaching is simply the application of learning principles to sport settings to better teach and train athletes. Effective behavioral coaching primarily employs operant learning principles (i.e., reinforcement and/or punishment), although modeling techniques have also been included (Allison & Ayllon, 1980). As for classical conditioning, although this work is both intriguing and informative, classical conditioning has a limited application to sport settings because this type of learning revolves around involuntary, reflexive responses. In sport, most responses are voluntary and within the control of the athlete, coach, or fan. As a result of the limitations of classical conditioning within sport, little research has investigated this topic in sport-related settings (LeUnes & Nation, 1989). However, because some responses in the sport world are reflexive in nature (such as the anxiety example described earlier in this chapter), more studies examining classical conditioning within sport settings are warranted.

Martin and Hryciako (1983, see also Donahue, Gillis, & King, 1980) suggest that a preliminary step in the use of EBC is to target the behaviors to be increased or decreased and transmit this information to the players. As Warren (1983) noted, to be successful, reinforcement programs "must begin with an understanding on the part of both player and coach as to what constitutes desired behavior" (pp. 91–92).

Several studies have examined the effectiveness of behavioral coaching techniques with the vast majority reporting encouraging results. Effective behavioral coaching has been discussed and/or has successfully improved the performance of athletes in swimming (Koop & Martin, 1983; McKenzie & Rushall, 1974; Rushall & Siedentop, 1972), basketball (Anshel, 1994; Siedentop, 1980), physical education classes (McKenzie, 1980), baseball (Anshel, 1994), football (Allison & Ayllon, 1980; Siedentop, 1980), and tennis (Buzas & Ayllon, 1981), as well as the behaviors of coaches (Smith, Smoll, & Curtis, 1978; Smoll et al., 1993; Rushall & Smith, 1979; Trudel & Gilbert, 1995; Ziegler, 1980a).

To illustrate how these programs operate, let us examine two of the above studies in detail. Siedentop's (1980) article is a good candidate for further examination because this manuscript describes how a football coach and a basketball coach used operant principles with their teams. The high school football coach began by targeting specific behaviors he wished to see either increased or decreased. These behaviors included more hustle and devotion during practice, fewer penalties during games, and fewer school-related behavior problems (such as absenteeism). The coach needed a reinforcement that would be desired by all teammates, and, therefore, decided to reward the players with a start in the next game (it was determined that starting was a strong incentive). Players received points for each of several categories reflecting the target behaviors. Those players earning all of the possible points for that week (referred to as the "100%ers") received a helmet decal and were placed into the pool of potential starters and team captains for the next game. This procedure was apparently quite successful in altering the players' behaviors.

The junior high school basketball coach wanted an increase in effort during practice. This coach awarded points during practice for performing routine drills and exhibiting "team player" attitudes and behaviors, and deducted points for demonstrating a negative attitude. The points were totaled and those players reaching a specific point were rewarded by having their name placed on an "Eagle Effort Board" conspicuously placed in the hallway leading to the gym. Once the system was implemented, players made more lay-ups, jump shots, and free throws; were more likely to hustle; and were less likely to display a poor attitude.

The work of Ziegler (1980a) also warrants further discussion because it provides an example of the use of EBC in the behaviors of coaches. Ziegler studied the effects of reinforcing the behavior of a women's volleyball coach. The coach's behaviors were recorded during practices for an entire season, and the coach was reinforced with verbal praise when one of several target behaviors were exhibited (e.g., on-task discussions, positive interactions with players, and positive interactions with feedback to players). Results indicated that each of the three target behaviors was increased when the coach was reinforced following the display of the behaviors.

Length and Spacing of Practice Sessions

Research in EBC and the psychology of learning has added valuable information concerning the length and spacing of practice sessions. Practice sessions are categorized into one of two types: distributed practice and massed practice. **Distributed practice** involves widely spaced practice sessions with long periods of rest, while **massed practice** has the team practicing on numerous occasions during a short time frame. A number of investigators have attempted to determine whether massed or distributed practice is better at facilitating learning. Sanderson (1983) argues that the best results are gained by using something in between the two; too much rest and too little rest can both be detrimental to learning. If the two types are compared directly, research has found that longer rest periods between trials (distributed practice) tend to be superior to no rest periods or shorter rest periods (massed practice, Doré & Hilgard, 1937; Lee & Genovese, 1988; Mazur, 1994). If too much effort is exerted in a single session, fatigue may set in, resulting in a decrease in performance (Chamberlin & Lee, 1993).

It should be noted, however, that the definitive answer to which type of practice is preferable is not available (Mazur, 1994). In fact, Chamberlin and Lee (1993, p. 220) concluded that, "there can be no absolute conclusions" concerning the length and distribution of practice sessions. One problem with the research in this area is that the trials and rest periods often involve seconds (e.g., Bourne & Archer, 1956; Chamberlin & Lee, 1993; Noble, Salazar, Skelley, & Wilkerson, 1979) as opposed to hours or days. Such small periods of practice may be of limited interest to coaches who are usually concerned with longer practice and rest periods.

Feedback, Knowledge of Results, and Knowledge of Performance

Research in the psychology of learning and EBC has found that motor learning is substantially facilitated by providing feedback to the learner concerning his or her progress in learning the task, especially when the feedback is precise and specific (Glencross, 1992; Magill & Wood, 1986). Feedback need not be presented to the athlete on every practice trial to garner these benefits. Indeed, Magill notes that it may be "comforting to the instructor to realize that he or she will not be causing the athlete harm by failing to provide feedback all the time" (p. 203). Magill (1993) states that feedback provides two benefits to athletes. First, it provides information concerning the success or failure of a behavior and, second, it may motivate the individual to continue to reach her or his goal. Black and Weiss (1992) note that feedback is also beneficial because athletes respond quite favorably to such information, regardless of whether the feedback focuses on successful or unsuccessful performances. These authors found that increases in beliefs that coaches provided high levels of feedback corresponded to higher levels of player enjoyment, competence, and perceived success.

Two types of feedback that are especially important to learning are knowledge of results and knowledge of performance. ***Knowledge of results*** (KR) involves providing information to a learner about the accuracy of his or her behavior (Mazur, 1994). Thomas et al. (1993) refer to KR as "outcome information" (p. 93), for example, providing information concerning how far a ball was thrown or how high an athlete jumped. Regarding observational learning, receiving KR of the model's behavior may enhance learning (McCullagh, 1993; Weir & Leavitt, 1990). That is, subjects may be more likely to reproduce a model's behavior accurately if they are given information about the accuracy of the model's performance. ***Knowledge of performance*** (KP) involves presenting an individual with information concerning one or more of the individual parts of the movement processes involved in the outcome. An example of this type of feedback would be providing information to a young basketball player about her footwork, grip, release, and stance. Providing information about both KR and KP may be the most effective feedback strategy (Schmidt & Young, 1991).

The Use of Punishment in Sport

Although punishment can be successful in teaching and altering behaviors (Schwartz, 1989), it may also present several problems for the coach employing this behavior modification strategy. As a result, reinforcing desired behaviors is preferable to punishing undesired ones. In fact, even Thorndike refined his theories to reflect the inadequacies of punishment (Thorndike, 1931). Research in the psychology of learning and sport psychology has identified a number of problems with punishment that render it less desirable.

First, punishment is often lacking in intensity (Schwartz, 1989). To be effective, punishment must be intense (Azrin & Holz, 1966). If not, the effects may be temporary, lasting only as long as the punishment itself. Choosing the appropriate intensity level is a tricky task. In sport settings, punishments often take the form of verbal reprimands because physical reprimands are never acceptable as avenues for punishing players (Warren, 1983). The result may be that the punishment is simply not severe enough to curtail the behavior.

Second, the undesirable behavior and the punishment are often separated by a substantial amount of time (Azrin & Holz, 1966; Schwartz, 1989). Remember, both reinforcements and punishments must be immediate to be effective. For example, let us assume that a football player has been benched for Friday's game because of a lack of effort during Tuesday's practice. There will be a 3-day time span between the behavior and the punishment and, as a result, the punishment will lose a great deal of its effectiveness.

A third problem with punishment is that it tells the individual what not to do but does not tell the person what to do (Mazur, 1994; Schwartz, 1989; Skinner, 1971; Warren, 1983). A football coach may begin to yell at his lineman for a poor block the player attempted, saying things such as, "How could you do that?" and "I don't want to ever see you block like that again!" Yet the player has not been told what the optimal behavior is and, thus, has not furthered his skills. The coach should accompany his complaints with an explanation of the correct blocking technique.

Finally, other problems with the use of punishment include: the inability to punish the behavior each time it is exhibited (Azrin & Holz, 1966), the failure to explain the reasons behind the punishment (Baron & Greenberg, 1990), the resulting negative emotions and aggressions that result from punishment (Azrin & Holz, 1966; Mazur, 1994), and that, for some players, the attention accompanying the punishment is actually quite rewarding. Because of the problems with using punishment, most sport psychologists view reinforcement as preferable to punishment (Buzas & Ayllon, 1981; LeUnes & Nation, 1989). In fact, Anshel (1994) goes so far as to say that punishments in sport settings are flatly an "incorrect" form of behavior modification (p. 188).

SPECIFIC RECOMMENDATIONS FOR ENHANCING LEARNING IN SPORT AND MOTOR SETTINGS

Based on the preceding discussion of the psychology of learning and effective behavioral coaching, it seems appropriate to offer several specific recommendations for enhancing learning in sport settings. These suggestions were derived from Siedentop (1980), Anshel (1994), Thompson (1993), Mazur (1994), Wolff (1993), and Glencross (1992), as well as my own coaching experiences.

1. Be very clear in the operational definitions of the target behavior. Define these behaviors in precise and observable terms.
2. Monitor the players' behaviors clearly such that each appropriate instance of the desired/undesired behavior is reinforced/punished.
3. Be consistent in the presentation of rewards and punishments. Each instance of the de-

sired behavior should be rewarded in the same way for each player and, likewise, each exhibition of the undesired behavior should be punished in the same manner for each player.

4. Praise the desired behavior, not the individual's personality. For example, if a player has completed a critical pass in a football game, don't say "You're a great player." Rather, offer behavior-specific praise such as, "That was a great play." Behavior-specific praise is more likely to reinforce the desired response.

5. Reward effort and improvement as well as the final behavioral outcome. In this way, lesser skilled players are reinforced.

6. Provide the appropriate models for demonstrating the desired behaviors.

7. If you are a coach, monitor and be careful of your own behaviors; with the players' attentional focus directed toward you, they may model both your positive *and* negative behaviors.

8. Let players make mistakes, especially younger players. When players do not feel overwhelmed by the fear of punishment, they may play more assertively, with more confidence, and with less anxiety. The fear of punishment may lead to an attempt to escape the situation altogether by leaving the team.

9. Avoid rewards that are incompatible with team spirit. For example, team most valuable player awards may promote individual play over team play.

10. Be sure to provide both knowledge of results and knowledge of performance. Further, be sure to provide information to the athlete that informs the player about what she or he should do next, that is, how to use the feedback.

11. Employ a partial reinforcement schedule to decrease the likelihood of extinction.

12. Reward and punish immediately.

13. When teaching new behaviors to athletes, employ shaping to assist in the training.

14. Finally, although it is recommended that punishment not be used, if this strategy is employed, be sure the punishment is at the appropriate intensity level, is done immediately, is accompanied by information identifying the appropriate behavior, and is done consistently. In addition, be sure an explanation for the punishment is provided. Further, you should never shout or scream at players (particularly young players), should never punish a child to make yourself feel better, and should always offer at least one warning to the athlete prior to implementing punishment.

A FINAL NOTE: THE IMPORTANCE OF COGNITION IN LEARNING

Before concluding this chapter, a word about the importance of cognition in sport learning is warranted. Although this chapter's focus has been on the learning of behaviors, recent investigations of learning have found that cognition is a vital aspect of motor learning (Glencross, 1992). In fact, two prominent authors on motor learning have incorporated cognition into their theories (Adams, 1971; Schmidt, 1975). The importance of cognition in learning can be seen in many situations. For example, (1) memory is a requirement for observational learning, (2) understanding and thinking about knowledge of results impacts learning, and (3) memories for past rewards and punishments are vital for these strategies to have maximum effects. Thus, although we have described the behavioral aspects of learning, cognitive aspects (such as attention, memory, and perception) are important as well. These topics will be discussed further in the chapter on information processing and attention in sport.

SUMMARY

Coaches spend a great deal of their time teaching skills to players. Thus, learning is an important area of study for sport psychologists. Three different types of learning are most relevant for sport: classical conditioning, operant conditioning, and observational learning.

Classical conditioning involves the pairing of a neutral stimulus (conditioned stimulus or CS) with another stimulus (the unconditioned stimulus or US) that elicits an automatic, reflexive response (the unconditioned response or UR). After several pairings of the CS followed by the US, the CS begins to elicit the response (now referred to as the conditioned response or CR). If the CS is continually presented to the organism without the accompanying US, after a short time the CS will no longer elicit the CR, a process known as extinction. A new CS may be substituted for the original CS. If the new CS elicits the CR, generalization has been demonstrated. Conversely, if the new CS does not elicit the CR, discrimination has been shown.

Operant conditioning, which involves voluntary behaviors, is reflected in Thorndike's law of effect. Coaches can alter the behaviors of players by applying a positive stimulus (positive reinforcement) or negative stimulus (punishment) after the player's behavior. Further, coaches can modify the players' behaviors by removing a positive stimulus (response cost) or negative stimulus (negative reinforcement). The training of athletes is often facilitated by the process of shaping. Schedules of reinforcement are also important and include immediate and delayed reinforcement, continuous and partial reinforcement, and fixed and variable ratio schedules. Superstitious behavior is found when an individual believes that a reward is based on a certain response (contingent reinforcement) when, in actuality, the reward was not based on anything (noncontingent reinforcement).

As for observational learning, Bandura presented a four-step model for this process. This model includes attention directed toward the model, memory for what the model did, the ability to reproduce the behavior, and the motivational desire to do so.

The application of learning principles to sport settings is accomplished by using effective behavioral coaching (EBC). Several important aspects of EBC were identified including the length of practice sessions (i.e., massed versus distributed practice), the importance of feedback through knowledge of results and knowledge of performance, and the problems and use of punishment in sporting environments.

GLOSSARY

Behaviorism   A subdiscipline of psychology reflecting the belief that psychology should be the science of observable behavior.

Classical Conditioning   A form of learning involving involuntary, reflexive responses.

Conditioned Response   The response elicited by the conditioned stimulus.

Conditioned Stimulus   A neutral stimulus that, after many pairings with the unconditioned stimulus, begins to elicit the conditioned response.

Contingent Reinforcement   Reinforcement that is based on a specific behavior.

Continuous Reinforcement   Rewarding a behavior each time it is exhibited.

Delayed Reinforcement   Reinforcement in which a substantial amount of time separates the target behavior and the reward.

Discrimination   The application of a new conditioned stimulus that is quite dissimilar from the original conditioned stimulus and, as a result, fails to elicit the conditioned response.

Distributed Practice   A practice schedule involving widely spaced practice sessions with long periods of rest.

Effective Behavioral Coaching   The application of learning principles to sport settings to teach and train athletes better.

Extinction   The elimination of a response through the removal of the unconditioned stimulus or reward.

Fixed Ratio   A schedule of reinforcement in which a reward is presented each time a specified number of responses has occurred.

Generalization   The eliciting of a conditioned response through the presentation of a new conditioned stimulus that is similar to the original conditioned stimulus.

Immediate Reinforcement   Reinforcement that immediately follows the target behavior.

Knowledge of Performance   Presenting an individual with information concerning one or more individual parts of the movement process involved in the outcome.

Knowledge of Results   Providing information to a learner about the accuracy of his or her behavior.

Law of Effect   Any behavior followed by a positive consequence will have an increased likelihood of being displayed in the future. Conversely, any behavior followed by a negative consequence will have a decreased likelihood of being displayed in the future.

Learning   Any relatively permanent change in behavior due to experience.

Massed Practice   A practice schedule involving numerous sessions during a short time.

Negative Reinforcement   The removal of a negative stimulus in an attempt to increase a desired behavior.

Noncontingent Reinforcement   Reinforcement that is not based on any particular behavior.

Observational Learning   The vicarious learning of behaviors through imitation and modeling.

Operant Conditioning   The strategic presentation of reinforcements and punishments in an attempt to increase desired voluntary behaviors while decreasing undesired voluntary behaviors.

Partial Reinforcement   Rewarding a behavior on only a subset of trials.

Positive Reinforcement   The application of a positive stimulus in an attempt to increase a desired behavior.

Punishment   The application of a negative stimulus in an attempt to decrease an undesired behavior.

Response Cost   The removal of a positive stimulus in an attempt to decrease an undesired behavior.

Self-Modeling   A procedure in which individuals view themselves correctly performing a task.

Shaping   Reinforcing successive approximations toward a goal behavior.

Unconditioned Response   The involuntary response elicited by the unconditioned stimulus.

Unconditioned Stimulus   The stimulus that automatically elicits the unconditioned response.

Variable Ratio   A schedule of reinforcement in which the number of responses required for reinforcement is an average of some number.

APPLICATION AND REVIEW QUESTIONS

1. Develop an example of classical conditioning. Include and identify the US, UR, CS, and CR, and extinction, generalization, and discrimination.
2. Explain the law of effect.
3. Describe the 2 × 2 matrix of operant conditioning, providing an example of each of the four strategies for increasing/decreasing behavior.
4. How is shaping used to teach new behaviors?
5. Explain the differences between continuous and partial schedules of reinforcement and between fixed ratio and variable ratio schedules of reinforcement.
6. Describe Bandura's four-step process of observational learning and develop a sport-specific example incorporating each of the four steps.
7. Assuming that you are the coach of a little league sport team, what suggestions would you offer to facilitate the players' learning of new skills?

SUGGESTED READINGS

GLENCROSS, D. J. (1992). Human skill and motor learning: A critical review. *Sport Science Review, 1,* 65–78. This article examines the importance of cognition in motor learning.

MAGILL, R. (1993). Augmented feedback in skill acquisition. In R. N. Singer, M. Murphy, & L. K. Tennant (Eds.), *Handbook of research on sport psychology* (pp. 891–900). New York: Macmillan. This chapter examines the types and effectiveness of feedback in sport, including such factors as the timing and frequency of the feedback.

MAZUR, J. E. (1994). *Learning and behavior* (3rd ed.). Englewood Cliffs, NJ: Prentice-Hall. This textbook provides the reader with a general overview of learning as well as the principles involved.

McCULLAGH, P. (1993). Modeling: Learning, developmental, and social psychological considerations. In R. N. Singer, M. Murphy, & L. K. Tennant (Eds.), *Handbook of research on sport psychology* (pp. 106–126). New York: Macmillan. As the title implies, this chapter reviews research on modeling in sport settings.

Chapter 6

INFORMATION PROCESSING AND ATTENTION IN SPORT

You may recall that our definition of sport psychology includes the players' (and spectators') cognitive reactions. Cognitions were described as mental processes such as thoughts and memories. After reading our definition of sport psychology, you may have wondered why mental processes are so important. To help answer this question, think about the times when you have been watching elite athletes on television. If you have watched even a small amount of televised sports, you have probably heard an announcer describe one or more of the participants as an "intelligent" player. Similarly, a successful coach is often seen as a "genius." This seems to indicate that intelligence and the ability to process information are key ingredients in athletic success. However, some successful players appear to be acting without thinking, simply letting their natural abilities take over. Indeed, when athletes are in a slump, they are often told that they are "thinking too much."

Thus, it is apparent that mental processes are indeed relevant to athletic success. For example, questions such as, "How do athletes process information given to them by coaches?", "How do they remember which play to run?", and "How do they remember how to execute the required skills (such as dribbling a basketball)?", are all important to sport psychologists. In this chapter, we will examine these and other topics related to the information processing of athletes (the knowledge of fans will be discussed in a later chapter). However, before discussing the sport-specific ramifications of information processing, it will be helpful to have a general understanding of the information processing system.

INFORMATION PROCESSING

In our review of information processing, we will examine how individuals remember and use information relevant to athletic performance. Throughout this presentation, it will be helpful to consider how a computer works because the operations of a computer and the information processing system of humans share many commonalties. Let us say an individual had begun work on a term paper for her sport psychology course. When she turned on the computer and inserted the floppy disk, there was, of course, no information on the disk. To write the paper, the student needed to put information onto the disk. Similarly, in information processing one must encode the information into memory. ***Encoding,*** the first stage of information processing, involves transforming information into a form suitable for memory storage. For example, before a basketball player can execute "play number 4," she must encode information about this play: where she should stand, to whom should she throw the ball, and so forth.

Information ***storage,*** the second stage of information processing, involves the storing of information in a permanent or nearly permanent fashion. Returning to our sport psychology student, let us imagine that this person had typed half of her paper when she was interrupted by an emergency. In response to the emergency, she quickly shut off the computer and left the room, forgetting to save her paper. When she returned later in the day to finish her assignment, she found nothing on the disk because her paper was not stored. A similar process is at work with human memory. If the basketball player's attention had been directed away from the coach when he was describing "play number 4," the information concerning this play may not have been stored in memory.

Let us return to the sport psychology student one more time. This time, let us assume that she did save the paper before leaving to deal with the emergency, but let us also imagine that this was the 18th paper she had written for this class. As a result, when she returned to work on her paper, she could not remember which of the 18 files contained the current paper. Thus, even though the information was properly encoded and stored on the disk, she still had trouble retrieving the information. ***Retrieval,*** the final stage in information processing, is the process of recalling and using information stored in long-term memory. For example, the basketball player may have been directing her attention to her coach during practice and may have correctly encoded and stored the information, yet, because she was nervous during a game, she might not have been able to retrieve the information properly. For information processing to work fully, the individual must successfully encode, store, and retrieve the information. The following section describes these processes in detail by examining the different types of memory involved in information processing.

Memory

Research in cognitive psychology has identified three different types of memory: sensory memory, short-term memory, and long-term memory, all of which are relevant to sport performance (Glencross, 1992). These different memories, although distinct, operate together to process information (Atkinson & Shiffrin, 1968; Best, 1992; Galotti, 1994). Figure 6.1 depicts this process, described in detail below.

Sensory Memory.   ***Sensory memory*** is the first step in the memory process. This type of memory involves the very brief storage of sensory information. Two forms of sensory memory with relevance for sport psychology are iconic sensory memory and echoic sensory memory. ***Iconic sensory memory*** involves the visual sense, while ***echoic sensory memory*** involves the auditory sense. Information reaching the visual and auditory senses is briefly stored in the iconic and echoic memories. For example, let us say a high school football quarterback, John, looks to the bench to see which play the coach would like to have run. As soon as John sees the coach, the image of the coach signaling for play number 4 and the players and spectators in the background enter John's iconic sensory memory. Had the coach verbally informed John of the play by yelling the number 4, the word "four" would have entered John's echoic sensory memory.

Research has found that the duration of sensory memory is extremely short. In fact, icons usually last less than a second, while echoes last only a few seconds (Best, 1992; Galotti, 1994; Sperling, 1960; Watkins & Watkins, 1980). Although the duration is short, the capacity of sensory memory is quite large (Best, 1992; Galotti, 1994). Remembering the football player discussed above, when he looked to the bench for the play there was a great deal of information in the image. The coach, the players, the uniforms, the fans, the members of the press, and many other components combined to form the icon.

Short-term Memory.   Much of the information entering sensory memory ends there. That is, the information remains in sensory memory and eventually is lost. This information is said to have ***decayed***, meaning that the memory trace has been completely erased (similar to erasing a file from a computer disk). However, information to which the individual pays close attention will usually be transferred to short-term memory. ***Short-term memory*** is the second step in the memory process and concerns the active, cognitive manipulation and use of information. For this reason, short-term memory is also called working memory. The duration of short-term memory is quite short (Best, 1992; Galotti, 1994). Research has indicated that information

FIGURE 6.1   The relationships between the three types of memory.

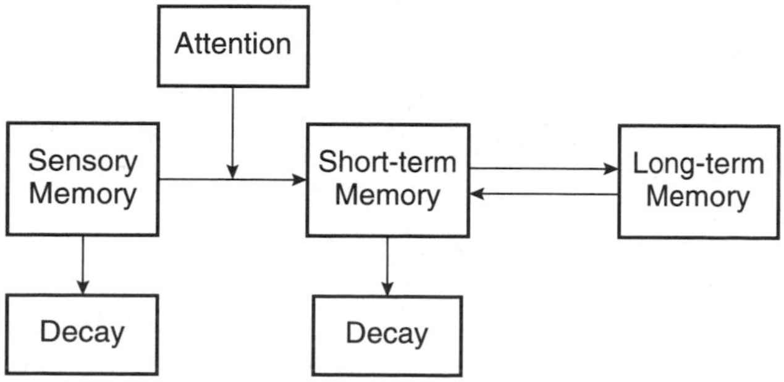

remains in short-term memory for only about half a minute (Brown, 1958; Peterson & Peterson, 1959). Individuals often use the technique of rehearsal to maintain information in short-term memory for longer periods. ***Rehearsal*** involves the constant repetition of information. For example, imagine that John and his football coach are meeting on the sideline during a time out to discuss the next play. If the coach tells John to run play 4, a reverse, John must remember this information for several more moments as he waits for the time out to end and after he has trotted back out onto the field. To be certain that he does not forget the play, John probably would repeat to himself "play 4, reverse; play 4, reverse; play 4, reverse." This rehearsal of the play can keep the information in short-term memory for a long time.

The capacity of short-term memory is quite small (Best, 1992; Galotti, 1994). Miller's (1956) research indicated that the capacity was approximately seven items of information. If the football coach asked John to run a series of plays, John would only be able to remember a list of approximately seven plays. However, individuals can increase the size of the items in short-term memory through the process of chunking. A ***chunk*** is a meaningful unit of information organized around a rule or pattern (Best, 1992). Thus, the coach could ask the quarterback to run all of the plays to his fullback (seven plays) and then all of the plays to his tight end (six plays). By chunking the information into meaningful units (plays directed toward certain individuals), John could keep a larger number of total plays in his short-term memory.

As shown in Figure 6.1, new information enters short-term memory from sensory memory, while old information (previously stored information) enters short-term memory from long-term memory. Let us first consider information entering from sensory memory; information re-entering short-term memory from long-term memory will be discussed shortly. When John saw his coach signal for play 4, this information was briefly stored in his iconic sensory memory. Of course, the game is continuing and John cannot continue to stare at his coach indefinitely. He will not actually begin the play for several seconds, a longer period than the duration of iconic sensory memory. Thus, the information must be transferred to short-term memory or it will be lost before the play can begin. John may have to rehearse the play to keep the information in short-term memory. With the information in short-term memory, he can run the play.

Long-term Memory.   Some of the new information housed in short-term memory will be transferred into ***long-term memory,*** the final stage of the memory process involving an apparently infinite capacity and seemingly permanent storage (Best, 1992; Galotti, 1994). Other items of information will be lost (i.e., decay). As depicted in Figure 6.1 and mentioned previously, information housed in long-term memory can be transferred to short-term memory to use the information actively and cognitively. Remember that it is for this reason that short-term memory is often referred to as working memory. Let us imagine that the information concerning play number 4 was successfully stored in John's long-term memory. Indeed, after the game he told numerous family members and friends that the coach called play number 4. Let us now jump in time 5 years to a conversation John is having with a former teammate, Larry. It has been years since John has thought about executing play number 4 in the game in question. Indeed, this information is far from his current thoughts and consciousness. When Larry asks John to recall the play, however, the information is transferred from its dormant state in long-term memory to an active state of processing in short-term memory. John and Larry can then discuss the details of the play, reliving the moment together.

It is important to note that, even though the information was correctly encoded and stored in John's long-term memory, he still might not have been able to retrieve the information successfully. This is because of a phenomenon known as interference. ***Interference*** is the inability to recall information due to other competing or conflicting items of information. Certainly, John would have been involved in many other plays both before and after the specific play in question. This large bulk of other information may block John's retrieval of play number 4. In fact, it is believed that interference is responsible for most, if not all, of the forgetting of information stored in long-term memory (Galotti, 1994). Thus, when we forget something that has been successfully stored in long-term memory, it is incorrect to assume the memory trace has decayed. Rather, the information is there but we simply cannot get to it due to interference.

Research in cognitive psychology has identified three types of long-term memory (Galotti, 1994; Solso, 1991; Tulving, 1985, 1986). One type, ***semantic memory,*** is our memory for the specifics of a language. For example, when the football coach asked John to run a reverse, John had an understanding of the meaning of the word "reverse." A second type of long-term memory, ***episodic memory*** (sometimes called autobiographical memory), contains information about personally experienced events. John's memory for the play described earlier is an episodic memory. Episodic memories are rarely complete and accurate. Rather, we tend to add information to our experiences unconsciously, making our memories of these events complete. John may not have a complete memory of a play that occurred 5 years earlier. As a result, he may have thought that the game was against Central High, while his friend, Larry, was convinced that their opponent was Northfield High. Both individuals could be highly certain of the accuracy of their retrieval because their memories have been reconstructed. Finally, ***procedural memory*** (also called perceptual-motor memory) concerns our memory for stimulus-response pairings. These memories involve the storage of information related to motor activities. For example, information concerning the procedures for walking, running, and sitting down is housed in procedural memory. In sport, a great deal of information is stored in this type of memory. Behaviors such as swinging a bat, holding a putter, throwing a football, and kicking a soccer ball are all examples of procedural memories.

ATTENTION AND ATHLETIC PERFORMANCE

Within sport psychology, most work examining information processing has investigated the attention of athletes. In 1890, James defined attention as "the taking possession by the mind, in clear and vivid form, of one out of what seem several simultaneously possible objects or trains of thought. Focalization, concentration, and consciousness are of its essence. It implies withdrawal from some things in order to effectively deal with others" (pp. 403–404). While this definition accurately incorporates all components of attention and is commonly cited, its length makes it a bit cumbersome. I tend to prefer Galotti's (1994) definition of ***attention***: "cognitive resources, mental effort, or concentration devoted to a cognitive process" (p. 477). Thus, attention involves actively and cognitively focusing on a topic (or topics). We attempt to attend to certain aspects of our environment while excluding others. In the following section, we will examine the general psychology research on attention. This section will be followed by a review of the sport-specific work targeting the attention of athletes.

General Psychology Research on Attention

Research on attentional processes was stimulated by Cherry's work in the early 1950s (Cherry, 1953; see also Wood & Cowan, in press). Cherry was interested in what he called the ***cocktail party phenomenon,*** which concerns people being able to carry on a conversation with one specific individual even though there are several other people talking nearby. Cherry wondered how it was possible to focus one's perceptual and cognitive attention on just this one individual. To examine this phenomenon, Cherry used a research technique called shadowing. In the ***shadowing*** procedure, a subject is presented with a different message in each ear and asked to repeat out loud (i.e., shadow) one of the two messages. Cherry (1953) found that subjects' memory of the information presented in the attended ear was quite good. Conversely, subjects reported little if any memory of the information presented in the unattended ear.

A few years later, Broadbent (1954, 1957) proposed a filter theory of attention to account for Cherry's findings. Broadbent's ***filter theory of attention*** proposes that unattended information is completely screened out of processing by a buffer. This theory is depicted in Figure 6.2. When a pair of balls are simultaneously placed in the tubes, only one of the balls can fit through the filter (the swinging hinge) at a time. According to Broadbent, the same phenomenon occurs in attention. When subjects are presented with information through two "tubes" at the same time (e.g., different messages simultaneously presented in each ear), only one item of information can pass through the filter at a given point in time.

Although some research supported Broadbent's theory, other work cast doubt about the notion that unattended information is completely screened out of processing. Rather, several studies indicated that some of the unattended information is processed, although the processing may occur at an unconscious level. For example, even while shadowing the information being presented in one ear, subjects often could recognize when their name was presented in the unattended ear (Moray, 1959). That information presented in the nonshadowed ear is at least partially processed was also demonstrated in a study performed by von Wright, Anderson, and Stenman (1975). In this research, subjects were asked to attend to a long list of words. Each time a target word was presented (the Finnish word for suitable), participants were given a mild electric shock. Subjects were then asked to shadow a list of words in one ear while they were presented with (and supposedly ignored) a dif-

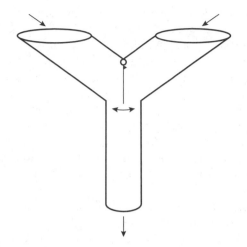

FIGURE 6.2 Broadbent's filter theory of attention. (Reprinted from: Broadbent, D. E. [1957]. A mechanical model for human attention and immediate memory. *Psychological Review,* 64: 205–215.)

ferent list in the other ear. When the Finnish word was presented in the unattended ear (the word to which subjects were shocked during the earlier stage of the research), there was a noticeable and significant increase in galvanic skin response, an indication of elevated physiological arousal. Thus, subjects were apparently processing some of the information being presented in the unattended ear.

As a result of studies finding that information presented in the unattended ear is at least partially processed, it became apparent that Broadbent's filter theory was too rigid. To accommodate the conflicting research, Treisman (1964) altered Broadbent's theory. Treisman's model, called the ***attenuation theory of attention,*** was similar to Broadbent's model, but Treisman's theory proposed that the unattended message was not completely blocked from processing. Rather, it was simply lower in strength than the information presented in the attended ear (Eysenck, 1984).

The Implications of Attention Research for Athletic Performance

The attention research of cognitive psychologists has many important implications for athletic performance. Indeed, this topic is so vital to sport psychology that sport researchers began to conduct sport-specific attention research and develop sport-specific instruments. In general, two areas of attention research have surfaced in sport psychology: the relationship between attention and performance and the attentional styles of athletes. Please note that these areas are not mutually exclusive. Rather, they are quite connected. For example, research on the attentional style has found that certain styles facilitate performance. These styles are reviewed later in this chapter.

Attention and Performance. With regard to athletic performance, the attention of athletes is important when athletes are learning a behavior and when they are performing a previously acquired skill. When learning a new skill, athletes must correctly direct their attention toward their coach or manager. For example, consider once again our high school quarterback, John. When John was young he most likely did not know the proper grip for throwing a pass. As a result, he had to be taught the grip by his prep football coaches. If John's attention had been divided during the demonstrations, he would not have properly encoded the information in sensory and short-term memory. As a result, the information concerning the proper grip would not have been transferred to long-term memory for John's use during practice and games. As for performing a skill during competition, athletes must be able to focus their attention on the task at hand. For example, if John is to execute a pass play optimally, he must have his attention focused on his target. If his attention is divided, John's performance will suffer.

Thus, there is a positive correlation between athletic performance and attention, both when learning a skill and when performing the skill in competition. Athletes with superior attention and concentration skills tend to be successful (e.g., Highlen & Bennett, 1980; Thomas & Over, 1994). This relationship occurs because our cognitive capacity is limited (Easterbrook, 1959; Galotti, 1994; Mandler, 1984). At any time, the amount of information we can process is limited. We cannot simultaneously devote our attention to an infinite number of stimuli. As a result, when our attention is highly divided, the quality of our performance on tasks will often decrease (Eysenck, 1984; Kahneman, 1973).

That performance quality decreases when athletes attend to and concentrate on too many stimuli at once has two major implications. First, athletes should learn their athletic skills to the point that they become automatic. Indeed, Thomas et al. (1993) state that "The goal of learning is to automate the skill" (p. 92). ***Automatic processes*** are behaviors that become so well ingrained in procedural memory that the execution of these behaviors can be done without consciousness and with few cognitive resources (Solso, 1991). Automatic processes can be contrasted with controlled processes (Boutcher, 1992). ***Controlled processes*** are behaviors that require careful and conscious thought, such as selecting the appropriate golf club or interpreting the sign being flashed by a third base coach. As an everyday example of an automatic process, think about when you sit down in a chair. As you move toward the chair, turn around, and bend your knees, are you conscious of these behaviors? In all likelihood you are not. This behavior, as well as many others such as opening a door, picking up a telephone, and starting a car, is so automatic that we need not think about this task when performing the actions involved. Indeed, it is because the act of sitting is automatic and done without conscious effort that others are able to surprise us by removing the chair from behind us! Because behaviors like these are automatic, we do not have to allocate much, if any, of our cognitive capacity to them. We are then able to devote the attentional capacity to other tasks.

The sport implications of this should be readily apparent. By regularly practicing the skills performed in their sport, athletes are able to store the information in procedural memory to the degree that performing the skill becomes automatic. As a result, athletes begin to trust their skill when executing the target behavior (Moore & Stevenson, 1991, 1994). By automating a skill, an athlete is then able to devote his or her attention to other aspects of the game. For example, consider the act of dribbling a basketball. If a point guard has not stored the act of dribbling in procedural memory to the point that it has become automatic, she will have to attend consciously to the act while competing. She will have to be conscious of the position of her hands, her feet, and the ball. As a result, she will be less able to attend to other aspects of the game such as the position of her teammates, the location of her opponents, and the suggestions of her coaches. Consequently, her performance will suffer. However, if she is able to learn to dribble so well that the behavior becomes automatic, she will no longer be forced to divide her attention.

The second sport implication of our limited attentional capacity is that athletes should try to convey as much extraneous information as possible to their opponents. Doing this will cause the opponent's attention to be divided, and their performance will subsequently decrease. If a football team never throws a pass to the tight end, the other team does not have to attend to this person on pass plays. Instead, they can focus their attention solely on the other receivers. On the other hand, if the tight end is incorporated into the passing offense, the defensive team must attend to and concentrate on this player as well, reducing the attention directed toward other players.

There are many real-life examples of attempts by athletes and fans to divide the attention of visiting teams. Many teams have developed complicated offenses to force their opponents to concentrate on many factors. At little league baseball games it is quite common to hear the fielders shouting in rhythm in an attempt to disrupt the batter's concentration. The "trash talking" that has become all too common in professional and college basketball is also designed to disrupt the opponent's concentration. As for spectators, many sport fans feel that it is their job to help disrupt the other team. At the University of California, Santa Barbara, for example, they have developed elaborate methods of diverting the attention of the visiting team. Fans seated at the end of the court spin spiralling pinwheels while the opposing players attempt free throws. They also have a "Thundermeter" to measure the noise level in the arena. When the noise gets to a certain level, lights begin to flash. Of course, the high noise level is designed to alter the concentration of the visiting team while psyching up the home team. As will be discussed later in this text, these attempts by spectators to influence the behaviors of athletes can be successful.

Attentional Style.   Within sport psychology, perhaps the greatest amount of research targeting the attention of athletes has been focused on the attentional style of sport participants. ***Attentional style*** involves an individual's tendency to attend to environmental cues in a personalized manner (Anshel et al., 1991). Thus, the attentional style of athletes is similar to a personality trait, with an athlete's attentional style remaining somewhat consistent across different situations (Nideffer, 1993a). Most often, research on the attentional style of athletes has examined their ***attentional focus,*** that is, their ability to focus in the most appropriate style and on the correct stimuli.

DIMENSIONS OF ATTENTIONAL FOCUS.   Robert Nideffer (1993a; see also Wachtel, 1967), a leader in sport attention research, suggests that there are two independent dimensions of attentional focus. The first dimension is attentional width. ***Attentional width*** concerns the number of stimuli on which an individual is focusing and ranges from narrow to broad. A ***narrow attentional focus*** involves focusing attention on just one or a few stimuli, while a ***broad attentional focus*** involves focusing attention on a large number of stimuli. At certain times, each of these styles should be employed. A bowler trying to convert a single-pin spare should use a narrow attentional focus (i.e., focus solely on the pin), while a point guard dribbling the ball and getting ready to run a set play would best be served by using a broad attentional focus (she needs to focus on several stimuli simultaneously, including the players, the basket, the ball, and the coach).

The second dimension of attentional focus is ***attentional direction.*** This dimension concerns the degree to which an individual's attention is focused internally or externally. An ***internal attentional focus*** is when an athlete directs his or her attention inwardly toward his or her own thoughts and feelings. An ***external attentional focus*** involves directing attention outwardly to environmental stimuli. As with attentional width, both forms of attentional direction can facilitate performance when used in the correct setting. The point guard described above should maintain an external focus, while a marathon runner should occasionally focus internally to monitor his or her body. The attentional focus of marathon runners has been of particular interest to sport psychologists as discussed in this chapter's "A Closer Look."

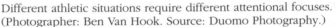

Different athletic situations require different attentional focuses. (Photographer: Ben Van Hook. Source: Duomo Photography.)

A CLOSER LOOK:
THE ATTENTIONAL FOCUS OF MARATHON RUNNERS

The attentional focus of marathon runners has gained a great deal of research attention from sport psychologists. The attentional focus of marathon runners can be categorized to include associaters and dissociaters (Morgan, 1978). ***Associaters*** tend to internalize their attentional focus to their bodies while ***dissociaters*** tend to externalize their attentional focus to outside stimuli. That is, dissociaters attempt to block out feedback from their bodies. For example, these runners may sing a song, think about work, wear headphones for listening to music, or admire the scenery. These dissociation tactics are designed to reduce feelings of exertion, fatigue, and pain.

Morgan and his colleagues (Morgan, 1978; Morgan & Pollack, 1977) have suggested that the best marathon runners use an associative strategy. According to Morgan, this strategy allows the athletes to monitor their physical states more effectively and, therefore, decreases the likelihood of injury. However, contrary to this perspective, research has failed to find a relationship between the use of an associative strategy and the likelihood of injury (Masters & Lambert, 1989; Masters & Ogles, 1992).

Knowing that research has found that elite marathoners tend to associate, you may be wondering why less gifted runners do not also try to adopt this attentional strategy. The answer is that there appears to be a benefit to the employment of dissociative techniques for many exercisers. As mentioned above, dissociative strategies take the athletes away from the pain and anguish of long distance sports. As a result, they may be able to train longer and harder because they perceive that they have lower levels of exertion. For example, Johnson and Siegel (1992) had subjects perform a 15-minute exercise session on a cycle ergometer. Some subjects were asked to associate, while others were asked to use a dissociate strategy. Subjects asked to associate during the session reported higher levels of exertion, even though their heart rates did not differ from the dissociaters (i.e., their actual effort was the same). Other research has also supported the finding that dissociative strategies allow for performance gains by decreasing perceptions of effort and fatigue (Morgan, Horstman, Cymerman, & Stokes, 1983; Pennebaker & Lightner, 1980), leaving Rose (1986) to conclude that "dissociative strategies are more appropriate for novice athletes, and a mixture of associative and dissociative strategies should be used by more elite athletes" (p. 235).

The four types of attentional focus can be combined to form four possible attentional strategies: broad-internal, broad-external, narrow-internal, and narrow-external (Nideffer, 1993a, 1993b). Individuals using a broad-internal focus of attention are usually analyzing a particular situation, such as focusing on the game plan or thinking about a new strategy. Martens (1987b) refers to players who tend to use this attentional strategy as "thinking players" (p. 143). Persons using a broad-external attentional focus are usually involved with assessing a particular situation, such as a point guard examining the positions of other players. Athletes employing a narrow-internal attentional strategy are often rehearsing their performance prior to the game. This strategy can be seen in athletes who "put on a game face" prior to competition, as well as golfers who mentally imagine a shot prior to swinging the club. Finally, athletes using a narrow-external strategy are usually in a position to act or react to specific components of the external environment, such as a batter getting ready to hit a pitch.

The ability to match the correct attentional strategies with the appropriate game situations is vital if an athlete is to achieve a top level of performance (Mahoney, Gabriel, & Perkins, 1987; Nideffer, 1993a). Sports such as golf require a narrow focus, while other sports, such as football, require the use of a broad attentional focus (see Figure 6.3 for a humorous look at what might happen when an athlete employs an inappropriate attentional focus). However, it is incorrect to state that one attentional style is preferable to another because most sports require the use of multiple attentional strategies. What is most critical for athletic performance is the ability to

FIGURE 6.3   Sometimes athletes employ the wrong attentional focus. In this humorous example, the player should have used an external focus instead of an internal focus. (Source: Universal Press Syndicate.)

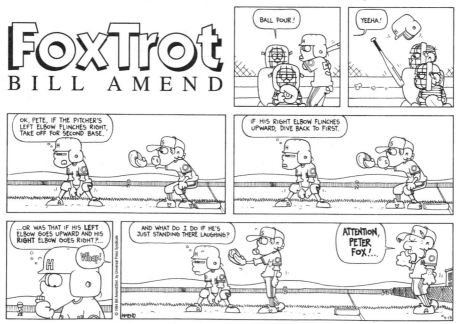

fluctuate back and forth from one attentional style to another (Nideffer, 1979). For example, Castiello and Umiltà (1992) found that professional volleyball players were faster than control subjects at recognizing the position of a stimulus (displayed on a video monitor), particularly if the stimulus appeared in an unexpected location. Castiello and Umiltà concluded that "expert athletes are characterized by higher attentional flexibility" (p. 307).

To assist athletes in developing the correct attentional strategies for specific situations, and to assist them in learning how to be flexible in their attentional style, many sport psychologists have developed attention control training programs. Because these programs concern an active intervention by a trained sport psychologist, this topic will be discussed in the intervention chapter.

MEASURING ATTENTIONAL STYLE. In 1976, Nideffer (1976a) published the Test of Attentional and Interpersonal Style (TAIS), a scale that has since become the standard instrument for assessing attentional style in sport settings. The TAIS consists of 144 Likert-scale items, approximately half of which assess attentional style. By summing subsets of these items, respondents receive scores on six different subscales. The first subscale, the broad-external subscale (BET), concerns the extent to which an individual can effectively deal with a large number of external stimuli. A second subscale is the broad-internal scale (BIT), which involves an athlete's ability to think about and concentrate on several items of information simultaneously. Respondents are also assigned a narrow effective focus score (NAR). This subscale assesses the extent to which a person can effectively narrow his or her attentional focus (i.e., move from a broad to narrow focus of attention). Another subscale is the external overload scale (OET). Scores on this subscale indicate the degree to which an athlete's performance begins to suffer when he or she is overloaded by external stimuli. Individuals scoring high on the OET subscale are unable to narrow their attentional focus effectively to block out environmental distractions. Respondents also receive an OIT score representing the degree to which they tend to become overloaded by internal stimuli such as thoughts and cognitions. Finally, there is a reduced attentional focus subscale (RED). Persons scoring high on this subscale have a difficult time broadening their attentional focus and, as a result, fail to attend to the necessary environmental stimuli in a given situation. Researchers and psychologists can also calculate a total attentional ability score by combining scores on the six subscales. Finally, it should be noted that, due to the lengthy nature of this scale, a shorter version was developed (Nideffer, 1976b). Because it contains only 12 items, this scale is particularly useful in applied settings.

Through his research with the six TAIS subscales, Nideffer (1980) identified several distinct attentional profiles. Figure 6.4 compares the ineffective and effective profiles. These two profiles have several differences. First, as indicated by high scores on the OET and OIT subscales and low scores on the NAR, individuals exhibiting an ineffective pattern tend to be overloaded and confused by large numbers of stimuli. Second, persons exhibiting an ineffective profile have difficulty shifting from an internal focus to an external focus. Figure 6.5 depicts the "choking" profile. Persons exhibiting this pattern of scores tend to have a chronically narrowed attentional focus (i.e., high NAR scores). As a result, they are unable to react quickly to changes

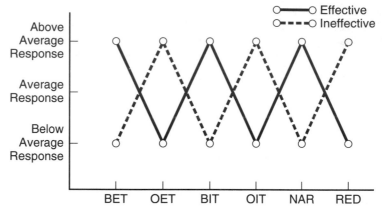

FIGURE 6.4   Effective and ineffective attentional profiles. (Adapted by permission from: Nideffer, R. M. [1980]. Attentional focus—self-assessment. In: R. Suinn [Ed.], *Psychology in sports: Methods and applications* [pp. 281–290]. Englewood Cliffs, NJ: Prentice Hall.)

in their environment, changes that require a broad external focus. As an example of such a person, Nideffer (1980) describes a basketball player who is unable to find an open teammate. A similar profile, shown in Figure 6.6, is termed the choking-high anxiety profile. These persons also have a chronically narrowed attentional focus, but they also have high OIT scores, indicating that they become overloaded by excessive amounts of internal stimuli. Nideffer states that these persons become their own worst enemies because they focus and dwell internally on their own mistakes, disregarding external stimuli. Finally, Figure 6.7 represents the external distractibility profile. Nideffer (1980) states that these individuals "are reactive rather than reflective" (p. 287). That is, they tend to respond automatically and instinctively to their

FIGURE 6.5   The "choking" attentional profile. (Adapted by permission from: Nideffer, R. M. [1980]. Attentional focus—self-assessment. In: R. Suinn [Ed.], *Psychology in sports: Methods and applications* [pp. 281–290]. Englewood Cliffs, NJ: Prentice Hall.)

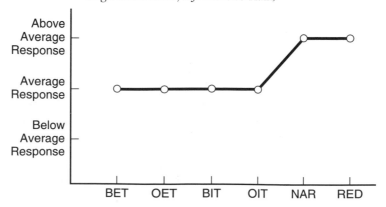

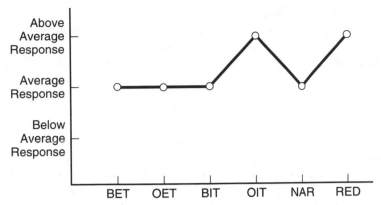

FIGURE 6.6 The "choking-high anxiety" attentional profile. (Adapted by permission from: Nideffer, R. M. [1980]. Attentional focus—self-assessment. In: R. Suinn [Ed.], *Psychology in sports: Methods and applications* [pp. 281–290]. Englewood Cliffs, NJ: Prentice Hall.)

environments (the high BET and OET scores indicate that these persons are chronically broad in their attentional focus). Yet, if a response fails, they do not reflect on this poor response and act in a similarly poor manner when the situation again presents itself. Also, as a result of their external focus, Nideffer notes that these persons can easily be psyched out by environmental stimuli.

In spite of its popularity among most sport psychologists, a handful of researchers have questioned the psychometric properties of the TAIS (see Abernethy, 1993, for a review, but see Nideffer, 1990, for arguments supporting the TAIS). As a result, the test may be more appropriate as a diagnostic tool than as an instrument for predicting athletic performance. To increase the quality of the TAIS, some inves-

FIGURE 6.7 The "external distractability" attentional profile. (Adapted by permission from: Nideffer, R. M. [1980]. Attentional focus—self-assessment. In: R. Suinn [Ed.], *Psychology in sports: Methods and applications* [pp. 281–290]. Englewood Cliffs, NJ: Prentice Hall.)

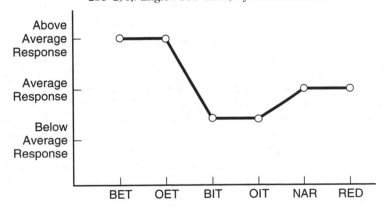

tigators have developed sport-specific measures of attentional focus, using the TAIS as a guide. For example, sport psychologists have constructed measures specific to tennis (the T-TAIS, Van Schoyck & Grasha, 1981), baseball/softball (the B-TAIS, Albrecht & Feltz, 1987), as well as field hockey, diving, and basketball (Taylor, 1986).

SUMMARY

Information processing is vitally important for athletic performance. Three steps are involved with information processing: encoding (transforming information into a form suitable for storage), storage (storing information in a permanent or near permanent fashion), and retrieval (the process of recalling and using information stored in long-term memory). Information is encoded, stored, and retrieved through a memory system involving three distinct but interacting memory types. Sensory memory has a large capacity but a very short duration. Short-term memory, which involves both information transferred from sensory memory and information recalled from long-term memory, has a small capacity and a short duration. The capacity of short-term memory may be expanded by chunking the information into meaningful units. Likewise, the duration may be expanded by using rehearsal. Long-term memory receives information from short-term memory and stores this information in an unlimited and permanent fashion. Long-term memory is further divided into three types: semantic memory (memory for the specifics of a language), episodic memory (memory for personally experienced events), and procedural memory (memory for motor activities).

Most work examining information processing in sport has focused on attention. Attention involves the cognitive resources, mental effort, or concentration devoted to a cognitive process. Using a research procedure called shadowing, Broadbent argued for a filter theory of attention. This theory states that unattended information is completely screened out of processing. However, because research tended to find that unattended information is occasionally processed, albeit sometimes at an unconscious level, future authors proposed an attenuation theory of attention, stating that unattended messages are not completely blocked from consciousness. Rather, they are lower in strength than messages to which a person attends.

Because our attentional capacity is limited, athletes should attempt to learn their athletic skills to the point at which they are automatic. Automatic processes are behaviors that have become so well ingrained in procedural memory that the execution of these behaviors can be done without consciousness and with few cognitive resources. By automating their athletic skills, athletes can attend to other important stimuli during competition.

The greatest volume of attentional research within sport psychology appears to have focused on attentional style (an individual's tendency to attend to environmental cues in a personalized manner) and attentional focus (an individual's ability to focus in the most appropriate style and on the correct stimuli). Two dimensions of attentional focus have been examined. Attentional width concerns the number of stimuli on which an individual is focusing and ranges from a narrow width to a broad width. Attentional direction concerns the degree to which an individual's attention is focused internally or externally. The ability to match the most appropriate strategy with the correct game situation and the ability to be flexible in one's attentional focus are key ingredients in athletic success.

Attentional style is most often assessed through the Test of Attentional and Interpersonal Style (TAIS). The TAIS contains six attentional subscales: broad-external, broad-internal, narrow effective focus, overloaded by external stimuli, overloaded by internal stimuli, and reduced attentional focus. Using the general TAIS, several sport-specific measures of attentional style have also been developed.

GLOSSARY

Associaters   Athletes who tend to internalize their attentional focus to their body.

Attention   Cognitive resources, mental effort, or concentration devoted to a cognitive process.

Attentional Direction   The degree to which an individual's attention is focused internally or externally.

Attentional Focus   An individual's ability to focus in the most appropriate style and on the correct stimuli.

Attentional Style   An individual's tendency to attend to environmental cues in a personalized manner.

Attentional Width   The number of stimuli on which an individual is focusing, which may range from a narrow width to a broad width.

Attenuation Theory of Attention   A theory of attention proposing that unattended messages are not completely blocked from consciousness but are lower in strength than information to which a person attends.

Automatic Processes   Behaviors that become so well ingrained in procedural memory that the execution of these behaviors can be done without consciousness and with few cognitive resources.

Broad Attentional Focus   The focusing of attention on a large number of stimuli.

Chunk   A meaningful unit of information organized around a rule or pattern.

Cocktail Party Phenomenon   The ability to carry on a conversation with one specific individual even though there are several other people talking at the same time.

Controlled Processes   Behaviors that require careful and conscious thought.

Decay   The process through which a memory trace is completely erased.

Dissociaters   Athletes who tend to externalize their attentional focus to outside stimuli.

Echoic Sensory Memory   The sensory memory for the auditory sense.

Encoding   The first stage of information processing, which involves transforming information into a form suitable for memory storage.

Episodic Memory   Long-term memory of information about personally experienced events.

External Attentional Focus   Directing attention outwardly to environmental stimuli.

Filter Theory of Attention   A theory of attention proposing that unattended information is completely screened out of processing.

Iconic Sensory Memory   Sensory memory for the visual sense.

Interference   The inability to recall information due to other competing or conflicting items of information.

Internal Attentional Focus   Directing attention inwardly toward one's own thoughts and feelings.

Long-term Memory   The final stage of the memory process involving an apparently infinite capacity and seemingly permanent storage.

Narrow Attentional Focus   Focusing attention on just one or a few stimuli.

Procedural Memory   Long-term memory for stimulus-response pairings, that is, the storage of information related to motor activities.

Rehearsal   The constant repetition of information in short-term memory.

Retrieval   The final stage in information processing, which involves the process of recalling and using information stored in long-term memory.

Semantic Memory   Long-term memory for the specifics of a language.

Sensory Memory   The first step in the memory process, this type of memory involves the large capacity, short duration storage of sensory information.

Shadowing   A research procedure in which a subject is presented with a different message in each ear and asked to repeat out loud one of the two messages.

Short-term Memory   The second step in the memory process, this short duration, small capacity type of memory concerns the active, cognitive manipulation and use of information.

Storage   The second stage of information processing, it involves the storing of information in a permanent or nearly permanent fashion.

APPLICATION AND REVIEW QUESTIONS

1. Describe the relationships among the three types of memory.
2. Compare and contrast the capacity and duration of the three types of memory.
3. Describe a sport-specific example of the three types of long-term memory.
4. What is the key difference between the filter theory of attention and the attenuation theory of attention?
5. Using examples from sport settings, compare and contrast internal, external, broad, and narrow attentional focus.

SUGGESTED READINGS

ABERNETHY, B. (1993). Attention. In R. N. Singer, M. Murphey, & L. K. Tennant (Eds.), *Handbook of research on sport psychology* (pp. 127–170). New York: Macmillan. This in-depth chapter examines the general notion of attention as well as the role of attentional processes in sport.

BOUTCHER, S. H. (1992). Attention and athletic performance: An integrated approach. In T. S. Horn (Ed.), *Advances in sport psychology* (pp. 251–265). Champaign, IL: Human Kinetics. This chapter covers a number of interesting topics relevant to attention in sport including attentional selectivity, automatic and controlled processes, and attentional capacity.

GALOTTI, K. M. (1994). *Cognitive psychology in and out of the laboratory.* Pacific Grove, CA: Brooks/Cole. This textbook includes several chapters on memory and attention. These chapters offer the reader a basic understanding of cognitive processes.

GLENCROSS, D. J. (1992). Human skill and motor learning: A critical review. *Sport Science Review, 1,* 65–78. This article, which also has relevance for learning in sport, presents the reader with an informative sport-specific discussion of sensory, short-term, and long-term memory.

NIDEFFER, R. M. (1992). *Psyched to win: How to master skills and improve your physical performance.* Champaign, IL: Leisure Press. This book focuses on several psychological aspects of athletic performance, including the attentional focus and style of sport participants. Written by a leader in the field of attention research, it is a valuable source for persons interested in a deeper understanding of the relationship between attention and athletic performance.

Chapter 7

AROUSAL, STRESS, AND ANXIETY IN SPORT

Consider the experiences of two amateur golfers, Jim and Joyce. These golfers both usually play in the low 80s. Although their average scores are quite adequate for the weekend golfer, both players could improve if they were better able to manage their arousal and anxiety while playing. Jim tends to become too anxious and "worked up" when faced with difficult shots. Before attempting such a shot he can feel his heart pounding, has trouble breathing, and has difficulty concentrating. Joyce's problem is just the opposite. She tends to be too relaxed and uninvolved when beginning a round. As she steps up to the first tee, she tends to be lackadaisical and uninterested. Although she "gets into it" after three or four holes, by then she has often played so poorly that a good round is not possible.

The problems Jim and Joyce are experiencing highlight the importance of arousal, stress, and anxiety in sport. Jim is suffering from detrimentally high levels of anxiety and arousal, while Joyce has an arousal level that is too low. The experiences of these golfers are far from rare. Many athletes struggle to control their anxiety and arousal. Because arousal, stress, and anxiety have an impact on the performances of athletes, it is not surprising that sport psychologists have studied these constructs. In this chapter, we will examine this work. We will begin our review by defining the constructs of interest. This section will be followed by an in-depth discussion of the relationships among anxiety, arousal, and performance.

DEFINING AROUSAL, STRESS, AND ANXIETY

Arousal

In sport psychology literature, physiological arousal has been described in a number of ways. Cox (1990) describes arousal as a "physiological state of readiness" (p. 88). LeUnes and Nation (1989) write that arousal involves "psychological activation" while Cratty (1989) defines arousal as "readiness to perform physically, intellectually, or perceptually" (p. 58). Warren (1983) states that arousal "refers to the amount of emotional involvement an athlete brings to competition" (p. 105). All of these descriptions contain an important common link: They view arousal as neither positive nor negative and as having both beneficial and detrimental effects on performance. Because it appears to be the most comprehensive definition, a description of arousal similar to Cratty's (1989) will be used in this text. Specifically, ***arousal*** will be defined as a nonemotional physiological state of readiness to perform physically, intellectually, or perceptually.

The neurophysiology of arousal involves the ***autonomic nervous system*** (ANS). The ANS controls automatic, involuntary bodily functions. This includes processes people normally do not think about such as heart rate, blood pressure, perspiration, and respiration. The ANS is composed of two divisions: the sympathetic and parasympathetic. The ***sympathetic division*** is the arousing division and prepares the body for action. Because of this, it is often called the "fight or flight" division. The ***parasympathetic division*** is the calming division. This division returns the body to its normal state of arousal. For humans, physiological arousal is a homeostatic process. ***Homeostasis*** is a state of physiological balance or stability. Each individual has an optimal level of arousal. When the sympathetic division is highly active, the individual is above this optimal level. It is the responsibility of the parasympathetic division to return the individual to his or her homeostatic level of arousal. For example, if a bench warmer is suddenly asked to pinch hit in a crucial baseball game, the sympathetic division is responsible for the flash of arousal the player will most likely experience. The player may begin to perspire, breathe heavily, and feel tense. If the coach then reconsiders her decision and returns the player to the bench, the parasympathetic division is responsible for returning the player to his normal state of arousal. Once the player has regained his normal state of arousal he is said to have regained homeostasis.

Stress

Stress is a nonemotional bodily response to an environmental demand. Thus, arousal and stress are similar in that both processes are nonemotional. These two processes are often correlated. When persons are highly stressed, they usually experience a high level of physiological arousal. However, arousal and stress are not interchangeable terms because an individual can be stressed and maintain a normal or even low level of arousal. Likewise, one may experience a high level of arousal without experiencing stress. In fact, the ingestion of drugs such as adrenaline can elevate physiological arousal in the complete absence of an environmental demand.

The Physiological Response to Stress: Selye's General Adaptation Syndrome.
Throughout the last several decades, Hans Selye (1956, 1974, 1982) has examined bodily responses to stressful situations. Using different animals and different stressors, Selye concluded that reactions to stressful environments are generally nonspecific. That is, he felt that an organism's responses to stress do not change with different stressors, and members of a species respond in a similar manner to stressful settings (Smith, 1993). Selye called this typical reaction to stress the ***general adap-***

tation syndrome (GAS). The GAS consists of three stages. The first stage, referred to as the *alarm stage,* begins with the onset of the stressor and is characterized by higher than normal levels of physiological arousal. It is during this stage that the organism prepares to combat the stressor. For example, imagine that a minor league baseball player, Brian, has been called up to the major leagues in the middle of a pennant race. As soon as Brian receives the phone call about the promotion, he enters the alarm stage. Brian will experience a rush of nervousness and adrenaline reflective of his heightened physiological arousal.

If the stressor continues, the organism will move into the next stage, the *resistance stage.* During this stage the organism tries to cope with the stressor. At first, the resistance stage is marked by higher than normal levels of arousal. However, as the stress continues, arousal begins to decline until it reaches lower than normal levels. Continuing with the example above, Brian will continue to experience stress as the pennant race wears on. To cope with the daily stress, Brian may choose to exercise and complete crossword puzzles. Brian's methods of coping with the stress are certainly not the only ones available. Rather, athletes perform many behaviors to cope with a lingering stressor. The most common methods athletes use to cope with the stress of sport are reviewed in Chapter 10.

If the stressor continues, the individual will eventually enter the third stage, the *exhaustion stage.* This stage of the GAS is characterized by low levels of arousal. As the individual's ability to cope with the stress wears down, the individual may begin to experience fatigue and illness. In the example above, because of the constant pressure of playing in his first pennant race, Brian may feel tired and even begin to experience headaches and ulcers. In fact, there are a number of physiological problems that may be triggered or intensified because of a continuing stressor including allergies, asthma, hypertension, insomnia, and arthritis (Schafer, 1992).

Before concluding our discussion of Selye's work, it should be noted that some investigators have challenged the notion that stress is nonspecific (Bernard & Krupat, 1994). These researchers argue that psychosocial factors cause various stressors to be nonequivalent. That is, some stressors elicit more intense stress responses than others. Several of the characteristics that render a stressor more or less anxiety-inducing are described below. There are also individual differences in responses to stress, including stressful situations in sport (Martens, Vealey, & Burton, 1990). Some people react more strongly to stressful settings than do others. Thus, although Selye's GAS model has received substantial support, the notions that stress is nonspecific and that different individuals react in the same manner to stressful environments are oversimplifications. While Selye's theory remains valid as a framework for many stressful reactions, to understand fully how an individual will react to a stressful event, one should consider the individual as well as the nature of the stressful setting. Thus, the usefulness of the interactional perspective described in previous chapters is again validated.

Valence of the Stress.   Although most people tend to view stress as a negative state, in actuality stress is neither positive nor negative. Rather, it is one's interpretation of the environmental demand that determines whether or not the stress will be positive, negative, or neutral (Rotella & Lerner, 1993; Schafer, 1992; Smith, 1993). Individuals who feel overwhelmed by an environmental demand will most likely view the stressor as negative and will be affected accordingly. Others who view the stress in a positive frame of mind (perhaps as a motivator or energizer) may welcome the stress and believe that it is both beneficial and pleasant. Still others may remain unaffected by the stress, rendering it neutral.

Thus, there are actually three different types of stress, each with a different valence and having a different impact. When stress is viewed in a positive manner, such as the excitement of an upcoming athletic event, it is called eustress (recall that eustress was discussed in Chapter 3). For example, a baseball player may enjoy the rush of excitement he feels as he steps to the plate with the game on the line. This player likes being in the spot light and enjoys the pressure of this stressful situation. That is, his cognitive interpretation of this situation is positive.

Stress can also be neutral, what Schafer (1992) calls neustress (i.e., neutral stress). **Neustress** occurs when environmental demands have neither positive nor negative effects on an individual. Schafer notes that neustress is actually quite common. During the course of a day, there are numerous environmental demands that do not impact our functioning. For example, consider a college basketball player participating in an away game in a hostile environment. Unlike some of his teammates, this player remains unaffected by the taunts of the opposing spectators. Although a stressor is most certainly present, the player's ability to ignore the stressor renders it neutral. Again, it is this player's cognitive interpretation of the stress that gives the stressor its valence.

The final type of stress involves negative reactions to an environmental demand. When individuals feel overwhelmed by a stressor and believe that they are unable to meet its demands, they experience negative stress. This negative form of stress is called distress and anxiety. As noted by Cox (1990), the terms distress and anxiety are used quite interchangeably in the sport and anxiety literatures. However, because the term anxiety is somewhat more common in sport research, this is the term used in this book. Specifically then, we can define **anxiety** as the negative interpretation of past, present, and future environmental demands. Although people generally think of sport anxiety in terms of fear and apprehension of an upcoming competition, athletes can also be anxious about a current game as well as past sporting events. In addition, athletes can feel anxious about facets of their life as an athlete that are far removed from the competition itself. For example, stressful travel schedules, negative media coverage, abusive fans, and contract negotiations may all produce feelings of anxiety.

Anxiety

Because anxiety is a negative state that can have highly detrimental effects on athletic performance, we will examine this construct in detail. We will review several components of anxiety that have relevance for sport settings. First, we will discuss the difference between state anxiety and trait anxiety. We will then examine several common methods of measuring sport anxiety. Next, we will review the importance of the timing of the stressor, the amount of stimulation involved in the stressor, and one's perception of control over the stimulus. The anxiety resulting from one's role as an athlete will then be discussed. Although the discussions to follow will focus on athlete anxiety, sport anxiety is not limited to athletes. Rather, coaches, sport officials, and fans may also experience high levels of anxiety. The anxiety of officials is reviewed in this chapter's "A Closer Look." The anxiety experienced by coach and spectators is discussed later in this text.

State Anxiety versus Trait Anxiety.   When discussing the anxiety of athletes, it is important to distinguish between state anxiety and trait anxiety. *State anxiety,* often abbreviated as A-state, involves a reaction to a current stressful condition. Because state anxiety involves temporary reactions, the anxiety should subside once the stressor has past. *Trait anxiety* (A-trait), on the other hand, involves a long-lasting, chronic predisposition to experience anxiety in stressful environments. Trait anxiety is similar to a personality variable. Individuals high in trait anxiety tend to perceive a variety of situational demands in a highly threatening way.

A CLOSER LOOK:
THE ANXIETY OF SPORT OFFICIALS

Players are not alone in their experiences of anxiety during athletic events. Rather, because their actions are closely scrutinized and evaluated, officials are also likely to experience high levels of anxiety. Weinberg and Richardson (1990) list three specific sources of anxiety for sport officials. First, they suggest that many officials experience a fear of failure. Indeed, research does indicate that the fear of making the wrong call is often one of the greatest sources of anxiety (Anshel & Weinberg, 1995), particularly among younger officials (Kaissidis & Anshel, 1993). A second source of anxiety listed by Weinberg and Richardson concerns the officials' feelings of inadequacy. That is, many officials experience qualitative overload, feeling they do not have the physical capabilities or the experience required to perform at an adequate level. They may also experience quantitative overload, believing that the time urgency required when making a call is a hindrance to their performance. Finally, Weinberg and Richardson state that an official's perception of a loss of control may lead to anxiety. For example, an official may feel that he or she is being controlled by the fans, players, or coaches, a feeling that will ultimately lead to feelings of anxiety.

Of course, these are not the only sources of anxiety for sport officials. Other research testing referees from a variety of sports and countries found that officials feel anxious for several additional reasons including: interpersonal conflicts, peer conflicts, role conflicts, fear of physical harm and injury, verbal abuse, game pressure, time pressure, and belief that they are no longer perceived as authority figures (Anshel & Weinberg, 1995; Goldsmith & Williams, 1992; Kaissidis & Anshel, 1993; Rainey, 1995a, 1995b; Rainey, Santilli, & Fallon, 1992; Taylor & Daniel, 1987).

It would be incorrect to assume that state and trait levels do not interact. In fact, Martens et al. (1990) presented a theory attempting to explain the relationship between state and trait anxiety using an interactional model. Martens' model is presented in Figure 7.1. The model begins by including the athlete's objective responses and interpretation of the situation. This includes the athlete's perceptions of the uncertainty and importance of the outcome. As will be discussed shortly, feelings of anxiety tend to increase as situations become more uncertain. Similarly, as a competition grows in importance, so too will feelings of anxiety. Perceptions of competition uncertainty and importance lead to one's perceptions of the threat of the competition. Highly uncertain yet important games yield high levels of threat while guaranteed victory or defeat in unimportant contests leads to low levels of threat. At this point in the model, trait anxiety is introduced. Research has shown that those with higher levels of trait anxiety perceive higher levels of threat in competitive environments (Martens et al., 1990). The combination of trait anxiety and perceptions of threat result in experiences of state anxiety. Thus, this model is truly consistent with an interactional perspective because it incorporates both personal variables (trait anxiety) and situational variables (the objective competitive situation).

Measuring Anxiety.   Research on anxiety in sport has used both general and sport-specific inventories. Three general inventories have gained extensive use: the

FIGURE 7.1   A theory of competitive anxiety. (Note: From *Competitive Anxiety in Sport* [p. 219] by Rainer Martins, Robin S. Vealey and Damon Burton. Champaign, IL: Human Kinetic Publishers. Copyright 1990 by Human Kinetic Publishers. Reprinted by permission.).

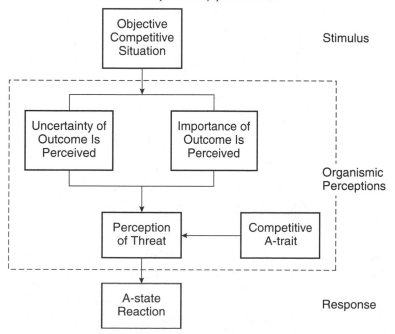

Affective Adjective Checklist (AACL), the Taylor Manifest Anxiety Scale (TMAS), and the State-Trait Anxiety Inventory (STAI). For research focusing on state levels of anxiety, investigators often use Zuckerman's (1960) AACL. This instrument presents the subject with 11 positive and 10 negative adjectives. Respondents are asked to check the adjective that describes their current emotion. The TMAS, which was developed from the MMPI, has been a common measure of trait anxiety. The TMAS contains 50 true/false items (Taylor, 1953). However, the general psychology anxiety scale receiving the greatest attention from sport researchers in recent years appears to be the STAI (Martens et al., 1990). This 20-item, Likert-scale measure is valuable because it assesses both trait and state anxiety (Spielberger, 1983; Spielberger, Gorsuch, & Lushene, 1970).

With regard to sport-specific inventories, two questionnaires developed by Rainer Martens and his colleagues (1990) have gained wide spread use: the Sport Competition Anxiety Test (SCAT) and the Competitive State Anxiety Inventory-2 (CSAI-2). The SCAT is aimed at identifying athletes who perceive competition as threatening in a variety of environments. Thus, the SCAT focuses on trait levels of sport-based anxiety. There are two 15-item forms of the SCAT, the SCAT-A for adults and the SCAT-C for children.

The CSAI-2 (a revision of the original CSAI) is used to examine state levels of anxiety. This 27-item inventory is a multidimensional measure of state anxiety. Nine of the items are designed to assess somatic anxiety. **Somatic anxiety** is the physiological element of anxiety and matches what we have termed arousal. In fact, the terms somatic anxiety and arousal will be used interchangeably throughout the remainder of this text. Examples of these items include "I feel nervous" and "My body feels tense." Nine other questions are designed to measure cognitive anxiety. Martens et al. (1990) view cognitive anxiety as "the mental component of anxiety caused by negative expectations" (p. 9). Thus, **cognitive anxiety** concerns fear, apprehension, and worry about an upcoming athletic event. Questions on this subscale include "I am concerned about this competition" and "I am concerned about losing." The final nine questions on the CSAI-2 are combined to form a state self-confidence subscale (e.g., "I'm confident I can meet the challenge."). As one might expect, scores on the CSAI-2 somatic anxiety and cognitive anxiety subscales are positively correlated (Smith, 1989; Martens et al., 1990). Martens and his associates note that the somatic subscale of the CSAI-2 is more strongly correlated with the SCAT than is the cognitive CSAI-2 subscale because the items on the SCAT tend to be somatic in nature. Finally, research has found that male athletes tend to score higher than female athletes on the self-confidence subscale but lower on the somatic anxiety subscale (Krane & Williams, 1994; Martens et al., 1990).

Although the SCAT and CSAI-2 inventories have received the greatest attention from sport researchers, other sport-specific measures of anxiety have been developed. In fact, Ostrow (1990) lists well over a dozen sport-specific anxiety inventories. For example, other trait anxiety measures such as the Sport Anxiety Scale (Smith, Smoll, & Schultz, 1990) and other state anxiety scales such as the Pre-Race Questionnaire (Jones, Swain, & Cale, 1990) and the Mental Readiness Form (MRF, Krane, 1994; Murphy, Greenspan, Jowdy, & Tammen, 1989) are available to researchers. Because it consists of only three items (one each measuring cognitive anxiety, somatic anxiety, and confidence), the MRF is especially useful in applied settings calling for an unobtrusive inventory.

The Timing of the Stressor.   Individuals may feel anxious about stressors that have already happened, are currently happening, or have yet to begin. When individuals feel anxious about events in the past they are experiencing ***residual anxiety.*** Many athletes feel anxious about past performances because of their own and/or their team's poor performance. In these situations, athletes are said to be experiencing ***postcompetition anxiety.*** Research has found that game outcome is one of the greatest predictors of postcompetition anxiety (Martens et al., 1990; Scanlan & Lewthwaite, 1984; Scanlan & Passer, 1977, 1978). Some athletes experience stress after a successful competition because of the pressure of meeting the high expectations stemming from their success (Gould, Jackson, & Finch, 1993). Athletes also experience residual anxiety that is not based on their performance. For example, an athlete may feel anxious about a past trade or relationships with former teammates.

At other times, individuals feel anxious about current environmental demands. These feelings of ***current anxiety*** are quite common among athletes. When feelings of current anxiety are due to a competition in progress, the anxiety is termed ***competition anxiety.*** An example of competition anxiety would include the rookie baseball player described previously. Because he is anxious about his current situation (being asked to perform in a pennant race), this player is experiencing competition anxiety. Some currently active environmental demands are not tied to a competition. Examples of these stressors include a player's first practice with a new team and his or her first meeting with a new coaching staff.

Athletes sometimes experience anxiety because of upcoming events. These feelings of anxiety, called ***anticipatory anxiety,*** are responses to future stressful situations. Often, the anxiety is elicited by an upcoming competition. These feelings are called ***precompetition anxiety.*** Research has found that precompetition anxiety usually takes the form of an inverted-V (Fenz, 1988; Gould, Horn, & Spreemann, 1983; Gould, Petlichkoff, & Weinberg, 1984; Jones, Swain, & Cale, 1991; Martens et al., 1990). Athletes tend to display low levels of anxiety several days prior to a competition. As the competition nears, their anxiety levels increase, peaking a few minutes prior to the beginning of the competition. Once the competition begins, their anxiety starts to decline. As a result, the anxiety experienced during a competition is often lower than precompetition anxiety experienced immediately prior to the event.

Research has found a number of ways athletes vary in their levels of precompetition anxiety. First, athletes differing in competitiveness have different anxiety patterns. Specifically, athletes low in competitiveness show a steady increase in cognitive anxiety as the competition nears, while those high in competitiveness exhibit stable levels of cognitive anxiety. Furthermore, low competitiveness athletes exhibit an earlier initial increase in precompetition somatic anxiety than do highly competitive persons (Swain & Jones, 1992). Second, athletes participating in different sports also have different precompetition anxiety levels. Athletes participating in endurance sports tend to experience low levels of precompetition anxiety, and the anxiety does not appear to inhibit their performances (Hammermeister & Burton, 1995). And, third, research by Jones and his colleagues (1991) indicates that there may be gender differences in tendencies to experience precompetition anxiety. These researchers found that, although male cognitive anxiety remained relatively stable prior to a competition, female cognitive anxiety increased significantly as a competition neared. Gender differences were not found for somatic anxiety.

Research has also found that athletes are well aware of their precompetition anxiety state, and they are able to recall their anxiety levels accurately several days after a competition. Harger and Raglin (1994; see also Raglin & Morris, 1994) asked university track and field athletes to complete the STAI 1 hour prior to a meet and then again 2 days after the meet. The correlations between the actual and recalled precompetition anxiety were highly positive. Further, even when the items on the STAI were rearranged on the posttest to reduce response bias, the high correlations were replicated with a second sample of track and field athletes.

Upcoming competitions are not the only future events that foster feelings of anticipatory anxiety among athletes. For example, many athletes experience anticipatory anxiety because of their impending retirement from professional or amateur athletics (Baillie, 1993; Parker, 1994; Taylor & Ogilvie, 1994). Other future events that cause feelings of anxiety include meeting with a team doctor to discuss an injury or meeting with a coach or the media to discuss a poor performance.

The Amount of Stimulation.   Anxiety can also be classified on the basis of the amount of stimulation involved in the setting. First, anxious situations can be classified as overload or underload settings. Second, stressful environments can be classified as either quantitative or qualitative. By combining these two dimensions, one arrives at four different settings: quantitative overload, qualitative overload, quantitative underload, and qualitative underload (Baron & Greenberg, 1990).

Quantitative overload situations are found when an individual is required to do more work than is possible in a given time. For example, a rookie quarterback may be asked to memorize a group of plays in a short time. If the player believes that the amount of time allotted is insufficient to learn the information, he will most likely experience quantitative overload anxiety. However, even if the quarterback is given an ample amount of time to learn the plays, he will still experience feelings of anxiety if he feels he does not have the ability necessary. Situations such as this involve ***qualitative overload.*** Much of the anxiety experienced by athletes can be classified as qualitative overload. For example, consider a female volleyball player who typically serves in a conservative, underhanded fashion. If this player were asked to attempt a difficult and unfamiliar overhead jump-serve, she would quite likely experience qualitative overload.

If a sample of sport participants and fans were asked to describe a typical situation causing anxiety for athletes, most of their responses would probably involve an overload setting. However, situations involving stimulation underload can be equally anxiety-inducing. Some of these situations involve ***quantitative underload.*** In these situations, an athlete feels anxious because he or she has too little to do, that is, too few tasks to fill the amount of time allotted. Perhaps the most obvious example of quantitative underload in sport settings involves the experiences of bench players (Petrie, 1993; Rotella & Newburg, 1989). Anyone who has performed in a backup role understands just how stressful this can be.

Other situations are characterized by qualitative underload. ***Qualitative underload*** settings are found when an individual feels anxious because he or she is required to perform a repetitive or boring task and, consequently, feels a lack of mental stimulation from the task. For example, imagine a place kicker on a football team. During practice, the player is simply asked to practice kicking field goals. He performs this same behavior dozens of times each day without doing anything else to break up the monotony. As a result, he may begin to experience qualitative underload.

Other Key Characteristics of the Stressor: Predictability and Control. Psychological research has identified other characteristics of the stressor that can increase the amount of anxiety experienced. One such characteristic is the predictability of the stressor (Fisher & Zwart, 1982; Smith, 1993; Taylor, 1991). Research has found that anxiety usually increases as the onset of a stressor becomes less predictable and more unexpected (Glass & Singer, 1972; Miller, 1981). It is for this reason that a loss against a weaker opponent (i.e., an unexpected stressor) might elicit higher levels of postcompetition anxiety than a loss against a superior opponent (i.e., an expected stressor). Research has also found that uncontrollable stressors often generate higher levels of anxiety than controllable stressors (Glass & Singer, 1972; Suls & Mullen, 1981). Players who believe they can influence the outcome of a stressful contest should be less anxious than those without such a perception. Quite possibly, it is the perception of uncontrollability that fosters the anxious reactions of bench and injured athletes.

Role Anxiety. Many athletes experience anxiety due to their role as athletes (Capel, Sisley, & Desertrain, 1987). Some individuals may experience role ambiguity (Baron & Greenberg, 1990). ***Role ambiguity*** occurs when an individual is uncertain about one or more components of a specific role. We have all been faced with the uncomfortable position of being newly hired or newly appointed to a position and being unsure of the expectations associated with that position. As an athletic example, imagine a player who has been elected to the position of team captain by her coaches. It is quite possible that she would be unclear about the responsibilities and duties of this position. Subsequently, this player may feel anxious about her role as team captain.

Other experiences of role anxiety fall under the general heading of ***role conflict*** (situations in which one's role conflicts with oneself or other roles, Baron & Greenberg, 1990). One form of role conflict is ***personality role conflict,*** which occurs when an individual's personality conflicts with a given role. For example, let us again consider the team captain described above. Usually, election or selection to this position is an honor and commands respect from teammates and coaches. However, if this player had an introverted personality and did not like being in the spotlight, her role of team captain would conflict with her personality. Most likely, the result would be feelings of anxiety, and she would actively attempt to be removed from this position.

A second type of role conflict, ***intrarole conflict,*** occurs when a single role has conflicting expectations. This form of role conflict may facilitate the anxiety experienced by the head coaches of professional sports teams, especially coaches working for a "hands on" team owner. On the one hand, an owner expects a coach to act in the owner's best interest. On the other hand, the players expect coaches to act in the players' best interest. As a result of these conflicting expectations, the coach may experience anxiety. In fact, this is precisely what happened during the 1994–1995 Major League baseball strike. Managers were caught in a no-win situation involving their loyalty to the owners and their loyalty to the players.

A third form of role conflict is called ***interrole conflict.*** This conflict occurs when an individual simultaneously possesses two incongruent roles. For a common example of this form of role conflict, let us return once again to the newly appointed team captain. This individual would now hold two distinct roles: player and captain. As a player, she is expected to act like other players by having fun and joking around. However, her role as team captain requires that she remain serious and attempt to motivate the other players to work harder. In certain situations, these two conflicting roles may cause anxiety. A second common form of interrole conflict occurs when college athletes attempt to balance the role of "student" with the role of "athlete" (Chartrand & Lent, 1987; Greenspan & Andersen, 1995).

In recent years, Britton Brewer and his colleagues have attempted to clarify further the importance of athletic role identification and its relationship to psychological health. To facilitate this research, Brewer, Van Raalte, and Linder (1993) developed the Athletic Identity Measurement Scale (AIMS). The AIMS consists of ten Likert-scale items measuring a person's degree of identification with his or her role as an athlete. For example, respondents are asked the extent to which they consider themselves to be athletes, the extent to which others see them as athletes, and the extent to which they have sport-related goals. The AIMS is appropriate for use with a wide variety of athletes, including both recreational athletes and elite performers.

Research conducted by Brewer and his associates has examined how the athletic role leads to negative psychological states such as anxiety. For example, it was predicted that highly identified athletes would report intense negative reactions to sustaining an injury (Brewer, 1993). The logic employed here was that athletes who base their identity exclusively or almost exclusively on their athletic role will be unable to rely on other roles to buffer the negative psychological impact of the injury. This line of reasoning is consistent with Linville's (1987) self-complexity theory, Thoits (1983) identity accumulation hypothesis, and Wann and Hamlet's (1994) social-complexity theory. Consistent with predictions, Brewer (1993) found that among injured athletes, high levels of identification with the role of athlete corresponded to high levels of depression (and one can reasonably assume anxiety). This finding was substantiated both for imagined injuries and actual injuries.

Brewer and his colleagues argue that one's role as an athlete may have two additional negative impacts on psychological well-being. First, sport psychologists have noted that high levels of anxiety often accompany retirement from professional and amateur sports (Baillie, 1993; Parker, 1994; Taylor & Ogilvie, 1994). Brewer et al. (1993) suggest that athletes with a high degree of identification with their athletic role will experience exceptionally high levels of anxiety on retirement. Second, in a study of several hundred college students, Good, Brewer, Petitpas, Van Raalte, and Mahar (1993) found that athletes who are highly identified with their athletic role tend to be less likely to explore and investigate alternative roles. It seems possible that this behavior is an attempt to avoid interrole conflict. That is, by refraining from actively seeking out and acquiring roles that may conflict with one's role of an athlete (such as being a "straight 'A' student"), athletes may avoid the corresponding anxiety.

THE RELATIONSHIPS AMONG AROUSAL, ANXIETY, AND ATHLETIC PERFORMANCE

In this section, we will examine the relationships among arousal, anxiety, and athletic performance. In the first section, we will review two standard and competing theories of the relationship between arousal and performance. This section will be followed by an analysis of the relationship between anxiety and performance. Finally, we will examine the reasons underlying the relationships.

Arousal and Athletic Performance

The relationship between physiological arousal and motor performance has been of interest to psychologists since the early 1900s. Research led to the development of two rather distinct theories: the inverted-U theory and drive theory.

The Inverted-U Theory.   Proponents of the ***inverted-U theory,*** depicted graphically in Figure 7.2, argue that the relationship between arousal and performance is nonlinear. They believe that the highest levels of performance occur when individ-

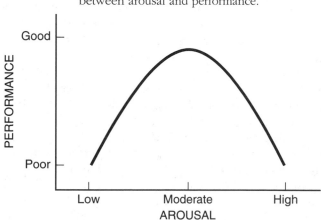

FIGURE 7.2 The inverted-U theory of the relationship between arousal and performance.

uals are moderately aroused, while the lowest levels of performance are associated with exceptionally low and high arousal. Because this pattern of effects was first presented in their research, the inverted-U theory is often referred to as the Yerkes-Dodson Law (Yerkes & Dodson, 1908).

The inverted-U theory has received a great deal of general psychology and sport psychology research support. Before reviewing a sample of these articles, it must be mentioned that many of the studies supporting the inverted-U theory operationally defined arousal as anxiety. Specifically, these authors were referring to somatic anxiety. Recall from our earlier discussion that somatic anxiety is the physiological arousal dimension of anxiety. The inverted-U theory predicts that moderate levels of somatic anxiety (i.e., arousal) are associated with the highest levels of performance, while exceptionally low and high levels of somatic anxiety result in lower levels of performance. This line of reasoning is consistent with the arguments of Martens et al. (1990) who note that arousal is often operationalized as somatic anxiety, and that in these instances the anxiety/performance relationship should resemble an inverted-U curve. The work of Martens and Landers (1970) offers further support for the notion that somatic anxiety and arousal are linked in their relationship with athletic performance. In this research, subjects were asked to complete a motor tracking task under one of three anxiety conditions. In the high anxiety condition, subjects were told that, if they failed at the tracking task, they would be given severe shocks. In the moderate condition, participants were told that task failure would lead to mild shocks. Finally, those in the low anxiety condition were told nothing about receiving shocks for poor performance. The authors assessed the physiological responses of subjects in the three conditions and found that arousal increased with increases in anxiety (i.e., the high anxiety group was higher in arousal than the low anxiety group). Thus, these authors were manipulating somatic anxiety. Consistent with the predictions of the inverted-U theory, these authors found that subjects in the moderate anxiety condition performed better than those in the low or high anxiety condition.

Perhaps the most widely cited study supporting the inverted-U theory is the work of Sonstroem and Bernardo (1982). These authors had female college basketball players complete both the SCAT and the CSAI (an earlier form of the CSAI-2 measuring A-state somatic anxiety). Sonstroem and Bernardo then compared the subjects' arousal scores for each game with their performance for that game (field goal shooting, rebounding, assists, and so on). The results indicated quite conclusively that the highest levels of performance were associated with moderate levels of arousal/somatic anxiety. Further, inverted-U relationships were found for high, moderate, and low trait anxiety players. In a different study, Klavora (1978) measured the precompetition anxiety levels of high school basketball players and compared these measures with their performance (as judged by the players' coaches). Consistent with the inverted-U theory, the highest levels of performance were found for the moderately anxious players. In addition to the works cited thus far, several other studies in sport settings have substantiated the inverted-U relationship between arousal/somatic anxiety and performance (Anderson, 1990; Brewer, Van Raalte, & Linder, 1990; Burton, 1988; Gould, Petlichkoff, Simons, & Vevera, 1987; Stennett, 1957).

Although several research endeavors have supported the inverted-U theory, the general conclusion that moderate levels of arousal result in the highest levels of performance is actually simplistic. To account for the inverted-U relationship, one must consider the difficulty of the task, the skill level of the player, and the type of activity involved. The importance of task difficulty is demonstrated in Figure 7.3. As shown in this diagram, the achievement of optimal levels of performance at easy tasks requires higher levels of arousal, than moderately difficult tasks. Moderately difficult tasks require higher levels of arousal than highly difficult tasks. For example, a college point guard would perform a simple dribbling task best under high arousal, while the more difficult task of shooting a free throw would be performed best under moderately arousing conditions. Finally, the difficult task of shooting a three-point field goal would require lower levels of arousal for optimal performance.

Closely related to task difficultly is a player's ability at the specific task. As depicted in Figure 7.4, the inverted-U theory predicts that players high in task ability will perform best in a state of high arousal. The logic here is that for such players the task should be quite simple and, as noted above, simple tasks are performed best under high arousal. Individuals who are moderately adept at a task will perform best under moderately arousing conditions (for these persons the task is moderately difficult). Individuals who are unskilled at a task will operate best when experiencing low levels of arousal. As an individual becomes more experienced and competent at a motor task, he or she will perform better at increasingly higher levels of arousal. For example, as the point guard mentioned above was first learning to dribble, she would have performed best at lower levels of arousal. However, as her ability to dribble improved, her optimal level of arousal would have risen at a corresponding rate until, as an experienced college player, her optimal level of arousal for this task would be quite high.

FIGURE 7.3   The relationships among task difficulty, arousal, and performance.

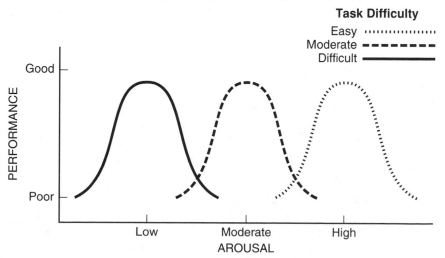

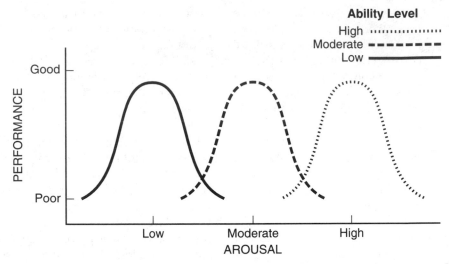

FIGURE 7.4   The relationships among ability level, arousal, and performance.

The third consideration concerns the type of sporting event being performed (see Figure 7.5). Sports involving high levels of concentration and fine motor movements warrant lower levels of arousal for peak performance. Examples of such events, called ***control sports*** by Cratty (1989), include putting in golf and executing a difficult shot in billiards. Other sports fitting Cratty's definition of ***speed-plus control sports*** (sports involving moderately high levels of strength, speed, and coordination) require moderate levels of arousal. This would include activities such as running the bases in baseball/softball and catching a football. Finally, certain sports seem best suited for situations involving high levels of arousal. These ***speed-power***

FIGURE 7.5   The relationships among sport type, arousal, and performance.

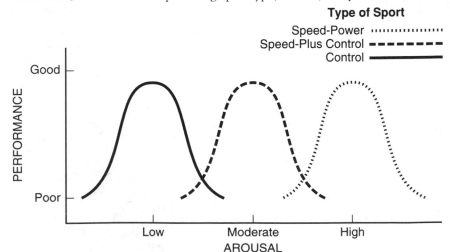

sports (Cratty, 1989) include gross motor activities such as weight lifting and tackling in football.

Drive Theory.   In contrast to the inverted-U hypothesis, supporters of ***drive theory*** argue that the relationship between arousal and performance is linear and in the form of a positive correlation (Hull, 1951; Spence, 1956). As seen in Figure 7.6, the lowest levels of performance are expected when the individual experiences low levels of arousal, moderate performance is associated with moderate arousal, and high performance is associated with high arousal. It is the prediction that high arousal is associated with top performance that is at odds with the inverted-U theory.

The relationship between arousal and performance as predicted by the drive theory is a function of the following formula:

$$\text{Performance} = \text{Habit Strength} \times \text{Drive}$$

Habit Strength refers to the individual's prior learning of the task, while Drive refers to the individual's degree of physiological arousal. Thus, an athlete's performance is thought to be a function of how well they have learned the specific task and their current level of arousal. Well learned tasks performed in a state of heightened arousal should result in the highest levels of performance. Conversely, performing a new behavior at a low level of arousal would lead to the lowest levels of performance. Because the performance is believed to be a multiplicative function of learning and arousal, if either learning or arousal is zero, performance will also be zero. One must have at least a minimal level of learning and arousal to perform a motor task.

Comparing the Inverted-U and Drive Theories.   It should be apparent that the inverted-U and drive theories are quite different in their depictions of the relationship between arousal and performance. Although some studies have been supportive of the drive model (e.g., Griffiths, Steel, & Vaccaro, 1979; Ryan, 1962; Spence,

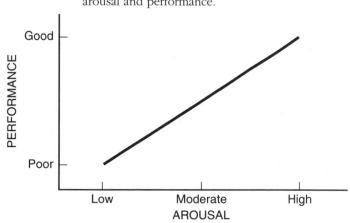

FIGURE 7.6   The drive theory of the relationship between arousal and performance.

Farber, & McFann, 1956), most research has supported the inverted-U model. In fact, the evidence has been strong enough to lead Cox (1990) to comment that "We can conclude that the relationship between arousal and athletic performance takes the form of an inverted-U" (p. 112), while LeUnes and Nation (1989) state that "Considering the great amount of support for the inverted-U position, there is reason to question . . . a single drive principle such as Hull's" (p. 104).

Although research tends to favor the inverted-U theory, it would be premature to dismiss the drive approach outright and incorrect to state that drive theory has not had an impact on sport psychology. Indeed, drive theory has lead to two major advances in sport psychology research. First, this theory added to our understanding of the relationship between learning (i.e., habit strength) and arousal. The inverted-U theory, on the other hand, is simply concerned with arousal and performance. Second, drive theory was influential in our understanding of the relationship between the audience-induced arousal and athletic performance. This area of research, termed social facilitation, is reviewed in the chapter devoted to the social nature of sport (Chapter 14).

Some authors have noted that research supporting drive theory can be incorporated in the inverted-U model (Cox, 1990; Cratty, 1989; Martens, 1974). To understand their thinking, it will be helpful to reexamine Figures 7.2 and 7.6. Notice that the predictions for drive theory (Figure 7.6) resemble the predictions for the first half of the inverted-U theory (Figure 7.2). That is, as arousal levels increase from low to moderate levels, both theories argue that there will be a corresponding increase in athletic performance. Thus, drive theory can be thought of as the first portion of the inverted-U hypothesis. Research supporting drive theory (research showing a positive correlation between arousal and performance) can, therefore, also be incorporated within the inverted-U framework. In this research, had the arousal been increased to a higher level, performance might have begun to decrease, thus supporting the inverted-U approach. However, this prediction often cannot be tested because inducing such high levels of physiological arousal is unethical.

Cognitive Anxiety and Athletic Performance

In the previous section, we examined the relationship between arousal and performance. Recall that arousal has been defined as a nonemotional state of readiness to perform physically, intellectually, or perceptually, and includes the somatic dimension of anxiety. In the current section, we will review the relationship between anxiety (e.g., negative stress) and performance. This discussion will focus on the cognitive dimension of anxiety. While somatic anxiety tends to form an inverted-U pattern in its relationship with performance, research has found that cognitive anxiety is negatively related to performance. As seen in Figure 7.7, this implies that the highest levels of performance are found in situations involving the lowest levels of cognitive anxiety, while the poorest performances are associated with the highest levels of cognitive anxiety.

Recent investigations incorporating the multidimensional CSAI-2 have supported the negative relationship between cognitive anxiety and performance (see Martens et al., 1990, for a review). For example, Burton (1988) asked competitive

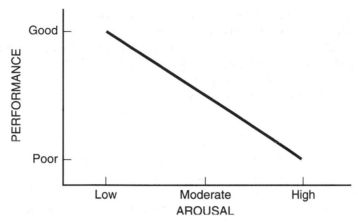

FIGURE 7.7 The relationship between cognitive anxiety and performance.

swimmers to complete the CSAI-2 and compared their anxiety scores to their performance. Consistent with expectations, cognitive anxiety was negatively related to performance, while somatic anxiety (i.e., arousal) formed an inverted-U pattern with performance. Similarly, in their study of male soccer players, Rodrigo, Lusiardo, and Pereira (1990) found a negative relationship between cognitive anxiety and sport performance. Recent work conducted in industrial/organizational psychology further substantiates the notion that small levels of cognitive anxiety can impair performance (e.g., Motowidlo, Packard, & Manning, 1986). However, because some studies have failed to find the expected negative relationship between cognitive anxiety and performance (Martens et al., 1990), and because the CSAI-2 is relatively new and few studies have incorporated this measure, future work is still needed to validate the cognitive anxiety-performance relationship.

Reasons Underlying the Relationships among Arousal, Anxiety, and Athletic Performance

With our understanding of anxiety, arousal, and performance, we can now examine the reasons underlying the relationships. First, let us examine the basis of the inverted-U theory. That is, why do moderate levels of arousal facilitate performance, while lower and higher levels do not? The primary reason responsible for this phenomenon is that physiological arousal reduces one's cognitive capacity. Several authors have noted that, because the human capacity to process cognitive information is limited, a reduction in that capacity will result in a reduction in performance (Broadbent, 1971; Easterbrook, 1959; Eysenck, 1976; Mandler, 1984). However, a moderate level of arousal can be beneficial because the reduction in cognitive capacity causes a person to pay less attention to irrelevant cues (such as the crowd), while focusing high levels of attention on relevant cues (i.e., the task at hand). Thus, as predicted by the inverted-U theory, a moderate increase in arousal will facilitate performance. If the arousal level increases too much and the person's cognitive capacity is too limited, she or he will begin to disregard relevant cues. As a result, the individual will begin to make mistakes, and his or her performance will suffer.

Let us now examine the reasons underlying the negative relationship between cognitive anxiety and performance. There are two main reasons behind this relationship. First, as noted by Baron and Greenberg (1990), low levels of cognitive anxiety can be distracting. As a result, individuals may begin to focus on their cognitive anxiety rather than on the task at hand, resulting in an increase in errors and a decrease in performance. To demonstrate this phenomenon, Bird and Horn (1990) asked 202 high school softball players to complete the CSAI-2 and asked the players' coaches to complete a questionnaire designed to assess the players' mental errors. After categorizing the players into low and high mental error groups, the authors examined the players' cognitive anxiety scores from the CSAI-2. As expected, players in the high mental errors group had higher cognitive anxiety scores than those in the low mental errors group.

Second, cognitive anxiety can interfere with one's health and sleep habits. Individuals suffering from poor health and sleep habits often exhibit impaired performance. As for the relationship between anxiety and health, several authors have shown that athletes experiencing high levels of anxiety tend to have higher numbers of injuries (Andersen & Williams, 1988; Coddington & Toxell, 1980; Hanson et al., 1992; Rotella & Heyman, 1993). Concerning the relationship between anxiety and sleep, Savis (1994) notes that highly anxious athletes may suffer from sleep disorders. As a result, athletes may experience health problems and fatigue, experiences that can ultimately inhibit their athletic performance.

ALTERNATIVE APPROACHES TO THE AROUSAL-PERFORMANCE RELATIONSHIP

In the previous section, we reviewed three standard approaches to the relationships among arousal, anxiety, and performance (the inverted-U hypothesis, drive theory, and the negative relationship between cognitive anxiety and performance). Although most researchers have examined the arousal-anxiety-performance relationship from one of these perspectives, some theorists have recently proposed alternative models. In this section, we will examine four of these newer approaches: reversal theory, zones of optimal functioning, catastrophe model, and the direction of an individual's experience of anxiety (i.e., debilitative versus facilitative).

Reversal Theory

Reversal theory reflects the belief that to understand the performance implications of arousal, an individual's subjective interpretation of the arousal must be considered (Kerr, 1985, 1990). Both high and low levels of arousal can be viewed as positive or negative experiences, depending on the particular situation. In an "anxiety-avoidance state" (Kerr, 1985, p. 173), the athlete will prefer a low level of arousal (e.g., during a precompetition relaxation period). Conversely, in an "arousal-seeking state" (p. 173), athletes actively search for excitement. Athletes can quickly reverse their interpretation of the arousal (hence, the name of the theory). That is, high or low levels of arousal may be perceived as pleasant one moment but unpleasant the next. Performance should be at top levels when there is little discrepancy between an athlete's preferred state of arousal (e.g., "I would like to feel relaxed") and actual state (e.g., "I feel relaxed").

Because reversal theory is still new, few studies have targeted the validity of the model. However, a recent investigation conducted by Raedeke and Stein (1994) does have relevance for the theory. In this study, recreational slalom skiers completed a self-report measure of their felt arousal (an individual's perception of his or her arousal state) and stated how they felt on an extremely negative to extremely positive continuum. Based on these scales, subjects were classified into four groups: high arousal-positive feelings, high arousal-negative feelings, low arousal-positive feelings, and low arousal-negative feelings. Participants were also asked to complete a scale measuring their subjective performance immediately after completing a slalom run but prior to receiving feedback about the actual performance. Because both high arousal and positive affect facilitate performance, Raedeke and Stein predicted that subjects experiencing a high level of arousal in a positive mood state would report the most positive subjective performance scores. As expected, skiers in the high arousal-positive feelings condition believed they had performed better than those in the other three groups. These findings are consistent with Kerr's (1990) contentions because arousal and the interpretation of the arousal (i.e., feelings) combined to influence subjective performance.

Zones of Optimal Functioning

Another alternative approach to the arousal-performance relationship was proposed by Hanin (1989). Hanin argues that athletes possess a ***zone of optimal functioning*** (ZOF). An athlete's ZOF is an optimal state of anxiety (i.e., arousal) that leads to high levels of performance. Poor performance is expected when an athlete's anxiety state falls below his ZOF or rises above his ZOF. Athletes with a high arousal ZOF will perform best when in a heightened state of arousal, while those with a low arousal ZOF will perform best with minimal levels of arousal. Hanin's theory differs from the traditional inverted-U perspective because an athlete's ZOF may or may not lie near the midpoint on the arousal continuum, as predicted by the inverted-U hypothesis. Recent investigations have supported the notion of a ZOF (Hanin, 1989; Hanin & Syrjä, 1995).

Catastrophe Model

Throughout this chapter we have made a distinction between somatic anxiety and cognitive anxiety. Hardy (1990) recently presented a theory designed to account for the performance implications of the interaction between somatic and cognitive anxiety. Hardy's perspective, called the ***catastrophe model,*** reflects the belief that somatic anxiety impacts performance in the form of an inverted-U curve, but only in situations involving low levels of cognitive anxiety. When moderately high levels of somatic anxiety are accompanied by high levels of cognitive anxiety, a catastrophic decrease in performance is predicted. This pattern is shown in Figure 7.8. This model differs from the traditional inverted-U perspective predicting a gradual drop-off in performance in all highly arousing situations. Several sport studies have supported the catastrophe model (see Hardy, 1990, for a review).

Hardy (1990) notes there are two important implications of the catastrophe model. First, because athletes tend to be high in cognitive and somatic anxiety prior to a competition, coaches should be cautious when attempting to "psych-up" their players. That is, players may already be at dangerously high levels of cognitive and somatic anxiety and the added anxiety from the psyching-up rituals may impair performance. Second, because the catastrophe model implies that both somatic and cognitive anxiety influence performance, coaches and sport psychologists should train athletes in the control of both somatic and cognitive anxiety (anxiety control techniques will be discussed in the interventions chapter).

The Direction of One's Anxiety Experience: Debilitative and Facilitative Anxiety

Throughout this chapter, I have stated that the relationship between somatic anxiety and performance is best described as an inverted-U, while the relationship between cognitive anxiety and performance is best described in terms of a negative linear pattern. These findings suggest that sport psychologists should increase an athlete's somatic anxiety to an optimal level while decreasing the athlete's cognitive anxiety. However, recent advances by Jones, Swain, and their colleagues seem to indicate that this interpretation is overly simplistic (Jones & Swain, 1992, 1995; Jones, Swain, & Hardy, 1993; Parfitt & Hardy, 1993). Rather, they argue that to understand the anxiety-performance relationship fully, sport psychologists must consider not only

FIGURE 7.8   According to the catastrophe model, high levels of somatic arousal will lead to gradual declines in performance. However, when the somatic arousal is accompanied by high levels of cognitive arousal, there will be a catastrophic decline in performance.

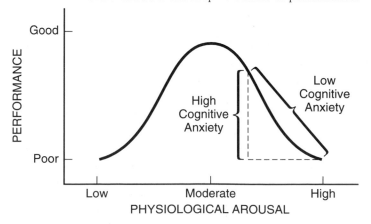

anxiety intensity (i.e., a low, moderate, or high anxiety level) but also anxiety direction. *Anxiety direction* concerns the athlete's cognitive interpretation of the anxiety, that is, whether the anxiety is viewed as debilitative or facilitative (i.e., inhibiting or enhancing athletic performance).

To demonstrate the importance of anxiety direction, Jones and Swain (1992) first altered the CSAI-2. Recall that this inventory measures the intensity of an athlete's somatic anxiety, cognitive anxiety, and self-confidence. Jones and Swain added a Likert-scale directionality question to each item, asking subjects to state the extent that the anxiety intensity was viewed as debilitative or facilitative. The modified CSAI-2 and a measure of competitiveness were given to a sample of athletes. The results indicated that, although athletes high and low in competitiveness did not differ in degree of anxiety intensity, highly competitive subjects reported a greater belief in the performance-enhancing effects of cognitive anxiety. Highly competitive persons also tended to view somatic anxiety as more facilitative than low competitiveness people (although the difference was not statistically significant). Perhaps the most interesting finding was that all subject groups viewed anxiety as facilitative rather than debilitative.

Subsequent studies have indicated that successful and unsuccessful athletes differ in their tendencies to interpret anxiety in a debilitative or facilitative fashion. For example, Jones et al. (1993) found that successful female gymnasts viewed their anxiety as more facilitative than unsuccessful gymnasts, even though the two groups did not differ on anxiety intensity. Similar results have been found for swimmers (Jones, Hanton, & Swain, 1994) and cricket players (Jones & Swain, 1995). In addition, Wiggins (1995) found that athletes with a facilitative view of anxiety report higher performance expectations than persons with a debilitative view of anxiety.

Thus, investigations employing the modified CSAI-2 have shown that researchers' beliefs about the anxiety-performance relationship may have been simplistic. Researchers need to consider the intensity of the anxiety *and* the direction of the anxiety. Assuming that anxiety will inhibit performance is incorrect. Rather, many athletes believe that anxiety enhances their performance. Future researchers should continue to address the directionality of anxiety, furthering our understanding of this construct.

SUMMARY

While they are often used interchangeably, arousal, stress, and anxiety are actually independent constructs. Arousal is a nonemotional physiological state of readiness to perform physically, intellectually, or perceptually. The maintenance of a homeostatic level of arousal is controlled by the sympathetic and parasympathetic divisions of the autonomic nervous system. Stress is a nonemotional bodily response to an environmental demand.

Anxiety is the negative interpretation of past, present, and future environmental demands. Individuals can experience both state and trait anxiety in response to stressful events. There have been several instruments used to measure anxiety in sport settings. The most popular tests are the Sport Competition Anxiety Test (measuring trait anxiety) and the Competitive State Anxiety Inventory-2 (measuring both somatic state anxiety and cognitive state anxiety). Athletes experience anxiety due to previous events (residual anxiety), current events (current anxiety), and future events (anticipatory anxiety). Anxiety can also be classified based on whether the stressor is qualitative or quantitative and whether the athlete is experiencing a stimulus overload or underload.

Many sport participants experience anxiety because of their role as athletes. Some athletes experience role ambiguity, a situation in which the athlete is unclear about the components of his or her athletic role. Other athletes experience one of three forms of role conflict. Personality role conflict occurs when an individual's personality conflicts with a given role. Intrarole conflict occurs when a single role has conflicting expectations. Interrole conflict is found when an individual simultaneously possesses two incongruent roles.

Two theories have been proposed to account for the relationship between arousal and performance. The inverted-U theory states that athletic performance will be facilitated by moderate levels of arousal. High and low levels of arousal are thought to be associated with lower levels of performance. Conversely, drive theory states that there is a positive relationship between arousal and performance. Higher levels of arousal are believed to be associated with higher levels of performance. To date, although studies have been supportive of both theories, most of research supports the inverted-U hypothesis. Concerning the relationship between cognitive anxiety and performance, research has found a negative linear relationship involving these variables. Higher levels of cognitive anxiety are associated with lower levels of performance.

Alternative approaches to the relationships involving arousal, anxiety, and performance have recently been advanced. Reversal theory reflects the belief that to understand the performance implications of arousal, an individual's subjective interpretation of the arousal must be considered. Zones of optimal functioning involve an athlete's optimal state of anxiety, a state that leads to high levels of performance. The catastrophe model reflects the belief that somatic anxiety affects performance in the form of an inverted-U curve but only in situations involving low levels of cognitive anxiety. When high levels of somatic anxiety are accompanied by high levels of cognitive anxiety, a sharp decrease in performance is predicted. Finally, to understand the relationship between anxiety and performance fully, psychologists must consider the direction of the anxiety. Successful athletes tend to view their anxiety as facilitating their performance.

GLOSSARY

Alarm Stage   The first stage of the GAS, this stage begins with the onset of the stressor and is characterized by higher than normal levels of physiological arousal.

Anticipatory Anxiety   Feelings of anxiety about future events.

Anxiety   The negative interpretation of past, present, and future environmental demands.

Anxiety Direction   An athlete's cognitive interpretation of anxiety (i.e., whether the anxiety is viewed as debilitative or facilitative).

Anxiety Intensity   The level of an individual's anxiety experience (i.e., low, moderate, or high).

Arousal   A nonemotional physiological state of readiness to perform physically, intellectually, or perceptually.

Autonomic Nervous System (ANS)   Involves the control of automatic, involuntary bodily functions.

Catastrophe Model   Reflects the belief that somatic anxiety affects performance in the form of an inverted-U curve, but only in situations involving low levels of cognitive anxiety. When moderately high levels of somatic anxiety are accompanied by high levels of cognitive anxiety, a catastrophic decrease in performance is predicted.

Cognitive Anxiety   Fear, apprehension, and worry about an upcoming athletic event.

Competition Anxiety   A form of current anxiety in which athletes experience anxiety about a current performance.

Control Sports   Sports involving high levels of concentration and fine motor movements that require lower levels of arousal for peak performance.

Current Anxiety   Feelings of anxiety about current events.

Drive Theory   A theory reflecting the belief that the relationship between arousal and performance is linear and in the form of a positive correlation.

Exhaustion Stage   The third stage of the GAS, this stage is characterized by low levels of arousal, fatigue, and illness.

General Adaptation Syndrome (GAS)   The hypothesis that individuals exhibit nonspecific reactions to stressors.

Homeostasis   A state of physiological balance or stability.

Interrole Conflict   Conflict occurring when an individual simultaneously possesses two incongruent roles.

Intrarole Conflict   Conflict occurring when a single role has conflicting expectations.

Inverted-U Theory   A theory reflecting the belief that the relationship between arousal and performance is nonlinear and that the highest levels of performance will be found when individuals are moderately aroused, while the lowest levels of performance will be associated with low and high levels of arousal.

Neustress   Neutral stress that occurs when environmental demands have neither positive nor negative effects.

Parasympathetic Division of the ANS   The calming division of the ANS that returns the body to its normal state of arousal.

Personality Role Conflict   Conflict occurring when an individual's personality conflicts with a given role.

Postcompetition Anxiety   A form of residual anxiety in which athletes experience anxiety about a past performance.

Precompetition Anxiety   A form of anticipatory anxiety in which athletes experience anxiety about a future performance.

Qualitative Overload   Occurs when an individual believes he or she does not have the ability to perform a task.

Qualitative Underload   Occurs when an individual is required to perform a repetitive and/or boring task and, consequently, feels a lack of mental stimulation from the task.

Quantitative Overload   Occurs when an individual is required to do more work than is possible in a given time.

Quantitative Underload   Occurs when an individual has too little to do.

Residual Anxiety   Feelings of anxiety about past events.

Resistance Stage   The second stage of the GAS, this stage is marked by higher than normal levels of arousal as the organism attempts to cope with the stressor. Arousal begins to decline as the stressor lingers.

Reversal Theory   Reflects the belief that to understand the performance implications of arousal, an individual's subjective interpretation of the arousal must be considered.

Role Ambiguity   Anxiety occurring when an individual is uncertain about one or more components of a specific role.

Role Conflict   Situation in which one's role conflicts with oneself or other roles.

Somatic Anxiety   The physiological element of anxiety.

Speed-Plus Control Sports   Sports involving moderately high levels of strength, speed, and coordination that require moderate levels of arousal for peak performance.

Speed-Power Sports   Sports involving gross motor activities that require high levels of arousal for peak performance.

State Anxiety   Acute reactions to a current stressful condition.

Stress   A nonemotional bodily response to an environmental demand.

Sympathetic Division of the ANS   The arousing division of the ANS that prepares the body for action.

Trait Anxiety   A long-lasting, chronic predisposition to experience anxiety in stressful environments.

Zone of Optimal Functioning   An optimal state of anxiety leading to high levels of performance.

APPLICATION AND REVIEW QUESTIONS

1. Define, compare, and contrast the terms arousal, stress, somatic anxiety, and cognitive anxiety.
2. Describe a sport example of Selye's General Adaptation Syndrome.
3. Describe a sport example of residual, current, and anticipatory anxiety.
4. Compare and contrast quantitative overload, qualitative overload, quantitative underload, and qualitative underload. Now give a sport example of each.
5. Give a sport example of each of the forms of role anxiety.
6. Compare and contrast the inverted-U and drive theories. Which theory is best supported by research?
7. Describe the relationship between cognitive anxiety and athletic performance.

SUGGESTED READINGS

GOULD, D., & KRANE, V. (1992). The arousal-athletic performance relationship: Current status and future directions. In T. S. Horn (Ed.), *Advances in sport psychology* (pp. 119–142). Champaign, IL: Human Kinetics. This chapter focuses on the relationships among anxiety, arousal, and athletic performance.

HANIN, Y. L. (1989). Interpersonal and intragroup anxiety in sports. In D. Hackfort & C. D. Spielberger (Eds.), *Anxiety in sports: An interactional perspective* (pp. 19–28). New York: Hemisphere. This chapter focuses on the relationship between zones of optimal functioning and athletic performance.

HARDY, L. (1990). A catastrophe model of performance in sport. In J. Graham & L. Hardy (Eds.), *Stress and performance in sport* (pp. 81–106). New York: Wiley. This chapter reviews the catastrophe model of anxiety and performance.

JONES, G., & SWAIN, A. (1995). Predispositions to experience debilitative and facilitative anxiety in elite and nonelite performers. *The Sport Psychologist, 9,* 201–211. This article examines the implications of perceptions of anxiety as either facilitative or debilitative.

KERR, J. H. (1990). Stress and sport: Reversal theory. In J. Graham & L. Hardy (Eds.), *Stress and performance in sport* (pp. 107–131). New York: Wiley. This chapter describes Kerr's reversal theory.

MARTENS, R., VEALEY, R. S., & BURTON, D. (1990). *Competitive anxiety in sport*. Champaign, IL: Human Kinetics. This book describes the processes used to validate the SCAT and CSAI-2. In addition, numerous articles employing these measures are discussed. Perhaps the finest feature of this book is that the text includes the entire SCAT and CSAI-2 questionnaires, and investigators are encouraged to incorporate these scales into their research.

SMITH, J. C. (1993). *Understanding stress and coping*. New York: Macmillan. This book presents the reader with an overview of stress and anxiety research. In addition, several chapters focus on the strategies used to combat or lessen the negative effects of stress.

Chapter 8

MOTIVATION IN SPORT

Please read the following scenarios. As you read the passages, try to find the common link between them.

1. The coach of a college football team requires that his players witness the castration of a bull.
2. The owner of a professional sports team has her players examine a picture of her dog's grave.
3. The coach of a little league baseball team offers $20 to any player who hits a home run.
4. The coach of a college football team makes his players watch him swallow a worm.
5. A college basketball coach leaves the bench in the middle of a game and sits in the stands, giving "high-fives" to spectators and the mascot.
6. Prior to a game against a top-ranked team, a college basketball coach shows his players a video of the college's football team upsetting a top-ranked opponent.
7. A college basketball coach vows to get his head shaved if his team wins five consecutive games.
8. A high school coach uses fake blood and blanks to stage his own shooting in the school cafeteria.

What do these scenarios have in common? Unbelievably, they are actual attempts by coaches and owners to increase the motivation of their players (for a more detailed discussion of these accounts, see Anderson, 1994b; McCallum, 1993; Telander, 1994; *The National Sports Review,* 1992; Warren, 1983; Wolff, 1993; Wolff, 1994). As these examples indicate, coaches will try almost anything to increase the motivation of their players.

In this chapter, we will examine several components of motivation relevant to sport settings. We will begin our examination by defining motivation and exploring the relationship between intrinsic and extrinsic motivation. We will then review the history of research on motivation. This section will be followed by a discussion of several theories and research endeavors aimed at understanding motivation in sport settings. Before beginning, however, it should be noted that the current chapter focuses on persons who have already chosen to participate in athletics. The motives influencing sport participation decisions were discussed in Chapter 3.

DEFINING MOTIVATION AND A COMPARISON
OF INTRINSIC AND EXTRINSIC MOTIVES

While many definitions of ***motivation*** have been advanced, I prefer to define motivation as a process of arousal within an organism that helps direct and sustain behavior. Motivation can be intrinsic or extrinsic. ***Intrinsic motives*** lie within an individual and involve the individual's interest and enjoyment of a task. A child who plays softball because she likes the sport is intrinsically motivated. ***Extrinsic motives*** lie outside an individual and involve the rewards and benefits of performing a task. Trophies, ribbons, money, and praise are all examples of extrinsic motivators. Contrary to popular belief, using extrinsic motives to enhance motivation is not always a good idea. In fact, in situations in which an individual is performing a task because of intrinsic motivation, presenting the individual with extrinsic rewards for performing the activity will often lower the person's intrinsic motivation (Deci, 1971; Deci & Ryan, 1985; Harackiewicz, 1979; Lepper, Greene, & Nisbett, 1973; Ross, 1975).

To explain this phenomenon, Deci and Ryan (1985; Deci & Olson, 1989; Frederick & Ryan, 1995) developed their cognitive evaluation theory. ***Cognitive evaluation theory*** states that rewards can be divided into two types: controlling rewards and informational rewards (some rewards are both controlling and informational). ***Controlling rewards,*** such as praise or trophies, are designed to influence (i.e., control) an individual's behavior while ***informational rewards*** convey informa-

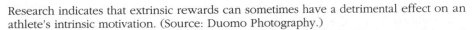

Research indicates that extrinsic rewards can sometimes have a detrimental effect on an athlete's intrinsic motivation. (Source: Duomo Photography.)

tion about an individual's competence at a task. Deci and Ryan argue that rewards perceived as controlling decrease intrinsic motivation, while rewards viewed as informational increase intrinsic motivation. If a player believes her coach's praise is designed to control her behavior, the praise will lower her intrinsic motivation for the task. If, on the other hand, the player believes that the praise is designed to provide information about her successful performance, her intrinsic motivation for the task would increase.

Because of the relationship between intrinsic and extrinsic motivation, coaches, parents, and league officials must think carefully about the rewards they offer to athletes. As discussed in the learning chapter, reinforcements should be used to increase desired behaviors, but these rewards may have a detrimental effect on intrinsic motivation. Thus, individuals must walk a fine line in their decisions to reward players, considering both the positive effects of rewards (i.e., the subsequent increase in desirable behavior) and the potential negative effects of rewards (i.e., the lowering of intrinsic motivation).

In addition to examining the relationship between intrinsic and extrinsic motivation, research has also focused on the relationship between intrinsic motivation and competition. Three findings have consistently been supported. First, in a comparison of competitive and noncompetitive settings, research has found that competition tends to increase one's intrinsic motivation (Reeve, 1992). Apparently, competition represents a challenge and allows the athlete to compare his or her skills with those of others. Second, in a comparison of competitive and mastery-oriented environments (mastery-oriented settings encourage the improvement of one's skills rather than defeating an opponent), mastery-oriented environments usually lead to higher levels of intrinsic motivation (Vallerand, Gauvin, & Halliwell, 1986). Finally, in a comparison of winning and losing, researchers have found that winning results in higher levels of intrinsic motivation (Reeve & Deci, 1996; Weinberg, 1979; Weinberg & Jackson, 1979; Weinberg & Ragan, 1980). Winning facilitates intrinsic motivation because success increases perceptions of competence, not because it gives one the feeling that he or she has defeated an opponent (McAuley & Tammen, 1989).

The Measurement of Intrinsic and Extrinsic Motivation in Sport

Recently, Pelletier and his associates (1995; Fortier, Vallerand, Brière, & Provencher, 1995) developed an instrument measuring intrinsic motivation, extrinsic motivation, and amotivation in sport settings. This scale, called the Sport Motivation Scale (SMS), contains 28 Likert-scale items categorized into seven motivation subscales. Three subscales measure components of intrinsic motivation. The "intrinsic motivation to know" subscale reflects the desire to participate in athletics as a means of fulfilling a curiosity and a desire to learn and understand the sport. The "intrinsic motivation toward accomplishments" subscale reflects the desire to master the task. The final intrinsic subscale measures "intrinsic motivation to experience stimulation" and involves the desire for excitement, eustress, aesthetic experiences, and enjoyment.

The SMS also contains three extrinsic motivation subscales. The "external regulation" subscale reflects the desire to receive external rewards through participation in athletics. The "introjection" subscale assesses the impact of formerly external sources of motivation that have been internalized (e.g., athletes who feel compelled to participate in athletics because they feel pressure to stay in shape). The third extrinsic subscale, labeled "identification," reflects an athlete's desire to participate in sport because he or she believes that participation fosters personal growth and development.

The seventh subscale is "amotivation." Amotivation occurs when individuals no longer perceive a link between actions and outcomes. Subsequently, they experience a sense of incompetence and a lack of control. The authors note that when athletes experience a state of amotivation, they are no longer able to cite reasons for participating in sport and are likely to discontinue their participation (Pelletier et al., 1995).

Because the SMS is still new, there is little empirical research documenting the reliability and validity of the scale. However, Pelletier et al. (1995) do cite preliminary evidence indicating the sound psychometric properties of the instrument. These authors asked more than 500 university athletes to complete the SMS and several potentially related scales (such as perceived competence and impressions of the coach). Correlations computed between the SMS subscales of the other scales revealed a pattern consistent with expectations. For example, a negative relationship was found between amotivation and perceived competence and effort. Also, positive correlations were found between the intrinsic subscales and effort. These scales were negatively related to distraction. Thus, although additional work is needed, current research using the SMS is encouraging.

A BRIEF REVIEW OF THE HISTORY OF MOTIVATION THEORY

A review of past research and theorizing about the origin of motivation in humans reveals that three general theories have been presented: instinctual models, drive models, and expectancy theories.

Instinctual Models of Motivation

During the early years of the 20th century, the notion that instincts guided the behavior of humans dominated psychology. ***Instinctual theories of motivation*** reflect the belief that behavior is motivated by innate or inherited predispositions and characteristics. Several prominent psychologists postulated instinctual theories. For example, William James (1890) argued that humans possess several instincts including instincts for sympathy, play, and curiosity. Sigmund Freud believed that behavior was primarily driven by two instincts: eros, the life instinct, and thanatos, the death instinct (see Weiner, 1989). Other prominent authors such as William McDougall (1908) and Charles Darwin (1859) also believed that motivation was primarily instinctual in origin.

Although a handful of theorists still favor instinctual models of motivation, the instinctual theories lost most of their support in the 1930s. Several problems with these theories led to their decline. First, the instinctual theorists were unable to agree on the number and types of instincts. While authors such as Freud argued that there were only a few powerful instincts, others such as McDougall and James believed that there were a dozen or more different instincts. Taken as a whole, the instinctual theorists suggested hundreds of different instincts (Bernard, 1924). Second, instinctual theories tend to be based on circular logic. For example, let us say a researcher believes that human aggression is instinctually motivated. If you were to ask this person to explain why humans behave aggressively, he or she would state that the aggressive behavior is due to an instinct. If you were to then ask this person how he or she knew that humans have an aggressive instinct, they would reply that humans must have an aggressive instinct because they are aggressive. Circular logic such as this is problematic because there is no starting point to the process and because these theories are often difficult or impossible to test.

Drive Models of Motivation

Because of the problems with the instinctual perspectives, many psychologists began to adopt drive theories of motivation. ***Drive theories*** represent the belief that human behavior is motivated by drives designed to reduce biological needs. Before proceeding further, it will be helpful to define two constructs involved in drive theories: drive and need. A ***drive*** is an internal state of tension. A ***need*** is a biological or psychological deficiency felt by an individual.

Perhaps the most famous and influential drive theory was presented by Hull (1943, 1951). A simplified version of Hull's drive reduction model is presented in Figure 8.1. When individuals experience a need, they have lost their homeostatic balance for that substance. For example, let us consider water. When an individual goes without water for several hours, he or she experiences a need for water because there is no longer an optimal balance of this substance in his or her system. This need leads to a drive. Hull believed that the drive energized the individual but that the drive did not direct the individual's behavior toward a goal. Recall from our discussion of drive theory in Chapter 7 that Performance = Habit Strength × Drive. Habit strength was equated with prior learning. As for Hull's drive reduction model of motivation, the selection of a goal to reduce a drive is a function of prior learning. The drive toward water energizes the individual, while his or her prior learning directs behavior toward a goal (e.g., a drinking fountain or a faucet). As indicated in

FIGURE 8.1   Hull's drive reduction model of motivation.

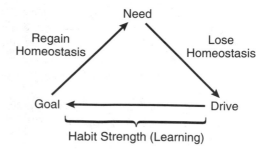

Figure 8.1, once the goal has been achieved, the individual has regained homeostasis. However, because the body continually needs water, the process is ongoing.

A sport-specific example of Hull's model may be helpful. Let us continue to use water as the substance in question. Imagine that an individual, John, has just spent the last 2 hours lifting weights at a gym. After his workout, John has a need for water. That is, because of the strenuous workout, John has lost his homeostatic balance of this substance. As a result, he is energized by a drive. In the past when he felt thirsty following a session at this particular gym, John would purchase a bottle of water at a convenience mart on the way home. He had learned that this behavior was successful in attaining the goal of water. Had this store not offered bottled water, his learning would have lead to a different goal (e.g., a different convenience mart or he may have brought his own water). Once John finishes drinking the water, he will regain his optimal, homeostatic level of this substance.

While drive reduction models such as Hull's were originally designed to explain biological motives (e.g., drinking, eating, and sexual behavior), it soon became apparent that these models could also accommodate learned drives. Learned drives involved motives such as the need for affiliation, achievement, and self-esteem. For example, consider an athlete, Sarah, who is motivated by a need for affiliation. When this person is alone, there is a deficiency in her need for affiliation. This need and the corresponding loss of homeostasis lead to an energizing drive. Her prior learning may have led Sarah to believe that she could satisfy her need for affiliation through athletic participation. That is, the drive arouses Sarah, while her past experiences with sport have taught her that these activities lead to social encounters. As a result, Sarah decides to go to the gym to work out with her friends. Once there, she achieves her goal and regains the homeostatic balance needed.

Expectancy Models of Motivation

Although many people preferred drive models of motivation during the mid-1900s, these theories also began to lose favor among researchers. Although authors found several problems with these models (Reeve, 1992), perhaps the greatest limitation of drive theories is one they share with the instinctual models. Both instinctual and drive theories of motivation tend to be "stick" theories. As with an individual trying to make a donkey move from point A to point B by swatting the donkey on the behind, the instinctual and drive theories argue that people are pushed into action by their drives and instincts. Although people are indeed motivated by "sticks" such as previous rewards, punishments, successes, and failures, recent work in motivation has found that individuals are also motivated by "carrots." These carrots, such as future goals and aspirations, dangle in front of people and pull them toward the future.

Becoming popular in the 1970s, expectancy theories were developed in an attempt to account for the vast amount of human behavior that is motivated by future events. ***Expectancy theories of motivation*** argue that future outcomes pull individuals into action. For example, consider an athlete who is in the middle of a strenuous 90-minute workout. This person is extremely tired, thirsty, and sore. Instinctual and drive theories would argue that this person would be driven (i.e., pushed) to return his body to a state of balance. Thus, these theories would predict that he will end his workout once he becomes tired. However, as most athletes know, this is not an accurate analysis of what happens during workout sessions. Because athletes are pulled by future goals and rewards (such as health, physique, or sport mastery), they continue to workout even though their bodies tell them to stop.

Although a carrot is used to describe expectancy theories, one should not be misled into believing that all future motives are positive. Rather, people are motivated to approach certain outcomes, while being motivated to avoid others. For example, athletes are motivated to approach and gain skill, self-esteem, and confidence while avoiding outcomes such as failure and ridicule. In addition, individuals are rarely if ever motivated by a single outcome at any given time. That is, humans tend to be multimotivational (motivated simultaneously by several outcomes) rather than unimotivational (motivated by a single outcome). In some instances, the motivations operating simultaneously within an individual come into conflict. Research has identified four such motivational conflicts.

Approach-approach motivational conflict occurs when an individual must choose between two or more positive outcomes. For example, a high school senior who is offered an athletic scholarship from two attractive colleges must choose only one of these schools. A second type of conflict, *avoidance-avoidance motivational conflict* occurs when an individual must choose between two or more negative outcomes. For example, imagine a young baseball player who desperately wants to be a pitcher. However, his coach has told him that he must choose between catcher and right fielder, neither of which he desires. *Approach-avoidance motivational conflict* occurs when an individual is presented with a single outcome having both positive and negative components. The conflict resides in the individual's decision to accept or reject the goal. For example, a young athlete may be given the opportunity to play in an all-star game after the season. The child wants to play in the game because he enjoys the sport and recognition, but at the same time he does not want to play in the all-star game because of the pressure. Finally, *double approach-avoidance motivational conflict* occurs when an individual is simultaneously presented with two or more outcomes, each having both positive and negative components. For example, consider an adolescent softball player who must choose between two different teams. Team A has the advantage of being a championship contender (a positive component), but in all likelihood the player will ride the bench on this team (a negative component). Team B is made up of many of the player's best friends (a positive component), but this team's games will be played on poor fields (a negative component). Because of the complexity involved in double approach-avoidance conflicts, these conflicts are often the most difficult to resolve.

SPECIFIC THEORIES AND APPROACHES TO MOTIVATION IN SPORT

For the remainder of this chapter, we will examine several specific approaches to motivation in sport. First, we will review the importance of self-efficacy and goal setting. We will then examine the achievement motivation, equity, and valence-instrumentality-expectancy theories of motivation.

Self-Efficacy

If you have spent even a small amount of time in sport settings, one thing has probably become clear to you: self-confidence is a very important part of motivation and success in sport. To help in their understanding of the influences of self-confidence, sport psychologists often turn to Bandura's self-efficacy theory (Bandura, 1977a, 1986). *Self-efficacy* refers to an individual's belief that he or she has the ability to perform at a specified level on a certain task. Unlike stable personality traits, self-efficacy is situation specific. An individual may have a high level of efficacy at one task or sport yet experience a low level of efficacy for a different task or sport. For example, athletes who are confident about their baseball skills will not necessarily be confident of their abilities in other sports.

Bandura (1986) believes that feelings of self-efficacy are the result of information gained from four sources. First and most important, individuals develop their perceptions of efficacy as a result of their successes and failures at the task in question. As people experience success at a task, they integrate information about their accomplishments. As a result, they begin to believe that they possess the abilities necessary to succeed at the task. Conversely, if individuals consistently fail at a task, this information will lead to the belief that they do not have the abilities necessary to perform the task. Second, people receive efficacy information vicariously through their social comparisons with others. Bandura (1986) states that when individuals see others succeed at a task, they "persuade themselves that if others can do it, they should (also) be able to achieve at least some improvement in performance" (p. 399). A third form of information concerns persuasion. For example, a coach or a parent may attempt to convince an individual that he or she has the ability to succeed at a task. Although these persuasive attempts have an effect on perceptions of efficacy, they will not be as important as the individual's actual experiences with the task. Finally, individuals receive efficacy information through their current physiological state. For example, imagine a baseball player who experiences a heightened level of arousal prior to important games. If he believes that the arousal is due to a lack of ability, he may come to believe that he does not possess the required skills.

Because of its obvious ramifications for athletic motivation, sport psychologists have examined the impact of self-efficacy in sport settings. Feltz (1992) notes that many of the studies targeting self-efficacy and sport confidence have tested the importance of the four sources of efficacy information described above. In general, these studies have strongly supported Bandura's belief that people develop their perceptions of efficacy through information provided by actual experience, vicarious experience, persuasion, and physiological arousal (see Feltz, 1992, for a review).

Other studies have been designed to test the relationship between perceptions of self-efficacy and athletic performance (e.g., Feltz, 1988, 1992; Feltz, Landers, & Raeder, 1979; George, 1994; Highlen & Bennett, 1980; Martin & Gill, 1991, 1995; Theodorakis, 1995; Weinberg, Gould, Yukelson, & Jackson, 1981). This research has consistently found that increases in perceptions of self-efficacy lead to better levels of performance. Thus, it appears that beliefs in the ability to succeed do enhance subsequent performance. In fact, the performance implications of self-confidence are so important that we will examine intervention strategies aimed at building self-confidence in Chapter 11.

Goal Setting in Sport

While many topics relevant to athletic motivation have attracted the attention of sport psychologists, only recently have researchers become interested in the impact and importance of goal setting. This line of work has indicated that to be beneficial, goals must be established in the correct manner. When goals are established in an improper fashion, they may actually inhibit motivation, effort, and performance. This is what Burton (1992b) refers to as the "Jekyll/Hyde nature of goals" (p. 268). How, then, should one go about setting proper goals? Based on research in industrial, organizational, academic, and sport settings, the answer appears to lie in the establishment of specific and difficult goals and in providing feedback about goal attainment (Burton, 1993; Locke & Latham, 1985).

Goal Specificity.   Research has found that specific goals lead to better performance than "do your best" goals (Baron & Greenberg, 1990; Latham & Lee, 1986; Weinberg, 1994). Coaches should not simply ask players to perform to their best ability. Instead, they should be specific and precise in what they want players to accomplish. For example, rather than telling an athlete to "do as many sit-ups as you can," the coach or physical educator should state an exact goal (for example, ask the athlete to do 50 sit-ups).

It is also important to link the players' practice goals with actual game conditions. When the players' practice goals match the behaviors found in actual games, the goals may be more effective. The importance of the consistency between practice goals and game conditions can be seen in the work of Kozar, Vaughn, Lord, and Whitfield (1995). These researchers examined college basketball players' practice free throw accuracy and game free throw accuracy. They found that the players had a better shooting accuracy in practice. However, they also found a large discrepancy between the number of free throws attempted during practice and during games. During practice sessions, the players attempted an average of 7.5 free throws each time they stepped to the foul line. However, players usually attempt only one or two free throws per trip during games. When the researchers compared the players' shooting accuracy for their first two practice shots with their game accuracy, they found no differences. Thus, this study suggests that coaches should set specific goals that reflect actual game conditions. For example, basketball coaches should require players to complete two consecutive free throws on five different trips to the foul line rather than asking players to hit 10 consecutive free throws on one trip. Although both of the goals are highly specific, the five-trip goal is a better approach because this goal more closely resembles actual game conditions.

Goal Difficulty.   Research indicates that goal specificity alone may not be sufficient for enhancing performance. To be effective, specific goals should be paired with difficult but attainable goals (Burton, 1993; Locke & Latham, 1990, 1994). Coaches should assign specific goals that force the athlete to exert a fairly large amount of effort. Brehm and his colleagues (Brehm, Wright, Solomon, Silka, & Greenberg, 1983; Wright & Brehm, 1989) proposed a theory accounting for the relationship between goal difficulty and performance, one they labeled energization theory.

Energization theory is a theory of motivation predicting that performance and goal attractiveness are enhanced by difficult but attainable goals. Proponents of energization theory argue that task difficulty determines the amount of arousal, energy, and effort mobilized for a task. The attractiveness of the goal is a function of the amount of energy mobilized. Higher levels of task difficulty correspond with higher levels of goal attractiveness until a task is perceived as unattainable. At this point, energy and attractiveness fall to zero. Thus, higher levels of effort and goal attractiveness are expected when persons are presented with difficult but attainable goals.

Another component of energization theory involves potential motivation. Potential motivation is a function of an individual's need for a goal, the incentive value of the goal, and the degree to which the individual expects to receive the goal if the task is completed. For example, consider the motivation of hunger, the task of walking to a restaurant, and the goal of a cheeseburger. Low potential motivation would be found in someone who is not hungry (a low level of need), does not like cheeseburgers (low incentive value), and does not expect to receive the cheeseburger if the task is completed (e.g., the individual believes the restaurant is closed). High potential motivation would be found in an individual who is hungry, likes cheeseburgers, and expects to receive the food if the task is completed.

A sport-specific application of energization theory has been diagramed in Figure 8.2. In this example, we will explore the situations of two female golfers participating in a high school tournament. Golfer A has a high level of potential motivation. She has never won a tournament but has a high need for achievement (i.e., golfer A has a high level of need and the goal is important to her). Further, this person believes that if she puts forth the effort, she will receive the goal of victory. Golfer B has a low level of potential motivation due to her lack of interest in athletic success and her belief that she cannot win regardless of how hard she tries. Because of her low level of potential motivation, energization theory would predict that golfer B's effort and attraction to the goal of victory will drop off drastically if the task is perceived as even slightly difficult. That is, because this person does not care if she wins, winning is not important to her (i.e., goal attractiveness is low), and her effort in attaining the goal will be low (i.e., she will have a low level of energy and arousal). Conversely, because golfer A possesses a high level of potential motivation, she will continue to exert a high level of effort and be attracted to the goal of victory so long as the goal is perceived as attainable.

Research testing the predictions of energization theory has been quite supportive (Brehm, Wright, Solomon, Silka, & Greenberg, 1983; Wright & Brehm, 1984; see Wright & Brehm, 1989, for a review). However, to date, energization theory has not been subjected to verification in sport settings. Although the predictions appear to be valid for sporting endeavors, the conclusion that energization effects operate in athletic environments must be reserved until the theory is tested with athletes. For example, it must be documented that athletes with a high level of motivation potential will continue to be energized by and attracted to a goal until the goal is viewed as impossible.

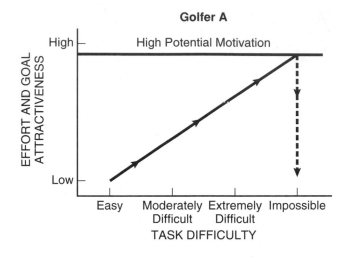

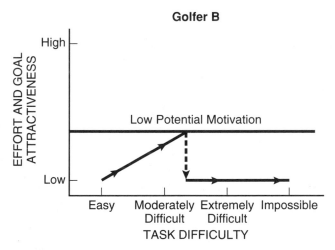

FIGURE 8.2   A sport-specific example of the energization theory of motivation.

Feedback.   A final important factor in the effectiveness of goal setting involves providing feedback about goal attainment. As discussed in the learning chapter and consistent with the theorizing of Locke and Latham (1990), providing feedback about goal attainment enhances the learning process. Because this topic has already been explored in detail, it will not be discussed further here. Simply put, when coaches provide goal attainment feedback to their players, athletes learn whether their performance was below, at, or above the stated goal.

Understanding the Relationship between Goal Setting and Performance.   The preceding pages have reviewed the relationship between goal setting and performance, noting that setting appropriate goals (i.e., specific, difficult, and providing feedback) can enhance performance. However, what has yet to be discussed are the reasons underlying the relationship between goal setting and performance. Reeve (1992) and Locke and Latham (1985) discuss four primary reasons responsible for the performance improvements provided by goal setting. First, goals direct an individual's attention to the task at hand. Setting a difficult and specific weightlifting goal, for example, forces the athlete to focus on the task to achieve the goal. Second, goals tend to mobilize effort. A weight lifter will increase her effort in proportion with the difficulty of the task. Third, goals lead to persistence because one's effort will continue until the goal is attained (the weight lifter will continue to perform until the goal is met). Finally, the presentation of goals often leads to the development of new strategies. For example, if the weight lifter is unable to reach the desired goal of bench pressing 225 pounds using her current workout regimen, she will be forced to try a new approach. The new approach may lead to better training skills and result in goal attainment.

Goal Setting in Sport: Is It Successful?   Most research endeavors testing the effectiveness of goal setting have been conducted in industrial, organizational, or academic settings (Weinberg, 1992). In contrast, relatively few studies within sport psychology have examined this phenomenon. Indeed, Burton (1993) found that fewer than 20 studies on goal setting had examined sport behaviors. In his examination of goal setting research in sport, Burton (1993) found that, although goal setting did appear to be beneficial (67% of the sport-relevant studies discovered that goal setting enhanced performance), the research was inconsistent and the benefits of goal setting did not appear to be as strong as in other areas. Weinberg (1992; see also Kyllo & Landers, 1995; Weinberg, 1994) echoed Burton's comments, stating that "results in the sport psychology literature concerning the effects of goal specificity and performance have been equivocal, with only a few of the studies supporting" past work and theorizing (p. 183). Thus, goal setting in sport situations appears to be beneficial, but not to the extent found in nonsport settings. Burton (1993) and Weinberg (1992) present several explanations to account for this finding (see also Locke, 1991).

SAMPLE SIZE.   Burton's review of sport-specific goal setting research indicated that many of the studies tested small samples. In fact, a third of the studies tested 30 or fewer subjects. However, the average sample size was 80 subjects, and most studies tested at least 20 subjects per condition (10–15 subjects per condition is usually considered adequate). Further, those studies with sample sizes of 30 or fewer tended to show the positive effects of goal setting. As a result, Burton rejected the notion that sample size is responsible for the inconsistent findings.

PERFORMANCE POTENTIAL.   Burton states that a second plausible explanation involves the fact that athletes operate close to their performance potential. The logic here is that if an individual is already performing at or near his or her top level, goal setting should not be expected to enhance the athlete's performance further. Burton's (1993) review of sport studies failing to find an enhancement of performance indicated that this "ceiling effect" explanation has merit. That is, those studies not finding an enhancing effect for goal setting could have been testing persons already operating at maximum levels of performance.

TASK COMPLEXITY.   The third possible explanation, discussed by both Burton and Weinberg, involves the complexity of the task. According to Locke and Latham

(1990), the impact of goal setting will be slower for complex tasks because it takes time to develop a high level of skill at these tasks. Burton reports that half of the studies failing to show the benefits of goal setting involved complex tasks (e.g., juggling and free throw shooting), tasks that may have needed more time for the goal setting to become effective. To allow for an adequate amount of time, researchers may want to examine goal setting over an entire season rather than only a few testing sessions. This was the strategy used by Weinberg, Stitcher, and Richardson (1994). These authors examined college lacrosse players for an entire season, randomly assigning some players to a goal setting condition and others to a "do your best" condition. The results of this longitudinal research clearly indicated benefits of setting specific and difficult goals. Those in the goal condition outperformed those in the "do your best" condition on several performance measures.

INDIVIDUAL DIFFERENCES.   Burton and Weinberg also argue that there are individual differences in responses to goal setting strategies. Burton specifically mentions one's level of self-efficacy. When receiving failure feedback on a task, high self-efficacy individuals should increase the quality of their goal attainment strategies and subsequently exert a greater level of effort and persistence. Conversely, low self-efficacy persons would be expected to attempt poorer strategies and exert less effort and persistence (Burton, 1993). Weinberg (1992) notes that one's motivational level may also be important. Many studies examining goal setting in sport test subjects drawn from university conditioning classes. Because they are volunteers, Weinberg argues that the subjects may be unusually high in motivation, resulting in an attenuation of the effects of goal setting.

The individual difference variable that may be most relevant involves personal preferences for certain types of goal setting strategies. Duda (1992; Duda & Nicholls, 1992) classifies athletic goal preferences into two types: task involvement goals (called learning goals by Dweck, 1986, and mastery goals by Ames, 1992) and ego involvement goals (called performance and ability goals by Dweck and Ames, respectively). ***Task involvement*** goals concern the mastery of a task and are found in persons interested in improving their own ability. ***Ego involvement*** involves the desire to be better than others at a task. Task involvement is self-referenced (competence is gained through the ability to master the task), while ego involvement is other-referenced (competence is gained through the ability to defeat opponents). For a more detailed comparison of task involvement and ego involvement goals, please read this chapter's "A Closer Look."

A CLOSER LOOK:
TASK INVOLVEMENT VERSUS EGO INVOLVEMENT
AS GOAL PERSPECTIVES

As noted in the text, some athletes prefer task involvement goals, while others prefer ego involvement goals. Duda developed the Task and Ego Orientation in Sport Questionnaire to assess task and ego involvement (Duda, 1989, 1992).

This scale contains 13 items. Seven of the items measure task involvement and six assess ego involvement. Initial research using the scale has documented its sound psychometric properties (Boyd & Callaghan, 1994; Duda, 1992; Duda, Chi, Newton, Walling, & Catley, 1995; Duda & White, 1992). Another scale, the 21-item Perceived Motivational Climate in Sport Questionnaire, was designed to assess the degree to which players feel their team has a task or ego orientation focus (Seifriz, Duda, & Chi, 1992).

Individuals with different goal perspectives are expected to behave in different ways (Duda, 1992; Duda et al., 1995; Duda, Fox, Biddle, & Armstrong, 1992; Duda & White, 1992; Williams & Gill, 1995). For example, those possessing a task orientation are expected to choose moderately difficult tasks, exert a high level of effort, have a high level of intrinsic motivation for the activity, feel competent at the activity, demonstrate a high level of persistence and task enjoyment, and believe that athletic success is the result of effort. These desirable behaviors and attributes are also indicative of ego oriented persons, but only if they are confident in their abilities (Duda, 1992). If an ego oriented person doubts his or her ability, he or she is likely to choose easy or impossible tasks, exert a low level of effort, feel incompetent at the task, have a lower level of persistence, and believe that athletic success is the result of ability. Research has supported these contentions. Solmon and Boone (1993) found that students in physical education classes were more likely to select challenging tasks if they were task oriented. In their research with bowlers, Newton and Duda (1993) found that task orientation was negatively correlated with worry and positively correlated with enjoyment. In their work with young athletes, Theeboom, De Knop, and Weiss (1995) also found that a mastery orientation was related to higher levels of enjoyment. These authors also found that a mastery orientation was related to high levels of intrinsic motivation. In further support of the distinctions between task and ego orientations, Williams (1994) found that athletes with an ego orientation prefer information associated with social comparisons, while those possessing a task orientation prefer information associated with task mastery, learning, and improvement.

Coaches and parents who emphasize scoring will likely facilitate the adoption of ego involvement strategies among their athletes, while coaches who stress effort will likely foster the adoption of task involvement perspectives (Ames, 1992). These different coaching philosophies may also lead to the adoption of different goal perspectives by the team. Seifriz et al. (1992) found that teams varied greatly in the extent to which they were task or ego oriented. Players who believed that their team was task oriented reported higher levels of enjoyment and intrinsic motivation compared with those believing that their team was ego oriented. In addition, players perceiving that their team was a task oriented team were more likely to believe that success was the result of effort. Those believing that their team was ego oriented reported that success is based on ability.

Because some athletes prefer task involvement goals, while others prefer ego involvement goals, coaches should be careful with the goals they assign. Goals that are incompatible with an athlete's personal preference may not be effective. For example, consider a weight lifter, Lewis, who has a preference for task involvement goals. Lewis is not interested in lifting more weight than others. Rather, he is only concerned with bettering his own performance. If his coach assigned Lewis an ego involvement goal, it might not be effective. For instance, if Lewis were told that he should focus his efforts on beating a teammate's best lift, Lewis might not feel motivated. On the other hand, Lewis may benefit from a task involvement goal. For example, the coach could tell Lewis to concentrate on beating his previous best lift. Likewise, athletes with a preference for ego involvement goals may perform better when assigned these goals than when assigned task involvement goals.

SPONTANEOUS GOAL SETTING.   Yet another problem with sport-specific research is that subjects in "no goal" conditions often spontaneously set their own goals (called participant-set or self-set goals; see Weinberg, 1994). In one study, 83% of subjects in the no goal condition developed their own goals (Weinberg, Bruya, & Jackson, 1985), while other studies found that greater than a third of the subjects spontaneously set their own goals (Bar-Eli, Levy-Kolker, Tenenbaum, & Weinberg, 1993; Hall & Byrne, 1988). If subjects in control groups are setting their own goals, the comparison between these groups and the goal setting conditions are rendered invalid because the control conditions are no longer no goal conditions. Rather, when subjects set their own goals, experimenters are simply comparing different types of goal setting strategies (i.e., assigned versus self-set goals).

CONCLUSIONS ABOUT GOAL SETTING IN SPORT: A DIFFERENCE OF OPINIONS.   As a result of the problems discussed above, Locke (1991) concluded that differences between goal setting in sport and goal setting in industrial, organizational, and academic settings were the result of methodological shortcomings of the sport research. If these shortcomings were eliminated, Locke felt that there would be no differences between sport research and other work. However, Weinberg and Weigand (1993) believe that it is an oversimplification to conclude that the inconsistent results are due entirely to methodologic flaws. Rather, although they agree with Locke that part of the difference may be due to methodology, Weinberg and Weigand (1993) state that "the challenge for researchers is not to simply attempt methodologically rigid experiments that lack any external validity" but instead to "determine what kind of goals are most effective for different individuals, performing different tasks, under different situations" (p. 95). That is, Weinberg and Weigand believe that we should not simply disregard the inconsistencies between sport and nonsport research targeting goal settings. They feel that we should explore the incongruencies and be open to the idea that there are real and important differences between sport and nonsport environments.

So what should we conclude? Does goal setting significantly increase athletic performance as Locke (1991) contends, or is sport a unique situation, one in which the benefits of goal setting are less powerful? Although a definitive answer to this question is unavailable, perhaps the best solution is found in the work of Kyllo and

Landers (1995). These authors conducted a meta-analysis of 36 studies testing the impact of goal setting in sport. They found that goal setting did indeed significantly increase athletic performance, particularly moderately difficult goals. In addition, their work indicated that sport goals are especially effective if the goals are absolute (i.e., based on outcome), if the goals are public, and if the athlete is allowed to participate in the goal setting process. Thus, based on research completed to date, it appears that goal setting in sport is a successful strategy for enhancing performance.

Achievement Motivation

As discussed in the socialization chapter, many individuals are motivated to begin participating in sport by their need for achievement (their desire to strive for success at certain tasks). However, once individuals have chosen to participate in athletics, their achievement motivation may continue to exert an influence on their behavior.

The McClelland-Atkinson Model.   Perhaps the most in-depth model of achievement motivation is the McClelland-Atkinson model (Arkes & Garske, 1982; McClelland, Atkinson, Clark, & Lowell, 1953; Reeve, 1992). The ***McClelland-Atkinson model*** (MAM) is a mathematical model of achievement motivation incorporating one's motivation to succeed and motivation to avoid failure. The MAM is presented in Figure 8.3 (several forms of the MAM have been offered; the one represented in Figure 8.3 is a general version). To determine one's need for achievement (n Ach), individuals are often asked to complete the Thematic Apperception Test (this test is described in the personality chapter). Based on their responses to the test, subjects are given scores for their motivation to achieve success (Ms) and their motivation to avoid failure (Maf). Ms and Maf are different constructs, and individuals can be high or low in both their Ms and their Maf. An individual's Ms pulls them toward competition, while their Maf pushes them away from competition. As a result, some persons find themselves in the approach-avoidance motivational conflict described earlier. They want to succeed at a certain task but at the same time they feel anxious about the prospect of failing. As seen in Figure 8.3, one's Maf score is subtracted from his or her Ms score. Therefore, higher positive numbers indicate a higher degree of Ms relative to Maf. Numbers near zero indicate a balance between one's Ms and Maf, while higher negative numbers indicate a higher degree of Maf relative to Ms.

The second calculation involved in the MAM involves the probability of success (Ps) and the incentive value of success (Is). One's Ps represents his or her belief about the chances of success at a task and ranges from 0.00 to 1.00. For example, if someone believes that she or he has little chance in defeating an opponent, the Ps would be a low number such as .10. If the individual feels that the chances of success are average, the Ps would be at or near .50. If the person believes that success is likely, the Ps would be a large number such as .80. One's

FIGURE 8.3   The McClelland-Atkinson model of achievement motivation.

$$\text{n Ach} = (\text{Ms} - \text{Maf})(\text{Ps} \times \text{Is}) + \text{Mext}$$

Is is calculated as $1 - Ps = Is$. Thus, as Ps goes up, Is goes down. For example, imagine a female professional tennis player who is currently ranked number 50 in the world. If this person were to play the number 1 ranked player, the probability of success (Ps) would be quite low, such as .20. As a result, the Is for defeating the top ranked player would be quite high ($1 - .20 = .80$). If, on the other hand, the 50th ranked player were to play the number 200 ranked player, the Ps would be quite high (e.g., .80) and the Is would be rather low (.20). Because this portion of the calculation for determining an individual's n Ach involves multiplying the person's Ps and Is, the highest level of n Ach is found in situations in which the individual believes that he or she has a 50% chance of success (Ps = .5, Is = .5, and, thus, $.5 \times .5 = .25$).

The final component of the MAM concerns the extrinsic rewards available to individuals should they succeed at the task (Atkinson, 1964). This is indicated by the letters Mext (motivation for extrinsic rewards). This component is important because some people who are low in Ms and high in Maf still enter competitive situations because of the rewards offered for success. For example, imagine an individual with an Ms of 3 and an Maf of 5 (on scales ranging from 1 to 10). Because this person's motivation to avoid failure is higher than his motivation to achieve success, it may be assumed that this person will tend to avoid competitive situations. However, this person may still seek out competitive environments if the extrinsic rewards are great enough. For example, if the individual believes that success would result in a large monetary reward, he may still be attracted to the competition.

Let us now examine a few examples demonstrating the entire MAM (the numbers presented are fictitious). For example 1, consider a high school tennis player, Jane, who has a high Ms (9) and a low Maf (2) based on scales ranging from 1 to 10. Because she believes that her opponent is a poor player, Jane feels the task is fairly easy resulting in a Ps of .80 and an Is of .20. The contest is a practice match so there are no extrinsic motivators present (i.e., Mext = .00). As a result, Jane's n Ach would be 1.12 [$(9 - 2) \times (.8 \times .2) + .00 = 1.12$]. For example 2, consider Jane's perceptions as she begins to play an opponent she thought was equal in ability. Although Jane still has an Ms of 9 and an Maf of 2, her Ps is .50 (as is her Is). In this situation, Jane's n Ach would equal 1.75 [$(9 - 2) \times (.5 \times .5) + .00 = 1.75$]. Thus, Jane's n Ach would be higher in the situation involving a moderate probability of success. Now, for example 3, consider the same situation as in example 2 with one change: instead of a practice match, the match is for the state championship and, therefore, has the extrinsic motivators of self-esteem, praise, and a trophy (Mext = 1.00). The result will be an even higher n Ach of 2.75 [$(9 - 2) \times (.5 \times .5) + 1.00 = 2.75$].

Differences between Persons High and Low in Need for Achievement. Research has indicated that there are several differences between individuals high in n Ach and those low in this trait. For example, those high in n Ach usually prefer moderately challenging tasks, and they will persist longer at these tasks, while those low in n Ach prefer easy or impossible tasks (Karabenick & Yousseff, 1968; Reeve, 1992). High n Ach people prefer difficult tasks because their chances of success at the task are good, yet these tasks are challenging. Persons low in n Ach prefer easy or impossible tasks because easy tasks allow for success with little or no effort, while impossible tasks give them an excuse for failure.

Although persons high in n Ach tend to perform better than those low in n Ach at difficult tasks (Karabenick & Yousseff, 1968), the precise relationship between n Ach and performance is somewhat more complex. In his examination of research testing the relationship between n Ach and performance, Carron (1980) noted an interesting trend. Carron found that persons high in n Ach tend to outperform those low in n Ach during the early stages of practice and learning, but not at later stages. As success at a task becomes more regular and expected with practice, high n Ach individuals become bored with the success and, thus, experience a reduction in motivation and performance. Conversely, the same successful experiences give confidence to those low in n Ach (remember, they prefer easy tasks) and, therefore, serve to increase their motivation.

Another difference between high and low n Ach individuals concerns their reactions to competition. As mentioned earlier, competition can increase intrinsic motivation. However, this effect is mediated by the n Ach of the individuals. Epstein and Harackiewicz (1992) found that competition tends to enhance the intrinsic interest of persons high in n Ach, while inhibiting the intrinsic motivation of those low in achievement needs. The authors also found that high n Ach people showed an increase in intrinsic motivation when they received information about their opponent (information leading to the expectancy of success or failure). Conversely, opponent information leads to a decrease in intrinsic motivation for those low in n Ach.

Equity Theory

Prior to the 1990 season, the Kansas City Royals professional baseball team gave a huge, $13 million contract to Mark Davis, a free agent pitcher. This action upset many current players, especially those who had been performing at or above the new player's level of performance but who were receiving much lower salaries. The former players were unable to see the fairness in management's decision to give the new player such a large contract. As a result, the motivation level of the players was greatly reduced (Antonen, 1991).

This real life event highlights the application of equity theory to sport settings. *Equity theory* is a theory of motivation examining the extent to which an individual believes that his or her ratio of outputs and inputs is equitable in comparison to the ratios of others (equity refers to just and fair relationships). Equity theorists believe that individuals are motivated to maintain perceived equitable relationships between themselves and others (Adams, 1963; Walster, Berscheid, & Walster, 1973). In sport settings, equity theorists argue that athletes are motivated to maintain perceived equitable relationships between themselves and their teammates, coaches, and fans. Two important aspects of equity theory must be mentioned. First, because individuals are motivated to maintain equitable relationships, when they encounter an inequitable relationship, they will attempt to restore equity to this relationship. The methods of equity restoration are described below. Second, this theory involves the *perceptions* of equity. Even if most individuals would state that a relationship is inequitable, so long as the individual involved believes that the relationship is equitable, this person will not attempt to alter the relationship.

As stated, equity theory argues that persons compare their ratio of outputs over inputs to the ratios of others (see Figure 8.4). ***Outputs*** involve the rewards and benefits individuals receive. In sport, outputs would include money, prestige, playing time, self-esteem, and trophies. ***Inputs*** are the contributions made by an individual and include effort and performance. In the examples to be presented in the discussion that follows, I will use an athlete's salary as the output and his or her performance as the input.

When persons compare their ratios to the ratios of others, they conclude that they are involved in one of three types of relationships: equitable, overpayment, or underpayment (see Figure 8.5). When a person believes that his or her ratio is fair in comparison to another person's ratio, he or she concludes that this is an ***equitable relationship.*** The emotional reaction to equitable relationships is satisfaction. For example, let us examine a pitcher (player A) for a professional baseball team who had a total of 10 victories (his input) and received a salary of $500,000 (his output). If player A learns that a teammate (player B) with 20 victories received a salary of $1,000,000, player A would believe that the relationship is equitable and would feel satisfied. Now imagine a situation in which player A, still being paid $500,000 for 10 victories, is informed that player B is being paid $250,000 for 10 victories. In situations like this in which an individual's ratio is more attractive than another's ratio (player A's ratio is more attractive than player B's), the individual (e.g., player A) experiences an ***overpayment inequity relationship.*** The emotional reaction to overpayment inequity is guilt. However, because player B's ratio is less attractive, this person would experience an ***underpayment inequity relationship*** to which the emotional reaction is anger.

As stated earlier, equity theory proposes that people are motivated to maintain equity in their relationships. When individuals realize they are involved in an inequitable relationship (both overpayment and underpayment), they attempt to restore equity to the relationship in one of two ways: by restoring actual equity and/or by restoring psychological equity. Restoring actual equity involves a behavioral change. Walster et al. (1973) stated that a person "can restore 'actual equity' by appropriately altering his own outcomes or inputs or the outcomes or inputs of the other participants" (p. 154). Restoring equity through psychological means involves a cognitive restoration. Regarding psychological equity, Walster et al. (1973) stated

FIGURE 8.4   Ratios involved in the equity theory of motivation.

Athlete's Ratio of: Teammate's Ratio of:

OUTPUTS   OUTPUTS
(salary and playing time)   (salary and playing time)
————————————————   **Compared**   ————————————————
INPUTS   **with:**   INPUTS
(effort and performance)   (effort and performance)

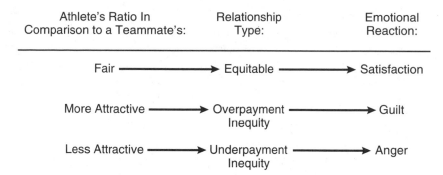

FIGURE 8.5   The types of relationships and emotional reactions involved in the equity theory of motivation.

that an individual "can restore 'psychological equity' by appropriately distorting his perception of his own or his partner's outcomes and inputs" (p. 154).

Let us first examine the restoration of equity to overpayment relationships by returning to the example described above. Recall that player A ($500,000 for 10 victories) was overpaid in comparison to player B ($250,000 for 10 victories). The guilt resulting from the overpayment would motivate player A to attempt to restore equity to the relationship. Player A may choose a behavioral restoration strategy and increase his effort and performance to justify his larger salary. Player A may also attempt to restore equity through psychological tactics. For example, he may convince himself that he is more valuable to the team, a more devoted player, and so on. Once player A believes that he has reestablished equity to the relationship (even if outsiders would disagree), he will feel satisfied.

Regarding the restoration of equity to underpayment relationships, let us examine the reactions expected of player B. Because his ratio is less favorable than that of player A, player B will experience anger. The anger will motivate player B to restore equity to the relationship. Player B could attempt to restore equity through behavioral means by exerting a lower level of effort, thereby justifying his lower salary. Or he could select a psychological strategy, such as convincing himself that the other player is simply a favorite of management or that he will have to wait until his next contract to restore equity. Similar to overpayment inequity, once player B believes the relationship is equitable, his emotional reaction will be satisfaction.

Equity Research in Sport Settings.   A large body of research has found support for the propositions of equity theory, including research targeting sport settings. Lord and Hohenfeld (1979) examined major league baseball players who played out their option during the 1976 season. The researchers thought that this group of players would experience underpayment inequity because they received a substantial pay cut, while two of their peers received large monetary contracts (due to the beginning of free agency). Consistent with their predictions, Lord and Hohenfeld found that the players experienced underpayment inequity. They attempted to restore equity through behavioral means as indicated by their poorer levels of performance. Once the players resigned with a team and their salaries reached equitable levels, their performances returned to normal. Although subsequent investigations tended to support Lord and Hohenfeld's findings (Bretz & Thomas, 1992; Duchon & Jago, 1981), Harder's (1991) work suggests that athletes are less willing to reduce underpayment inequity by lowering performance in areas leading to future rewards. For example, in professional baseball salary is linked more closely to power statistics (e.g., home runs) than to other offensive statistics such as batting average. Consistent with Harder's expectations, home runs were not an accurate measure of behavioral restoration of underpayment inequity because a player's lowering of home run output would be counterproductive for future rewards. Rather, batting average was a better predictor of behavioral restoration because this type of restoration would not inhibit future rewards.

Research examining the impact of equity in sport settings has focused almost exclusively on underpayment inequity situations while ignoring the motivational implications of overpayment relationships. A colleague and I attempted to fill this research void by testing equity theory in situations in which athletes may believe they are overpaid (Wann & Fortner, 1995). We expected athletes to show an improvement in performance when they felt the need to justify a situation that is highly favorable. To test our predictions, we examined the premove and postmove records of major league baseball teams constructing new stadiums since 1960. We expected these teams to show improvement because players on these teams may have felt the need to justify the expense of the new stadium (that is, they were overpaid relative to players performing in older stadiums). Our hypothesis was strongly supported. Prior to the moves, the 16 teams in our sample had an average winning percentage of .479 and .475 for the previous 3 years and previous 1 year, respectively. However, the winning percentages jumped to .516 and .505 after the moves.

Our study examining overpayment inequity in sport leads to an interesting suggestion for coaches. Coaches usually strive for equitable and harmonious relationships between players. Indeed, cohesion among players can have many positive effects (Widmeyer, Carron, & Brawley, 1993). However, our results indicate that coaches who are able to establish overpayment relationships may subsequently increase their players' performances. In fact, as Fortner and I note, "statements such as 'If you want to continue to start, you had better perform' appear to be an attempt to place the player in a position where he/she feels the need to justify the reward of starting, and hence, increase performance" (Wann & Fortner, 1995). Coaches employing this tactic must allow the players the opportunity to restore equity through behavioral means. If players were to use a psychological restoration tactic, no performance increases would be found. We argue that the best way to insure a behavioral method of restoration is to implement a sound goal setting program incorporating the factors described earlier in this chapter.

Valence-Instrumentality-Expectancy Theory

A final theory with ramifications for sport motivation is valence-instrumentality-expectancy theory (VIE theory). While many variations of this theory exist (Pinder, 1991), most share common themes. The presentation here will reflect the general state of the theory.

Originating primarily with the work of Vroom (1964) and Porter and Lawler (1968), *valence-instrumentality-expectancy (VIE) theory* represents the belief that motivation is a multiplicative function of valence, instrumentality, and expectancy (see Figure 8.6). *Expectancy* concerns an individual's belief that effort will result in performance. For example, consider the behavior of Eddie, a junior varsity baseball player. Expectancy involves the degree that Eddie believes that practicing and working out (i.e., effort) will lead to increases in his ability (i.c., performance). The term instrumentality should be familiar. Remember from the learning chapter that another term for operant conditioning is instrumental conditioning. It should also be remembered that instrumental conditioning involves the strategic presentation of rewards in an attempt to increase the occurrence of desired behaviors. Thus, *instrumentality* concerns an individual's belief that performance will be rewarded. Continuing with the example above, instrumentality would involve Eddie's belief that if he improves his performance, he will be rewarded with reinforcements such as praise, making the varsity team, playing time, and trophies. The final component of the VIE model of motivation is valence. *Valence* involves an individual's perception of the value of the rewards being offered for performance. That is, to what extent does the individual desire or need these rewards? For Eddie, perhaps his performance will be rewarded with verbal praise from his coach. Valence would involve the value of the praise for Eddie (Does he desire the praise or does he wish to receive another reward such as playing time?).

As noted earlier, VIE theory predicts that motivation is a multiplicative function of valence, instrumentality, and expectancy. As a result, if any of the three components is zero, the individual's overall motivation will also be zero. As an example of this process, let us return to the junior varsity baseball player. Let us first assume that Eddie has a high level of expectancy because he is high in self-efficacy and believes that if he practices hard he will improve. Let us also imagine that Eddie has a high level of instrumentality. That is, he firmly believes that if he improves he will be rewarded with verbal praise. However, because this reward has absolutely no value to Eddie (he wants to be rewarded with playing time), VIE theory would predict that Eddie's level of motivation will be zero. Imagine now a slightly different set of circumstances. In this scenario, Eddie again believes that his effort will result in performance (i.e., expectancy). Further, because the coach has told his players that if their performances improve, they will be rewarded with increased playing time Eddie also desires the reward (i.e., valence). However, because Eddie plays the same position as the coach's son, Eddie is convinced that even if he plays better, his performance will never be rewarded. Rather, the coach will continue to play his son. Again, VIE theory would predict that Eddie would not be motivated. Finally, con-

$$\text{Motivation} = \begin{array}{c} \text{Valence} \\ \times \\ \text{Instrumentality} \\ \times \\ \text{Expectancy} \end{array}$$

FIGURE 8.6 The valence-instrumentality-expectancy (VIE) theory of motivation.

sider a situation in which Eddie believes that the coach will reward him (i.e., instrumentality), and he desires the reward of increased playing time (i.e., valence). However, because Eddie is low in both achievement motivation and self-efficacy, he is convinced that his effort will not result in increased performance. Once again, VIE theory would predict a zero level of motivation for Eddie.

The preceding examples highlight an important suggestion for coaches, sport psychologists, and physical educators. These persons should not necessarily be concerned that each athlete has a high level of valence, instrumentality, and expectancy. Rather, what VIE theory suggests is that these persons must insure that the players have at least a minimum belief that their effort will result in performance, that their performance will be rewarded, and that the reward is valued. It must also be noted that VIE theory has yet to be tested in sport settings. Although the predictions of this theory appear to be relevant to athletics, research is needed to test the validity of the theory in sport environments.

SUMMARY

Research on motivation has found that athletes can be motivated by intrinsic and extrinsic rewards. When athletes are intrinsically motivated to perform a task, the addition of extrinsic rewards often lowers their intrinsic motivation. Cognitive evaluation theory was developed to explain this phenomenon. This theory argues that there are two types of rewards: controlling and informational. Controlling rewards are thought to decrease intrinsic motivation, while informational rewards are believed to increase intrinsic motivation.

Historically, theorizing about motivational processes passed through three phases. Originally, most psychologists believed that humans were motivated by instinctual desires. However, these theories fell out of favor and were replaced by drive reduction models. Drive reduction models suggest that human motivation is a result of the desire to reduce biological needs. Expectancy theories are the newest approaches to motivation. These theories argue that humans can be motivated by future goals as well as by events from the past.

Self-efficacy refers to an individual's belief that he or she has the ability to perform a certain task. Individuals receive information about efficacy from four sources. The most important source of efficacy information comes from personal accomplishments, successes, and failures. When individuals succeed at a task, they begin to believe they have the abilities required to perform the task. Individuals also receive efficacy information through social comparisons, through persuasion, and through physiological arousal.

Research in industrial, organizational, and academic settings has consistently found that providing individuals with specific and difficult goals and providing feedback about goal attainment increases performance. However, research in sport settings has been less consistent. That is, although sport research has found that goal setting is effective, the benefits are not as strong as they are in other environments. Several problems may be contributing to the inconsistent sport research. For example, (1) athletes may already be performing at top levels and, as a result, goal setting could not possibly facilitate performance; (2) complex tasks such as those found in sport settings may require more time for goal setting to take effect; (3) there may be individual difference variables mediating the effect; and (4) many subjects set their own goals when they are in a "no goal" condition.

The McClelland-Atkinson model is a mathematical theory suggesting that n Ach $= (Ms - Maf) (Ps - Is) + Mext$, where n Ach is need achievement, Ms is the motive to achieve success, Maf is the motive to avoid failure, Ps is the probability of success, Is is the incentive value of success, and Mext is extrinsic motivation. Research has found that high n Ach people prefer difficult tasks and persist at these tasks, while those low in n Ach prefer easy or impossible tasks. As for the relationship between n Ach and performance, research has found that high n Ach people tend to outperform low n Ach people, although the performance differences are most prominent during the early stages of learning.

Equity theory states that persons are motivated to maintain equitable relationships between themselves and others. When individuals encounter an equitable relationship, their emotional reaction is satisfaction. Individuals feel guilty when they encounter overpayment inequitable relationships. Individuals feel anger in response to underpayment inequitable settings. Individuals can restore equity to overpayment and underpayment relationships through both behavioral and psychological means.

The valence-instrumentality-expectancy theory suggests that motivation is a multiplicative function of expectancy (the belief that effort will lead to performance), instrumentality (the belief that performance will be rewarded), and valence (the value of the reward).

GLOSSARY

Approach-Approach Motivational Conflict   A situation in which an individual must choose between two or more positive outcomes.

Approach-Avoidance Motivational Conflict   A situation in which an individual is presented with a single outcome having both positive and negative components.

Avoidance-Avoidance Motivational Conflict   A situation in which an individual must choose between two or more negative outcomes.

Cognitive Evaluation Theory   A theory of intrinsic motivation stating that rewards perceived as controlling decrease intrinsic motivation, while rewards viewed as informational increase intrinsic motivation.

Controlling Rewards   Rewards such as praise or trophies that are designed to influence (i.e., control) an individual's behavior.

Double Approach-Avoidance Motivational Conflict   A situation in which an individual is simultaneously presented with two or more outcomes, each having both positive and negative components.

Drive   An internal state of tension.

Drive Theories   Theories reflecting the belief that human behavior is motivated by drives designed to reduce biological needs.

Ego Involvement   An other-referenced goal perspective in which an individual is concerned with the desire to be better than others at a task.

Energization Theory   A theory of motivation predicting that performance and goal attractiveness are enhanced by difficult but attainable goals.

Equitable Relationship   A relationship found when a person believes that his or her ratio is fair in comparison to another person's ratio.

Equity Theory   A theory of motivation that examines the extent to which an individual believes that his or her ratio of outputs and inputs is equitable in comparison to the ratios of others.

Expectancy   An individual's belief that effort will result in performance.

Expectancy Theories of Motivation   Theories reflecting the belief that future outcomes pull individuals into action.

Extrinsic Motives   Motives lying outside an individual that involve the rewards and benefits for performing a task.

Informational Rewards   Rewards designed to convey information about an individual's competence at a task.

Inputs   Contributions made by an individual.

Instinctual Theories of Motivation   Theories reflecting the belief that behavior is motivated by innate or inherited predispositions and characteristics.

Instrumentality   An individual's belief that performance will be rewarded.

Intrinsic Motives   Motives lying within an individual involving the individual's interest and enjoyment of a task.

McClelland-Atkinson Model   A mathematical model of achievement motivation incorporating an individual's motivation to succeed and motivation to avoid failure.

Motivation   The process of arousal within an organism that helps direct and sustain behavior.

Need   A biological or psychological deficiency felt by an individual.

Outputs   Rewards and benefits received by an individual.

Overpayment Inequity Relationship   A relationship found when a person believes that his or her ratio is more attractive than another person's ratio.

Self-Efficacy   An individual's belief that he or she has the ability to perform at a specified level on a certain task.

Task Involvement   A self-referenced goal perspective in which an individual is concerned with mastering a task.

Underpayment Inequity Relationship   Relationship found when a person believes that his or her ratio is less attractive than another person's ratio.

Valence An individual's perception of the value of the rewards being offered for performance.

Valence-Instrumentality-Expectancy Theory A theory of motivation representing the belief that motivation is a multiplicative function of valence, instrumentality, and expectancy.

APPLICATION AND REVIEW QUESTIONS

1. Describe the differences between intrinsic and extrinsic motives and the impact of using extrinsic rewards with intrinsically motivated people.
2. Trace the history of motivation theory.
3. Apply Hull's drive reduction model to a sport setting.
4. Give a sport-specific example of each motivational conflict.
5. Describe the importance of goal specificity, goal difficulty, and goal feedback and discuss the relationship between goal setting and performance in sport environments.
6. Apply your own sport experiences to each of the following theories: McClelland-Atkinson model of achievement motivation, equity theory, and valence-instrumentality-expectancy theory.

SUGGESTED READINGS

Burton, D. (1993). Goal setting in sport. In R. N. Singer, M. Murphey, & L. K. Tennant (Eds.), *Handbook of research on sport psychology* (pp. 467–491). New York: Macmillan. This chapter gives an in-depth look at goal setting including an examination of the effectiveness of goal setting in sport. In addition, this article reviews individual differences in goal setting and presents a model of competitive goal setting.

Deci, E. L., & Olson, B. C. (1989). Motivation and competition: Their role in sports. In J. H. Goldstein (ed.), *Sports, games, and play: Social and psychological viewpoints* (2nd ed., pp. 83–110). Hillsdale, NJ: Erlbaum. This chapter describes the relationships among intrinsic motivation, extrinsic motivation, and competition. Further, the authors provide a detailed description of cognitive evaluation theory.

Roberts, G. C. (Ed.). (1992). *Motivation in sport and exercise*. Champaign, IL: Human Kinetics. This book presents the reader with an up-dated examination of many issues relevant to sport motivation. The chapters on goal setting, self-efficacy, and achievement are especially informative.

Thrill, E., & Vallerand, R. J. (Eds.). (1995). Motivation and emotion in the sport context [Special issue]. *International Journal of Sport Psychology, 26*(1). This issue of the *International Journal of Sport Psychology* focuses on current topics in motivation relevant to sport settings. Leading researchers in the area of sport motivation examine a number of interesting phenomena including cognitive evaluation theory, task/ego orientations, achievement, and self-efficacy.

Weinberg, R. S. (1994). Goal setting and performance in sport and exercise settings: A synthesis and critique. *Medicine and Science in Sports and Exercise, 26*, 469–477. This short article contains a brief synopsis of critical issues in goal setting including goal specificity, goal difficulty, and spontaneous goal setting (self-set goals).

Chapter 9

PLAYER ATTRIBUTIONS IN SPORT

In sport, one of the most frequently asked questions is "Why?" Sport reporters, players, coaches, and fans are all interested in finding out why players and teams acted and performed a certain way. For example, when Chris Webber cost his team a chance to win a college basketball championship by calling an illegal time out, everyone wanted to know why he called the time out. Did he forget the number of time outs his team had remaining? Did he misunderstand his teammates shouting to him from the bench? Similarly, when the Buffalo Bills lost four consecutive Super Bowls, everyone wanted to know why they lost those games. Were they a team composed of "chokers"? Were they less skilled than their opponents from the other conference? These "why" questions point to the importance of attributional processes in sport. **Attributions** are estimates of the causes of our own or someone else's behavior. In this chapter, we will investigate the attributional process in sport by examining the causes that players assign to their own behaviors and to the behaviors of their teammates (we will examine the attributions of sport spectators in Chapter 15).

EXPECTED VERSUS UNEXPECTED AND SUCCESSFUL VERSUS UNSUCCESSFUL OUTCOMES

Because this chapter focuses on the explanations athletes give for the outcomes of sport competitions, it is appropriate to review the situations that most often lead to attributional formation. Previous research had indicated that negative and unexpected outcomes lead to the greatest amount of attributional thinking (Kanazawa, 1992; Weiner, 1985; Wong & Weiner, 1981). For example, athletes who lose when expecting to win (negative and unexpected outcome) and athletes who win when expecting to lose (unexpected outcome) should form the greatest number of attributions to explain the outcome.

However, Kanazawa (1992) challenged this line of thinking because the vast majority of studies had confounded the expectancy and success manipulations. That is, the studies were conducted in such a way that the two variables were dependent on one another. For example, if an athlete who believed she would win a competition was defeated, this athlete would experience a negative *and* unexpected outcome. Thus, although it may appear that both factors are important, it is possible that only one was responsible for the effect. Kanazawa believed that if the success and expectancy outcomes were examined independently, only the expectancy outcome would be related to attributional thinking. Kanazawa's research supported this hypothesis. Subjects in an academic role-playing study revealed that unexpected outcomes (success when failure was expected and vice versa) led to more attributional statements than did expected outcomes. However, also as predicted, there was no difference in the number of attributions formed in successful and unsuccessful settings. Based on these findings, one would expect a victorious athlete who had expected to lose and a defeated athlete who expected to win to produce the greatest number of attributional explanations to account for the outcome. However, if an athlete expected to lose and did, he or she would not be predicted to list a large number of reasons for the outcome.

ATTRIBUTIONAL DIMENSIONS

A large body of research has been directed at identifying and understanding the various dimensions involved in the attributional process. Several attributional dimensions have been identified. In the following sections, we will examine the dimensions with the greatest relevance to sport.

The Locus of Causality Dimension and Kelley's Covariation Model

While several different attributional dimensions have been discovered, the greatest amount of attention has been devoted to the locus of causality dimension. Indeed, the vast majority of attribution theories include this dimension (e.g., Heider, 1958; Jones & Davis, 1965; Kelley, 1967, 1973; Weiner, 1982, 1989). The *locus of causality attributional dimension* concerns the extent to which an individual believes that the cause of a behavior is internal or external. *Internal attributions* (sometimes referred to as dispositional attributions) reflect the belief that a behavior was caused by the individual. For example, if a tennis player won a match, she may believe that the outcome was due to her skill or effort. *External attributions* (sometimes called situational attributions) reflect the belief that a behavior was caused by the environment or setting. For example, the tennis player may have felt that fate caused her victory.

One final example may help in understanding the distinction between internal and external attributions. Let us say a baseball player, Kevin, is sitting on the bench watching his team participate in a critical game. In the final inning, with the game on the line, the manager asks Kevin to pinch hit. On the first pitch, Kevin smacks a home run that was aided by a 30 mile per hour wind. When a reporter asks Kevin's coach to explain the cause of Kevin's success, the coach states that Kevin hit the home run because he has great hand–eye coordination and upper body strength. Was the coach's attribution internal or external? Further, imagine that when the opposing coach was asked to explain Kevin's hit, he said the home run was due to the wind. What type of attribution is this? If you said that Kevin's coach formed an internal attribution, while the opposing coach formed an external attribution, you were correct.

At this point, you may be wondering what determines whether individuals form an internal or external attribution. The answer to this question lies at the heart of Kelley's (1967, 1973) covariation theory (see Zebrowitz, 1990). ***Covariation theory*** argues that when individuals attempt to determine the locus of causality for a behavior, they try to acquire information about three aspects of the behavior: consistency, distinctiveness, and consensus (if information concerning one or more of these items is missing, individuals will rely on the information available). ***Consistency*** refers to the frequency with which an individual exhibits the behavior in a particular setting. ***Distinctiveness*** refers to the degree to which an individual exhibits the behavior in other settings. ***Consensus*** refers to the number of other individuals exhibiting the behavior in a particular setting. According to Kelley and as depicted in Figure 9.1, when individuals conclude that a behavior lacks consistency, they tend to form an external attribution. If persons feel that a behavior is consistent, the situation is distinct, and there is consensus, they also tend to form an external attribution. This type of attribution is called a target/entity attribution (i.e., another person or an inanimate entity is believed to be the cause of the behavior). When individuals decide that a behavior is consistent but the situation is not distinct and there is no consensus, they usually form an internal attribution. This type of attribution is also called an actor attribution (i.e., the actor is perceived to be the cause of the behavior). Kelley's theory has stood up well to empirical testing (e.g., McArthur, 1972; Pruitt & Insko, 1980).

Let us examine Kelley's theory through the use of a concrete example. Imagine that a volleyball player, Jennifer, has just been thrown out of a match because she swore at an official (the official made a call that went against her). Certainly, Jennifer's coach will want to determine the cause of Jennifer's actions. That is, was Jennifer's behavior due to her disposition (an internal attribution) or was it caused by the setting (an external attribution). According to Kelley, to ascertain the locus of causality for Jennifer's actions, her coach will seek out information about consistency, distinctiveness, and consensus. As for information concerning the consistency of Jen-

FIGURE 9.1   Kelley's covariation theory of attribution.

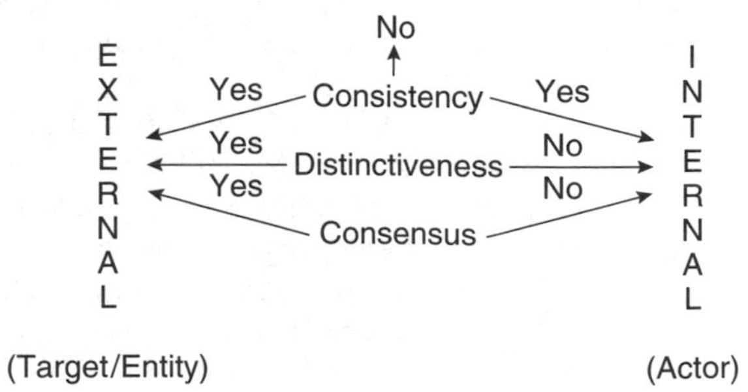

(Target/Entity)   (Actor)

nifer's abusive behavior, her coach will consider whether or not she has acted this way in this situation before. For our example, let us assume that, based on her past experiences with Jennifer, the coach decides that, yes, Jennifer does usually act this way in this situation. In other words, Jennifer is consistently abusive at volleyball games when an official's call does not go her way.

Jennifer's coach will also want to know the distinctiveness of the behavior, that is, does Jennifer exhibit abusive behaviors in other settings. For the moment, let us assume that the coach decides that this situation is not distinct. That is, the coach re- members that during an intramural basketball game Jennifer was also quite abusive to the officials and that she gets very upset when she receives poor grades on class assignments. Thus, it appears to the coach that there is nothing unique, special, or distinct about the volleyball situation. Rather, Jennifer exhibits abusive behaviors in a variety of settings.

The last bit of information the coach needs to estimate the locus of causality for Jennifer's abusive behavior concerns consensus. For now, let us imagine that none of the other players on Jennifer's team became abusive after the questionable call. Only Jennifer began to swear at the official. As a result, Jennifer's coach has de- cided that there is no consensus.

To recap, Jennifer's coach has concluded that Jennifer's abusive behavior is consistent with her past behavior in this setting, that the situation is not distinct be- cause Jennifer is abusive in other settings, and there is no consensus because none of Jennifer's teammates exhibited the abusive behavior. Based on this set of circum- stances, can you determine whether the coach's attribution for Jennifer's behavior will be internal or external? A glance back at Figure 9.1 may help. Because of the pattern of answers to the consistency (yes), distinctiveness (no), and consensus (no) questions, Kelley's (1973) covariation theory would predict that the coach would form an internal (i.e., actor) attribution.

Now consider a different set of circumstances. Again, imagine that the coach has determined that there is a high level of consistency to Jennifer's abusive behav- ior. However, in contrast to the last example, let us now assume that the coach has concluded that this situation is distinct because in other settings Jennifer does not exhibit abusive behaviors. Further, imagine that the coach has determined that there is a high level of consensus because all of Jennifer's teammates also became upset and abusive after the questionable call. Thus, the coach has determined that there is a high level of consistency, distinctiveness, and consensus in Jennifer's behavior. Us- ing Kelley's (1973) theory as a framework, we would expect the coach to form an external (i.e., target/entity) attribution concerning Jennifer's actions. For example, the coach may conclude that the call was so bad that it warranted Jennifer's reaction or that Jennifer was stressed because it was finals week.

The Stability and Controllability Dimensions

Although Weiner (1979, 1980a) also believed that the internal/external locus of causality dimension was important, he thought that to understand the attributional process fully, other dimensions must be considered as well. Weiner felt that attribu- tions are formed on the basis of two more dimensions: stability and controllability. The ***stability attributional dimension*** concerns the extent to which an individual believes that the cause of a behavior was due to features that are variant. ***Stable attributions*** reflect the belief that a behavior was caused by permanent or near permanent personality traits or environmental features. For example, an athlete may state that her success at a task was due to her ability or the ease of the task, both of which are invariant. ***Unstable attributions*** reflect the belief that a behavior was caused by variable traits or environmental features. For example, an athlete may feel that her success was due to her effort or mood.

The third dimension discussed by Weiner (1979, 1980a), the ***controllability attributional dimension,*** concerns the extent to which an individual believes that the cause of a behavior was under the voluntary control of the actor. ***Controllable attributions*** reflect the belief that a behavior was under the voluntary control of the actor, while ***uncontrollable attributions*** reflect the belief that a behavior was beyond the control of the actor. For example, because athletes can control their level of effort, attributions such as "she succeeded because she exerted a great deal of effort" are controllable attributions. Conversely, because athletes cannot control their inherited athletic ability, attributions such as "she succeeded because she has a high level of natural ability" are uncontrollable attributions.

By combining each of Weiner's three attributional dimensions (locus of causality, stability, and controllability), we can make predictions about the types of attributions expected for successful and unsuccessful outcomes. Each different combination results in a different attribution. These combinations are presented in Table 9.1 (Weiner, 1980b). For example, if an individual believes that her or his success was due to an internal, controllable, and unstable cause, she or he likely will feel that the success was due to individual effort. Conversely, if someone feels that her or his success is due to an internal, uncontrollable, and unstable cause, she or he will probably believe that the success was due to such factors as fatigue or mood.

Measuring Attributional Dimensions in Sport

Researchers interested in testing attributional processes in sport have the option of using a general attribution inventory or a sport-specific measure. The general inventory gaining widespread use in sport is the Causal Dimension Scale (CDS) con-

TABLE 9.1   A Three-Dimensional Taxonomy of the Perceived Causes of Success and Failure

| | Controllable | | Uncontrollable | |
	Stable	Unstable	Stable	Unstable
Internal	Stable effort of self	Unstable effort of self	Ability of self	Fatigue, mood, and fluctuations in skill of self
External	Stable effort of others	Unstable effort of others	Ability of others, task difficulty	Fatigue, mood, and fluctuations in skill of others, luck

(Figure from *Human Motivation* by Bernard Weiner, copyright © 1980 by Holt, Rinehart & Winston, Inc. Reprinted by permission of the publisher. [Adapted from Rosenbaum, 1972, p. 21.])

structed by Russell in 1982. The CDS consists of nine Likert-scale items, three each assessing the attributional dimensions of locus of causality, stability, and controllability. Several authors have used the CDS in their research investigating sport attributions (e.g., Mark, Mutrie, Brooks, & Harris, 1984; McAuley & Gross, 1983).

However, the CDS has been criticized regarding its psychometric properties, particularly the control dimension (Russell, McAuley, & Tarico, 1987; Vallerand & Richer, 1988). In an attempt to rectify the problems with the original CDS, McAuley, Duncan, and Russell (1992) revised the original scale and developed the CDS-II. To improve the control dimension, the authors separated the single controllability subscale into two different subscales. One subscale was designed to measure personal control (e.g., "The cause of your performance was something over which you have power/over which you have no power."), while the other subscale was designed to assess external control (e.g., "The cause of your performance was under the power of other people/not under the power of other people."). The results of their research using the CDS-II indicated that the changes were effective in strengthening the psychometric quality of the instrument (McAuley et al., 1992).

A sport-specific measure of attributional style is the Sport Attributional Style Scale (SASS) developed by Hanrahan, Grove, and Hattie (1989). This instrument presents athletes with 16 positive and negative sport events (e.g., "You perform very well in a competition."). Athletes are asked to state what they believe to be the most likely cause of the event and to answer several specific questions about the event. The questions assess five attributional dimensions. Three of the dimensions (locus, stability, and controllability) match those found on the CDS. The other dimensions included in the SASS are intentionality (Is the cause intentional?) and globality (Does the cause influence other areas of life?). Thus, each event is examined using all five attributional dimensions. Hanrahan et al. (1989) found that the SASS was both a reliable and valid sport-specific test of sport-related attributions.

ATTRIBUTIONAL ERRORS

Our discussion thus far probably leaves the impression that individuals go to great lengths to determine the causes of behavior. Indeed, people do put forth a great deal of effort in this endeavor. Consequently, you may have come to the conclusion that the attributions formed are quite accurate. However, research has found that individuals often form erroneous attributions, concerning both their own behaviors and those of others.

The Fundamental Attribution Error

Regarding attributions about the actions of others, research has found that individuals often exhibit the fundamental attribution error (Jones, 1979; Ross, 1977; Snyder & Jones, 1974). The *fundamental attribution error* is a biased, other-directed attributional pattern in which an individual overemphasizes the importance of internal causes and underemphasizes the importance of external causes. For example, consider a group of athletes discussing the reasons responsible for the tardy behavior of a teammate. Based on the fundamental attribution error, we would expect the teammates to attribute the player's tardiness to an internal cause, such as laziness, or to a lack of motivation, rather than to an external cause such as car trouble or traffic.

Research has found two reasons for the fundamental attribution error. One reason concerns attentional focus. When individuals view another person executing a behavior, their attentional focus is usually narrowly directed toward the actor rather than broadly directed toward the surrounding setting and environment. As a result, they tend to believe that the person caused the outcome (Storms, 1973).

A second factor responsible for the fundamental attribution error involves the amount of effort required to form internal and external attributions. This factor is a major component of the three-stage model of attribution proposed by Gilbert and colleagues (Gilbert, 1995; Gilbert, Pelham, & Krull, 1988). This model, depicted in Figure 9.2, involves a one-stage identification phase (see also, Trope, 1986) and a two-stage attribution phase. The identification phase concerns the fact that, "before we can ask *why* a person behaved in a certain way, we must first know *what* the person is doing" (Gilbert, 1995, p. 117). Once individuals have determined what a person is doing (e.g., they have identified the behavior), they move to the attribution stages involving the "why" of the behavior. Gilbert et al. (1988) believe that the first step in the attribution phase involves forming internal attributions because these attributions tend to be automatic. The second step, forming external attributions, tends to require greater effort. This theory predicts that persons will form effortful, external attributions only when (1) they have good information about the situation or (2) their attention is not directed toward other tasks (remember from the attention chapter that our attentional capacity is limited). Thus, this theory argues that the fundamental attribution error is a function of the ease with which we form internal attributions. Because individuals tend to prefer simple cognitive tasks, they will usually not put forth the effort required to form an external attribution.

Thus, the fundamental attribution error may be due to two factors: focus of attention and the amount of effort required to form internal and external attributions. It appears that each of these factors may be relevant to different sport populations. The focus of attention explanation may be particularly relevant for sport spectators. When viewing sporting events, spectators tend to focus attention on the athlete in possession of the ball rather than the setting surrounding this person. As a result of this focus of attention, they are likely to believe that the athlete was responsible for

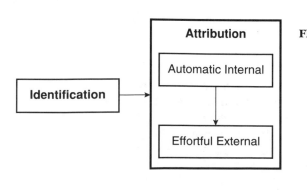

FIGURE 9.2   The three-stage model of attribution. (Adapted by permission from: Gilbert, D. T. [1995]. Attribution and interpersonal perception. In: A. Tesser [Ed.], Advanced social psychology [pp. 99–147]. New York: McGraw Hill.)

her behavior. This line of thinking is developed further in an upcoming chapter on sport spectators (Chapter 15). On the other hand, the amount of effort required to form internal and external attributions may be most relevant to the attributions formed by athletes and coaches. The logic here is that, during competition, athletes and coaches must devote most or all of their attentional capacity and effort to the competition at hand. As a result, they are unable to take the time and expend the energy necessary to form external attributions. As a result, they become susceptible to the fundamental attribution error.

Because most research examining sport attributions has examined self-directed attributions (attributions athletes form about their own behavior) rather than other-directed attributions (attributions assigned to the behaviors of others), researchers have yet to document the fundamental attribution error among athletes. However, because several researchers have suggested a need for more sport studies focusing on other-directed attributions (Biddle, 1993; Brawley & Roberts, 1984; Rejeski, 1979), future research may begin to explore these types of attributions.

However, there are two lines of research that have investigated other-directed attributions in sport. First, as discussed in this chapter's "A Closer Look," researchers have examined how head and assistant coaches tend to form different attributions about their players' performances. Second, several studies have examined the attributions that sport fans formulate concerning team and individual performances. We will explore the attributions of sport fans toward the end of this text.

The Self-Serving Bias

Concerning self-focused attributions, research has consistently demonstrated the self-serving bias (Miller & Ross, 1975; Snyder, Stephan, & Rosenfield, 1978). The ***self-serving bias*** is a self-directed attributional pattern in which individuals externalize their failures while internalizing their successes. For example, suppose a tennis player has just defeated a talented opponent. When asked to explain her success, the self-serving bias would predict that she would present an internal attribution. For instance, she may suggest that her ability and effort led to her victory. However, if she were to have lost, she would use an external attribution to explain her behavior, such as the weather or her opponent's ability. Thus, the self-serving bias has two parts. The first part concerns the ego-enhancing strategy of attributing one's successes to internal causes (e.g., believing that success in tennis is due to ability and effort). The second part concerns the ego-protecting strategy of attributing failures to external causes (e.g., believing that failure at tennis is due to the weather or performance of an opponent).

There appear to be two reasons underlying the self-serving bias. First, as discussed by Myers (1993), the self-serving bias can be due to a conscious desire to make oneself look better. Such an explanation for the self-serving bias argues that there is a motivational reason behind the error. Specifically, it is believed that individuals are motivated to maintain a positive self-image, and one way to accomplish this goal is through the use of the self-serving bias. While the motivational argument assumes an intentional effort on the part of the individual, the second possible explanation for the self-serving bias lies purely at the cognitive level. This explanation,

A CLOSER LOOK:
THE DIFFERENTIAL ATTRIBUTIONS OF HEAD COACHES
AND ASSISTANT COACHES: ABILITY VERSUS EFFORT

Although most studies examining sport attributions have investigated the players' self-directed attributions, Carver, DeGregorio, and Gillis (1980) went against this trend by examining the other-directed attributions of head and assistant coaches. These researchers conducted a field study testing the prediction that coaches exhibit a bias in their attributions concerning the players' performances. Carver et al. believed that a coach's role will influence the nature of the bias. Specifically, these authors argued that "It is the role of the head coach to plan recruitment and plot the team's course over the years. The role of the assistant, on the other hand, is to work intensively with a few players, building their motivation, and polishing what skills the players have" (p. 45). Based on these roles, it was expected that beliefs that the players lacked talent would be threatening to the head coach because he or she is in charge of player selection and recruitment. Conversely, perceptions that the players were not demonstrating the desired level of effort were expected to be threatening to assistant coaches.

Carver and his colleagues tested their reasoning by asking the head and assistant coaches of a football team to complete a questionnaire prior to the start of the season and again at midseason. The questionnaire asked the coaches to rate the ability and effort of the players. The head coach rated all players, while the assistant coaches rated the players under their direction. The target team was quite unsuccessful during the first half of the season. As a result, Carver et al. expected the head coach to protect his self-esteem by attributing the team's failures to a lack of effort by the players. Conversely, assistant coaches were expected to protect their image by attributing the team's poor performance to the players' lack of abilities. Indeed, this is what the researchers found. The head coach rated the players' higher in ability at midseason but lower in effort, while the assistant coaches reported lower midseason ratings for ability but higher ratings of effort. Had these researchers tested the coaches of a successful team, we would have expected a different set of findings. The head coach of a winning team should believe that the team's success was due to ability (an attribution indicating the head coach's abilities), while the assistant coaches should attribute the team's success to the players' effort (an attribution indicating the assistants' abilities).

often referred to as the information-processing approach (Myers, 1993), states that the self-serving bias is simply a bi-product of how individuals cognitively perceive their world (Fiske & Taylor, 1991; Miller & Ross, 1975). Supporters of the information processing approach do not believe that people are consciously motivated to use the self-serving bias to maintain their positive self-image. Rather, they feel that

We tend to attribute our successes to internal causes, while attributing our failures to external causes. This attributional pattern is termed the *self-serving bias*. (Photographer: Paul J. Sutton. Source: Duomo Photography.)

people naturally view themselves in a positive light and, therefore, automatically (i.e., without effort) process information about their behaviors in a positively biased manner. Because research has supported both the motivation and information processing approaches to the self-serving bias, both viewpoints appear to have merit (Fiske & Taylor, 1991).

In contrast to the lack of sport research on the fundamental attribution error, several studies have examined the prevalence of the self-serving bias in athletic settings. In general, this research has found that sport winners are more likely to form internal attributions than losers, a finding that has been replicated with a number of different sports and athlete populations (Bird & Brame, 1978; Lau & Russell, 1980; Peterson, 1980; Riordan, Thomas, & James, 1985; Santamaria & Furst, 1994; Spink & Roberts, 1980; Watkins, 1986). Further, in their investigation of table tennis players, McAuley and Gross (1983) found that winners formed more internal, stable, and controllable attributions than did losers. McAuley's (1985) research with gymnasts replicated the results of McAuley and Gross, as have other studies (e.g., Duncan & McAuley, 1987; Tenenbaum & Furst, 1985). In their work with squash players, Mark and his colleagues (1984) also found that winners reported more controllable and stable attributions than did losers. However, in this research, winners and losers did not differ on the locus of causality dimension. Lalonde (1992) found that, although the members of a last place hockey team did report that the other teams were more skilled, the players were able to maintain a positive self-identity by attributing their lack of success to the dirty play of the other teams. Finally, in their research testing young athletes, Weiss, McAuley, Ebbeck, and Wiese (1990) found that children high in self-esteem were especially likely to form internal and stable attributions.

Thus, it appears that sport winners are more likely to form internal, stable, and controllable attributions than are losers. To test the magnitude of the self-serving bias in sport, Mullen and Riordan (1988) conducted a metaanalysis of 22 studies testing the self-serving bias in sport environments. Their research found that successful athletes did tend to attribute their success to internal causes, thus substantiating the self-serving bias. However, the effect was only moderately powerful and some studies did not find the self-serving bias. For example, the work of Mark et al. (1984) did not find that competition winners internalized the success to a greater degree than competition losers, a finding that was replicated by Grove, Hanrahan, and McInman (1991).

To help explain why some sport studies have failed to find the self-serving bias, Mark et al. (1984; see also Scanlan, 1977) suggested that there may be a unique norm operating in some sport settings. This norm, called the **sport outcome responsibility norm,** encourages athletes to accept responsibility for their actions and outcomes. As a result of this norm, athletes feel compelled to internalize their failures as well as their successes. Subsequently, the impact of the self-serving bias is reduced or eliminated. Consistent with this reasoning, some studies have found that players formed a high level of internal attributions, regardless of whether they were successful or unsuccessful (e.g., Duncan & McAuley, 1987; Grove et al., 1991; Mark et al., 1984; McAuley & Gross, 1983).

So what should we conclude about the prevalence of the self-serving bias in sport? By examining the evidence, it appears that the self-serving bias is a real and active phenomenon in sport settings, although the magnitude of the phenomenon may be less than originally believed. Further, it may be that the sport outcome responsibility norm is at least partially responsible for the attenuated impact of the self-serving bias in athletics. Perhaps future research will attempt to manipulate the importance of the sport outcome responsibility norm. By comparing athletes participating in settings involving this norm and participants performing in settings not impacted by this norm, we may learn more about the self-serving bias in sport.

ATTRIBUTIONAL DIFFERENCES BASED ON SPORT TYPE

A handful of researchers have explored the attributions of athletes participating in different sports. These investigations have examined whether or not participants in certain sports favor one or more of the attributional dimensions described above. A study conducted by Tenenbaum and Furst (1985) indicated that there may be attributional differences based on sport type. These authors assessed the attributions of 44 athletes participating in individual sports (boxing, table tennis, and track and field) and 94 athletes participating in team sports (soccer, team handball, and basketball). They found that athletes participating in individual sports formed more internal attributions than did persons involved with team sports. Apparently, because the individual sport athletes were solely responsible for their performances, they were less likely to believe that outside forces had an impact on their behavior.

In an attempt to build on the work of Tenenbaum and Furst (1985), Leith and Prapavessis (1989) compared the attributions of athletes participating in subjective sports with the attributions of persons involved with objective sports. **Subjective sports** are sports in which the final outcome is based on the subjective evaluations and scoring of one or more judges. Examples of subjective sports include diving, gymnastics, and figure skating. **Objective sports** are sports in which the outcome is determined by quantifiable units and direct competition. Track and field events and bowling would be classified as objective sports. Because the outcomes of subjective sports are based on external factors (i.e., the judges' ratings), Leith and Prapavessis thought that participants in these sports may report an especially high level of external attributions. To test their prediction, Leith and Prapavessis asked 52 teenage athletes to complete a survey designed to measure their attributions for competition outcomes. Approximately half of the subjects participated in objective sports, while the other half participated in subjective sports. To the researchers' surprise, the data indicated no differences between athletes involved in subjective and objective sports. Thus, Leith and Prapavessis (1989) were left to conclude that for athletes, "the same factors are seen as important regardless of whether the outcome is determined by objective or subjective means" (p. 230).

So what then should we conclude about the attributional differences of athletes participating in various sports? Quite frankly, because so few studies have addressed this issue, we are left to conclude that we currently can form no conclusions! Rather, much additional research is required before we will arrive at an understanding of the sport-type differences in athlete attributions.

GENDER, AGE, AND RACE DIFFERENCES IN SPORT ATTRIBUTIONS

In this section, we will examine research targeting how the attributional process is affected by three subject variables: gender, age, and race.

Gender Differences in Attributional Processes

A number of authors have compared the attributions exhibited by male and female athletes. In early thinking on the topic, some authors thought that females and female athletes were less likely to exhibit the self-serving bias than males and male athletes (Deaux, 1984; Lenney, 1977; McHugh, Duquin, & Frieze, 1978). These authors argued that, because success in sport violates the stereotypical female gender role, women who succeed in sport may tend to form external attributions, while women who fail report internal attributions. Several studies supported the notion that female athletes are less likely than male athletes to display the self-serving bias (e.g., Bird & Williams, 1980; Duquin, 1978; Murray & Matheson, 1993; Tenenbaum & Furst, 1985; White, 1993). However, an equal if not larger set of studies found no differences between the attributions of male and female athletes (e.g., Blucker & Hershberger, 1983; Croxton, Chiacchia, & Wagner, 1987; Gill, 1980; Hendy & Boyer, 1993; Riordan et al., 1985; Scanlan & Passer, 1980). In fact, the large number of studies failing to indicate gender differences in sport-related attributions led Biddle (1993) to conclude that the "assumption . . . that males and females attribute success and failure in different ways in sport has not been supported with confidence" (p. 445).

To explain the apparent lack of attributional differences between male and female athletes, it may be helpful to recall our discussion of the fear of success. In the personality chapter, we noted that female athletes tend not to experience the fear of success because success is consistent with their roles acquired through athletic participation. A similar phenomenon may be occurring with the attributional patterns of female athletes. Rather than showing a negative, nonbiased pattern, female athletes exhibit a pattern similar to male athletes because female athletes do not believe that athletic success violates their gender roles.

Age Differences in Attributional Processes

While a few researchers have focused their attention on age differences in attributions, research examining this topic has been quite scarce (Biddle, 1993; Rejeski & Brawley, 1983). In fact, the lack of research on this topic discourages one from drawing overall conclusions about the relationship between age and sport-based attributions. However, a couple of studies have been conducted, with each revealing some interesting patterns.

The most complete study on the relationship between age and attributional processes in sport was conducted by Bird and Williams (1980). These authors examined the attributions of 192 male and 192 female children from four age groups (7–9, 10–12, 13–15, and 16–18 years). Subjects were asked to read a series of sport-related stories. In some stories the feature character was a male, while in others this person was a female. Further, in some stories the target character was successful at an athletic endeavor, while in others the target failed at the task. After reading the stories, subjects were asked to state the extent to which they believed the outcome was due to ability, hard work, task difficulty, and luck. Bird and Williams found that the three youngest age groups did not form differential attributions based on the gender of the target. However, gender stereotypes did emerge in the oldest age group (16–18 years). Subjects in this age group reported that success of a male was due to effort, while success of a female was due to luck. It should be mentioned that this study assessed the children's other-directed attributions. The children's self-directed attributions were not tested.

In another study examining age differences in sport attributions, White (1993) assessed the causality, stability, and controllability dimensions for the attributions of junior varsity and adult softball players. Subjects were asked to complete the CDS after the first game of a tournament (all players had won the game). The two age groups did not differ on the causality or controllability dimensions. However, the younger players were more likely to form stable attributions.

Race and the Attributional Process

In the current section, rather than examine the self-directed attributions of different races, we will examine the other-directed attributions individuals form to explain the behaviors of white and black athletes. One of the most informative studies in this area was conducted by Murrell and Curtis (1994). These authors examined the magazine coverage of six different professional quarterbacks, three white and three black. The three black quarterbacks were selected because they were the only black starting quarterbacks during the 3 years examined. The white quarterbacks were selected because their performance ratings were similar to those of the black quarterbacks. The five magazines contained 38 articles on one or more of the quarterbacks. The articles contained more than 250 explanations of the quarterbacks' behaviors. The behavioral explanations were coded based on their locus of causality, stability, and controllability. It was found that the locus of causality dimension of the writers' attributions did not differ by race. In general, attributions were internal for both white and blacks athletes. However, differences were found for both the stability and controllability dimensions. The performances of white quarterbacks were thought to be less stable but more controllable than the performances of black athletes. Thus, attributions for the behaviors of white athletes were internal, unstable, and controllable, indicating that their performances were believed to be due to hard work and effort (see Table 9.1). Conversely, attributions for the behaviors of black athletes were internal, stable, and uncontrollable, indicating that their performances were thought to be the result of natural ability.

The results of the Murrell and Curtis (1994) research highlight the stereotypical attributions used to explain the successes of black athletes. Many people believe that the success of African-American sport performers is due simply to their high level of natural ability. On the other hand, white athletes are thought to be successful because of their hard work, diligence, and intelligence. This substantiates the arguments of Harris (1993). This author states that many individuals stereotypically believe that, "Without inborn talent, where would the black athlete be?" while simultaneously thinking that the success of white athletes is due to "intelligence, industriousness, and other unspecified intangibles" (p. 62). To support his propositions, Harris (1993) quotes the descriptions of four top collegiate point guards. The descriptions for two of the players included their instincts and lack of thinking skills, while the descriptions of the other two players noted their genius and how the intangibles outweighed their lack of ability. Can you determine which pair of athletes was black? As you probably guessed, it was the first group.

Thus, it appears that the successes of white athletes are perceived as being a function of effort, while the successes of black athletes are viewed as being a result of natural ability. This pattern of attributions can lead to unfair evaluations of performance. Previous research has indicated that individuals are more impressed when they attribute a person's success to effort than when they believe the success is due to ability (Baron & Greenberg, 1990; Mitchell, Green, & Wood, 1982). For example, if the performances of black and white athletes with equal credentials were to be evaluated, the white athlete would probably receive greater accolades and rewards for his performance. This is because coaches, fans, and reporters would attribute his success to effort, while the black athlete's success would be attributed to his natural ability. This is yet another example of the challenges facing minority athletes as they strive to compete on an even playing field.

SUMMARY

There are several different attributional dimensions. The dimension receiving the most attention concerns the locus of causality of the behavior. Individuals decide that behaviors are caused by either external forces or internal forces. Kelley's covariation theory was an attempt to explain the process individuals use when determining if a behavior was due to external or internal forces. This theory argues that when people believe that a behavior is consistent, the situation is distinct, and there is consensus among others, they conclude that the behavior was caused by external factors. Conversely, when individuals believe that the behavior is consistent, the situation is not distinct, and there is no consensus among others, they conclude that the behavior was caused by the internal disposition of the actor. Two other attributional dimensions that have gained a fair amount of attention are stability and controllability.

Although individuals appear to feel confident in the accuracy of their attributions, research has indicated that people tend to make errors in their attributions. Regarding other-directed attributions, research has found that people tend to overemphasize internal causes while underemphasizing external causes. This tendency has been labeled the fundamental attribution error. As for self-directed attributions, research has indicated that people tend to internalize their successes while externalizing their failures, an attributional pattern referred to as the self-serving bias. It appears that sport competition winners tend to form more internal, stable, and controllable attributions for their own behavior than do sport competition losers. This pattern appears to be rather self-serving. However, some athletes may not exhibit the self-serving bias in sport settings because of the sport outcome responsibility norm.

Research investigating sport differences in attributions has found that athletes participating in individual sports tend to form more internal attributions than do those involved with team sports. However, participants in subjective and objective sports do not exhibit differential patterns of attributions. Research has also found that male and female athletes do not differ in their attributions. Research on age and attributions has found that gender role attributional stereotypes begin in the late teens. Concerning race, the successes of black athletes tend to be stereotypically attributed to their ability, while the successes of white athletes are thought to be the result of their effort. This attributional pattern is unfair because attributions of effort are more likely to be rewarded than are attributions of ability.

GLOSSARY

Attributions   Estimates of the causes of our own or someone else's behavior.

Consensus   The number of other individuals exhibiting a behavior in a particular setting.

Consistency   The frequency with which an individual exhibits a behavior in a particular setting.

Controllability Attributional Dimension   The extent to which an individual believes that the cause of a behavior was under the voluntary control of the actor.

Controllable Attributions   The belief that a behavior was under the voluntary control of the actor.

Covariation Theory   A theory arguing that when individuals attempt to determine the locus of causality for a behavior, they try to acquire information about consistency, distinctiveness, and consensus.

Distinctiveness   The degree to which an individual exhibits a behavior in other settings.

External Attributions   The belief that a behavior was caused by the environment or setting.

Fundamental Attribution Error   A biased, other-directed attributional pattern in which an individual overemphasizes the importance of internal causes and underemphasizes the importance of external causes.

Internal Attributions   The belief that a behavior was caused by the individual.

Locus of Causality Attributional Dimension   The extent to which an individual believes that the cause of a behavior is internal or external.

Objective Sports   Sports in which the outcome is determined by quantifiable units and direct competition.

Self-Serving Bias   A self-directed attributional pattern in which an individual externalizes failures while internalizing successes.

Sport Outcome Responsibility Norm   A norm that encourages athletes to accept responsibility for their actions and outcomes.

Stability Attributional Dimension   The extent to which an individual believes that the cause of a behavior was due to features that are variant.

Stable Attributions   The belief that a behavior was caused by permanent or near permanent personality traits or environmental features.

Subjective Sports   Sports in which the final outcome is based on the subjective evaluations and scoring of one or more judges.

Uncontrollable Attributions   The belief that a behavior was beyond the control of the actor.

Unstable Attributions   The belief that a behavior was caused by variable personality traits or environmental features.

APPLICATION AND REVIEW QUESTIONS

1. Using an example from sport, explain the differences between an internal and an external attribution.
2. Describe Kelley's covariation theory of attributions.
3. Using an example from sport, explain the differences between a stable and an unstable attribution.
4. Using an example from sport, explain the differences between a controllable and an uncontrollable attribution.
5. Develop a sport-specific example of the fundamental attribution error and the self-serving bias.
6. With regard to the attributional dimensions of locus of causality, stability, and controllability, what is the typical attributional pattern found among athletes? Is this pattern self-serving?
7. Do male and female athletes differ in their sport attributions?

SUGGESTED READINGS

BIDDLE, S. (1993). Attribution research and sport psychology. In R. N. Singer, M. Murphey, & L. K. Tennant (Eds.), *Handbook of research on sport psychology* (pp. 437–464). New York: Macmillan. This chapter presents an in-depth look at the attributional processes in sport. Several important topics are discussed including gender and age differences, the relationship between attributions and emotions, and the self-serving bias.

MCAULEY, E. (1992). Self-referent thought in sport and physical activity. In T. S. Horn (Ed.), *Advances in sport psychology* (pp. 101–118). Champaign, IL: Human Kinetics. This chapter examines both attribution and self-efficacy research in sport.

ZEBROWITZ, L. A. (1990). *Social perception* (chapter 5). Pacific Grove, CA: Brooks/Cole. This chapter gives a basic overview of attribution processes, including a description of Kelley's covariation theory and the fundamental attribution error.

Chapter 10

INTERVENTIONS TARGETING AROUSAL/ANXIETY REGULATION AND ATHLETIC INJURY MANAGEMENT

At the beginning of this book, I noted that one of the major goals of sport psychology is to enhance athletic performance. In the following two chapters, we will examine several performance enhancement intervention strategies employed by sport psychologists to achieve this goal. The current chapter focuses on the regulation of arousal and anxiety and interventions designed to assist the recovery of injured athletes. The second chapter examines self-confidence, imagery, attention, and psychological skills training.

Although the primary goal of sport psychology interventions is the enhancement of performance, athletes, coaches, and sport psychologists may use intervention strategies for other reasons as well. For example, although the anxiety control tactics described in the next two chapters are primarily designed to improve performance, they may also increase personal well-being and satisfaction. Similarly, the intervention strategies used with injured athletes are not only designed to expedite their recovery but also to help athletes deal with their injuries. Thus, consistent with the purpose of applied sport psychology discussed in Chapter 1, sport psychology interventions really have two goals: performance enhancement and increasing psychological well-being.

THE REGULATION OF AROUSAL AND ANXIETY

As discussed in Chapter 7, there is a strong relationship among arousal, anxiety, and athletic performance. The arousal (i.e., somatic anxiety) and performance relationship takes the form of an inverted-U, while cognitive anxiety and performance are negatively related. Because of the strong relationship between anxiety and performance, it is not surprising that sport psychologists have developed or modified several techniques designed to regulate the arousal and anxiety of athletes. However, before we examine the specific techniques, two important points must be mentioned.

First, sport psychologists need to consider somatic and cognitive anxiety as separate entities and employ different intervention strategies for these forms of anxiety (Burton, 1990). To assist in this endeavor, sport consultants should use the anxiety matching hypothesis (Maynard, Hemmings, & Warwick-Evans, 1995; Maynard, Smith, & Warwick-Evans, 1995). The ***anxiety matching hypothesis*** implies that cognitive intervention strategies will be most effective and should be used with individuals experiencing problematic levels of cognitive anxiety, while somatic intervention strategies will be most effective and should be used with individuals experiencing problematic levels of somatic anxiety. Because a moderate level of somatic anxiety facilitates performance, sport psychologists should attempt to lower the arousal of athletes who are "too pumped up" while raising the arousal of athletes who are "too low-keyed." On the other hand, because research has found that even small levels of cognitive anxiety can hinder athletic performance, in most cases, sport psychologists should attempt to decrease the cognitive anxiety of the athletic participants (Martens et al., 1990).

However, a second point that must be mentioned qualifies the first point. Recently, several authors have become interested in the direction of somatic and cognitive anxiety (debilitative to facilitative, see Maynard et al., 1995). As discussed in Chapter 7, not all athletes believe that a high level of cognitive and somatic anxiety is harmful to performance. Rather, some athletes gain strength and are encouraged by high levels of both forms of anxiety. Thus, to understand how an athlete's anxiety will impact his or her performance, a sport psychologist must consider both the intensity and the direction of the athlete's anxiety. Although an athlete may appear to experience a detrimentally high level of cognitive or somatic anxiety, a sport psychologist should not attempt to reduce this anxiety if the athlete perceives the anxiety as facilitating his or her performance.

Anxiety Reduction

In this section, we will examine a number of intervention strategies designed to reduce the cognitive and somatic anxiety of athletes. The strategies described below are not intended to be an exhaustive list. In fact, Martens et al. (1990) list almost a dozen different anxiety reduction techniques. Rather, this section is designed to give the reader a general feel for the types of anxiety/arousal interventions used by sport psychologists. Further, athletes are not the only members of a team who suffer from anxiety. Rather, coaches are also under a high level of stress. Please see this chapter's "A Closer Look" for a description of an intervention strategy designed to assist coaches in lowering their anxiety.

Personal Tactics for Coping with Anxiety in Sport.   Consider a college basketball player who is experiencing a detrimentally high level of anxiety prior to games. Because of her anxiety, she has concluded that something must be done to reduce the anxiety. Initially, to whom would this person turn for help? A teammate or coach? A sport psychologist? In actuality, the athlete would most likely first solicit suggestions from herself. Because athletes are aware of their anxiety and its consequences, they usually attempt to cope and manage the anxiety themselves prior to seeking outside help. That is, athletes employ certain coping strategies without the assistance of others.

A CLOSER LOOK:
STRESS MANAGEMENT FOR COACHES

Taylor (1992) recently published an article that included the phrase "Coaches are people too" in the title (p. 27). Taylor's title acknowledges that, although sport psychologists pay a great deal of attention to the anxiety of athletes, the stress of coaches is often ignored. However, coaching can be as stressful as athletic involvement, particularly at the college and professional levels. Because coaches experience high levels of anxiety, Taylor believes they will benefit from anxiety-reducing intervention strategies. To this end, he fashioned an anxiety reduction program specifically for coaches. Unfortunately, because Taylor's program is quite new, researchers have yet to document its effectiveness empirically (although case study reports have been encouraging, see Taylor, 1992).

Taylor's (1992) intervention, called ***stress management for coaches,*** includes five components (see Figure 10.1). The first component, perceptions of coaching, reflects the notion that one's cognitive appraisal of a stressor influences the impact of the stressor. Thus, coaches are first asked to describe their perceptions, beliefs, and motivations about coaching. An individual's perceptions of coaching can be reflected in a variety of ways, including their personal values, their quality of life, their perceptions of the benefits and detriments of coaching, and their personal and career goals.

The second component involves the identification of primary stressors. Taylor (1992) groups stressors faced by coaches into three categories: personal, social, and organizational. Personal stressors include self-doubts, poor physical health, and inadequate skills. Examples of social stressors include lack of social support, team conflict, and pressure from fans and the media. Third, Taylor lists long hours, travel, and time pressures as examples of organizational stressors. In addition to these three forms of stress, coaches may experience stress from outside the professional setting through major life events (e.g., a death in the family) or daily hassles (e.g., living out of hotels).

Once the psychologist and coach understand the particular stressors impacting the coach, they must identify the ways the stressors are manifested in the coach's cognitions, emotion/physiology, and behaviors. That is, simply identifying the specific stressors is not enough: The coach must also achieve an understanding of the impact of the stressor on his or her thinking, feelings, and actions. Taylor lists negative thinking as a common cognitive manifestation; anger, fatigue, and illness as common emotional/physiological manifestations; and tardiness, isolation, and reduced efficiency as typical behavioral manifestations.

The fourth stage in Taylor's model involves the development of coping skills. During this phase of the program, the psychologist should initiate one or more intervention strategies targeting the coach's specific needs. For example, if the stressors are manifested cognitively, the psychologist may want to begin a cognitive restructuring program. On the other hand, if the stressors result in emotional/physiological changes, the psychologist should use a different form of intervention such as relaxation training. Behavior modification programs (such as time management and assertiveness training) would be prescribed for stressors leading to behavioral problems.

The final stage in Taylor's model involves social support. As mentioned in an earlier chapter, social support can serve as a buffer against stress and anxiety. If coaches are able to establish a social support network, they will be better able to cope with the anxiety of coaching. Taylor lists a variety of individuals who can potentially become a part of a coach's social support system including upper-level management (for college and professional teams), the coaching staff, the sport psychologist, and family and friends.

In his research with athletes from a variety of competition levels and sports, Crocker (1992; see also Crocker & Graham, 1995) was able to identify the strategies used by athletes to manage their anxiety. Crocker asked the athletes to describe their most anxious athletic situation in the past 3 weeks. Participants then completed a Ways of Coping checklist containing 68 Likert-scale items. This checklist asked subjects to report the methods they had used to cope with the anxiety. Responses revealed that there were eight general methods athletes used to manage their anxiety. These strategies are described in Table 10.1. As seen in the table, the most common strategies involved self-blame and active coping, while the least common strategies involved seeking social support and practicing self-control. Research by Madden, Summers, and Brown (1990) and Madden, Kirkby, and McDonald (1989) also found that active coping was a common strategy for athletes, particularly those experiencing exceptionally high levels of stress. However, contrary to Crocker's work, these studies found that seeking social support was a common factor, indicating that it may be an important personal coping strategy for athletes.

Rathus and Nevid (1989) note that some anxiety management strategies are preferable to others. These authors state that ***active coping strategies*** are prefer-

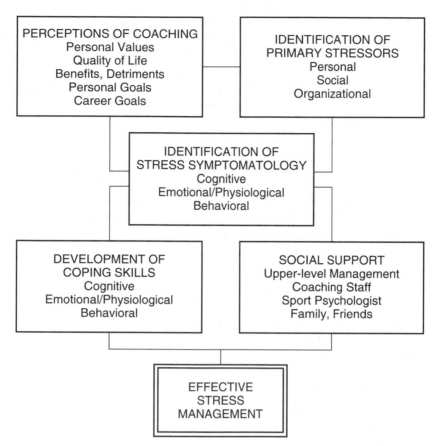

FIGURE 10.1 Applied model of stress management for coaches. (Reprinted by permission from: Taylor, J. [1992]. Coaches are people too: An applied model of stress management for sport coaches. *Journal of Applied Sport Psychology*, 4: 27–50.)

TABLE 10.1 Personal Anxiety Management Strategies Used by Athletes

Strategy	*Sample Item*	*Rank*[*]
Active Coping	"I knew what I had to do, so I doubled my efforts to make things work."	2
Problem-Focused	"I mentally pictured myself handling the situation better."	3
Social Support	"I asked a relative or friend I respected for advice."	7
Reappraisal	"I tried to reevaluate the situation to see or gain something positive from the situation."	4
Wishful Thinking	"I wished that the situation would go away or somehow be better"	5 (tie)
Self-Control	"I waited to see what would happen before doing anything."	8
Detachment	"I tried to keep my feelings to myself."	5 (tie)
Self-Blame	"I criticized or lectured myself."	1

*A rank of 1 indicates that the strategy was the most common, while a rank of 8 indicates the strategy was the least common.

able because these strategies reflect attempts to change, alter, or remove the stressor, thereby reducing or eliminating its impact. Of the athletic anxiety management strategies found in Crocker's (1992) work, the active and problem-focused tactics reflect active coping strategies. In most cases, these strategies will be highly successful because they actively engage the problem. Other anxiety management strategies are called passive strategies (these strategies are called defensive strategies by some authors; Rathus & Nevid, 1989). *Passive coping strategies* reflect attempts to deal with or manage the anxiety in a temporary manner without confronting the stressor itself. Although these tactics may offer temporary relief from the stressor, they are less than optimal because they do not change, alter, or remove the stressor. As a result, when one stops using a passive strategy, the stressor is still present. In Crocker's research, the most obvious example of a passive coping strategy was wishful thinking. Although wishful thinking and daydreaming may temporarily relieve anxiety, these are stop-gap approaches because the stressor remains intact.

Relaxation Training.   In some cases, athletes are unable to cope with athletic anxiety on their own. It is at this point that they should seek the assistance of a sport psychologist trained in anxiety reduction. Sport psychologists have altered or developed several techniques designed to reduce the anxiety experienced by athletes. Many of these techniques fall under the general heading of relaxation training. *Relaxation training* refers to a number of techniques designed to lower somatic and cognitive anxiety. In the following sections, we will examine three relaxation techniques: progressive relaxation, biofeedback, and meditation. We will also review the relationship between these strategies and athletic performance.

PROGRESSIVE RELAXATION.   Progressive relaxation is a technique originally developed by Jacobson (1929, 1976; see also Berstein & Borkovec, 1973). *Progressive relaxation* involves the systematic tension and relaxation of muscle groups in an attempt to reduce anxiety. In this procedure, athletes are asked to lie or sit in a comfortable position. The environment is kept peaceful, quiet, and free of distractions. Athletes are then asked to inhale and tense a specific muscle group for approximately 5 seconds. The athlete then exhales and releases the tension from the specified muscle group, concentrating on the feelings of relaxation. This procedure is repeated for a number of muscle groups. A sample progressive relaxation exercise is presented in Table 10.2.

Using progressive relaxation for the entire body can be a lengthy process, often lasting up to an hour. However, after a few weeks of training, the athlete is usually capable of tensing and relaxing several muscle groups simultaneously (e.g., she may tense both feet and both legs at the same time). This shortens the amount of time needed to complete the process. Once the athlete becomes highly skilled at the technique, the tension phase of the procedure can be eliminated and the athlete will simply relax the targeted muscle groups, a process that may only take a few minutes. However, to practice progressive relaxation during a competition, the athlete must be able to relax the key muscle groups in only a few seconds. For example, a point guard who is about to shoot a free throw can take no more than 5 or 6 seconds to relax. Thus, although progressive relaxation can easily be used prior to a

TABLE 10.2   A Sample Progressive Relaxation Exercise

Step 1:   Find a quiet and peaceful location.
Step 2:   Dim the lighting.
Step 3:   Loosen all tight and binding clothing and remove shoes.
Step 4:   Sit or lie in a comfortable position.
Step 5:   For each of the muscle groups listed below, inhale deeply, squeeze the muscle group for 5 seconds, then relax the muscle group while exhaling deeply. Pause for 15 seconds between muscle groups. Be sure to focus on the specific muscle group, that is, tighten only the target group and maintain a state of relaxation throughout the rest of your body. Pay particular attention to the different sensations and feelings in the tension and relaxation states.

Muscle Group 1:   Right hand and fingers (make a fist)
Muscle Group 2:   Right forearm
Muscle Group 3:   Right upper arm
Muscle Group 4:   Left hand and fingers (make a fist)
Muscle Group 5:   Left forearm
Muscle Group 6:   Left upper arm
Muscle Group 7:   Head and face
Muscle Group 8:   Shoulders
Muscle Group 9:   Chest
Muscle Group 10:   Stomach and abdomen
Muscle Group 11:   Right upper leg
Muscle Group 12:   Right lower leg
Muscle Group 13:   Right foot and toes
Muscle Group 14:   Left upper leg
Muscle Group 15:   Left lower leg
Muscle Group 16:   Left foot and toes

competition, athletes must diligently practice and perfect their progressive relaxation skills before they can be implemented during a competition.

Several studies have documented the performance benefits of progressive relaxation (e.g., Carlson & Hoyle, 1993; Greenspan & Feltz, 1989; Maynard et al., 1995; Onestak, 1991). Some researchers have used the case study method to demonstrate the benefits of this exercise. Nideffer and Deckner (1970) examined the impact of progressive relaxation on the performance of a 20-year-old collegiate shot-putter. Although the subject was a competent athlete (he was the conference shot-put record holder), he had ceased to improve and his coaches felt that he might have reached his performance limit. However, after receiving relaxation training, he went on to set two new conference records. In a different study, Horton and Shelton (1978) were able to improve the performances of a small group of collegiate wrestlers by providing the athletes with progressive relaxation exercises.

Other researchers have used the experimental method to document the benefits of progressive relaxation. For example, Lanning and Hisanaga (1983) implemented a modified progressive relaxation program with a group of female high school volleyball players. The players were randomly assigned to either a treatment condition or a control condition. Subjects in the treatment condition received seven 30-minute relaxation training sessions. Lanning and Hisanaga then examined the players' service performance. The results showed that players receiving the relaxation training exhibited an increase in service performance. No such improvement was found among those in the control group.

In another study, Broucek, Bartholomew, Landers, and Linder (1993) examined the effects of progressive relaxation on pain tolerance. These authors hypothesized that subjects receiving progressive relaxation training and given a cue shortly before the onset of a painful stimulus would be able to withstand a larger amount of pain than subjects receiving progressive relaxation training who were *not* given a cue and subjects in a control group not receiving the training. The cue was expected to produce the pain tolerance effect because cued subjects would be able to begin the relaxation procedure prior to the onset of pain, while those not receiving the cue would only be able to begin the relaxation procedure after the pain had begun. The results supported the predictions. Physical education students receiving the training and given a cue were able to withstand the pain of a rubber cleat pressed against their lower leg better than the other subjects. Thus, progressive relaxation appears to benefit athletes in at least three ways: by lowering arousal, by increasing performance, and by increasing pain tolerance (when accompanied by a cue).

BIOFEEDBACK. Biofeedback is another technique used to reduce anxiety. **Biofeedback** involves the use of instruments that monitor autonomic processes, thereby allowing individuals to develop some control over these processes. Biofeedback instruments can monitor several different biological processes including heart rate, blood pressure, respiration rate, skin temperature, muscles, and brain waves. These instruments allow the individual to learn behaviors and thoughts that lead to a state of tension, as well as those leading to a state of relaxation. Once the individual has learned the behaviors and thoughts that lead to anxiety and relaxation, he or she can learn to control the anxiety.

Research examining the performance implications of biofeedback has been positive (Blais & Vallerand, 1986; Costa, Bonaccorsi, & Scrimali, 1984; De Witt, 1980; French, 1978; Zaichkowsky & Fuchs, 1988), particularly with heart rate and respiration biofeedback (Blais & Vallerand, 1986; Petruzzello, Landers, & Salazar, 1991). One of the more involved sets of studies investigating biofeedback in athletics was carried out by Daniels and Landers (1981). These authors examined the impact of biofeedback on the shooting performances of eight high-level junior shooters. The subjects completed 40 warm-up shots, while the experimenters simultaneously monitored their physiological responses. By examining the relationship between performance and physiology for the warm-up trials, the authors were able to determine inhibitory and facilitatory physiology patterns for each subject (e.g., one subject performed poorly when his heart rate was greater than 100 beats per minute). This information was used to develop an individualized target physiological response pattern that was described to each subject. Half of the subjects were then assigned to a biofeedback condition, while the other subjects were placed into a control group.

Participants in the biofeedback group received biofeedback information while performing a 40-shot posttest. The biofeedback information was designed to help the athletes perform within the parameters of their target physiological response pattern. Subjects in the control condition were asked to perform within the range of their target response pattern without the benefit of biofeedback information. The results of the 40-shot posttest revealed that the performances of subjects in the biofeedback group improved and became more consistent. These beneficial changes were not exhibited by subjects in the control condition.

MEDITATION. Meditation is a relaxation training technique that has been in use for thousands of years. **Meditation** involves the use of mental focus to calm the body (Schafer, 1992). While some researchers have found that meditation can result in a state of relaxation similar to that achieved from other relaxation training techniques (Benson, 1975; Wallace & Benson, 1972), other authors have challenged the notion that meditation lowers arousal (Holmes, 1984).

Although there are many different forms of meditation (Zaichkowsky & Takenaka, 1993), most forms share several commonalities. As a result, the meditation described here is a general synopsis of various types (particularly transcendental meditation). When meditating, individuals usually sit in a comfortable position in a quiet and dark environment, breathing slowly and deeply. The individual then concentrates on a single stimulus. For example, the individual may focus on a candle flame or picture. Some persons prefer to repeat a certain sound or word called a mantra (such as repeating the sound "ulm"). By concentrating on the single stimulus, the individual attempts to eliminate all thoughts from consciousness, thereby relaxing the body.

Researchers have found that meditation can facilitate athletic performance (Layman, 1980; Reddy, Bai, & Rao, 1977; Schafer, 1992). However, this effect may be limited to activities involving gross motor movements such as running and weight lifting. Meditation appears to be less effective with activities involving fine motor movements. This pattern of effects was shown in a series of studies by Williams in the 1970s (Williams, 1978; Williams, Lodge, & Reddish, 1977; Williams & Vickerman, 1976; see also Hall & Hardy, 1991). For example, Williams and Herbert (1976) asked a group of skilled meditators and a group of nonmeditators to complete a fine motor skill activity (a rotary pursuit tracking task). Prior to attempting the task, the meditation subjects were allowed to meditate for 20 minutes, while the nonmeditation subjects sat quietly with their eyes closed for 20 minutes. The results revealed no differences in scores for the two groups, thus supporting the notion that the performance enhancing benefits of meditation are limited to gross motor activities.

Stress Management Training. Another strategy used to combat anxiety is called **stress management training** (SMT). Stress management training is a comprehensive stress management program that teaches individuals to relax and control their anxiety. Through SMT programs, individuals learn about stress in general as well as their own personal tendencies and reactions to stressors. As a result, individuals can identify events and situations that typically lead to anxiety and learn new coping strategies to handle the stress better. It should be noted that SMT programs are quite similar to stress inoculation training (SIT) programs. Although subtle distinctions between these two anxiety reduction strategies can be found (see Burton, 1990, for a detailed comparison), they share a number of similarities. In fact, research by Ziegler, Klinzing, and Williamson (1982) found that while both strategies were more effective in controlling anxiety than a control condition, no differences emerged between the SMT and SIT conditions. Therefore, I will discuss each strategy under the general heading of SMT, with the understanding that SIT and SMT programs are slightly different.

AN SMT PROGRAM FOR SPORT.   An SMT program for use in sport settings was developed by Smith (1980). Smith's program contains five phases:

1. Pretreatment/assessment
2. Treatment rationale
3. Skill acquisition
4. Skill rehearsal
5. Posttreatment evaluation

Phase 1: Pretreatment/Assessment.   Phase 1 in Smith's (1980) program is the pretreatment/assessment phase. During this phase, the sport psychologist and athlete discuss the athlete's typical reactions to stressful events, attempting to identify events leading to the highest levels of anxiety. The psychologist also determines the athlete's particular methods of coping with anxiety. For example, does the athlete adopt active or passive coping strategies? Does the athlete seek social support, employ problem-focused strategies, or withdraw from the stressor? Based on the discussions taking place during this phase, the psychologist and athlete develop an individualized SMT program addressing the particular needs and concerns of this athlete.

Phase 2: Treatment Rationale.   The second phase is the treatment rationale phase. This phase is the educational section of the program. During this portion of the program, athletes receive information about anxiety in general and typical responses to anxiety. For example, athletes are given information about the different forms of anxiety (i.e., somatic and cognitive) and the physiology involved in stressful reactions. They also learn about the relationship between anxiety and performance and the relationship between anxiety and psychological and physiological health. Basically, athletes are presented with the type of information appearing in Chapter 7 of this textbook.

Phase 3: Skill Acquisition.   The third phase in Smith's (1980) SMT program, labeled the skill acquisition phase, involves training the athletes to cope with stress and anxiety in a positive manner. Essentially, participants are trained in the use of active coping strategies. This involves training in two separate but related areas: muscle relaxation and cognitive restructuring. As for the muscle relaxation training, athletes receive progressive relaxation training (see above). With regard to cognitive restructuring, athletes are taught to identify self-defeating, negative, and irrational thoughts. Specifically, athletes are trained in the art of positive self-talk (see Bunker, Williams, & Zinsser, 1993). **Positive self-talk** involves reassuring oneself with positive and rational thoughts and statements. For example, consider an athlete facing an anxious situation, such as a key late-inning at bat. When faced with this situation, the athlete usually presents himself with negative and self-defeating thoughts and statements (i.e., ***negative self-talk***) such as "I'm not ready for this" or "I'm unable to handle this pressure and I'm going to choke." In the skill acquisition phase, athletes are trained to restructure these negative thoughts into positive self-statements such as "I'm all right, I'm ready, physically fit, and I can perform well at this task."

A number of studies have indicated that positive self-talk is associated with successful performance (e.g., Kirschenbaum, Ordman, Tomarken, & Holtzbauer, 1982; Rushall, Hall, Roux, Sasseville, & Rushall, 1988), while negative self-talk is associated with poorer performance (e.g., Van Raalte, Brewer, Rivera, & Petitpas, 1994). For example, consider the work of Van Raalte and her colleagues (1995) investigating the impact of positive and negative self-talk on dart throwing. These researchers randomly assigned college undergraduates to one of three conditions: positive self-talk, negative self-talk, or control. Prior to attempting 15 actual dart throws (each subject was also given 15 practice throws), subjects in the positive self-talk condition were asked to repeat to themselves "you can do it," while those in the negative self-talk group were asked to repeat to themselves "you cannot do it." Subjects in the control group were not given any particular self-talk instructions. After the throwing task was completed, the researchers calculated the mean number of centimeters separating the dart and the bull's-eye. The results supported the performance enhancing effects of positive self-talk and the performance inhibiting effects of negative self-talk. Subjects in the control group missed the target by an average of 85 cm, while those in the positive self-talk group missed by an average of only 70 cm. Those in the negative self-talk condition performed the poorest, missing by an average of 93 cm.

Phase 4: Skill Rehearsal. The fourth phase is the skill rehearsal phase. In this portion of the program, the athlete practices the muscle relaxation and cognitive restructuring skills learned in the previous phase. Smith (1980) notes that "Stress coping skills are no different than any other kind of skill. In order to be most effective, they must be rehearsed and practiced under conditions which approximate the 'real life' situations in which they will eventually be employed" (p. 65). Thus, to facilitate the use of the coping strategies learned in the previous stage, the psychologist guides the athlete through progressively more stressful situations by asking the athlete to imagine real-life, anxiety-inducing settings. For example, consider a pitcher who experiences a detrimentally high level of anxiety when he is pitching with a runner on third base. To help the athlete learn to deal with this situation, the player would be asked to imagine himself in this setting with the game on the line. He would be asked to visualize the setting, to see the runner and the batter, to hear the crowd murmur, and to feel his tension mounting. These images will cause the player to feel anxious. When the anxiety begins, the player is told to use the tools (muscle relaxation and cognitive restructuring) learned in Phase 3. As a result, the pitcher will learn to handle this situation effectively.

Phase 5: Posttreatment Evaluation. The last phase, called the posttreatment evaluation phase, involves analyzing the effectiveness of the SMT program. It is extremely important to evaluate an intervention program after a set time. The evaluation can provide the athlete and sport psychologist with a great deal of important information regarding the program's effectiveness. Based on the evaluation, the consultant can determine if the program is having a beneficial impact on the athlete's anxiety and performance. In addition, the evaluation can be used to highlight portions of the program that should be deleted, altered, or enhanced.

THE EFFECTIVENESS OF SMT PROGRAMS.   Stress management training programs have been found to be successful in lowering anxiety and improving performance (Crocker, 1989; Long, 1980; Ziegler et al., 1982). For example, Crocker, Alderman, and Smith (1988) had a group of volleyball players complete a service reception task. After completing this pretest measure, some of the players participated in eight 1-hour SMT sessions. A control group of players did not receive the SMT training. A posttest of the service reception task indicated that the SMT group exhibited a marked increase in performance, while the performance of the control group did not change. In a separate study, Mace and Carroll (1985; see also Mace, Carroll, & Eastman, 1986) had subjects complete an anxiety-inducing task (lowering themselves down a rope). Some of the subjects completed an SMT program, while a control group of subjects did not receive the training. Compared with control subjects, participants who had received SMT exhibited lower levels of anxiety prior to attempting the task. In yet another test of SMT, Smith (1980) documented the skill enhancing effects of an SMT program on the efforts of a figure skater. Prior to receiving SMT, the athlete had struggled, never placing above eighth place. However, after completing an SMT program she won three of her next four competitions, placed second in the other, and exhibited a decrease in sport competition anxiety.

The Reduction of Acute Anxiety: Anshel's COPE Model.   Another program designed to help athletes cope with anxiety is Anshel's (1990) COPE model. The **COPE model** is a cognitive and behavioral strategy for coping with acute sport anxiety that focuses on *c*ontrolling emotions, *o*rganizing input, *p*lanning the next response, and *e*xecuting the response. It is important to note that the COPE model focuses on acute stressors, that is, stressors that are temporary. Examples of these stressors include a bad call by an official, a verbal reprimand by a coach, and committing an error in baseball. Thus, the COPE model is different from the previously reviewed anxiety reduction techniques. Techniques such as relaxation exercises and stress management training are designed to assist athletes with chronic levels of anxiety. If a basketball player consistently experienced detrimental levels of anxiety prior to games, she should attempt to reduce her chronic anxiety through one of the methods described above. However, if the player is typically low in anxiety but is currently feeling anxious because of a temporary negative stimulus, she should use the COPE model to lower the acute anxiety.

STAGES IN THE COPE MODEL.   The COPE model contains four stages (Anshel, 1990):

1. Controlling emotions
2. Organizing input
3. Planning the next response
4. Executing the response

Stage 1: Controlling Emotions.   The first stage, controlling emotions, is initiated when the athlete is confronted with an anxiety-inducing stimulus. This stage begins with the onset of acute stressors such as criticism from a coach, negative perfor-

The COPE model can be used to lower an athlete's anxiety response to an acute stressor such as a bad call, a fight with a coach, or a poor play execution. (Source: Duomo Photography.)

mances, hostile fans, and confrontations with opponents, teammates, or officials. The controlling emotions stage involves two cognitive-behavioral objectives. First, athletes must prevent what Anshel (1990) calls "emotional upheaval" (p. 63). That is, athletes must not become overwhelmed by their emotional reactions to the stressor. They must attempt to lower their physiological arousal and control their thoughts and emotions. To facilitate their control, athletes may wish to take a few deep breaths or attempt other short-term relaxation exercises. By controlling their physiological arousal levels and emotional reactions, athletes are able to think more clearly and rationally (recall from earlier chapters that physiological arousal can reduce an individual's cognitive capacity). The second cognitive-behavioral objective involves taking responsibility for and accurately perceiving the causes of performance.

Stage 2: Organizing Input. The second stage involves organizing inputs into meaningful and nonmeaningful categories. Anshel (1990) states that this may be the most difficult portion of the model. In this stage, the athlete consciously attempts to filter out meaningless, irrelevant, and negative information. The negative information (e.g., "My coach hates me.") should be replaced by positive information (e.g., "My coach is only trying to make me a better athlete."). Because it is impossible to filter out information without first analyzing it, all information must be processed. Athletes cannot simply discard all items of information because this would result in the loss of beneficial information. On the other hand, athletes cannot keep all information because this will result in the use of negative information. Thus, athletes must learn to make judgments about the value of specific items of information. Once the athlete has determined the positive and negative aspects of the information, he or she should focus on and rehearse the useful positive information while discarding the detrimental negative information.

Essentially, the second stage of the COPE model asks athletes to become "virtually impervious to negative input or an unpleasant experience" (Anshel, 1990, p. 69). However, because individuals have a desire to see themselves in a positive manner and wish to be perceived by others in a positive way, ignoring negative information and experiences can be quite difficult. Anshel (1990) believes that four cognitive strategies will assist athletes in properly categorizing information into meaningful and nonmeaningful units. First, athletes can use a technique called fogging. Fogging involves actively agreeing with a critic through the use of a reflective statement (e.g., "You are correct coach, I should have caught the ball."). Second, players may want to use a technique Anshel calls negative assertion. This technique goes beyond merely agreeing with a critic by involving self-criticism (e.g., "I really am lacking in effort today."). Third, athletes may wish to try negative inquiry. This procedure involves seeking information that will help relieve the anxiety (e.g., "I know I should have caught that ball. Can you show me what I am doing wrong?"). This strategy is especially useful because it can lead to the use of active coping strategies. Finally, athletes may want to distance themselves from the source of the anxiety. For example, athletes may attempt to reduce the impact of a coach's verbal reprimands by challenging the credibility of the source. However, because most coaches are seen as credible, this strategy may be difficult and ineffective.

Stage 3: Planning the Next Response.   The third stage involves planning the response. In this stage the athlete attempts to use cognitive strategies that assist in selecting their next response. Athletes should attempt to put the stressor behind them as quickly as possible and begin to respond in a positive fashion. A main objective of this stage is to avoid self-reflection. That is, rather than dwelling on the stressor and its impact (e.g., "I hate it when the coach yells at me."), players should direct their attention toward the future. This will be facilitated by positive self-talk, keeping thought processes under control, using self-deprecating humor (this tends to help one relax), and setting a short-term goal.

Stage 4: Executing the Response.   The final stage involves executing the planned response. Anshel (1990) states that the ultimate goal of this stage is for the athlete to return to performing at top efficiency as soon as possible. By initiating the first three stages, the athlete will quickly be able to return to his or her previous level of performance and execute the task without a great deal of thinking. Ideally, the athlete's behavior will again become automatic and the athlete will have forgotten about the acute stressor.

AN EXAMPLE OF THE COPE MODEL.   Let us now examine the use of the COPE model in a concrete example. Imagine that a volleyball player, Emily, was caught out of position during a point and, as a result, her team lost the first game of a match. During the break between games, Emily's coach verbally reprimanded her, telling Emily that she had better increase her performance or she would find herself on the bench. Although Emily is typically quite low in anxiety, the coach's harsh comments caused a great deal of acute anxiety. To reduce her anxiety, Emily decided to employ Anshel's COPE model (she was trained in the use of the model by the team's sport psychologist).

Emily knew that the first step was to control her emotions. Thus, she attempted to relax by taking a few deep breaths and quickly employing a muscle relaxation technique. By doing this, she prevented an emotional upheaval. Emily was also aware of the second aspect of controlling emotions: She took full responsibility for her mistake. Emily now moved to the second stage of the COPE program. In her attempt to classify the coach's remarks into meaningful and nonmeaningful units, Emily determined that the coach's statement that she must "stay at home" in her area of the court was correct (and hence meaningful), but the coach's comment about "finding herself on the bench" was irrelevant (and thus nonmeaningful). As a result, she repeated the coach's meaningful comments to herself several times. Emily now felt ready to move to the third stage and plan her next response. She decided that in the next game she was going to make a conscious effort to cover her area of the court. And, finally, as the second game began, Emily implemented her planned response.

THE EFFECTIVENESS OF THE COPE MODEL.   Anshel has tested his model with collegiate tennis, baseball, and softball players. In his work with tennis players, Anshel (1990) asked 12 athletes to hit a series of forehand and backhand ground strokes at a target on the opposite side of the court. The task was completed under stressful conditions (the players were asked to perform while receiving verbal reprimands from a coach). Anshel then measured the players' hitting accuracy and affective reactions to the stressor. Players were then given a 6-hour COPE intervention program. They then returned to the court to attempt to hit the same targets in the same stressful environment. As seen in Table 10.3, the athletes showed improved performance, lower anxiety and depression, and higher positive affect after receiving the COPE training. In their work with baseball and softball players, Anshel, Gregory, and Kaczmarek (1990) again found success for the COPE model. In this research, athletes were assigned to one of three conditions: a COPE treatment condition, members of which received the COPE program; a placebo treatment group, members of which watched sport videotapes; and a no treatment control group. The authors found that subjects receiving the COPE treatment were less fearful of negative evaluations and felt more in control of the situation than athletes in the other two conditions.

Increasing Anxiety and Arousal: Psyching-Up Strategies

In the previous section, we examined several techniques designed to lower anxiety/arousal and subsequently increase athletic performance. However, for some athletes the problem is not detrimentally high levels of anxiety or arousal but rather a

**TABLE 10.3   Performance and Affective Benefits
of the COPE Model**

Measure	Pretreatment	Posttreatment
*Performance**	3.12	4.24
Affect†		
Anxiety	44.37	40.67
Depression	51.20	40.23
Positive Affect	36.17	48.50

*Because subjects were awarded points for successfully hitting the target, higher scores on the performance measure reflect better performance.
†Higher scores on the affect measures reflect greater mood intensity.

lack of these states. For these athletes to improve performance, sport psychologists and consultants must increase the athlete's level of anxiety and arousal prior to competition. Strategies and techniques designed to increase an athlete's anxiety/arousal are referred to as ***psyching-up strategies.***

Psyching-up strategies tend to be the opposite of relaxation training techniques. While relaxation training is used to lower anxiety and arousal to optimal levels, psyching-up strategies are designed to increase somatic anxiety (but not cognitive anxiety) to optimal levels. Some psyching-up strategies are initiated by the athletes themselves, while others are initiated by a coach or sport psychologist. As for athlete-initiated strategies, researchers have identified six common techniques used by athletes to increase their arousal (Caudill, Weinberg, & Jackson, 1983; Dorney, Goh, & Lee, 1992; Murphy, Woolfolk, & Budney, 1988; Shelton & Mahoney, 1978; Weinberg, 1984; Weinberg, Gould, & Jackson, 1980). Some athletes psych-up by increasing their attentional focus on the task at hand. Other athletes actually psych-up by relaxing their muscles. A third method involves an attempt to increase confidence and self-efficacy. A fourth method involves preparatory arousal. For example, some athletes attempt to increase their arousal directly, often by becoming angry (baseball fans may remember Al Hrabosky, a pitcher who readily used this psyching-up strategy). Others prefer to use imagery, visualizing themselves succeeding at a task (imagery is discussed further below and in the next chapter). Finally, some athletes attempt to psych-up by listening to inspirational music prior to competition.

There are also several psyching-up strategies that can be initiated by coaches and sport psychologists. Sometimes coaches' attempts to psych-up their players border on the bazaar. For example, as discussed at the beginning of the motivation chapter, coaches have tried anything from faking their own deaths to the castration of a bull in an attempt to psych-up their players. Thankfully, coaches and sport consultants also use more reasonable strategies. For example, many coaches implement a strategic goal setting plan to energize their players. Recall from Chapter 8 that difficult but attainable goals lead to the highest levels of arousal. Thus, when coaches set these types of goals, they are in effect psyching-up their athletes. Other coaches use pep talks and visual cues such as signs and bulletin boards in an attempt to psych-up their teams. In fact, the pregame pep talks of coaches such as Knute Rockne, Vince Lombardi, and Red Auerbach have become legendary. Because some members of a team may already be operating at high levels of arousal, these team-directed pep talks may be harmful. That is, coaches should not attempt to psych-up players who are already at their optimal level of arousal because the additional arousal may be detrimental to performance.

During the past 20 years, researchers have attempted to document empirically the performance benefits of psyching-up strategies. Shelton and Mahoney (1978) conducted one of the first investigations. This study consisted of three trials. Weight lifters were first asked to squeeze a hand dynamometer to determine a baseline measure of their hand strength. Subjects were then asked to count backwards by seven from a four-digit number, after which their hand strength was again assessed. This trial served as a measure of the effect of distraction. At this point, half of the subjects were assigned to a psyching-up group, while the other half were placed in a control group. Prior to the third (and most critical) trial, the psyching-up group was asked to "think about ways of psyching yourself up for your best effort" (Shelton & Mahoney, 1978, p. 278). The control group was again asked to count backwards. The results showed the beneficial effects of the psyching-up strategies. Although the control showed a slight decrease in performance from trial 2 to trial 3 (-1.46 Kg), the psyching-up group showed a dramatic increase in performance ($+3.47$ Kg). Psyching-up strategies have also been found to improve performance at leg strength exercises (Weinberg et al., 1980), track and field (Caudill et al., 1983), and calisthenics such as sit-ups, push-ups, and pull-ups (Weinberg, Jackson, & Seabourne, 1985). Thus, it appears that psyching-up strategies are an effective intervention tactic for increasing the arousal and performance of athletes.

ATHLETIC INJURY MANAGEMENT

As noted in a previous chapter, several studies have found a positive relationship between anxiety and athletic injury. Furthermore, athletic injuries often foster feelings of anxiety. Therefore, the relationship between anxiety and injury appears to be reciprocal (see Figure 10.2). Anxious athletes are more likely to suffer an injury than nonanxious athletes, and the injury itself will most likely lead to anxiety. Thus, to have a complete grasp of the interventions involving anxious athletes, an understanding of the types of interventions used with injured players is necessary.

For all athletes, sport injury is an unwanted possibility. Unfortunately for many participants, this possibility becomes a reality. As a result of the large number of injured athletes, interest in the psychology of sport injuries has expanded. Some psychologists are interested in furthering our understanding of the psychological and personality correlates of sport injuries (such as anxiety). This line of research was discussed in the personality chapter. Other sport psychologists have devoted their attention to the benefits of providing psychological intervention strategies to injured athletes. These strategies are the focus of this section.

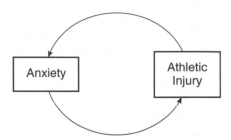

FIGURE 10.2 The reciprocal relationship between anxiety
and athletic injury.

The Treatment Team

Team approaches are becoming quite popular in the treatment of sport injuries because this approach allows for a wider range of services (Heil, 1993a). The treatment
team typically consists of a physician (who often specializes in sports medicine), an
athletic trainer (and sometimes a physical therapist), a clinical psychologist, and a
sport psychologist. As for the physician's role on the treatment team, this person must
serve as an educator, explaining the situation to the athlete and presenting the athlete with the pros and cons of the various treatment options (Heil, Bowman, & Bean,
1993; Petrie, 1993). Because the athlete may feel unsure of his or her condition, confused about treatment options, and anxious about the treatment, the educator role
is especially important. Ultimately, the athlete will base any treatment decisions on
the information provided by the physician. As a result, physicians must be honest,
be thorough, and speak in laymen's terms when describing treatment possibilities.

Because the athletic trainer often has a large amount of contact and positive
rapport with the injured athlete, this individual is an extremely important member of
the treatment team (Henderson & Carroll, 1993; Wiese-Bjornstal & Smith, 1993). The
high amount of contact allows the trainer to monitor the behaviors and psychological disposition of the athlete closely. If the athlete begins to exhibit a high level of
distress, it will probably be the trainer who first notices the situation. Heil et al. (1993)
note that, because athletic trainers often lack psychological and counseling training,
they are often "left to their own devices when it comes to treating 'bruised' egos or
'wounded' pride" (p. 245). Because trainers are a vital part of the treatment team, the
lack of an educational background in psychology is unfortunate. It is hoped that athletic trainers will realize the importance of sport psychology in treating injured athletes and subsequently seek to educate themselves. The texts listed in the Suggested
Readings section at the end of this chapter will be helpful in this endeavor.

Of course, sport psychologists are the most important members of the treatment team from a psychological perspective. If the sport psychologist is a clinical
sport psychologist, then another clinician may not be necessary. However, if the sport
psychologist is an educational sport psychologist, a licensed clinical psychologist will
be necessary to deal with the athlete's emotional problems. This is not meant to imply that the work of an educational sport psychologist is unwanted or unnecessary

when dealing with injured athletes. On the contrary, the performance enhancement training of these individuals is extremely important.

The athlete, coaches, teammates, and parents should also be considered extensions of the treatment team (Heil, 1993a; Wiese-Bjornstal & Smith, 1993). The athlete's impressions are important because he or she has a unique vantage point and may best understand his or her current psychological state. Parents, coaches, and teammates are important because they, too, may have insight into the patient's physiological and psychological state and because they are the primary members of the athlete's social support network.

Psychological Responses to Sport Injuries

Athletes display a wide variety of psychological responses to injury including negative reactions such as depression, low self-esteem, and stress (Brewer, Linder, & Phelps, 1995; Brewer & Petrie, 1995; Leddy, Lambert, & Ogles, 1994). Factors such as the magnitude of the injury, the success of the rehabilitation program, the athlete's personality, and level of competition have an impact on the athlete's responses, rendering the responses somewhat idiosyncratic (May & Sieb, 1987; Wiese & Weiss, 1987). However, some generalities across different populations and settings can be found. To help in the understanding of psychological responses to athletic injuries, a few authors have developed comprehensive theories of reactions to injuries. In the following sections, we will examine two such theories: affective cycle theory and cognitive appraisal theory. We will then examine a few specific factors that affect an athlete's responses to injury.

Affective Cycle Theory of Responses to Athletic Injury.   In an attempt to account for athletes' responses to injury, Heil (1993b) presented an ***affective cycle theory of responses to injury.*** This perspective argues that an athlete's reaction to injury is comprised of three different responses: distress, denial, and determined coping (see Figure 10.3). Distress (similar to what we have termed anxiety) involves the negative emotional impact of the injury and includes shock, anger, guilt, humiliation, and helplessness. Denial includes feelings of disbelief and possibly an "outright failure to accept the severity of injury" (Heil, 1993b, p. 37). Denial itself is nei-

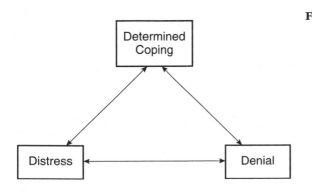

FIGURE 10.3 The affective cycle theory of responses to injury. (Adapted by permission from J. Heil, 1993, "A Psychologist's View of the Personal Challenge of Injury." In *Psychology of Sport Injury,* edited by J. Heil [Champaign, IL: Human Kinetics], 37.)

ther positive nor negative. Rather, it is the use of denial that is important. For example, a temporary period of denial may provide the athlete with a tool for holding back many distressing emotions. Denial becomes a hindrance to rehabilitation when it completely blocks the athlete's negative emotional responses and, as a result, these emotions are never released and replaced with determined coping. Determined coping involves the athlete's level of acceptance of the injury's severity and his or her use of positive coping strategies. Heil argues that distress and denial are foremost during the early stages of injury recovery and that athletes slowly begin to move toward determined coping as the recovery and interventional process proceeds. The psychological intervention programs initiated by the sport psychologists should facilitate movement toward determined coping. Heil believes that shifts among the three response types are quite common and that the shifts can be a function of events in the athlete's life. Although the recovery process may be proceeding nicely and an athlete may be responding with determined coping, an environmental or situational factor may lead to a shift in his response pattern. For example, if an athlete were to watch a video tape of the injury, he may return to a distress or denial response pattern.

Cognitive Appraisal Model of Responses to Athletic Injury.   Brewer (1994) suggests a different approach to understanding an athlete's reaction to injury. He believes that an athlete's reaction to a sport injury can best be understood through a ***cognitive appraisal model of responses to athletic injury*** (see Figure 10.4). Proponents of this model view an injury as an anxiety-causing stressor. As discussed in the anxiety chapter, an individual's reaction to a stressor will reflect his or her cognitive interpretation (i.e., appraisal) of the stressor. Thus, "the fact that an injury has *occurred* is considered less critical to understanding emotional reactions than is the way in which the injury is *perceived*" (Brewer, 1994, p. 90).

As shown in Figure 10.4, Brewer (1994) believes that an athlete's cognitive appraisal of an injury is a function of an individual's personality and the situation. The cognitive appraisal then influences the athlete's emotional response to the injury, and the emotional response impacts the athlete's behavioral responses (behaviors such

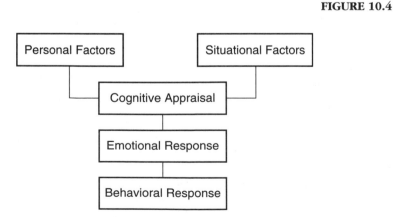

FIGURE 10.4   Cognitive appraisal model of psychological adjustment to athletic injury. (Reprinted by permission from: Brewer, B. W. [1994]. Review and critique of models of psychological adjustment to athletic injury. *Journal of Applied Sport Psychology,* 6: 87–100.)

as adherence to a rehabilitation program). Brewer suggests a number of personality characteristics that can influence an individual's cognitive appraisal of an injury. For example, athletes with a high level of self-esteem and well-developed coping skills will be more positive in their appraisal than persons low in self-esteem and lacking in coping skills. Similarly, persons who are high in trait anxiety or who have a majority of their identity invested in their athletic role may be especially negative in their appraisals. Brewer also lists a variety of situational factors that can potentially influence the athlete's cognitive appraisal. For instance, the presence of a social support network and recovery progress can lead to better adjustment and more positive appraisals, while injury severity and life stress can retard adjustment and foster negative appraisals.

Specific Factors Impacting Responses to Athletic Injury.

In this section, we will review the impact of three specific factors on responses to athletic injury. Specifically, we will examine the length of time since the injury, the athlete's attributions about the injury, and the athlete's coping skills.

LENGTH OF TIME SINCE THE INJURY.   A few studies have found that the immediate reactions to athletic injuries are highly negative, but reactions become more positive with the passage of time (Leddy et al., 1994; McDonald & Hardy, 1990). For example, Quackenbush and Crossman (1994) examined the positive and negative emotional responses during four postinjury stages: immediately after sustaining the injury, the following day, during rehabilitation, and when returning to practice. Previously injured athletes were presented with a set of four checklists, each containing 36 negative and 12 positive emotions. The four checklists reflected the four postinjury stages. The athletes were asked to check the emotions they experienced during each of the four periods. The authors found that the athletes were likely to experience negative emotions shortly after sustaining the injury and unlikely to experience positive emotions during this period. However, the athletes reported experiencing fewer negative emotions and more positive emotions as time passed. For instance, 64% of the respondents reported feeling angry when initially sustaining the injury. However, only 8% reported feeling angry when returning to practice. As for the positive emotions, none of the athletes reported feeling enthusiastic or good when the injury occurred, but 48% reported these emotions when returning to practice.

THE IMPACT OF ATTRIBUTIONS.   The attributional process can also be a factor in an athlete's psychological reaction to injury. Recall from the previous chapter that attributions are estimates of the causes of behavior. An athlete's psychological response to an injury will vary depending on how and to whom the athlete assigns blame for the injury (i.e., to what does the athlete attribute the cause of her injury). If the athlete blames herself for the injury, she is quite likely to react with feelings of guilt, particularly if she feels as though she has let her teammates down (Heil, 1993c). On the other hand, the athlete is more likely to respond with anger if she believes that another individual is responsible for her injury (such as a coach, teammate, or competitor).

THE IMPACT OF COPING SKILLS.   An athlete's psychological response to an injury is also influenced by his or her coping abilities (Heil, 1993b). Athletes with better coping strategies (i.e., strategies that tend to be active) and athletes with a strong social support network will likely exhibit better psychological responses to the injury than those with poor coping strategies and poor support systems. It is for this reason that psychological interventions are important to injured athletes: They help the athlete develop adaptive coping strategies and establish a social support network. In the following section, we will examine several intervention strategies that can aid the psychological and physiological rehabilitation of injured athletes.

Psychological Intervention for Injured Athletes

Psychological interventions are a vital component of an athlete's recovery from injury. Without psychological interventions, athletes are unlikely to obtain a speedy and optimal recovery (Steadman, 1993). The benefits of intervention strategies are not limited to the elite or professional athlete. Rather, the weekend athlete is also likely to incur a sport injury. In fact, Steadman (1993, p. 25) refers to sport injuries as "the great equalizer," implying that, although their talent levels may be quite different, the challenges facing novice and elite injured athletes are identical. As such, psychological interventions are equally important for both groups.

Injury interventions involve two distinct steps. First, the psychologist must complete a clear and precise assessment of the psychological ramifications of the injury. Second, based on the assessment, psychologists can recommend and begin implementing a player-specific psychological intervention program. We will now examine each of these steps.

Assessing the Psychological Impact of Sport Injuries.   Heil (1993c) states that the purpose of the psychological assessment of an injured athlete is twofold. First, the sport psychologist must determine the subjective cost of the injury to the athlete. That is, the psychologist must assess the psychological impact of the injury. This assessment should not be limited to those factors associated with the injury. Rather, the psychologist should also examine factors preceding the injury and factors following the injury. Important preinjury factors include the athlete's medical and psychological history, an assessment of various life stressors, and the approach of a major competition. Postinjury factors include compliance with treatment, perceived effectiveness of the treatment, and the impact of fans and the media (Heil, 1993c). These and other preinjury and postinjury factors can have a large impact on the effectiveness of the rehabilitation process. For example, because researchers have found that athletic injuries become more likely as a major competition approaches (Kerr & Minden, 1988), an understanding of the athlete's current schedule of competition may shed some light on the psychological impact of the injury. This understanding may assist in the selection of the intervention strategies most appropriate for this particular athlete.

The second purpose of the psychological assessment is to develop an understanding of the athlete's coping strategies and abilities. Each athlete will cope with an injury in a different fashion. Only through an understanding of the athlete's coping styles and abilities will the psychologist be able to prescribe an intervention strategy that uses the athlete's coping strengths and assists the athlete with his or her coping weaknesses.

THE INTERVIEW.   The main component of the assessment process is the personal interview. Interviews should be conducted alone (to help insure confidentiality) and in comfortable surroundings (Wiese-Bjornstal & Smith, 1993). Interviews should provide the information needed to form an accurate diagnosis of the psychological impact of the injury. However, as Heil (1993d) notes, the psychologist must weigh the information-gathering benefit of asking highly personal questions against the cost of making the athlete feel uncomfortable. Interviews that are conducted in a caring and nonobtrusive manner may facilitate the psychologist–athlete relationship. The athlete will begin to trust the psychologist and experience a reduction in anxiety. Therefore, the psychologist must be aware of the athlete's reactions to the interview process. If the athlete appears to be highly distressed by the line of questioning, the psychologist should begin a less intrusive set of questions. If the answers to the current questions are necessary to assess the athlete's reaction to the injury, the psychologist should temporarily end the session and allow the athlete to regroup. The length of the break will be a function of the athlete's level of distress and resistance to the questioning.

PSYCHOLOGICAL TESTING.   The psychologist may want to supplement the interview process by asking the athlete to complete a battery of psychological tests (Heil, 1993d). A number of tests are available. For example, the Minnesota Multiphasic Personality Inventory (Hathaway & McKinley, 1943), the Cattell 16 Personality Factor Questionnaire (Cattell et al., 1970), and the Profile of Mood States (McNair et al., 1971) are all general psychological inventories that may shed light on the athlete's current psychological state (see Chapter 4 for a discussion of these tests). Sport-specific inventories may also be useful. For example, the Sport Competition Anxiety Test and the Competitive State Anxiety Inventory-2 can assist in the assessment of the athlete's current level of anxiety (Martens et al., 1990, see Chapter 7).

Intervention Strategies.   Based on the information gained from the assessment, the psychologist (in collaboration with the other members of the treatment team) can develop a treatment plan incorporating one or more intervention strategies. A number of interventions have proven to be effective with injured athletes. In the following sections, we will review several of these strategies.

PROACTIVE INTERVENTIONS.   **Proactive interventions** are designed to intervene before an injury occurs (Sachs, Sitler, & Schwille, 1993). As noted, because some personal and psychological factors may predispose athletes to injury, it can be beneficial to identify those athletes who are at risk prior to the injury. Identification usually involves interviews and a rather substantial amount of psychological testing. Ideally, the interviews and tests will review the athlete's background, level of and responses to stress and anxiety, physical health, psychological state, and coping abilities (Grove, 1993; Sachs et al., 1993). After identifying athletes with a personality and psychological profile indicative of injury occurrence, the psychologist and other

A number of psychological intervention strategies can be used to help injured athletes. (Source: Gamma-Liaison, Inc.)

members of the treatment team can initiate an intervention package designed to prevent the injury. For example, imagine an athlete who was identified as a high risk individual because of her extremely high level of stress and anxiety. Once the athlete's risk was identified, the sport psychologist could begin working with the athlete to reduce her anxiety before she incurs an injury. Such a program would be welcomed by athletes and seems to be a pleasant alternative to programs beginning after an injury.

SOCIAL SUPPORT.   Social support interventions are based on the premise that social support can serve as a buffer to negative emotions and anxiety. As discussed in Chapter 7, this reasoning is well supported by research (e.g., Brewer, 1993; Linville, 1987; Thoits, 1983; Wann & Hamlet, 1994). Because of its buffering qualities, social support can facilitate recovery from athletic injuries (Duda, Smart, & Tappe, 1989; Wiese & Weiss, 1987). As such, social support is viewed as an effective intervention strategy, one that can be used in combination with other interventional programs.

Social support interventions begin with an assessment of the nature of the distress. Next, the psychologist and treatment team members match the needs of the athlete (based on the athlete's distress) with the appropriate source (i.e., "who") and form (i.e., "what") of social support (Hardy & Crace, 1993). As for the "who" of support, a number of individuals can become members of a social support network.

Coaches, teammates, parents, friends, and members of the treatment team can all provide valuable support (Heil, 1993e). For example, coaches can provide support by allowing and encouraging the injured athlete to attend practices and participate in team meetings. This should help the athlete reestablish or maintain her or his athletic identity. Further, coaches, athletic trainers, and teammates can establish support groups comprised of currently and formerly injured athletes. The groups can focus their discussions on the rehabilitation process and provide reassurance to one another.

Hardy and Crace (1993) list three different forms of social support: emotional, tangible, and informational. Emotional support involves "being there" for the injured athlete and is the most important form of support immediately following the injury. Typically, emotional support is accomplished through active listening and genuine feelings of empathy. Tangible support is a materialistic form of assistance. An example of a tangible support would be providing a ride for the injured athlete. Informational support is an educational form of support and involves instructional feedback and assisting in the athlete's understanding of his or her injury.

MODELING.   Modeling has also been successfully employed as an intervention tactic (Weiss & Troxel, 1986). Flint (1993) states that there are two types of modeling programs for use with injured athletes: informal and formal. Informal modeling strategies occur naturally during the rehabilitation process. When psychologists or athletic trainers describe others who have successfully recovered from an athletic injury, they are using an informal strategy. Formal modeling tactics are deliberate attempts to provide the athlete with a suitable model. The model then provides the injured person with pertinent information. The model may be presented in live form (for instance, a roommate in the hospital) or on videotape. Because formal modeling procedures are more structured, the amount of information presented is usually greater and, therefore, more beneficial to the athlete.

Regardless of whether a psychologist employs a formal strategy, an informal strategy, or both, the key to the success of the modeling intervention lies in (1) satisfying each component of the modeling process and (2) the information presented. Recall from Chapter 5 that Bandura (1986) proposed a four-stage process of modeling. The four steps are: (1) attention, (2) memory, (3) behavior reproduction, and (4) motivation. For a model's behavior to be reproduced, the individual must pay attention to the model; remember the model's behavior; have the physical, psychological, and cognitive abilities to reproduce the behavior; and be motivated to reproduce the behavior. If one of these components is missing, the individual will not imitate the model's actions. Thus, for the modeling intervention strategy (formal or informal) to be effective, the sport psychologist must insure that the components have been met. For example, the psychologist can increase the attention toward the model by using attractive, nurturing, or prestigious models (see Chapter 5 for further discussion of Bandura's model).

However, successfully including each of the four components does not insure a sound modeling interventional strategy. Rather, the psychologist must allow (or even train) the model to present the correct information to the injured athlete (Flint,

1993). For example, imagine that a sport consultant has decided to implement a formal modeling intervention system for an athlete having difficulty with her rehabilitation program. The consultant has decided to have the athlete continue her rehabilitation program in the presence of a model who has successfully completed a similar program. However, unbeknownst to the consultant, the model is extremely dissatisfied with the recovery program. As a result, when the model and athlete converse, the model provides the athlete with negative information, a situation that will most likely disrupt the athlete's recovery. To eliminate this possibility, psychologists must monitor the information being provided to the injured person. Several different types of information are beneficial to the injured athlete and, therefore, should be provided by the model. For example, athletes should receive information concerning successful coping strategies, medical information about upcoming surgeries or treatment programs, methods of managing and increasing adherence to rehabilitation programs, and pain management strategies. When the injured athlete is provided with this type of useful information, the modeling intervention strategy will be beneficial to the recovery process and the athlete's psychological well-being.

GOAL SETTING.   As discussed in the motivation chapter, specific and difficult goals and providing feedback about goal attainment can facilitate performance. Thus, it should come as no surprise that effective goals can help an athlete recover from an injury (Wiese & Weiss, 1987). The goals should be developed through the joint efforts of the treatment team and the injured athlete. In addition, the goals should target a variety of time frames, including daily, weekly, and monthly progress (Ievleva & Orlick, 1993). Daily goals can be especially effective because athletes will view these goals as more attainable than long-term goals (Ievleva & Orlick, 1991). For example, if the sport psychologist simply says "Your goal is to return to your former level of performance," the goal may be rejected because it is perceived as impossible.

It is also important to set a wide variety of goals, rather than to focus solely on the athlete's physical recovery (Heil, 1993e). Additional goals should focus on taking medication and wearing/using support devices in the prescribed manner and on the athlete's coping abilities and psychological recovery. For instance, athletes may be asked to reduce their negative thinking to a certain number of thoughts per day while simultaneously increasing their positive self-statements. In this way, the benefits of goal setting can be extended beyond the athlete's physical rehabilitation process to include the athlete's psychological rehabilitation.

A recent investigation by Brewer, Jeffers, Petitpas, and Van Raalte (1994) revealed that athletes rate goal setting as the most effective psychological intervention for injuries. In this research, two groups of athletes were asked to rate the effectiveness of three injury intervention tactics: goal setting, imagery (see below), and counseling (asking open-ended questions and providing support in a counseling atmosphere). The first group of subjects was comprised of college students. These subjects read a scenario describing an injured athlete working with a sport psychologist. Subjects read that the athlete was receiving either a goal setting, imagery, or counseling intervention. Subjects were then asked to provide their estimates of the success of the intervention. The authors found that while all three tactics were thought to be beneficial, subjects believed the goal setting strategy to be most useful. The second group of subjects was comprised of injured athletes. These participants were presented with a short presentation describing each of the three intervention strategies. Subjects were then asked to rate the strategies. Consistent with the first group of subjects, the injured athletes gave positive ratings to all three tactics and the highest rating to the goal setting approach.

IMAGERY. **Imagery** involves the mental visualization of a task prior to or while engaging in the task. Green (1992) lists three main uses of imagery relevant to sport injuries, each use being tied to the chronology of the injury (the use of imagery as a performance enhancement strategy for noninjured athletes will be described in the next chapter). First, imagery may be used prior to injury occurrence. As noted, psychological states such as stress and anxiety may facilitate athletic injury. Imagery used prior to injury may reduce stress and anxiety, thereby reducing the likelihood of injury. Therefore, imagery can be used as a proactive intervention strategy.

The second use of imagery with injured athletes involves intervention immediately after the injury has occurred but prior to surgery or rehabilitation (Green, 1992). This form of imagery is designed to assist the athlete in developing an understanding of the nature of the injury. Athletes should be encouraged to produce images of upcoming surgery and rehabilitation, the maintenance of a positive attitude, and the effective control of emotions.

The third use of imagery occurs during the rehabilitation process (Green, 1992; Porter & Foster, 1986). Green (1992) refers to this use as "creating the mind set for recovery" (p. 209). This use of imagery is founded on the notion of a mind-body relationship. The mind-body relationship involves the ability of the mind to affect bodily functioning. Several research endeavors have supported the idea of a mind-body link by indicating a relationship between one's mental state and recovery from illness and injury (Achterberg, Matthews-Simonton, & Simonton, 1977; Epstein, 1986; Fiore, 1988; Siegel, 1986, 1989). Based on these findings, an athlete should be able to facilitate his progress by imagining himself successfully recovering from the injury. Green (1992) lists several images that should assist the athlete's maintenance of a positive outlook. For example, athletes should imagine themselves (1) reaching their rehabilitation goals, (2) reaching performance levels, and (3) successfully coping with pain. Also, athletes should mentally picture the injured body part recovering quickly and completely. An example of this strategy, referred to as rehabilitative imagery (Green, 1992) and healing imagery (Ievleva & Orlick, 1991), would include an athlete with a broken arm mentally picturing the bone healing and the swelling and pain subsiding.

SUMMARY

A variety of psychological intervention strategies have been used to enhance athletic performance. One set of strategies involves the control of anxiety and arousal. Some of these strategies are designed for use with athletes suffering from a detrimentally high level of somatic and cognitive anxiety. Intervention tactics for chronic anxiety include personal coping strategies (such as active coping and seeking social support), relaxation training procedures (such as progressive relaxation, biofeedback, and meditation), and stress management training. The COPE model may be the most useful strategy for the reduction of acute anxiety. This model involves controlling emotions, organizing inputs into meaningful and nonmeaningful categories, planning the next response, and executing the response. Research has found each of these strategies can successfully lower anxiety and improve athletic performance, although meditation appears to be beneficial for gross motor activities rather than fine motor activities. A second subset of anxiety control strategies, referred to as psyching-up strategies, involves attempts to increase the athlete's arousal to an optimal level.

Because research has indicated a relationship between stress/anxiety and athletic injury, it is important to discuss the psychological interventions designed to assist injured athletes with their recovery. Most frequently, these interventions are executed using a treatment team consisting of a physician, an athletic trainer, a clinical psychologist, and a sport psychologist. A number of interventions are available for use with injured athletes including proactive intervention strategies, social support, modeling, goal setting, and imagery.

GLOSSARY

Active Coping Strategies   Strategies for coping with anxiety that attempt to change, alter, or remove the stressor, thereby reducing or eliminating its impact.

Affective Cycle Theory of Responses to Injury   A perspective arguing that an athlete's reaction to injury is comprised of three different responses: distress, denial, and determined coping.

Anxiety Matching Hypothesis   A perspective reflecting the belief that cognitive intervention strategies will be most effective and should be used with individuals experiencing problematic levels of cognitive anxiety, while somatic intervention strategies will be most effective and should be used with individuals experiencing problematic levels of somatic anxiety.

Biofeedback   The use of instruments that monitor autonomic processes, thereby allowing individuals to develop some control over these processes.

Cognitive Appraisal Model of Responses to Athletic Injury   A model reflecting the belief that an athlete's emotional and behavioral responses to an injury will be a function of his or her cognitive appraisal of the injury.

COPE Model   A cognitive and behavioral strategy for coping with acute sport anxiety that focuses on controlling emotions, organizing input, planning the next response, and executing the response.

Imagery   The mental visualization of a task prior to or while engaging in the task.

Meditation   The use of mental focus to calm the body.

Negative Self-Talk   Self-defeating and negative thoughts and statements.

Passive Coping Strategies   Strategies for coping with anxiety that attempt to deal with or manage the anxiety in a temporary manner without confronting the stressor itself.

Positive Self-Talk   Reassuring oneself with positive and rational thoughts and statements.

Proactive Interventions   Intervention strategies designed to intervene before an injury occurs.

Progressive Relaxation   The systematic tension and relaxation of muscle groups in an attempt to reduce anxiety.

Psyching-Up Strategies   Strategies and techniques designed to increase an athlete's arousal.

Relaxation Training   Techniques designed to lower somatic and cognitive anxiety.

Stress Management for Coaches   A model of stress management designed for coaches that includes five stages: perceptions of coaching, identification of primary stressors, identification of stress symptomatology, development of coping skills, and social support.

Stress Management Training   A comprehensive stress management program teaching individuals to relax and control their anxiety.

APPLICATION AND REVIEW QUESTIONS

1. Describe progressive relaxation, biofeedback, and meditation.
2. Imagine that you had a teammate who suffered from a detrimentally high level of anxiety. Develop a stress management training program for this individual, being sure to discuss each of the five phases.
3. Use the COPE model to help a hypothetical teammate who becomes upset when confronted with a bad call from an official.
4. Describe the appropriate use of psyching-up strategies.
5. Imagine that you are an educational sport psychologist beginning to work with a seriously injured athlete. Who would make up your treatment team? How would you assess the psychological impact of the injury? What intervention strategies would you suggest?

SUGGESTED READINGS

HEIL, J. (Ed.). (1993). *Psychology of sport injury*. Champaign, IL: Human Kinetics. This book provides the reader with a general background on the relationship between psychology and injury. Several suggestions for dealing with injured athletes are given. The discussions of a team-oriented approach to injury care and the information on pain and pain management are especially noteworthy.

Pargman, D. (Ed.). (1993). *Psychological bases of sport injuries*. Morgantown, WV: Fitness Information Technology. A second valuable source on the psychological aspects of sport injury, this text is particularly useful for individuals with an athletic training background. The chapters focusing on various intervention strategies (such as imagery and modeling) are quite informative.

Note: A number of the suggested readings listed in the next chapter involve anxiety and arousal regulation strategies.

Chapter 11

INTERVENTIONS TARGETING SELF-CONFIDENCE, IMAGERY, ATTENTION CONTROL TRAINING, AND PSYCHOLOGICAL SKILLS TRAINING

In the previous chapter, we reviewed several intervention techniques designed to regulate arousal and anxiety. In addition, because of the interactive relationship between anxiety and athletic injury, we also examined a number of intervention strategies for use with injured athletes. In the current chapter, we will review several other interventions designed to facilitate athletic performance. Specifically, we will discuss self-confidence building, imagery, attention control training, and comprehensive programs designed to improve psychological skills.

SELF-CONFIDENCE

As with most psychological traits, athletes vary in their degree of self-confidence. Some athletes can be classified as diffident (Martens, 1987b). **Diffidence** is a lack of self-confidence. These athletes believe that they do not possess the ability to complete a task successfully (i.e., they are low in self-efficacy). Because their confidence is low and, therefore, easily shaken, one small mistake can be catastrophic to these athletes. The mistake reinforces the athlete's self-doubts and subsequently leads to poorer performance (see Figure 11.1). In this way, the low level of self-confidence becomes a self-fulfilling prophecy (Martens, 1987b). The athlete's low self-confidence leads to an expectation of poor performance, the expectations lead to poor performance, and the poor performance leads to an even lower level of self-confidence.

Other athletes are overconfident (what Martens, 1987b, calls false confident). Overconfident athletes possess an inaccurate and overinflated belief about their athletic abilities. The overconfidence can be general in nature (i.e., believing one is a more gifted all-around athlete than is actually the case) or task-specific (i.e., believing one is better at a specified activity than is actually the case). Overconfidence can also be a detriment to performance (see Figure 11.1). Because of their inaccurate beliefs in their abilities, these athletes may be less likely to practice and may exert a lower level of effort during competition, both of which can impede performance. Furthermore, because overconfident athletes believe that failure is highly unlikely, they may be highly disturbed by a mistake. That is, because the mistake is unexpected, it may shock the athlete and disrupt his or her concentration and performance.

Some athletes possess an optimal level of self-confidence, a trait associated with successful performance (see Figure 11.1). These players have a realistic view of their athletic abilities. Athletes who are optimally self-confident are usually able to handle mistakes in a positive manner. Rather than viewing a mistake as another example of their inability (as with diffident athletes) or being shocked and disturbed by the mistake (as with overconfident athletes), optimally confident athletes try to learn from their mistakes, using mistakes as an indication of the limits of their ability. Other benefits of self-confidence include better concentration and positive emotional reactions (Weinberg & Gould, 1995).

FIGURE 11.1   The relationship between self-confidence and performance.

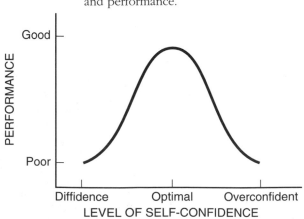

Sport psychologists and coaches can assist athletes in the development of optimal levels of self-confidence. Because an athlete's optimal level of self-confidence is based on his or her ability, it is important to develop individualized self-confidence intervention programs. For example, consider two youth baseball players, Eric and Drew. Eric's athletic skills are advanced for his age, and he is the best player on the team. Drew, on the other hand, possesses an average level of athletic ability. If the coach were to develop the same level of self-confidence in both players, one of the players would suffer. For example, if the coach wanted both players to be highly self-confident, a level that is optimal for the advanced player Eric, Drew would become overly confident and disturbed by his unexpected mistakes. Conversely, if the coach attempted to foster a level of self-confidence in both players that was optimal for Drew (the player with average ability), Eric might develop diffidence and have a less than optimal level of self-confidence.

Promoting Self-Confidence in Athletes

Athletes often incorrectly assume that their current level of confidence is unchangeable. In reality, there are several intervention strategies designed to adjust an athlete's self-confidence to an optimal level. These interventions may be especially important for young athletes because these participants are still developing their athletic confidence. Table 11.1 lists several suggestions for achieving an optimal level of self-confidence. Most of the suggestions are applicable to athletes with diffidence and those that are overconfident. For example, the suggestion that she be realistic in her abilities can help a diffident athlete increase her confidence or an overconfident athlete lower her confidence. Table 11.1 also offers several suggestions for coaches who want to enhance the self-confidence of their players (see Schunk, 1995).

IMAGERY

As discussed in the previous chapter, imagery (also called mental rehearsal and mental practice), involves the mental visualization of a task prior to or while engaging in the task. Imagery can be used in two different, but related, situations. Sometimes, imagery involves precompetition practice. In these instances, athletes mentally picture themselves performing a task in a specific setting. For example, a golfer may devote 30 minutes a day to mentally practicing her swing. Other instances involve ongoing competitions, either immediately prior to or during a contest. For example, a basketball player may visualize a successful free throw before attempting the shot. In their work with athletes from a variety of sports, Hall, Rodgers, and Barr (1990) found that athletes are more likely to use imagery in conjunction with competition than with practice, indicating that athletes appear to "consider imagery to be more important as a technique for enhancing performance than . . . as a learning aid" (p. 7). The finding that athletes are more likely to use imagery during a competition than as a form of practice has been replicated in other studies (Barr & Hall, 1992; Salmon, Hall, & Haslam, 1994). However, because both strategies can facilitate performance,

TABLE 11.1   Suggestions for Reaching an Optimal Level of Self-Confidence in Sport

Suggestions for Athletes

1. Be realistic about your athletic abilities relative to the task at hand.
2. Consider your past experiences (both successes and failures) when determining your ability at a task.
3. Use goal setting in your athletic endeavors. By setting and reaching difficult but attainable goals, your self-confidence will increase.
4. Imagine yourself thinking and acting in a confident manner while performing the task in question. (See the description of imagery later in this chapter.)
5. Be prepared. In this way, you will feel you are ready to compete, a belief that will increase your level of confidence.
6. Consider each of the four sources of efficacy information. That is, develop your confidence through your own experiences, through modeling, through persuasion, and through your own physiological state (return to Chapter 8 for a discussion of self-efficacy theory).
7. Remove catastrophic thinking and use positive self-talk. If you make a mistake, remind yourself that it is only one small part of the overall competition, attempt to learn from the mishap, and then put the error behind you.

Suggestions for Coaches

1. Similar to Item 3 above, set specific and difficult goals. Also, be sure to provide feedback concerning goal attainment.
2. Present yourself as a confident role model. If you express a lack of confidence in your players, they will continue to experience a low level of self-confidence.
3. Point out athletes who have an optimal level of confidence and use these athletes as role models.
4. Continually praise your athletes. Offer only constructive criticism and do so in private.
5. Offer quality instruction and drilling.
6. Encourage positive self-talk.
7. Construct a highlight video for each player that includes clips of their outstanding performances and inspirational music (see Leavitt, Young, & Connelly, 1989).

sport psychologists should encourage athletes to use imagery both prior to and during a competition.

Internal and External Imagery

Imagery can be classified as internal or external. When using ***internal imagery,*** athletes imagine their surroundings and behaviors from their own vantage point. If a basketball player were to picture a free throw from his own perspective (i.e., as if he were looking at the backboard and the other players through his own eyes), he would be using internal imagery. On the other hand, if this player were to imagine the situation from the perspective of someone else and see himself in the image, he would be using ***external imagery.*** Some researchers have suggested that internal imagery is more likely to enhance performance (Hale, 1982; Harris & Robinson, 1986; Mahoney & Avener, 1977; Smith, 1987). In fact, a metaanalysis conducted by Hinshaw (1991–1992) found that internal imagery produced greater performance gains than external imagery. However, other researchers have questioned the superiority of internal imagery (Meyers et al., 1979; Mumford & Hall, 1985). For example, Gordon, Weinberg, and Jackson (1994) found that the performances of cricket bowlers did not differ as a function of whether they were instructed to adopt an internal versus an external perspective. Because many athletes switch back and forth between the two forms of imagery (Gordon et al., 1994; Murphy, 1994; Ungerleider & Golding, 1991; Wang & Morgan, 1992), the ability to use both styles is probably best, particularly if one is able to match a style with a particular setting.

Individual Differences in Imagery Ability

Research has found that individuals differ in the ability to produce mental images (Clark, 1960; Harris & Robinson, 1986; Murphy, 1994; Richardson, 1994). For example, people vary in their ability to form vivid and controllable images (Murphy & Jowdy, 1992). However, imagery skills can be improved through practice (Rodgers, Hall, & Buckolz, 1991). Athletes already possessing strong imagery abilities can perfect their skills, while those lacking in imagery ability are able to acquire at least a basic level of imagery skill. Some writers have suggested techniques for assisting athletes in enhancing their imagery skills (Hickman, 1979; Nideffer, 1992; Smith, 1987). A general list of suggestions can be found in Table 11.2.

Imagery and Performance

A number of studies have examined the relationship between imagery and athletic performance. Taken as a whole, these studies show that imagery can be highly beneficial to performance (Hinshaw, 1991–1992), although as discussed in this chapter's "A Closer Look," researchers have disagreed on the reasons underlying the perfor-

---

TABLE 11.2   Suggestions for Developing Imagery Skills in Sport

1. Find a quiet setting and become as relaxed as possible.
2. Develop vivid images. Images that are sharp, include color, and realistically reflect one's surroundings are most beneficial.
3. When possible, use past experiences to shape the image.
4. Use as many senses as possible. For example, if you are imagining a free throw, attempt to see the basket, hear the crowd, feel the texture of the ball, and feel the perspiration running down your face.
5. Use positive rather than negative imagery. That is, control your image in a way that leads to a successful outcome.
6. Imagine the situation from both an internal and an external perspective. Determine the perspective that works best for you. Remember that a combination of internal and external viewpoints may be best and that you should not feel compelled to choose only one perspective.
7. Adopt the proper attitude. Like most mental and psychological skills, imagery is limited by the user's belief in the usefulness of the process. If you begin an imagery training program with doubts about its effectiveness, the imagery will be less successful.
8. Practice your imagery skills. Your imagery ability will improve over time and the performance benefits will grow accordingly.
9. Perhaps most important, evaluate your progress. Be prepared to alter your imagery program as indicated by your evaluation.

A CLOSER LOOK:
HOW IMAGERY ENHANCES ATHLETIC PERFORMANCE:
TWO DISTINCT THEORIES

As stated in the text, a number of research endeavors have documented the performance benefits of imagery. However, while researchers do not dispute the effectiveness of imagery, they do disagree on the reasons underlying the benefits. Although several theories have been proposed to account for the performance-enhancing effects of imagery, we will limit our discussion to two of the more popular theories: psychoneuromuscular theory and symbolic learning theory. Both theories have gained research support, indicating that both approaches may be correct.

Psychoneuromuscular theory reflects the belief that imagery facilitates performance by producing innervation (i.e., stimulation) in an individual's muscles that is similar to actual physical movements. That is, as athletes imagine themselves engaging in a physical activity, there are small and typically undetectable muscular impulses reflecting the imagined activity. For instance, this theory postulates that if a baseball player were to imagine himself hitting a ball, the muscles involved in the execution of the swing would be stimulated. Several studies have supported the psychoneuromuscular theory, particularly those investigating internal imagery (e.g., Hale, 1982; Harris & Robinson, 1986; Jacobson, 1931; Wang & Morgan, 1992). For example, consider the work of Suinn (1976) with downhill skiers. In this research, skiers were asked to imagine skiing a downhill course while the experimenter monitored the electrical activity in their leg muscles. Muscle activity was highest when subjects imagined skiing a difficult section of the course. Because the difficult section would require the greatest muscle activity in an actual run, Suinn's findings support the psychoneuromuscular theory.

A second theory accounting for the benefits of imagery is symbolic learning theory (Sackett, 1934). *Symbolic learning theory* reflects the belief that imagery facilitates performance by providing individuals with a mental code and plan of their movements, thus making the movements more familiar and automatic. For example, this theory states that in the baseball example described above, the mental image of the swing will result in a mental code that will facilitate performance. Like the psychoneuromuscular theory, symbolic learning theory has received empirical support (e.g., Hird et al., 1991; Ryan & Simons, 1981, 1983). Most support lies in the finding that imagery is most successful with activities containing a cognitive component. This finding is consistent with symbolic learning theory because tasks with a high cognitive component should result in the most detailed and informative mental code and plan, resulting in an automatic behavior.

mance improvements. Research has found that, while imagery may not be quite as effective as physical practice (Clark, 1960; Corbin, 1967; Grouios, 1992; Hird, Landers, Thomas, & Horan, 1991), it is certainly better than no practice at all (Grouios, 1992; Feltz & Landers, 1983; Richardson, 1967a, 1967b). In fact, imagery has been found to enhance performance in a number of different sports including endurance tasks (Dorney et al., 1992; Lee, 1990), basketball (Meyers, Schleser, & Okwumabua, 1982; Predebon & Docker, 1992; Templin & Vernacchia, 1995), dart throwing (Vandell, Davis, & Clugston, 1943), soccer (Salmon et al., 1994), diving (Grouios, 1992), juggling (Corbin, 1967), volleyball (Shick, 1970), golf (Meacci & Price, 1985; Murphy & Woolfolk, 1987; Woolfolk, Parrish, & Murphy, 1985), skating (Rodgers et al., 1991), gymnastics (Lee & Hewitt, 1987), track and field (Ungerleider & Golding, 1991), SCUBA diving (Griffiths, Steel, Vaccaro, Allen, & Karpman, 1985), and downhill skiing (Suinn, 1972, 1976).

It may be possible to increase the effectiveness of imagery by combining imagery with self-modeling (Templin & Vernacchia, 1995). Recall from Chapter 5 that self-modeling involves videotaping an athlete's exceptional performances and then allowing the player to model her or his own successful behaviors (rather than the successful behaviors of a stranger). By viewing her or his own successful performances, an athlete should be able to develop a highly vivid and personally relevant image for use in a mental practice routine. These types of images are especially effective in enhancing sport performance.

Although imagery can be beneficial to performance, the positive effects are limited in three ways. First, a handful of studies have indicated that imagery is only successful for persons who are somewhat skilled at the task in question (e.g., Clark, 1960; Corbin, 1967; Epstein, 1980; Gray, 1990). For example, imagine a teenager who has never shot a basketball. If one were to ask this person to practice a free throw mentally, the imagery would not be helpful because the person has no prior knowledge or experience to serve as the basis of his mental practice.

Second, the greatest benefits of imagery appear to be limited to certain types of activities. Activities involving cognitive and visual components appear to be best suited for imagery (Andre & Means, 1986; Feltz & Landers, 1983). For example, figure skating, long jumping, and gymnastics all include the cognitive component of the memorization of foot placements. Likewise, activities such as hitting in baseball/softball and putting in golf are ideal for imagery strategies because they can be easily visualized. In these and similar activities, imagery will be quite effective. However, imagery will be less effective in activities that are based on gross motor movements that are not easily visualized (such as weightlifting, push-ups, and sit-ups). For example, in a study of runners, Burhans, Richman, and Bergey (1988) found that subjects in imagery conditions did not perform better than those in a control condition.

Third, research has indicated that simply imagining a behavior is not enough to produce an increase in performance. Rather, the athlete should also imagine the outcome of the behavior. The type of outcome imagined is extremely important. Research has found that, while ***positive imagery*** (i.e., imagining a successful outcome) will enhance performance, ***negative imagery*** (i.e., imagining a negative/unsuccessful outcome) can be detrimental to performance (Martin & Hall, 1995;

Murphy, 1994; Powell, 1973; Woolfolk et al., 1985). The performance inhibiting effects of negative imagery were documented by Woolfolk, Murphy, Gottesfeld, and Aitken (1985). These authors examined the putting performances of college undergraduates. Subjects were given imagery instructions prior to attempting their putts. Some subjects were asked to form negative images, imagining that the ball was "rolling, rolling, toward the cup, but at the last second narrowly missing" (p. 193). Other subjects were asked to form positive images, mentally picturing the ball "rolling, rolling, right into the cup" (p. 193). Woolfolk and his colleagues found that, while the positive imagery subjects displayed a modest improvement in performance, the negative imagery subjects exhibited a drastic decrease in performance.

Combining Imagery with Relaxation Training: Visuo-Motor Behavior Rehearsal

In the 1970s, Suinn (1972, 1976) developed a motor performance enhancement program titled *visuo-motor behavior rehearsal* (VMBR). Visuo-motor behavior rehearsal involves two steps (Suinn, 1993). First, the athlete receives relaxation training through one of the methods described in Chapter 10. Second, the athlete is trained in the use of positive imagery. The images should be as real and game-like as possible such that the athlete mentally experiences the event. When the athlete uses imagery in a relaxed state, the result will be images that are real enough to resemble dreams (Suinn, 1993). However, because the athlete remains in control of the image, VMBR has obvious advantages over dreams.

A number of case studies have documented the advantages of VMBR. One study, described by Titley (1976), involved a college football place kicker who was given VMBR training. During the season prior to the training, the kicker had missed several crucial late-game field goals. However, the player's performance showed a dramatic improvement after the VMBR training, and he even kicked an NCAA record 63-yard field goal. Another study was conducted by Kearns and Crossman (1992). These authors examined the pre-VMBR treatment and post-VMBR treatment free throw shooting of three collegiate basketball players. After receiving the VMBR training, the players' performances improved during both practices and games. Suinn (1993) summarizes other case studies using VMBR in which individual performances have improved in bowling, tennis, basketball, golf, and baseball.

There have also been a number of experimental studies documenting the effectiveness of VMBR (e.g., Gray, 1990; Hall & Erffmeyer, 1983; Hall & Hardy, 1991; Lane, 1980). Weinberg, Seabourne, and Jackson (1981) conducted one of the first controlled experimental studies examining VMBR. These authors investigated the performances of students in a karate club. Subjects were placed into one of four groups: relaxation and imagery (VMBR), relaxation only, imagery only, or control (neither relaxation nor imagery). After a 6-week training period, the subjects' performances were rated by karate experts. The ratings indicated that subjects in the VMBR group outperformed subjects in each of the other three conditions. Seabourne, Weinberg, and Jackson (1984) were able to replicate this effect. Noel (1980) examined effects of VMBR on the service skills of tennis players. Noel found that high ability tennis players receiving VMBR training outperformed a control group not receiving the training. However, performance was not facilitated in players who were low in ability. Apparently, similar to other imagery tactics, VMBR may be best suited for individuals who are somewhat skilled at the task in question.

Based on the reports cited above, it appears that VMBR is an effective intervention tactic. However, Suinn (1993) notes that there may be factors that influence the overall effectiveness of VMBR. These factors are depicted in Figure 11.2. First, there may be training factors that influence the usefulness of the VMBR procedure. Suinn states that the length and content of the VMBR training sessions are extremely important. As for the length of the VMBR sessions, programs with multiple training sessions (versus a one session format) seem to be most effective (Weinberg, Seabourne, & Jackson, 1982). Concerning the content of the training, Suinn notes that little research has examined this factor. For example, should VMBR encourage internal or external imagery? What is the role of arousal in the imagery process (i.e., is there an optimal level of arousal for imagery procedures)? These and other questions linking the content of the imagery and the effectiveness of VMBR need to be addressed in future studies.

Second, Suinn (1993) notes that characteristics of the user influence the effectiveness of VMBR. For example, athletes with higher levels of athletic or task-specific ability are more likely to benefit from VMBR training. Also, as noted above, some athletes possess better imagery skills than others. For these persons, VMBR training will most likely be highly effective.

Finally, Suinn feels that job demands impact the effectiveness of VMBR training. Suinn (1993) defines job demands as "the overall level of demands facing the athlete using imagery" (p. 508). If an athlete is in a highly demanding environment, the demands may overwhelm the athlete, thereby lessening the effectiveness of VMBR. For example, a novice athlete may be overwhelmed by situational demands such as learning the proper technique, remembering instructions, and maintaining

FIGURE 11.2   Factors influencing the effects of VMBR on performance. (From: R. Suinn, "Imagery." Reprinted with permission of Macmillan Reference USA, a Division of Simon & Schuster, from *Handbook of Research on Sport Psychology*, Robert N. Singer, Milledge Murphey, and L. Keith Tennant (Eds.) pp. 492–510. Copyright © 1993 by The International Society of Sport Psychology.)

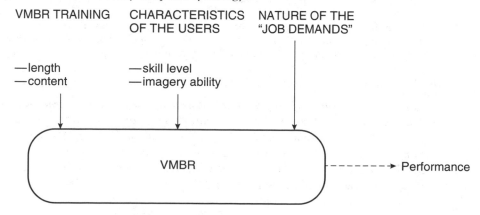

concentration. These demands may reduce the effectiveness of VMBR training. Perhaps it is for this reason that novice athletes do not show the performance benefits of VMBR that are evident in more skilled athletes (Noel, 1980).

ATTENTION CONTROL TRAINING

In this section, we will examine ***attention control training*** (ACT). Attention control training (also called attentional focus training) is a comprehensive program designed to improve an athlete's attentional skills. Before discussing the specifics of ACT, it is necessary to remind the reader of two issues discussed in previous chapters. First, there are two different attentional dimensions: width (broad and narrow) and direction (internal and external). Second, arousal can have a detrimental impact on an individual's attentional abilities. If a person is too highly aroused, he or she may disregard relevant situational and performance cues. If a person is too low in arousal, he or she may pay attention to and analyze numerous irrelevant cues. To perform at peak levels, athletes must be able to match the appropriate attentional dimension and level of arousal to a specific situation.

An ACT Program

Before beginning an ACT program, it is important for athletes to possess an understanding of the basics of the attentional process (Martens, 1987b). That is, athletes should be provided with the information found in Chapters 6 and 7 of this text. For example, athletes should be given an explanation of the various attentional dimensions, the relationship between arousal and attention, and the relationships among attention, arousal, and performance. If athletes do not receive this educational experience, they will be unable to assist the coach and sport psychologist in identifying their attentional strengths and weaknesses.

According to Nideffer (1993a, 1993b; see also Nideffer & Sharpe, 1978), ACT programs should contain five stages:

1. Assessment of the athlete's attentional strengths and weaknesses.
2. Assessment of the attentional demands of the performance setting.
3. Assessment of situational and interpersonal characteristics that impact arousal (and, subsequently, performance).
4. Identification of task-relevant and task-irrelevant informational cues.
5. The implementation of one or more situationally specific intervention strategies to correct any problems identified in Stages 1 through 4.

In the following sections, we will examine each of the five stages.

Stage 1: Assessment of the Athlete's Attentional Strengths and Weaknesses.
Before an athlete can correct his or her attentional deficiencies, it is necessary to assess the athlete's current attentional skills. Several procedures may be used to determine an athlete's attentional strengths and weaknesses. These procedures are not mutually exclusive and more than one procedure should be used to acquire a well-rounded perspective of the athlete's abilities.

To determine his or her attentional abilities, the athlete should complete Nideffer's (1976a) Test of Attentional and Interpersonal Style (see Chapter 6). Because this inventory was designed "to provide a non-situation-specific, self-report measure of attentional strengths and weaknesses" (Nideffer, 1993a, p. 544), an athlete's score on this inventory can be used in a diagnostic fashion. A picture of an athlete's attentional strengths and weaknesses may also be acquired through verbal consultation with a sport psychologist. By asking the athlete to describe his or her typical attentional patterns, the psychologist can gain a feel for the individual's attentional skills. An athlete may want to practice or participate in his or her athletic activity in the presence of a sport psychologist. In this way, the psychologist can observe the athlete's attentional processes in action. Again, this should provide the consultant with a general picture of the athlete's attentional strengths and weaknesses.

Stage 2: Assesssment of the Attentional Demands of the Performance Setting.

Different athletic tasks place different attentional demands on an athlete. As a result, it is important to identify the attentional needs specific to the task in question. Once the situational demands have been identified, the coach and sport psychologist can assist the athlete in maintaining the correct attentional perspective. For example, consider the tasks of bowling and playing the position of point guard in basketball. The attentional demands of these activities are quite different. For a bowler to perform well, he must operate primarily with a narrow external focus of attention (i.e., his attention should be focused on the pins or his "mark"). Conversely, a point guard must be able to shift her focus of attention. When she is moving up the court looking to pass the ball, she must maintain a broad external focus. However, when she goes to the free throw line to attempt a foul shot, she needs to operate with a narrow external focus. Helping the point guard perfect a broad external focus of attention and enhancing this athlete's ability to shift her attentional focus quickly should be beneficial to her performance. However, because this information would be of little use to the bowler, the coach and sport consultant should spend their time helping this athlete perfect a different attentional focus.

In some situations, a task actually requires that an athlete attempt to reduce his or her attentional focus on the task. These situations involve motor tasks that have become automatic through practice. When players learn a motor task so well that the task is incorporated into their procedural memory (i.e., perceptual-motor memory), focusing attention on the task can inhibit the smooth execution of the task. For example, consider a pitcher who has successfully encoded the correct arm motion for a curveball. If this person attempts to focus his attention on his arm position and movement while throwing this pitch, the attention will interfere with the natural execution of the activity resulting in decreased performance. Thus, athletes must be allowed and encouraged to trust their ability to execute well-learned tasks without consciously focusing their attention on the task (Moore & Stevenson, 1991, 1994).

Stage 3: Assessment of Situational and Interpersonal Characteristics that Impact Arousal.

Because of the relationship between arousal and attention (i.e., attention can be impaired by arousal levels that are too high or too low), it is necessary to determine those situational and interpersonal characteristics that may impact the athlete's arousal level. Regarding situational characteristics, some athletic events tend to be more arousing than others. For example, a ski jumper about to begin a run will probably be higher in arousal than a golfer about to attempt a putt. However, because there are large individual differences in arousal, coaches and sport psychologists must also consider the athlete's interpersonal tendencies. For example, it is possible that because she is low in trait anxiety, the ski jumper may actually have a lower level of arousal than the golfer. Thus, to understand an athlete's arousal and its effects on performance, one must consider both the situation and the person. This reflects the interactional perspective mentioned throughout this book.

Stage 4: Identification of Task-Relevant and Task-Irrelevant Informational Cues.

The next stage concerns the identification of the task-relevant and task-irrelevant informational cues found in an athlete's competitive environment. Athletes should pay attention to the relevant cues while ignoring those that are irrelevant. By teaching the athlete to focus solely on task-relevant cues, coaches and sport psychologists are able to enhance the athlete's attentional effectiveness. For example, consider a baseball player who has been struggling to hit with a runner on base. Through a discussion with his coach, it has become apparent that when the batter is faced with this situation, his attention is inappropriately diverted to the runner (a task-irrelevant cue) rather than focused on the pitched ball (the task-relevant cue). That is, the player has adopted an incorrect broad external focus of attention rather than the more appropriate narrow external perspective. By teaching the player to direct his attentional focus on the pitch rather than the runners, the coach and sport psychologist will improve the player's attentional ability.

Stage 5: The Implementation of a Situationally Specific Intervention Strategy.

Once the first four stages have been completed, it is time to implement a situationally specific intervention strategy designed to correct the athlete's attentional deficiencies. Sometimes, these strategies involve interventions discussed earlier. For example, the use of imagery may help the athlete maintain the appropriate attentional focus. Likewise, a relaxation procedure may lower the athlete's arousal to a level that does not disrupt his or her attentional processes.

Other strategies involve procedures yet to be discussed. For example, athletes may want to use an attentional cue word (or phrase). **Attentional cue words** are words or short phrases that remind the athlete of the proper attentional focus for a given situation (Ravizza & Hanson, 1995). For example, a basketball player may want to repeat the words "relax and follow through" prior to each free throw. The cue centers the athlete's attention to the task at hand, thereby increasing concentration and performance.

Another intervention strategy is thought stopping (Ziegler, 1980b). **Thought stopping** involves eliminating negative thinking and refocusing attention on relevant informational cues. This tactic should be employed when athletes feel themselves losing their attentional control. Consider a golfer who is about to attempt a difficult, but makeable, 15-foot putt. To perform at her highest level, the golfer should maintain a low level of arousal (recall that a low arousal level facilitates performance at tasks involving fine motor movements). She should also maintain a narrow external attentional focus. However, as the golfer approaches the ball she begins to feel herself losing her attentional focus. She feels herself being distracted by the crowd and other players, notices that her heart is racing, and begins to think to herself, "I know I'm going to choke" and "I just can't seem to concentrate today." It is at this point that she should employ the thought stopping procedure. She should say to herself, "No! I'm a good putter and I know it! Now clear your head of these negative thoughts and concentrate on the putt." By removing the negative thoughts and centering her attentional focus, the golfer will perform at a higher level.

One pointing is a third attention control intervention strategy (Schmid & Peper, 1993). This exercise, employed prior to competition, requires the athlete to examine an object in a photograph depicting his or her particular sport (for example, for a football player the object could be a football). The athlete should attempt to maintain his or her focus on the object. If distracting thoughts enter the athlete's consciousness, the thoughts should be redirected back to the object. This exercise should be successful in training athletes to refocus their attention toward proper cues.

ACT and Performance

As noted by Nideffer (1993a), few studies have directly tested the impact of ACT programs on athletic performance. While several studies have documented the performance benefits of using ACT as a component of multiple-component intervention packages (see Nideffer, 1993a, for a review), it is not possible to determine if the ACT was responsible for the performance improvements or if another of the components was responsible. It is also possible that the benefits resulted from an interaction among the various components. Future researchers should attempt to isolate the impact of the ACT component and document its independent contribution to the performance gains.

One study that did directly test the impact of attention control training was recently conducted by Efran, Lesser, and Spiller (1994). In this research, 69 young and talented tennis players were introduced to the ***metaphor method of attention control.*** This technique presents an athlete with a metaphor designed to insulate the athlete from distractions (such as a coach's verbal abuse). Subjects were divided into three age groups. The groups were roughly equivalent to late grade-school-age, middle-school-age, and high-school-age. The athletes were further divided into control and experimental groups. Subjects in the experimental groups were presented with the metaphor method. The metaphors were selected and labeled based on the age groups. Those in the youngest group were asked to imagine that they were in a "bubble" while performing. Subjects in the middle-school group were asked to place themselves in an imaginary "cocoon," while those in the oldest group were asked to enclose themselves in a "chrysalis." The players were told that, "Self-doubts and evaluations of all sorts, as well as extraneous noises, distractions, and comments, were to be left outside the shell" (Efran et al., 1994, p. 353). Thus, irrelevant cues were to be left outside the shell while relevant cues were let inside.

To assess the effectiveness of the program, subjects completed a questionnaire once a week during the 3-week program. The players' tennis skills were also rated at these times. The results, presented in Table 11.3, show the dramatic success of the program. As for the players' concentration (the result most relevant to the discussion here), the experimental subjects reported continued improvement in concentration

**TABLE 11.3   A Comparison of Subjects in the Metaphor
(i.e., Experimental) and Control Conditions**

Measure	Week 1	Week 2	Week 3
Concentration			
Experimental Group	11.02	12.95	13.78
Control Group	11.93	11.75	11.00
Skill Improvement			
Experimental Group	1.12	2.71	4.17
Control Group	0.61	0.93	0.96
Enjoyment			
Experimental Group	13.93	15.49	16.56
Control Group	14.29	14.64	14.25
Motivation			
Experimental Group	2.85	3.12	3.32
Control Group	3.00	3.07	2.67

(Adapted by permission from: Efran, J. S., Lesser, G. S., & Spiller, M. J. [1994].
Enhancing tennis coaching with youths using a metaphor method. *The Sport
Psychologist*, 8: 349–359.)

skills throughout the program. No such improvement was found in the control subjects. Further, the performances of subjects using the metaphor method improved
dramatically, while the skills of the control subjects showed little change. The experimental subjects also reported increases in enjoyment and motivation. Thus, the
preliminary evidence indicates that attention training programs not only result in better concentration and performance, but also lead to increases in enjoyment and motivation, at least in the case of young athletes.

A COMPREHENSIVE INTERVENTION PROGRAM
FOR ATHLETES: PSYCHOLOGICAL SKILLS TRAINING

In the current chapter and in Chapter 10, I have described a variety of psychological intervention strategies designed to improve athletic performance. In this final section, I would like to discuss **psychological skills training** (PST) programs. Psychological skills training programs are comprehensive intervention packages
designed to educate and train athletes in mental preparation. They incorporate some
or all of the intervention tactics described in Chapters 10 and 11, as well as information presented in other chapters such as effective goal setting strategies, building
leadership skills, and videotape modeling. Goal setting (discussed in Chapter 8) is
an especially common and important component of PST programs (Porter & Foster,
1986; Vealey, 1994).

The exact make-up of PST programs varies because programs should be tailored to meet the specific needs of an individual, team, or sport. For example, con-

sider Gary and Dan, doubles partners on a university tennis team. Gary is able to keep his anxiety and arousal at an optimal level but tends to suffer from a lack of self-confidence and appears to lack the motivation necessary to reach his self-set goals. Conversely, although Dan's self-confidence and motivation are adequate, he suffers from precompetition anxiety and has poor imagery skills. If these two athletes were presented with the same PST program, the benefits would be limited because these athletes have contrasting needs. Gary needs a program centered around improving his self-confidence and goal-setting skills, while Dan's PST should focus on anxiety control strategies and imagery training.

Although both clinical and educational sport psychologists may provide PST programs, these packages are usually developed by individuals with an educational sport psychology background. Recall from Chapter 1 that clinical sport psychologists help athletes with their emotional and psychological abnormalities, while educational sport psychologists provide athletes with the psychological training necessary to increase their performance. Often, this training is presented in the form of a PST program.

Implementation of a PST Program

Although differences exist between various PST programs, implementation of a PST program usually involves five stages:

1. Education.
2. Development of an individualized PST program based on an assessment of the athlete's psychological skills.
3. Acquisition of psychological skills.
4. Practicing the newly acquired psychological skills.
5. Evaluation of the PST program.

In the following sections, we will examine each of these stages.

Stage 1: Education.   It is unreasonable to expect athletes to accept and become dedicated to a PST program without possessing an understanding of the relationships between psychological skills and athletic performance. If a sport psychologist initiates a PST program without educating the athlete on the importance of psychological skills, the athlete may not be willing to expend the time and effort necessary to make the program a success. Therefore, education is an important starting point in any PST program.

The educational phase often involves providing the athlete with the type of information found in Section 3 of this text. That is, athletes receive information on psychological processes such as attention, arousal/anxiety, and motivation. Once the athletes possess a general understanding of these processes, information concerning the relationships between these constructs and athletic performance should be provided. For example, athletes should be educated on the attentional process (e.g., memory systems, attentional style, dimensions of attentional focus) and then be given information on the relationship between attention and athletic performance (e.g., adopting the correct attentional focus for a specific situation).

Stage 2: Development of an Individualized PST Program Based on an Assessment of the Athlete's Psychological Skills.   Once an athlete has acquired a basic understanding of the psychological principles involved in PST, the sport psychologist's next task is to determine the athlete's psychological strengths and weaknesses (Boutcher & Rotella, 1987; Taylor, 1995). In this way, the psychologist can determine which psychological skills need improvement and develop a PST program tailored specifically for a particular athlete. When determining an athlete's psychological strengths and weaknesses, the consultant should consider not only input from the athlete, but also suggestions from the athlete's coach. Grove and Hanrahan (1988) offer several reasons for considering a coach's perspective when designing a PST program. First, because they are often "the point of entry" (p. 228) for sport psychologists, coaches are quite accessible. Second, because coaches are often responsible for hiring the sport consultant, they probably have perceived a deficiency in their players' mental abilities. These perceptions will be quite valuable to the psychologist. Third, because the coach and athlete may disagree on the athlete's particular strengths and weaknesses, discussions between these two parties may clarify the discrepancy.

   DEVELOPING A PST PROGRAM USING PSYCHOLOGICAL TESTS.   A variety of tests can assist in the development of a PST program by identifying the player's strengths and weaknesses. For example, the Sport Competition Anxiety Test and the Competitive State Anxiety Inventory-2 (Martens et al., 1990, see Chapter 7) will provide the sport consultant with information concerning the athlete's typical trait and state anxiety responses. The Competitive State Anxiety Inventory-2 will also provide information about the athlete's level of self-confidence, as will scores derived from the State Sport-Confidence Inventory and the Trait Sport-Confidence Inventory (Vealey, 1986). Scores on the Profile of Mood States (McNair et al., 1971, Chapter 4) and the Nideffer's (1976a) Test of Attentional and Interpersonal Style (Chapter 6) are also helpful.
   In an attempt to construct a single measure to assess an athlete's overall psychological skills strengths and weaknesses, Mahoney and his colleagues (1987) developed the Psychological Skills Inventory for Sports (PSIS). The PSIS contains 45 Likert-scale items (Mahoney, 1989; the original version contained 51 true/false questions, see Mahoney et al., 1987). The PSIS measures six different psychological skills/constructs: anxiety control, mental preparation, team focus, concentration, self-confidence, and motivation. To test the validity of the PSIS, Mahoney et al. (1987) asked elite and nonelite athletes from a number of sports to complete the scale. Mahoney and his associates found that elite and nonelite athletes scored differently on a number of items, with elite athletes exhibiting better psychological skills. In general, compared with nonelite athletes, elite athletes were better able to (1) control their anxiety, (2) concentrate, (3) remain self-confident, (4) mentally prepare, (5) focus on their own rather than their team's performance, and (6) maintain a high level of motivation. As a result, Mahoney et al. (1987) concluded that "The PSIS did prove to be a useful pilot instrument for assessing psychological skills relevant to athletic training and performance" (p. 195).

However, subsequent research by Chartrand, Jowdy, and Danish (1992) revealed a number of psychometric problems with the PSIS. First, the structure of the scale was incompatible with the data (i.e., the data did not reflect the predicted six factors). Furthermore, most of the subscales showed a poor level of internal consistency. Because of these problems, Chartrand et al. (1992) concluded that additional research and validation of the PSIS are required before this inventory should be used in applied and research settings. It is hoped this research will lead to a refinement of the PSIS, resulting in a more psychometrically sound assessment tool.

In an attempt to develop a more psychologically sound alternative to measuring an athlete's overall psychological skills, Smith, Schutz, Smoll, and Ptacek (1995) recently constructed the Athletic Coping Skills Inventory-28 (ACSI-28). This instrument assesses psychological skills in seven areas: coping with adversity (i.e., maintaining control and a positive attitude when faced with adversity), peaking under pressure (i.e., viewing pressure as facilitating performance), goal setting/mental preparation, concentration, freedom from worry, confidence and achievement motivation, and coachability. Scores on the seven subscales can be combined to acquire a total psychological skills score. Initial research on the measure indicated that the data did indeed fit the model, indicating the measure was accurately assessing seven separate dimensions of psychological skill. Further, by correlating the subscale and total scores with other measures of psychological skills (e.g., measures of self-esteem, self-efficacy, and sport anxiety), Smith and his colleagues were able to demonstrate the validity of the scale.

As a further indication of the scale's validity, Smith et al. (1995) were able to use the ACSI-28 to differentiate between overachieving and normal achieving/underachieving high school athletes. The athletes were asked to complete the ACSI-28 prior to the start of their season. At the conclusion of the season, coaches were asked to rate the players. The results indicated that the players with the highest ratings (i.e., the overachievers) had better psychological skills than athletes receiving lower ratings (i.e., normal achieving/underachieving players). Overachievers had particular high scores on the coping with adversity, concentration, and coachability subscales. In a related study involving professional baseball players, Smith and Christensen (1995) found that ACSI-28 scores were positively correlated with batting and pitching performance and career longevity. Thus, based on the data gathered to date, it appears that the ACSI-28 is an attractive alternative to the PSIS.

DEVELOPING A PST PROGRAM USING PERFORMANCE PROFILING.   Performance profiling is a second method that can assist in the development of an individualized PST program. **Performance profiling** is a technique that uses input from the athlete and coach to arrive at an understanding of the player's skills (see Butler & Hardy, 1992; Butler, Smith, & Irwin, 1993). In this way, the athlete and coach are better able to articulate the player's physical and psychological strengths and weaknesses. This is an important task because a player and coach may have conflicting perceptions of the player's psychological skills and profile (Huddleston, Ahrabi-Fard, & Garvin, 1995; Smith & Christensen, 1995). Once the athlete's psychological skills have been determined, the information can then be used to develop an individualized PST program.

Dale and Wrisberg (1995a, 1995b) provided a detailed description of the performance profiling technique. Their version of the technique involves four stages:

1. A meeting between the coaches and the sport psychologist.
2. An initial meeting between the players and the sport psychologist.
3. A second meeting between the players and the sport psychologist.
4. Athlete/coach comparisons and player, coach, and sport psychologist meetings.

Stage 1: A Meeting between the Coaches and the Sport Psychologist.   The first stage involves a meeting between the coaches and the sport psychologist (Dale & Wrisberg, 1995a, 1995b). During this meeting, coaches are given a description of the performance profiling technique. This description should include the procedures to be used, the time constraints involved, and the benefits of the technique.

Stage 2: An Initial Meeting between the Players and the Sport Psychologist.   The second stage is the initial meeting between the players and the sport psychologist (Dale & Wrisberg, 1995a, 1995b). To insure that players feel free to be honest and open during this meeting, coaches are asked not to attend. This initial player/psychologist meeting is divided into two sections. During the first section, players are provided with information about the performance profiling technique, information similar to that given to the coaches in the previous stage. During the second portion of this stage, the players are asked to construct an individual profile. The individual profiles should be constructed in small groups organized around a particular position (for example, in baseball, the pitchers, catchers, infielders, and outfielders should form separate groups). Once players are in their groups, they are to suggest and discuss the characteristics indicative of an elite performer at their position, listing the characteristics on a sheet of paper titled "Characteristics of an Elite Performer." Once the group has a complete list, the players are to rate themselves individually on the characteristics on a 1 ("this is not me") to 10 ("this is me") scale.

It should be noted that players may also be asked to construct team and coach profiles. Although these profiles are effective in facilitating the communication between the coaches and the players, because they are only peripherally related to the development of a personalized PST program, these profiles are not discussed here. Information on the application of team and coach profiles is provided by Dale and Wrisberg (1995a, 1995b).

Stage 3: A Second Meeting between the Players and the Sport Psychologist.   The second meeting between the players and the sport psychologist should take place approximately 1 week after the initial meeting (Dale & Wrisberg, 1995a, 1995b). At the beginning of the second meeting, each player is given a graph reflecting the individual profile ratings developed during the initial meeting. The graph is designed to provide the athlete with a visual record of his or her profile. Players are asked to examine the graph carefully to insure that it reflects their beliefs. Any discrepancies are discussed and the items and ratings are altered as needed. Figure 11.3 depicts a sample graph of a profile for a baseball pitcher.

Stage 4: Athlete/Coach Comparisons and Player, Coach, and Sport Psychologist Meetings. During the fourth stage, coaches are asked to rate the players using the same 1 to 10 scale employed by the players themselves. A second bar graph is then constructed,

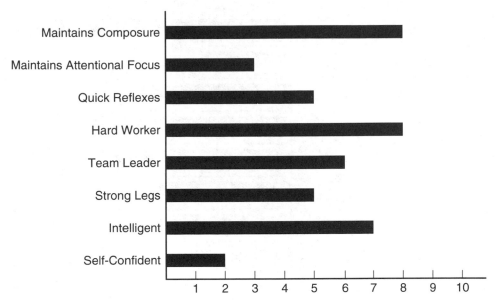

FIGURE 11.3 A sample bar graph depicting the individual performance profile ratings for a baseball pitcher.

one that includes the player's ratings and the coach's ratings. An example of such a graph is shown in Figure 11.4. Meetings involving the player, coach, and sport psychologist are then scheduled. During these meetings, the player and coach openly discuss the graph, noting both the players' physical and psychological strengths as well as the player's weaknesses. In addition, the player and coach are asked to resolve any large discrepancies in their ratings. Based on these discussions, the player and coach are able to develop an individualized PST program.

For example, consider the athlete depicted in Figure 11.4. Based on an examination of this graph, it is apparent that the player and coach share some similar viewpoints about the player's abilities. However, the player and coach also have a number of discrepancies in their perceptions. As for similarities, the player and coach agree that maintaining attentional focus and a high level of confidence is difficult for the player, that the player is an average team leader, and that the player possesses quick reflexes, is a hard worker, and is intelligent. Based on this information, the sport psychologist, player, and coach would want to develop a PST program that emphasizes attentional training and self-confidence building. Concerning discrepancies between the player's and coach's ratings, there is one incongruency that is readily apparent: The player feels that he is able to maintain composure, while the coach feels that the player is unable to maintain his composure. The player and coach (with the assistance of the sport psychologist) must discuss the discrepancy and arrive at a congruent rating. For instance, after a lengthy discussion the player may conclude that the coach is correct, that is, the player does have a difficult time maintaining composure. As a result, a set of relaxation exercises targeting both acute and chronic forms of anxiety should be added to the PST program.

FIGURE 11.4   A sample bar graph depicting the individual performance profile ratings for a baseball pitcher. This graph includes both the athlete's ratings and the coach's ratings.

Stage 3: Acquisition of Psychological Skills.   Based on the information gained in the assessment stage, the sport psychologist is now ready to design and implement an individualized PST program. In the acquisition stage, the athlete is introduced to intervention strategies that address his or her needs. For example, if the assessment stage revealed that the athlete suffered from a detrimentally high level of anxiety and a lack of concentration, the psychologist would present the athlete with interventions targeting these areas. The specific interventions used may vary, although the tactics described in the past two chapters are all quite common. The length of time required for the acquisition stage will also vary, depending on the number of psychological skills to be introduced and the athlete's prior knowledge and understanding of the processes involved.

Stage 4: Practicing the Newly Acquired Psychological Skills.   Similar to physical skills, mental skills must be practiced regularly before they can be improved. Thus, once an athlete has been introduced to a psychological skill, he or she must work to perfect the skill. It is important that the psychologist assist the athlete during this stage rather than simply presenting the player with the intervention strategies in Stage 3 and then leaving him or her to practice the skills alone. Although the athlete will most certainly need to practice individually before the skill can be acquired, the sport psychologist should remain available to assist the athlete should he or she hit a road block. Martens (1987b) recommends the use of a PST journal to help in this stage of the process. By writing down their PST successes and failures, athletes will be able to monitor their progress, discussing the progress with the sport consultant.

Stage 5: Evaluation of the PST Program.   The final step in a PST program involves the evaluation of the athlete's progress and the program's effectiveness (Boutcher & Rotella, 1987). Evaluation of a PST program does not have to be an elaborate process. Rather, simply repeating the assessment stage can serve this purpose. For example, imagine that an athlete was receiving a PST program centered around self-confidence and concentration because her PSIS scores acquired during the assessment stage revealed a weakness in these areas. After a specified time, the sport psychologist could evaluate the athlete's progress and the program's usefulness simply by asking the athlete to retake the PSIS. After examining the athlete's new set of scores, the psychologist could alter the program as needed or conclude the program if it were apparent that the athlete had acquired the psychological skills.

The Effectiveness of PST Programs

While sport psychologists have worked with athletes on topics such as anxiety and imagery for decades, only recently have they begun to examine and implement PST programs. In fact, most of the literature describing PST programs has been published since the mid-1980s. Although PST programs are relatively new, enough research evidence has been collected to warrant the conclusion that PST programs are extremely effective and can lead to significant increases in athletic performance. Rather than being limited to a small sample of sport types or a particular athletic population, the benefits of PST programs have been documented in a large variety of sports and with a diverse array of athletes. For example, a review of the literature reveals that PST programs have improved athletic performance in basketball (Hughes, 1990; Kendall, Hrycaiko, Martin, & Kendall, 1990), football (Fenker & Lambiotte, 1987; Hughes, 1990), gymnastics (Cogan & Petrie, 1995), ice hockey (Anderson, Crowell, Doman, & Howard, 1988), field hockey (Bakker & Kayser, 1994), cricket (Bull, 1995), shooting (Prapavessis, Grove, McNair, & Cable, 1992), skiing (Hellstedt, 1987), tennis (Daw & Burton, 1994), table tennis (Li-Wei, Qi-Wei, Orlick, & Zitzelsberger, 1992), and wrestling (Gould, Petlichkoff, Hodge, & Simons, 1990; Jefferies & Esparza, 1992). Further, PST programs have been used successfully with young (Li-Wei et al., 1992; Orlick & McCaffery, 1991; Weiss, 1991), interscholastic (Anderson et al., 1988; Hellstedt, 1987; Hughes, 1990), intercollegiate (Daw & Burton, 1994; Fenker & Lambiotte, 1987; Meyers & Schleser, 1980), elite (Gould et al., 1990), physically challenged (Asken, 1991; Clark & Sachs, 1991), and mentally challenged (Travis & Sachs, 1991) athletes, as well as athletes from different cultures (Cox & Liu, 1993).

Although an in-depth review of each of the studies listed above would be excessive, it may be informative to review two of the works in detail. I have chosen to examine the works of Daw and Burton (1994) and Bakker and Kayser (1994) because (1) these research endeavors incorporated many of the more common components of PST programs, (2) the results are straightforward, and (3) one study involved the case study approach (Daw & Burton, 1994) while the other involved an experimental approach (i.e., Bakker & Kayser, 1994).

The Daw and Burton (1994) research examined the impact of a PST program designed for collegiate tennis players. Although 12 players participated in the PST program, we will review the author's case study discussion of two players: Doug and Jenny (the names are fictitious). Through individualized and group consultation sessions, it was determined that Doug needed to increase his attentional focus and imagery skills. Jenny needed an effective goal-setting program to help her stay in shape and assistance in maintaining control during matches. The consultants then initiated individualized PST packages for the athletes, addressing each player's specific concerns. The results of the study were extremely encouraging. Doug's imagery and attentional skills continued to improve throughout the program, as did his performance. In fact, his first-serve percentage increased from 72% during preseason play (the beginning of the program) to 85% at postseason. His double-fault percentage decreased from 13% to 2%, while his unforced-error percentage dropped from 24% to 12%. As for Jenny, although her first-serve percentage did not change from preseason to postseason, her double-fault percentage dropped from 4% to 1% and her unforced-error percentage dropped from 39% to 28%.

The Bakker and Kayser (1994) investigation reviewed the impact of a PST program on the performances of 29 late adolescent and young adult field hockey players. The athletes were divided into three groups: a mental training group receiving audio and videotape information on concentration, relaxation, and imagery; a placebo-control group receiving audio and videotape information about field hockey; and a control group that did not receive any information. Subjects met with the experimenters on three occasions. During the first meeting, all subjects completed an anxiety inventory and were then taken to a hockey field and asked to attempt 12 penalty shots. After attempting the shots, the control group was excused. The mental training group was asked to listen to an audiotape containing information on concentration, relaxation, and imagery, while the placebo-control group listened to an audiotape containing information about field hockey. Subjects in these two conditions took the tapes home and were instructed to listen to the tapes once a day. During the second meeting, this procedure was repeated (i.e., subjects attempted the penalty shots and listened to the audiotapes). In addition, subjects in the mental training group watched a videotaped model to assist in the mental training, while those in the placebo-control group watched a videotaped field hockey match. At the third meeting, subjects were again asked to attempt the 12 penalty shots.

The results of the program were very encouraging. Although the penalty shooting of subjects in the control and placebo-control groups did not improve from the first meeting to the second or from the second to the third, scores of subjects in the mental training group improved dramatically. The mental training group's shooting improved approximately 10% from the first testing date to the second, and approximately 20% from the second occasion to the third, resulting in an overall improvement of around 30%. After the third meeting, subjects were asked if they felt more relaxed, self-confident, and able to concentrate during the third testing date (compared with the first). As for subjects in the mental training condition, 89%, 56%, and 67% reported feeling more relaxed, self-confident, and able to concentrate, respectively. For those in the placebo-control group, the percentages were only 50%, 10%, and 20%, and for those in the control group, only 40%, 40%, and 20%.

SUMMARY

Strategies designed to foster an optimal level of self-confidence can be useful for athletes suffering from diffidence or overconfidence. These strategies include maintaining a realistic appraisal of one's abilities, using effective goal setting procedures, and considering a variety of sources of efficacy information.

Imagery can be either internal (from one's own perspective) or external (from the perspective of another individual). Research has indicated that, although imagery does not facilitate performance as well as physical practice, it is more effective than no practice at all. In addition, imagery works best with (1) individuals who are at least moderately skilled at the task, (2) tasks that are at least partially cognitive in nature, and (3) images involving positive outcomes. A special form of imagery, called visuo-motor behavior rehearsal, is particularly effective because it combines imagery with relaxation training.

Attention control training (ACT) programs usually contain five stages: (1) assessment of the athlete's attentional strengths and weaknesses, (2) assessment of the attentional demands of the performance setting, (3) assessment of situational and interpersonal characteristics that impact arousal, (4) identification of task-relevant and task-irrelevant informational cues, and (5) the implementation of one or more situationally specific intervention strategies such as attentional cue words and thought stopping. Although only a few studies have examined the efficacy of ACT programs, research to date indicates that these strategies are beneficial to performance.

Comprehensive psychological intervention programs, called psychological skills training (PST), involve packaging a number of intervention strategies into one program. These programs involve five stages: (1) education, (2) assessment of the athlete's psychological skills, (3) acquisition of psychological skills, (4) practicing the newly acquired psychological skills, and (5) evaluation of the PST program. Research has found that PST programs can enhance athletic performance in a variety of sports and with a variety of athletic populations.

GLOSSARY

Attention Control Training   A comprehensive program designed to improve an athlete's attentional skills.

Attentional Cue Words   Words or short phrases that remind the athlete of the proper attentional focus for a given situation.

Diffidence   A lack of self-confidence.

External Imagery   Imagining one's surroundings and behaviors from the perspective of another individual.

Internal Imagery   Imagining one's surroundings and behaviors from one's own vantage point.

Metaphor Method of Attention Control   A technique according to which an athlete is presented with a metaphor designed to insulate the athlete from distractions.

Negative Imagery   Imagining a negative outcome.

One Pointing   An attention control exercise requiring the athlete to examine an object in a photograph and maintain his or her focus on the object.

Performance Profiling   A technique that uses input from the athlete and coach to arrive at an understanding of the player's skills.

Positive Imagery   Imagining a successful outcome.

Psychological Skills Training   A comprehensive intervention package designed to educate and train athletes in mental preparation.

Psychoneuromuscular Theory   A theory reflecting the belief that imagery facilitates performance by producing innervation in one's muscles that is similar to actual physical movements.

Symbolic Learning Theory   A theory reflecting the belief that imagery facilitates performance by providing individuals with a mental code and plan of their movements, thus making the movements more familiar and automatic.

Thought Stopping   Eliminating negative thinking and refocusing attention on relevant informational cues.

Visuo-Motor Behavior Rehearsal   A motor performance enhancement program that integrates imagery and relaxation training.

APPLICATION AND REVIEW QUESTIONS

1. Explain the differences among diffidence, overconfidence, and optimal confidence. Which term best describes you?
2. Imagine that you had a teammate who was suffering from diffidence. What suggestions would you give her or him to boost her or his self-confidence?
3. What is the difference between internal and external imagery? Develop an example of both.
4. Develop a hypothetical attention control training program. Be sure to include each of the five stages.
5. What is a PST program?
6. Consider what you feel are your own psychological skill strengths and weaknesses. Now, based on your analysis, develop a PST program for yourself that includes each of the five stages.

SUGGESTED READINGS

MARTENS, R. (1987). *Coaches guide to sport psychology*. Champaign, IL: Human Kinetics. This text discusses several sport psychology intervention strategies including anxiety control, attention control, imagery, and psychological skills training. Because this book was written with coaches in mind, it is especially helpful for this population.

MURPHY, S. M. (Ed.) (1995). *Sport psychology interventions*. Champaign, IL: Human Kinetics. This textbook is a valuable source for all individuals interested in furthering their understanding of sport psychology intervention strategies. A number of topics in Murphy's book are not covered in this text, including interventions with children, gender issues, and marital therapy. Perhaps the best feature of this text is the "hands-on" case study approach taken by the authors.

NIDEFFER, R. M. (1992). *Psyched to win*. Champaign, IL: Leisure Press. This book provides athletes with valuable suggestions for improving their psychological skills. Specifically, readers are presented with information on improving concentration, attentional focus, and imagery.

NIDEFFER, R. M. (1993). Attention control training. In R. N. Singer, M. Murphey, & L. K. Tennant (Eds.), *Handbook of research on sport psychology* (pp. 542–556). New York: Macmillan. As noted in the chapter's title, this work discusses the importance of attention control training.

ORLICK, T. (1993). *Free to feel great: Teaching children to excel at living*. Carp, Ontario, Canada: Creative Bound. This book offers a number of suggestions for enhancing the psychological skills of young athletes.

PORTER, K., & FOSTER, J. (1986). *The mental athlete*. New York: Ballantine. This short book examines the importance of mental training for athletic success. The authors describe several activities designed to enhance one's mental skills, including activities involving relaxation, goal setting, and coping with an injury.

SUINN, R. (1993). Imagery. In R. N. Singer, M. Murphey, & L. K. Tennant (Eds.), *Handbook of research on sport psychology* (pp. 492–510). New York: Macmillan. This chapter gives a detailed description of imagery, with a particular focus on visuo-motor behavior rehearsal.

SYER, J., & CONNOLLY, C. (1987). *Sporting body sporting mind: An athlete's guide to mental training*. Englewood Cliffs, NJ: Prentice Hall. This book provides the reader with a number of activities to improve his or her psychological skills, including concentration, imagery, and relaxation skills.

Chapter 12

PLAYER AGGRESSION IN SPORT

The following excerpts were each taken from newspaper and magazine articles published in the 1990s.

1. Houston Rockets guard Vernon Maxwell could be charged with simple assault, a misdemeanor punishable by a year in jail and a $2,500 fine, for allegedly punching a fan Monday night in Portland Ore. Witnesses say Maxwell charged into the stands during the third quarter of the Rockets' 120-82 loss to the Trail Blazers and hit Steve George in the face (Nance, 1995, p. 4C).

2. The injury to the New York Jets' Dennis Byrd occurred two weeks ago and broadcasters and columnists still have this curious catch in their voices. . . . It's guilt. . . . We may rhapsodize about teamwork and strategy, about the inner strength of coaches and the self-discipline of stars, but the principal selling point of football is bone-jarring violence (Brown, 1992, p. 10C).

3. Football fields, basketball courts, and baseball diamonds were literally battle grounds for high school sports in 1992. . . . Oran Curry, whose son Jason played for the Tabiona (Utah) boys basketball team, hit coach Lee Gines at practice because Curry thought his son was not getting enough playing time. . . . Matt Griffin, Tulsa Bixby soccer coach, was beaten and kicked by opposing players after Tulsa Hale's 3-0 victory. Griffin's eye socket, cheek-bone, and jaw were broken (Dorsey, 1992, p. 14C).

4. Leave it to Houston Oilers defensive coordinator Buddy Ryan to add intrigue to the New York Jets' death march at the Astrodome. Irritated by a Cody Carlson sack and fumble during a passing play just before halftime, Ryan punched (Oiler) offensive coordinator Kevin Gilbride in the jaw to protest the call (Bell, 1994, p. 4C).

5. Jimmy Boni, a hockey player being tried for causing the death of an opponent during a game, pleaded guilty to a reduced manslaughter charge (Weisman, 1994, p. 7C).

6. The coach of a North Carolina Little League team, (Richard) Blackwell was arrested May 20 after he slashed the throat of a rival coach, Marty Butler, with a knife during an argument over a game their teams had played a few days earlier (*National Sports Review*, 1992, p. 33).

7. An American Legion baseball player, (Timothy) Daurity was arrested on felony assault charges in Fuquay-Varina, N.C., after whacking umpire Glenn Barham in the chest

with a bat. Barham's crime: He had mistakenly called Daurity out on a second strike (*National Sports Review,* 1992, p. 33).

8. In response to scuffles between opposing players at several recent high school basketball games, the Marmonte League in Southern California has outlawed postgame handshakes (O'Brien, 1994, p. 22).

9. On Sunday, Temple's John Chaney got into a violent exchange with UMass coach John Calipari. Chaney interrupted Calipari's postgame news conference to denounce Calipari's complaining, and within moments Chaney had to be restrained from charging Calipari. The irate Temple coach was clearly heard to say "I'll kill you. You remember that" (Telander, 1994, pp. 78, 80).

10. Basketball and baseball have a problem. They can release statistics about fighting being down, and they can whine that the media are exaggerating the unruly incidents, and they can suggest that their games used to be rougher and tougher in the old days. But perception nowadays is reality, and right now the perception is that both great American pastimes end in *brawl,* not *ball* (McCallum, 1994a, pp. 26, 28).

Each of these stories depicts the aggressive nature of sport today. Because of the prominence of sport violence, it is not surprising that the causes and consequences of aggression in sport have been common topics of research. In this chapter, we will examine this research. We will begin our review by defining aggression and examining the most common methods of measuring aggressive behavior. We will then examine three classic theories of aggression and their application to sport. Several situational and game factors that promote aggression will then be discussed. This chapter concludes with suggestions for curbing player violence. It should be noted that this chapter focuses on player aggression rather than spectator aggression. Spectator violence is discussed in the final chapter of this text.

DEFINING AGGRESSION

A widely accepted definition of aggression was suggested by Baron and Richardson (1994). These authors contend that aggression is "any form of behavior directed toward the goal of harming or injuring another living being who is motivated to avoid such treatment" (p. 7). This definition implies that aggression involves goal-directed behavior, there must be an intent to inflict pain, aggression is not limited to behaviors causing physical pain (aggression may also involve psychological injury), and to be considered an act of aggression, a behavior must be directed at a living being who is motivated to avoid such treatment.

For the most part, I agree with Baron and Richardson's definition of aggression. However, to account fully for the aggressive behaviors of athletes, it is necessary to alter their definition and define ***aggression*** as the intent to physically, verbally, or psychologically harm someone who is motivated to avoid such treatment and/or the physical destruction of property when motivated by anger. Obviously, there are several commonalties between their definition and mine: both definitions include the notion of intent, concur that aggression can be verbal or psychological, and agree that the behavior should not be considered an aggressive act if the recipient of the violence was not motivated to avoid the treatment. The key difference between the definitions is that Baron and Richardson's version does not consider the destruction of property to be an aggressive act. For example, consider the behavior of a base-ball player who has just struck out with the game on the line. Due to his anger, this player walks back into the clubhouse and smashes a clubhouse toilet. Baron and Richardson's stance is that unless this behavior harmed another person, it should not be considered an aggressive act. Conversely, based on the working definition of aggression that we will be employing in this text, because the act was motivated by anger, it would be considered an example of aggression.

Types of Aggression in Sport: Hostile Aggression, Instrumental Aggression, and Assertiveness

An inspection of the aggressive actions of athletes reveals that players behave violently for a variety of reasons. Because of this, it is helpful to classify the forms of aggression found in athletics (Silva, 1980a). Hostile aggression is one type of aggression found in

FIGURE 12.1   The types of aggressive and assertive behaviors found in sport settings. (Note: From "Assertive and Aggressive Behavior in Sport" by John M. Silva. In: *Psychology of Motor Behavior and Sport—1979* [p. 205] by Claude H. Nadeau, et al. [Eds.]. Champaign, IL: Human Kinetics Publishers. Copyright 1980 by Human Kinetic Publishers. Reprinted by permission.)

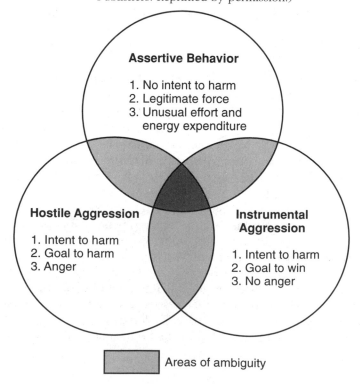

sport (see Figure 12.1). ***Hostile aggression*** refers to aggressive actions motivated by anger that have the intent and goal of harming another person (or object). For instance, imagine that a quarterback threw a touchdown pass that embarrassed and angered a defensive back. Later in the game, the defensive back retaliated by punching the quarterback with the sole intent of hurting him. Because the violent act was motivated by anger and designed to harm the target, this is an example of hostile aggression.

A second form of aggression is instrumental aggression (see Figure 12.1). ***Instrumental aggression*** refers to aggressive actions intended to harm another person, with the goal of achieving a result other than the victim's suffering, such as victory in an athletic contest. This form of aggression is not motivated by anger and a desire to hurt another individual. Rather, the aggressive act is a means to an end. Returning to our football example, imagine that the defensive back attempted to execute an illegal tackle by using his helmet to spear the quarterback. However, rather than being motivated by anger and the desire to harm the quarterback, the defensive back wanted to cause the quarterback to fumble the ball, thereby increasing his team's chances of winning. Because his violent action was directed toward the goal of victory, the defensive back's behavior is an example of instrumental aggression.

As a real-life example of instrumental aggression, consider the comments made by John Starks of the New York Knicks professional basketball team. Starks had been accused of committing several aggressive acts during a playoff series with the Chicago Bulls. When asked to explain his aggressive actions, Starks replied "Yeah, I intentionally tripped Scottie (Pippen) to stop a fast break. I saved two points by doing it. I wasn't trying to hurt anyone. I was trying to win and I'll do whatever it takes" (Taylor, 1994, p. 21). Apparently, Starks felt that his aggressive actions would facilitate his team's success. He may have been correct because his team won the playoff series 4 games to 3. Thus, in this case it appears that instrumental aggression was successful in accomplishing the goal of victory. However, rather than relying on anecdotal evidence such as this to understand the relationship between aggression and performance, sport psychologists have conducted several empirical studies examining the relationship. This line of research is the focus of this chapter's "A Closer Look."

Assertiveness is a third category of behavior with relevance to aggression in sport (see Figure 12.1). ***Assertiveness*** is the use of legitimate force and strategy to achieve a goal. Unlike actions defined as aggressive, the intent to harm is absent from assertive behaviors. Assertive behaviors are instances when individuals exhibit a high level of energy and expenditure of effort to achieve a goal. The key difference between assertive and aggressive behaviors is that assertive behaviors lie within the legal bounds of the game, while aggressive behaviors do not. For example, each of the previous descriptions of the defensive back's behavior were illegal (punching and spearing are illegal tactics in football). If the defensive back were to have executed a hard but legal tackle on the quarterback without the intent to inflict harm or injury, he would have been committing an assertive act.

Although assertiveness is not an act of aggression, it is included in Figure 12.1 and discussed here because these behaviors are often inappropriately described as aggressive. For example, consider the following statement by Porter and Foster (1986). In describing the benefits of the *aggressive* actions of athletes, these authors write, "Rushing the net, rebounding for the ball, surging in a race, and intercepting

A CLOSER LOOK:
THE RELATIONSHIP BETWEEN SPORT AGGRESSION AND PERFORMANCE

Several researchers have found a positive relationship between sport aggression and performance. For example, in their studies examining ice hockey players, McCarthy and Kelly (1978a, 1978b) found that higher numbers of penalty minutes corresponded with increased scoring. Russell (1974) found similar results in his work with hockey players. However, the straightforward conclusion that aggression facilitates athletic success may be an oversimplification of a complex phenomenon. A more accurate account of the relationship may need to consider the timing of the aggression. For example, research conducted by Widmeyer and Birch (1984) found that aggression was positively related to performance in the first period of play but not in the last period.

However, some researchers do not believe there is a positive relationship between sport aggression and performance (e.g., Silva, 1979, 1980b; Widmeyer & Birch, 1979). Silva believes that aggression will be detrimental to athletic performance for two reasons. First, he argues that as athletes focus their attention toward harming their opponent, their attention to the task at hand suffers. The result of the reduced attentional focus is a decrement in performance. Second, Silva believes that the arousal accompanying the display of aggression may push the athlete beyond his optimal level. Again, the result is a reduction in performance.

Although Silva's arguments contradict the work of McCarthy and Kelly (1978a, 1978b) and Russell (1974), his thinking appears to be sound and is consistent with research presented throughout this text. Cox (1990) feels that it may be possible to reconcile the differences. He argues that the reconciliation lies in the inverted-U theory. Recall that arousal tends to facilitate performance until it reaches a peak. At this point, further increases in arousal are detrimental to performance. Cox suggests that the moderate levels of arousal associated with moderate levels of aggression may lead to performance enhancement. However, if the aggression and violence become too intense, the accompanying arousal will become too great and the player's performance will suffer.

a shot are all examples of assertive and aggressive behavior" (p. 119). These authors are confusing *assertive* actions with *aggressive* actions.

A glance back to Figure 12.1 indicates an important point in the demarcations among hostile aggression, instrumental aggression, and assertiveness. As shown in the figure, there is an overlap among these behaviors. Because it is often difficult to ascertain an athlete's true motivation and intention for a behavior, we are often unable to label the action accurately. For example, consider a pitcher who hits a batter in the head with a fastball. Was this act aggressive and, if so, was it an example of hostile or instrumental aggression? Or was this an act of assertiveness? The answer lies in the motivations and intentions of the pitcher. If the pitcher was simply trying to throw inside (a legal behavior) and was not trying to hit the batter, then this action should be labeled as assertive. If, on the other hand, he did intend to harm the batter, then the action was indeed aggressive. If the pitcher believed that hitting the batter would send a message to the other players and subsequently increase his chances of winning, the behavior should be classified as instrumental aggression. Conversely, if the pitcher was not concerned about the game outcome and simply wanted to hurt the batter, the action should be classified as hostile aggression.

MEASURING AGGRESSION

Several methods of measuring aggression have been developed. Some of the methods are general in nature and some are sport-specific.

General Methods of Measuring Aggression

The Buss-Durkee Hostility Inventory (BDHI, Buss & Durkee, 1957) has probably been the most popular general inventory of aggression (Baron & Richardson, 1994). The BDHI contains 75 true-false items measuring seven different components of aggression: assault, indirect aggression, irritability, negativism, resentment, suspicion, and verbal aggression. A different general method of measuring aggression uses an aggression machine (Buss, 1961). An aggression machine is a metal box with approximately 20 buttons. Subjects are told that, when the buttons are depressed, a specified level of shock will be delivered to a "victim" (in actuality, no shocks are delivered). By recording the intensity level and duration of the shocks, researchers are able to acquire a behavioral measure of aggression.

Sport-Specific Methods of Measuring Aggression

Sport psychologists have also been active in developing measures of aggression. Bredemeier has constructed a pair of sport-specific inventories. The Bredemeier Athletic Aggression Inventory (BAAGI) contains 100 Likert-scale items (Bredemeier, 1978, Wall & Gruber, 1986). Half of the BAAGI items measure hostile aggression and half measure instrumental aggression. To assess the aggression of younger athletes, Bredemeier and her colleagues developed the Scale of Children's Action Tendencies in Sport (SCATS, Bredemeier, 1994; Bredemeier, Weiss, Shields, & Cooper, 1986). The SCATS presents subjects with a set of ten sport-specific stories focusing on physically or nonphysically hostile situations. For example, subjects read that, "You're running in a long distance race, and one of the other runners comes up from behind, trips you, and runs on ahead" (Bredemeier, 1994, p. 6). Respondents are presented with a list of response options reflecting aggressive, assertive, and submissive behaviors. Subjects are asked to circle the option best reflecting their normal reaction to this type of situation. For the item described above, agreeing with "Try to catch up and get that runner back" would indicate an aggressive reaction, while marking "Forget about it" would indicate a submissive reaction. Responses to the ten items are summed to reveal four scores: physical aggression, nonphysical aggression, assertion, and submission.

CLASSIC THEORIES OF AGGRESSION

Although the history of psychology has seen the development of a diverse array of theories designed to account for human aggression, most theories can be classified into one of three types: instinctual theories, drive reduction models, or social learning theories.

Instinctual Theories

Popular in the early years of the 20th century, ***instinctual theories of aggression*** reflect the belief that humans possess an inherited predisposition to act aggressively (see Figure 12.2). Sigmund Freud and Konrad Lorenz are recognized as having made the primary contributions to this line of thinking. Freud believed that people are motivated toward self-destruction through a death instinct he called thanatos (Freud, 1920, 1930; Hall & Lindzey, 1968). Freud also thought that humans possess a life instinct he called eros and that the thanatos and eros instincts were in conflict. The conflict could be resolved by redirecting the self-destructive, aggressive energy outwardly toward others (thus satisfying both instincts). In a similar approach, Lorenz (1966) argued that humans (and other organisms) possess a fighting instinct. Lorenz believed that the instinct is triggered by negative environmental stimuli. The display of overt aggression is thought to be the result of an interaction between the amount of accumulated aggressive energy and the presence and strength of the aggression-releasing environmental stimulus (Lorenz, 1974).

Perhaps the aspect of instinctual theories gaining the most attention is the notion of catharsis (see Figure 12.2). ***Catharsis*** is the release of aggression through aggression. There are actually two forms of catharsis: aggression catharsis and symbolic catharsis (Geen, 1990). ***Aggression catharsis*** involves the release of aggression through one's own aggressive responses. Because this form of catharsis involves the aggressive actions of players, it is relevant to the current chapter. ***Symbolic***

FIGURE 12.2   According to instinctual theories of aggression, innate aggressive urges can be released through aggression catharsis (i.e., overt aggressive) or symbolic catharsis (i.e., viewing aggression).

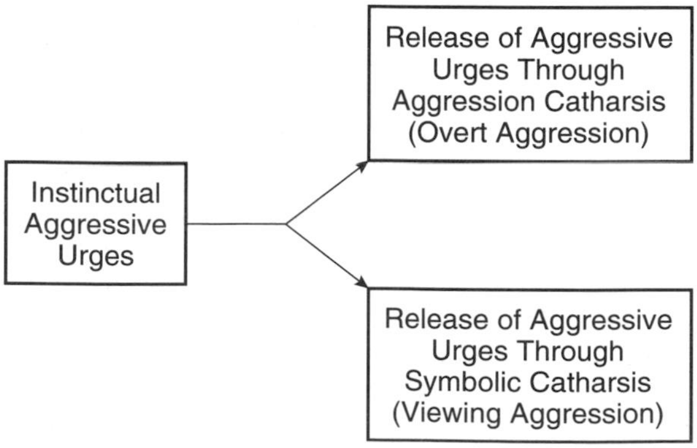

catharsis involves the release of aggression by viewing the aggressive actions of others. Because this form of catharsis is most relevant to the aggressive responses of sport fans and spectators, discussion of this topic will be reserved for a later chapter.

Both Freud and Lorenz believed that sport is beneficial for society because of its cathartic qualities (Sipes, 1973). For example, Lorenz (1966) stated that, "the main function of sports today lies in the cathartic discharge of aggressive urges" (p. 280). Other theorists extended this line of thinking by suggesting that the cathartic nature of sport decreases the likelihood of war (Mead, 1955; Murdock, 1949; Tiger, 1969). However, a number of studies have refuted the notion of aggression catharsis (see Baron & Richardson, 1994). In fact, not only does participation in aggressive sports fail to lower the players' aggression, participation often leads to an increase in aggressive tendencies (although aggressive actions may lower one's level of physiological arousal, see Geen, 1990; Hokanson, 1970; Hokanson & Burgess, 1962). For example, consider the work of Patterson published in 1974. This investigator asked scholastic football players and physical education students to complete a hostility inventory before and after a football season. In direct contradiction to aggression catharsis, the football players displayed an increase in aggression from the beginning to the end of the season, while students in the physical education classes showed no change in aggression. Zillmann, Johnson, and Day (1974a) compared the aggressive tendencies of athletes participating in aggressive sports, athletes participating in nonaggressive sports, and nonathletes. The results indicated no differences in aggressive tendencies among the groups. Again, this contradicts the theory of aggression catharsis because subjects participating in the aggressive sports should have been less hostile. In another study refuting the notion of aggression catharsis, Frintner and Rubinson (1993) examined the behaviors of male college students and found that athletes were more likely than nonathletes to commit violent acts against women. Had the cathartic perspective been correct, we would have expected the athlete population to commit fewer crimes because their aggressive urges were released on the playing field. Several other studies have also failed to support the belief that aggressive actions lead to a lowering of an individual's aggressive tendencies (e.g., Collins, Hale, & Loomis, 1995; Crosset, Benedict, & McDonald, 1995; Husman, 1955; Ryan, 1970; Sipes, 1973; Zillmann, Katcher, & Milavsky, 1972).

Although a large body of research has refuted the notion of aggression catharsis, a number of individuals continue to believe in this perspective, including athletic coaches (Bennett, 1991) and psychologists (Biaggio, 1987). Russell (1983; see also Russell, Arms, & Bibby, 1995) found that the general public also tends to support the catharsis viewpoint. Russell asked more than 500 college students if they felt that "Participating in combatant or aggressive sports is a good way for people to get rid of their aggressive urges" (p. 159). He found that 63% of the respondents agreed with the statement.

Evaluating the Instinctual Approaches.   A number of problems with the instinctual perspectives have been identified. For example, because constructs such as "thanatos" and a "fighting instinct" are difficult or impossible to document empirically, they are difficult to prove or disprove. Also, as mentioned in the motivation chapter, instinctual theories tend to be based on circular logic. In his review of the literature, Berkowitz (1969a) argued for a rejection of the instinctual perspectives because these theories lacked control, included poor operational definitions, were oversimplified, and made inappropriate comparisons between the behaviors of lower animals and the actions of humans. Due to these and other problems, instinctual approaches to aggression fell out of favor.

Drive Reduction Models and the Frustration-Aggression Hypothesis

In the 1930s, drive reduction models began to replace the instinctual viewpoints. ***Drive reduction models of aggression*** reflect the belief that aggression stems from an aggressive drive that has been triggered by an external stimulus (recall that a drive is an internal state of tension). The most popular drive reduction model is the frustration aggression hypothesis proposed by Dollard, Doob, Miller, Mowrer, and Sears (1939). The ***frustration-aggression hypothesis*** argues that the inability to attain a goal leads to frustration. The frustration then triggers an aggressive drive, which facilitates overt aggression. This pattern of effects is depicted graphically in Figure 12.3. While instinctual theorists clearly predicted that aggression is inherited rather than learned, supporters of the frustration-aggression hypothesis seemed to avoid taking sides on this issue. For example, Miller et al. (1941) stated that "no assumptions are made as to whether the frustration-aggression relationship is of innate or of learned origin" (p. 340). Likewise, Berkowitz (1969b, p. 4) argues that "the frustration-aggression hypothesis may be *learnable* without being entirely *learned*," indicating that the hostile effects of frustration can be inherited, learned, or both.

In their original formulation of the frustration-aggression hypothesis, Dollard and his colleagues (1939) proposed that frustration always leads to aggression and aggression always follows frustration. Although the simplicity of this perspective enhanced its attractiveness, in reality this was an oversimplification of the process. That is, although frustration often leads to aggression, it may also lead to other behaviors

FIGURE 12.3   According to the original frustration-aggression hypothesis, frustration from the inability to attain a goal leads to an aggressive drive that is reduced through aggression catharsis (i.e., overt aggression) or symbolic catharsis (i.e., viewing aggression).

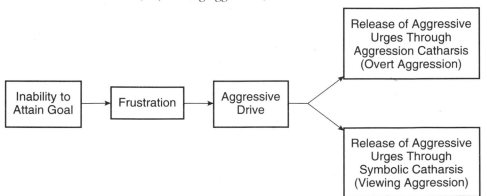

such as depression and "giving up." Likewise, while aggression can follow frustration, individuals behave in a hostile fashion for other reasons as well. Because they had obviously overstated the importance of the frustration-aggression link, Miller (one of the original authors) softened the theory, arguing that frustration often leads to aggression and aggression is often the result of frustration (Miller et al., 1941).

Although the frustration-aggression theory presented by Dollard and his associates differed immensely from the instinctual perspectives, these viewpoints both shared the notion of catharsis. In fact, Dollard et al. (1939) believed that almost any form of aggression lowered the individual's disposition toward further aggressive actions (see Figure 12.3). Thus, one's aggressive drive could be reduced through aggression aimed at the source of the frustration or through the displacement of aggression directed toward another person or inanimate object. When choosing the target of displacement, Miller (1948) felt that frustrated individuals search for targets similar to the source of the frustration.

The Aggressive Cue/Neoassociation Theory of Aggression. Throughout the past several decades, Leonard Berkowitz has authored a series of papers modifying the original frustration-aggression hypothesis (Berkowitz, 1969b, 1974, 1983, 1988, 1989). Berkowitz's reformulation has been called the ***aggressive cue/cognitive neoassociation theory*** (see Figure 12.4). According to Berkowitz (1989), frustration resulting from the inability to attain a goal leads to aggressive inclinations because the frustration is perceived as aversive (i.e., the frustration leads to anger). Further, this theory asserts that the presence of aggressive cues increases the likelihood of an overt aggressive response. ***Aggressive cues*** are objects, settings, or persons previously or presently associated with aggression. Although Berkowitz (1989) does not view aggressive cues as necessary for aggressive behavior, their presence is thought to enhance the likelihood that the frustrated individual will respond in an aggressive fashion. In contradiction to the stance of Dollard et al. (1939), Berkowitz (1964, 1981) does not agree with the catharsis hypothesis.

In 1988, Frank and Gilovich published a series of studies examining the cuing effects of black athletic uniforms. They argued that, because "Black is viewed as the color of evil and death in virtually all cultures" (p. 74), there may be a high level of

FIGURE 12.4 This diagram reflects Berkowitz's reformulation of the frustration-aggression hypothesis (the aggressive cue/neoassociation theory of aggression). Berkowitz believes that the inability to attain a goal leads to frustration. The frustration then leads to negative affect which, in turn, leads to an aggressive drive. The presence of an aggressive cue increases the likelihood of overt aggression.

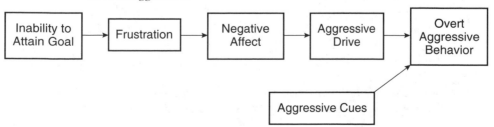

aggressiveness associated with football and hockey teams wearing black uniforms. In the first study, 25 subjects possessing no knowledge of football and hockey were presented with slides depicting the uniforms of the National Football League (NFL) and National Hockey League (NHL) teams. Participants were asked to rate the aggressiveness of the uniforms. As expected, subjects believed the black uniforms found in both the NFL ($n = 5$, e.g., the Los Angeles Raiders and Pittsburgh Steelers) and the NHL ($n = 5$, e.g., the Boston Bruins and Chicago Blackhawks) were more aggressive than nonblack uniforms. In a second study, Frank and Gilovich (1988) examined the penalty records of the NFL and NHL teams. Their logic in this analysis was that penalties may indicate the aggressiveness of a team (penalty records appear to be a good indication of aggression in sport, see Vokey & Russell, 1992). The sample included the NFL penalty yards and NHL penalty minutes between 1970 and 1986. The authors found that the five NFL teams (ranked 1st, 3rd, 7th, 8th, and 12th out of 28 teams) and the five NHL teams (ranked 1st, 2nd, 3rd, 6th, and 10th out of 21 teams) with black uniforms were among the most penalized teams.

The work of Frank and Gilovich (1988) points to the powerful cuing effects of black uniforms. It is conceivable that three different groups of individuals may receive the aggressive cuing effects of black uniforms: spectators, officials, and players. The implications of aggressive cuing for spectators will be reviewed in a future chapter. As for officials, Frank and Gilovich noted that the increased penalties found in football and hockey may be due to the sensitivity of referees to black uniforms. To test this possibility, the authors asked 20 high school and college football referees to view two mildly violent football plays in which the defensive team wore either a black or white uniform (the offensive team wore a red uniform). The plays were staged by former football players, and the black and white uniform versions were identical except for the color of the defensive team's jersey. When asked to rate the likelihood that they would penalize the play of the defensive team, referees viewing the black uniform version were more likely to call a penalty than those watching the white uniform version.

To test the notion that the players are cued to act aggressively by black uniforms, Frank and Gilovich (1988) conducted a final study. In this experiment, small groups of subjects were told that they would be competing with another group in a series of activities. Subjects were given a list of activities varying in aggressiveness from highly aggressive (e.g., a dart gun fight) to not at all aggressive (e.g., a putting contest) and asked to choose, individually, the five most preferable activities. The group members were then asked to wear either a black or white uniform and to reevaluate their activity preferences as a team. Consistent with predictions, teams became more aggressive in their activity preferences when wearing black uniforms, while no such increase was found in subjects wearing white uniforms. Thus, Frank and Gilovich (1988) concluded that "the excessive penalties amassed by black-uniformed teams in professional sports stem from two distinct processes—their own aggressiveness and harsher treatment by the referees" (p. 83).

Evaluating the Frustration-Aggression Approach.   In its original state, the frustration-aggression hypothesis overstated the relationship between frustration and ag-

Research indicates that athletes wearing predominantly black uniforms are more aggressive than athletes wearing uniforms featuring a different color. (Photographer: Mitchell Layton. Source: Duomo Photography.)

gression. As a result, this version of the theory was lacking in merit. However, the newer perspective that frustration often (rather than always) leads to aggression and aggression often follows frustration is substantiated by research, and Berkowitz's adaptations have increased the validity of the theory. For example, in their study of aggression in Belgium soccer, Lefebvre and Passer (1974) found a tendency for players on a losing team to commit more fouls than players on a winning team (presumably, losing players are more frustrated than winning players). In a different study, Ryan (1970) found that subjects losing a nail hammering competition were more aggressive than those winning the competition. Other authors have also found that losers tend to be more aggressive than winners (Leith, 1989; Martin, 1976). Thus, it appears as though the current form of the frustration-aggression hypothesis is a useful framework for understanding sport aggression.

Social Learning Theory

Social learning theory is a third major approach to understanding human aggression. Proposed by Bandura (1973, 1977b, 1983), ***social learning theory*** reflects the belief that aggressive behaviors are learned through operant conditioning and observational learning. As for operant conditioning, recall from the learning chapter that reinforcing a behavior increases the likelihood that the behavior will be repeated. For example, coaches, parents, and fans who reward the aggression and hostility of players are increasing the attractiveness of this style of play. Similarly, when an athlete behaves in an aggressive manner and subsequently wins a competition, he or she will most likely continue to act aggressively.

Although Bandura acknowledges the importance of operant conditioning in the acquisition of aggressive behavior, he believes that observational learning plays an equal or greater role in the learning of aggression (remember that observational learning involves vicarious learning through modeling). As we discussed in the learning chapter, Bandura (1986) believes there are four steps in the observational learning process: attention, memory, ability, and motivation. For example, consider a young basketball player who is watching her favorite team on television. During the game, her favorite player commits a flagrant foul against the opposing team's best player, injuring him to the point at which he can no longer play. Without the services of their top player, the opposing team is defeated by a large margin. As a result, the young athlete begins to believe that injuring a talented opponent can facilitate one's chances of victory. Bandura's theory posits that before the young player will reproduce the aggressive act, she must attend to the behavior, remember the behavior, possess the abilities to imitate the behavior, and be motivated to do so. If her attention had been diverted when her favorite player committed the foul, she would not be able to reproduce the behavior. Likewise, if she did not remember the player's illegal actions when she was playing in her next game, she could not imitate the aggression. Further, if she did not possess the ability to repeat the behavior (perhaps because she had not reached the cognitive level of development needed to comprehend the action), she would not be able to imitate the athlete. Finally, if she were not motivated to act aggressively, it would not be expected that she would reproduce the player's hostile actions.

Evaluating Social Learning Theory.   A major premise of Bandura's social learning theory is that viewing aggression leads to further aggression. Thus, the social learning perspective lies in direct opposition to the principle of catharsis. A number of investigations have found that viewing aggression facilitates subsequent hostile actions, thus supporting Bandura's contentions (Bandura, 1973). Social learning theory argues that young players can learn to act aggressively by watching the aggression of older players. Congruent with the social learning perspective, research has substantiated this logic. For example, consider the work of Russell (1979). In this research, 205 young Canadian hockey players were asked to state their favorite National Hockey League teams. When the teams' penalties were correlated with team selections, a positive relationship emerged. That is, players preferred the more aggressive teams. Further, Smith (1980) notes that young athletes often model the aggressive play of parents, even if the parents are no longer active in sport but describe themselves as formerly aggressive players.

Comparing the Classic Theories: A Concrete Example

Perhaps the best way to delineate the classic theories of aggression is through a concrete example. Imagine that a little league baseball team is batting in the final inning of a game they are losing by 10 runs. The first batter of the inning, Eric, has just charged the mound after being hit by a pitch. The instinctual, frustration-aggression, and social learning theories would present vastly different arguments to account for Eric's hostile actions. As for the instinctual perspective, supporters of this viewpoint would argue that Eric's behavior reflects his innate need to act aggressively. In addition, supporters of these theories would argue that Eric's aggression could be reduced through catharsis.

Supporters of the frustration-aggression hypothesis would argue that Eric's aggressive display was the result of the frustration of losing the game. The frustration, in turn, initiated the aggressive drive. Consistent with individuals adopting an instinctual viewpoint, individuals supporting the original frustration-aggression hypothesis would argue that Eric could have reduced his aggressive drive through catharsis. Berkowitz's stance, however, would argue for a different pattern of effects. Supporters of Berkowitz's reformulation of the frustration-aggression hypothesis would argue that the frustration of losing led to negative affect. The negative affect then initiated the aggressive drive. Further, because the situation was accompanied by several aggressive cues (e.g., the bat and the hostile cries of the spectators), the likelihood of an aggressive response was enhanced. Unlike the instinctual perspective and the original statement of the frustration-aggression hypothesis, researchers adopting Berkowitz's approach would not feel that Eric's aggression could have been reduced through catharsis.

Finally, theorists following Bandura's social learning approach would hypothesize that Eric's aggression was the result of operant conditioning, observational learning, or both. As for operant conditioning, these theorists would note that Eric's attempt to start a fight during a previous game was verbally rewarded by his coach. Regarding the process of observational learning, Bandura's supporters would point to the high level of media attention given to a number of professional baseball players who had charged the mound after being hit by a pitch.

SITUATIONAL FACTORS PROMOTING PLAYER AGGRESSION

Research has consistently found that situational factors can promote aggression (Baron & Richardson, 1994; Berkowitz, 1993; Geen, 1990). In this section, we will review several situational factors found at sporting events that increase the likelihood of player aggression.

Physiological Arousal

Some situational factors facilitate aggressive behavior because they lead to increases in physiological arousal (e.g., increases in heart rate, blood pressure, respiration). Research has found that increases in arousal can intensify negative emotional responses, thereby increasing the likelihood of overt aggressive actions (Baron & Richardson, 1994; Geen, 1990; Rule & Nesdale, 1976). Zillmann's (1971, 1988) *excitation transfer theory* was designed to account for this effect. According to Zillmann's theory, residual arousal from one setting can be misattributed to a subsequent emotional setting, thereby intensifying the emotional response. For example, imagine that a softball player, Mary Jo, has just completed a 15-minute base running exercise. Within a few minutes of finishing, Mary Jo is unfairly accused of selfish play by a teammate. The likelihood of Mary Jo responding to the accusation in an aggressive fashion is enhanced because she is aroused from the running exercise. However, the residual arousal from the jogging exercise must be misattributed to the unkind remarks of the teammate. If the residual arousal were correctly attributed to the exercise, the transfer effect would not occur because Mary Jo would assume that her arousal was due to the exercise, not because of her teammate's harsh remarks (Zillmann & Bryant, 1974). A number of studies have supported Zillmann's hypothesis (e.g., Cantor, Zillmann, & Einsiedel, 1978; Christy, Gelfand, & Hartmann, 1971; O'Neal, McDonald, Hori, & McClinton, 1977), including several using exercise to induce arousal (e.g., Bryant & Zillmann, 1979; Zillmann, Johnson, & Day, 1974b; Zillmann et al., 1972).

Zillmann's hypothesis predicts that situational forces at sporting events leading to heightened physiological arousal can facilitate player aggression. In sport settings, heat and noise are two situational factors that are especially likely to increase the arousal and aggression of players.

The Relationship between Heat and Aggression.   Several investigators have found a positive correlation between heat and aggression. Some of the studies were field/archival in nature, examining the relationship between daily high temperatures and riots (Anderson, 1989; Baron & Ransberger, 1978; Carlsmith & Anderson, 1979). In these studies, the relationship between heat and aggression appeared to be linear (see Figure 12.5). However, research in the laboratory has been less clear (Baron & Richardson, 1994). In laboratory settings, the relationship between heat and ag-

FIGURE 12.5   The conflicting findings of laboratory and field/archival research examining the heat-aggression relationship.

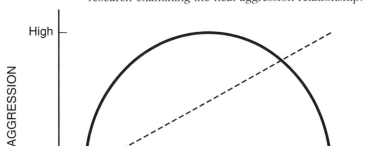

gression has appeared to be curvilinear (see Figure 12.5). For example, Baron and his colleagues found that aggression increased with higher temperatures initially, but when the temperature got too high, aggression began to decline (Baron & Bell, 1975, 1976; Baron & Ransberger, 1978). To account for this pattern of effects, Baron hypothesized that when temperatures reach a high level, they become extremely uncomfortable. At this point, individuals focus their attention on escaping the situation rather than being aggressive toward others (Baron & Richardson, 1994).

Although the pattern of results from field/archival research and laboratory studies is inconsistent, the differences can be reconciled. In the real world, escape from high temperatures is often difficult or impossible. As a result, a linear relationship between heat and aggression emerges. On the other hand, subjects in laboratory experiments realize that they have the right to terminate their participation at anytime. If they act aggressively, they may prolong the study and remain in the uncomfortably hot environment. As a result, individuals may lessen their aggressive responses, thus shortening the study and escaping the uncomfortable setting more quickly.

Thus, research suggests that player aggression should increase with a moderate rise in temperature. However, if the temperature reaches a critically high level and the player has the option of escaping the situation, we would expect a decrease in aggression. Research conducted by Reifman, Larrick, and Fein (1991) is relevant to these hypotheses. These authors examined more than 800 Major League baseball games from 1986 to 1988 and recorded the number of hit batters and the high temperature for the home city for each game. Consistent with predictions, these investigators found a positive relationship between temperature and the number of hit batsmen, even when controlling for variables such as pitcher wildness, errors, home runs, and attendance. The pattern of results revealed a linear relationship between heat and aggression, a finding that is consistent with the logic outlined above. That is, because the pitchers were unable to escape the heat (unless they removed themselves from the game), the heat continued to facilitate their aggression. Had the pitchers been able to escape the heat, one would have expected a lower rate of aggression on extremely hot days.

The Relationship between Noise and Aggression.   Noise is another arousal-inducing situational factor present at sporting events. Several studies have found that high decibel noise facilitates aggressive responses, particularly when the noise is uncontrollable (Donnerstein & Wilson, 1976; Geen, 1978; Geen & O'Neal, 1969; Glass & Singer, 1972). Within sport settings, researchers have yet to examine empirically the relationship between crowd noise and aggression. However, because the research from general psychology has consistently found that loud noise encourages aggressive behavior, it is likely that crowd noise is a contributing factor to player aggression.

Intent

Individuals are more likely to retaliate against someone if they believe the other person's aggressive actions were intentional (Betancourt & Blair, 1992; Dodge, Murphy, & Buchsbaum, 1984; Epstein & Taylor, 1967; Zillmann & Cantor, 1976). Harrell (1980) examined the relationship between intent and aggression in sport. In this study, the actions of 45 high school basketball players were recorded. Specifically, observers noted a number of potential predictors of aggression including (1) the number of aggressive actions exhibited by the target player; (2) the number of turnovers the target committed; (3) the amount of time the target played; (4) the number of aggressive actions directed toward the target by members of the opposing team; (5) the target's number of field goals and free throws; and (6) the target's height, weight, and position. The results indicated that the best predictor of player aggression was prior intentional aggression from an opponent. Players were most likely to behave aggressively when they themselves were the initial target of aggression.

Competition Outcome and Point Differential

As noted earlier, losers of athletic competitions tend to be more aggressive than winners. However, some studies have not found this pattern of effects (e.g., Cullen & Cullen, 1975; Wankel, 1973; Worrell & Harris, 1986), leading to some disagreement on the impact of competition outcome. Russell (1983) hypothesized that clearer results could be obtained if researchers examine the point differential of the final score rather than simply dichotomizing the outcome variable. Russell studied the relationship between penalty minutes and final score point differential for winners and losers of 430 hockey games. He found that losers were more likely to display aggression when they lost by three or more goals, while winners were most likely to be aggressive when they had been victorious by three or more goals. Relatively few penalties occurred when the final score was close (i.e., two or fewer goals separating the teams). Other research has substantiated Russell's findings (Rainey & Cherilla, 1993; Russell & Drewry, 1976; Wankel, 1973).

Thus, player aggression appears to be most likely when the point spread is large. Russell and others have attempted to account for this finding by examining the cognitions of players (Russell, 1983; Russell & Drewry, 1976; Wankel, 1973). Because aggressive actions are against the rules of the game, players realize that their hostile actions may be penalized. If the penalty occurs at a critical point in the contest (i.e., when the game is close), it may damage the team's chances for victory. As a result, players are more likely to be aggressive when their team is comfortably ahead or hopelessly behind.

Game Location

As most sport fans know, home teams tend to outperform visiting teams (a topic we will examine in Chapter 14). In an attempt to explain this phenomenon, Edwards (1979) argued that home teams perform better because they are attempting to protect their territory. Based on this logic, we would expect home teams to act more aggressively than visiting teams. However, in his review of the literature, Russell (1981a) found little support for this line of thinking. Russell's survey revealed that several studies found no differences in the aggressiveness of the home and visiting teams. In addition, some studies that did find aggressive differences revealed that the away team was more likely to act aggressively than the home team. Russell's work was replicated by McGuire, Courneya, Widmeyer, and Carron's (1992) research on professional ice hockey. Thus, contrary to Edwards' (1979) contentions, it appears as though there are no differences in the aggression of home and away teams.

League Standings

Based on the frustration-aggression hypothesis, one would expect first place teams to display lower levels of aggression than lower place teams. That is, because they are attaining their goal of leading the league and, therefore, are not frustrated, first place teams should not display a high level of aggression. Teams not currently in first place should be frustrated by their league standing and, as a result, exhibit higher levels of aggression. Studies by Russell and Drewry (1976) and Volkamer (1971) confirm this pattern of effects. However, although both studies found that teams trailing the league leader were higher in aggression than the leader, the pattern of aggression differed among the trailing teams. Russell and Drewry found that, as teams moved up the standings, they exhibited higher levels of aggression. These authors argued that, as teams get closer to first place, the frustration of not being the league leader became more salient. As a result, the second place team was the most aggressive team in the league. Volkamer, on the other hand, found that the lowest place teams exhibited the highest levels of aggression. Volkamer states that frustration increases as teams get further from their goal of winning the league. Therefore, the last place team should be the most aggressive team in the league. Thus, although these authors agree that the first place team should be the least aggressive team in the league, they disagree on which team should display the highest level of aggression. Future research is needed to clarify the frustration and aggression of teams not currently in first place.

Point in Time during Competition

Some researchers have examined the relationship between the point in time during the competition and the level of aggression among the players. Russell's (1981a, 1983) review of this literature led him to conclude that aggression tends to increase as the contest progresses. For example, in their 7-year investigation of aggression in university ice hockey, Kelly and McCarthy (1979) found that the players exhibited more aggression in the second and third periods than in the first period.

However, stating that aggression increases for all teams as the game continues is an oversimplification. Rather, successful and unsuccessful teams may display a different pattern of effects. Cullen and Cullen (1975) found this to be true in their investigation of hockey players. In this research, aggression increased in a linear fashion for winners but in a curvilinear fashion for losers (losing teams tended to display the highest level of aggression in the middle of a contest). It is likely that losing players cease their aggressive actions because these behaviors are not being rewarded or are perceived as inhibiting their performance. Losing players may also refrain from aggressive behavior later in the game because they believe any penalties resulting from the aggression will hurt or eliminate any remaining chances for success. On the other hand, winning players most likely continue to be aggressive because aggression is perceived as a successful strategy.

Steroid Use and Aggression

A final situational factor that can facilitate player aggression involves the use of anabolic steroids. While other individual differences such as Machiavellianism, locus of control, conservatism, and moral reasoning may be related to aggression (Bredemeier, 1985, 1994; Bredemeier & Shields, 1986; Russell, 1974, 1981b), I have chosen to focus on steroids because of the dangerous ramifications of steroid use.

Steroids are drugs designed to allow athletes to train longer and increase their muscle mass. Research has indicated that an increase in aggression is a major negative side effect of these drugs (Gregg & Rejeski, 1990; Lubell, 1989). For example, Yates, Perry, and Murray (1992) asked 37 weight lifters to complete the Buss-Durkee Hostility Inventory. The sample consisted of 12 current or former steroid users and 25 controls who had never used steroids. The results indicated that the steroid users were higher in aggression than nonusers, particularly on the assault, indirect aggression, and verbal aggression subscales. Because of the dangers accompanying the use of anabolic steroids, both for users in terms of physical damage and for others due to the user's heightened aggression, the International Society of Sport Psychology (1993) published a position statement encouraging the prohibition of steroid use. Coaches, particularly those involved with youth, scholastic, or collegiate athletes, should actively discourage steroid use among their players and severely punish, or even suspend, those players found to be using these dangerous drugs.

SUGGESTIONS FOR REDUCING PLAYER AGGRESSION

I would like to end this chapter by offering several suggestions for reducing player aggression. These suggestions were developed from a combination of my own research and the remarks of other authors (Cratty, 1989; Cox, 1990; Goldstein, 1989; LeUnes & Nation, 1989).

1. It is important to provide young players with nonaggressive role models. Coaches who act aggressively themselves or allow older players to behave aggressively are in essence suggesting that these behaviors are acceptable.
2. Coaches should not reward aggressive behavior. While assertive behavior should be encouraged, athletes displaying aggressive behavior should be removed from the field and suspended from future games if they repeat the hostile actions. Coaches encouraging aggressive and violent play should be asked or forced to resign their positions.
3. Spectators whose presence encourages player aggression should be removed from the area.
4. Because a large amount of player aggression arises out of perceptions of injustice (Mark, Bryant, & Lehman, 1983), leagues should hire qualified officials. Leagues relying on inexperienced officials are inviting trouble because these individuals will not be perceived as authority figures (see Chapter 13 for a further discussion of this point). Officials who instigate hostilities between themselves and players or coaches should be replaced.
5. Coaches and officials should receive formal training in dealing with and curtailing aggression.

6. Players who choose not to act aggressively when confronted with a potentially hostile situation should be rewarded and used as role models.
7. Fair play and enjoyment should be stressed while winning should be deemphasized (especially for younger athletes). Because winning is no longer the central goal of the competition, losing athletes will be less frustrated and less likely to act aggressively.
8. Reduce or eliminate the presence of alcohol.

SUMMARY

Aggression is one of the most pervasive negative aspects of sport today. Whether players commit the aggressive act because of a desire to hurt the target or because they want to improve their chances of victory, many athletes resort to violence during competition. Most theorists have adopted one of three classic approaches in their attempt to understand the origins of aggression. Early psychologists usually sided with an instinctual perspective, arguing that aggressive urges are innate. Later, many psychologists adopted the notion of an aggressive drive. The most prominent drive reduction model is the frustration-aggression hypothesis. This approach reflects the belief that aggression is a result of frustration from the inability to attain a desired goal. While different in many ways, instinctual theories and the frustration-aggression hypothesis share the notion of catharsis. However, research has consistently contradicted the catharsis hypothesis. Berkowitz recently reformulated the frustration-aggression hypothesis by stating that frustration leads to negative affect and that aggressive cues facilitate the likelihood of aggressive responses. The third general model of aggression, the social learning approach, reflects the belief that individuals learn to behave aggressively through operant conditioning and observational learning.

Research has found that (1) the physiological arousal accompanying noisy and/or uncomfortably hot environments can facilitate aggression; (2) if athletes believe that the aggressive actions of others were intentional, they are more likely to be aggressive themselves; (3) aggression is most likely to occur in lopsided games and later in the contest; (4) home and visiting teams do not appear to exhibit a differential amount of aggression; (5) first place teams appear to be less aggressive than teams not leading the league; and (6) steroid use facilitates player aggression.

GLOSSARY

Aggression   The intent to physically, verbally, or psychologically harm someone who is motivated to avoid such treatment or the physical destruction of property when motivated by anger.

Aggression Catharsis   The release of aggression through one's own aggressive responses.

Aggressive Cues   Objects, settings, or persons previously or presently associated with aggression.

Aggressive Cue/Cognitive Neoassociation Theory   A theory reflecting the belief that frustrations resulting from the inability to attain a goal lead to aggressive inclinations because the frustrations are perceived as aversive, and that aggressive cues increase the likelihood of an overt aggressive response.

Assertiveness   The use of legitimate force and strategy to achieve a goal.

Catharsis   The release of aggression through aggression.

Drive Reduction Models of Aggression   Theories reflecting the belief that aggression stems from an aggressive drive that has been triggered by an external stimulus.

Excitation Transfer Theory   A theory reflecting the belief that residual arousal from one setting can be misattributed to a subsequent emotional setting, thereby intensifying the emotional response.

Frustration-Aggression Hypothesis   A theory reflecting the belief that the inability to attain a goal leads to frustration. The frustration then triggers an aggressive drive which facilitates overt aggression.

Hostile Aggression   Aggressive actions motivated by anger that have the intent and goal of harming another person (or object).

Instinctual Theories of Aggression   Theories reflecting the belief that humans possess an inherited predisposition to act aggressively.

Instrumental Aggression   Aggressive actions intended to harm another person with the goal of achieving a result other than the victim's suffering.

Social Learning Theory   A theory reflecting the belief that aggressive behaviors are learned through operant conditioning and observational learning.

Symbolic Catharsis   The release of aggression by viewing the aggressive actions of others.

APPLICATION AND REVIEW QUESTIONS

1. Describe the differences among hostile aggression, instrumental aggression, and assertiveness. Construct a sport-specific example of each.
2. Describe the aggressive behavior of a former teammate or opponent. Analyze and account for the behavior using (1) the instinctual approach, (2) the original frustration-aggression hypothesis, (3) Berkowitz's reformulation of the frustration-aggression hypothesis (i.e., the aggressive cue/cognitive neoassociation model), and (4) the social learning perspective.
3. Describe the principle of catharsis. Does research support this principle?
4. It was noted that noise and heat may facilitate aggressive responses because these factors increase physiological arousal. Can you think of other situational factors found at sporting events that could raise the arousal level of players?
5. How does (1) intent, (2) point differential, (3) league standing, and (4) the point in time during a competition impact player aggression?

SUGGESTED READINGS

Baron, R. A., & Richardson, D. R. (1994). *Human aggression* (2nd ed.). New York: Plenum Press. This book is the second edition to Baron's classic text on human aggression. The text covers most of the important topics related to aggressive behavior including the classic theories of aggression, social and personality factors related to aggression, and the biological bases of aggression.

Geen, R. G. (1990). *Human aggression.* Pacific Grove, CA: Brooks/Cole. Similar to the Baron and Richardson book, Geen's text provides the reader with a general overview of human aggression. However, because Geen's book is approximately half the size of the Baron and Richardson text, some readers may find Geen's book a bit less cumbersome.

Goldstein, J. H. (Ed.). (1983). *Sport violence.* New York: Springer-Verlag. This book is recommended to anyone interested in sport aggression. Written by leading authors and researchers in sport violence, the chapters in this volume cover many interesting phenomena, including player and spectator aggression, psychological issues related to sport aggression, and perceptions of injustice.

Chapter 13

LEADERSHIP
IN SPORT

Like most organizations, sport teams need qualified leaders to be successful. Thus, leadership is extremely important. **Leadership** is a behavioral process in which one group member influences the other members regarding the attainment of the group's goals. The importance of leadership in sport is reflected in the performance implications of managerial and coaching changes. Although performance may increase for a short period subsequent to a change (Fabianic, 1994; McTeer, White, & Persad, 1995), frequent changes can be detrimental to team performance because they disrupt the flow and stability of team leadership (Grusky, 1963). For example, consider the research of Allen, Panian, and Lotz (1979) on the influence of professional baseball managerial changes. These authors correlated managerial changes and winning percentages for more than 50 seasons and found a negative relationship. That is, as the number of managerial changes increased, performance decreased. The harmful effects of leadership changes in sport appear to be most powerful during the season when leadership stability is most important (Allen et al., 1979; Brown, 1982).

In this chapter, we will examine the causes and consequences of leadership in sport. We will begin our investigation by examining the sources of power possessed by leaders. This section will be followed by a review of the common traits and behaviors of leaders. We will end this chapter by examining several theories of leadership and their application to sport settings.

LEADERSHIP POWER

Power is defined as the ability to influence or change the attitudes or behaviors of others (Baron & Greenberg 1990; Keys & Case, 1990; Ragins & Sundstrom, 1989). Players, coaches, owners, sport reporters, and fans all have power if they are able to influence or change the behaviors of others. However, because they most likely have the greatest impact on team and individual performances, we will focus our attention on the power of players and coaches.

Sources of Power

French and Raven (1959) identified five different sources of power: expert, legitimate, referent, reward, and coercive. These sources of power are briefly described in Table 13.1.

Expert Power.   Expert power is a common source of power in sport settings. ***Expert power*** is the ability to change another individual's attitude or behavior because a person is believed to be knowledgeable, skillful, or talented in a certain area. For example, young baseball players are especially likely to follow the suggestions of a coach who is a former professional athlete. Similarly, running backs are more likely to comply with the demands of the running back coach than the quarterback coach. An individual's expert power is limited in scope. For instance, offensive players will follow the offensive coordinator's suggestions concerning the offense because this coach is viewed as an expert in this area. However, the offensive coordinator will not be able to enlist the players' compliance with his demands concerning defensive tactics because he is not seen as an expert in this phase of the game.

Legitimate Power.   Another common source of power in sport settings is legitimate power. ***Legitimate power*** is the ability to change another individual's attitude or behavior because of a person's position within the organization or group. The individual's position within the organizational framework justifies the request. For example, many players follow the requests of a coach simply because this individual is recognized as an authority figure. Consider a baseball player whose coach has asked him to change his batting stance. Even if the player disagrees with the coach's suggestions, he will probably comply with the request because the coach possesses legitimate power. Likewise, because of the length of their tenure with the organization, veteran players possess a certain degree of legitimate power. Younger players often follow the suggestions of older players because of their position within the team's informal hierarchical structure.

TABLE 13.1   A General Summary of the Five Sources of Leadership Power

Source	*Description*
Expert Power	The ability to change another individual's attitude or behavior because a person is believed to be knowledgeable, skillful, or talented in a certain area.
Legitimate Power	The ability to change another individual's attitude or behavior because of a person's position in the organization.
Referent Power	The ability to change another individual's attitude or behavior because a person is liked and respected by the group members.
Reward Power	The ability to change someone's attitude or behavior because a person controls access to one or more desired rewards.
Coercive Power	The ability to change someone's attitude or behavior because a person controls access to one or more punishments.

Referent Power. ***Referent power*** is a third source of power found in athletic situations. This is the ability to change another individual's attitude or behavior because a person is liked and respected by the group members. Players are more likely to follow the directions of coaches they respect, like, and admire. A well-liked coach may be able to induce compliance simply because her players are loyal. Referent power can be very important to coaches involved with young athletes because these coaches often do not possess other sources of power. For example, these coaches may not be viewed as experts or legitimate authority figures. As a result, they must encourage loyalty and interpersonal attraction to get the players to comply with their demands.

Reward Power. ***Reward power*** is relevant to our discussion of the psychology of learning in Chapter 5. This form of power involves the ability to change someone's attitude or behavior because one controls access to desired rewards. For example, a player will follow the requests of a coach because the coach has the power to reward the player with playing time, verbal praise, and other rewards. Similarly, coaches and players comply with the requests of ownership because owners control the distribution of monetary rewards.

Coercive Power. A final source of power is coercive power. ***Coercive power*** is the ability to change someone's attitude or behavior because a person controls access to one or more punishments. Thus, this power source is also relevant to the psychology of learning. Not only can coaches increase playing time, they can also decrease playing time. Other punishments controlled by coaches include verbal reprimands, forcing a player to play a different and possibly less glamorous position, and making players run laps. Owners also control certain punishments (such as firing a coach and releasing a player) and, therefore, also possess a certain degree of coercive power.

The Effective Use of Power

In most situations, leaders possess more than one type of power. For example, coaches can increase and decrease an athletes playing time and, therefore, possess both reward and coercive power. Similarly, officials possess both expert and legitimate power, although, as discussed in this chapter's "A Closer Look," athletes of different ages have different beliefs about the power of officials. Because leaders often have multiple forms of power at their disposal, they should use the source of power most appropriate for a specific situation.

To help in this endeavor, Yukl (1989) offered several suggestions for increasing the effectiveness of the various forms of power. When using expert power, Yukl suggests that leaders make the subordinates aware of their educational background, previous experience, and relevant accomplishments. However, it is important for leaders to be subtle when informing the subordinates about their qualifications. If the information is presented in a boastful manner, subordinates are likely to believe the leader is a braggart. Leaders using expert power must keep informed and up-to-date concerning changes and advances in their area of expertise. For example, when

A CLOSER LOOK:
AGE DIFFERENCES IN PERCEPTIONS OF THE EXPERT
AND LEGITIMATE POWER OF SPORT OFFICIALS

Because of their position of authority, prior experience, and knowledge, sport officials usually possess a high level of expert and legitimate power. That is, they are able to change the attitudes and behaviors of coaches and players, and their decisions are not challenged simply because of their position as an official. In 1992, Rainey, Santilli, and Fallon conducted a study examining age differences in perceptions of the power possessed by baseball umpires.

Rainey and his colleagues asked 80 male baseball players to complete a questionnaire packet assessing their age and beliefs about the power of umpires (such as why they follow the directions and decisions of umpires, why the umpires are allowed to make the calls, and whether or not they would argue with an umpire). The subjects were classified into four age groups: 6 to 9 years, 10 to 13 years, 14 to 17 years, and 18 to 22 years. The authors then examined the relationships between age and perceptions of power.

The results indicated a strong relationship between age and perceptions of power. Players from the youngest age group reported following the umpires' decision because of their emotional relationships with the umpires. For example, they felt that if they did not follow the umpire's decision, he would become angry. Subjects from the middle age groups tended to believe in the legitimate power of the officials. These subjects stated that they would go along with the umpires' calls because "He's in charge" or "He's the boss" (p. 401). This group of subjects also believed the umpires possessed a high level of expert power, as did the oldest subjects. Those in the oldest group stated that the umpires' decisions should stand because "He knows what an umpire should do" or because "He's gone to umpire school" (p. 401). Thus, it appears that teenage athletes view officials as having the greatest level of legitimate power, while teenage and older athletes share the belief in the officials' expert power. However, very young athletes have not yet developed a belief in the legitimate or expert power of sport officials.

players feel that their coach is no longer an expert in his or her area of interest, the coach will no longer be able to enforce his or her decisions based on expert power.

As for legitimate power, Yukl suggests that individuals with this form of power should be polite and cordial when making requests. Requests phrased in an abrasive or confrontational manner can lead to resentment because subordinates may believe that the leader is simply trying to display his or her power. In addition, requests based on legitimate power should be accompanied by the reasons underlying the request. For example, when a player questions the rationale behind a coach's decision or request, the coach should never tell the player, "Because I told you so." If players do not feel that there is a sufficient reason for the request, they may conclude that the request is no more than a show of power and authority.

Regarding the use of referent power, Yukl notes that leaders can increase the effectiveness of this power base by treating the subordinates fairly and by giving the impression that they are concerned about the subordinates' welfare. Coaches can increase the effectiveness of their referent power by backing the players during the players' confrontations with management, fans, and reporters. In addition, leaders wanting to increase the effectiveness of their referent power should attempt to hire subordinates who are similar to themselves. For example, a "no nonsense" head coach will most likely have a better rapport with assistant coaches and players who possess a similar attitude. Conversely, a coach who is rather laid back in his approach to discipline will build better relationships with subordinates who are also laid back.

Concerning the effectiveness of reward power, leaders must insure that the request is successfully completed before rewarding the subordinate. If subordinates are rewarded when they have only completed a portion of the request, they will begin to believe that they do not have to comply fully with the leader's demands prior to reinforcement. For example, imagine a coach who tells a football player that he will start Friday's game if he completes his workout regimen each day from Monday to Thursday. Imagine further that, even though the player only completed his workout on Monday and Tuesday, the coach decided that this was close enough and allowed the player to start Friday's game. During the next week of workouts, do you think that the player will complete two or four workouts? Because he was rewarded for only two workouts during the previous week, it is likely that the player will complete only two workouts the following week.

Regarding coercive power, leaders must be certain that the request was not completed. If subordinates are punished unjustly, they will feel resentment and anger toward the leader. As a result, the leader's referent power will be diminished. However, leaders possessing coercive power can increase their referent power by warning subordinates prior to punishment and by punishing them in private. Other suggestions that can assist coaches in their use of reward and coercive power were listed at the end of the learning chapter.

THE TRAITS AND BEHAVIORS OF SUCCESSFUL LEADERS

During the past several decades, researchers have attempted to identify the traits and behaviors indicative of successful leadership. Originally, this work focused on the personality and physical characteristics of the leaders. Because this work was unsuccessful, researchers began to document the behaviors exhibited by successful leaders. In the following sections, we will examine both lines of research.

The Trait Approach to Leadership

During the early and middle years of this century, a large number of researchers tried to identify the traits and characteristics of successful leaders. These researchers believed in the ***trait approach to leadership.*** This approach reflects the belief that successful leaders possess traits that are lacking in less successful leaders. Good leaders were believed to be born with traits that facilitated their leadership success. Because these traits were thought to be enduring, leaders who were successful in one situation were expected to be successful in other situations as well. Although this line of reasoning appears to be intuitively sound, research testing the trait approach failed to find support for this model because a consistent pattern of attributes characteristic of leadership success was not found (Baron & Greenberg, 1990; Geier, 1969; Hellriegel, Slocum, & Woodman, 1992; Stogdill, 1948; Yukl, 1989).

Although the trait approach to leadership was generally abandoned by the 1960s, this was not the case in sport psychology. Rather, throughout the 1960s and early 1970s, sport researchers continued their efforts to identify psychological and physiological characteristics associated with successful sport leadership, particularly the success of coaches (e.g., Oligvie & Tutko, 1966). However, in his review of the sport personality literature, Sage (1975) found that, similar to the work in general psychology, the results of the sport endeavors revealed a rather fragmented pattern of traits. He concluded that the evidence for the trait approach in sport settings was weak. As a result of Sage's review, most of the work testing the trait approach in sport was discontinued.

The Behavioral Approach to Leadership

Because the trait approach was unsuccessful, researchers turned their attention to the behaviors of leaders. That is, investigators became interested in what good leaders do, not who they are. This ***behavioral approach to leadership*** reflects the belief that successful leaders exhibit behaviors not displayed by less successful leaders. Thus, this approach stressed that "leaders are made, not born" (Cox, 1990, p. 378). This approach to research was much more successful than the trait approach. In fact, several different successful leader behaviors have been identified. In the following sections, we will examine several of these behaviors.

The Autocratic/Democratic Behavioral Dimension.   One behavioral dimension of leadership concerns the degree to which a leader allows subordinates to participate in the decision making process. This dimension is referred to as the autocratic/democratic leadership dimension (Baron & Greenberg 1990; Muczyk & Reimann, 1987). Some leaders are autocratic in their leadership style. ***Autocratic leaders*** tend to make decisions alone. In athletics, an autocratic head coach would tend to choose her line-up, roster, practice schedule, and plays with little input from the players and assistant coaches. Autocratic leadership behaviors can be advantageous because they often lead to increases in productivity and they tend to speed up the decision making process. However, the autocratic style has the disadvantage of reduced employee satisfaction. Furthermore, leaders who make decisions alone are not fully using the skills, resources, and knowledge of their subordinates. In sport, assistant coaches and players offer valuable suggestions regarding the decisions facing head coaches.

Democratic leaders prefer to consult with subordinates when making decisions. For example, head coaches often converse with their assistant coaches when deciding on a starting line-up. This leadership style is advantageous because it often leads to increased job satisfaction on the part of subordinates. However, when leaders employ this pattern of leadership, subordinates may begin to doubt the leader's competence. That is, they may begin to question the leader's ability because he seems unable to make decisions on his own.

The Directive/Permissive Behavioral Dimension.   The directive/permissive dimension is a second pattern of leadership (Baron & Greenberg 1990; Muczyk & Reimann, 1987). This dimension concerns the extent to which a leader directs the behaviors of the subordinates. ***Directive leaders*** tend to watch closely over their subordinates, telling them what to do, making certain they are following instructions, and so on. A directive wrestling coach, for example, would stroll around the weight room, making sure the players are working out as instructed. Other leaders tend to be rather lenient in their leadership style. These ***permissive leaders*** prefer to give subordinates a task and then let them carry out the task on their own. These leaders trust the subordinates to complete the task successfully without being monitored. If the wrestling coach described above were permissive in his leadership approach, he would simply inform his wrestlers of the weightlifting routine and leave the players to complete the regimen on their own.

An advantage of being a directive leader is that the task will often get done better and faster than if the leader exhibits a permissive style. However, a disadvantage of the directive style is that subordinates may feel that the leader believes that they are incompetent. An advantage of using a permissive style of leadership is that this pattern often provides subordinates with a feeling of accomplishment and responsibility. Furthermore, this style allows the leader to deal with more important activities. For example, if the wrestling coach allowed the players to work out on their own, he would have more time to work on strategy and pairings for upcoming meets.

Combining the Autocratic/Democratic and Directive/Permissive Dimensions.   Muczyk and Reimann (1987) note that, by combining the dimensions just described, one arrives at four different and distinct behavioral patterns. Each of the combinations has advantages and disadvantages. Depending on the characteristics of the situation and subordinates, each combination can be the most appropriate and, therefore, the most effective.

One type of leader, called a directive autocrat, tends to monitor the subordinates' work closely and prefers to make decisions without consultation. While this may sound like a poor and unnecessarily harsh leadership style, in reality, it is appropriate in some settings. In fact, this is the preferred style of leadership when dealing with unskilled subordinates. For example, consider a pee-wee football team. Because the children do not yet understand the rules and fundamentals of the sport, they need to be watched closely. In addition, because the children do not know how to run a football team, the coaches should not rely on the input of the youths when making decisions.

Permissive autocrats also tend to make decisions alone, but instead of monitoring the activities of subordinates, these individuals allow the subordinates to carry out tasks on their own. This pattern tends to be effective when dealing with subordinates who are highly skilled but do not care to get involved in the decision making process. For example, many professional athletes do not want to be involved in the player and strategy decisions made by coaches. Rather, they wish to be allowed to concentrate their energies on their physical efforts.

Another group of leaders are referred to as directive democrats. These persons tend to keep a close eye on their subordinates, but they do let them have a say when decisions are being made. This style of leadership is best suited for subordinates who have not learned the standard operating procedures of a specific organization but may have valuable suggestions from their previous experiences with other organizations. For example, imagine an assistant athletic director who has recently been hired by a college. Because the assistant is not familiar with the operations and methods of the new school, the head athletic director must closely guide and direct her behavior. However, because this individual brings valuable information and experience from her former position, the head athletic director should welcome any suggestions she has to offer.

Finally, other leaders are classified as permissive democrats. These leaders tend to leave their subordinates alone while gaining their input prior to making a decision. As with the other combinations, there are certain settings in which this style is appropriate. For example, this type of leadership can sometimes be seen in the behaviors of certain owners of professional sport franchises. Some owners prefer to leave the subordinates to do their jobs (i.e., they do not interfere in the daily operations of the team), but when an important decision must be made they consult the necessary individuals (for example, they will confer with the general manager on player transactions).

The Task-Oriented and Person-Oriented Dimensions.   A third leadership dimension concerns the extent that a leader is task-oriented and person-oriented (Baron & Greenberg, 1990; Fleishman, Harris, & Burtt, 1955). ***Task-oriented leaders*** (also called production-oriented leaders) are primarily concerned with production and getting the job done correctly and efficiently. Because individuals with this orientation tend to be concerned with setting goals, making sure that rules and regulations are being followed, and making certain that subordinates know their roles, this dimension is often referred to as the initiating structure dimension. Coaches who believe in the "winning is everything" philosophy are task-oriented leaders.

Person-oriented leaders, on the other hand, tend to be concerned with establishing good relationships between themselves and their subordinates. These leaders are more likely to perform favors for the subordinates and insure that they are safe and satisfied. As a result, this dimension has been referred to as the consideration dimension. Coaches who are a "player's coach" are high on the person-oriented dimension.

It is important to note that the task-oriented and person-oriented styles are separate leadership dimensions. Thus, individuals can be high on one dimension and low on the other, high on both dimensions, or low on both dimensions. Some coaches are concerned about both the welfare of their players and the success of the team, while other coaches care only about either the players' welfare or the team's performance and some coaches appear not to care about either the players' welfare or the team's performance. Tjosvold (1984) studied the effectiveness of the four possible orientation combinations. Tjosvold's research found that leaders with a high task and high person orientation tend to be the most effective. Can you guess which pattern was least effective? Contrary to what many persons predict, Tjosvold found that the least effective leaders were those exhibiting a low task orientation and a high person orientation. Thus, coaches stressing both positive relationships with their players and the team's performance are likely to be successful, while those stressing only positive relationships are likely to be less successful. Apparently, when they are coached by someone with the relationship-only pattern, players feel that they do not have to exert a high level of effort.

THEORIES OF LEADERSHIP

In the previous section, we examined some of the specific traits and behaviors found among leaders. For the remainder of this chapter, we will examine several general theories of leadership. That is, rather than focusing on one or a few factors, we will now review the work of authors testing the overall leadership process. We will review four different theories: contingency theory, normative theory, attributional theory, and the multidimensional model.

The Contingency Theory of Leadership

In the 1960s and 1970s, Fiedler (1967, 1978) proposed a ***contingency theory of leadership.*** This theory predicts that a leader's effectiveness is determined by the leader's traits and the leader's control of the situation. As for the leader's traits, this theory proposes that the key trait of the leader is his or her liking of the least preferred co-worker (LPC). To determine their LPC score (that is, their rating of the LPC), leaders are asked to think about all of the people with whom they have worked. They are then asked to imagine the individual they least preferred. This individual is the LPC. Leaders then answer questions about the LPC. For example, they are asked to rate this person in terms of friendliness, pleasantness, and efficiency. Based on this scale, leaders are classified as either a high LPC or a low LPC leader. A high LPC leader is one who views the LPC in positive terms. That is, although they like this person less than others with whom they have worked, they do like this individual. A low LPC leader is one who views the LPC in negative terms. For example, imagine a coach who has been asked to consider all of her former players and to focus on the player she liked the least. Let us assume that the coach feels that Carrie was her least favorite player. However, the coach liked Carrie, just not as much as the other players. In this scenario, the coach would be considered a high LPC leader. If, on the other hand, the coach disliked Carrie, she would be considered a low LPC leader.

With regard to leadership control, this model contains three situational factors that combine to determine the leader's situational control: group atmosphere, task structure, and the leader's position power. Group atmosphere refers to the feelings subordinates have for the leader. For example, are the players behind the coach, do they like the coach, are they loyal to her? When the leader has the backing of the subordinates, the group atmosphere is defined as good. Conversely, when the leader does not have the subordinates' support, the group atmosphere is considered to be poor. Task structure concerns the extent to which the task is routine. Routine tasks are those that are highly repetitive, the goals are clearly defined, and the task itself is easily understood. Nonroutine tasks are nonrepetitive, are not clearly defined, and are complex. In sport, adding weight to a bar bell would be a routine task, while constructing an opening day line-up would be considered a nonroutine task. Task structure is defined as either high (routine tasks) or low (nonroutine tasks). Position power concerns the leader's ability to force the workers to comply with his or her demands. A leader's position power is defined as being either strong (having the ability to force the players into compliance) or weak (lacking the ability to do so). A leader's position power is likely to be higher in a professional organization than in a volunteer setting. For example, managers of professional baseball teams have a high level of position power because they can fine or release players. Conversely, managers of little league teams do not have these options at their disposal. As a result, they must rely on other types of power such as expert and referent power.

With this basic understanding of the trait and situational control factors involved in Fiedler's model, let us examine how the pieces fit together. Fiedler argues that to facilitate the group's performance, leaders must be placed in the correct situation. High LPC leaders are expected to work better in some situational control settings, while low LPC persons are thought to be better suited for others (see Figure 13.1). As seen in this illustration, Fiedler's contingency theory predicts that, for situations involving high or low leadership control, group performance will be highest when the leader is a low LPC individual. In high control environments, low LPC leaders are preferable because they will not attempt to change an already successful setting by attempting to establish social relationships with the subordinates. Low LPC leaders are well suited for low control settings because they are likely to provide the necessary direction and guidance. For situations involving moderate leadership control, Fiedler's model hypothesizes that high LPC leaders will lead to the highest level of group per-

FIGURE 13.1   The contingency theory of leadership.

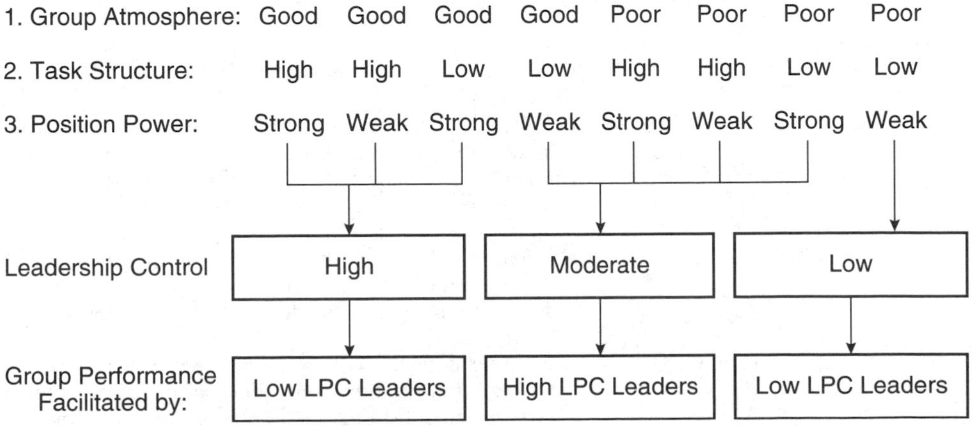

1. Group Atmosphere:	Good	Good	Good	Good	Poor	Poor	Poor	Poor
2. Task Structure:	High	High	Low	Low	High	High	Low	Low
3. Position Power:	Strong	Weak	Strong	Weak	Strong	Weak	Strong	Weak

| Leadership Control | High | Moderate | Low |

| Group Performance Facilitated by: | Low LPC Leaders | High LPC Leaders | Low LPC Leaders |

formance. In these situations, leaders with sound interpersonal skills can often foster the interest and subsequently the effort of the subordinates. In contrast, because they may be viewed as autocratic and authoritarian, low LPC leaders are often unable to motivate the subordinates and are, therefore, unsuccessful in these situations.

More than 100 different investigations have tested the validity and accuracy of Fiedler's theory. The results of these investigations have been mixed. Although some studies have supported Fiedler's model, others have not (Peters, Hartke, & Pohlmann, 1985; Strube & Garcia, 1981). In their examination of the literature on contingency theory, Peters et al. (1985) found that although the model appears to hold up rather well in laboratory investigations, field tests of the theory have not been as supportive. The problem is that many of the components of Fiedler's theory are easily quantifiable in the laboratory but difficult to quantify in field settings. For example, in laboratory research an investigator is able to manipulate the precise level of group atmosphere, task structure, and position power. However, in real-world settings these situational factors are not nearly so simplistic as the model predicts.

Sport-specific tests of contingency theory have also faired poorly. Reviews of sport-oriented research testing this theory have found little support for the model (Carron, 1980). In fact, based on his examination of the literature, Cox (1990) concluded that "it would appear that Fiedler's contingency theory is not applicable to sport settings" (p. 393). It should be noted, however, that few studies have tested this theory in sporting environments (most likely, less than a dozen studies have been completed). As a result, before we conclude that contingency theory is useless from a sport perspective, more research should be completed.

The Normative Theory of Leadership

Normative theory is another approach to leadership developed in the 1970s. Proposed by Vroom and his colleagues (Vroom & Jago, 1978, 1988; Vroom & Yetton, 1973), the **normative theory of leadership** is designed to examine the decision making of leaders. This theory provides a model suggesting the proper amount of subordinate input for various types of decisions. Vroom's theory proposes five different methods of reaching a decision. The methods vary in the amount of input given to the subordinates:

Autocratic I (AI): The leader makes the decision alone with the information already available.

Autocratic II (AII): The leader acquires information from subordinates and then makes the decision alone, using the information gathered.

Consultative I (CI): The leader consults with subordinates individually, acquiring information and their suggestions/comments. The leader then makes the decision alone, using the information gathered.

Consultative II (CII): The leader consults with subordinates in a group meeting, acquiring information and their suggestions/comments. The leader then makes the decision alone, using the information gathered.

Group Decision (GII): The leader consults with subordinates in a group meeting, acquiring information and their suggestions/comments. The leader and subordinates then make the decision together.

A concrete example will help differentiate the decision methods. Let us assume that the manager of a professional baseball team must decide whether or not to start a rookie pitcher for a crucial game. If this manager simply uses information already available to him (for example, by looking at past performances and other statistics already on file in his office) and then makes the decision alone, he is using the AI method. If he instead asked his assistant coaches to provide the information (but not their personal input and suggestions), he is using the AII approach. In reality, however, it is likely that the manager would ask for input and suggestions from his assistant coaches. If he approached them individually for their suggestions before making the decision alone, the manager would be making a CI decision. If he asked the assistant coaches to come to a meeting and then elicited their input (prior to making the decision alone), he would be employing the CII method. Finally, if at the meeting he asked the coaches to vote on whether or not to start the pitcher, the manager would be using the GII approach.

Depending on the situation, each of the methods just described can be the most effective approach. To determine the type of decision they should use, leaders are asked to answer the questions found on the decision tree depicted in Figure 13.2. The answers to the questions lead to suggested decision methods. For example, imagine that a manager is faced with the decision of whether or not to change a light bulb in his office. He wants to know if he should involve others in the decision making process. To assist in this endeavor, he has decided to follow Vroom's decision tree (it will be helpful if you follow the decision tree as well). The first question concerns the level of technical quality involved. Because the technical quality of changing a light bulb is low, he answers as such and follows the path to the next question. This question concerns the degree of subordinate commitment to the decision. In this situation the degree of subordinate commitment required is low. By following the path to the end of the decision tree, the manager would find that, to make the most effective and expeditious decision, he should decide on his own (i.e., AI).

Now imagine that the manager must decide whether or not to purchase a new and expensive pitching machine. Again, to assist in the decision making process he has decided to consult Vroom's decision tree. As for the first question, the current decision is highly technical. Thus, the manager follows this path to the next question. As for the second question, subordinate commitment, commitment to the decision is important because other coaches and players will be using the new machine. Concerning the next two questions, let us assume that the manager does have sufficient information to make a high-quality decision, but if he were to make the decision alone the other players and coaches would not be committed to it. However, the other coaches and players do share the manager's goals and they do have sufficient information to form a quality decision. As a result, the manager should use the GII method of decision making, perhaps by allowing the players and coaches to vote on whether or not to buy the machine.

The results of research testing the validity of the normative theory of leadership have been encouraging. For example, studies by Field (1982) and Heilman, Hornstein, Cage, and Herschlag (1984) each found strong support for the model. Within sport settings, research has indicated that athletes tend to prefer the AI style,

QR	QUALITY REQUIREMENT:	How Important Is the Technical Quality of This Decision?
CR	COMMITMENT REQUIREMENT:	How Important Is Subordinate Commitment of This Decision?
LI	LEADER'S INFORMATION:	Do You Have Sufficient Information to Make a High-Quality Decision?
ST	PROBLEM STRUCTURE:	Is The Problem Well Structured?
CP	COMMITMENT PROBABILITY:	If You Were to Make the Decision by Yourself, is it Reasonably Certain That Your Subordinate(s) Would Be Committed to the Decision?
GC	GOAL CONGRUENCE:	Do Subordinates Share the Organizational Goals to be Attained in Solving This Problem?
CO	SUBORDINATE CONFLICT:	Is Conflict Among Subordinates Over Preferred Solutions Likely?
SI	SUBORDINATE INFORMATION:	Do Subordinates Have Sufficient Information to Make a High-Quality Decision?

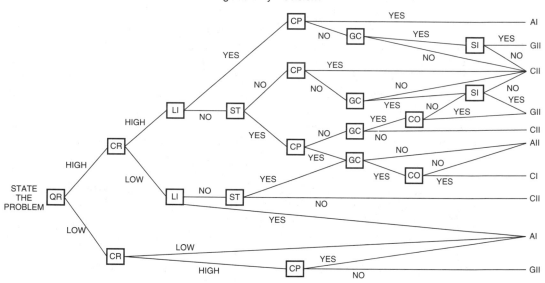

FIGURE 13.2   Time-driven decision tree—group problems. (From: Vroom, V. & Jago, A. [1988]. The new leadership: Managing participation in organizations. Englewood Cliffs, NJ: Prentice Hall. Reprinted by permission.)

and this is the most common form of decision making in sport (Chelladurai & Quek, 1995; Chelladurai, Haggerty, & Baxter, 1989). The importance of the AI decision making style may indicate that this style is more consistent with the operations and norms of a sport team.

Chelladurai and Haggerty (1978; see also Chelladurai, 1993) developed a normative model of decision styles in coaching fashioned after the works of Vroom and his colleagues. Rather than using five decision styles in the manner of Vroom, Chelladurai and Haggerty's model includes three methods of decision making: autocratic, participative, and delegative. The autocratic decision style occurs when the coach makes the decision alone, whether or not he consulted with others prior to doing so. The participative decision style is seen when the decision is ultimately made by a group of individuals, one of whom is the coach. Finally, the delegative decision style is found when the coach delegates the decision making responsibilities to others (e.g., assistant coaches and players).

As with Vroom's theory, coaches are asked to answer several questions found on a decision tree. The final result of the answers reveals the suggested decision style. Instead of being general and applicable to a variety of situations, some of the questions comprising Chelladurai and Haggerty's (1978) decision tree are sport-specific. Several studies testing the validity of this model have indicated its usefulness as a theoretical and diagnostic tool (e.g., Chelladurai & Arnott, 1985; see Chelladurai, 1993, for a review). One conclusion that can be drawn from this research is that delegation is quite rare in sport decision making. That is, few coaches are willing to share the decision making responsibility with their players, and players do not wish to have the authority delegated (Chelladurai, 1993; Chelladurai & Arnott, 1985).

The Attributional Theory of Leadership

Another theory with relevance to sport settings is the ***attributional theory of leadership*** (Hellriegel et al., 1992; McElroy, 1982; Meindl & Ehrlich, 1987; Mitchell & Wood, 1979). This theory focuses on leaders' evaluations of the performances of subordinates and how the attributional process impacts the evaluations. Proponents of this theory argue that a leader's attributions of a subordinate's performance and the actual performance combine to determine the final evaluation (Hellriegel et al., 1992). This implies that a coach's evaluation of a player will not always be impartial and objective. Rather, the coach's attributions will impact the process.

The attributional theory of leadership is diagramed in Figure 13.3. The process originates with a player's behavior (i.e., performance). For example, imagine that a college basketball player missed two crucial free throws in the final minute of an important game. It is the coach's responsibility to determine the reasons underlying the player's poor performance. The coach must decide if the player's behavior was due to the player herself (an internal attribution) or due to the situation (an external attribution). Recall from Chapter 9 that individuals tend to focus on three types of information when determining if another individual's behavior was the result of internal or external factors. The three types of information are consistency (the frequency

FIGURE 13.3   The attributional theory of leadership.

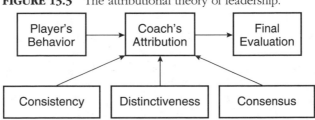

with which an individual exhibits the behavior in this particular setting), distinctiveness, (the degree to which an individual exhibits the behavior in other settings), and consensus (the number of other individuals exhibiting the behavior in this particular setting). Imagine that the coach decided that (1) the behavior was consistent because this player had performed poorly against this team in the past, (2) it was a distinct setting because the player had not choked in other sports or against other teams, and (3) there was consensus because the entire team had shot poorly that night. As a result of this line of thinking, the coach would most likely form an external attribution (you may want to review Figure 9.1 from Chapter 9 if this is unclear).

However, if the coach had determined that the behavior was consistent with this player's past performances, that the situation was not distinct because this player had choked in a variety of settings, and there was no consensus because the other players had shot well that night, the coach would have come to a different conclusion. Specifically, she would have formed an internal attribution (see Figure 9.1).

Whether the coach forms an internal or external attribution has implications for the coach's evaluation of the player's performance (see Figure 13.3). For example, if the coach concluded that the player's performance was due to an outside force (i.e., an external attribution), she may blame the long bus ride to the game or the hostile fans. On the other hand, if the coach felt that the behavior was due to an internal factor, her evaluation would be different. For example, she may decide that the player simply cannot handle the pressure of close games. In addition, it should be remembered that a coach's evaluation will be based in part on whether he feels that the performance was due to effort or ability (Baron & Greenberg, 1990; Mitchell et al., 1982). Recall that effort tends to be rewarded more than ability. Thus, if two players achieve the same level of performance, they will not necessarily receive the same evaluation from their coach. Rather, the player who succeeded because of effort will receive a more favorable evaluation. Likewise, if a player fails and the coach attributes the failure to a lack of effort, the evaluation will likely be more harsh than if the coach had attributed the poor performance to the player's lack of skill.

The Multidimensional Model of Leadership:
A Sport-Specific Approach

Yet another approach to leadership is the multidimensional theory proposed by Chelladurai (Chelladurai, 1978, 1984, 1990, 1993). The ***multidimensional theory of leadership*** is a sport-specific model focusing on the congruence among three leadership behavioral states: required, actual, and preferred. This model predicts that as the congruence among these states increases, so too will group performance and member satisfaction (see Figure 13.4). The antecedents of these leadership behaviors are situational, leader, and member characteristics.

Required leader behaviors reflect the demands and constraints placed on the leader by the situation and member characteristics. For example, the required behaviors of a coach involved with young players (such as insuring equitable playing time) are different from those of coaches working with professional athletes. Actual leader behaviors are actions the leader exhibits regardless of the situational and subordinate constraints. Actual leader behaviors often reflect the leader's personal disposition and

ANTECEDENTS   LEADER BEHAVIOR   CONSEQUENCES

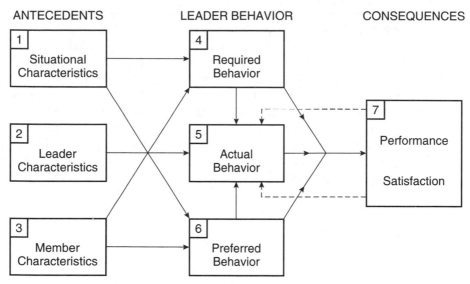

FIGURE 13.4 The multidimensional model of leadership. (Reprinted by permission from: Chelladurai, P. [1990]. Leadership in sports: A review. *International Journal of Sport Psychology*, 21: 328–354.)

leadership style. Preferred leader behaviors are behaviors desired by the subordinates, preferences that may change with changes in the situation. As noted, Chelladurai's model predicts that group performance and member satisfaction will be highest when the required, actual, and preferred leader behaviors are congruent. That is, the team will perform best and with the highest level of enjoyment when the coach's behaviors match those desired by the players and match the situational requirements.

To assist in the testing of the multidimensional model of leadership, Chelladurai and Saleh (1978, 1980) developed the Leadership Scale for Sports (LSS). The LSS consists of 40 items measuring five different dimensions of leader behavior: training and instruction (behaviors aimed at improving performance and providing instruction), democratic behavior (allowing athletes to participate in decision making), autocratic behavior (the coach makes decisions unilaterally), social support behavior (concern for the welfare of the athletes), and rewarding behavior (using positive feedback). Several studies have successfully used this scale (Chelladurai, 1984; Chelladurai & Saleh, 1980; see Chelladurai, 1993, for a review).

Research on the multidimensional model of leadership has been encouraging. For example, in his study of college basketball athletes, Chelladurai (1984) found that as a player's perception of the coach's behavior became more incongruent with the player's preferences, the player's satisfaction decreased, a finding consistent with the multidimensional model. Similarly, in their research with intercollegiate coach-athlete dyads, Horne and Carron (1985) found that discrepancies between an athlete's preferred leadership behaviors and perceived leadership behaviors were related to satisfaction and performance. Other researchers have also found support for the model (e.g., Chelladurai, Imamura, Yamaguchi, Oinuma, & Miyauchi, 1988; Gar-

land & Barry, 1990; Laughlin & Laughlin, 1994; Riemer & Chelladurai, 1995; Schliesman, 1987; Weiss & Friedrichs, 1986).

Thus, research to date indicates that the multidimensional model of leadership
proposed by Chelladurai is a valid and useful model for understanding the leadership process in sport. However, thus far investigators have tested only a portion or
portions of the model rather than the model as a whole (Chelladurai, 1993; Horn,
1992). Hopefully, by using advanced statistical techniques that examine the links between each portion of the model, future researchers will be able to comment on the
validity of the whole model rather than its individual parts (see Schutz & Gessaroli,
1993). Such an examination will lead to refinements and improvements in the model's
structure, thus furthering its validity.

SUMMARY

Leaders attempt to influence others through the strategic use of power. Five different forms of power are common in sport settings: expert, legitimate, referent, reward,
and coercive.

Early work on the leadership process tended to focus on the traits possessed
by successful leaders. However, because this line of research was unsuccessful, investigators turned their attention to the behaviors of leaders. Several dimensions of
leader behaviors have been identified. First, leaders can be categorized as being either autocratic or democratic. Autocratic leaders prefer to make decisions alone,
while democratic leaders prefer to involve the subordinates in the decision making
process. Second, leaders can be classified as directive because they prefer to watch
subordinates closely and monitor their behavior or as permissive because they let
subordinates carry out tasks on their own. Third, some leaders are task-oriented and
tend to be concerned with production and getting the job done efficiently, while others are person-oriented and tend to be concerned with establishing good social relationships between themselves and their subordinates.

The contingency theory of leadership predicts that a leader's effectiveness will
be determined by the leader's traits and the leader's control of the situation. The leadership trait involved in this theory is the leader's LPC score, that is, the leader's liking of the LPC. Leaders who like the LPC are called high LPC leaders, while those
who dislike the LPC are called low LPC leaders. The leader's control of the situation
is a function of the group atmosphere, the task structure, and the leader's position
power. This theory argues that group performance will be highest when high LPC
leaders are matched with situations involving moderate control and low LPC leaders
are matched with situations involving high or low control.

The normative theory of leadership examines the decision making process and
five methods of reaching a decision: Autocratic I (leader makes the decision alone
with the information currently available), Autocratic II (leader acquires information
from subordinates and then makes decision alone), Consultative I (leader consults
with subordinates individually, acquiring information and suggestions, then makes
decision alone), Consultative II (leader consults with subordinates in a group meet-

ing, acquiring information and suggestions, then makes decision alone), and Group Decision (leader consults with subordinates in a group meeting, acquiring information and suggestions, then leader and subordinates reach a decision together). By answering the questions found on a decision tree, leaders are provided with a suggested decision making strategy.

The attributional theory of leadership focuses on the impact of the attributional process on leaders' evaluations of subordinate performance. When a coach determines that a performance was due to an external cause (i.e., the coach forms an external attribution), his or her evaluation will be different than if he or she had determined that the performance was due to an internal factor (i.e., an internal attribution).

The multidimensional theory of leadership is a sport-specific theory. This theory examines the leadership process by focusing on the congruence among three leadership behavioral states: required, actual, and preferred. This model proposes that as the required, actual, and preferred leader behavior becomes more congruent, the team will exhibit an increase in performance and group members will become more satisfied.

GLOSSARY

Attributional Theory of Leadership   A theory of leadership focusing on leaders' evaluations of the performances of subordinates and how the attributional process impacts the evaluations.

Autocratic Leaders   Leaders who tend to make decisions alone.

Behavioral Approach to Leadership   An approach to leadership reflecting the belief that successful leaders exhibit behaviors not displayed by less successful leaders.

Coercive Power   The ability to change someone's attitude or behavior because a person controls access to one or more punishments.

Contingency Theory of Leadership   A theory of leadership predicting that a leader's effectiveness is determined by the leader's traits and the leader's control of the situation.

Democratic Leaders   Leaders who prefer to consult with subordinates when making decisions.

Directive Leaders   Leaders who tend to watch closely over their subordinates, telling them what to do, making certain they are following instructions, and so on.

Expert Power   The ability to change another individual's attitude or behavior because a person is believed to be knowledgeable, skillful, or talented in a certain area.

Leadership   A behavioral process in which one group member influences the other members regarding the attainment of the group's goals.

Legitimate Power   The ability to change another individual's attitude or behavior because of a person's position within the organization or group.

Multidimensional Theory of Leadership   A theory of leadership focusing on the congruence among three leadership behavioral states: required, preferred, and actual.

Normative Theory of Leadership   A theory of leadership examining the decision making process.

Permissive Leaders   Leaders who prefer to give subordinates a task and then let them carry out the task on their own.

Person-Oriented Leaders   Leaders who tend to be concerned with establishing good relationships between themselves and their subordinates.

Power   The ability to influence or change the attitudes or behaviors of others.

Referent Power   The ability to change another individual's attitude or behavior because a person is liked and respected by the group members.

Reward Power   The ability to change someone's attitude or behavior because a person controls access to desired rewards.

Task-Oriented Leaders   Leaders who are primarily concerned with production and getting the job done correctly and efficiently.

Trait Approach to Leadership   An approach to leadership reflecting the belief that successful leaders possess traits that are lacking in less successful leaders.

APPLICATION AND REVIEW QUESTIONS

1. Compare and contrast the five sources of power and give an example of each from the sport world.
2. What are the differences between the trait and behavioral approaches to leadership? Which approach is the most accurate?
3. Describe the differences between autocratic and democratic leaders. In your experiences with coaches, have they tended to be autocratic or democratic in their leadership styles? Which style did/do you prefer and why?
4. Describe the differences between directive and permissive leaders. In your experiences with coaches, have they tended to be directive or permissive in their leadership styles? Which style did/do you prefer and why?
5. Describe the differences between task-oriented and person-oriented leaders. In your experiences with coaches, have they tended to be task-oriented or person-oriented in their leadership styles? Which style did/do you prefer and why?
6. Describe the contingency theory of leadership. Now, describe the LPC score of a hypothetical coach and, based on the contingency approach, describe the situational control setting(s) in which this leader should be most effective.
7. Describe the five methods of reaching a decision as presented in the normative theory of leadership.
8. Describe the components of the multidimensional model of leadership. Now discuss the model's predictions concerning group performance and member satisfaction.

SUGGESTED READINGS

CHELLADURAI, P. (1993). Leadership. In R. N. Singer, M. Murphey, & L. K. Tennant (Eds.), *Handbook of research on sport psychology* (pp. 647–671). New York: Macmillan. This chapter is written by one of the leading authors in sport leadership research. In addition to providing general coverage of leadership in sport, this article includes an in-depth discussion of the normative and multidimensional models of leadership.

HORN, T. S. (1992). Leadership effectiveness in the sport domain. In T. S. Horn (Ed.), *Advances in sport psychology* (pp. 181–199). Champaign, IL: Human Kinetics. This chapter presents a detailed description of the multidimensional model of leadership and also poses several suggestions for future research in the area of sport leadership.

RUSSELL, G. W. (1993). *The social psychology of sport* (ch. 3). New York: Springer-Verlag. This chapter focuses on leadership issues in sport. Included in this chapter are discussions of the impact of coaching changes, the trait and behavioral approaches to leadership, and the importance of coaching experience.

Chapter 14

THE SOCIAL NATURE OF SPORT: TEAM COHESION, AUDIENCE EFFECTS, AND SELF-PRESENTATION

In most cases, athletes do not perform in isolation. Rather, they participate in sport as a member of a team, in competition with other athletes, or while being observed by one or more spectators (and sometimes by millions of television viewers). In this chapter, we will examine how the presence of others impacts the performances, behaviors, and attitudes of athletes, a major area of investigation throughout the history of sport psychology (Brawley & Martin, 1995). First, we will examine the nature and impact of team cohesion. Next, we will review the effects of sport audiences. Finally, we will examine self-presentational concerns in sport.

TEAM COHESION

Phrases such as "we won as a team" and "there is no 'I' in the word team" are quite common in sport. These statements reflect the general belief that team cohesion can be an important factor in athletic success. To test the accuracy of this belief, a number of sport psychologists have investigated team cohesion. However, before we discuss this line of research, it is important to articulate precisely what is meant by team cohesion. In this text, I will use Carron's (1982) definition of team cohesion. Carron defined **team cohesion** as "a dynamic process which is reflected in the tendency for a group to stick together and remain united in the pursuit of goals and objectives" (p. 124).

The Nature of Cohesion

Originally, most researchers viewed cohesion as a unidimensional construct (e.g., Festinger, Schachter, & Back, 1950; see Cota, Evans, Dion, Kilik, & Longman, 1995, for a review). However, because research indicated that there were a number of facets to group cohesion, many authors became disillusioned with the unidimensional approach and began to adopt multidimensional perspectives (Cota et al., 1995; Gill, 1978; Hagstrom & Selvin, 1965). Two common dimensions of cohesion found in sport settings are task cohesion and social cohesion. **Task cohesion** refers to the extent that group members work together and remain united in their attempt to complete a specific task. **Social cohesion** refers to the degree of interpersonal attraction among the group's members. Task and social cohesion are independent dimensions. A team member could feel driven to maintain her involvement with a team because of the team's tasks, the social nature of the group, or both.

Cota and his colleagues (1995) make a further distinction between primary and secondary dimensions of cohesion. **Primary dimensions of cohesion** are dimensions applicable to most or all groups. **Secondary dimensions of cohesion** are dimensions applicable to a subset of groups. Cota argues that task and social cohesion are examples of primary dimensions because they are common to most groups. The authors state that normative viewpoints of group members and resistance to disruptive forces are additional primary dimensions. The authors list the hierarchical structure of military-style groups and group-specific roles as examples of secondary dimensions. It is important to reiterate that primary dimensions such as task and social cohesion are common to most groups. Thus, groups found in most types and levels of sport, as well as most levels within a single sport (e.g., players, management, fans) will be influenced by task and social cohesion. However, secondary dimensions will be found in only a specific type of group. For example, the secondary dimension of group-specific roles will often be found in player groups but less often among fan groups.

Measuring Team Cohesion

Researchers have developed several methods of assessing team cohesion. One of the earliest instruments developed was the Sports Cohesiveness Questionnaire (SCQ, Martens & Peterson, 1971). The SCQ contains eight Likert-scale items, with most questions focusing on social cohesion. This measure of cohesion has been in use for several years and is one of the most common tools for assessing team cohesion. However, because this scale lacks documented reliability and validity, its popularity may be unwarranted. In the 1980s, Gruber and Gray (1981, 1982) published a second scale for measuring team cohesion. Their instrument, labeled the Team Cohesiveness Questionnaire (TCQ), contains 13 Likert-scale items. The TCQ measures both task and social cohesion. A third questionnaire, the Multidimensional Sport Cohesion Instrument (MSCI), was developed by Yukelson, Weinberg, and Jackson (1984). This instrument contains 22 Likert-scale items measuring four dimensions of team cohesion: attraction to the group, unity of purpose, quality of teamwork, and the value of one's role on the team. The attraction to the group dimension is similar to social cohesion, while the quality of teamwork dimension reflects task cohesion.

A final measure of cohesion is the Group Environment Questionnaire (GEQ) developed by Carron, Widmeyer, and Brawley (1985; Carron & Spink, 1992; Widmeyer, Brawley, & Carron, 1985). The GEQ contains 18 Likert-scale items focusing on the task/social cohesion dimension and an individual attraction/group integration dimension. Individual attraction involves a "team member's personal attractions to the group" (Carron et al., 1985, p. 248). This dimension involves the member's role in the group and their involvement with the group. Group integration involves "a member's perceptions of the group as a totality" (p. 248). This dimension involves group closeness, bonding, and similarity. Thus, the GEQ measures four dimensions of team cohesion: individual attraction/task (individual is attracted to the team to satisfy task completion needs), individual attraction/social (individual is attracted to the team to satisfy social needs), group integration/task (individual is bonded to the team as a unit to satisfy task completion needs), and group integration/social (individual is bonded to the team as a unit to satisfy social needs). Any of the four dimensions can encourage an athlete to maintain his or her association with the team, although the combined effect of the four dimensions is probably more influential (Widmeyer et al., 1993). Within the past decade, a number of studies have documented the strong reliability and validity of the GEQ (e.g., Brawley, Carron, & Widmeyer, 1987; Carron, Widmeyer, & Brawley, 1988).

Causes of Team Cohesion

As most athletes realize, sport teams differ in their degree of cohesion. Certain teams appear to be comprised of a close-knit group of players with strong emotional and psychological ties, while other teams seem to lack this sense of unity. To understand better why some teams become cohesive and others do not, researchers have attempted to identify the factors involved in the development of team cohesion. In this section, we will examine several of these variables.

Intragroup Cooperation and Intergroup Conflict.   In 1961, Sherif, Harvey, White, Hood, and Sherif published a report describing their work with young adolescent boys attending a summer camp. When the boys arrived, they were divided into two groups and assigned separate living quarters. During the first few weeks of camp, the groups worked as separate units on various tasks. As the children cooperated, they began to exhibit signs of cohesiveness within their group, even naming their group. The groups then began challenging each other to competitive activities. Sherif and his colleagues noticed that as the competition between the groups escalated, their sense of team cohesion continued to increase. The groups began to develop into cohesive units to deal with the threat of a common opponent (Baron & Greenberg, 1990). Thus, both intragroup cooperation (working together within the group) and intergroup competition (competition between two rival groups) facilitated cohesion.

The work by Sherif and his associates (1961) has two interesting implications for the cohesiveness of sport teams. First, because cooperation leads to feelings of cohesiveness, coaches should develop cooperative activities for their teams. For example, rather than allowing players to work out individually, coaches should place athletes into work-out teams. In addition, because competition and external threats lead to cohesiveness, coaches may want to facilitate the perception that it is "us versus the world." If players feel that other groups such as rival teams and the media are working against them, they may begin to unite into a cohesive group in an attempt to combat the external threat. For the New York Yankees, such a situation developed during the 1995 baseball season. The season was marked by several external threats to the team including a beanball incident with Seattle pitcher Randy Johnson, rumors linking seven-time league drug offender Steve Howe with the distribution of amphetamines in the clubhouse, and unsuspected coaching changes. Of interest, the players reported that the team was able to gain strength from these incidents. In fact, team captain Don Mattingly stated that, "When all this stuff happens off the field there's always the chance we'll band together and win games" (Callahan, 1995, p. 47). Thus, external threats led to an increase in the cohesiveness of the team.

Team Stability. Research has also found that group stability is related to cohesion (Forsyth, 1990). Teams that have been together longer (i.e., teams that have had little turnover in player personnel) should be more cohesive. Teams with a large number of personnel changes and absenteeism will most likely be unable to develop the sense of unity necessary for feelings of cohesion.

Team Homogeneity. Cox (1990) suggests that team homogeneity can play a role in a team's sense of unity. ***Team homogeneity*** refers to the degree of similarity among a team's players. Cox believes that homogeneous teams comprised of individuals with similar characteristics (e.g., ethnicity, socioeconomic status) will tend to be cohesive. Conversely, heterogeneous teams ("melting pot" teams comprised of individuals from a variety of backgrounds) are expected to exhibit lower levels of cohesion. Cox notes that the empirical evidence for his hypothesis is slight. In fact, a recent study conducted by Widmeyer and Williams (1991) failed to find a relationship between homogeneity and cohesion. Anecdotally, one can recall teams that support Cox's contentions and teams that refute his idea. For example, the cultural homogeneity of Olympic teams may foster feelings of cohesion among team members. On the other hand, professional teams can be cohesive even though they are comprised of highly dissimilar individuals. Perhaps in these situations it is the goal of team success that is important. That is, although professional teams are heterogeneous in most aspects, the players are homogeneous in their goal of victory. It is plausible that this common goal fosters cohesiveness. Future researchers should more closely examine the relationship between team homogeneity and cohesion for a better understanding of this phenomenon.

Team Size.   Team size is another factor related to cohesion. Research has found that as the size of a group increases, the group's cohesion decreases (Baron & Greenberg, 1990; Schultz & Schultz, 1994). Widmeyer, Brawley, and Carron (1990) examined the team size-team cohesion relationship by measuring the perception of cohesion among participants in volleyball and three-on-three basketball leagues. The basketball teams contained 3, 6, or 9 members, while the volleyball teams were comprised of 3, 6, or 12 players. As expected, Widmeyer and his colleagues found an inverse relationship between team size and team cohesion.

Coaches dealing with large teams may want to develop the cohesiveness of subunits (Davis, 1969). For example, a football coach could divide his or her players into a defensive unit, an offensive unit, and a special teams unit, and then attempt to develop the cohesion of these smaller and more personal groups. However, coaches must be concerned with the degree of intergroup rivalry and competition they encourage between the subunits. Although the competition may foster feelings of subunit cohesion, it may disrupt the players' perceptions of overall team unity and ultimately have a negative impact on team performance (Murrell & Gaertner, 1992; Spink, 1992).

Severe Initiation.   In 1959, Aronson and Mills conducted a study requiring subjects to exert a high level of effort to join a discussion group. Other subjects exerted a moderate amount of effort to join the group, while a third group exerted no effort. After taking part in the discussion, subjects were asked about their impressions of the group. Aronson and Mills found that subjects who exerted the greatest amount of effort were most favorably disposed toward the group, while those exerting no effort were least favorably disposed. Participants exerting a moderate amount of effort reported moderate favorability ratings.

The research of Aronson and Mills (1959) highlights the impact of severe initiation on group cohesion. The more effort required to join a group, the greater the cohesion of that group. This finding suggests that when athletes are required to exert a high level of effort to join a team, they feel more allegiance and cohesion toward that team. For example, consider a scholastic athlete who has worked extremely hard to move up from the sophomore and junior varsity teams. Finally, in his senior year he makes the varsity squad. Now consider a second player who makes the varsity team his junior year with relatively little effort. Based on the work of Aronson and Mills, we would expect the first player to experience a higher level of team cohesion because he exerted a higher level of effort to become a member of the team.

The notion that effort enhances cohesion has implications for professional sport as well. Recently, there has been a tendency for college players to waive their final year of eligibility and enter the National Basketball Association draft after their junior year. Because these players are highly skilled, they tend to be drafted very early, receive multimillion dollar contracts, and are given starting roles on the team. Compared to players who earned their way onto the professional team through 4 years of college and a few years on the professional team's bench, we would expect players entering the NBA early to exhibit lower levels of team cohesion. Consistent with this logic, authors have claimed that these players have little or no sense of team loyalty and cohesion (e.g., Taylor, 1995).

Consequences of Team Cohesion

Once teams have established a cohesive environment, cohesion can have an influence on the players' behaviors and attitudes. Sport psychologists have been particularly interested in two consequences of team cohesion: performance and satisfaction.

The Relationship between Team Cohesion and Performance.   Although sport psychologists have been interested in a number of aspects of team cohesion, perhaps the greatest amount of research has examined the relationship between team cohesion and performance. Research has found a positive correlation between team cohesion and performance in a variety of sports and at different levels of competition (e.g., Arnold & Staub, 1973; Landers, Wilkinson, Hatfield, & Barber, 1982; Murrell & Gaertner, 1992; Slater & Sewell, 1994; Williams & Hacker, 1982; Williams & Widmeyer, 1991). In fact, in their review of the cohesion-performance literature, Widmeyer et al. (1993) found that approximately 80% of the studies indicated that higher levels of team cohesion corresponded with better performance (17% found a negative relationship, while 3% indicated no relationship).

Thus, it appears that cohesion is associated with increased performance. However, because a small minority of the studies examined by Widmeyer and his colleagues (1993) found a negative cohesion-performance relationship, it appears that, in certain situations, cohesion may actually be detrimental to performance. One such situation has been identified by researchers working in industrial/organizational psychology. These researchers have found that the relationship between leaders and subordinates can be an important determinant of whether cohesion will help or hinder performance (Seashore, 1954; Schriescheim, 1980; Tziner & Vardi, 1982). When group members believe that leaders are supportive of their efforts, cohesion will enhance performance (see Figure 14.1). However, when leaders are not supportive of the group's efforts, cohesion will impair performance. For example, imagine a baseball team comprised of a highly cohesive group of players. If the relationship between the players and manager is supportive (i.e., the players and manager agree on the team's goals, the group atmosphere is positive), the players will work together as a unit to accomplish the manager's goals. However, if the player-manager relationship is not supportive, the players will view the setting as hostile and will not be motivated to perform and produce for the manager. In fact, because the players are highly cohesive, the team may band together in an attempt to have the manager replaced.

Another factor that can impact the cohesion-performance relationship is the type of sport in question. In his investigation of the team cohesion-performance literature, Cox (1990) found a positive relationship between cohesion and performance in sports involving a high level of interaction among the teammates (such as football, volleyball, and basketball). However, in sports with little or no interaction (such as bowling and archery), there was a negative relationship between cohesion and performance.

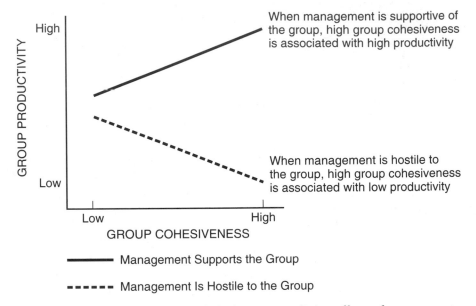

FIGURE 14.1   Group cohesion and productivity: mediating effects of management. (Reprinted by permission from: Baron, R. A., & Greenberg, J. [1990]. Behavior in organizations: Understanding and managing the human side of work (3rd ed.). Needham Heights, MA: Allyn & Bacon.).

The Direction of the Relationship between Team Cohesion and Athletic Performance. The research described above highlights the positive correlation between team cohesion and athletic performance. However, we have yet to discuss the causal pattern involving these variables. As you may recall from Chapter 2, a positive correlation simply points to the relationship between two variables and does not allow for a determination of causation. While it is possible that higher levels of team cohesion cause better performance, it is also possible that better performance leads to higher levels of cohesion.

Widmeyer et al. (1993) reviewed three studies examining the causal relationship between cohesion and performance (Carron & Ball, 1977; Landers et al., 1982; Williams & Hacker, 1982). Each of these studies employed a cross-lagged panel methodology (see Chapter 2). In their critical review of these studies, Widmeyer et al. (1993) found that the average correlation from early performance measures to later cohesion measures was greater than the average correlation from early cohesion measures to later performance measures (see Table 14.1). As a result, Widmeyer et al. state that the "data support the conclusion that the causal link between performance and cohesion is somewhat stronger than the causal link between cohesion and performance" (p. 677).

Before concluding our discussion of the causal pattern involving cohesion and performance, an important point must be mentioned. Widmeyer et al. (1993) concluded that performance tends to cause cohesion to a greater extent than cohesion causes performance. This conclusion does not imply that cohesion does not impact performance. Increased cohesion can result in better performance, but the relation-

TABLE 14.1   Cohesion-Performance Relationships Across Time*

Authors	*Early to Mid-season*	*Mid-to Postseason*	*Early to Postseason*
Relationship of Early Cohesion Measures to Later Performance Measures			
Carron & Ball (1977)	.225	.391	.072
Landers et al. (1982)	.800	.720	.810
Williams & Hacker (1982)	.720	.720	.620
Average[†]	.633	.632	.566
Relationships of Early Performance Measures to Later Cohesion Measures			
Carron & Ball (1977)	.528	.770	.790
Landers et al. (1982)	.850	.640	.750
Williams & Hacker (1982)	—	.870	.870
Average[†]	.726	.776	.810

*Cohesion was assessed by a composite index comprising measures of friendship, influence, enjoyment, sense of belonging, value of membership, closeness, and teamwork.
[†]Z-transformations were used to compute averages.

ship is circular, with successful performance, in turn, causing greater cohesion (see Slater & Sewell, 1994). In fact, simply providing feedback about team cohesion may facilitate performance (Vergina & Dugoni, 1993). Thus, it may be concluded that, although team cohesion is both a cause *and* consequence of performance, cohesion is *predominantly* a consequence of performance.

The Relationship between Team Cohesion and Satisfaction.   Another aspect of team cohesion that has interested researchers is the relationship between cohesion and player satisfaction. In 1971, Martens and Peterson presented their viewpoint concerning the interaction between cohesion and satisfaction. These authors argued for a circular relationship involving cohesion, satisfaction, and team performance. Specifically, they stated that (1) team cohesion leads to successful performance, (2) successful performance leads to higher levels of satisfaction, and (3) higher levels of satisfaction lead to higher degrees of cohesiveness. A different model was proposed by Williams and Hacker (1982). These researchers felt that (1) successful performance leads both to higher levels of team cohesion and higher levels of satisfaction, and (2) increases in cohesion also result in higher levels of satisfaction. Although these two models are different in their predictions of the causal patterns involving team cohesion and satisfaction, they agree that a positive relationship exists between these variables. Consistent with these theories, research has found that individuals do enjoy being a member of cohesive groups (Baron & Greenberg, 1990; Cartwright, 1968), and members who perceive their team as cohesive are particularly likely to continue their participation (Spink, 1995).

An Overall Picture of Team Cohesion in Sport

Before leaving this section, it may be helpful to integrate the research described above, thus providing an overall picture of team cohesion. Figure 14.2 is designed

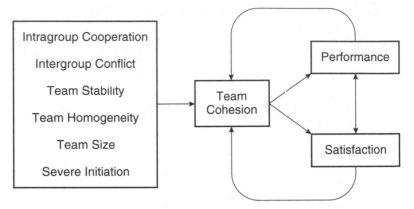

FIGURE 14.2   The antecedents and consequences of team cohesion in sport.

to provide this integration, depicting both the antecedents and consequences of team cohesion. As seen in the figure, several factors can cause team cohesion. These factors include intragroup cooperation, intergroup conflict, team factors (such as stability, homogeneity, and size), and severe initiation. Higher levels of team cohesion lead to higher levels of performance and team member satisfaction. Performance and satisfaction are shown to have a bidirectional influence. Finally, successful performance and higher levels of satisfaction may, in turn, lead to higher levels of team cohesion. Thus, the relationship among cohesion, performance, and satisfaction is both interactive and circular. Changes in any of the three variables could alter one or both of the other two.

AUDIENCE EFFECTS

This section examines the impact of sport audiences on athletic performance. In particular, we will examine social facilitation and the home field advantage. However, before proceeding into our examination of these phenomena, it is necessary to identify the types of audiences found in sport settings (see Figure 14.3). One type of sport audience, the **spectating audience,** consists of sport spectators. **Inactive-spectating audiences** include passive spectators who do not interact with the athletes. A **reactive-spectating audience,** on the other hand, consists of spectators who react either positively or negatively to the athletes' actions. Another type of audience, the **coactive audience,** consists of other athletes. Coactive audiences include one's own teammates as well as players on the opposing team and can be divided into two subtypes. An **interactive-coactive audience** consists of players from one's own team and the opposing team who actively interact while performing. A **noninteractive-coactive audience** is comprised of individuals performing simultaneously in the same setting who do not interact with one another. A final type of audience, the **regulatory audience,** consists of individuals such as referees, judges, and officials who regulate the procedures and outcomes of a competition. Regulatory audiences

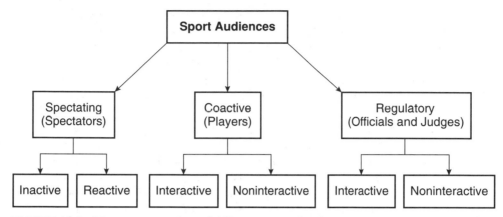

FIGURE 14.3 There are a number of different types of audiences present at sporting events.

can be divided into interactive-regulatory and noninteractive-regulatory audiences. ***Interactive-regulatory audiences*** include referees, judges, and officials who interact with players while the competition is in progress (such as football, basketball, and baseball officials). ***Noninteractive-regulatory audiences*** include referees, judges, and officials who do not interact with players while the competition is in progress (such as diving and figure skating judges).

An example may help differentiate the types of audiences described above. Imagine that a hockey player, Gary, is preparing for tonight's championship game. To settle his nerves, Gary arrives at the rink before the other competitors. As he begins to practice his slap shot, a few janitors begin cleaning the stands for the upcoming game. Although the janitors notice and occasionally watch Gary, because they do not interact with him they would be considered an inactive-spectating audience. However, if the janitors began to applaud (or boo), they would be considered a reactive-spectating audience. Imagine now that a few of Gary's competitors began to practice on the same rink as Gary without interacting with him. These individuals would comprise a noninteractive-coactive audience. Gary's teammates who make their way onto the ice and begin practicing with Gary comprise an interactive-coactive audience. When the contest begins, the referees are an interactive-regulatory audience. If Gary were in a figure skating contest, the judges would be a noninteractive-regulatory audience.

Social Facilitation

When athletes are asked if they prefer to compete alone or against other athletes, the vast majority indicate their preference for competing against another individual. Apparently, athletes believe that coactive audiences enhance their performance. Similarly, many athletes feel they perform better when competing in the presence of a spectating audience (inactive and reactive). In what is generally accepted as the first attempt to examine this phenomenon scientifically, Triplett (1898) studied the performances of bicycle racers. He found that cyclists performed better when they competed against another cyclist than when they competed alone. To examine the phenomenon in the laboratory, Triplett asked children to wind a reel as fast as possible. Some children were asked to complete the task alone, while others competed in a dyad. Similar to findings on the times of the cyclists, Triplett found that the children wound the reels faster when they competed against another individual. As a result, Triplett concluded that the presence of an audience facilitated performance.

Although the straightforward nature of Triplett's findings were attractive, some researchers were unable to replicate the performance enhancing effects of an audience (e.g., Pessin, 1933). In 1965, Zajonc published a paper designed to integrate the conflicting research findings. Zajonc's paper outlined his **social facilitation theory** (a term coined by Allport in 1924). This theory reflects the belief that audiences are arousing and arousal leads to the dominant response (see Figure 14.4). If a task is easy or someone is highly skilled at a task, his or her dominant response is successful task performance. Conversely, if an individual is attempting a difficult task or is unskilled at a task, his or her dominant response is failure. For example, the dominant response of a professional golfer attempting a 4-foot putt would be successfully sinking the putt, while the dominant response for someone who has never played golf would be missing the putt.

Numerous studies have supported Zajonc's theory (e.g., Geen & Gange, 1977; Hunt & Hillery, 1973; Landers, Brawley, & Hale, 1978; Landers & McCullagh, 1977; Martens, 1969). For example, consider Singer's (1965) investigation of university athletes and nonathletes. On the first day of the study, subjects were allowed to practice a balancing task. The nonathletes outperformed the athletes on these practice trials, indicating that the nonathletes had a more successful dominant response. The following day, participants were asked to perform six additional trials of the balancing task. The first three trials were performed alone, while the last three were performed in front of an audience. Consistent with Zajonc's theory, the nonathlete group performed better than the athlete group during the final three trials (i.e., the nonathletes performed better in front of the audience). Thus, the subjects with a successful dominant response (the nonathletes) exhibited an increase in performance when behaving in the presence of an audience. No such performance improvement was displayed by individuals with an unsuccessful dominant response (the athletes).

Davis and Harvey (1992) also conducted a sport-specific study testing social fa-

FIGURE 14.4   The theory of social facilitation.

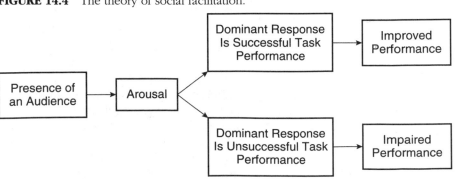

cilitation theory. These authors examined the ability of Major League players to perform in several pressure situations (such as batting with two outs and players in scoring position). They reasoned that because the dominant response in hitting is failure (most hitters fail over 70% of the time), performance should decrease in pressure situations due to the increased arousal accompanying these settings. The results supported the predictions. For example, consider the performances of players batting with teammates in scoring position. In these situations, players had a batting average of .262 when hitting with less than two outs in the inning (low pressure and low arousal). However, their average was only .231 when there were two outs (high pressure and high arousal).

Reasons Underlying the Arousing Qualities of an Audience. A number of investigators have focused on the arousing nature of audiences. This work has lead to the development of three theories accounting for the arousal-inducing qualities of audiences: evaluation apprehension, mere presence, and distraction (see Figure 14.5).

EVALUATION APPREHENSION. Several authors have suggested that audiences are arousing because individuals are concerned with the ability of the audience to evaluate their performance, a perspective referred to as the ***evaluation apprehension theory of audience arousal*** (Cottrell, 1972; Haas & Roberts, 1975; Henchy & Glass, 1968; Martens & Landers, 1972; Monteleone & White, 1994; Sasfy & Okun, 1974). For example, consider a study conducted by Worringham and Messick (1983). In this research, runners jogging alone were timed as they moved along a path. The subjects' times in two different 45-yard sections were recorded. All subjects ran the first section alone. In the second section, the experimenters set up three different conditions. In one condition, subjects were left to run the second section alone (the alone condition). In the second condition, a female confederate sat near the second section of track facing away from the runners (the mere presence condition). In a final condition, the confederate sat near the second section facing the runners (the

FIGURE 14.5 A variety of factors may be responsible for the arousing nature of audiences.

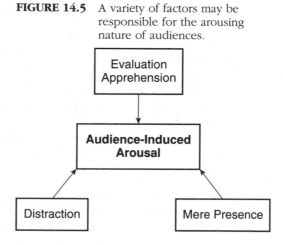

evaluation apprehension condition). By comparing the runners' times in the two sections, Worringham and Messick were able to show support for Zajonc's theory and highlight the importance of evaluation apprehension. Because the subjects were volunteer runners, we would expect their dominant response to be success at the task. As a result, Zajonc would predict that the runners' times would decrease in the mere presence and evaluation apprehension conditions (i.e., they would run faster). The results indicated that, although the times in these two conditions did decrease for the second portion of the path, only the decrease exhibited by joggers in the evaluation apprehension condition reached statistical significance. Thus, Worringham and Messick's (1983) research supports Zajonc's theory and demonstrates the importance of the evaluative nature of an audience.

MERE PRESENCE.   In describing his theory of social facilitation, Zajonc (1965, 1980) articulated his belief that individuals become aroused by the mere presence of an audience. The ***mere presence theory of audience arousal*** states that the mere presence of another member of one's species is sufficient to trigger an arousal response. Several studies have substantiated Zajonc's belief. For example, animals such as monkeys, chickens, armadillos, and even roaches display a social facilitation effect by performing better in the presence of other members of their species (Clayton, 1978; Zajonc, Heingartner, & Herman, 1969). Because it is unlikely that members of these species would have been concerned about how the audience was evaluating them, it appears that their increased performance was due to the mere presence of others. Two additional lines of evidence favor the mere presence theory of audience arousal. First, individuals often exhibit their dominant response even though members of the audience are unable to evaluate the target's behavior (Schmitt, Gilovich, Goore, & Joseph, 1986; Towler, 1986). For example, when individuals perform in front of a blind-folded audience, they still exhibit a small social facilitation effect (Haas & Roberts, 1975). Second, there can be a facilitation effect for behaviors such as getting dressed (Markus, 1978). In these and similar behaviors (such as eating and drinking), it is unlikely that the subjects are concerned with the evaluations of the audience and, as such, it seems that the mere presence of the audience was again responsible for the social facilitation effect.

DISTRACTION.   Distraction is another attempt to explain the arousing effects of audiences. The ***distraction theory of audience arousal*** represents the belief that audiences produce an attentional conflict within the performer by forcing the individual to attend to both the audience and the task (Baron, 1986). The presence of others distracts the performer. The individual becomes aroused as he or she attempts to remain focused on the task. Anyone who has attempted to study for an exam while being distracted by others understands the process underlying distraction theory. The distraction perspective has been supported by several studies (e.g., Groff, Baron, & Moore, 1983; Landers & McCullagh, 1977; Sanders, Baron, & Moore, 1978).

Evaluating the Theories of Audience Arousal.   Each theory described above has empirical evidence to substantiate its position. As a result, researchers have begun to discard the notion that one approach is superior to the others and instead favor the idea that arousal may result from any or all of the three possibilities (Forsyth, 1990). For example, Baron and Greenberg (1990) conclude that "all the explanations . . . provide some important insight into the social facilitation process" (p. 280). However, some authors maintain that one stance is more valid than the others. For example, in an attempt to determine the most accurate perspective on audience arousal, Bond and Titus (1983) conducted a meta-analysis of more than 200 social facilitation studies testing almost 24,000 subjects. Based on their analysis, Bond and Titus concluded that the evidence favored the mere presence theory of audience arousal.

A theory that assists in integrating the evaluation apprehension, mere presence, and distraction approaches was presented by Chapman (1974). Chapman argued in favor of a ***psychological presence theory of audience arousal.*** This theory states that a performer's arousal increases as an audience becomes more psychologically present. An audience that is unable to evaluate the actor's performance is more psychologically present than no audience at all. However, an audience that is able to evaluate the actor's performance is more psychologically present than an audience without this ability. Thus, Chapman's theory predicts that merely present audiences will result in higher levels of arousal than no audience but that evaluative audiences will result in the highest levels of arousal and the greatest social facilitation effect. Chapman's research supports his hypothesis as does the Worringham and Messick (1983) research discussed earlier. Recall that these investigators found that runners performing alone ran slower than those in a mere presence condition (i.e., a confederate with her back turned to the runners). Further, runners in the mere presence condition ran slower than those in the evaluation apprehension condition (i.e., a confederate facing the runners). The confederate in the evaluation apprehension condition was more psychologically present than the confederate in the mere presence condition. As for the distraction theory of audience arousal, we would predict that, as audiences become increasingly psychologically present, they also become more distracting. Again, Worringham and Messick's subjects would be expected to show the greatest facilitation effect in the highly distracting evaluation apprehension condition, which is precisely what the authors found.

The Home Field Advantage

A second topic relevant to sport audiences (particularly reactive-spectating audiences) is the home field advantage. Since the early stages of organized sport, players, coaches, and fans have subscribed to the belief that home teams perform better than visiting teams. However, it was not until the latter part of this century that researchers began to document the home field advantage empirically.

The first major piece of research testing the home field advantage in sport was conducted by Schwartz and Barsky (1977). These authors examined the outcomes of 1,880 professional baseball, 182 professional football, 910 collegiate football, and 542 professional hockey games played in 1971 (the hockey data were taken from the 1971–1972 season). They found that a home field advantage existed in each sport as home teams in professional baseball (53%), professional football (55%), collegiate football (59%), and hockey (53%) won a higher percentage of games than visiting teams. Support for the home field advantage in these sports was also found by Edwards (1979; Edwards & Archambault, 1989), Pollard (1986), and Irving and Goldstein (1990). Subsequent research has shown that the home field advantage generalizes to many sports and levels of competition. For example, a home field advantage has been found in college basketball (Snyder & Purdy, 1985; Varca, 1980), alpine skiing (Bray & Carron, 1993), the summer and winter Olympics (Leonard, 1989), junior ice hockey (Agnew & Carron, 1994), minor league baseball (Courneya & Carron, 1991), cricket (Pollard, 1986), women's collegiate basketball and field hockey (Gayton, Mutrie, & Hearns, 1987), high school sports (McCutcheon, 1984), and soccer (Pollard, 1986).

Courneya and Carron (1992) recently conducted an extensive review of the home field advantage literature. Based on their in-depth investigation, these authors concluded that the home field advantage is a real and measurable phenomenon, that college and professional teams do not differ in the degree of the home field advantage, and that the advantage is different for various sports. Their review found the greatest home field advantage for soccer, basketball, and hockey. Home teams had the least advantage in baseball. Of interest, this finding corresponds with the work of Donzelli and Edwards (1994) who found that baseball players were less likely than players from other sports to believe in the home field advantage. Thus, it appears that home teams do tend to have an advantage over visiting teams. However, as discussed in this chapter's "A Closer Look," when a championship is on the line the visiting team may have the advantage.

The Reasons Underlying the Home Field Advantage.   Because the home field advantage is so well documented, many researchers have shifted their attention away from documenting the existence of the phenomenon and are now attempting to identify the factors responsible for the effect. Research has indicated that there may be several different factors underlying the home field advantage.

THE SUPPORTIVE HOME AUDIENCE.   Several authors have argued that the home field advantage is the result of a supportive home audience. For example, Cox (1990) stated that, "While many variables might help create the home court or field advantage, none seem to be as important as the presence of a supportive audience" (p. 304). Cox's sentiment was echoed by Iso-Ahola and Hatfield (1986) who stated that "We submit that the home-field advantage exists mainly because the partisan crowd enhances the home-team members' motivation" (p. 315). Research tends to support these arguments (Mizruchi, 1985). In their analysis of Major League baseball, Zeller and Jurkovac (cited in Horn, 1988) found that home teams playing in domed stadiums had a greater advantage than teams playing in open air stadiums. The authors believe the increased success is due to the ability of domed stadiums to hold in noise and give a greater impression of a supportive audience. Similarly, Pollard (1986) found a positive relationship between crowd density (the number of fans in attendance relative to the size of the stadium) and team performance among professional baseball players. Agnew and Carron (1994) found a similar result in their investigation of junior hockey teams. In this work, although crowd density was related to the home field advantage, absolute crowd size (i.e., the raw number of fans in attendance) was not. Thus, it appears that the number of spectators in attendance

A CLOSER LOOK:
THE HOME FIELD DISADVANTAGE IN SPORT

Although a large body of research has found that home teams perform better than visiting teams, Baumeister and Steinhilber (1984; Baumeister, 1995) identified a situation that may lead to a reversal of this effect. According to these authors, when a team is close to achieving a highly desired goal, the increased self-focus and self-attention associated with a supportive audience may be detrimental to performance. Baumeister and Steinhilber suggest two reasons for this home field disadvantage effect. First, the increased self-focus reduces one's ability to focus on environmental cues that are critical for success. Second, the increased self-attention directed at previously automatic behaviors may disrupt the smooth execution of these behaviors. To test their hypothesis, Baumeister and Steinhilber (1984) examined the outcomes of the baseball World Series from 1924 to 1982. They found that home teams were victorious in 60% of the first two games of the series, replicating the home field advantage research. However, in the final game the visiting team was more likely to be victorious, winning 59% of the contests. In addition, in the game with the greatest amount of self-focus, a seventh game played at home (the World Series is a best of seven series), the visiting team won 61% percent of the time. This finding was replicated using data from championships in the National Basketball Association.

To determine if the final game home field disadvantage was due to the visiting team improving their performance or the home team's tendency to display a "championship choke" (Heaton & Sigall, 1989, p. 1019), Baumeister and Steinhilber compared the fielding errors from games 1 and 2 with the errors committed in game 7. They found that the visiting team displayed a slight and nonsignificant tendency to commit fewer errors in the final game. However, in support of the notion of a championship choke, the home team committed significantly more errors in the final game. Heaton and Sigall (1989) provided further evidence that the home field disadvantage is a function of the home team's impaired performance. Reexamining the baseball data from the Baumeister and Steinhilber research, Heaton and Sigall found that, in the final game, home teams had difficulty maintaining a lead when ahead or gaining the lead when behind. For example, when the home team scored first in games 1 through 6, they held the lead 70% of the time. However, when scoring first in the 7th game, the home team held the lead only 30% of the time. When home teams fell behind in the first six games, they were able to take the lead 51% of the time, but when they fell behind in game 7 they could take the lead only 25% of the time.

Some authors have challenged the generalizability and validity of the home field disadvantage. In particular, Courneya and Carron (1992) were critical of the evidence supporting a championship choke. First, they noted that the samples examined by Baumeister and Steinhilber (1984) and Heaton and Sigall

(1989) included only a small number of games. In fact, when Schlenker, Phillips, Boniecki, and Schlenker (1995a, 1995b) updated the Baumeister and Steinhilber (1984) data set by including the baseball championships played in the decade following the Baumeister and Steinhilber analysis, the home field disadvantage was no longer present. Second, Courneya and Carron (1992) noted that other researchers have failed to replicate the effect in other sports. For example, Gayton, Matthews, and Nickless (1987) were unable to find a home field disadvantage for National Hockey League championships (although Wright, Jackson, Christie, McGuire, & Wright, 1991, did find a home course disadvantage in professional golf). Third, when the dominant team is eliminated from the analysis, the home field disadvantage is attenuated (Benjafield, Liddell, & Benjafield, 1989).

A final problem in determining the scope of the home field disadvantage, one not mentioned by Courneya and Carron (1992), lies in the lack of consistency in data analyses. As mentioned, Gayton et al. (1987) did not find a home field disadvantage for National Hockey League championships in their comparison of games 1 through 4 with the last and seventh game of the series. Conversely, Wright, Voyer, Wright, and Roney (1995) did find a home field disadvantage in the National Hockey League. These authors operationally defined early/noncritical games as contests 1 and 3, comparing the outcomes of these contests with the last game of the series. A further discrepancy between the two studies is that the Gayton et al. work included the semifinal and final series, while the Wright et al. study was limited to the final series. The inconsistency in the results is probably a function of the inconsistent methods used to define the noncritical and critical games as well as the different notions of a "championship" series. As a result, even though some studies have supported the notion of a home field disadvantage in championship games, before we can conclude that the home field disadvantage exists, more research is needed, particularly research maintaining consistent operational definitions of the important constructs.

is not a critical factor in facilitating an advantage for the home team. Rather, it is crowd density that enhances the home team's performance. Dense crowds give the appearance of a sold-out arena. Quite likely, it is the impression that the arena is at or near capacity that encourages the home team.

A recent investigation by Donzelli and Edwards (1994) indicates that players overwhelmingly feel that a supportive audience enhances performance. These authors asked 388 athletes from a variety of sports to report their expectations for performance, self-confidence, and belief in the home field advantage. The respondents indicated that they expected to perform better in front of supportive home audiences and they were more confident in front of these audiences.

THE DISRUPTIVE AWAY AUDIENCE.   Other authors believe that the home field advantage is a result of the away audience's ability to disrupt the performance of the visiting team (see Laird, 1923). For example, consider Greer's (1983) research examining spectator booing at college basketball games. Greer examined the players' actions subsequent to sustained crowd protests (booing lasting a minimum of 15 seconds) and compared these actions to those occurring during normal crowd conditions. The results showed that the home team played slightly better (as indicated by points, turnovers, and fouls) after a period of sustained protest. However, the visiting team played much worse subsequent to fan protests.

Silva and Andrew (1987) also examined the "away court disadvantage" (p. 196). These authors examined data from more than 400 college basketball games played between 1971 and 1981. They recorded the home and visiting teams' field goal percentage, free throw percentage, fouls, turnovers, and rebounds. To determine a standard for performance comparisons, coaches were asked to state numerical values reflecting good, average, and poor performance. For example, the coaches reported that a field goal percentage of 51.4 was good, 49.2 was average, and 46.0 was poor (these are averages across several coaches). Silva and Andrew then compared the performance standards with the actual performances of the home and away teams. They found that, although the visiting team performances fell within the poor performance standards, the home team performances did not resemble the good performance standards. For example, home teams had an average field goal percentage of just under 50%, which was similar to the standard reflecting an average performance (see above). However, the visiting team had an average field goal percentage of 47.7%, which was similar to the standard set for poor performance. As a result, Silva and Andrew concluded that the superior performances displayed by home teams may be a function of the home crowd's disruptive effect on the visiting team.

The research of Thirer and Rampey (1979) indicates that the hostile actions of the home crowd may have a negative effect on the home team as well. These authors examined the antisocial behaviors of spectators attending several collegiate basketball games. Antisocial behaviors included throwing objects on the court, fighting, and verbal aggression (i.e., swearing at the opponents or officials). Because it is quite common at sporting events, booing was not considered to be an antisocial act. Thirer and Rampey compared the onset of antisocial behaviors with the subsequent performances of the home and visiting teams. The results indicated that abusive behavior had a detrimental effect on the performance of the home team. Although the number of infractions (e.g., fouls) committed per minute by the visiting team was consistent regardless of crowd behavior, the home team committed more infractions during antisocial crowd reactions.

ASSERTIVENESS. There are also nonaudience factors that can be responsible for the improved performance of home teams. One nonaudience factor is the assertive play of the home team. Although home and away teams do not appear to differ in their aggressiveness (see Chapter 12), they may differ in their assertiveness. A study by Varca (1980) supports this line of reasoning. Varca hypothesized that the home field advantage is a function of the home team's tendency to display functionally aggressive behavior, while the visiting team tends to display dysfunctionally aggressive behavior. However, because Varca used rebounds, steals, and blocked shots as an indication of functionally aggressive play, it appears that he was assessing the level of assertive play rather than aggressive play (recall that actions are only considered aggressive if they lie beyond the rules of the game). Dysfunctional aggression was viewed as behavior that impaired the team's performance (such as personal fouls). As seen in Table 14.2, Varca's predictions were confirmed as home teams performed better on the assertiveness measures, while the visiting teams exhibited higher levels of dysfunctional aggression (i.c., they committed more personal fouls).

Although I have described assertiveness as a potential nonaudience explanation for the home field advantage, it should be noted that audiences can play a role in the players' assertive behavior and ultimately their performance. At certain sporting events, spectators may actively cheer and encourage the assertive play of the home team. The cheering and support from the home audience may reinforce the assertive play. As a result, the audience facilitates the performance of the home team by encouraging assertive actions.

OTHER NONAUDIENCE FACTORS.   Assertiveness is not the only nonaudience factor playing a role in the home field advantage. Additional factors that have caught the research attention of sport psychologists include stadium familiarity, travel, biased officiating, and game rules. Concerning the impact of familiarity, intuitively it seems likely that as players become more familiar with the nuances of their stadium (e.g., the "green monster" at Fenway Park in Boston), their performance at home will almost certainly improve. Indeed, Donzelli and Edwards (1994) found that athletes strongly believe that stadium familiarity gives them an advantage. However, Courneya and Carron (1992) note that few studies have examined the impact of stadium familiarity, leaving the importance of this variable in doubt. A major reason for the scarcity of research concerns the lack of opportunities to observe a team's performance on multiple home courts. However, Moore and Brylinsky (1995) recently had an opportunity to do just this. During the 1992–1993 basketball season, the Western Michigan University men's and women's teams had to play their home games at five

TABLE 14.2   Means for Assertive and Dysfunctionally Aggressive Actions by Game Location

	Game Location	
Performance Variable	*Home*	*Away*
Assertiveness		
Steals	6.6	5.3
Blocked Shots	2.8	2.3
Rebounds	37.5	34.4
Dysfunctional Aggression		
Fouls	20.6	21.9

Note: Means reflect per game averages. All means are significantly different.

different unfamiliar arenas while construction on their new home arena was being completed. Moore and Brylinsky found that both teams still had better records at home than on the road. Thus, the teams had a home field advantage even though they were not familiar with the home stadiums and facilities, implying that stadium familiarity may not be as great a factor in the home field advantage as previously believed.

As for the impact of travel, common sense may lead one to believe that the fatigue and disruption of daily routines associated with extended road trips will impair the visiting team's performance. However, research has not supported this contention (Courneya & Carron, 1991; Edwards & Archambault, 1989; Pollard, 1986).

Regarding the impact of biased officiating, several studies have found that officials' calls tend to favor the home team (Greer, 1983; Lehman & Reifman, 1987). For example, Allen (1994) examined the calls of 20 National Hockey League referees and found that 18 of the officials awarded the home team more power play opportunities than the road team. Allen concluded that "referees have different stripes when it comes to administering justice" (p. 5C). It should be noted that similar to the impact of assertiveness on the home field advantage, an official's decision may be an audience-related factor if his or her decision is influenced by the crowd.

Finally, concerning the rules governing athletics, in certain sports the home team is given an apparent advantage. For example, in baseball and softball the home team has the final at bat. Courneya and Carron (1990) tested the impact of this rule by examining the results of 1,120 softball double-headers. The analysis of double-header competitions was advantageous because each team served as the home team for one game, and this format controlled for factors such as personnel and weather conditions. The authors found no outcome differences based on batting first versus last. Thus, although much additional work is needed, differential rules for the home and visiting teams might not be as important as previously believed.

SELF-PRESENTATIONAL CONCERNS IN SPORT

I once talked to an individual who enjoyed jogging alone but was afraid to run after dark. It seemed to me that the most straightforward solution to her problem was for her to begin jogging during the daylight hours. However, she stated that she could never jog during the day because she thought she looked awkward when running and did not want to be seen by others. This individual's behavior is an excellent example of the impact of self-presentational concerns in sport. **Self-presentation** (sometimes called impression management) involves one's desires and efforts to present oneself in a positive way to others (e.g., spectators, teammates, opponents). Because self-perception is a function of social interactions, it is yet another process relevant to the social nature of sport.

In his 1992 keynote address to the North American Society for the Psychology of Sport and Physical Activity, Leary discussed three areas in which self-presentational processes play a role in sport activities: motivation to participate in athletics, choice of activities and settings, and performance quality.

Self-Presentation and the Motivation to Participate in Athletics

In the socialization chapter, we discussed a number of different motives for participating in sport, including the fitness benefits gained from athletics. Leary (1992) notes that, because many people equate fitness benefits with a healthier and more attractive appearance, this motivational factor often reflects an athlete's self-presentational concerns. Also, because individuals who feel embarrassed by their physical appearance often shy away from athletic endeavors, self-presentational concerns also may act as a motivation to refrain from or discontinue athletic participation (see Hart, Leary, & Rejeski, 1989).

Self-Presentation and the Selection of Activities and Settings

Leary (1992) also notes that desires to present oneself in a positive manner can influence decisions involving athletic activities and settings. Most individuals have the option of choosing between a variety of sport activities and settings. Concerning ac-

Some athletes choose to participate in a particular sport because they want to be associated with the traits of others who participate in that sport. (Photographer: Sunstar. Source: Photo Researchers, Inc.)

tivity choices, individuals often possess stereotypes about people engaging in certain athletic endeavors. For example, what traits do you think best describe a "typical" bowler and a "typical" surfer. Are the traits similar for these two athletes? Most likely, they are not. Rather, we tend to assume that people participating in particular sports possess specific traits and characteristics (Colley, Nash, O'Donnell, & Restorick, 1987; Germone & Furst, 1991; Pedersen & Kono, 1990; Sadalla et al., 1988). Leary argues that some individuals choose an athletic activity because they want to be associated with the stereotypical traits of those participating in the chosen sport. Individuals wanting to present themselves as "rough," "carefree," or "conservative" will probably choose different sports. As a result, activity choices become a function of the self-presentational desire to be perceived in a particular way (e.g., as a carefree surfer) or to avoid being perceived in a certain way (e.g., some women may avoid certain sports because they fear they will be viewed as masculine or aggressive).

Concerning an athlete's choice of settings, consider the jogging example discussed earlier. Because she was worried about her appearance, the woman described in this example chose not to exercise during daylight hours. Thus, her self-presentational concerns dictated her choice of exercise settings. Leary (1992) notes that the impression management concerns of some athletes may be so intense that they never exercise in public. Other athletes, because they feel unskilled at a certain sport, may choose to participate only in a limited environment.

Self-Presentation and Performance

Performance quality is a third area of sport impacted by self-presentation. Leary (1992) states that self-presentational concerns can alter performance in a number of ways. First, self-presentation may impact effort and exertion. In sports such as bicycling, jogging, and weightlifting, an individual's performance is closely related to his or her effort. When individuals participate in these sports in front of others, performance tends to increase as individuals attempt to present themselves in a positive manner (Bond, 1982; Worringham & Messick, 1983).

The performance implications of self-presentation become more involved when dealing with team sports. In many team situations, individuals exert a lower level of effort compared to situations in which they are acting alone. This process is known as ***social loafing.*** Social loafing has its greatest impact when the efforts of the group's members cannot be identified and, thus, they are no longer motivated by self-presentational concerns. Studies have found social loafing effects on a variety of tasks including clapping/cheering (Latané, Williams, & Harkins, 1979) and rope pulling (Ingham, Levinger, Graves, & Peckham, 1974). Social loafing has also been found in sports such as swimming and rowing (Anshel, 1995; Hardy, 1990; Hardy & Crace, 1991; Williams, Nida, Baca, & Latané, 1989).

Social loafing research predicts that team members will often lower their effort if they feel that their contributions to the team cannot be singled out. Consequently, the most effective strategy for countering the effects of social loafing can be to arrange the team environment in such a manner that each member's contribution is identifiable (Williams, Harkins, & Latané, 1981; Williams et al., 1989). Other successful techniques for reducing social loafing include increasing commitment to success (Brickner, Harkins, & Ostrom, 1986) and strengthening the team's cohesiveness (Baron & Byrne, 1994; Everett, Smith, & Williams, 1992).

Leary (1992) states that a second way self-presentational concerns impact performance is through self-handicapping (Berglas & Jones, 1978; Jones & Berglas, 1978). ***Self-handicapping*** involves protecting one's self-image by systematically creating an excuse for failure. This self-esteem maintenance tactic arises when an individual is concerned about his or her ability to perform a task successfully. The individual does not wish to be perceived as a failure and, as a result, constructs obstacles impeding performance, obstacles that allow for an excuse for failure (usually in the form of an external attribution). Because self-handicapping is more likely to occur when others are aware of the excuse, these behaviors are partially motivated by self-presentational concerns (Kolditz & Arkin, 1982). Two important points must be mentioned. First, although individuals who initiate self-handicapping strategies are afraid of failure, this does not necessarily imply that they want to fail. Second, there are actually two forms of self-handicapping (Boris & Hirt, 1994). Behavioral self-handicapping involves behavioral changes such as reducing one's practice time. Verbal self-handicapping involves excuse making (e.g., "I was too stressed out." or "I wasn't feeling well."). Both forms of self-handicapping are common among athletes.

A straightforward method of self-handicapping in sport involves reducing one's practice time. For example, if a diver were concerned about his performance at an upcoming meet, he might reduce his practice time during the weeks prior to the competition. Should he perform poorly at the meet, he can explain to others that his performance was due to his lack of practice rather than his lack of ability. Leary (1992) points out that for endurance sports (e.g., long distance running), individuals may actually self-handicap by practicing too much. Should they fail, they can blame the poor performance on a lack of energy rather than a lack of talent.

If an individual should succeed in spite of the handicap, he or she will receive an especially powerful ego boost. If the diver were to have won the meet without practicing, he would feel especially proud of his accomplishment and would be able to present himself in an exceptionally positive manner (e.g., "I am so talented at diving that I can win without practicing."). Thus, athletes can self-handicap for two reasons: to provide an excuse for failure and thus protect one's image or to provide an ego-enhancing boost to one's image.

Research indicates that self-handicapping behaviors do exist in sport settings. For example, consider Rhodewalt, Saltzman, and Wittmer's (1984) research examining university swimmers. Two weeks prior to the first meet, subjects were asked to complete a scale assessing their self-handicapping tendencies. Subjects also completed the scale on the day prior to 11 competitions. The subjects' practice attendance was recorded. Rhodewalt and his colleagues found that, although low and high self-handicappers did not differ in their attendance prior to an unimportant meet, high self-handicappers were less likely to attend practice prior to an important meet. Evidently, the high self-handicapping swimmers were attempting to use lower levels of practice as an excuse for potential failure. A second study found similar results with professional golfers (Rhodewalt et al., 1984).

Carron, Prapavessis, and Grove (1994) took a different approach in their investigation of self-handicapping in sport. These authors attempted to link research on self-handicapping tendencies with work on team cohesion. To test the relationship between self-handicapping and cohesion, Carron and his associates asked 221 males participating in team sports to complete the Group Environment Questionnaire (GEQ) and a measure of self-handicapping tendencies. The results indicated a significant negative correlation between handicapping and perceptions of team cohesiveness. That is, athletes with a tendency toward self-handicapping felt that their team was relatively low in task cohesion. Apparently, beliefs that the team was low in task cohesion gave the athletes an excuse for failure. That is, the perception that the team was not cohesive was itself a verbal self-handicapping strategy designed to explain a poor performance (e.g., "We would have performed better if we were a more cohesive group.").

Additional Influences of Self-Presentation

Although Leary's (1992) description of self-presentation in sport was quite in-depth, there are other important components of self-presentational processes in athletics. In this final section, we will explore three additional factors related to self-presentation: team selection, social facilitation, and aggression.

Self-Presentation and the Selection of a Team.   In some sport settings, individuals are allowed to select their team. For instance, in many recreational softball and bowling leagues, new players can choose from several different teams. Often, the choices are a function of self-presentational concerns. For example, some athletes want to be associated with a winning team because they believe the association will assist in their attempt to present a positive image (Cialdini & Di Nicholas, 1989). These individuals will most likely choose to join a successful team. Others may want a noncompetitive team because this is the image they wish to project. In each of these settings, team selection reflects self-presentational concerns.

Self-Presentation and Social Facilitation.   Another way self-presentational concerns alter the behavior of athletes is reflected in Bond's ***self-presentational analysis of social facilitation*** (Bond, 1982; Bond & Titus, 1983). This theory states that performers have a desire to present themselves in a positive manner to onlookers. When individuals feel they are skilled at a given task, an audience will facilitate their efforts as the performers attempt to project an image of competence. However, if individuals believe they are unskilled at a task, they will become embarrassed and aroused by the prospect of performing in front of an audience. The result will be an impairment of performance.

Self-Presentation and Aggression.   Aggressive behavior is a final area of sport that may be influenced by athletes' self-presentational concerns. Individuals may act aggressively toward others simply to present themselves in a particular manner to their own teammates. As an example of this process, consider Foley's (1990) description of Texas high school football. He notes that the dominant males often abused their weaker classmates. However, Foley states that it was the males who emulated the athletes and wanted to gain the athletes' approval who were most abusive. It appears that these individuals were using aggression as a self-presentational strategy (see also Bryan & Horton, 1976). Laboratory research has substantiated Foley's notion of the relationship between self-presentation and aggression (Noel, Wann, & Branscombe, 1995).

SUMMARY

Research examining the impact of team cohesion has identified several factors that promote feelings of cohesiveness, including intragroup cooperation, intergroup conflict, team stability, team homogeneity, team size, and severe initiations. Consequences of team cohesion include increased performance and satisfaction.

Two lines of research have focused on the impact of an audience: social facilitation and the home field advantage. The theory of social facilitation argues that the presence of an audience leads to arousal which, in turn, leads to the dominant response. If an athlete is skilled at a task, he or she should perform better in front of others, while an athlete who is unskilled at the task will most likely exhibit an impairment of performance. Research has found that audiences are arousing for a variety of reasons. Regarding the home field advantage, a number of studies have found that home teams perform better than visiting teams (with the possible exception of championship games). Several factors may account for this robust phenomenon including the supportive home audience; the disruptive away audience; and nonaudience factors such as player assertiveness, travel, and fatigue.

The behaviors of athletes may be impacted by their self-presentational desire to present themselves to others in a positive manner. For example, athletes may alter their sporting activities and settings because of impression management concerns. Similarly, self-presentation can impact performance. Although individuals may perform better in public to enhance their image, persons performing in a group may exert a reduced level of effort because they no longer feel compelled to display a positive image. Other athletes may attempt the self-presentational tactics of (1) self-handicapping, (2) strategically selecting a successful team, or (3) displaying a high level of aggression toward opponents.

GLOSSARY

Coactive Audience   Audience consisting of other athletes.

Distraction Theory of Audience Arousal   The belief that audiences produce an attentional conflict within the performer by forcing this individual to attend to both the audience and the task.

Evaluation Apprehension Theory of Audience Arousal   The belief that audiences are arousing because individuals are concerned with the ability of the audience to evaluate their performance.

Inactive-Spectating Audience   Audience consisting of passive spectators who do not interact with the athletes.

Interactive-Coactive Audience   Audience consisting of players from an athlete's own team and the opposing team who actively interact while performing.

Interactive-Regulatory Audience   Audience consisting of referees, judges, and officials who interact with players while the competition is in progress.

Mere Presence Theory of Audience Arousal   The belief that the mere presence of another member of one's species is sufficient for triggering an arousal response.

Noninteractive-Coactive Audience   Audience consisting of individuals performing simultaneously in the same setting who do not interact with one another.

Noninteractive-Regulatory Audience   Audience consisting of referees, judges, and officials who do not interact with players while the competition is in progress.

Primary Dimensions of Cohesion   Dimensions applicable to most or all groups.

Psychological Presence Theory of Audience Arousal   The belief that a performer's arousal increases as an audience becomes more psychologically present.

Reactive-Spectating Audience   Audience consisting of spectators who react either positively or negatively to the actions of athletes.

Regulatory Audience   Audience consisting of individuals such as referees, judges, and officials who regulate the procedures and outcomes of a competition.

Secondary Dimensions of Cohesion   Dimensions that are applicable to a subset of groups.

Self-Handicapping   Protecting one's self-image by systematically creating an excuse for failure.

Self-Presentation   Desires and efforts to present oneself in a positive way to others.

Self-Presentational Analysis of Social Facilitation   A theory reflecting the belief that performers want to present themselves in a positive manner. If they are skilled at a task, an audience will facilitate their performances as they attempt to project an image of competence. If they are unskilled at a task, they will become embarrassed by the prospect of performing poorly in front of an audience and will suffer an impairment of performance.

Social Cohesion   The degree of interpersonal attraction among the group's members.

Social Facilitation Theory   A theory reflecting the belief that audiences are arousing and arousal leads to the dominant response.

Social Loafing   The tendency for individuals to exert a lower level of effort when participating in a team setting.

Spectating Audience   Audience consisting of sport spectators.

Task Cohesion   The extent that group members work together and remain united in their attempt to complete a specific task.

Team Cohesion   A dynamic process reflected in the tendency for a group to stick together and remain united in the pursuit of goals and objectives.

Team Homogeneity   The degree of similarity among a team's players.

APPLICATION AND REVIEW QUESTIONS

1. What is the difference between task cohesion and social cohesion?
2. Using your own experiences in sport, recall a team that you felt was highly cohesive. What were the factors causing the high level of cohesion? Do they match the factors discussed in the text?
3. What is the relationship between team cohesion and performance and between team cohesion and satisfaction?
4. List and describe the different types of audiences found at sporting events.
5. Describe Zajonc's social facilitation theory. How does his theory compare to the work of Triplett?
6. Why are audiences arousing? How and why are you aroused by audiences?
7. Why does the home team perform better than the visiting team?
8. Describe social loafing and construct an example from the world of sport.
9. Describe self-handicapping and construct an example from the world of sport.
10. Can you recall how a fellow athlete altered his or her behavior because of self-presentational concerns?

SUGGESTED READINGS

COURNEYA, K. S., & CARRON, A. V. (1992). The home advantage in sport competitions: A literature review. *Journal of Sport & Exercise Psychology, 14,* 13–27. This short article provides an analysis of the home field advantage.

EDWARDS, J., & ARCHAMBAULT, D. (1989). The home-field advantage. In J. H. Goldstein (Ed.), *Sports, games, and play: Social and psychological viewpoints* (2nd ed., pp. 333–370). Hillsdale, NJ: Erlbaum. This chapter provides the reader with a general overview of support for the home field advantage.

LEARY, M. R. (1992). Self-presentational processes in exercise and sport. *Journal of Sport & Exercise Psychology, 14,* 339–351. This article describes Leary's thoughts on self-presentational processes in sport.

WIDMEYER, W. N., CARRON, A. V., & BRAWLEY, L. R. (1993). Group cohesion in sport and exercise. In R. N. Singer, M. Murphey, & L. K. Tennant (Eds.), *Handbook of research on sport psychology* (pp. 672–692). New York: Macmillan. This chapter, written by the leading researchers in the area of sport cohesion, discusses a variety of important topics including the measurement of cohesion, the cohesion-performance relationship, and issues for future research.

Chapter 15

THE PSYCHOLOGY OF SPORT FANS AND SPORT SPECTATORS

Think about your involvement with sport. Most likely, some of your involvement reflects your athletic participation in sport. However, it is also likely that a large portion of your participation reflects your involvement as a sport fan. If you find that a large percentage of your sport involvement concerns your role as a fan, you are not alone. In fact, a survey conducted in the mid-1980s found that 71% of the subjects considered themselves to be sport fans (Thomas, 1986). In the final two chapters of this text, we will examine this group of individuals. In the first chapter, we will examine the psychology of sport fans and spectators. The second chapter focuses on the emotional and aggressive reactions of sport spectators.

Before we begin our examination, two important points must be made. First, it is important to distinguish between a sport fan and a sport spectator (Wann, 1995). Although these terms are often used interchangeably, they actually have slightly different meanings. A ***sport fan*** is an individual who is interested in and follows a sport, athlete, or team. A ***sport spectator*** (also called a sport consumer) is an individual who, at that moment, is watching or listening to a sporting event. Sport spectators can be further divided into ***direct sport consumers*** and ***indirect sport consumers*** (Kenyon, 1969; McPherson, 1975). Direct sport consumers are individuals attending a sporting event in person, while indirect sport consumers are individuals who spectate through television and radio broadcasts. In this text, I will use the term sport fan as a general description of someone who is interested in sport while reserving the term sport spectator to describe an individual who is viewing or listening to a sporting event.

A second point is that, because so few studies have examined sport fans, our understanding of these individuals is incomplete. Three lines of evidence indicate the lack of research on sport fans. First, in a study of articles published in sport psychology and sport sociology journals between 1987 and 1991, a colleague and I found that only 4% of the articles examined fans (Wann & Hamlet, 1995). Second, the paucity of research on sport fans can be seen in Ostrow's (1990) collection of sport-specific questionnaires. Although Ostrow's book lists more than 100 different inventories, only one scale was designed for use with sport fans (there have been a few additional fan scales developed since Ostrow's book was published). Third, although the *Handbook of Research in Sport Psychology* (Singer, Murphey, & Tennant, 1993) contains 44 chapters and is just shy of 1,000 pages, only one 20-page chapter is devoted to sport fans.

SPORT FANS AND SPECTATORS: WHO ARE THEY?

One method of understanding sport fans is through the construction of a psychological profile of these individuals. In this section, we will attempt to develop such a profile. This analysis will be framed around fans' (1) demographic characteristics, (2) socialization and motivation, (3) team identification, and (4) reasons for attending sporting events.

An Analysis of Fan and Spectator Demographics

One of the first studies to document the characteristics of sport fans was conducted by Schurr, Ruble, and Ellen (1985). These authors compared the demographic characteristics of more than 900 college students attending a basketball game with the characteristics of a sample comprised of students not attending the game. Thus, this research compared the characteristics of direct sport consumers and nonspectators. Unfortunately, there is no way of knowing how many persons in the nonattendance group were sport fans who simply did not attend that particular game. Further, because this research was limited to college students, the results should only be generalized to that population.

Subjects in the Schurr et al. (1985) research were asked to answer a variety of demographic items. The items assessed characteristics such as academic major, distance traveled to the arena, and distance from one's hometown. The results revealed six interesting demographic patterns. First, of the 44 physical education majors included in the overall sample, 75% attended the game, indicating that the spectators tended to have a general interest in sport. Second, those in attendance were disproportionately likely to be male. These two findings have also been found in a number of other studies (Doyle, Lewis, & Malmisur, 1980; Freischlag & Hardin, 1975; Lee & Zeiss, 1980; Murrell & Dietz, 1992; Prisuta, 1979; Yergin, 1986). Third, those in attendance often listed an active major such as business and radio/television. Fourth, those attending the game were disproportionately likely to be black. Fifth, students living in dormitories were especially likely to attend (see also, Doyle et al., 1980;

McPherson, 1975). Finally, students whose hometowns were furthest from the university were most likely to attend the game. Apparently, because these persons were separated from past associations, they were seeking to form new group memberships through sport spectating.

In 1988, Schurr, Wittig, Ruble, and Ellen conducted a second study examining the demographic characteristics of college students attending or not attending a basketball game. Based on their attendance at two different games, subjects were classified as persistent attenders (attended both games), occasional attenders (attended one game), or nonattenders (did not attend either game). Similar to the first study (Schurr et al., 1985), subjects were asked to complete a demographics questionnaire. Also consistent with the first study, it is impossible to determine the degree to which persons in the nonattendance group were sport fans who did not attend that particular game. In addition, because the sample was limited to college students, the results should not be generalized beyond this population.

The results of the second study replicated the first project. For example, subjects classified as attenders (i.e., those attending one or both games) were more likely to list an active major than subjects classified as nonattenders. Also consistent with the first study, attenders were disproportionately likely to be black, male, and from a hometown that was distant from the university. Further, attenders were especially likely to reside in residential halls and attend in groups, indicating that convenience and a desire for social support may have been important. In the comparison of persistent and occasional attenders, two demographic differences were found. Relative to occasional attenders, persistent attenders were disproportionately likely to be male and live in a residence hall.

A different demographic variable was studied by Mashiach (1980). This author examined the socioeconomic status (SES) of spectators attending the 1976 Summer Olympic Games. The results indicated that spectators were especially high in SES. Due to the prohibitive costs of traveling to and attending the Olympic Games, the generalizability of Mashiach's findings is a concern. However, because other studies using different populations have replicated Mashiach's results (Prisuta, 1979; Waldrop, 1989; Yergin, 1986), we can be relatively certain of the positive relationship between SES and sport spectating.

Although it would be nice to offer a complete demographic profile of sport spectators, this is not possible because of the scarcity of studies conducted in this area. Furthermore, because the studies described above targeted the demographics associated with direct and indirect sport consumption rather than with sport "fandom," generalizations are limited. Based on the studies completed to date, we may only conclude that *spectators* (1) often prefer active pastimes, (2) tend to be involved with sport as an athlete as well as a spectator, (3) are disproportionately likely to be black and male, and (4) appear to be higher in SES than nonspectators. It is also important not to infer causation from the results cited above. Rather, these studies simply indicate a relationship between certain demographic variables and sport spectating. They do not provide information about the directionality of the relationships. For example, it would be inappropriate to conclude that a preference for active pastimes causes one to enjoy sport spectating. It is equally likely that enjoyment of sport spectating causes a preference for active pastimes and even more likely that a third variable causes both sport spectating and pastime preferences.

The Socialization and Motivations of Sport Fans

In this section, we will attempt to ascertain how and why people become a sport fan. To understand the reasons underlying an individual's involvement as a fan, one must consider a process incorporating the individual's socialization into the sport follower role and his or her particular motives for becoming a fan. This process is represented graphically in Figure 15.1.

Socialization into the Role of Sport Fan.   Perhaps the most important work on sport fan socialization was conducted by McPherson (1976). In a study of high school students, McPherson examined the impact of four socialization agents (family, peers, school, and community) on sport consumption. Sport consumption was viewed as a combination of three factors: behavioral (i.e., attending games and buying tickets), affective (i.e., loyalty to a team and mood changes while consuming the sport), and cognitive (i.e., knowledge of the individuals, teams, and rules of the sport). McPherson found that both male and female fans were influenced by their families and peers (see also Smith, Patterson, Williams, & Hogg, 1981). For males, the peer group was the single greatest influence, while the family was the primary influence for female subjects. However, schools were influential only in the socialization of males, while the community was influential only in the socialization of females.

It is important to note that McPherson's (1976) data were collected two decades ago. Because researchers have found that gender differences in sport fan socialization can change with the passage of time (Anderson & Stone, 1981), it would be informative to replicate McPherson's research with a current sample. As gender-role stereotypes for activities such as sport fandom are reduced, gender differences in the socialization process may diminish.

FIGURE 15.1   The process leading to involvement with sport as a fan or spectator.

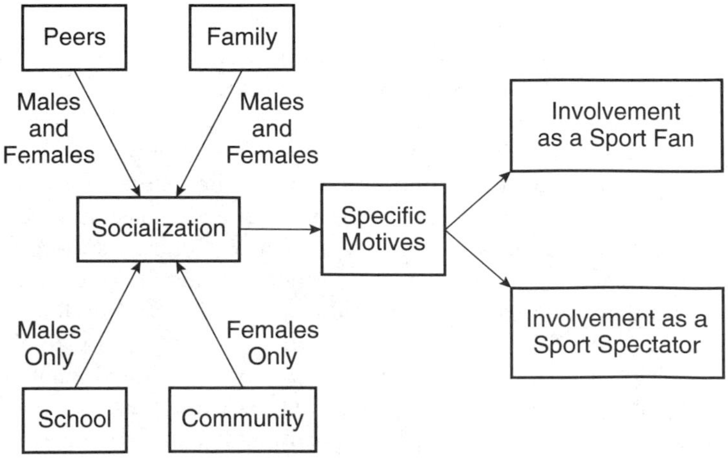

The Motives of Sport Fans.   Similar to participation in sport as an athlete, an individual's contact with socialization agents does not guarantee that he or she will become a sport fan. Rather, the socialized person will only become a fan if he or she is motivated to do so. In this section, we will examine the motives of sport fans. We will begin by reviewing the most prominent motives. We will then examine the measurement of the various forms of motivation.

SPECIFIC MOTIVES OF SPORT FANS.   Theorists have argued that fans are typically motivated by one or more of the following eight factors: group affiliation, family needs, escape, entertainment, eustress, aesthetics, self-esteem, and economics. Although this is not an exhaustive list, each of these factors has been a part of the research of one or more authors, lending credibility to each motive.

Group Affiliation.   Several authors have suggested that the desire to establish group affiliations can be a primary motivational influence for sport fans (Beisser, 1967; Branscombe & Wann, 1991; Gantz & Wenner, 1995; Guttmann, 1986; Karp & Yoels, 1990; Melnick, 1993; Sloan, 1989; Smith, 1988; Stein, 1977). This motive involves a fan's need for belongingness. By becoming a fan of a sport team, an individual is able to share the experience with other fans of the same team. In this way, he or she can become attached to and identify with something larger than the self, such as other fans, a college, a community, or even a nation. This motive is substantiated by the finding that spectators are particularly likely to attend a sporting event as a member of a group (Aveni, 1977; Mann, 1969), and other members of the group can influence the fan's enjoyment of the contest (Wakefield, 1995).

Many individuals enjoy sport spectating because they enjoy rooting with their friends. (Photographer: William R. Sallaz. Source: Duomo Photography.)

Family. A similar motive involves a fan's desire to spend time with his or her family (Gantz, 1981; Gantz & Wenner, 1995; Guttmann, 1986; Wenner & Gantz, 1989). Some fans view their sport consumption as a family activity. For example, consider a typical summer evening for my family. Although my older brother and I were too old to play recreational baseball, my younger brother was still active in his summer league. Each game night, my family would gather up the lawn chairs and a few snacks and go to my younger brother's game. The games gave my family the opportunity to spend time together. In fact, when the season was over, we missed the family interaction as much as the excitement of the games.

Escape. The use of sport fandom as an escape from everyday life is a third common motive (Lever & Wheeler, 1984; McPherson, 1975; Meier, 1979; Sloan, 1989; Smith, 1988; Stein, 1977). Fans who are disgruntled by their home-life, work, college experience, and so on may be able to forget about their troubles temporarily through sport fandom. As Smith (1988) notes, by participating in sport as a fan, individuals may be able to escape their "humdrum daily routines" (p. 58). In a similar fashion, Meier writes that the poor New York Mets teams of the early 1960's "provided . . . a temporary suspension of the problems and irritations of the everyday world" (p. 293).

The escape motive may be particularly important during difficult times. For example, many individuals use sport spectating as a diversion during war (McGuire, 1994). In fact, President Franklin D. Roosevelt's decision to allow professional baseball to continue during World War II was an attempt to provide an escape for North Americans. In explaining his decision, Roosevelt stated that Americans "ought to have a chance for recreation and for taking their minds off their work" (see McGuire, 1994, p. 66).

Entertainment. Some fans view sport spectating as a pastime similar to watching movies or television, listening to music, and so on. These fans are influenced by the entertainment motive (Gantz, 1981; Gantz & Wenner, 1995; Lahr, 1976; Sloan, 1989; Zillmann, Bryant, & Sapolsky, 1989). This motive may be especially prominent among fans of pseudosports. **Pseudosports** are staged sports that contain a scripted outcome, such as professional wrestling and roller derby. Even though fans of these sports readily admit that the outcomes are fixed (Stone, 1971), they are still attracted to these events because of their entertainment value.

Eustress. Other fans are motivated by eustress (Branscombe & Wann, 1994a; Bryant, Rockwell, & Owens, 1994; Elias & Dunning, 1970; Gantz & Wenner, 1995; Prisuta, 1979; Sloan, 1989; Wenner & Gantz, 1989). It should be recalled that eustress is a positive form of stress that stimulates and energizes an individual. Although fans can experience a high level of stress while watching an athletic contest, because they can control their level of involvement with the game, their stress remains positive. For example, a portion of my wife's enjoyment of our university's basketball games is the excitement the games provide. However, if the excitement becomes too great (i.e., the stress moves from eustress to anxiety), she simply removes herself from the arena until her excitement and arousal return to a more comfortable level.

Aesthetics. A sixth motive involves the aesthetic value of athletic events. Some fans are attracted to sport because of the beauty and grace found in athletic performances (Duncan, 1983; Guttmann, 1986; Sloan, 1989; Smith, 1988). For example, sports such as figure skating, diving, and gymnastics are attractive to many fans because of the artistic expression of the athletes. However, the aesthetic motive is not limited to these sports. Rather, fans of baseball, basketball, football, and hockey may also view the athletes' performances as an art form. For example, a fan may enjoy the beauty and grace of a wide receiver diving to make a catch.

Self-Esteem. Another group of fans are motivated by a desire to enhance their self-esteem (Branscombe & Wann, 1991, 1994a; Gantz, 1981; Sloan, 1989). Sport fanship helps many individuals create and maintain a positive self-concept. When a fan's team is successful, he or she gains a feeling of achievement and accomplishment. In fact, some sport fans increase their association with successful teams for this reason (Cialdini et al., 1976). It is important to note that team success is not a requirement for fans to gain self-esteem through their association with a team. Rather, because it leads to a sense of belonging, identifying with the team can be related to higher levels of self-esteem regardless of the team's record (Branscombe & Wann, 1991).

Economics. A final motive is an economic one. Some sport fans are motivated by the potential financial gains of sport wagering (Chorbajian, 1978; Frey, 1992; Gantz & Wenner, 1995; Guttmann, 1986; McPherson, 1975). These individuals become and stay involved with sport spectating because of the opportunities to gamble on the events. College students appear to be particularly likely to be motivated by gambling opportunities (Layden, 1995).

MEASURING THE MOTIVES OF SPORT FANS. Until recently, a questionnaire designed to measure the relative importance of the aforementioned motives was unavailable to researchers. In an attempt to fill this void, I recently developed the Sport Fan Motivation Scale (SFMS, Wann, 1995). The SFMS is a 23-item Likert-scale instrument containing eight independent subscales. The subscales reflect the eight motives described above. Preliminary work using the SFMS has indicated that the scale is both valid and reliable. In addition, research indicates that there are gender differences in the importance of several motives. Males report being highly motivated by eustress, self-esteem, escape, entertainment, and aesthetics, while females are more influenced by family needs (Wann, 1995). Gender differences have not been found for the economic and group affiliation motives. As for the relative importance of each motive, the highest scores have been found on the entertainment and eustress subscales. The economic motive has been found to be the least important factor (Wann, 1995).

Team Identification

Team identification is another important component in the psychology of sport fans (Branscombe & Wann, 1992a; Hirt, Zillmann, Erickson, & Kennedy, 1992; Real & Mechikoff, 1992; Smith et al., 1981; Tajfel, 1981; Wakefield, 1995; Zillmann et al., 1989). **Team identification** concerns the extent that a fan feels psychologically connected to a team (team identification is also being used to describe identification with athletes participating in individual sports). Fans who are highly identified with a team view the team as an extension of themselves. For these fans the team's successes, the feelings of comradery felt with other fans, and the self-perception that "I am a fan of this team" are all central to their self-concept. Further, they feel that other supporters of their team are better people than supporters of rival teams (Wann & Branscombe, 1995a, 1995b; Wann & Dolan, 1994a). Conversely, low identified fans have only a minimal amount of their social identity invested in the team. Although they may follow the team to a limited degree, their involvement remains peripheral.

Highly identified fans exhibit a variety of bizarre behaviors reflecting their fanaticism. For example:

1. A San Jose Shark fan removed her brassiere and threw it on the ice after a Shark player recorded a hat trick (Murphy, 1994).
2. A fan at Wrigley Field in Chicago heeded the final request of his recently deceased father by leaning over the outfield wall and spreading his father's ashes onto the field (Beaton, 1995).
3. A University of Kentucky basketball fan impersonated a deputy so he could provide an escort for the team on their road trips (Harris, 1993). It is not surprising that the fan's license plate was NO1 CAT (the school's mascot is a wildcat).
4. A St. Louis Cardinals fan used a small transistor radio and an ear plug hidden behind his hair to listen to a Cardinal's game during his own wedding. The fan stated that "I had the best man clued in on what I was doing just in case I missed a strategic answer or something" (*USA Today Baseball Weekly,* 1993).
5. A Boston Red Sox fan paid $99,000 for the original contract that sent Babe Ruth from the Red Sox to the New York Yankees (Antonen, 1994). The fan wanted to destroy the curse that supposedly has haunted the Red Sox since the sale of Ruth by burning the contract at home plate on opening day of the following season.
6. In 1993, the Houston Rockets offered a pair of tickets to a game against the Phoenix Suns to any male fan willing to shave his head in a Charles Barkley look-a-like contest. Female fans willing to shave their heads were offered a pair of tickets to all remaining games. Two hundred people, including a dozen women, were willing to go bald for the tickets (*The National Sports Review,* 1993).
7. A Dallas Cowboys fan was arrested for stealing a television so he could watch the Cowboy's playoff game against the San Francisco 49ers. The thief was arrested when he returned to the scene of the crime to steal the remote control (*The National Sports Review,* 1993).

Although the vignettes presented above attest to the fanaticism of highly identified fans, it is incorrect to assume that these fans will blindly support their team in all situations. While most highly identified fans remain loyal even when the team is playing poorly (Wann & Branscombe, 1990a), these same fans can become upset by activities occurring beyond the playing field (Wakefield, 1995). For example, consider the impact of the 1994–1995 baseball strike. Many fans were upset by the strike and distanced themselves from Major League baseball (a similar effect resulted from the 1981 strike; see Chaiy & Extejt, 1982). For example, attendance at Major League games was down 21% by mid-June (Gildea, 1995), and lesser-known sports such as Arena Football were outdrawing baseball in some cities (Wolff & Stone, 1995a). Owners tried unsuccessfully to lure fans back with special discounts and events (for a humorous look at the owners' efforts, see Figure 15.2). For example, even though the Houston Astros gave away each seat for a Friday night game, only 30,000 spectators attended the game: more than 20,000 fans less than the stadium's capacity (Mihoces,

TANK M^cNAMARA®   **by Jeff Millar & Bill Hinds**

FIGURE 15.2 This comic strip illustrates the negative fan reactions to the 1994–1995 baseball strike and the owners' attempts to bring the fans back. (Source: Universal Press Syndicate.)

1995). Attendance at the baseball Hall of Fame was also down substantially (Kekis, 1995). This finding is especially noteworthy because the Hall of Fame is typically frequented by highly identified fans, adding support to the notion that, although highly identified fans will allow their *team* to "go down the tubes," they might not be willing to hang around to watch the deterioration of their *sport*.

In the following paragraphs, we are going to take a closer look at team identification. We will begin our examination by reviewing a recently developed measure of team identification. We will then investigate the relationship between identification and sport knowledge. We will conclude with a look at the origin of team identification.

Measuring Team Identification.   Recently, Branscombe and I developed a questionnaire designed to assess sport team identification (Wann & Branscombe, 1993). This scale, titled the Sport Spectator Identification Scale (SSIS), contains seven Likert-scale items. Research indicates that the scale is reliable and valid (research by Straub, 1995, indicates that the scale is reliable and valid with German sport fans as well). For example, college basketball fans were asked to complete the SSIS on two different occasions separated by approximately 1 year. The test-retest correlation comparing the Time 1 and Time 2 scores was highly significant, indicating a high level of consistency between the administration dates. This finding appears to suggest that team identification is a fairly stable trait. This possibility is explored further in this chapter's "A Closer Look."

To test the measure's validity, another sample of basketball fans was asked to complete the SSIS and a set of items assessing their involvement with the team, investment in the team, and the degree to which they believed fans of the team were special. Subjects were divided into three groups based on their SSIS scores: high identification, moderate identification, or low identification. We then compared the three groups' scores on the investment, involvement, and "fans are special" items. As seen in Table 15.1, highly identified fans were the most involved and invested group and were most likely to believe that fans of the team were special. The low identification fans scored lowest on these items.

A CLOSER LOOK:
THE STABILITY OF SPORT TEAM IDENTIFICATION

An interesting aspect of team identification concerns the stability of this trait. That is, to what degree does a fan's identification fluctuate from week to week, over the course of a season, or from year to year? A handful of studies have investigated the stability of fan identification. Taken as a whole, this research indicates that fan identification is remarkably stable. For example, the 1-year test-retest data collected by Wann and Branscombe (1993) indicated a high level of consistency in SSIS scores. That is, fans' identification scores remained quite consistent from one season to the next. A somewhat more elaborate investigation of identification stability was conducted by Wann, Dolan, McGeorge, and Allison (1994; see also Wann & Schrader, 1996). This research tested the impact of game outcome on identification stability. It seemed possible that identification might drop after a team had been defeated and rise after the team had been victorious. To test this possibility, we used the SSIS to assess the identification of spectators attending one of four college basketball games. Two of the games were losses and two were victories. The results indicated no differences in the identification scores after wins and losses, suggesting that fan identification is a relatively stable phenomenon.

While the Wann et al. (1994) study provided information on the stability of fan identification, the design of this study was rather simplistic. That is, fans were assessed on only a single occasion. A more comprehensive analysis of identification stability would be derived from an investigation assessing the identification of a group of fans across an entire season. Recently, I conducted such an investigation (Wann, 1996; see also Dietz-Uhler & Murrell, 1995). This research involved two separate studies, one involving a historically successful college basketball team and one involving a historically unsuccessful college football team. In each study, subjects were asked to complete the SSIS during the class period following games by the team in question. The results revealed that, although identification for both teams remained quite stable, identification scores for the basketball team were higher after wins than after losses. However, identification scores for the football team did not differ based on competition outcome. These differential reactions are best understood in terms of the fans' expectations and their motivations for following the team. In all likelihood, fans of the historically successful basketball team expected the team to play well. Indeed, many of these fans may have been motivated by the self-esteem boosts that resulted from following this team. As a result, their identification with the team was at least partially tied to the team's success. In contrast, fans of the historically unsuccessful football team probably did not expect to gain self-esteem from following this team. Rather, they were motivated by other factors, such as group affiliation or eustress. As a result, these fans were less likely to base their identification on the performances of the team and, as a result, their identification scores were not influenced by game outcome.

TABLE 15.1   A Comparison of the Involvement, Investment, and Perceptions of Highly, Moderately, and Lowly Identified Fans

Item	Identification Level		
	High	*Moderate*	*Low*
Involvement			
Number of years has been a fan of this team	7.42	3.76	1.17
Number of home games attended each year	11.82	7.80	2.20
Likelihood of attending an away game	3.92	3.04	1.50
Investment			
Amount willing to pay for a regular season ticket*	27.56	15.23	8.42
Amount willing to pay for a playoff ticket*	65.75	31.68	16.98
Amount willing to pay for a championship ticket*	125.57	64.64	26.23
Amount of time willing to wait in line for a ticket†	4.29	3.43	1.97
Fans of this Team Are Special			
Percentage of friends who are fans of this team	75.79	70.21	51.41
Believe that fans of this team are special‡	5.65	4.47	3.03
Believe that fans of this team are bonded‡	6.39	5.67	4.64

Higher numbers represent more of each item.
*dollar amounts.
†hours.
‡Likert-scale responses ranging from 1 (agree) to 7 (disagree).
(Adapted by permission from: Wann, D. L., & Branscombe, N. R. [1993]. Sports fans: Measuring degree of identification with their team. *International Journal of Sport Psychology*, 24: 1–17.)

The Origination, Continuation, and Cessation of Team Identification.   Pause for a moment to think about your favorite sport team. What were the reasons that caused you to identify with this team? What are the reasons causing you to continue identifying with this team? Now consider a team that you used to support but no longer care for. What were the reasons that caused you to stop identifying with this team? These were the questions that colleagues and I recently asked a sample of college sport fans (Wann, Tucker, & Schrader, 1996; see also Shaw, 1978). These questions were designed to assess the most common reasons underlying the origination, continuation, and cessation of sport team identification. Dozens of different reasons were given (for a complete list, see Wann et al., 1996). The five most commonly listed reasons are presented in Table 15.2. As seen in the table, there was a large amount of overlap in the reasons for beginning, continuing, and ceasing to identify with the teams. The success of the team, the players, and geographic reasons were particularly important. The finding that team success plays a major role in the origin of team identification is paralleled by the finding that athletes' abilities are prominent in fans' choices of their favorite players (Russell, 1979; Smith, 1976).

Team Identification and Knowledge.   Because highly identified fans are more invested in and involved with the team, and because they are more likely to be exposed to the team (Wann & Branscombe, 1993), it stands to reason that these fans

TABLE 15.2   The Most Common Reasons Underlying the Origination, Continuation, and Cessation of Team Identification

	Reasons For		
Rank	*Origination*	*Continuation*	*Cessation*
1	Family followed team	Team was successful	Team was unsuccessful
2	The players	The players	Too many other commitments
3	Geographical reasons	Geographical reasons	Loss of certain players
4	Friends followed team	Friends followed team	Geographical reasons
5	Team was successful	Family followed team	Friends stopped following team

are more knowledgeable about the team than less identified fans. This hypothesis was recently tested in a study of college basketball fans (Wann & Branscombe, 1995b). Students at the University of Kansas were asked to complete the SSIS with the university's men's basketball team as the target. Subjects then completed a 35-item test assessing their knowledge of the team's players, the team's history, and the sport of basketball (e.g., history of the game, rules of the game). The results supported the prediction that highly identified fans possess a greater sport knowledge base than fans classified as low in identification (Wann & Branscombe, 1995b).

In an earlier study examining the knowledge of highly identified fans, Tannenbaum and Noah (1959) examined the level of understanding of sport terminology, a terminology they labeled "sportugese" (p. 164). Using several hundred newspaper game reports, Tannenbaum and Noah identified verbs used to describe the final point spread in basketball games (e.g., squeaked, defeated, humiliated). Their investigation lead to the identification of 84 different verbs. The authors then presented high and low identification fans with the 84 verbs and asked the fans to estimate the point spread described by the verbs. Tannenbaum and Noah then correlated the fans' point spread estimates with the actual point spreads. The results indicated that highly identified fans possessed a much greater knowledge of the sportugese terminology than lowly identified individuals. Specifically, the correlation between the estimated scores and the actual scores was .86 for high identification fans but only .33 for low identification fans.

Factors Influencing Attendance

Now that we have established an understanding of the "who" and "why" of sport fandom, let us turn our attention to the act of sport spectating. Several studies have investigated the factors involved in a fan's decision to attend a particular sporting event (see Figure 15.3).

The Impact of Team Performance.   A number of studies have found that home team performance and attendance are positively related (Schofield, 1983). This pattern has been noted in a number of sports including professional football (Noll, 1974), professional hockey (Jones, 1969; Noll, 1974), and soccer (Hart, Hutton, & Sharot, 1975), although most studies have targeted professional baseball (e.g., Baade & Tiehen, 1990; Fullerton & Merz, 1982; Greenstein & Marcum, 1981; Porter & Scully,

FIGURE 15.3 There are a variety of factors influencing an individual's decision to attend a sporting event.

1982; Whitney, 1988). Research conducted by Hay and Rao (1982) indicates that head coaches are well aware of the positive relationship between performance and attendance. These authors asked several high school and college coaches to rate the importance of factors impacting attendance at their games. The coaches reported that producing a winning team was far more likely to put spectators in the stands than any other factor.

Research by Iso-Ahola (1980) reveals that the visiting team's recent performance and fans' attributions of the home and visiting teams' performances also influence attendance decisions (see also Fullerton & Merz, 1982; Hansen & Gauthier, 1989; Wann, 1996). Iso-Ahola had subjects read descriptions of an upcoming game and indicate the probability that they would attend the contest. The game descriptions contained four variables: the home team's past performance, reasons for the home team's performance (i.e., internal or external), the visiting team's past performance, and reasons for the visiting team's performance. For example, some subjects read that the home team had experienced a great deal of recent success but that the success appeared to be due to external factors such as luck and games against easy opponents. In addition, these subjects read that the visiting team also had experienced a great deal of recent success and that the success appeared to be due to internal factors such as highly skilled players. This scenario is an example of the home team success/external attribution—visiting team success/internal attribution description. Other subjects read one of the other 15 combinations. The results revealed an interaction between game outcome and attribution. Subjects reported that they were least likely to attend a game when the home team had been unsuccessful and the visiting team had been successful and these outcomes were attributed to internal causes. In this situation, fans believe that the home team is playing poorly because they lack skill, while the visiting team is playing well because they possess a high level of skill. As a result, fans infer that the home team will be soundly defeated and, therefore, they are less likely to attend this game. Subjects reported that they were most likely to attend a contest involving two successful teams whose successes were believed to be the result of internal causes. Apparently, these types of games have two advantages: There is a good chance for a home team victory and the game promises to be a close and exciting contest.

Nonperformance Factors.   Although performance plays a major role in attendance decisions, research has indicated that nonperformance factors are important as well. One such factor involves the population of the host community, with larger communities generating larger audiences (Baade & Tiehen, 1990; Hansen & Gauthier, 1989; Marcum & Greenstein, 1985). The presence of a "star" player (Baade & Tiehen, 1990; Chaiy & Extejt, 1982; Fullerton & Merz, 1982; Schurr et al., 1988), a "homecoming" game (Wann, 1996), and promotions/special events (Hansen & Gauthier, 1989; Marcum & Greenstein, 1985) can also increase attendance. Other factors involve the accessibility of the event (Hansen & Gauthier, 1989; Marcum & Greenstein, 1985). These factors include weather (Siegfried & Hinshaw, 1977), distance to the arena (Schurr et al., 1988), the availability of parking (Hay & Rao, 1982), and the day of the game (higher levels of attendance have been found for weekend games; see Fullerton & Merz, 1982; Marcum & Greenstein, 1985). In addition, some individuals (such as league officials and team owners) believe that the television accessibility of a game can negatively impact attendance (see Jones, 1969). However, research has found that televising a home game does not significantly reduce attendance at that contest (Siegfried & Hinshaw, 1977).

SPORT FANDOM: A WORTHWHILE PASTIME OR A WASTE OF TIME?

For almost a century, social scientists have debated the merits of sport fandom. For example, consider the following descriptions of sport fans and spectators offered at the beginning of the 20th century:

> A singular example of mental perversion, an absurd and immoral custom tenaciously held fast in mod-mind, has its genesis in the partisan zeal of athletic spectator-crowds. I refer to the practice of organized cheering, known in college argot as "rooting." From every aspect it is bad (Howard, 1912, p. 46).

> The spectators, under the excitement of a great game, become hoodlums, exhibiting violent partisanship and gross profanity, bestowing idiotic adulations upon the victors and heaping abuse upon the referee, restrained oftentimes only by the players themselves from inflicting upon him actual bodily harm (Patrick, 1903, p. 104).

Although these negative viewpoints of fans and spectators are almost a century old, they reflect the beliefs of a number of current social scientists. In fact, Zillmann and his colleagues (1989) write that there is "nearly a universal condemnation of sport spectatorship" on the part of social scientists (p. 246). Hughes (1987) concurs with this viewpoint, stating that everyone seems to like sport except the social scientists conducting research on the topic.

A number of arguments have been levied against the sport fan role. One of the most common arguments concerns the supposed laziness of sport fans and spectators. Perhaps Guttmann (1980) best articulated this stance when he wrote, "Although it is unusual to denounce museum-goers for not painting still-lifes and bad form to fault concert audiences for not playing the violin, it is quite common . . . to criticize spectators for athletic inactivity" (p. 275).

Other authors have argued against spectating because they believe this activity serves as an opiate for the masses (Meier, 1989; see Guttmann, 1980). This line of reasoning implies that not only are fans inactive and lazy, they are actually anesthetized by sport. That is, fans are perceived to be wasting their time and should instead become active in more worthwhile pursuits. In support of this position, Meier (1989) wrote that sport spectating "will deplete the available resources and reservoirs of money, time, and critical thought which could be utilized . . . to attempt to effect productive political and positive, meaningful social transformation" (pp. 113–114).

Other arguments against sport fandom have been centered around the aesthetics, aggression, and values of sport. For instance, some writers do not believe that sport is a form of art (Maheu, 1962; Meier, 1989; see also Morgan & Meier, 1988). Others have suggested that sport spectators are violent individuals seeking a place to release their aggression (e.g., Howard, 1912; Patrick, 1903; see also Proctor & Eckerd, 1976). Still others have argued that sport fandom leads to the adoption of distorted values such as racism, sexism, cheating, and greed (Brohm, 1978; Cullen, 1974; Hoch, 1972). Finally, some individuals feel that sport spectating (particularly televised sport viewing) may be disruptive to intimate relationships (i.e., the "football widow"; see Gantz, Wenner, Carrico, & Knorr, 1995a, 1995b).

Now consider the comments of Brill, written in 1929:

> . . . the average man, for perfectly simple psychological reasons, just will not muster much enthusiasm for the idea of getting out and playing instead of watching the game. On the other hand, through the operation of the psychological laws of identification and catharsis, the thorough-going fan is distinctly benefited mentally, physically, and morally by spectator-participation in his favorite sport (Brill, 1929, p. 430).

Brill's position, also over a half century old, reflects the thoughts of other social scientists who have taken the position that sport fandom is a worthwhile pastime. These writers argue that this activity can have positive benefits for the individual and society (e.g., Guttmann, 1980; Smith et al., 1981; Zillmann et al., 1989). For example, writers have listed a reduction in feelings of alienation, escape from the monotony of everyday life, and the aesthetic experience as benefits of sport fandom (Guttmann, 1986; Kovich, 1971; Maheu, 1962; Melnick, 1993; Smith, 1988; Spinrad, 1981). Other authors have suggested that sport teaches the values of fair play and justice (Zillmann et al., 1989). At the societal level, Smith (1988) wrote that "Society benefits from the sports follower role too, because an interest in sport promotes personal interaction which leads to social cohesion and a strengthening of major social values" (p. 59).

The sport fandom debate heated up during the late 1980s when Smith and

Meier published a series of articles debating the issue. Smith's (1988) original article, titled "The Noble Sports Fan," argued that there are a number of personal and societal benefits to sport fandom. A few months later, Meier (1989) countered with an article titled "The Ignoble Sports Fan." Meier's contention was that sport fanship and spectatorship are not beneficial and should be considered as a hindrance to personal and societal growth. Smith (1989) followed Meier's (1989) article with a paper titled "The Noble Sports Fan Redux" in which he challenged Meier's contentions and reaffirmed his position that sport fandom and spectating can be beneficial to individuals and society.

Smith and Meier were unable to reach an agreement, holding steadfastly to their original positions. Their lack of a resolution should not be surprising because these authors based much of their arguments on theory rather than research. That is, while each author was able to present an articulate and logical line of reasoning to underscore his position, the reasoning often lacked the backing of empirical data. To examine the debate over the virtue of sport fandom, one should collect and analyze data from fans themselves. If the data indicate that there are benefits to the sport follower role, then the debate can be resolved in a much more effective manner. A few empirical studies have attempted to gather such data. It should be noted that it is much easier to assess the individual benefits of sport fanship than to assess societal benefits. As a result, the studies reviewed below focus primarily on personal benefits.

A handful of empirical studies have addressed the sport fan debate. For example, at the beginning of this chapter I noted that research has found a positive correlation between sport spectating and active sport involvement as an athlete (see Guttmann, 1986). This relationship tends to invalidate the argument that sport fans and spectators are passive, lazy creatures. Research has also challenged the assumption that sport teaches negative values. For example, sport fans tend to be against cheating and dirty play (Smith, 1988; Smith et al., 1981). The belief that sport fans are hostile individuals can also be countered with research showing that these individuals are not unusually high in trait aggression (Russell & Goldstein, 1995; Wann, 1994a). Finally, the notion that sport spectating tends to disrupt intimate relationships was refuted by Gantz and his colleagues (1995a, 1995b). These researchers found that few couples reported negative effects of televised sport spectating.

Another study examining a potential benefit of sport fandom was conducted by Schurr, Wittig, Ruble, and Henriksen (1993). These authors predicted that students attending their university's basketball games would benefit from the social integration of attendance. To test this hypothesis, Schurr and his colleagues compared the grade point averages (GPA) and graduation rates of college students attending and not attending university basketball games. Although the two groups did not differ in their expected college performances (based on high school GPA and college entrance scores), the attending group had a higher average GPA (2.55) and a higher graduation rate (.64) than the nonattending group (GPA = 2.36, graduation rate = .48).

Branscombe and I conducted another set of studies examining the potential benefits of sport fandom (Branscombe & Wann, 1991). In this research, we investigated the relationship between university basketball team identification and psychological health. In the first two studies, we asked college students to complete a questionnaire packet containing the SSIS and various measures of psychological health. By correlating the identification scores with the measures of psychological health, we were able to detect several positive benefits to sport fandom. Specifically, we found that higher levels of identification were related to (1) higher levels of personal self-esteem, (2) a greater tendency to experience positive emotions, (3) a reduced tendency to experience negative emotions, and (4) lower levels of depression and alienation. In a subsequent study, I found that higher levels of team identification were also related to higher levels of collective (i.e., group-level) self-esteem (Wann, 1994a; see also Murrell & Dietz, 1992).

Thus, research to date indicates that there are personal benefits to the sport follower role. As a result, it appears that Smith (1988) was correct when he coined the term "the noble sports fan" (p. 54). However, empirical research on the benefits of sport fandom and sport spectating is still in its infancy. As a result, a number of questions remain to be answered including the causal direction of the relationships and the possibility of societal benefits.

THE BIASES OF SPORT FANS AND SPECTATORS

It should be apparent that sport fans and spectators care a great deal about the performances of their team. Because of their desire to view their team in a positive manner, many fans become biased in their analyses of their team's efforts. In this section, we will examine two areas of fan bias: (1) attributions and (2) predictions/recollections of past and future performance.

Biased Attributions

In Chapter 9, we examined two common attributional biases: the self-serving bias and the fundamental attribution error. The self-serving bias is a self-directed attributional pattern in which individuals externalize failures while internalizing successes. The fundamental attribution error is an other-directed attributional pattern in which persons overemphasize the importance of internal causes and underemphasize the importance of external causes. In the following sections, we will examine how each of these biases is reflected in the attributional patterns exhibited by sport spectators.

The Self-Serving Bias and Spectator Attributions. In the early 1990s, a sport fan wrote a letter to the editor of my university's newspaper titled "Racer fans let team down" (Webber, 1993). In this letter, the fan described her "shame" in the way the university's fans had let the team down during a crucial conference match-up, a game the team lost to the eventual league champion. The writer, disappointed by the lack of noise and enthusiasm from the home crowd, stated that "Guys (men's basketball team), you didn't disappoint us as much as we disappointed you" (p. 4). This letter is an excellent example of the self-serving attributional bias of sport fans. In this case, the fan did not want to place the blame for the loss on the players (an internal attribution). Rather, she wanted to blame the fans (an external attribution). In this way, she could still believe that her team was as talented as their opponent and might have won if the fans had been more supportive.

One of the first empirical examinations of the self-serving nature of spectator attributions was conducted by Hastorf and Cantril (1954). These authors asked Dartmouth and Princeton students to describe a football game between these schools. During the game, Princeton's star player and All-American candidate was severely injured, resulting in the accusation that the Dartmouth team had intentionally injured the player. The spectators' descriptions of the game revealed a biased pattern of attributions. For example, while 25% of the Dartmouth supporters classified the game as "rough but fair," only 2% of the Princeton fans viewed the game in this manner. Rather, the Princeton fans classified the game as "rough and dirty." Further, when asked about the belief that Dartmouth had intentionally injured Princeton's star player, only 10% of the Dartmouth supporters agreed with the accusation. Conversely, 55% of the Princeton fans reported that the injury was intentional. Hastorf and Cantril concluded that supporters of the two teams seemed to have been observing two different games, with each blaming the other for the rough play.

A second study highlighting the self-serving biases of sport spectators was conducted by Mann (1974). Mann's research is important because it was an early attempt to examine the internal and external attributions of sport spectators. Mann interviewed spectators following a championship contest in the Australian Football League. Consistent with the findings of Hastorf and Cantril (1954), supporters of the two teams seemed to be witnessing a different contest. Relative to supporters of the winning team, fans supporting the losing team were more likely to report that the outcome was due to external factors. For example, 27% of supporters of the losing team reported that the outcome was caused by poor officiating and luck while none of the winning fans reported this attribution.

The Hastorf and Cantril (1954) and Mann (1974) articles indicate that sport fans can exhibit self-serving attributional patterns, forming internal attributions when their team is victorious and external attributions when they are defeated. This pattern has been found in other studies as well. For instance, sport writers tend to offer internal attributions when describing their team's successes while offering external explanations of their team's failures (Dietz-Uhler, 1995; Lau, 1984; Lau & Russell, 1980). Also, spectators often report defensive attributions when attempting to explain the unsportsmanlike behaviors of a favorite player (Tanner, Sev'er, & Ungar, 1989; Ungar & Sev'er, 1989). However, some authors have been unable to replicate this pattern of effects (e.g., Burger, 1985). For example, Grove et al. (1991) did not find a statistically significant self-serving attributional pattern among spectators witnessing a recreational basketball game.

An important distinction can be drawn between spectators participating in the Grove et al. (1991) research and those participating in the other studies described above. This distinction involves the subjects' identification with the target team. Hastorf and Cantril's investigation tested students attending one of the two schools, while subjects tested in Mann's research were spectators attending the football contest. As a result, spectators in these studies were probably highly identified with their team (this is also true for Lau's research on writers). Conversely, participants in the Grove et al. research were simply asked to view a recreational basketball game and were probably low in identification with the team. Had the subjects been highly identified with one of the basketball teams, their attributions might have been self-serving.

Highly identified subjects should be especially likely to report biased attributions for game outcomes because these subjects have the most to gain from biased perceptions. For these fans, the role of team supporter is central to their self-concept. By reporting a self-serving attributional pattern, highly identified fans are able to maintain a positive identity (Tajfel, 1981; Tajfel & Turner, 1979). That is, they can feel better about themselves by feeling better about their team. Conversely, the team's performances are only minimally relevant to those low in team identification (Crocker & Major, 1989; Harter, 1986). As a result, these spectators should be less likely to report a biased attributional pattern.

A colleague and I recently tested this prediction of the relationship between team identification and attributional bias (Wann & Dolan, 1994b; see also Dietz-Uhler & Murrell, 1995; Wann & Branscombe, 1993). We asked university students to meet in a predetermined room prior to one of two university men's basketball games (a home team win and a home team loss). Subjects were asked to complete the SSIS and were then escorted to the basketball arena. After watching the game, subjects were asked to meet in a predetermined location inside the arena to complete a questionnaire assessing their attributions of the game's outcome. The questionnaire contained items assessing both internal attributions and external attributions. The results supported the hypothesized relationship between level of team identification and biased attributions. As expected, spectators formed internal attributions following a win and external attributions after a loss, and the attributional differences were more pronounced in highly identified fans. Lowly identified fans exhibited only a small tendency toward self-serving attributions.

The Fundamental Attribution Error and Spectator Attributions.   The fundamental attribution error is a second attributional bias with relevance to sport spectators. Based on this attributional bias, we would expect fans to overestimate the importance of internal factors when determining the causes of players' and teams' performances. A number of studies have substantiated this pattern. For example, spectators have overemphasized the internal causes for sport outcomes in professional football (Lau, 1984; Winkler & Taylor, 1979), professional baseball (Lau & Russell, 1980), and college basketball (Burger, 1985; Wann & Dolan, 1994b). Thus, it appears that the fundamental attribution error does impact the attributions of sport spectators.

There is some indication that spectators become increasingly more susceptible to the fundamental attribution error with the passage of time. Burger (1985) telephoned subjects who had attended a recent college basketball contest and asked the subjects to state their perceptions of the reasons for the team's performance. The subjects' attributions were classified as either internal or external and the percentages of internal/external attributions were calculated. Some subjects were contacted on the morning following the game (the immediate condition), while others were contacted 4 or 5 days after the game (the delayed condition). The results indicated that subjects' attributions became more dispositional over time. For subjects in the immediate condition, 56% of the attributions were classified as internal. However, 76% of the explanations offered by those in the delayed condition reflected internal attributions.

In Chapter 9, I noted that some authors believe that the fundamental attribution error is at least partially due to attentional focus. That is, individuals overemphasize internal causes because their attention is directed toward the person performing the behavior rather than the situation surrounding this person. This logic appears quite reasonable when applied to sport spectators. When spectators watch a team in action, their attention is more likely to be directed toward the players than to the environment (e.g., the stadium, weather, officials). For example, imagine that you are watching a football game on television and one of the team's star running backs has just completed a dazzling touchdown run. When you attempt to determine the reasons for the running back's behavior, it is likely that you will emphasize internal reasons because your attention was focused on the player as he completed his run. You can actually experience this process first hand. The next time you are watching a sporting event, ask yourself if you are directing your attention toward the player with the ball or toward the other players involved in the competition. Most likely, you will find that your attention has been directed toward the player in possession of the ball.

A second factor that may partially explain the fundamental attribution error in spectators is the notion of the sport outcome responsibility norm (Duncan & McAuley, 1987; Mark et al., 1984; McAuley & Gross, 1983). Recall that this norm encourages athletes to accept responsibility for competitive outcomes. As a result, they report internal attributions for their failures as well as their successes. It seems reasonable that spectators also subscribe to this belief (Grove et al., 1991). That is, because spectators typically have a sound understanding of sport, they are probably aware of the athletes' beliefs that they are responsible for their performances. Consequently, spectators may also begin to adopt this perspective.

Biased Recollections and Predictions of Team Performance

In this section, we will examine sport fans' biased recollections and predictions of their team's performance. Because fans are motivated to evaluate their team in a positive fashion, they often believe that their team's past performances were better than the team's actual record demonstrates. Further, fans also predict that their team will perform exceptionally well in future contests. Similar to the attributional biases described above, fans' tendencies to embellish their team's performances are particularly common among highly identified fans.

Several recent studies have documented the biased recollections and predictions of highly identified sport fans (Hirt & Ryalls, 1994; Hirt et al., 1992; Murrell & Dietz, 1992; Wann, 1996; Wann & Branscombe, 1993). For instance, a colleague and I recently asked fans of a college basketball team to complete the SSIS and to estimate the number of games the team had won in the previous season and the number of games the team would win in the current season (Wann & Dolan, 1994c). Subjects were asked to base their estimates on a 30-game season. The historically successful team had a record of 4 and 1 at the time of testing. The team had won 17 games in the previous season and would go on to win 18 games in the current season. The results indicated that highly identified subjects were more biased in their estimates than were lowly identified subjects. Specifically, those high in identification stated that the team had won 20.4 games during the previous season and would win 19.1 games in the current season (both estimates were higher than the actual number of wins). However, those low in identification estimated the wins to be only 18.7 and 17.6 for the past and current seasons, respectively. This biased pattern of effects for highly identified fans was replicated using supporters of a historically unsuccessful college football team (Wann, 1994b).

It should be noted that fans' predictions of their team's future performances can be negative if the predictions are given immediately after watching their team perform poorly (Hirt & Ryalls, 1994; Hirt et al., 1992). Evidently, the negative affect and low self-esteem resulting from the poor performance temporarily clouds the fans' predictions in a negative manner. However, when the negative affect subsides and self-esteem returns to normal, fans again become positively biased in their estimates of the team's future performances (Wann, 1994b).

SUMMARY

An important first step in an understanding of the psychology of the sport fan is to construct a psychological profile of sport consumers. This profile has been based on fan demographics, socialization and motivation, team identification, and reasons for attendance at sporting events. As for demographics, research has found that spectators (1) often prefer active pastimes, (2) tend to be involved with sport as an athlete as well as a spectator, (3) are disproportionately likely to be black and male, and (4) may be somewhat higher in SES than nonspectators. However, it is not possible to provide a complete demographic profile because of the small number of studies conducted in this area.

It appears that four socialization agents play a role in fan socialization: family, peers, school, and the community. Eight common motives have been identified: group affiliation, family needs, escape, eustress, aesthetics, self-esteem, entertainment, and economics. Recent investigations have indicated that the entertainment and eustress motives are quite common, while the economic motive is rather rare.

The success of the team, the players, and geographical factors play a prominent role in the origination, continuation, and cessation of team identification. Highly identified fans tend to have a greater sport knowledge base than persons low in team identification. In fact, highly identified sport fans have even developed their own terminology for describing sport behaviors and outcomes.

A number of factors can influence attendance at sporting events. A major factor is team performance. Several studies have found a positive relationship between team performance and attendance levels. Individuals are especially likely to attend a competition involving two successful teams when the success is attributed to internal factors. Nonperformance factors such as the presence of a star player, special promotions, a talented opponent, and the accessibility of the event also play a role in attendance decisions.

Throughout the past century, social scientists have debated the merits and evils of sport fandom. Some authors have arued that sport spectating is a waste of time. These individuals contended that sport fans are lazy, that the activity serves as an opiate to the masses, and that sport teaches a distorted set of values. Other authors have refuted this stance. These persons argued that sport fans are a "noble" group and that the activity can benefit both the individual fan and society as a whole. Research has tended to support the latter perspective, finding that there are several benefits of sport fandom including higher self-esteem and decreased alienation.

Sport fans are often biased in their assessment of their team. These biases are most common among highly identified fans. For example, spectators tend to report biased attributions about their team's performance. These attributions often reflect the self-serving bias with fans offering internal attributions to account for their team's successes while offering external attributions to explain their team's failures. Fans also report biased recollections and predictions of their team's performance.

GLOSSARY

Direct Sport Consumers   Individuals who are attending a sporting event in person.

Indirect Sport Consumers   Individuals who are spectating through television or radio broadcasts.

Pseudosports   Staged sports that contain a scripted outcome.

Sport Fan   An individual who is interested in and follows a sport, athlete, or team.

Sport Spectator   An individual who is watching or listening to a sporting event.

Team Identification   The extent to which a fan feels psychologically connected to a team.

APPLICATION AND REVIEW QUESTIONS

1. What distinguishes sport spectators and sport fans?
2. What are some demographics that characterize sport spectators?
3. Describe the process of socialization into the role of sport fan including the motives of sport fans. Now, apply this process to your own experiences as a sport fan.
4. What is team identification? Would you consider yourself to be highly identified with a particular sport team? If so, what were the origins of the identification and what factors affect your continuing to follow this team?

5. What factors tend to promote attendance at athletic events? What factors are most likely to promote your attendance?
6. Do you feel that sport fandom is a waste of time or a worthwhile pastime?
7. Describe the common biases of sport spectators. How does team identification play a role in these biases?

SUGGESTED READINGS

GOLDSTEIN, J. H. (Ed.). (1989). *Sports, games, and play: Social and psychological viewpoints.* Hillsdale, NJ: Erlbaum. Goldstein's edited work includes a number of interesting chapters including work by Sloan on fan motivation and by Zillmann, Bryant, and Sapolsky on sources of enjoyment for fans.

GUTTMANN, A. (1986). *Sports spectators.* New York: Columbia University Press. This text is extremely important for anyone interested in the psychology of the sport spectator. A number of interesting topics are reviewed including the history of sport spectating and spectator motives.

MELNICK, M. J. (1989). The sports fan: A teaching guide and bibliography. *Journal of Sport and Social Issues, 6,* 167–175. The value of this article lies in its extensive bibliography of articles, books, and chapters relevant to the psychology and sociology of the sport fan. More than 100 works are included in the bibliography.

Chapter 16

THE EMOTIONAL AND AGGRESSIVE REACTIONS OF SPORT SPECTATORS

In his book on sport violence, Atyeo (1979) discusses a distraught Denver Broncos fan who was so depressed by the team's inept play that he attempted suicide (thankfully, he was unsuccessful). When the police arrived, they found a note that read "I have been a Broncos fan since the Broncos were first organized, and I can't stand their fumbling anymore" (p. 245). Although most fans do not react in the drastic manner of this fan, their emotional responses to their team's performances can be quite intense. In this chapter, we will explore these responses. First, we will examine the positive and negative emotional responses of sport spectators. We will then examine the causes and consequences of spectator aggression.

THE POSITIVE AND NEGATIVE EMOTIONAL RESPONSES OF SPORT FANS AND SPECTATORS

Sloan (1979, 1989) conducted one of the first examinations of the emotional reactions of sport fans. In this study, basketball spectators were asked to complete a questionnaire assessing their current emotional state. The questionnaire addressed both positive emotions (e.g., pleased, happy) and negative emotions (e.g., angry, discouraged). Subjects completed the questionnaire prior to or following one of three different basketball contests: an easy win, a difficult win, or a loss. The results indicated that spectators' emotions changed considerably from pregame to postgame and that the changes were a function of game outcome. Following a loss, subjects reported an increase in negative emotions and a decrease in positive emotions. Conversely, subjects exhibited an increase in positive emotions after the difficult win. Spectators did not display a change in positive or negative emotions following an easy win. Kimble and Cooper (1992) were able to replicate Sloan's research.

Gantz and Wenner (1995; Wenner & Gantz, 1989) also examined spectator emotions. In this study, adults from large metropolitan areas were telephoned and asked to respond to a set of questions assessing their emotional reactions during and after watching sport on television. Subjects reported experiencing a high level of positive emotions *during and after* watching their favorite team perform well. A slightly different pattern of effects was found when spectators watched their team perform poorly. In these instances, although subjects reported experiencing a high level of negative emotions *while* watching their team, they were less likely to experience negative emotions *after* the contest. This last finding seems to be at odds with Sloan's (1979, 1989) research finding that spectators experience a high level of negative emotions after a loss. Perhaps the difference lies in the methods used to gather the data. Sloan collected his data from subjects attending a sporting event. Thus, the negativity of the loss was fresh in the minds of these subjects. Subjects in the Wenner and Gantz study were telephoned and asked to recall their affective reactions. As a result, these subjects had to rely on their memory and may have been unable to recall the intensity of their negative reactions. Because memory for life events tends to be incomplete (Myers, 1993), this logic seems reasonable.

Think about your own emotional reactions to sporting events. It is likely that some events cause you to become highly emotional (positively and negatively), while other events leave you relatively unaffected. Are the events that lead to intense emotional reactions different from those that do not? It is possible that your intense emotional reactions occur in response to the efforts of one of your favorite teams. Conversely, the nonemotional events probably did not involve one of your favorite teams. Recently, some colleagues and I tested this hypothesis. Specifically, we predicted that the most intense emotional reactions to sporting events are exhibited by spectators who are highly identified with one of the competing teams (Wann et al., 1994; see also Tannenbaum & Gaer, 1965). To test this prediction, we replicated Sloan's (1979, 1989) study while taking into consideration the spectators' level of team identification. Similar to Sloan, we asked college students to attend one of three university men's basketball games: an easy win, a difficult win, or a loss. Prior to the contests, subjects met in a university building to complete the SSIS and a pretest questionnaire assessing their current emotional state. Subjects were then escorted to the basketball arena to watch one of the contests. Immediately following the game, respondents were asked to meet in a predetermined section of the arena to complete a posttest measure of their current emotional state (the pretest and posttest measures were identical). The results supported the prediction. Subjects reported increased negative affect and decreased positive affect after the loss. However, these reactions were much more pronounced for highly identified spectators. Subjects exhibited an increase in positive emotions and a decrease in negative emotions after the difficult win. Again, these reactions were most intense for the highly identified spectators. The easy win had little effect on fans high or low in team identification.

The results of the Wann et al. (1994) research are consistent with the ***disposition theory of sport spectatorship*** developed by Zillmann and his colleagues (1989; Sapolsky, 1980). This perspective reflects the belief that a spectator's emotional reaction to a team is largely a function of his or her alliance with the team. Two predictions can be derived from this theory. First, one's enjoyment from watching a team succeed should increase with positive sentiments toward the team and decrease with negative sentiments toward the team. Second, one's enjoyment from watching a team lose should increase with negative sentiments and decrease with positive sentiments. Thus, spectators are expected to be happiest when their favorite teams succeed and their least favorite teams fail, and least happy when their favorite team fails and their least favorite team succeeds. In discussing their theory, Zillmann and Paulas (1993) state that "seeing an allied athletic party succeed and win will produce more euphoria the stronger the alliance" (p. 604). This statement is supported by the Wann et al. (1994) finding that highly identified fans (i.e., fans with a high level of team alliance) exhibit the most intense positive and negative emotional reactions to their team's performance.

Research has indicated that a team's performance can even impact fans' general outlook on life. For example, Lever (1969) reported that production in one Brazilian city rose by 12% when the city's most popular soccer team was victorious. When the team was defeated, accidents in the work place rose by 15%. In a more recent study, Schwarz, Strack, Kommer, and Wagner (1987) contacted German residents immediately prior to and after their country's team participated in two contests during the 1982 Soccer World Championships. In one game the team was victorious by a score of 4 to 1, while the other game ended in a tie (0–0). Subjects were asked a variety of questions assessing their outlook on life, including items measuring their global well-being and job and income satisfaction. The results indicated that game outcome had a pronounced effect on the respondents' outlook on life as subjects' global well-being, and satisfaction with work and income increased after the victory but decreased following the tie.

Another study investigating the life-outlook consequences of sporting events was conducted by Schweitzer, Zillmann, Weaver, and Luttrell (1992). These researchers investigated the impact of a sporting event on fans' expectations of a war between Iraq and America. Undergraduate fans of two rival schools were asked to view a football contest between the universities. After the contest, participants were asked to state their estimates of the likelihood of war between Iraq and America and, in the event of war, the number of American casualties. The results revealed that fans of the losing team were more likely to believe that the Gulf War was imminent. In addition, fans of the losing team predicted a greater number of American casualties (69,300) than did fans of the winning team (22,800). Schweitzer et al. (1992) concluded that "postgame emotions are indeed capable of influencing the perception and evaluation of feared future events" (p. 81).

Subjects can also react emotionally to activities that are not based on team performance. For example, Branscombe and I recently tested fans' emotional responses to reading the sports page (Wann & Branscombe, 1992). We hypothesized that fans' emotional reactions to the sports page would be influenced by a number of factors including their level of identification with the team, the game's outcome, and characteristics of the article's author. To test this prediction, we used the SSIS to assess students' identification with their university's men's basketball team. Subjects were then asked to read a brief article describing a basketball contest involving the university's team. The article contained a summary section and an author's commentary section. The summary section described an overtime contest between the home school and a conference rival. Some subjects read that the home team had won the contest while others read that the home team had been defeated. The commentary section indicated the author's group membership (i.e., a supporter of the home team or a supporter of the rival team) as well as the author's loyalty to the team (i.e., loyal or disloyal). After reading the article, subjects were asked to complete a scale assessing their current emotional state. The results revealed an interesting pattern of effects. The most positive emotional responses were exhibited by highly identified fans reading a loyal home team fan's description of a victory. This version resulted in a highly positive reaction because fans were happy about the team's success and because the author validated the fans' beliefs about the team (i.e., the author was also a loyal home team fan). The most negative reactions were found in highly identified subjects reading a disloyal home team fan's description of a loss. This version elicited intense negative responses because fans were upset by the team's poor performance, and by the statements of the "traitor" author. Thus, true to our hypothesis, fans' affective responses to reading the sports page are influenced by their level of identification with the team, the game's outcome, and characteristics of the article's author.

Trujillo and Krizek (1994) were interested in a different nonperformance emotional response of sport spectators. These authors investigated fans' reactions to the closing of their favorite team's ballpark. They conducted interviews with spectators attending the final series at two Major League baseball stadiums: Old Comisky Park in Chicago, Illinois (former home of the Chicago White Sox) and Arlington Stadium in Arlington, Texas (former home of the Texas Rangers). The interviews revealed strong emotional reactions to the closing of the parks. For example, consider the statements of a 30- to 35-year-old female fan. When asked to comment on the closing of Arlington Stadium, she said, "I started cryin' when we parked the car. We came out here a week ago, but I said we got to come back [for the last game]. I've got a lot of memories here, all good, with friends, and a friend at the time who became my husband. I have mixed feelings about losing this stadium. I know I'll like the new one. But there are lots of good memories here" (p. 303). Another fan said "I've been coming here since the Rangers came here back in '72. This place has been a big part of me for 22 years. It's like losing an old friend. It's hard to tell an old friend goodbye" (p. 305).

SPORT FAN AND SPORT SPECTATOR AGGRESSION

In the previous section, we discussed how the emotional reactions of sport fans and spectators can reach highly intense levels. In this section, we will examine how fans' negative emotional reactions can become so intense that they lead to aggressive behaviors. Examples of spectator aggression and attempts to curb it are not hard to find. For instance, consider the following:

1. As early as 1897, a Major League baseball crowd became violent. In a contest between the Cincinnati Red Stockings and Washington Senators, female Senator fans stormed the field and threw bricks at an umpire who had ejected their favorite player (Wolff & Stone, 1995b).
2. A 1974 "Beer Night" Major League baseball game between the Cleveland Indians and Texas Rangers resulted in the players for both teams protecting themselves from a mob of fans who had poured onto the field (Lewis, 1982).
3. Disgruntled high school basketball spectators fought after a New Jersey playoff game. The fight was so extensive that one of the teams was banned from the following season's playoff games (Gregg, 1992).
4. Mitch Williams, former pitcher for the Philadelphia Phillies, received death threats and had eggs thrown at his house by fans who were upset by his poor performance in the 1993 World Series (Bodley, 1993). On a similar note, former Boston Red Sox Bill Buckner was forced to move because of the abuse he and his family received after his error in the 1986 World Series (Brown, Brady, Patrick, & DiSimone, 1993).
5. The organizers of the 1994 World Cup Soccer Championship were so concerned about fan violence that their largest budgetary item involved security. In fact, the organizers asked that alcohol not be sold in or around the arenas and reporters had to allow the FBI and police to conduct background checks (Hersch, 1994).
6. During a recent Brazilian soccer season, spectators were so afraid of the potential for violence in the stands that they refused to attend the games (Wolff & O'Brien, 1995). One stadium that typically attracted more than 100,000 spectators drew only 640 fans for one match.
7. Renovations on the University of Wisconsin's football stadium included more than $200,000 to build holding cells for spectators who break the law (Lidz & Kennedy, 1995).

Before we begin our examination of spectator aggression, two points must be mentioned. First, similar to the aggressive actions of athletes, the violence of sport spectators can be verbal (e.g., yelling obscenities) and physical (e.g., fighting and the destruction of property). Second, although some spectators' verbal assaults on players and officials are obvious examples of hostile aggression, it is less clear if spectator hostilities should, on occasion, be classified as instances of instrumental aggression. If spectators' do attempt to enhance their team's chances through instrumentally aggressive actions, we should find that spectators tend to believe that they have the ability to influence athletic events. The possibility that spectators truly believe that they can alter the outcome of a sporting event is discussed in this chapter's "A Closer Look."

Theories of Spectator Aggression

Recall that sport fans and nonfans do not differ in their trait aggressiveness (Russell & Goldstein, 1995; Wann, 1994a). Thus, sport fans probably do not enter the athletic arena in an aggressive state. Rather, "something" happens during the event that triggers their aggressive responses. It has been the goal of a number of social scientists to identify these "somethings." That is, researchers have attempted to determine the factors leading to spectator aggression and, ultimately, to answer the question posed by the character depicted in Figure 16.1. In the following sections, we will examine

Spectators can become so involved in the contest that they become violent.
(Photographer: Phillipe Crochet. Source: Gamma-Liaison, Inc.)

the work of these authors. We will conclude with a list of suggestions for curbing spectator aggression.

Revisiting the Classic Theories of Aggression.   In the player aggression chapter, we examined three classic theories of the origin of human aggression: instinctual theories, the frustration-aggression hypothesis, and social learning theory. In the following paragraphs, we will apply each of these theories to the aggressive behaviors of sport spectators.

INSTINCTUAL THEORIES AND SPECTATOR AGGRESSION.   As noted in Chapter 12, instinctual theories of aggression reflect the belief that aggressive tendencies are the result of inherited predispositions (Freud, 1920, 1930; Lorenz, 1966). The innate aggressive desires are released either through aggressive actions or through catharsis. As for their explanation of sport spectator aggression, instinctual theorists argue that sport spectating is a natural and safe method of releasing aggression. In fact, some clinical psychologists have encouraged their patients to attend violent sporting events so they may benefit from catharsis (Proctor & Eckerd, 1976).

Although sport fans do enjoy the violent and combative content of athletic events (Bryant, Brown, Comisky, & Zillmann, 1982; Bryant, Comisky, & Zillmann, 1981; Bryant & Zillmann, 1983; Russell, 1979), research indicates that viewing sport violence does not reduce one's aggressive tendencies. In fact, a number of sport studies have refuted the notion of symbolic catharsis, finding instead that spectators become more aggressive after viewing a violent sporting event (Gilbert & Twyman, 1984; Goranson, 1980; Russell, 1993b). For example, research has found an increase

A CLOSER LOOK:
SPECTATORS ROOT BUT DO THEY THINK IT MATTERS?

It is conceivable that spectators become verbally abusive to players and officials because they believe these actions can increase their team's chances of victory. However, before we can assume that spectators behave in an instrumentally aggressive manner, it must be demonstrated that spectators feel they can influence the outcome of sporting events. That is, it is unreasonable to assume that spectators' verbally aggressive acts are instances of instrumental aggression if fans do not feel they can impact an athletic contest.

A handful of studies have examined spectators' beliefs in their ability to influence athletic events. Crossman (1986a, 1986b) recorded the behaviors of spectators attending minor league hockey and minor league baseball games. She found that a fairly substantial number of verbalizations were directed toward the athletes and officials, a finding replicated by researchers studying other sports (Faucette & Osinski, 1987; Randall & McKenzie, 1988; Walley, Graham, & Forehand, 1982). However, although this study indicates that spectators perform behaviors that *could* influence players and officials, it does not assess the degree that the behaviors were *intended* to influence the outcome or the degree to which spectators *believe* that the behaviors successfully influenced the outcome.

I recently directed a study designed to answer these questions (Wann et al., 1994). In this research, subjects completed the SSIS for their favorite college basketball, college football, professional basketball, professional football, and professional baseball teams. Subjects then answered questions assessing their perceptions of influence for the five target sports. They were asked to state their perception of the extent to which spectators, in general, can influence the outcome of the target sports and the degree to which they personally attempted to influence the target sports.

The results indicated that fans do believe that spectators can influence the outcome of sporting events and that they themselves often attempt these behaviors. In addition, there was a strong positive correlation between the subjects' degree of team identification and their belief in influencing and attempts to influence sporting events. Thus, we may conclude that in certain situations, the verbally aggressive actions of sport spectators should be classified as instrumental aggression, particularly the behaviors of highly identified fans. That is, because spectators believe they can alter the outcome of sporting events, it is likely that some of their negative verbalizations directed toward the players and officials are aimed at increasing the chances of the home team.

in spectator aggression following exposure to boxing (Leith, 1982; Russell, 1992; Turner & Berkowitz, 1972), professional wrestling (Arms, Russell, & Sandilands, 1979; Russell, Horn, & Huddle, 1988), basketball (Leuck, Krahenbuhl, & Odenkirk, 1979; Turner, 1970), hockey (Arms et al., 1979; Celozzi, Kazelskis, & Gutsch, 1981; Harrell,

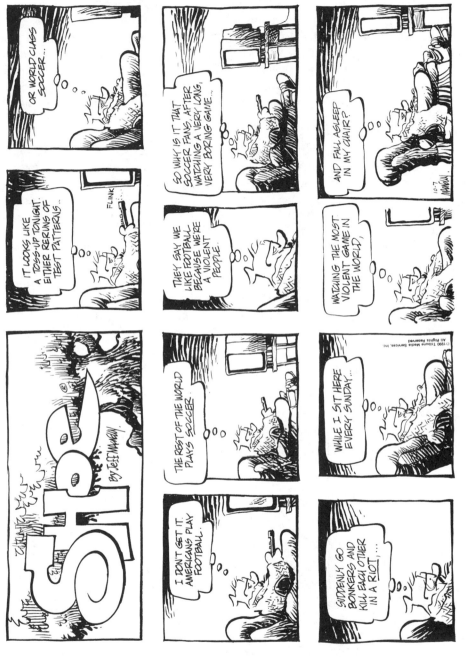

FIGURE 16.1 A number of sport psychologists and sport sociologists have attempted to answer the question posed by the character in this cartoon. (Reprinted by permission: Tribune Media Services.)

1981; Russell, 1981c; Russell, Di Lullo, & Di Lullo, 1988–89), and football (Goldstein & Arms, 1971; Lennon & Hatfield, 1980; Turner, 1970). For example, consider the work of Goldstein and Arms published in 1971. These researchers presented a hostility questionnaire to spectators attending the 1969 Army–Navy football game and to fans attending a gymnastics meet between Army and Temple University. The questionnaires were completed both before and after the contests. The results indicated that, although hostility did not change for spectators watching the nonviolent gymnastics meet, those watching the football contest exhibited a significant increase in hostility from pregame to postgame.

Another study refuting the notion of symbolic catharsis was conducted by Russell (1981c). This researcher measured the aggression and arousal of spectators attending a particularly violent minor league hockey game. The game involved 184 minutes of penalties, almost three standard deviations above the league average of 56 minutes per game. Questionnaires were completed at the beginning of the contest, at the end of the first and second periods, and immediately after the game. As shown in Figure 16.2, aggression and arousal followed similar patterns, increasing

FIGURE 16.2   Spectator aggression and arousal in relation to (violent) game features. (Reprinted by permission from G. W. Russell, 1981, "Spectator Moods at an Aggressive Sports Event." *Journal of Sport Psychology,* 3(3): 221.)

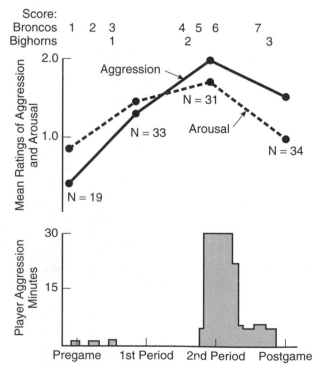

up to the conclusion of the second period and then decreasing after the game. Because the end of the second period was characterized by the most violent play (as indicated in penalty minutes, see Figure 16.2), the finding that this period also produced the highest levels of aggression contradicts the catharsis hypothesis.

THE FRUSTRATION-AGGRESSION HYPOTHESIS AND SPECTATOR AGGRESSION.   As noted in the aggression chapter, the frustration-aggression hypothesis is a drive reduction model of aggression reflecting the belief that the inability to attain a goal leads to frustration. The frustration then triggers an aggressive drive. The aggressive drive can be reduced through aggressive actions or through catharsis (which, as noted above, is an invalid assumption). This theory leads to the prediction that supporters of a losing team should be more aggressive than fans of a winning team. However, empirical research testing this prediction has been equivocal (Russell, 1983). Some studies have found that spectators of the losing team were highly aggressive (e.g., Sloan, 1979). For example, in a study of professional football playoff games, White (1989) found that homicides increased in the losing teams' cities. This increase was not found for the winning teams' cities. However, other studies have not found that losing fans were more aggressive than winning fans (e.g., Goldstein & Arms, 1971; Leuck et al., 1979; Randall & McKenzie, 1988). Russell (1981c, 1983) believes that the inconclusive findings may be explained by a methodological problem plaguing these studies. Russell notes that many researchers administer the posttest measures of aggression at the conclusion of the contest. However, the outcome of many contests is decided prior to the conclusion of the game. In these situations, although spectators may have been frustrated when they initially realized that their team was going to lose, by the end of the contest they had come to terms with their team's defeat and were no longer aggressive. A better assessment of spectator aggression could be obtained if fans completed the questionnaires at the moment the outcome is no longer in question, regardless of when that moment comes.

In Chapter 12, we discussed Berkowitz's reformulation of the frustration-aggression hypothesis (the aggressive cue/cognitive neoassociation theory). A major component of Berkowitz's theory concerns the notion of aggressive cues. Berkowitz (1983, 1988, 1989) believes that the presence of aggressive cues can increase the likelihood of an overt aggressive response. Two aggressive cues relevant to sport spectators have been examined. First, recall that Frank and Gilovich (1988) found that black uniforms cued aggressive thinking in both athletes and officials. It is reasonable to assume that spectators are also susceptible to the aggressive cuing effects of black uniforms.

A second aggressive cue involves the spectators' perceptions of the sport. Branscombe and I hypothesized that individuals primed with aggressive sport names would respond in a more aggressive fashion than persons primed with nonaggressive sport names (Wann & Branscombe, 1990b). To test this hypothesis, we asked subjects to unscramble a set of four-word sentences. Some subjects were presented with sentences containing aggressive sport names (e.g., hockey, rugby), while others were given sentences containing nonaggressive sport names (e.g., golf, billiards). After completing the unscrambling task, subjects were asked to interpret the ambiguous behaviors of a target individual. The results revealed that the interpretations of subjects reading the aggressive sport names were more hostile than the interpretations of those reading the nonaggressive sport names. Thus, spectators may be cued to act aggressively simply by thinking about and discussing sports that are perceived as aggressive.

SOCIAL LEARNING THEORY AND SPECTATOR AGGRESSION   Social learning theory is a third approach to aggression. According to this perspective, individuals learn to behave aggressively through operant conditioning and observational learning (Bandura, 1973, 1983). This theory leads to the prediction that spectators will exhibit an increase in aggression after viewing a violent sporting event. Aggression would not be expected to increase after viewing a nonviolent sport. Several studies have supported this pattern of effects (e.g., Arms et al., 1979; Dunand, Berkowitz, & Leyens, 1984; Lennon & Hatfield, 1980; Russell, 1992).

Three studies supporting Bandura's theory warrant special mention. First, let us return to Russell's (1981c) study of spectator reactions to a violent hockey game. As seen in Figure 16.2, the highest levels of spectator aggression occurred simultaneously with the highest levels of athlete aggression. It is possible that spectators were learning to behave aggressively by observing the athletes, a finding that is consistent with Bandura's theory.

Smith (1976) also conducted a study relevant to spectators' observational learning of aggression. Smith examined a Toronto newspaper for incidents of crowd violence. An incident was considered an episode of crowd violence if it involved 10 or more persons and led to violent actions against individuals or property. A total of 27 individual episodes of violence were identified (Smith's search spanned a 10-year period). Smith then examined the degree of violence characterizing the matches. That is, he recorded whether or not the event involved had an abnormally high level of player violence. The results indicated that 74% of the incidents of crowd violence were preceded by one or more violent acts among the athletes, leading Smith (1976) to conclude that most episodes of crowd violence are "ignited by player violence" (p. 127). This conclusion supports the social learning perspective.

Phillips (1983) conducted a third study supporting Bandura's theory of observational learning. This investigator examined the impact of championship heavyweight boxing matches on homicide rates in the United States. His investigation led to the identification of 18 championship matches between 1973 and 1978. Phillips then compared the number of homicides occurring during the 3-day period following the fight with the number of homicides expected if the match had not occurred. The results indicated a sharp increase in homicides following the boxing matches. In fact, homicides rose by 6.98 incidents for the period following the contests. Further, by comparing fights receiving a large amount of media attention with those not receiving media attention, Phillips was able to test Bandura's theory. If homicide increases were greater following matches receiving extensive coverage, one could conclude that observational learning played a role in the increase. This is precisely what Phillips found. The 3-day homicide increase following prize fights receiving a substantial amount of media coverage was 11.13, but the homicide rate was only 2.83 subsequent to matches not receiving extensive coverage.

Sport-Specific Theories of Spectator Aggression.   In this section, we will examine a number of sport-specific theories designed to account for the violence of sport fans and spectators. The first set of theories are typologies designed to classify the different forms of spectator violence. The second set of theories examine spectator aggression from a social psychological viewpoint. It should be noted that sport sociologists have also developed theories of spectator violence. However, because these theories focus on the collective behaviors of large numbers of fans rather than psychological processes, they are beyond the scope of this text. Readers interested in the sociological perspectives should consult a sociology of sport text such as those authored by Vogler and Schwartz (1993) and Leonard (1993).

USING TYPOLOGIES TO CATEGORIZE SPECTATOR AGGRESSION.   We will examine two typologies used to categorize instances of spectator aggression: Eitzen's three-category typology and Mann's five-category FORCE typology.

Eitzen's Typology of Spectator Aggression.   In 1979, Eitzen proposed a typology of spectator aggression containing three classifications of violence: rowdyism, sport riots, and exuberant celebrations. **Rowdyism** involves interpersonal and property damage associated with sporting events. Rowdyism can occur regardless of the outcome. In these instances, the sporting event simply serves as an outlet for existing hostilities and frustrations. **Sport riots,** on the other hand, are incidents of spectator aggression resulting from events occurring on the playing field. Eitzen believes that this type of aggression often is linked to social strains between different groups of fans, such as conflicts involving economic, political, or religious differences.

The third form of spectator aggression, ***exuberant celebrations,*** refers to celebrations that have resulted in violence and vandalism. A common example of this form of aggression is the tradition of tearing down football goal posts following a victory. One of the more intriguing reactions to an exuberant celebration occurred following the Arkansas Razorbacks' 1994 NCAA basketball championship (McCallum, 1994b). Although the fact that more than 100 people were arrested during the celebration was not unusual, the judge's ruling on the violations was quite unique. The judge lowered the normal fine of $100 per person to $76.72, the final score in the Razorbacks' 76 to 72 victory over Duke.

Mann's FORCE Typology of Spectator Aggression.   Mann (1989) proposed a different typology of spectator aggression. Mann's classification scheme, called the ***FORCE typology,*** contains five forms of spectator riots: **f**rustration, **o**utlawry, **r**emonstrance, **c**onfrontation, and **e**xpressive. Mann uses the term ***frustration*** to identify spectator hostilities stemming from deprivation or perceived injustice. Deprivation occurs when fans are deprived of a particular service, for example, when legitimate ticket holders are not allowed into a stadium. Perceived injustice occurs when spectators believe that a contest was fixed or officials' decisions were unjust. It is important to note that Mann's category of frustration does not involve frustrations resulting from a loss. Rather, his frustration category includes frustrations resulting from nonscore factors.

A second form of spectator riot, termed ***outlawry,*** concerns attacks on authority, the destruction of property, and the intimidation of rivals. In this form of spectator riot, on-field actions and game outcomes do not matter. Rather, the athletic event is an excuse for individuals to cause trouble. This form of violence includes the actions of the hooligans attracted to European soccer matches. These individuals move from contest to contest causing a great deal of destruction and violence (for a detailed review of soccer hooliganism, see Dunning, Murphy, & Williams, 1986; Guttmann, 1986; Lewis, 1980; Roadburg, 1980; Webb, 1986).

Remonstrance is a third form of spectator aggression. **Remonstrance** involves violent incidents based on political protests. The individuals use the athletic arena to express their political grievances or promote their particular ideologies. Mann (1989) feels that as sport has become more politicized, this form of riot has become more common. As an example of this form of violence, Mann describes the protests occurring when South African sport teams visited a number of countries during the 1970s and 1980s. During these events, some members of the crowd used the contests to protest apartheid and racial discrimination in South Africa.

Confrontation is a fourth form of spectator aggression. This type of violence involves groups of individuals with a history of bad relations. As a result, these individuals are especially likely to become involved in a riot. An infamous example of this form of aggression was the 1969 war between El Salvador and Honduras. These countries had a history of tense relations, tensions that were exacerbated by a soccer match between the two countries. The match took place in El Salvador and was won by the host country. This resulted in Honduran crowds attacking Salvadoreans, forcing them to flee for their lives. Shortly after, the two countries went to war.

The fifth form of spectator violence included in Mann's typology is called expressive violence. **Expressive** outbursts are the direct result of sport outcomes. This form of violence includes riots resulting from expressions of extreme euphoria after a team's victory and expressions of anger and depression after a team's loss.

SOCIAL PSYCHOLOGICAL APPROACHES TO SPECTATOR AGGRESSION.   In this section, we will review two social psychological approaches to spectator violence. These theories are considered social psychological in nature because of their focus on the social setting surrounding the athletic event and individual psychological processes.

The Psychosocial Model of Spectator Aggression.   In 1992, Simons and Taylor presented a **psychosocial model of spectator aggression.** Simons and Taylor hypothesized that spectator aggression is the result of a number of social psychological factors (see Figure 16.3). The initial set of factors are potentiating factors. These factors involve social variables that can predispose individuals toward violent actions, factors such as low socioeconomic status, political ideologies, and media coverage. The second factor in the model is team identification. These authors argue that if one's identification with a team becomes excessive, the team's losses become the individual's losses, increasing the likelihood of aggressive behaviors (see also Gilbert & Twyman, 1984; Turner & Berkowitz, 1972). According to Simons and Taylor, high levels of team identification lead to group solidarity. The group solidarity stage contains two major components. First, spectators begin to develop a "feeling of togetherness, belonging, and support" (p. 216). That is, the group begins to evolve into a cohesive unit. Second, a perception of intergroup hostility begins to develop as spectators adopt an "us versus them" perspective.

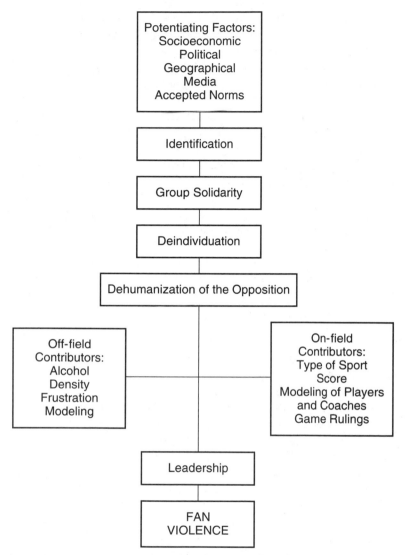

FIGURE 16.3 Psychosocial model of fan violence. (Reprinted by permission from: Simons, Y., & Taylor, J. [1992]. A psychosocial model of fan violence in sports. *International Journal of Sport Psychology*, 23: 207–226.)

Once spectators feel a sense of group solidarity, Simons and Taylor (1992) believe they are likely to experience deindividuation. ***Deindividuation*** is a mental state characterized by membership in a group, feelings of anonymity, and a loss of self-awareness (Deiner, 1976; Festinger, Pepitone, & Newcomb, 1952; Johnson & Downing, 1979; Zimbardo, 1970). When individuals are in a deindividualized state, they often display behaviors they would normally not exhibit. According to Simons and Taylor, high team identification, strong group solidarity, and feelings of deindividuation result in the dehumanization of the opposition. Fans and players representing the opposing team are viewed as less than human and, as a result, deserve to be treated in a negative fashion.

At this stage in the process, several on-field and off-field contributing factors come into play. These factors are not necessary for spectator aggression. Rather, Simons and Taylor (1992) believe that the presence of these factors simply enhances the likelihood that spectators will act violently. Concerning off-field factors, Simons and Taylor state that alcohol consumption, a dense crowd, frustration from a team's performance, and modeling the aggressive behaviors of other spectators can all enhance the likelihood of spectator aggression. Regarding on-field factors, the authors list the type of sport (i.e., aggressive versus nonaggressive), modeling the behavior of players, and the current score as potential facilitators of aggression.

At this point in the model, the importance of leadership is introduced. Simons and Taylor (1992) argue that the key component in their model is the emergence of a leader. Indeed, these authors state that "it is presently proposed that the appearance of a leader is the most critical factor in whether fan violence will occur" (p. 218). According to these authors, during the preliminary stages of the model, one simply has the potential for spectator aggression. This potential becomes a reality with the emergence of a leader. Further, these authors suggest that leaders do not simply develop in a random fashion. Rather, they believe that certain individuals attend athletic contests hoping to instigate aggressive incidents.

The Self-Esteem Regulation Model of Spectator Aggression. During a 1993 tennis match in Germany, professional tennis player Monica Seles was brutally attacked by a spectator, Gunter Parche (Smith, 1993). Parche's goal was to injure Seles to the point at which she could no longer play. His favorite player, Steffi Graf, could then regain the world number one ranking. Follow-up interviews with Parche revealed that he was a highly identified Graf fan who "could not bear" that Seles, rather than Graf, was ranked number one (Jenkins, 1993, p. 18).

Individual acts of spectator aggression such as this do not fit into Simons and Taylor's framework because these situations do not involve a leader. To provide a model accounting for this and similar forms of spectator violence, I recently authored a paper describing a different perspective of spectator aggression (Wann, 1993). This perspective, termed the **self-esteem regulation model of spectator aggression,** reflects the belief that spectator aggression is often the function of a highly identified fan's attempt to regain self-esteem.

The self-esteem regulation theory is based on a fan's desire to maintain a positive level of self-esteem. According to this model, individuals employ three self-esteem regulation strategies in order to maintain their self-esteem. The first strategy is **basking in reflected glory** (BIRGing). BIRGing involves increasing one's association with a successful group or individual to enhance self-esteem. The BIRGing phenomenon was first identified in a pair of studies conducted by Cialdini and his associates in 1976. In the first study, experimenters recorded the proportion of college students wearing apparel identifying their university. As predicted by BIRGing, the proportion of students wearing university-identifying apparel increased following a win by the university's football team. In a second study, Cialdini and his colleagues telephoned subjects and asked them to describe a recent contest involving their university's football team. Consistent with the BIRGing phenomenon, subjects were more likely to use the pronoun "we" to describe a recent win while using "non-we" responses to describe a defeat (e.g., "they"). A number of additional studies have replicated Cialdini's work on BIRGing (e.g., Burger, 1985; Cialdini & De Nicholas, 1989; Kimble & Cooper, 1992; Sloan, 1989).

Cutting off reflected failure (CORFing) is a second self-esteem regulation strategy. First identified by Snyder, Lassegard, and Ford (1986), CORFing involves decreasing one's association with an unsuccessful group or individual to protect self-esteem. Snyder and his colleagues were able to demonstrate the CORFing phenomenon empirically. These authors asked subjects to complete a cognitive task and then presented the subjects with bogus feedback about their performances. Subjects received positive, negative, or no feedback. After receiving the feedback, subjects were given the opportunity to take and wear badges identifying their group. In support of the CORFing phenomenon, subjects were reluctant to take and wear the team badges after receiving negative feedback because they attempted to distance themselves from the unsuccessful group. In support of the BIRGing phenomenon, subjects were more than willing to take and wear the badges following positive feedback.

The third strategy is called *blasting.* This tactic involves derogating an individual or group to restore lost self-esteem. By acting in a derogatory fashion toward outgroup members, persons may acquire the perception that they are better than the outgroup, thereby increasing their self-esteem (Greenberg & Pyszczynski, 1985; Oakes & Turner, 1980; Pelham, 1993; Wills, 1981). To demonstrate the blasting strategy, Cialdini and Richardson (1980) asked university students to complete a bogus creativity test. After the task, subjects were given either negative feedback (i.e., they were described as low in creativity) or no feedback. Subjects were then asked to rate a rival university. Consistent with the notion of blasting, subjects gave more negative evaluations of the rival school after suffering damage to their self-esteem.

With this understanding of BIRGing, CORFing, and blasting, we can now examine the self-esteem regulation model of spectator aggression. The model is diagramed in Figure 16.4. As depicted in the figure, separate processes are expected of spectators high and low in team identification. With respect to BIRGing, all spectators should attempt to use this strategy to enhance their self-esteem. That is, even persons who are only minimally identified with the team will increase their association when the team is performing well. These persons are often said to be "jumping on the band-wagon." However, the spectator must be at least minimally identified with a team to bask in the team's success. It is unreasonable to expect persons to bask in the success of a team that is completely unimportant to them or is perceived as a rival team (for example, citizens of the United States would not be expected to bask in the victory of Olympic teams from other countries).

Although both high and low identified fans BIRG, research has indicated that CORFing is a strategy used only by fans low in team identification (Sloan, 1979; Wann & Branscombe, 1990a; Wann, Hamlet, Wilson, & Hodges, 1995; Wenner & Gantz, 1989). Fans who are highly identified with a team tend to maintain their allegiance even when the team performs poorly. These fans are unable to distance themselves

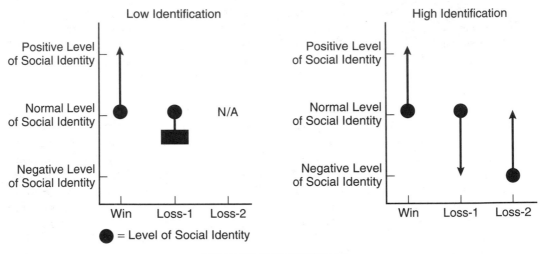

COMPETITION OUTCOME

Note: Loss-1 indicates the initial reaction to the loss.
Loss-2 represents the subsequent reaction to the loss.

FIGURE 16.4   The proposed pattern of use of the social identity maintenance tactics as a function of degree of identification with the team and competition outcome. (From: Wann, D. L. (1993). Aggression among highly identified spectators as a function of their need to maintain positive social identity. *Journal of Sport & Social Issues,* 17: 134–143. Reprinted by permission of Sage Publications, Inc.)

from their team because the role of team follower is too central to their identity to be discarded. The relationship between identification level and CORFing tendencies is shown in Figure 16.4 (see Loss-1). Fans low in identification with the team will use the CORFing strategy to protect their self-esteem. However, highly identified fans do not employ this strategy and, as a result, their self-esteem is lowered.

Because highly identified fans are unable to protect their self-esteem through CORFing, they must employ a strategy designed to restore their lost self-esteem. This strategy is blasting (see Figure 16.4, Loss-2). Highly identified fans may resort to verbal and physical aggression to regain their lost self-esteem. The aggression can be directed at a number of individuals including players, officials, and fans of the rival team. Branscombe and I demonstrated this process in an experiment using the movie Rocky IV (Branscombe & Wann, 1994b). We had subjects high and low in identification with America watch the final boxing scene from the movie. Although Rocky, an American boxer, won the fight in the real version, subjects in our study watched an edited version in which Rocky loses to Ivan Drago, a Russian boxer. Because none of the subjects had previously seen the movie, this alteration did not arouse their suspicions. After subjects had finished watching the fight scene, they completed a questionnaire packet containing the first half of a self-esteem measure, a derogation measure, and the second half of the self-esteem measure. The results were consistent with the self-esteem regulation model of spectator aggression. First, because the highly identified subjects refused to CORF, they displayed a reduction in self-esteem after watching Rocky lose. Subjects low in identification did not exhibit a reduction in self-esteem because of their ability to CORF. Second, subjects with the greatest damage to their self-esteem (i.e., the high identification subjects) were particularly likely to derogate relevant (i.e., Russians) and irrelevant outgroups (e.g., Mexicans, Canadians, Chinese). That is, when the self-esteem of the highly identified respondents was reduced because of Rocky's failure, they attempted to restore their lost self-esteem by blasting outgroup persons. However, derogation was only successful when the target was the relevant outgroup. When subjects derogated Russians, their self-esteem returned to normal. Self-esteem restoration was not found for attempts to derogate irrelevant outgroups.

At the beginning of this section, I described an example of spectator aggression involving Gunter Parche and tennis player Monica Seles. To understand the components of the self-esteem regulation model better, let us examine this incident in further detail. First, it is obvious that Parche was highly identified with his favorite tennis player, Steffi Graf. As a result, he was unable to CORF when she lost her number one ranking, resulting in a reduction in his self-esteem. Although he may have tried to restore his lost self-esteem by derogating members of irrelevant outgroups (such as court officials and those in charge of the rankings), these strategies would have been unsuccessful. Therefore, he attempted the ultimate form of derogation on the relevant outgroup—he violently attacked Seles. It is interesting and unfortunate to note that Parche's attempt was successful as Graf dominated tennis until Seles returned 2 years later.

Suggestions for Reducing Spectator Aggression

I would like to conclude our examination of spectator aggression by offering several suggestions for reducing these behaviors. These suggestions are derived from the thoughts of LeUnes and Nation (1989), Cratty (1989), and Coalter (1985), as well as suggestions derived from my own work on spectator violence (Branscombe & Wann, 1992a; Wann, 1993).

1. Limit the sale of alcoholic beverages, especially late in the contest. A number of studies indicate that alcohol can increase spectator aggression (Cavanaugh & Silva, 1980; Gilbert & Twyman, 1984; Lewis, 1982).
2. Because crowding can lead to aggression (Baron & Richardson, 1994), stadiums should not be filled beyond capacity.
3. Media should not accentuate the hate and animosity between competitors because these types of portrayals can lead to hostility between fans of the rival teams. Also, media should not focus unnecessarily on the violence of an event because glorification of sport violence may incite spectator violence. In fact, research indicates that even the descriptions of commentators can influence spectators' perceptions of the violence in a sporting event (Sullivan, 1991).
4. Stadium security should deal swiftly and firmly with acts of spectator violence, removing those involved.
5. Monitor the behaviors of players and managers, thus reducing the likelihood that spectators will model their aggression.
6. For reasons similar to those noted in Number 5, monitor the behaviors of cheerleaders.
7. Hire qualified officials, thereby reducing unjust calls (recall from Chapter 12 that unjust calls can lead to aggression, see Mark et al., 1983). This will make spectators less likely to become frustrated by the officiating.

8. Promote the idea that a team's effort is more important than a game's outcome. In this way, fans will be less frustrated by a team's defeat.

9. Do not arouse spectators to unnecessary and dangerous levels. Recall from Chapter 12 that high levels of arousal can facilitate aggression. Factors such as heat, noise, crowded stadiums, and standing room only seating can increase spectators' arousal (Baron & Richardson, 1994; Branscombe & Wann, 1992a; Dewar, 1980; Russell, 1993a). High levels of team identification can also lead to increased arousal (Branscombe & Wann, 1992b). Arousal from any of these sources can facilitate the aggression of sport spectators.

10. If possible, seat supporters of the opposing teams (particularly highly identified fans) in different sections of the arena.

11. A final suggestion derived from my self-esteem regulation theory would be to reduce the fans' team identification. However, this suggestion seems unreasonable, at least for professional and college teams, the existence of which is based in part on highly identified fans. However, this suggestion may be reasonable for spectators watching youth sports.

SUMMARY

Studies have shown that fans experience positive emotions when their team wins and negative emotions when their team loses. These emotional reactions, which are particularly intense for highly identified spectators, can even alter the fans' outlook on life. The emotional responses of spectators are not limited to situations involving their team's performance. Rather, spectators can also experience an emotional reaction when reading about their team in the sports page and/or in response to the closing of their team's home stadium.

Spectator aggression can be examined from the classic approaches to aggression: instinctual theories, the frustration-aggression hypothesis, and social learning theory. Supporters of the instinctual viewpoints argue that spectator aggression reflects an innate predisposition to behave aggressively. According to these theorists, one's aggressive urges can be cathartically discharged by viewing violent sporting events. However, research has refuted the notion of symbolic catharsis. Supporters of the frustration-aggression hypothesis predict that the fans of the losing team will be more aggressive than fans of the winning team. Research testing this perspective has been equivocal. However, research has found that aggressive cues can enhance the likelihood of spectator aggression. Finally, the social learning perspective reflects the belief that viewing violent sports will increase an individual's aggression. A number of studies have supported this viewpoint.

Typologies can be useful in classifying the various forms of spectator aggression. Eitzen's typology includes three categories of spectator violence: rowdyism, sports riots, and exuberant celebrations. Mann's FORCE typology includes five categories of spectator riots: frustration, outlawry, remonstrance, confrontation, and expressive.

The psychosocial model of spectator aggression argues that spectator violence is often a function of a number of sequentially related social psychological factors. These factors include potentiating factors such as socioeconomic status and political unrest, team identification, group solidarity, deindividuation, dehumanization of the opposition, off-field and on-field contributing factors, and leadership. Supporters of this model argue that the emergence of a leader is the key factor triggering spectator aggression.

The self-esteem regulation model of spectator aggression reflects the belief that spectator violence is often a function of an individual's need to maintain a positive social identity. This theory incorporates three self-esteem regulation strategies: basking in reflected glory (BIRGing), cutting off reflected failure (CORFing), and blasting. Although most fans will BIRG when their team succeeds, only those low in identification will CORF when their team fails. Highly identified people do not employ this self-esteem protection strategy. As a result, the self-esteem of highly identified fans is lowered. In an attempt to restore their lost self-esteem, these fans may resort to blasting and even assaulting outgroup persons (e.g., officials, fans of the other team).

GLOSSARY

Basking in Reflected Glory   A self-esteem regulation strategy that involves increasing one's association with a successful group or individual to enhance self-esteem.

Blasting   A self-esteem regulation strategy that involves derogating an individual or group to restore lost self-esteem.

Confrontation   From Mann's typology, spectator aggression involving two groups of individuals with a history of bad relations.

Cutting Off Reflected Failure   A self-esteem regulation strategy that involves decreasing one's association with an unsuccessful group or individual to protect self-esteem.

Deindividuation   A mental state characterized by membership in a group, feelings of anonymity, and a loss of self-awareness.

Disposition Theory of Sport Spectatorship   The belief that a spectator's emotional reaction to a team is largely a function of his or her alliance with the team.

Expressive   From Mann's typology, spectator aggression that is the direct result of sport outcomes.

Exuberant Celebrations   From Eitzen's typology, celebrations that have resulted in violence and vandalism.

FORCE Typology   A classification of spectator aggression that includes five forms of spectator riots: frustration, outlawry, remonstrance, confrontation, and expressive.

Frustration   From Mann's typology, spectator aggression stemming from deprivation or perceived injustice.

Outlawry   From Mann's typology, spectator aggression involving attacks on authority, the destruction of property, or the intimidation of rivals.

Psychosocial Model of Spectator Aggression   A model of spectator aggression reflecting the belief that a number of social and psychological factors play a role in spectator aggression, including the key factor, the emergence of a leader.

Remonstrance   From Mann's typology, spectator aggression based on political protests.

Rowdyism   From Eitzen's typology, interpersonal and property damage associated with sporting events that occurs regardless of the outcome.

Self-Esteem Regulation Model of Spectator Aggression   A model of spectator violence reflecting the belief that spectator aggression is often the function of a highly identified fan's attempt to regain self-esteem.

Sport Riots   From Eitzen's typology, spectator aggression resulting from events occurring on the playing field.

APPLICATION AND REVIEW QUESTIONS

1. What are spectators' typical emotional responses to their team in competition? How does team identification play a role in the responses?
2. It was noted that sport fans and spectators exhibit strong emotional reactions to their team in situations that are unrelated to the team's performance. Specifically, we examined reactions to reading the sports page and to the closing of a stadium. From your own experiences in sport, can you identify other non-competitive situations leading to emotional reactions?
3. Describe spectator aggression from each of the following perspectives: instinctual, frustration-aggression, and social learning. Develop an example of spectator aggression and apply each model to the example. Which theory do you feel is most accurate in accounting for spectator aggression?
4. What is symbolic catharsis? Does research support catharsis?
5. Describe the components of Mann's typology, giving an example of each.
6. Describe the psychosocial model of fan violence. Develop an example of spectator aggression and apply the model to the example.
7. Describe the self-esteem regulation model of fan violence. Develop an example of spectator aggression and apply the model to the example.

SUGGESTED READINGS

MANN, L. (1989). Sports crowds and the collective behavior perspective. In J. H. Goldstein (Ed.), *Sports, games, and play: Social and psychological viewpoints* (pp. 299–331). Hillsdale, NJ: Erlbaum. This chapter examines spectator violence from a sociological perspective.

RUSSELL, G. W. (1993a). *The social psychology of sport* (ch. 9). New York: Springer–Verlag. This chapter provides an in-depth examination of catharsis in sport.

SIMONS, Y., & TAYLOR, J. (1992). A psychosocial model of fan violence in sports. *International Journal of Sport Psychology, 23,* 207–226. This article describes the psychosocial model of spectator aggression.

WANN, D. L. (1993). Aggression among highly identified spectators as a function of their need to maintain positive social identity. *Journal of Sport and Social Issues, 17,* 134–143. This article describes the self-esteem regulation model of spectator aggression.

REFERENCES

ABERNETHY, B. (1993). Attention. In R. N. Singer, M. Murphey, & L. K. Tennant (Eds.), *Handbook of research on sport psychology* (pp. 127–170). New York: Macmillan.

ACHTERBERG, J., MATTHEWS-SIMONTON, S., & SIMONTON, O. C. (1977). Psychology of the exceptional cancer patient: A description of patients who outlive predicted life expectancies. *Psychotherapy: Theory, Research, and Practice, 14,* 416–422.

ACOSTA, R. V. (1993). The minority experience in sport: Monochromatic or technicolor. In G. L. Cohen (Ed.), *Women in sports: Issues and controversies* (pp. 204–213). New York: Sage.

ACOSTA, R. V., & CARPENTER, L. J. (1992). *Women in intercollegiate sport: A longitudinal study— fifteen-year update 1977–1992.* Unpublished manuscript, Brooklyn College, Brooklyn, New York.

ADAMS, J. A. (1971). A closed-loop theory of motor learning. *Journal of Motor Behavior, 3,* 111–149.

ADAMS, J. S. (1963). Toward an understanding of inequity. *Journal of Abnormal and Social Psychology, 67,* 422–436.

AGNEW, G. A., & CARRON, A. V. (1994). Crowd effects and the home advantage. *International Journal of Sport Psychology, 25,* 53–62.

ALBRECHT, R. R., & EWING, S. J. (1989). Standardization of the administration of the Profile of Moods States: Development of alternative word lists. *Journal of Personality Assessment, 53,* 31–39.

ALBRECHT, R. R., & FELTZ, D. L. (1987). Generality and specificity of attention related to competitive anxiety and sport performance. *Journal of Sport Psychology, 9,* 231–248.

ALDERMAN, R. B. (1978). Strategies for motivating young athletes. In W. Straub (Ed.), *Sport psychology: An analysis of athlete behavior* (1st ed., pp. 49–61). Ithaca NY: Mouvement Publications.

ALDERMAN, R. B. (1980). Sports psychology: Past, present, and future dilemmas. In P. Klavora (Ed.), *Psychological and sociological factors in sport* (pp. 3–19). Toronto: University of Toronto Press.

ALDERMAN, R. B., & WOOD, N. L. (1976). An analysis of incentive motivation in young Canadian athletes. *Canadian Journal of Applied Sport Sciences, 1,* 169–175.

ALLEN, K. (1994, January 12). The officials' words: We're trying. *USA Today,* p. 5C.

ALLEN, M. P., PANIAN, S. K., & LOTZ, R. E. (1979). Managerial succession and organizational performance: A recalcitrant problem revisited. *Administrative Science Quarterly, 24,* 167–180.

ALLISON, M. G., & AYLLON, T. (1980). Behavioral coaching in the development of skills in football, gymnastics, and tennis. *Journal of Applied Behavioral Analysis, 13,* 297–314.

ALLPORT, F. H. (1924). *Social psychology.* Cambridge, MA: Riverside Press.

AMERICAN PSYCHOLOGICAL ASSOCIATION. (1974). *Standards for educational and psychological tests.* Washington, DC: American Psychological Association.

AMERICAN PSYCHOLOGICAL ASSOCIATION. (1979). *Ethical standards for psychologists.* Washington, DC: American Psychological Association.

AMES, C. (1992). Achievement goals, motivational climate, and motivational processes. In G. C. Roberts (Ed.), *Motivation in sport and exercise* (pp. 161–176). Champaign, IL: Human Kinetics.

ANASTASI, A. (1988). *Psychological testing* (6th ed.). New York: Macmillan.

ANDERSEN, M. B., DENSON, E. L., BREWER, B. W., & VAN RAALTE, J. L. (1994). Disorders of personality and mood in athletes: Recognition and referral. *Journal of Applied Sport Psychology, 6,* 168–184.

ANDERSEN, M. B., & WILLIAMS, J. M. (1988). A model of stress and athletic injury: Prediction and prevention. *Journal of Sport & Exercise Psychology, 10,* 294–306.

ANDERSON, C. A. (1989). Temperature and aggression: Ubiquitous effects of heat on occurrence of human violence. *Psychological Bulletin, 106,* 74–96.

ANDERSON, D., & STONE, G. P. (1981). Responses of male and female metropolitans to the commercialization of professional sport 1960 to 1975. *International Review of Sport Sociology, 16*(3), 5–20.

ANDERSON, D. C., CROWELL, C. R., DOMAN, M., & HOWARD, G. S. (1988). Performance posting, goal setting, and activity-contingent praise as applied to a university hockey team. *Journal of Applied Psychology, 73,* 87–95.

ANDERSON, K. (1994a, March 7). Tip-ins. *Sports Illustrated,* p. 87.

ANDERSON, K. (1994b, January 31). Coach gets cut by players. *Sports Illustrated,* p. 83.

ANDERSON, K. J. (1990). Arousal and the inverted-U hypothesis: A critique of Neiss's "reconceptualizing arousal." *Psychological Bulletin, 107,* 96–100.

ANDRE, J. C., & MEANS, J. R. (1986). Rate of imagery in mental practice: An experimental investigation. *Journal of Sport Psychology, 8,* 124–128.

ANDRE, T., & HOLLAND, A. (1995). Relationship of sport participation to sex role orientation and attitudes toward women among high school males and females. *Journal of Sport Behavior, 18,* 241–253.

ANSHEL, M. H. (1987). Psychological inventories used in sport psychology research. *The Sport Psychologist, 1,* 331–349.

ANSHEL, M. H. (1990). Toward validation of a model for coping with acute stress in sport. *International Journal of Sport Psychology, 21,* 58–83.

ANSHEL, M. H. (1994). *Sport psychology: From theory to practice* (2nd ed.). Scottsdale, AZ: Gorsuch Scarisbrick.

ANSHEL, M. H. (1995). Examining social loafing among elite female rowers as a function of task duration and mood. *Journal of Sport Behavior, 18,* 39–49.

ANSHEL, M. H., FREEDSON, P., HAMILL, J., HAYWOOD, K., HORVAT, M., & PLOWMAN, S. A. (1991). *Dictionary of the sport and exercise sciences.* Champaign, IL: Human Kinetics.

ANSHEL, M. H., GREGORY, W. L., & KACZMAREK, M. (1990). The effectiveness of a stress training program in coping with criticism in sport: A test of the COPE model. *Journal of Sport Behavior, 13,* 194–217.

ANSHEL, M. H., & WEINBERG, R. S. (1995). Sources of acute stress in American and Australian basketball referees. *Journal of Applied Sport Psychology, 7,* 11–22.

ANTONEN, M. (1991, May 23). Royals could use a new start. *USA Today,* p. 3C.

ANTONEN, M. (1994, July 1). Ending the curse. *USA Today,* p. 3C.

ARKES, H. R., & GARSKE, J. P. (1982). *Psychological theories of motivation* (2nd ed.). Monterey, CA: Brooks/Cole.

ARMS, R. A., RUSSELL, G. W., & SANDILANDS, M. L. (1979). Effects on the hostility of spectators of viewing aggressive sports. *Social Psychology Quarterly, 42,* 275–279.

ARNOLD, G. E., & STRAUB, W. F. (1973). Personality and group cohesiveness as determinants of success among interoscholastic basketball teams. In I. D. Williams & L. M. Wankel (Eds.), *Proceedings of the Fourth Canadian Psycho-Motor Learning and Sport Psychology Symposium* (pp. 346–352). Ottawa, Canada: Fitness and Amateur Sport Directorate.

ARONSON, E., BREWER, M., & CARLSMITH, J. M. (1985). Experimentation in social psychology. In G. Lindzey & E. Aronson (Eds.), *Handbook of social psychology* (Vol. 1, pp. 441–486). Hillsdale, NJ: Erlbaum.

ARONSON, E., ELLSWORTH, P. C., CARLSMITH, J. M., & GONZALES, M. T. (1990). *Methods of research in social psychology* (2nd ed.). New York: McGraw-Hill.

ARONSON, E., & MILLS, J. (1959). The effects of severity of initiation on liking for a group. *Journal of Abnormal and Social Psychology, 59,* 177–181.

ASKEN, M. J. (1991). The challenge of the physically challenged: Delivering sport psychology services to physically disabled athletes. *The Sport Psychologist, 5,* 370–381.

ATKINSON, J. W. (1964). *An introduction to motivation.* New York: Van Nostrand.

ATKINSON, R. C., & SHIFFRIN, R. M. (1968). Human memory: A proposed system and its control processes. In W. K. Spence & J. T. Spence (Eds.), *The psychology of learning and motivation: Ad-*

vances in research and theory (Vol. 1, pp. 89–195). New York: Academic Press.

ATYEO, D. (1979). *Blood & Guts: Violence in sports.* New York: Paddington Press.

AVENI, A. F. (1977). The not-so-lonely crowd: Friendship groups in collective behavior. *Sociometry, 40,* 96–99.

AZRIN, N. H., & HOLZ, W. C. (1966). Punishment. In W. K. Honig (Ed.), *Operant behavior: Areas of research and application* (pp. 380–447). Englewood Cliffs, NJ: Prentice Hall.

BAADE, R. A., & TIEHEN, L. J. (1990). An analysis of Major League baseball attendance, 1969–1987. *Journal of Sport & Social Issues, 14,* 14–32.

BAILEY, C. I., & SAGE, G. H. (1988). Values communicated by a sports event: The case of the Super Bowl. *Journal of Sport Behavior, 11,* 126–143.

BAKKER, F. C., DE KONING, J. J., SCHENAU, G. J. V. I., & DE GROOT, G. (1993). Motivation of young elite speed skaters. *International Journal of Sport Psychology, 24,* 432–442.

BAKKER, F. C., & KAYSER, C. S. (1994). Effect of a self-help mental training programme. *International Journal of Sport Psychology, 25,* 158–175.

BAILLIE, P. H. F. (1993). Understanding retirement from sports: Therapeutic ideas for helping athletes in transition, *The Counseling Psychologist, 21,* 399–410.

BALAZS, E. V. (1975). Psycho-social study of outstanding female athletes. *Research Quarterly, 46,* 267–273.

BANDURA, A. (1969). *Principles of behavior modification.* New York: Holt, Rinehart, & Winston.

BANDURA, A. (1973). *Aggression: A social learning analysis.* Englewood Cliffs, NJ: Prentice-Hall.

BANDURA, A. (1977a). Self-efficacy: Toward a unifying theory of behavioral change. *Psychological Review, 84,* 191–215.

BANDURA, A. (1977b). *Social learning theory.* Englewood Cliffs, NJ: Prentice-Hall.

BANDURA, A. (1983). Psychological mechanisms of aggression. In R. E. Geen & E. I. Donnerstein (Eds.), *Aggression: Theoretical and empirical reviews* (Vol. 1, pp. 1–40). New York: Academic Press.

BANDURA, A. (1986). *Social foundations of thought and action: A social cognitive theory.* Englewood Cliffs, NJ: Prentice-Hall.

BANDURA, A., & HUSTON, A. C. (1961). Identification as a process of incidental learning. *Journal of Abnormal and Social Psychology, 63,* 311–318.

BAR-ELI, M., LEVY-KOLKER, N., TENENBAUM, G., & WEINBERG, R. S. (1993). Effect of goal difficulty on performance of aerobic, anaerobic and power tasks in laboratory and field settings. *Journal of Sport Behavior, 16,* 17–32.

BARON, R. A. (1970). Attraction toward the model and model's competence as determinants of adult imitative behavior. *Journal of Personality and Social Psychology, 14,* 345–351.

BARON, R. A., & BELL, P. A. (1975). Aggression and heat: Mediating effects of prior provocation and exposure to an aggressive model. *Journal of Personality and Social Psychology, 31,* 825–832.

BARON, R. A., & BELL, P. A. (1976). Aggression and heat: The influence of ambient temperature, negative affect, and a cooling drink on psychical aggression. *Journal of Personality and Social Psychology, 33,* 245–255.

BARON, R. A., & BYRNE, D. (1994). *Social psychology: Understanding human interaction* (7th ed.). Boston: Allyn and Bacon.

BARON, R. A., & GREENBERG, J. (1990). *Behavior in organizations: Understanding and managing the human side of work* (3rd ed.). Needham Heights, MA: Allyn and Bacon.

BARON, R. A., & RANSBERGER, V. M. (1978). Ambient temperature and the occurrence of collective violence: The "long, hot summer" revisited. *Journal of Personality and Social Psychology, 36,* 351–360.

BARON, R. A., & RICHARDSON, D. R. (1994). *Human aggression* (2nd ed.). New York: Plenum Press.

BARON, R. S. (1986). Distraction-conflict theory: Progress and problems. In L. Berkowitz (Ed.), *Advances in experimental social psychology* (Vol. 19, pp. 1–40). New York: Harcourt Brace Jovanovich.

BARR, K., & HALL, C. (1992). The use of imagery by rowers. *International Journal of Sport Psychology, 23,* 243–261.

BAUMEISTER, R. F. (1995). Disputing the effects of championship pressures and home audiences. *Journal of Personality and Social Psychology, 68,* 644–648.

BAUMEISTER, R. F., & STEINHILBER, A. (1984). Paradoxical effects of supportive audiences on performance under pressure: The home field disadvantage in sports championships. *Journal of Personality and Social Psychology, 47,* 85–93.

BEATON, R. (1995, May 5). Remains to be seen. *USA Today,* p. 5C.

BECKER, D. (1994, January 25). Coaches' pay sees gender gap. *USA Today,* p. 1C.

BECKER, J. (1975). Superstition in sport. *International Journal of Sport Psychology, 6,* 148–152.

BEISSER, A., (1967). *The madness in sports: Psychosocial observations on sports.* New York: Appleton-Century-Crofts.

BELL, J. (1994, January 3). Ryan adds punch to Oilers'. *USA Today,* p. 4C.

BEM, S. L. (1974). The measurement of psychological androgyny. *Journal of Consulting and Clinical Psychology, 42,* 155–162.

BENJAFIELD, J., LIDDELL, W. W., & BENJAFIELD, I. (1989). Is their a home field disadvantage in professional sports championships? *Social Behavior and Personality, 17,* 45–50.

BENNETT, J. C. (1991). The irrationality of the catharsis theory of aggression as justification for educators' support of interscholastic football. *Perceptual and Motor Skills, 72,* 415–418.

BENSON, H. (1975). *The relaxation response.* New York: William Morrow.

BERGLAS, S., & JONES, E. E. (1978). Drug choice as a self-handicapping strategy in response to noncontingent success. *Journal of Personality and Social Psychology, 36,* 405–417.

BERKOWITZ, L. (1964). Aggressive cues in aggressive behavior and hostility catharsis. *Psychological Review, 71,* 104–122.

BERKOWITZ, L. (1969a). Simple views of aggression: An essay review. *American Scientist, 57,* 372–383.

BERKOWITZ, L. (1969b). The frustration-aggression hypothesis revisited. In L. Berkowitz (Ed.), *Roots of aggression* (pp. 1–28). New York: Atherton.

BERKOWITZ, L. (1974). Some determinants of impulsive aggression: Role of mediated associations with reinforcements for aggression. *Psychological Review, 81,* 165–176.

BERKOWITZ, L. (1981). The concept of aggression. In P. F. Brain & D. Benton (Eds.), *Multidisciplinary approaches to aggression research* (pp. 3–15). New York: Elsevier/North Holland Biomedical Press.

BERKOWITZ, L. (1983). The experience of anger as a parallel process in the display of impulsive, "angry" aggression. In R. E. Geen & E. I. Donnerstein (Eds.), *Aggression: Theoretical and empirical reviews* (Vol. 1, pp. 103–133). New York: Academic Press.

BERKOWITZ, L. (1988). Frustrations, appraisals, and aversively stimulated aggression. *Aggressive Behavior, 14,* 3–11.

BERKOWITZ, L. (1989). Frustration-aggression hypothesis: Examination and reformulation. *Psychological Bulletin, 106,* 59–73.

BERKOWITZ, L. (1993). *Aggression: Its causes, consequences, and control.* New York: McGraw-Hill.

BERNARD, L. C., & KRUPAT, E. (1994). *Health psychology: Biopsychosocial factors in health and illness.* New York: Harcourt Brace Jovanovich.

BERNARD, L. L. (1924). *Instinct: A study in social psychology.* New York: Holt.

BERNSTEIN, D. A., & BORKOVEC, T. D. (1973). *Progressive relaxation training: A manual for the helping professional.* Champaign, IL: Research Press.

BEST, J. B. (1992). *Cognitive psychology* (3rd ed.). New York: West.

BETANCOURT, H., & BLAIR, I. (1992). A cognitive (attribution)-emotion model of violence in conflict situations. *Personality and Social Psychology Bulletin, 18,* 343–350.

BIAGGIO, M. K. (1987). A survey of psychologists' perspective on catharsis. *The Journal of Psychology, 121,* 243–248.

BIDDLE, S. J. (1993). Attribution research and sport psychology. In R. N. Singer, M. Murphey, & L. K. Tennant (Eds.), *Handbook of research on sport psychology* (pp. 437–464). New York: Macmillan.

BIRD, A. M., & BRAME, J. M. (1978). Self versus team attributions: A test of the "I'm OK, but the team's so-so" phenomenon. *Research Quarterly, 49,* 260–268.

BIRD, A. M., & HORN, M. A. (1990). Cognitive anxiety and mental errors in sport. *Journal of Sport & Exercise Psychology, 12,* 217–222.

BIRD, A. M., & WILLIAMS, J. M. (1980). A developmental-attributional analysis of sex role stereotypes for sport performance. *Developmental Psychology, 16,* 319–322.

BIRRELL, S. (1987). The woman athlete's college experience: Knowns and unknowns. *Journal of Sport & Social Issues, 11,* 82–96.

BIVENS, S., & LEONARD, W. M. II (1994). Race, centrality, and educational attainment: An NFL perspective. *Journal of Sport Behavior, 17,* 24–42.

BLACK, S. J., & WEISS, M. R. (1992). The relationship among perceived coaching behaviors, perceptions of ability, and motivation in competitive age-group swimmers. *Journal of Sport & Exercise Psychology, 14,* 309–325.

BLAIS, M. R., & VALLERAND, R. J. (1986). Multimodal effects of electromyographic biofeedback: Looking at children's ability to control precompetitive anxiety. *Journal of Sport Psychology, 8,* 283–303.

BLINDE, E. M., GREENDORFER, S. L., & SANKNER, R. J. (1991). Differential media coverage of men's and women's intercollegiate basketball: Reflection of gender ideology. *Journal of Sport & Social Issues, 15,* 98–114.

BLUCKER, J. A., & HERSHBERGER, E. (1983). Causal attribution theory and the female athlete: What conclusions can we draw? *Journal of Sport Psychology, 5,* 353–360.

BLUM, D. E. (1992, June 17). Big Ten chiefs vote for sex-equity plan and will push for cap in team sizes. *The Chronicle of Higher Education, 38,* A35.

BODLEY, H. (1993, October 25). Williams' life target of threats. *USA Today,* p. 1C.

BOND, C. F. (1982). Social facilitation: A self-presentational view. *Journal of Personality and Social Psychology, 42,* 1042–1050.

BOND, C. F., & TITUS, L. J. (1983). Social facilitation: A meta-analysis of 241 studies. *Psychological Bulletin, 94,* 265–292.

BORIS, H. I., & HIRT, E. R. (1994, May). *Audience reaction to self-handicapping.* Paper presented at the meeting of the Midwestern Psychological Association, Chicago.

BOUCHARD, C., & MALINA, R. M. (1983). Genetics of physiological fitness and motor performance. *Exercise and Sport Science Reviews, 11,* 306–339.

BOUCHARD, C., & MALINA, R. M. (1984). Genetics and Olympic athletes: A discussion of methods and issues. *Medicine and sport science, 18,* 28–38.

BOURNE, L. E., & ARCHER, E. J. (1956). Time continuously on target as a function of distribution of practice. *Journal of Experimental Psychology, 51,* 25–33.

BOUTCHER, S. H. (1992). Attention and athletic performance: An integrated approach. In T. S. Horn (Ed.), *Advances in sport psychology* (pp. 251–265). Champaign, IL: Human Kinetics.

BOUTCHER, S. H., & ROTELLA, R. J. (1987). A psychological skills educational program for closed-skill performance enhancement. *The Sport Psychologist, 1,* 127–137.

BOYD, M., & CALLAGHAN, J. (1994). Task and ego goal perspectives in organized youth sports. *International Journal of Sport Psychology, 22,* 411–424.

BRANSCOMBE, N. R., & WANN, D. L. (1991). The positive and self concept consequences of sports team identification. *Journal of Sport & Social Issues, 15,* 115–127.

BRANSCOMBE, N. R., & WANN, D. L. (1992a). Role of identification with a group, arousal, categorization processes, and self-esteem in sports spectator aggression. *Human Relations, 45,* 1013–1033.

BRANSCOMBE, N. R., & WANN, D. L. (1992b). Physiological arousal and reactions to outgroup members that implicate an important social identity. *Aggressive Behavior, 18,* 85–93.

BRANSCOMBE, N. R., & WANN, D. L. (1994a). Sport psychology. In *Magill's survey of social sciences: Psychology* (pp. 2363–2368). Pasadena, CA: Salem Press.

BRANSCOMBE, N. R., & WANN, D. L. (1994b). Collective self-esteem consequences of outgroup derogation when a valued social identity is on trial. *European Journal of Social Psychology, 24,* 641–657.

BRANSCOMBE, N. R., WANN, D. L., NOEL, J. G., & COLEMAN, J. (1993). In-group or out-group extremity: Importance of the threatened social identity. *Personality and Social Psychology Bulletin, 19,* 381–388.

BRAWLEY, L. R., CARRON, A. V., & WIDMEYER, W. N. (1987). Assessing the cohesion of teams: Validity of the Group Environment Questionnaire. *Journal of Sport & Exercise Psychology, 9,* 275–294.

BRAWLEY, L. R., & MARTIN, K. A. (1995). The interface between social and sport psychology. *The Sport Psychologist, 9,* 469–497.

BRAWLEY, L. R., & ROBERTS, G. C. (1984). Attributions in sport: Research foundations, characteristics, and limitations. In J. M. Silva & R. S. Weinburg (Eds.), *Psychologial foundations of sport* (pp. 197–213). Champaign, IL: Human Kinetics.

BRAY, S. R., & CARRON, A. V. (1993). The home advantage in alpine skiing. *The Australian Journal of Science and Medicine in Sport, 25*(4), 76–81.

BREDEMEIER, B. J. (1978). The assessment of reactive and instrumental athletic aggression. *Pro-*

ceedings of the International Symposium on Psychological Assessment in Sport (pp. 136–149). Netanya, Israel: Wingate Institute for Psychical Education and Sport.

BREDEMEIER, B. J. (1985). Moral reasoning and the perceived legitimacy of intentionally injurious sport acts. *Journal of Sport Psychology, 7,* 110–124.

BREDEMEIER, B. J. (1994). Children's moral reasoning and their assertive, aggressive, and submissive tendencies in sport and daily life. *Journal of Sport & Exercise Psychology, 16,* 1–14.

BREDEMEIER, B. J., & SHIELDS, D. L. (1986). Athletic aggression: An issue of contextual morality. *Sociology of Sport Journal, 3,* 15–28.

BREDEMEIER, B. J., WEISS, M. R., SHIELDS, D. L., & COOPER, B. A. B. (1986). The relationship of sport involvement with children's moral reasoning and aggression tendencies. *Journal of Sport & Exercise Psychology, 8,* 304–318.

BREHM, J. W., WRIGHT, R. A., SOLOMON, S., SILKA, L., & GREENBERG, J. (1983). Perceived difficulty, energization, and the magnitude of goal valence. *Journal of Experimental Social Psychology, 19,* 21–48.

BRETZ, R. D., & THOMAS, S. L. (1992). Perceived equity, motivation, and final-offer arbitration in major league baseball. *Journal of Applied Psychology, 77,* 280–287.

BREWER, B. W. (1993). Self-identity and specific vulnerability to depressed mood. *Journal of Personality, 61,* 343–364.

BREWER, B. W. (1994). Review and critique of models of psychological adjustment to athletic injury. *Journal of Applied Sport Psychology, 6,* 87–100.

BREWER, B. W., JEFFERS, K. E., PETITPAS, A. J., & VAN RAALTE, J. L. (1994). Perceptions of psychological interventions in the context of sport injury rehabilitation. *The Sport Psychologist, 8,* 176–188.

BREWER, B. W., LINDER, D. E., & PHELPS, C. M. (1995). Situational correlates of emotional adjustment to athletic injury. *Clinical Journal of Sport Medicine, 5,* 241–245.

BREWER, B. W., & PETRIE, T. A. (1995, Spring). A comparison between injured and uninjured football players on selected psychosocial variables. *The Academic Athletic Journal,* 11–18.

BREWER, B. W., VAN RAALTE, J. L., & LINDER, D. E. (1990). Effects of pain on motor performance. *Journal of Sport & Exercise Psychology, 12,* 353–365.

BREWER, B. W., VAN RAALTE, J. L., & LINDER, D. E. (1993). Athletic identity: Hercules' muscles or Achilles' heel? *International Journal of Sport Psychology, 24,* 237–254.

BRICKNER, M. A., HARKINS, S. G., & OSTROM, T. M. (1986). Effects of personal involvement: Thought-provoking implications for social loafing. *Journal of Personality and Social Psychology, 51,* 763–769.

BRILL, A. A. (1929). The why of the fan. *North American Review, 228,* 429–434.

BROADBENT, D. E. (1954). The role of auditory localization in attention and memory span. *Journal of Experimental Psychology, 47,* 191–196.

BROADBENT, D. E. (1957). A mechanical model for human attention and immediate memory. *Psychological Review, 64,* 205–215.

BROADBENT, D. E. (1971). *Decision and stress.* New York: Academic Press.

BROHM, J. M. (1978). *Sport—A Prison of measured time.* London: Ink Links.

BROOKS, D. D., & ALTHOUSE, R. C. (1993). Racial imbalance in coaching and managerial positions. In R. C. Althouse & D. D. Brooks (Eds.), *Racism in college athletics: The African-American athlete's experience* (pp. 101–142). Morgantown, WV: Fitness Information Technology.

BROUCEK, M. W., BARTHOLOMEW, J. B., LANDERS, D. M., & LINDER, D. E. (1993). The effects of relaxation with a warning cue on pain tolerance. *Journal of Sport Behavior, 16,* 239–250.

BROWN, B. (1992, December 12). We scream for blood, then criticize violence. *USA Today,* p. 10C.

BROWN, B., BRADY, E., PATRICK, D., & DISIMONE, B. (1993, July 15). Adios, Beantown. *USA Today,* p. 2C.

BROWN, J. (1958). Some tests of the decay theory of immediate memory. *Quarterly Journal of Experimental Psychology, 10,* 12–21.

BROWN, J. M. (1982). Are sport psychologists really psychologists? *Journal of Sport Psychology, 4,* 13–18.

BROWN, M. C. (1982). Administrative succession and organizational performance: The succession effect. *Administrative Science Quarterly, 27,* 1–16.

BRYAN, C., & HORTON, R. (1976). School athletics and fan aggression. *Educational Researcher, 5,* 2–11.

BRYANT, J., BROWN, D., COMISKY, P. W., & ZILLMANN, D. (1982). Sports and spectators: Commentary and appreciation. *Journal of Communication, 32,* 109–119.

BRYANT, J., COMISKY, P. W., & ZILLMANN, D. (1981). The appeal of rough-and-tumble play in televised professional football. *Communication Quarterly, 29,* 256–262.

BRYANT, J., ROCKWELL, S. C., & OWENS, J. W. (1994). "Buzzer beaters" and "barn burners": The effects on enjoyment of watching the game go "down to the wire." *Journal of Sport & Social Issues, 18,* 326–339.

BRYANT, J., & ZILLMANN, D. (1979). Effect of intensification of annoyance through unrelated residual excitation on substantially delayed hostile behavior. *Journal of Experimental Social Psychology, 15,* 470–480.

BRYANT, J., & ZILLMANN, D. (1983). Sports violence and the media. In J. H. Goldstein (Ed.), *Sports violence* (pp. 195–211). New York: Springer-Verlag.

BUHRMANN, H. G., & ZAUGG, M. K. (1981). Superstition among basketball players: An investigation of various forms of superstitious beliefs and behavior among competitive basketball at the junior high school to university level. *Journal of Sport Behavior, 4,* 163–174.

BULL, S. J. (1995). Reflections on a 5-year consultancy program with the England women's cricket team. *The Sport Psychologist, 9,* 148–163.

BUNKER, L., WILLIAMS, J. M., & ZINSSER, N. (1993). Cognitive techniques for improving performance and building confidence. In J. M. Williams (Ed.), *Applied sport psychology: Personal growth to peak performance* (2nd ed., pp. 225–242). Mountain View, CA: Mayfield.

BUONAMANO, R., CEI, A., & MUSSINO, A. (1995). Participation motivation in Italian youth sport. *The Sport Psychologist, 9,* 265–281.

BURGER, J. M. (1985). Temporal effects on attributions for academic performances and reflected-glory basking. *Social Psychology Quarterly, 48,* 330–336.

BURHANS, R. S. III, RICHMAN, C. L., & BERGEY, D. B. (1988). Mental imagery training: Effects on running speed performance. *International Journal of Sport Psychology, 19,* 26–37.

BURROUGHS, A., ASHBURN, L., & SEEBOHM, L. (1995). "Add sex and stir": Homophobic coverage of women's cricket in Australia. *Journal of Sport & Social Issues, 19,* 266–284.

BURTON, D. (1988). Do anxious swimmers swim slower? Reexamining the elusive anxiety-performance relationship. *Journal of Sport & Exercise Psychology, 10,* 45–61.

BURTON, D. (1990). Multimodal stress management in sport: Current status and future directions. In

J. E. Jones & L. Hardy (Eds.), *Stress and performance in sport* (pp. 171–201). New York: Wiley.

BURTON, D. (1992a). Why young wresters "hang up" their singlet: An exploratory investigation comparing two models of sport attrition. *Journal of Sport Behavior, 15,* 209–226.

BURTON, D. (1992b). The Jekyll/Hyde nature of goals: Reconceptualizing goal setting in sport. In T. S. Horn (Ed.), *Advances in sport psychology* (pp. 267–297). Champaign, IL: Human Kinetics.

BURTON, D. (1993). Goal setting in sport. In R. N. Singer, M. Murphey, & L. K. Tennant (Eds.), *Handbook of research on sport psychology* (pp. 467–491). New York: Macmillan.

BURTON, D., & MARTENS, R. (1986). Pinned by their own goals: An exploratory investigation into why kids drop out of wrestling. *Journal of Sport Psychology, 8,* 183–197.

BUSS, A. H. (1961). *The psychology of aggression.* New York: Wiley.

BUSS, A. H., & DURKEE, A. (1957). An inventory for assessing different kinds of hostility. *Journal of Consulting Psychology, 21,* 343–349.

BUTLER, R. J., & HARDY, L. (1992). The performance profile: Theory and application. *The Sport Psychologist, 6,* 253–264.

BUTLER, R. J., SMITH, M., & IRWIN, I. (1993). The performance profile in practice. *Journal of Applied Sport Psychology, 5,* 48–63.

BUTT, D. S., & COX, D. N. (1992). Motivational patterns in Davis Cup, university and recreational tennis players. *International Journal of Sport Psychology, 23,* 1–13.

BUZAS, H. P., & AYLLON, T. (1981). Differential reinforcement in coaching tennis skills. *Behavior Modification, 5,* 372–385.

CALLAHAN, G. (1995, August 14). Rebirth in the Bronx. *Sports Illustrated,* p. 44–48.

CAMPBELL, D. T., & STANLEY, J. C. (1963). *Experimental and quasi-experimental designs for research.* Boston: Houghton Mifflin.

CANTOR, J. R., ZILLMANN, D., & EINSIEDEL, E. F. (1978). Female responses to provocation after exposure to aggressive and erotic films. *Communication Research, 5,* 395–412.

CAPEL, S. A., SISLEY, B. L., & DESERTRAIN, G. S. (1987). The relationship of role conflict and role ambiguity to burnout in high school basketball coaches. *Journal of Sport Psychology, 9,* 106–117.

CARLSMITH, J. M., & ANDERSON, C. A. (1979). Ambient temperature and the occurrence of collective violence: A new analysis. *Journal of Personality and Social Psychology, 37,* 337–344.

CARLSON, C. R., & HOYLE, R. H. (1993). Efficacy of abbreviated progressive muscle relaxation training: A quantitative review of behavioral medicine research. *Journal of Consulting and Clinical Psychology, 61,* 1059–1067.

CARRON, A. V. (1975). Personality and athletics: A review. In B. Rushall (Ed.), *The status of psychomotor learning and sport psychology research* (pp. 5.1–5.12). Dartmouth, Nova Scotia: Sport Science.

CARRON, A. V. (1980). *Social psychology of sport.* Ithaca, New York: Mouvement.

CARRON, A. V. (1982). Cohesiveness in sport groups: Interpretations and considerations. *Journal of Sport Psychology, 4,* 123–138.

CARRON, A. V., & BALL, J. R. (1977). Cause-effect characteristics of cohesiveness and participation motivation in intercollegiate hockey. *International Review of Sport Sociology, 12,* 40-60.

CARRON, A. V., PRAPAVESSIS, H., & GROVE, J. R. (1994). Group effects and self-handicapping. *Journal of Sport & Exercise Psychology, 16,* 246–257.

CARRON, A. V., & SPINK, K. S. (1992). Internal consistency of the Group Environment Questionnaire modified for an exercise setting. *Perceptual and Motor Skills, 74,* 304–306.

CARRON, A. V., WIDMEYER, W. N., & BRAWLEY, L. R. (1985). The development of an instrument to assess cohesion in sport teams: The Group Environment Questionnaire. *Journal of Sport Psychology, 7,* 244–266.

CARRON, A. V., WIDMEYER, W. N., & BRAWLEY, L. R. (1988). Group cohesion in individual adherence to physical activity. *Journal of Sport & Exercise Psychology, 10,* 127–138.

CARTWRIGHT, D. (1968). The nature of group cohesiveness. In D. Cartwright & A. Zander (Eds.), *Group dynamics: Research and theory* (3rd. ed., pp. 91–109). New York: Harper & Row.

CARVER, C. S., DEGREGORIO, E., & GILLIS, R. (1980). Field-study evidence of an ego-defensive bias in attribution among two categories of observers. *Personality and Social Psychology Bulletin, 6,* 44–50.

CASTIELLO, U., & UMILTÀ, C. (1992). Orienting of attention in volleyball players. *International Journal of Sport Psychology, 23,* 301–310.

CATTELL, R. B., ERBER, H. W., & TATSOUKA, M. M. (1970). *Handbook for the Sixteen Personality Factor Questionnaire.* Champaign, IL: Institute for Personality and Ability Testing.

CAUDILL, D., WEINBERG, R. S., & JACKSON, A. (1983). Psyching-up and track athletes: A preliminary investigation. *Journal of Sport Psychology, 5,* 231–235.

CAVANAUGH, B. M., & SILVA, J. M. III. (1980). Spectator perceptions of fan misbehavior: An attitudinal inquiry. In C. H. Nadeau, W. R. Halliwell, K. M. Newell, & G. C. Roberts (Eds.), *Psychology of motor behavior and sport—1979* (pp. 189–198). Champaign, IL: Human Kinetics.

CELOZZI, M. J., KAZELSKIS, R., & GUTSCH, K. U. (1981). The relationship between viewing televised violence in ice hockey and subsequent levels of personal aggression. *Journal of Sport Behavior, 4,* 157–162.

CHAIY, S., & EXTEJT, M. M. (1982). The impact of player strikes on Major League spectator attendance: The case of the 1981 baseball season. In M. Etzel & J. Gaski (Eds.), *Applying marketing technology to spectator sports* (pp. 109–120). South Bend, IN: University of Notre Dame Press.

CHAMBERLIN, C., & LEE, T. D. (1993). Arranging practice conditions and designing instruction. In R. N. Singer, M. Murphey, & L. K. Tennant (Eds.), *Handbook of research on sport psychology* (pp. 213–241). New York: Macmillan.

CHAPMAN, A. J. (1974). An electromyographic study of social facilitation: A test of the 'mere presence' hypothesis. *British Journal of Psychology, 65,* 123–128.

CHARTRAND, J. M., JOWDY, D. P., & DANISH, S. J. (1992). The Psychological Skills Inventory for Sports: Psychometric characteristics and applied implications. *Journal of Sport & Exercise Psychology, 14,* 405–413.

CHARTRAND, J. M., & LENT, R. W. (1987). Sports counseling: Enhancing the development of the student-athlete. *Journal of Counseling and Development, 66,* 164–167.

CHEEK, W. H., & BURCH, W. R. (1976). *The social organization of leisure in human society.* New York: Harper & Row.

CHELLADURAI, P. (1978). *A contingency model of leadership in athletics.* Unpublished doctoral dissertation, University of Waterloo, Waterloo, Canada.

CHELLADURAI, P. (1984). Discrepancy between preferences and perceptions of leadership behavior and satisfaction of athletes in varying sports. *Journal of Sport Psychology, 6,* 27–41.

CHELLADURAI, P. (1990). Leadership in sports: A review. *International Journal of Sport Psychology, 21,* 328–354.

CHELLADURAI, P. (1993). Leadership. In R. N. Singer, M. Murphey, & L. K. Tennant (Eds.), *Handbook of research on sport psychology* (pp. 647–671). New York: Macmillan.

CHELLADURAI, P., & ARNOTT, M. (1985). Decision styles in coaching: Preferences of basketball players. *Research Quarterly for Exercise and Sport, 56,* 15–24.

CHELLADURAI, P., & HAGGERTY, T. R. (1978). A normative model of decision-making styles in coaching. *Athletic Administrator, 13*(1), 6–9.

CHELLADURAI, P., HAGGERTY, T. R., & BAXTER, P. R. (1989). Decisions style choices of university basketball coaches and players. *Journal of Sport & Exercise Psychology, 11,* 201–215.

CHELLADURAI, P., IMAMURA, H., YAMAGUCHI, Y., OINUMA, Y., & MIYAUCHI, T. (1988). Sport leadership in a cross-national setting: The case of Japanese and Canadian university athletes. *Journal of Sport & Exercise Psychology, 10,* 374–389.

CHELLADURAI, P., & QUEK, C. B. (1995). Decision style choices of high school basketball coaches: The effects of situational and coach characteristics. *Journal of Sport Behavior, 18,* 91–108.

CHELLADURAI, P., & SALEH, S. D. (1978). Preferred leadership in sports. *Canadian Journal of Applied Sport Sciences, 3,* 85–92.

CHELLADURAI, P., & SALEH, S. D. (1980). Dimensions of leader behavior in sports: Development of a leadership scale. *Journal of Sport Psychology, 2,* 34–45.

CHERRY, E. C. (1953). Some experiments on the recognition of speech, with one and with two ears. *The Journal of the Acoustical Society of America, 25,* 975–979.

CHORBAJIAN, L. (1978). The social psychology of American males and spectator sports. *International Journal of Sport Psychology, 9,* 165–175.

CHRISTY, P. R., GELFAND, D. M., & HARTMANN, D. P. (1971). Effects of competition-induced frustration of two classes of modeled behavior. *Developmental Psychology, 5,* 104–111.

CIALDINI, R. B., BORDEN, R. J., THORNE, A., WALKER, M. R., FREEMAN, S., & SLOAN, L. R. (1976). Basking in reflected glory: Three (football) field studies.

Journal of Personality and Social Psychology, 34, 366–375.

CIALDINI, R. B., & DE NICHOLAS, M. E. (1989). Self-presentation by association. *Journal of Personality and Social Psychology, 57,* 626–631.

CIALDINI, R. B., & RICHARDSON, K. D. (1980). Two indirect tactics of image management: Basking and blasting. *Journal of Personality and Social Psychology, 39,* 406–415.

CICCHETTI, C. J. (1972). A multivariate statistical analysis of wilderness users in the United States. In J. V. Krutilla (Ed.), *Natural environments: Studies in theoretical and applied analysis.* Baltimore: Johns Hopkins University Press.

CLARK, L. V. (1960). Effect of mental practice on the development of a certain motor skill. *Research Quarterly, 31,* 560–569.

CLARK, R. A., & SACHS, M. L. (1991). Challenges and opportunities in psychological skills training in deaf athletes. *The Sport Psychologist, 5,* 392–398.

CLARK, W. (1980). Socialization into the role of college and junior A hockey player. In P. Klavora (Ed.), *Psychological and sociological factors in sport* (pp. 362–366). Toronto: University of Toronto Press.

CLAYTON, D. A. (1978). Socially facilitated behavior. *The Quarterly Review of Biology, 53,* 373–392.

CLOUGH, P., SHEPHERD, J., & MAUGHAN, R. (1989). Motives for participating in recreational running. *Journal of Leisure Research, 21,* 297–309.

COAKLEY, J. (1982). *Sport in society: Issues and controversies.* St. Louis: Mosby.

COAKLEY, J. (1993). Socialization and sport. In R. N. Singer, M. Murphey, & L. K. Tennant (Eds.), *Handbook of research on sport psychology* (pp. 571–586). New York: Macmillan.

COALTER, F. (1985). Crowd behaviour at football matches: A study in Scotland. *Leisure Studies, 4,* 111–117.

CODDINGTON, R. D., & TROXELL, J. R. (1980). The effect of emotional factors on football injury rates—A pilot study. *Journal of Human Stress, 6,* 3–5.

COGAN, K. D., & PETRIE, T. A. (1995). Sport consultation: An evaluation of a season-long intervention with female collegiate gymnasts. *The Sport Psychologist, 9,* 282–296.

COHEN, G. L. (Ed.). (1993a). *Women in sports: Issues and controversies.* New York: Sage.

COHEN, G. L. (1993b). Media portrayal of the female athlete. In G. L. Cohen (Ed.), *Women in sports: Issues and controversies* (pp. 171–185). New York: Sage.

COHN, P. J. (1990). An exploratory study on sources of stress and athlete burnout in youth golf. *The Sport Psychologist, 4,* 95–106.

COLEMAN, J. S. (1970). Athletics in high school. In G. H. Sage (Ed.), *Sport and American society: Selected readings* (pp. 84–98). Reading, MA: Addison-Wesley.

COLLEY, A., EGLINTON, E., & ELLIOTT, E. (1992). Sport participation in middle childhood: Association with styles of play and parental participation. *International Journal of Sport Psychology, 23,* 193–206.

COLLEY, A., NASH, J., O'DONNELL, L., & RESTORICK, L. (1987). Attitudes to the female sex role and sex-typing of physical activities. *International Journal of Sport Psychology, 18,* 19–29.

COLLEY, A., ROBERTS, N., & CHIPPS, A. (1985). Sex-role identity, personality, and participation in team and individual sports by males and females. *International Journal of Sport Psychology, 16,* 103–112.

COLLINS, D., HALE, B., & LOOMIS, J. (1995). Differences in emotional responsivity and anger in athletes and nonathletes: Startle reflex modulation and attributional response. *Journal of Sport & Exercise Psychology, 17,* 171–184.

COOPER, L. (1969). Athletics, activity, and personality: A review of the literature. *Research Quarterly, 40,* 17–22.

CORBETT, D., & JOHNSON, W. (1993). The African-American female in collegiate sport: Sexism and Racism. In R. C. Althouse & D. D. Brooks (Eds.), *Racism in college athletics: The African-American athlete's experience* (pp. 179–204). Morgantown, WV: Fitness Information Technology.

CORBIN, C. B. (1967). Effects of mental practice on skill development after controlled practice. *Research Quarterly, 38,* 534–538.

CORBIN, C. B. (1977). The reliability and internal consistency of the motivation rating scale and the general trait rating scale. *Medicine and Science in Sports, 91,* 208–211.

COSTA, A., BONACCORSI, M., & SCRIMALI, T. (1984). Biofeedback and control of anxiety preceding athletic competition. *International Journal of Sport Psychology, 15,* 98–109.

COTA, A. A., EVANS, C. R., DION, K. L., KILIK, L., & LONGMAN, R. S. (1995). The structure of group cohesion. *Personality and Social Psychology Bulletin, 21,* 572–580.

COTTELL, N. B. (1972). Social facilitation. In C. G. McClintock (Ed.), *Experimental social psychology.* New York: Holt, Rinehart, & Winston.

COURNEYA, K. S., & CARRON, A. V. (1990). Batting first versus last: Implications for the home advantage. *Journal of Sport & Exercise Psychology, 12,* 312–316.

COURNEYA, K. S., & CARRON, A. V. (1991). Effects of travel and length of home stand/road trip on the home advantage. *Journal of Sport & Exercise Psychology, 13,* 42–49.

COURNEYA, K. S., & CARRON, A. V. (1992). The home advantage in sport competitions: A literature review. *Journal of Sport & Exercise Psychology, 14,* 13–27.

COX, R. H. (1990). *Sport psychology: Concepts and applications* (2nd ed.). Dubuque, IA: Brown.

COX, R. H., & LIU, Z. (1993). Psychological skills: A cross-cultural investigation. *International Journal of Sport Psychology, 24,* 326–340.

COX, R. H., QUI, Y., & LIU, Z. (1993). Overview of sport psychology. In R. N. Singer, M. Murphey, & L. K. Tennant (Eds.), *Handbook of research on sport psychology* (pp. 3–31). New York: Macmillan.

CRAIGHEAD, D. J., PRIVETTE, G., VALLIANOS, F., & BYRKIT, D. (1986). Personality characteristics of basketball players, starters and non-starters. *International Journal of Sport Psychology, 17,* 110–119.

CRATTY, B. J. (1959). Athletic and physical experiences of fathers and sons who participated in physical fitness testing at Pomona College, 1925–1959. *California Journal of Educational Research, 10,* 207–211.

CRATTY, B. J. (1960). A comparison of fathers and sons in physical ability. *Research Quarterly, 31,* 12–15.

CRATTY, B. J. (1989). *Psychology in contemporary sport* (3rd. ed.). Englewood Cliffs, NJ: Prentice Hall.

CREER, T. L., & MIKLICH, D. R. (1970). The application of a self-modeling procedure to modify inappropriate behavior: A preliminary report. *Behavior Research and Therapy, 8,* 91–92.

CROCKER, J., & MAJOR, B. (1989). Social stigma and self-esteem: The self-protective properties of stigma. *Psychological Review, 96,* 608–630.

CROCKER, P. R. E. (1989). Evaluating stress management training under competition conditions. *International Journal of Sport Psychology, 20,* 191–204.

CROCKER, P. R. E. (1992). Managing stress by competitive athletes: Ways of coping. *International Journal of Sport Psychology, 23,* 161–175.

CROCKER, P. R. E., ALDERMAN, R. B., & SMITH, F. M. R. (1988). Cognitive-affective stress management training with high performance youth volleyball players: Effects on affect, cognition, and performance. *Journal of Sport & Exercise Psychology, 10,* 448–460.

CROCKER, P. R. E., BOUFFARD, M., & GESSAROLI, M. E. (1995). Measuring enjoyment in youth sport settings: A confirmatory factor analysis of the Physical Activity Enjoyment Scale. *Journal of Sport & Exercise Psychology, 17,* 200–205.

CROCKER, P. R. E., & GRAHAM, T. R. (1995). Coping by competitive athletes with performance stress: Gender differences and relationships with affect. *The Sport Psychologist, 9,* 325–338.

CROSSET, T. W., BENEDICT, J. R., & MCDONALD, M. A. (1995). Male student-athletes reported for sexual assault: A survey of campus police departments and judicial affairs offices. *Journal of Sport & Social Issues, 19,* 126–140.

CROSSMAN, J. E. (1986a). Age of spectators as a factor influencing behavior at minor league hockey and baseball games. *Perceptual and Motor Skills, 62,* 639–648.

CROSSMAN, J. E. (1986b). Spectators' behavior at minor league hockey games: An exploratory study. *Perceptual and Motor Skills, 62,* 803–812.

CROXTON, J. S., CHIACCHIA, D., & WAGNER, C. (1987). Gender differences in attitudes toward sports and reactions to competitive situations. *Journal of Sport Behavior, 10,* 167–177.

CULLEN, F. T. (1974). Attitudes of players and spectators toward norm violation in ice hockey. *Perceptual and Motor Skills, 38,* 1146.

CULLEN, J. B., & CULLEN, F. T. (1975). The structural and contextual conditions of group norm violations: Some implications from the game of ice hockey. *International Review of Sport Sociology, 10*(2), 69–79.

DAISS, S., LEUNES, A. D., & NATION, J. (1986). Mood and locus of control of a sample of college and professional football players. *Perceptual and Motor Skills, 63,* 733–734.

DALE, G. A., & WRISBERG, C. A. (1995a, September). *The utilization of a performance profiling technique in a team situation to promote effective coach-athlete communication.* Workshop presented at the meeting of the Association for the Advancement of Applied Sport Psychology, New Orleans.

DALE, G. A., & WRISBERG, C. A. (1995b). *Utilization of the performance profiling technique to enhance coach-athlete communication and team goal setting.* Manuscript submitted for publication.

DANIELS, F. S., & LANDERS, D. M. (1981). Biofeedback and shooting performance: A test of disregulation and systems theory. *Journal of Sport Psychology, 4,* 271–282.

DANISH, S. J., & HALE, B. D. (1981). Toward an understanding of the practice of sport psychology. *Journal of Sport Psychology, 3,* 90–99.

DARWIN, C. (1859). *On the origin of species.* London: Murray.

DAVIS, C., & MOGK, J. P. (1994). Some personality correlates of interest and excellence in sport. *International Journal of Sport Psychology, 25,* 131–143.

DAVIS, J. H. (1969). *Group performance.* Reading, MA: Addison-Wesley.

DAVIS, M. H., & HARVEY, J. C. (1992). Declines in Major League batting performance as a function of game pressure: A drive theory analysis. *Journal of Applied Social Psychology, 22,* 714–735.

DAVIS, S. F., HUSS, M. T., & BECKER, A. H. (1995). Norman Triplett and the dawning of sport psychology. *The Sport Psychologist, 9,* 366–375.

DAW, J., & BURTON, D. (1994). Evaluation of a comprehensive psychological skills training program for collegiate tennis players. *The Sport Psychologist, 8,* 37–57.

DEAUX, K. (1984). From individual differences to social categories: Analysis of a decade's research on gender. *American Psychologist, 39,* 105–116.

DECI, E. L. (1971). Effects of externally mediated rewards on intrinsic motivation. *Journal of Personality and Social Psychology, 18,* 105–115.

DECI, E. L., & OLSON, B. C. (1989). Motivation and competition: Their role in sports. In J. H. Goldstein (Ed.), *Sports, games, and play: Social and psychological viewpoints* (2nd ed., pp. 83–110). Hillsdale, NJ: Erlbaum.

DECI, E. L., & RYAN, R. M. (1985). *Intrinsic motivation and self-determination in human behavior.* New York: Plenum Press.

DEINER, E. (1976). Effects of prior destructive behavior, anonymity, and group presence on deindividuation and aggression. *Journal of Personality and Social Psychology, 33,* 497–507.

DEWAR, A., & HORN, T. S. (1992). A critical analysis of knowledge construction in sport psychology. In T. S. Horn (Ed.), *Advances in sport psychology* (pp. 13–22). Champaign, IL: Human Kinetics.

DEWAR, C. K. (1980). Spectator fights at professional baseball games. *Review of Sport and Leisure, 1,* 12–25.

DE WITT, D. J. (1980). Cognitive and biofeedback training for stress reduction with university students. *Journal of Sport Psychology, 2,* 288–294.

DIETZ-UHLER, B. (1995). *Biases in the "objective" reporting of sporting events.* Unpublished manuscript, Miami University, Miami, OH.

DIETZ-UHLER, B., & MURRELL, A. (1995). *The effects of social identity on reactions to sporting events: A structural components analysis.* Unpublished manuscript, Miami University, Miami, OH.

DISHMAN, R. K. (1983). Identity crises in North American sport psychology: Academics in professional issues. *Journal of Sport Psychology, 5,* 123–134.

DODGE, K. A., MURPHY, R. R., & BUCHSBAUM, K. (1984). The assessment of intent-cue detection skills in children: Implications for developmental psychopathology. *Child Development, 55,* 163–173.

DOLLARD, J., DOOB, L. W., MILLER, N. E., MOWRER, O. J., SEARS, R. R. (1939). *Frustration and aggression.* New Haven, CT: Yale University Press.

DONAHUE, J. A., GILLIS, J. H., & KING, K. (1980). Behavior modification in sport and physical education: A review. *Journal of Sport Psychology, 2,* 311–328.

DONNERSTEIN, E., & WILSON, D. W. (1976). Effects of noise and perceived control on ongoing and subsequent aggressive behavior. *Journal of Personality and Social Psychology, 34,* 774–781.

DONZELLI, G. J., & EDWARDS, J. D. (1994, May). *Athletes' perceptions of reasons for the home advantage in team sports.* Paper presented at the meeting of the Mid-American Psychological Association, Chicago, IL.

DORÉ, L. R., & HILGARD, E. R. (1937). Spaced practice and the maturation hypothesis. *The Journal of Psychology, 4,* 245–259.

DORNEY, L., GOH, E. K. M., & LEE, C. (1992). The impact of music and imagery on physical performance and arousal: Studies of coordination and endurance. *Journal of Sport Behavior, 15,* 21–33.

DORSEY, V. L. (1992, December 9). Violence grabs growing share of spotlight away from events. *USA Today,* p. 14C.

DOWRICK, P. W. (1991). Feedforward and self-modeling. In P. W. Dowrick (Ed.), *Practical guide to using video in the behavioral sciences* (pp. 109–126). New York: Wiley.

DOWRICK, P. W., & DOVE, C. (1980). The use of self-modeling to improve the swimming performance of spina bifida children. *Journal of Applied Behavioral Analysis, 13,* 51–56.

DOYLE, R. C., LEWIS, J. M., & MALMISUR, M. (1980). A sociological application of Rooney's fan region theory. *Journal of Sport Behavior, 3*(2), 51–60.

DUBOIS, P. E. (1986). The effect of participation in sport on the value orientations of young athletes. *Sociology of Sport Journal, 3,* 29–42.

DUCHON, D., & JAGO, A. G. (1981). Equity and the performance of major league baseball players: An extension of Lord and Hohenfeld. *Journal of Applied Psychology, 66,* 728–732.

DUDA, J. L. (1989). Relationship between task and ego orientation and the perceived purpose of sport among high school athletes. *Journal of Sport & Exercise Psychology, 11,* 318–335.

DUDA, J. L. (1992). Motivation in sport settings: A goal perspective approach. In G. C. Roberts (Ed.), *Motivation in sport and exercise* (pp. 57–91). Champaign, IL: Human Kinetics.

DUDA, J. L., CHI, L., NEWTON, M. L., WALLING, M. D., & CATLEY, D. (1995). Task and ego orientation and intrinsic motivation in sport. *International Journal of Sport Psychology, 26,* 40–63.

DUDA, J. L., FOX, K. R., BIDDLE, S. J., & ARMSTRONG, N. (1992). Children's achievement goals and beliefs about success in sport. *British Journal of Educational Psychology, 62,* 313–323.

DUDA, J. L., & NICHOLLS, J. G. (1992). Dimensions of achievement motivation in schoolwork and sport. *Journal of Educational Psychology, 84,* 290–299.

DUDA, J. L., SMART, A. E., & TAPPE, M. K. (1989). Predictors in adherence in the rehabilitation of athletic injuries: An application of personal investment theory. *Journal of Sport & Exercise Psychology, 11,* 367–381.

DUDA, J. L., & WHITE, S. A. (1992). Goal orientations and beliefs about the causes of sport success among elite skiers. *The Sport Psychologist, 6,* 334–343.

DUNAND, M., BERKOWITZ, L., & LEYENS, J. P. (1984). Audience effects when viewing aggressive movies. *British Journal of Social Psychology, 23,* 69–76.

DUNCAN, M. C. (1983). The symbolic dimensions of spectator sport. *Quest, 35,* 29–36.

DUNCAN, M. C. (1990). Sports photographs and sexual difference: Images of women and men in the 1984 and 1988 Olympic Games. *Sociology of Sport Journal, 7,* 22–43.

DUNCAN, M. C., & HASBROOK, C. A. (1988). Denial of power in televised women's sports. *Sociology of Sport Journal, 5,* 1–21.

DUNCAN, M. C., MESSNER, M. A., WILLIAMS, L., & JENSEN, K. (1990). *Gender stereotyping in televised sports.* Los Angeles: Amateur Athletic Foundation.

DUNCAN, T., & MCAULEY, E. (1987). Efficacy expectations and perceptions of causality in motor performance. *Journal of Sport Psychology, 9,* 385–393.

DUNNING, E., MURPHY, P., & WILLIAMS, J. (1986). Spectator violence at football matches: Towards a sociological explanation. *British Journal of Sociology, 37,* 221–244.

DUQUIN, M. E. (1978). Attributions made by children in coeducational sport settings. In D. M. Landers & R. W. Christina (Eds.), *Psychology of motor behavior and sport—1977* (pp. 462–469). Champaign, IL: Human Kinetics.

DUQUIN, M. E. (1980). Social comparison processes in sport: The motivating power of similarity. In C. H. Neadeau, W. R. Halliwell, K. M. Newell, & G. C. Roberts (Eds.), *Psychology of motor behavior and sport—1979* (pp. 147–156). Champaign, IL: Human Kinetics.

DWECK, C. S. (1986). Motivational processes affecting learning. *American Psychologist, 41,* 1040–1048.

EASTERBROOK, J. A. (1959). The effect of emotion on cue utilization and the organization of behavior. *Psychological Review, 66,* 183–201.

EDWARDS, H. (1973). *Sociology of Sport.* Homewood, IL: Dorsey.

EDWARDS, J. (1979). The home-field advantage. In J. H. Goldstein (Ed.), *Sports, games, and play: Social and psychological viewpoints* (1st ed., pp. 409–438). Hillsdale, NJ: Erlbaum.

EDWARDS, J., & ARCHAMBAULT, D. (1989). The home-field advantage. In J. H. Goldstein (Ed.), *Sports, games, and play: Social and psychological viewpoints* (2nd ed., pp. 333–370). Hillsdale, NJ: Erlbaum.

EFRAN, J. S., LESSER, G. S., & SPILLER, M. J. (1994). Enhancing tennis coaching with youths using the metaphor method. *The Sport Psychologist, 8,* 349–359.

EITZEN, D. S. (1979). Sport and deviance. In D. S. Eitzen (Ed.), *Sport in contemporary society: An anthology* (pp. 73–89). New York: St. Martin's.

EITZEN, D. S., & SAGE, G. H. (1986). *Sociology of North American sport* (3rd ed.). Dubuque, IA: Brown.

ELIAS, N., & DUNNING, E. (1970). The quest for excitement in unexciting societies. In G. Luschen (Ed.), *The cross-cultural analysis of sport and games* (pp. 31–51). Champaign, IL: Stipes.

ELMES, D. G., KANTOWITZ, B. H., & ROEDIGER, H. L. (1992). *Research methods in psychology* (4th ed.). New York: West.

EPSTEIN, G. (1986). The image in medicine: Notes of a clinician. *Advances, 3,* 22–31.

EPSTEIN, J. A., & HARACKIEWICZ, J. M. (1992). Winning is not enough: The effects of competition and achievement orientation on intrinsic interest. *Personality and Social Psychology Bulletin, 18,* 128–138.

EPSTEIN, M. L. (1980). The relationship of mental imagery and mental rehearsal to performance of a motor task. *Journal of Sport Psychology, 2,* 211–220.

EPSTEIN, S., & TAYLOR, S. P. (1967). Instigation to aggression as a function of degree of defeat and perceived aggression intent of the opponent. *Journal of Personality, 35,* 265–289.

ESTRADA, A. M., GELFAND, D. M., & HARTMANN, D. P. (1988). Children's sport and the development of social behaviors. In F. Smoll, R. A. Magill, & M. J. Ash (Eds.), *Children in sport* (3rd ed., pp. 251–262. Champaign, IL: Human Kinetics.

Ethical standards for provision of services by NASPSPA members. (1982, Fall). *NASPSPA Newsetter, 7,* ii–vi.

EVANS, J., & ROBERTS, G. C. (1987). Physical competence and the development of children's peer relations. *Quest, 39,* 23–35.

EVERETT, J. J., SMITH, R. E., & WILLIAMS, K. D. (1992). Effects of team cohesion and identifiability on social loafing in relay swimming performance. *International Journal of Sport Psychology, 23,* 311–324.

EWERT, A., & HOLLENHORST, S. (1989). Testing the adventure model: Empirical support for a model of risk recreation participation. *Journal of Leisure Research, 21,* 124–139.

EYSENCK, M. W. (1976). Arousal, learning, and memory. *Psychological Bulletin, 83,* 389–404.

EYSENCK, M. W. (1984). *A handbook of cognitive psychology.* Hillsdale, NJ: Erlbaum.

FABIANIC, D. (1994). Managerial change and organizational effectiveness in Major League baseball: Findings for the eighties. *Journal of Sport Behavior, 17,* 135–147.

FAUCETTE, N., & OSINSKI, A. (1987). Adult spectator verbal behavior during a Mustang League World Series. *Journal of Applied Research in Coaching and Athletics, 2,* 141–152.

FELTZ, D. L. (1988). Self-confidence and sports performance. In K. B. Pandolf (Ed.), *Exercise and sport sciences reviews* (Vol. 16, pp. 423–457). New York: Macmillan.

FELTZ, D. L. (1992). Understanding motivation in sport: A self-efficacy perspective. In G. C. Roberts (Ed.), *Motivation in sport and exercise* (pp. 93–105). Champaign, IL: Human Kinetics.

FELTZ, D. L., & LANDERS, D. M. (1983). The effects of mental practice on motor skill learning and performance: A meta-analysis. *Journal of Sport Psychology, 5,* 25–57.

FELTZ, D. L., LANDERS, D. M., & RAEDER, U. (1979). Enhancing self-efficacy in high-avoidance motor tasks: A comparison of modeling techniques. *Journal of Sport Psychology, 1,* 112–122.

FELTZ, D. L., & PETLICHKOFF, L. (1983). Perceived competence among interscholastic sport participants and dropouts. *Canadian Journal of Applied Sport Science, 8,* 231–235.

FENKER, R. M., & LAMBIOTTE, J. G. (1987). A performance enhancement program for a college football team: One incredible season. *The Sport Psychologist, 1,* 224–236.

FENZ, W. D. (1988). Learning to anticipate stressful events. *Journal of Sport & Exercise Psychology, 10,* 223–228.

FESTINGER, L., PEPITONE, A., & NEWCOMB, T. (1952). Some consequences of deindividuation in a group. *Journal of Abnormal and Social Psychology, 47,* 382–389.

FESTINGER, L., SCHACHTER, S., & BACK, K. (1950). *Social pressures in informal groups: A study of human factors in housing.* New York: Harper Row.

FIEDLER, F. E. (1967). *A theory of leadership effectiveness.* New York: McGraw-Hill.

FIEDLER, F. E. (1978). The contingency model and the dynamics of the leadership process. In L. Berkowitz (Ed.), *Advances in experimental social psychology* (Vol. 11, pp. 59–112). New York: Academic Press.

FIELD, R. H. G. (1982). A test of the Vroom-Yetton Normative model of leadership. *Journal of Applied Psychology, 67,* 523–532.

FIORE, N. A. (1988). The inner healer: Imagery for coping with cancer and its therapy. *Journal of Mental Imagery, 12,* 79–82.

FISHER, A. C., & ZWART, E. F. (1982). Psychological analysis of athletes' anxiety responses. *Journal of Sport Psychology, 4,* 139–158.

FISKE, S. T., & TAYLOR, S. E. (1991). *Social cognition.* New York: McGraw-Hill.

FLEISHMAN, E. A., HARRIS, E. F., & BURTT, H. E. (1955). *Leadership and supervision in industry: An evaluation of a supervisory training program.* Columbus, OH: The Ohio State University.

FLINT, F. A. (1993). Seeing helps believing: Modeling in injury rehabilitation. In D. Pargman (Ed.), *Psychological bases of sport injuries* (pp. 183–198). Morgantown, WV: Fitness Information Technology.

FLOOD, S. E., & HELLSTEDT, J. C. (1991). Gender differences in motivation for intercollegiate athletic participation. *Journal of Sport Behavior, 14,* 159–167.

FOGARTY, G. J. (1995). Some comments of the use of psychological tests in sport settings. *International Journal of Sport Psychology, 26,* 161–170.

FOLEY, D. E. (1990). The great American football ritual: Reproducing race, class, and gender inequality. *Sociology of Sport Journal, 7,* 111–135.

FORSYTH, D. R. (1990). *Group dynamics* (2nd. ed.). Pacific Grove, CA: Brooks/Cole.

FORTIER, M. S., VALLERAND, R. J., BRIÈRE, N. M., & PROVENCHER, P. J. (1995). Competitive and recreational sport structures and gender: A test of their relationship with sport motivation. *International Journal of Sport Psychology, 26,* 24–39.

FRANK, M. G., & GILOVICH, T. (1988). The dark side and self- and social perception: Black uniforms and aggression in professional sports. *Journal of Personality and Social Psychology, 54,* 74–85.

FRANKS, I. M., & MAILE, L. J. (1991). The use of video in sport skill acquisition. In P. W. Dowrick (Ed.), *Practical guide to using video in the behavioral sciences* (pp. 231–243). New York: Wiley.

FREDERICK, C. M., & RYAN, R. M. (1995). Self-determination in sport: A review using cognitive evaluation theory. *International Journal of Sport Psychology, 26,* 5–23.

FREEDSON, P. S., MIHEVIC, P. M., LOUCKS, A. B., & GIRANDOLA, R. N. (1983). Physique, body composition, and psychological characteristics of competitive female body builders. *The Physician and Sportsmedicine, 11,* 85–93.

FREISCHLAG, J., & HARDIN, D. (1975). The effects of social class and school achievement on the composition of sport crowds. *Sport Sociology Bulletin, 4,* 36–46.

FREIXANET, M. G. (1991). Personality profile of subjects engaged in high physical risk sports. *Personality and Individual Differences, 12,* 1087–1093.

FRENCH, J. R. P., & RAVEN, B. (1959). The bases of social power. In D. Cartwright (Ed.), *Studies in social power* (pp. 150–167). Ann Arbor, MI: Institute for Social Research.

FRENCH, K. E., & THOMAS, J. R. (1987). The relation of knowledge development to children's basketball performance. *Journal of Sport Psychology, 9,* 15–32.

FRENCH, S. N. (1978). Electromyographic biofeedback for tension control during gross motor skill acquisition. *Perceptual and Motor Skills, 47,* 883–889.

FREUD, S. (1920). *A general introduction to psychoanalysis.* New York: Boni and Liveright.

FREUD, S. (1961). *Civilization and its discontents* (J. Strachey, Trans.). New York: Norton. (Original work published 1930).

FREY, J. H. (1992). Gambling on sport: Policy issues. *Journal of Gambling Studies, 8,* 351–360.

FRIES, M. E., & WOOLF, P. J. (1953). Some hypotheses on the role of the congenital activity type in personality development. *Psychoanalytic Study of the Child, 8,* 48–62.

FRINTNER, M. P., & RUBINSON, L. (1993). Acquaintance rape: The influence of alcohol, fraternity membership, and sports team membership. *Journal of Sex Education and Therapy, 19,* 272–284.

FULLERTON, S., & MERZ, G. R. (1982). An assessment of attendance at Major League baseball games. In M. Etzel & J. Gaski (Eds.), *Applying marketing technology to spectator sports* (pp. 77–94). South Bend, IN: University of Notre Dame Press.

GALOTTI, K. M. (1994). *Cognitive psychology in and out of the laboratory.* Pacific Grove, CA: Brooks/Cole.

GANTZ, W. (1981). An exploration of viewing motives and behaviors associated with television sports. *Journal of Broadcasting, 25,* 263–275.

GANTZ, W., & WENNER, L. A. (1995). Fanship and the television sports viewing experience. *Sociology of Sport Journal, 12,* 56–74.

GANTZ, W., WENNER, L. A., CARRICO, C., & KNORR, M. (1995a). Assessing the football widow hypothesis: A coorientation study of the role of televised sports in long-standing relationships. *Journal of Sport & Social Issues, 19,* 352–376.

GANTZ, W., WENNER, L. A., CARRICO, C., & KNORR, M. (1995b). Televised sports and marital relationships. *Sociology of Sport Journal, 12,* 306–323.

GARLAND, D. J., & BARRY, J. R. (1990). Personality and leader behaviors in collegiate football: A multidimensional approach to performance. *Journal of Research in Personality, 24,* 355–370.

GAUVIN, L., & RUSSELL, S. J. (1993). Sport-specific and culturally adapted measures in sport and exercise psychology research: Issues and strategies. In R. N. Singer, M. Murphey, & L. K. Tennant (Eds.), *Handbook of research on sport psychology* (pp. 891–900). New York: Macmillan.

GAYTON, W. F., MATTHEWS, G. R., & NICKLESS, C. J. (1987). The home field disadvantage in sports championships: Does it exist in hockey? *Journal of Sport Psychology, 9,* 183–185.

GAYTON, W. F., MUTRIE, S. A., & HEARNS, J. F. (1987). Home advantage: Does it exist in women's sports? *Perceptual and Motor Skills, 65,* 653–654.

GEEN, R. G. (1978). Effects of attack and uncontrollable noise on aggression. *Journal of Research in Personality, 12,* 15–29.

GEEN, R. G. (1990). *Human aggression.* Pacific Grove, CA: Brooks/Cole.

GEEN, R. G., & GANGE, J. J. (1977). Drive theory of social facilitation: Twelve years of theory and research. *Psychological Bulletin, 84,* 1267–1288.

GEEN, R. G., & O'NEAL, E. C. (1969). Activation of cue-elicited aggression by general arousal. *Journal of Personality and Social Psychology, 11,* 289–292.

GEIER, J. G. (1969). A trait approach to the study of leadership in small groups. *Journal of Communication, 17,* 316–323.

GEORGE, T. R. (1994). Self-confidence and baseball performance: A causal examination of self-efficacy theory. *Journal of Sport & Exercise Psychology, 16,* 381–399.

GERMONE, K. E., & FURST, D. M. (1991). Social acceptability of sport for young women. *Perceptual and Motor Skills, 73,* 323–326.

GERON, E., FURST, D., & ROTSTEIN, P. (1986). Personality of athletes participating in various sports. *International Journal of Sport Psychology, 17,* 120–135.

GILBERT, B., & TWYMAN, L. (1984). Violence: Out of hand in the stands. In D. S. Eitzen (Ed.), *Sport in contemporary society* (pp. 112–212). New York: St. Martin's.

GILBERT, D. T. (1995). Attribution and interpersonal perception. In A. Tesser (Ed.), *Advanced social psychology* (pp. 99–147). New York: McGraw-Hill.

GILBERT, D. T., PELHAM, B. W., & KRULL, D. S. (1988). On cognitive busyness: When person perceivers meet persons perceived. *Journal of Personality and Social Psychology, 54,* 733–740.

GILDEA, W. (1995, June 15). Betrayed baseball fans take themselves out of ballgame. *The Paducah Sun,* pp. 1B, 2B.

GILL, D. L. (1978). Cohesiveness and performance in sport groups. In R. S. Hutton (Ed.), *Exercise and sport science reviews* (Vol. 5, pp. 131–155). Santa Barbara, CA: Journal Publications Affiliates.

GILL, D. L. (1980). Success-failure attributions in competitive groups: An exception to egocentrism. *Journal of Sport Psychology, 2,* 106–114.

GILL, D. L. (1992). Gender and sport behavior. In T. S. Horn (Ed.), *Advances in sport psychology* (pp. 143–160). Champaign, IL: Human Kinetics.

GILL, D. L. (1993). Competitiveness and competitive orientation in sport. In R. N. Singer, M. Murphey, & L. K. Tennant (Eds.), *Handbook of research on sport psychology* (pp. 314–327). New York: Macmillan.

GILL, D. L. (1995). Women's place in the history of sport psychology. *The Sport Psychologist, 9,* 418–433.

GILL, D. L., & DEETER, T. E. (1988). Development of the Sport Orientation Questionnaire. *Research Quarterly for Exercise and Sport, 59,* 191–202.

GILL, D. L., DZEWALTOWSKI, D. A., & DEETER, T. E. (1988). The relationship of competitiveness and achievement orientation to participation in sport and nonsport activities. *Journal of Sport & Exercise Psychology, 10,* 139–150.

GILL, D. L., GROSS, J. B., & HUDDLESTON, S. (1983). Participation motivation in youth sports. *International Journal of Sport Psychology, 14,* 1–14.

GLASS, D. C., & SINGER, J. E. (1972). *Urban stress: Experiments on noise and social stressors.* New York: Academic Press.

GLENCROSS, D. J. (1992). Human skill and motor learning: A critical review. *Sport Science Review, 1,* 65–78.

GOLDSMITH, P. A., & WILLIAMS, J. M. (1992). Perceived stressors for football and volleyball officials from three rating levels. *Journal of Sport Behavior, 15,* 106–118.

GOLDSTEIN, J. H. (1989). Violence in sports. In J. H. Goldstein (Ed.), *Sports, games, and play: Social and psychological viewpoints* (2nd ed., pp. 279–297). Hillsdale, NJ: Erlbaum.

GOLDSTEIN, J. H., & ARMS, R. L. (1971). Effects of observing athletic contests on hostility. *Sociometry, 34,* 83–90.

GOOD, A. J., BREWER, B. W., PETITPAS, A. J., VAN RAALTE, J. L., & MAHAR, M. T. (1993, Spring). Identity foreclosure, athletic identity, and college sport participation. *The Academic Athletic Journal,* 1–12.

GORANSON, R. E. (1980). Sports violence and the catharsis hypothesis. In P. Klavora (Ed.), *Psychological and sociological factors in sport* (pp. 131–138). Toronto: University of Toronto Press.

GORDON, S., WEINBERG, R. S., & JACKSON, A. (1994). Effect of internal and external imagery on cricket performance. *Journal of Sport Behavior, 17,* 60–75.

GOULD, D., FELTZ, D., HORN, T., & WEISS, M. R. (1982). Reasons for attrition in competitive youth swimming. *Journal of Sport Behavior, 5,* 155–165.

GOULD, D., FELTZ, D., & WEISS, M. R. (1985). Motives for participating in competitive youth swimming. *International Journal of Sport Psychology, 16,* 126–140.

GOULD, D., FELTZ, D., WEISS, M. R., & PETLICHKOFF, L. (1982). Participation motives in competitive youth swimmers. In T. Orlick, J. T. Partington, & J. H. Salmela (Eds.), *Mental training for coaches and athletes* (pp. 57–59). Ottawa: Coaching Association of Canada.

GOULD, D., HORN, T., & SPREEMANN, J. (1983). Competitive anxiety in junior elite wrestlers. *Journal of Sport Psychology, 5,* 58–71.

GOULD, D., JACKSON, S., & FINCH, L. (1993). Sources of stress in national champion figure skaters. *Journal of Sport & Exercise Psychology, 15,* 134–159.

GOULD, D., PETLICHKOFF, L., HODGE, K., & SIMONS, J. (1990). Evaluating the effectiveness of a psychological skills educational workshop. *The Sport Psychologist, 4,* 249–260.

GOULD, D., PETLICHKOFF, L., SIMONS, J., & VEVERA, M. (1987). Relationship between Competitive State Anxiety Inventory-2 subscale scores and pistol shooting performance. *Journal of Sport Psychology, 9,* 33–42.

GOULD, D., PETLICHKOFF, L., & WEINBERG, R. S. (1984). Antecedents of, temporal changes in, and relationships between CSAI-2 subcomponents. *Journal of Sport Psychology, 6,* 289–304.

GOULD, D., & PICK, S. (1995). Sport psychology: The Griffith Era, 1920–1940. *The Sport Psychologist, 9,* 391–405.

GOULD, D., WEISS, M., & WEINBERG, R. S. (1981). Psychological characteristic of successful and nonsuccessful Big Ten wrestlers. *Journal of Sport Psychology, 3,* 69–81.

GRABE, M. (1981). School size and the importance of school activities. *Adolescence, 16,* 21–31.

GRANITO, V. J., & WENZ, B. J. (1995). Reading list for professional issues in applied sport psychology. *The Sport Psychologist, 9,* 96–103.

GRAY, S. W. (1990). Effect of visuomotor rehearsal with videotaped modeling on racquetball performance of beginning players. *Perceptual and Motor Skills, 70,* 379–385.

GREEN, L. B. (1992). The use of imagery in the rehabilitation of injured athletes. *The Sport Psychologist, 6,* 416–428.

GREEN, T. S. (1993). The future of African-American female athletes. In R. C. Althouse & D. D. Brooks (Eds.), *Racism in college athletics: The African-American athlete's experience* (pp. 205–223). Morgantown, WV: Fitness Information Technology.

GREENBERG, J., & PYSZCZYNSKI, T. (1985). Compensatory self-inflation: A response to the threat to self-regard of public failure. *Journal of Personality and Social Psychology, 49,* 273–280.

GREENDORFER, S. L. (1977). Role of socialization agents in female sport involvement. *Research Quarterly, 48,* 304–310.

GREENDORFER, S. L. (1983). Shaping the female athlete: The impact of the family. In M. A. Boutilier & L. San Giovanni (Eds.), *The sporting women: Feminist and sociological dilemmas* (pp. 145–155). Champaign, IL: Human Kinetics.

GREENDORFER, S. L. (1992). Sport socialization. In T. S. Horn (Ed.), *Advances in sport psychology* (pp. 201–218). Champaign, IL: Human Kinetics.

GREENDORFER, S. L. (1993). Gender role stereotypes and early childhood socialization. In G. L. Cohen (Ed.), *Women in sport: Issues and controversies* (pp. 3–14). Newbury Park, CA: Sage.

GREENDORFER, S. L., & EWING, M. A. (1981). Race and gender differences in children's socialization into sport. *Research Quarterly for Exercise and Sport, 52,* 301–310.

GREENDORFER, S. L., & LEWKO, J. H. (1978). Role of family members in sport socialization of children. *Research Quarterly, 49,* 146–152.

GREENSPAN, M., & ANDERSEN, M. B. (1993). Providing psychological services to student athletes: A developmental psychology model. In S. M. Murphy (Ed.), *Sport psychology interventions* (pp. 177–191). Champaign, IL: Human Kinetics.

GREENSPAN, M., & FELTZ, D. L. (1989). Psychological interventions with athletes in competitive situations: A review. *The Sport Psychologist, 3,* 219–236.

GREENSTEIN, T. N., & MARCUM, J. P. (1981). Factors affecting attendance of Major League Baseball: I. Team Performance. *Review of Sport and Leisure, 6*(2), 21–34.

GREER, D. L. (1983). Spectator booing and the home advantage: A study of social influence in the basketball arena. *Social Psychology Quarterly, 46,* 252–261.

GREGG, B. G. (1992, June 16). Ballgames become embattled. *USA Today,* p. 10C.

GREGG, E., & REJESKI, W. J. (1990). Social psychobiologic dysfunction associated with anabolic steroid abuse: A review. *The Sport Psychologist, 4,* 275–284.

GREGORY, C. J., & PETRIE, B. M. (1975). Superstitions of Canadian intercollegiate athletes: An intersport comparison. *International Review of Sport Sociology, 10,* 59–66.

GRIFFITH, C. R. (1926). *The psychology of coaching.* New York: Scribners.

GRIFFITH, C. R. (1928). *The psychology of athletes.* New York: Scribners.

GRIFFITHS, T. J., STEEL, D. H., & VACCARO, P. (1979). Relationship between anxiety and performance in scuba diving. *Perceptual and Motor Skills, 48,* 1009–1010.

GRIFFITHS, T. J., STEEL, D. H., VACCARO, P., ALLEN, R., & KARPMAN, A. M. (1985). The effects of relaxation and cognitive rehearsal on the anxiety levels and performance of SCUBA students. *International Journal of Sport Psychology, 16,* 113–119.

GROFF, B. D., BARON, R. S., & MOORE, D. L. (1983). Distraction, attentional conflict, and drivelike behavior. *Journal of Experimental Social Psychology, 19,* 359–380.

GROUIOS, G. (1992). The effect of mental practice on diving performance. *International Journal of Sport Psychology, 23,* 60–69.

GROVE, J. R. (1993). Personality and injury rehabilitation among sport performers. In D. Pargman (Ed.), *Psychological bases of sport injuries* (pp. 99–120). Morgantown, WV: Fitness Information Technology.

GROVE, J. R., & HANRAHAN, S. J. (1988). Perceptions of mental training needs by elite field hockey players and their coaches. *The Sport Psychologist, 2,* 222–230.

GROVE, J. R., HANRAHAN, S. J., & McINMAN, A. (1991). Success/failure bias in attributions across involvement categories in sport. *Personality and Social Psychology Bulletin, 17,* 93–97.

GROVE, J. R., & PRAPAVESSIS, H. (1992). Preliminary evidence for the reliability and validity of an abbreviated profile of mood states. *International Journal of Sport Psychology, 23,* 93–109.

GRUBER, J. J., & GRAY, G. R. (1981). Factor patterns of variables influencing cohesiveness at various levels of basketball competition. *Research Quarterly for Exercise and Sport, 52,* 19–30.

GRUBER, J. J., & GRAY, G. R. (1982). Responses to forces influencing cohesion as a function of player status and level of male varsity basketball competition. *Research Quarterly for Exercise and Sport, 53,* 27–36.

GRUSKY, O. (1963). Managerial succession and organizational effectiveness. *American Journal of Sociology, 69,* 21–31.

Guidelines for psychological testing within sport and other physical activity settings. (1982, Fall). *NASPSPA Newsletter, 7,* vi–viii.

GUTTMANN, A. (1980). On the alleged dehumanization of the sports spectator. *Journal of Popular Culture, 14,* 275–282.

GUTTMANN, A. (1986). *Sports spectators.* New York: Columbia University Press.

HAAS, J., & ROBERTS, G. C. (1975). Effect of evaluative others upon learning and performance of a complex motor task. *Journal of Motor Behavior, 7,* 81–90.

HAGSTROM, W. O., & SELVIN, H. C. (1965). Two dimensions of cohesiveness in small groups. *Sociometry, 28,* 30–43.

HALE, B. D. (1982). The effects of internal and external imagery on muscular and ocular concomitants. *Journal of Sport Psychology, 4,* 379–387.

HALL, C. R., RODGERS, W. M., & BARR, K. A. (1990). The use of imagery by athletes in selected sports. *The Sport Psychologist, 4,* 1–10.

HALL, C. S., & LINDZEY, G. (1968). The relevance of Freudian psychology and related viewpoints for the social sciences. In G. Lindzey & E. Aronson (Eds.), *The handbook of social psychology* (Vol. 1, 2nd ed., pp. 245–319). New York: Addison-Wesley.

HALL, E. G., & ERFFMEYER, E. S. (1983). The effect of visuo-motor behavior rehearsal with videotaped modeling on free throw accuracy of intercollegiate female basketball players. *Journal of Sport Psychology, 5,* 343–346.

HALL, E. G., & HARDY, C. J. (1991). Ready, aim, fire . . . Relaxation strategies for enhancing pistol marksmanship. *Perceptual and Motor Skills, 72,* 775–786.

HALL, H. K., & BYRNE, A. T. J. (1988). Goal setting in sport: Clarifying recent anomalies. *Journal of Sport & Exercise Psychology, 10,* 184–198.

HAMMER, W. M., & TUTKO, T. A. (1974). Validation of the Athletic Motivation Inventory. *International Journal of Sport Psychology, 5,* 3–12.

HAMMERMEISTER, J., & BURTON, D. (1995). Anxiety and the ironman: Investigating the antecedents and consequences of endurance athletes' state anxiety. *The Sport Psychologist, 9,* 29–40.

HANIN, Y., & SYRJÄ, P. (1995). Performance affect in junior ice hockey players: An application of the individual zones of optimal functioning model. *The Sport Psychologist, 9,* 169–187.

HANIN, Y. L. (1989). Interpersonal and intragroup anxiety in sports. In D. Hackfort & C. D. Spielberger (Eds.), *Anxiety in sports: An interactional perspective* (pp. 19–28). New York: Hemisphere.

HANRAHAN, S. J., GROVE, J. R., & HATTIE, J. A. (1989). Development of a questionnaire measure of sport-related attributional style. *International Journal of Sport Psychology, 20,* 114–134.

HANSEN, H., & GAUTHIER, R. (1989). Factors affecting attendance at professional sport events. *Journal of Sport Management, 3,* 15–32.

HANSON, S. J., McCULLAGH, P., & TONYMON, P. (1992). The relationship of personality characteristics, life stress, and coping resources to athletic injury. *Journal of Sport & Exercise Psychology, 14,* 262–272.

HARACKIEWICZ, J. H. (1979). The effects of reward contingency and performance feedback on intrinsic motivation. *Journal of Personality and Social Psychology, 37,* 1352–1363.

HARDER, J. W. (1991). Equity theory versus expectancy theory: The case of major league baseball free agents. *Journal of Applied Psychology, 76,* 458–464.

HARDY, C. J. (1990). Social loafing: Motivational losses in collective performance. *International Journal of Sport Psychology, 21,* 305–327.

HARDY, C. J., & CRACE, R. K. (1991). The effects of task structure and teammate competence on social loafing. *Journal of Sport & Exercise Psychology, 13,* 372–381.

HARDY, C. J., & CRACE, R. K. (1993). The dimensions of social support when dealing with sport injuries. In D. Pargman (Ed.), *Psychological bases of sport injuries* (pp. 121–144). Morgantown, WV: Fitness Information Technology.

HARDY, L. (1990). A catastrophe model of performance in sport. In J. Graham & L. Hardy (Eds.), *Stress and performance in sport* (pp. 81–106). New York: Wiley.

HARGER, G. J., & RAGLIN, J. S. (1994). Correspondence between actual and recalled precompetition anxiety in collegiate track and field athletes. *Journal of Sport & Exercise Psychology, 16,* 206–11.

HARNICK, F. S. (1978). The relationship between ability level and task difficulty in producing imitation in infants. *Child Development, 49,* 209–212.

HARRELL, W. A. (1980). Aggression by high school basketball players: An observational study of the effects of opponents' aggression and frustration-inducing factors. *International Journal of Sport Psychology, 11,* 290–298.

HARRELL, W. A. (1981). Verbal aggressiveness in spectators at professional hockey games: The effects of tolerance of violence and amount of exposure to hockey. *Human Relations, 34,* 643–655.

HARRIS, D. V., & ROBINSON, W. J. (1986). The effects of skill level on EMG activity during internal and external imagery. *Journal of Sport Psychology, 8,* 105–111.

HARRIS, G. (1993, April 10). A true salesman. *The Courier-Journal,* p. 1.

HARRIS, O. (1993). African-American predominance in collegiate sports. In D. Brooks & R. Althouse (Eds.), *Racism in college athletics: The African-American athlete's experience* (pp. 51–74). Morgantown, WV: Fitness Information Technology.

HARRISON, R. P., & FELTZ, D. L. (1980). The professionalization of sport psychology: Legal considerations. In W. Straub (Ed.), *Sport psychology: An analysis of athlete behavior* (2nd ed., pp. 26–34). Ithaca NY: Mouvement Publications.

HART, B. A., HASBROOK, C. A., & MATHES, S. A. (1986). An examination of the reduction in the number of female interscholastic coaches. *Research Quarterly for Exercise and Sport, 57,* 68–77.

HART, E. A., LEARY, M. R., & REJESKI, W. J. (1989). The measurement of social physique anxiety. *Journal of Sport & Exercise Psychology, 11,* 94–104.

HART, R. A., HUTTON, J., & SHAROT, T. (1975). A statistical analysis of association football attendances. *Applied Statistics, 24,* 17–27.

HARTER, S. (1981a). The development of competence motivation in the mastery of cognitive and physical skills: Is there still a place for joy? In G. C. Roberts & D. L. Landers (Eds.), *Psychology of motor behavior and sport—1980* (pp. 3–29). Champaign, IL: Human Kinetics.

HARTER, S. (1981b). A model of mastery motivation in children: Individual differences and developmental change. In W. A. Collins (Ed.), *Minnesota symposium on child psychology* (Vol. 14, pp. 215–255). Hillsdale, NJ: Erlbaum.

HARTER, S. (1986). Processes underlying the construction, maintenance, and enhancement of the self-concept in children. In J. Suls & A. G. Greenwald (Eds.), *Psychological perspectives on the self* (Vol. 3, pp. 136–182). Hillsdale, NJ: Erlbaum.

HARTER, S. (1993). Causes and consequences of low self-esteem in children and adolescents. In R. F. Baumeister (Ed.), *Self-esteem: The puzzle of low self-regard* (pp. 87–116). New York: Plenum.

HASTORF, A. H., & CANTRIL, H. (1954). They saw a game: A case study. *Journal of Abnormal and Social Psychology, 49,* 129–134.

HATHAWAY, S. R., & MCKINLEY, J. C. (1943). *Manual for the Minnesota Multiphasic Personality* Inventory. New York: Psychological Corporation.

HAY, R. D., & RAO, C. P. (1982). Factors affecting attendance at football games. In M. Etzel & J. Gaski (Eds.), *Applying marketing technology to spectator sports* (pp. 65–76). South Bend, IN: University of Notre Dame Press.

HEATON, A. W., & SIGALL, H. (1989). The "championship choke" revisited: The role of fear of acquiring a negative identity. *Journal of Applied Social Psychology, 19,* 1019–1033.

HEIDER, F. (1958). *The psychology of interpersonal relations.* New York: Wiley.

HEIL, J. (1993a). Sport psychology, the athlete at risk, and the sports medicine team. In J. Heil (Ed.), *Psychology of sport injury* (pp. 1–13). Champaign, IL: Human Kinetics.

HEIL, J. (1993b). A psychologist's view of the personal challenge of injury. In J. Heil (Ed.), *Psychology of sport injury* (pp. 33–46). Champaign, IL: Human Kinetics.

HEIL, J. (1993c). A framework for psychological assessment. In J. Heil (Ed.), *Psychology of sport injury* (pp. 73–87). Champaign, IL: Human Kinetics.

HEIL, J. (1993d). Diagnostic methods and measures. In J. Heil (Ed.), *Psychology of sport injury* (pp. 89–112). Champaign, IL: Human Kinetics.

HEIL, J. (1993e). A comprehensive approach to injury management. In J. Heil (Ed.), *Psychology of sport injury* (pp. 137–149). Champaign, IL: Human Kinetics.

HEIL, J., BOWMAN, J. J., & BEAN, B. (1993). Patient management and the sports medicine team. In J. Heil (Ed.), *Psychology of sport injury* (pp. 237–249). Champaign, IL: Human Kinetics.

HEILMAN, M. E., HORNSTEIN, H. A., CAGE, J. C., & HERSCHLAG, J. K. (1984). Reactions to prescribed leader behavior as a function of role perspective: The case of the Vroom-Yetton model. *Journal of Applied Psychology, 69,* 50–60.

HELLRIEGEL, D., SLOCUM, J. W., & WOODMAN, R. W. (1992). *Organizational behavior* (6th ed.). St. Paul, MN: West.

HELLSTEDT, J. C. (1987). Sport psychology at a ski academy: Teaching mental skills to young athletes. *The Sport Psychologist, 1,* 56–68.

HELLSTEDT, J. C. (1995). Invisible players: A family systems model. In S. M. Murphy (Ed.), *Sport psychology interventions* (pp. 117–146). Champaign, IL: Human Kinetics.

HENCHY, T., & GLASS, D. C. (1968). Evaluation apprehension and the social facilitation of dominant and subordinate responses. *Journal of Personality and Social Psychology, 10,* 446–454.

HENDERSON, J., & CARROL, W. (1993). The athletic trainer's role in preventing sport injury and rehabilitating injured athletes: A psychological perspective. In D. Pargman (Ed.), *Psychological bases of sport injuries* (pp. 15–31). Morgantown, WV: Fitness Information Technology.

HENDY, H. M., & BOYER, B. J. (1993). Gender differences in attributions for triathlon performance. *Sex Roles, 29,* 527–543.

HENSCHEN, K. P. (1993). Athletic staleness and burnout: Diagnosis, prevention, and treatment. In J. M. Williams (Ed.), *Applied sport psychology: Personal growth to peak performance* (2nd ed., pp. 328–337). Mountain View, CA: Mayfield.

HERSCH, H. (1994, May 9). A saucy start. *Sports Illustrated,* (p. 66–70).

HERWIG, C. (1993, April 9). Title IX spurs rise in women's programs. *USA Today,* p. 8C.

HERWIG, C. (1994, January 25). Equality of salary exception, not rule. *USA Today,* p. 8C.

HICKMAN, J. L. (1979). How to elicit supernormal capabilities in athletes. In P. Klavora & J. V. Daniel (Eds.), *Coach, athlete, and the sport psychologist* (pp. 113–132). Champaign, IL: Human Kinetics.

HIGGS, C. T., & WEILLER, K. H. (1994). Gender bias and the 1992 Summer Olympic games: An analysis of television coverage. *Journal of Sport & Social Issues, 18,* 234–246.

HIGHLEN, P. S., & BENNETT, B. (1980). Predicting performance of elite athletes: The importance of cognitive mediators. In P. Klavora (Ed.), *Psychological and sociological factors in sport* (pp. 257–269). Toronto: University of Toronto Press.

HIGHLEN, P. S., & BENNETT, B. B. (1983). Elite divers and wrestlers: A comparison between open- and closed-skill athletes. *Journal of Sport Psychology, 5,* 390–409.

HINSHAW, K. E. (1991–1992). The effects of mental practice on motor skill performance: Critical evaluation and meta-analysis. *Imagination, Cognition and Personality, 11,* 3–35.

HIRD, J. S., LANDERS, D. M., THOMAS, J. R., & HORAN, J. J. (1991). Physical practice is superior to mental practice in enhancing cognitive and motor task performance. *Journal of Sport & Exercise Psychology, 13,* 281–293.

HIRT, E. R., & RYALLS, K. R. (1994). Highly allegiant fans and sports team evaluation: The mediating role of self-esteem. *Perceptual and Motor Skills, 79,* 24–26.

HIRT, E. R., ZILLMANN, D., ERICKSON, G. A., & KENNEDY, C. (1992). Costs and benefits of allegiance: Changes in fans' self-ascribed competencies after team victory versus defeat. *Journal of Personality and Social Psychology, 63,* 724–738.

HOCH, P. (1972). *Rip of the big game: The exploitation of sports by the power elite.* Garden City, NY: Doubleday.

HOGSHEAD, N. (1992, June 16). Women deserve equal praise for obtaining athletic bodies. *USA Today,* p. 12C.

HOKANSON, J. E. (1970). Psychophysiological evaluation of the catharsis hypothesis. In. E. L. Megargee & J. E. Hokanson (Eds.), *The dynamics of aggression* (pp. 74–86). New York: Harper Row.

HOKANSON, J. E., & BURGESS, M. (1962). The effects of three types of aggression on vascular processes. *Journal of Abnormal and Social Psychology, 64,* 446–449.

HOLMES, D. S. (1984). Meditation and somatic arousal reduction: A review of the experimental literature. *American Psychologist, 39,* 1–10.

HORN, J. C. (1988, October). Dome-inating the game. *Psychology Today,* p. 20.

HORN, T. S. (1992). Leadership effectiveness in the sport domain. In T. S. Horn (Ed.), *Advances in sport psychology* (pp. 181–199). Champaign, IL: Human Kinetics.

HORNE, T., & CARRON, A. V. (1985). Compatibility in coach-athlete relationships. *Journal of Sport Psychology, 7,* 137–149.

HORNER, M. S. (1972). Toward an understanding of achievement-related conflicts in women. *Journal of Social Issues, 28,* 157–175.

HORTON, A. M., & SHELTON, J. K. (1978). The rational wrestler—A pilot study. *Perceptual and Motor Skills, 46,* 882.

HOWARD, G. E. (1912). Social psychology of the spectator. *American Journal of Sociology, 18,* 33–50.

HUDDLESTON, S., AHRABI-FARD, I., & GARVIN, G. W. (1995). Self-evaluation compared to coaches' eval-uation of athletes' competitive orientation. *Journal of Sport Behavior, 18,* 209–214.

HUGHES, R. H. (1987). Response to "An Observer's View of Sport Sociology." *Sociology of Sport Journal, 4,* 137–139.

HUGHES, S. (1990). Implementing psychological skills training program in high school athletics. *Journal of Sport Behavior, 13,* 15–22.

HULL, C. L. (1943). *Principles of behavior.* New York: Appleton.

HULL, C. L. (1951). *Essentials of behavior.* New Haven, CT: Yale University Press.

HUNT, P. J., & HILLERY, J. M. (1973). Social facilitation in a coaction setting: An examination of the effects over learning trials. *Journal of Experimental Social Psychology, 9,* 563–571.

HUSMAN, B. F. (1955). Aggression in boxers and wrestlers as measured by projective techniques. *Research Quarterly, 26,* 421–425.

IEVLEVA, L., & ORLICK, T. (1991). Mental links to enhanced healing: An exploratory study. *The Sport Psychologist, 5,* 25–40.

IEVLEVA, L., & ORLICK, T. (1993). Mental paths to enhanced recovery from a sports injury. In D. Pargman (Ed.), *Psychological bases of sport injuries* (pp. 219–245). Morgantown, WV: Fitness Information Technology.

INGHAM, A. G., LEVINGER, G., GRAVES, J., & PECKHAM, V. (1974). The Ringlemann effect: Studies of group size and group performance. *Journal of Experimental Social Psychology, 10,* 371–384.

International Society of Sport Psychology. (1993). The use of anabolic-androgenic steroids (AAS) in sport and physical activity: A position statement. *International Journal of Sport Psychology, 24,* 74–78.

IRVING, P. G., & GOLDSTEIN, S. R. (1990). Effect of home-field advantage on peak performance of baseball pitchers. *Journal of Sport Behavior, 13,* 23–27.

ISO-AHOLA, S. E. (1980). Attributional determinants of decisions to attend football games. *Scandinavian Journal of Sports Sciences, 2,* 39–46.

ISO-AHOLA, S. E., & HATFIELD, B. (1986). *Psychology of sports: A social psychological approach.* Dubuque, IA: Brown.

JACKSON, D. W., JARRETT, H., BAILEY, D., KAUSEK, J., SWANSON, J., & POWELL, J. W. (1978). Injury prediction in the young athlete: A preliminary report. *The American Journal of Sport Medicine, 6,* 6–14.

JACOBSON, E. (1929). *Progressive relaxation.* Chicago: University of Chicago Press.

JACOBSON, E. (1931). Electrical measurements of neuromuscular states during mental activities. *American Journal of Physiology, 96,* 115–121.

JACOBSON, E. (1976). *You must relax.* New York: McGraw-Hill.

JAKUBCZAK, L. F., & WALTERS, R. H. (1959). Suggestibility as dependency behavior. *Journal of Abnormal and Social Psychology, 59,* 102–107.

JAMES, W. (1890). *Principles of psychology.* New York: Holt.

JEFFERIES, S. C., & ESPARZA, R. (1992). Effects of imagery, relaxation, and self-talk on competitive interscholastic wrestling performance. *Research Quarterly for Exercise and Sport, 63* (Supplement), A–79.

JENKINS, S. (1993, May 10). Savage assault. *Sports Illustrated,* pp. 18–21.

JOHNSON, B. D., & JOHNSON, N. R. (1995). Stacking and "stoppers": A test of the outcome control hypothesis. *Sociology of Sport Journal, 12,* 105–112.

JOHNSON, J. H., & SIEGEL, D. S. (1992). Effects of association and dissociation on effort perception. *Journal of Sport Behavior, 15,* 119–129.

JOHNSON, R. D., & DOWNING, L. L. (1979). Deindividuation and valence of cues: Effects on prosocial and antisocial behavior. *Journal of Personality and Social Psychology, 37,* 1532–1538.

JONES, E. E. (1979). The rocky road from acts to dispositions. *American Psychologist, 34,* 107–117.

JONES, E. E., & BERGLAS, S. (1978). Control of attributions about the self through self-handicapping strategies: The appeal of alcohol and the role of underachievement. *Personality and Social Psychology Bulletin, 4,* 200–206.

JONES, E. E., & DAVIS, K. E. (1965). From acts to dispositions: The attribution process in person perception. In L. Berkowitz (Ed.), *Advances in experimental social psychology* (Vol. 2, pp. 219–266). New York: Academic Press.

JONES, G., HANTON, S., & SWAIN, A. (1994). Intensity and interpretation of anxiety symptoms in elite and non-elite sports performers. *Personality and Individual Differences, 17,* 657–663.

JONES, G., & SWAIN, A. (1992). Intensity and direction as dimensions of competitive state anxiety and relationships with competitiveness. *Perceptual and Motor Skills, 74,* 467–472.

JONES, G., & SWAIN, A. (1995). Predispositions to experience debilitative and facilitative anxiety in elite and nonelite performers. *The Sport Psychologist, 9,* 201–211.

JONES, G., SWAIN, A., & CALE, A. (1990). Antecedents of multidimensional competitive state anxiety and self-confidence in elite intercollegiate middle-distance runners. *The Sport Psychologist, 4,* 107–118.

JONES, G., SWAIN, A., & CALE, A. (1991). Gender differences in precompetition temporal patterning and antecedents of anxiety and self-confidence. *Journal of Sport & Exercise Psychology, 13,* 1–15.

JONES, G., SWAIN, A., & HARDY, L. (1993). Intensity and direction dimensions of competitive state anxiety and relationships with performance. *Journal of Sport Sciences, 11,* 525–532.

JONES, J. C. H. (1969). The economics of the National Hockey League. *Canadian Journal of Economics, 2,* 1–20.

JONES, J. G., & POOLEY, J. C. (1986). Cheating in sport: A comparison of attitudes toward cheating of Canadian and British rugby players. In M. L. Krotee & E. M. Jaeger (Eds.), *Comparative physical education and sport* (vol. 3, pp. 335–345). Champaign, IL: Human Kinetics.

KAHNEMAN, D. (1973). *Attention and effort.* Englewood Cliffs, NJ: Prentice-Hall.

KAISSIDIS, A. N., & ANSHEL, M. H. (1993). Sources and intensity of acute stress in adolescent and adult Australian basketball referees: A preliminary study. *The Australian Journal of Science and Medicine in Sport, 25,* 97–103.

KAMAL, A. F., BLAIS, C., KELLY, P., & EKSTRAND, K. (1995). Self-esteem attributional components of athletes versus nonathletes. *International Journal of Sport Psychology, 26,* 189–195.

KANAREFF, V. T., & LANZETTA, J. T. (1960). Effects of success-failure experiences and probability of reinforcement upon the acquisition and extinction of an imitative response. *Psychological Reports, 7,* 151–166.

KANAZAWA, S. (1992). Outcome or expectancy? Antecedent of spontaneous causal attribution. *Personality and Social Psychology Bulletin, 18,* 659–668.

KANE, J. E. (1980). Personality research: The current controversy and implications for sports studies. In W. Straub (Ed.), *Sport psychology: An analysis of athlete behavior* (2nd ed., pp. 228–240). Ithaca NY: Mouvement Publications.

KARABENICK, S. A., & YOUSSEF, Z. (1968). Performance as a function of achievement motive level and perceived difficulty. *Journal of Personality and Social Psychology, 10,* 414–419.

KARP, D. A., & YOELS, W. C. (1990). Sport and urban life. *Journal of Sport & Social Issues, 14,* 77–102.

KEARNS, D. W., & CROSSMAN, J. (1992). Effects of a cognitive intervention package on the free-throw performance of varsity basketball players during practice and competition. *Perceptual and Motor Skills, 75,* 1243–1253.

KEKIS, J. (1995, July 28). Hall feels fans' reaction to infamous strike. *The Paducah Sun,* p. 3B.

KELLEY, H. H. (1967). Attribution theory in social psychology. In. D. Levine (Ed.), *Nebraska Symposium on Motivation* (Vol. 15, pp. 192–238). Lincoln: University of Lincoln Press.

KELLEY, H. H. (1973). The process of causal attribution. *American Psychologist, 28,* 107–128.

KELLY, B. R., & MCCARTHY, J. F. (1979). Personality dimensions of aggression: Its relationship to time and place of action in ice hockey. *Human Relations, 32,* 219–225.

KENDALL, G., HRYCAIKO, D., MARTIN, G. L., & KENDALL, T. (1990). The effects of an imagery rehearsal, relaxation, and self-talk package on basketball game performance. *Journal of Sport & Exercise Psychology, 12,* 157–166.

KENYON, G. S. (1969). Sport involvement: A conceptual go and some consequences thereof. In G. S. Kenyon (Ed.), *Sociology of sport* (pp. 77–99). Chicago: The Athletic Institute.

KERR, G., & MINDEN, H. (1988). Psychological factors related to the occurrence of athletic injuries. *Journal of Sport & Exercise Psychology, 10,* 167–173.

KERR, J. H. (1985). The experience of arousal: A new basis for studying arousal effects in sport. *Journal of Sports Sciences, 3,* 169–179.

KERR, J. H. (1990). Stress and sport: Reversal theory. In J. Graham & L. Hardy (Eds.), *Stress and performance in sport* (pp. 107–131). New York: Wiley.

KEYS, B., & CASE, T. (1990). How to become an influential manager. *Academy of Management Executive, 4,* 38–51.

KIMBLE, C. E., & COOPER, B. P. (1992). Association and dissociation by football fans. *Perceptual and Motor Skills, 75,* 303–309.

KIMBLE, G. A. (1961). *Hilgard and Marquis' conditioning and learning.* New York: Appleton.

KIRSCHENBAUM, D. S., ORDMAN, A. M., TOMARKEN, A. J., & HOLTZBAUER, R. (1982). Effects of differential self-monitoring and level of mastery on sports performance: Brain power bowling. *Cognitive Therapy and Research, 6,* 335–342.

KLASS, E. T. (1979). Relative influence of sincere, insincere, and neutral symbolic models. *Journal of Experimental Child Psychology, 27,* 48–59.

KLAVORA, P. (1978). An attempt to derive inverted-U curves based on the relationship between anxiety and athletic performance. In D. M. Landers & R. W. Christina (Eds.), *Psychology of motor behavior and sport—1977* (pp. 369–377). Champaign, IL: Human Kinetics.

KLEIN, S. B. (1987). *Learning: Principles and applications.* New York: McGraw-Hill.

KLINT, K. A., & WEISS, M. R. (1986). Dropping in and dropping out: Participation motives of current and former youth gymnasts. *Canadian Journal of Applied Sport Sciences, 11,* 106–114.

KLINT, K. A., & WEISS, M. R. (1987). Perceived competence and motives for participating in youth sports: A test of Harter's competence motivation theory. *Journal of Sport Psychology, 9,* 55–65.

KNOPF, R. C. (1987). Human behavior, cognition, and affect in the natural environment. In D. Stokols & I. Altman (Eds.), *Handbook of environmental psychology, Vol. 1* (pp. 783–825). New York: Wiley.

KNOPPERS, A., MEYER, B. B., EWING, M., & FORREST, L. (1989). Gender and the salaries of coaches. *Sociology of Sport Journal, 6,* 348–361.

KOLDITZ, T. A., & ARKIN, R. M. (1982). An impression management interpretation of the self-handicapping strategy. *Journal of Personality and Social Psychology, 43,* 492–502.

KONZAK, B. (1980). Some comments on the field of sport sociology and its relation to sport psychology: Toward an integration of sport sociology and sport psychology. In P. Klavora (Ed.), *Psychological and sociological factors in sport* (pp. 337–361). Toronto: University of Toronto Press.

KOOP, S., & MARTIN, G. L. (1983). Evaluation of a coaching strategy to reduce swimming stroke errors with beginning age-group swimmers. *Journal of Applied Behavioral Analysis, 16,* 447–460.

KOVICH, M. (1971). Sport as an art form. *Journal of Health, Physical Education, and Recreation, 42*(8), 42.

KOZAR, B., VAUGHN, R. E., LORD, R. H., & WHITFIELD, K. E. (1995). Basketball free-throw performance. Practice implications *Journal of Sport Behavior, 18,* 123–129.

KRANE, V. (1994). The mental readiness form as a measure of competitive state anxiety. *The Sport Psychologist, 8,* 189–202.

KRANE, V., & WILLIAMS, J. M. (1994). Cognitive anxiety, somatic anxiety, and confidence in track and field athletes: The impact of gender, competitive level and task characteristics. *International Journal of Sport Psychology, 25,* 203–217.

KRAUS, J. F., & CONROY, C. (1984). Mortality and morbidity from injuries in sports and recreation. *Annual Review of Public Health, 5,* 163–192.

KROLL, W. (1976). Current strategies and problems in personality assessment of athletes. In A. C. Fisher (Ed.), *Psychology of sport* (pp. 371–390). Palo Alto, CA: Mayfield.

KROLL, W., & LEWIS, G. (1980). America's first sport psychologist. In W. Straub (Ed.), *Sport psychology: An analysis of athlete behavior* (2nd ed., pp. 13–16). Ithaca NY: Mouvement Publications.

KYLLO, L. B., & LANDERS, D. M. (1995). Goal setting in sport and exercise: A research synthesis to resolve the controversy. *Journal of Sport & Exercise Psychology, 17,* 117–137.

LAHR, J. (1976). The theater of sports. In M. Hart (Ed.), *Sport in the sociocultural process* (2nd ed., pp. 199–209). Dubuque, IA: Brown.

LAIRD, D. A. (1923). Changes in motor control and individual variations under the influence of 'razzing.' *Journal of Experimental Psychology, 6,* 236–246.

LAKIE, W. L. (1962). Personality characteristics of certain groups of intercollegiate athletes. *Research Quarterly, 33,* 566–573.

LALONDE, R. N. (1992). The dynamics of group differentiation in the face of defeat. *Personality and Social Psychology Bulletin, 18,* 336–342.

LAMB, M. (1986). Self-concept and injury frequency among female college field hockey players. *Athletic Training, 21,* 220–224.

LANDERS, D. M. (1995). Sport psychology: The formative years, 1950–1980. *The Sport Psychologist, 9,* 406–417.

LANDERS, D. M., BRAWLEY, L. R., & HALE, B. D. (1978). Habit strength differences in motor behavior: The effects of social facilitation paradigms and subject sex. In D. M. Landers & R. W. Christina (Eds.), *Psychology of motor behavior and sport—1977* (pp. 420–433). Champaign, IL: Human Kinetics.

LANDERS, D. M., & LANDERS, D. M. (1973). Teacher versus peer models: Effects of model's presence and performance level on motor behavior. *Journal of Motor Behavior, 5,* 129–139.

LANDERS, D. M., & McCULLAGH, P. D. (1977). Social facilitation of motor performance. In J. Keogh & R. S. Hutton (Eds.), *Exercise and sport science reviews* (vol. 4, pp. 125–162). Santa Barbara, CA: Journal Publishing Affiliates.

LANDERS, D. M., WILKINSON, M. O., HATFIELD, B. D., & BARBER, H. (1982). Causality and the cohesion-performance relationship. *Journal of Sport Psychology, 4,* 170–183.

LANE, J. F. (1980). Improving athletic performance through visuo-motor behavior rehearsal. In R. Suinn (Ed.), *Psychology in sport—methods and applications* (pp. 316–320). Minneapolis, MN: Burgess.

LANNING, W., & HISANAGA, B. (1983). A study of the relation between the reduction of competition anxiety and an increase in athletic performance. *International Journal of Sport Psychology, 14,* 219–227.

LAPCHICK, R. E., & BENEDICT, J. R. (1993). 1993 racial report card. *CSSS Digest, 5*(1), 1, 8.

LATANÉ, B., WILLIAMS, K. D., & HARKINS, S. (1979). Many hands make light work: The causes and consequences of social loafing. *Journal of Personality and Social Psychology, 37,* 822–832.

LATHAM, G. P., & LEE, T. W. (1986). Goal setting. In E. Locke (Ed.), *Generalizing from laboratory to field settings* (pp. 101–117). Lexington, MA: Lexington Books.

LAU, R. R. (1984). Dynamics of the attribution process. *Journal of Personality and Social Psychology, 46,* 1017–1028.

LAU, R. R., & RUSSELL, D. (1980). Attributions in the sports pages. *Journal of Personality and Social Psychology, 39,* 29–38.

LAUGHLIN, N., & LAUGHLIN, S. (1994). The relationship between the similarity in perceptions of teacher/coach leader behavior and evaluations of their effectiveness. *International Journal of Sport Psychology, 22,* 396–410.

LAYDEN, T. (1995, April 3). Bettor education. *Sports Illustrated,* pp. 68–74, 76–78, 80, 82–86, 90.

LAYMAN, E. M. (1980). Meditation and sport performance. In W. Straub (Ed.), *Sport psychology: An analysis of athlete behavior* (2nd ed., pp. 266–273). Ithaca NY: Mouvement Publications.

LEARY, M. R. (1992). Self-presentational processes in exercise and sport. *Journal of Sport & Exercise Psychology, 14,* 339–351.

LEATH, V. W., & LUMPKIN, A. (1992). An analysis of sportswomen on the covers and in the feature articles of *Women's Sports and Fitness* magazine, 1975–1989. *Journal of Sport & Social Issues, 16,* 121–126.

LEAVITT, J., YOUNG, J., & CONNELLY, D. (1989). The effects of videotape highlights on state self-confidence. *Journal of Applied Research in Coaching and Athletics, 4,* 225–232.

LEDDY, M. H., LAMBERT, M. J., & OGLES, B. M. (1994). Psychological consequences of athletic injury among high-level competitors. *Research Quarterly for Exercise and Sport, 65,* 347–354.

LEDERMAN, D. (1992a, March 18). Men get 70% of money available for athletic scholarships at colleges that play big-time sports, new study finds. *The Chronicle of Higher Education, 38,* A44–A46.

LEDERMAN, D. (1992b, April 8). Men outnumber women and get most of money in big-time sports programs. *The Chronicle of Higher Education, 38,* A36–A40.

LEDERMAN, D. (1993, May 26). Abide by U.S. sex-bias laws, NCAA panel urges colleges. *The Chronicle of Higher Education, 39,* A31–A34.

LEE, A. B., & HEWITT, J. (1987). Using visual imagery in a flotation tank to improve gymnastic performance and reduce physical symptoms. *International Journal of Sport Psychology, 18,* 223–230.

LEE, B. A., & ZEISS, C. A. (1980). Behavioral commitment to the role of sport consumer: An exploratory analysis. *Sociology and Social Research, 64,* 405–419.

LEE, C. (1990). Psyching up for a muscular endurance task: Effects of image content on performance and mood state. *Journal of Sport & Exercise Psychology, 12,* 66–73.

LEE, T. D., & GENOVESE, E. D. (1988). Distribution of practice in motor skill acquisition: Learning and performance effects reconsidered. *Research Quarterly for Exercise and Sport, 59,* 277–287.

LEFEBVRE, L. M., & PASSER, M. W. (1974). The effects of game location and importance on aggression in team sport. *International Journal of Sport Psychology, 5,* 102–110.

LEHMAN, D. R., & REIFMAN, A. (1987). Spectator influence on basketball officiating. *The Journal of Social Psychology, 127,* 673–675.

LEITH, L. M. (1982). An experimental analysis of the effect of vicarious participation in physical activity on subject aggressiveness. *International Journal of Sport Psychology, 13,* 234–241.

LEITH, L. M. (1989). The effect of various physical activities, outcome, and emotional arousal on subject aggression scores. *International Journal of Sport Psychology, 20,* 57–66.

LEITH, L. M., & PRAPAVESSIS, H. (1989). Attributions of causality and dimensionality associated with sport outcomes in objectively evaluated and subjectively evaluated sports. *International Journal of Sport Psychology, 20,* 224–234.

LENNEY, E. (1977). Women's self-confidence in achievement settings. *Psychological Bulletin, 84,* 1–13.

LENNON, J. X., & HATFIELD, F. C. (1980). The effects of crowding and observation of athletic events on spectator tendency toward aggressive behavior. *Journal of Sport Behavior, 3,* 61–68.

LEONARD, W. M. II (1987). Stacking in college basketball: A neglected analysis. *Sociology of Sport Journal, 4,* 403–409.

LEONARD, W. M. II (1989). The "home advantage": The case of the modern Olympiads. *Journal of Sport Behavior, 12,* 227–241.

LEONARD, W. M. II (1991). Socialization into an avocational subculture. *Journal of Sport Behavior, 14,* 169–185.

LEONARD, W. M. II (1993). *A sociological perspective of sport* (4th ed.). New York: Macmillan.

LEPPER, M. R., GREENE, D., & NISBETT, R. E. (1973). Undermining children's intrinsic interest with extrinsic reward: A test of the "overjustification" hypothesis. *Journal of Personality and Social Psychology, 28,* 129–137.

LEUCK, M. R., KRAHENBUHL, G. S., & ODENKIRK, J. E. (1979). Assessment of spectator aggression at intercollegiate basketball contests. *Review of Sport and Leisure, 4,* 40–52.

LEUNES, A. D., & HAYWARD, S. A. (1990). Sport psychology as viewed by chairpersons of APA-approved clinical psychology programs. *The Sport Psychologist, 4,* 18–24.

LEUNES, A. D., HAYWARD, S. A., & DAISS, S. (1988). Annotated bibliography on the Profile of Mood States in sport, 1975–1988. *Journal of Sport Behavior, 11,* 213–239.

LeUnes, A. D., & Nation, J. R. (1982). Saturday's heroes: A psychological portrait of college football players. *Journal of Sport Behavior, 5,* 139–149.

LeUnes, A. D., & Nation, J. R. (1989). *Sport psychology: An introduction.* Chicago: Nelson-Hall.

Lever, J. (1969). Soccer: Opium of the Brazilian people. *Trans-Action, 7,* 36–43.

Lever, J., & Wheeler, S. (1984). *The Chicago Tribune* sports page, 1900–1975. *Sociology of Sport Journal, 1,* 299–313.

Lewis, J. M. (1980). The structural dimensions of fan violence. In P. Klavora (Ed.), *Psychological and sociological factors in sport* (pp. 148–155). Toronto: University of Toronto Press.

Lewis, J. M. (1982). Fan violence: An American social problem. *Research in Social Problems and Public Policy, 2,* 175–206.

Lidz, F., & Kennedy, K. (1995, August 21). Scorecard. *Sports Illustrated,* p. 14.

Linville, P. W. (1987). Self-complexity as a cognitive buffer against stress related illness and depression. *Journal of Personality and Social Psychology, 52,* 663–676.

Linville, P. W., & Jones, E. E. (1980). Polarized appraisals of out-group members. *Journal of Personality and Social Psychology, 38,* 689–703.

Lister, V. (1994a, January 28). Beach volleyball: More than a bikini show. *USA Today,* p. 10C.

Lister, V. (1994b, January 28). Debate focuses on gender as selling point. *USA Today,* p. 10C.

Livengood, J. (1992, May 14). Wash. St. member of vangaurd. *USA Today,* p. 14C.

Li-Wei, Z., Qi-Wei, M. Orlick, T. & Zitzelsberger, L. (1992). The effect of mental imagery training on performance enhancement with 7–10-year-old children. *The Sport Psychologist, 6,* 230–241.

Lobmeyer, D. L., & Wasserman, E. A. (1986). Preliminaries to free throw shooting: Superstitious behavior? *Journal of Sport Behavior, 9,* 70–78.

Locke, E. A. (1991). Problems with goal-setting research in sports—and their solution. *Journal of Sport & Exercise Psychology, 13,* 311–316.

Locke, E. A., & Latham, G. P. (1985). The application of goal setting to sports. *Journal of Sport & Exercise Psychology, 7,* 205–222.

Locke, E. A., & Latham, G. P. (1990). *A theory of goal setting task performance.* Englewood Cliffs, NJ: Prentice Hall.

Locke, E. A., & Latham, G. P. (1994). Goal setting theory. In H. F. O'Neil, Jr. & M. Drillings (Eds.), *Motivation: Theory and research* (pp. 13–29). Hillsdale, NJ: Erlbaum.

Locksley, A., & Colten, M. E. (1979). Psychological androgyny: A case of mistaken identity? *Journal of Personality and Social Psychology, 37,* 1017–1031.

Lois, G. (1992, June 16). Portrayals 'stunning' but performances draw the most notice. *USA Today,* p. 12C.

Long, B. C. (1980). Stress management for the athlete: A cognitive behavioral model. In C. H. Neadeau, W. R. Halliwell, K. M. Newell, & G. C. Roberts (Eds.), *Psychology of motor behavior and sport—1979* (pp. 73–83). Champaign, IL: Human Kinetics.

Lopiano, D. A. (1993). Political analysis: Gender equity strategies for the future. In G. L. Cohen (Ed.), *Women in sports: Issues and controversies* (pp. 104–116). New York: Sage.

Lord, R. G., & Hohenfeld, J. A. (1979). Longitudinal field assessment of equity effects on the performance of major league baseball players. *Journal of Applied Psychology, 64,* 19–26.

Lorenz, K. (1966). *On aggression.* New York: Harcourt Brace Jovanovich.

Lorenz, K. (1974). *Civilized man's eight deadly sins.* New York: Harcourt Brace Jovanovich.

Lubell, A. (1989). Does steroid abuse cause—or excuse—violence? *The Physician and Sportsmedicine, 17*(2), 176–180, 185.

Lufi, D., & Tenenbaum, G. (1991). Persistence among young male gymnasts. *Perceptual and Motor Skills, 72,* 479–482.

Lumpkin, A., & Williams, L. D. (1991). An analysis of *Sports Illustrated* feature articles, 1954–1987. *Sociology of Sport Journal, 8,* 16–32.

Lydon, M. C. (1993). Secondary school programs: Diversity in practice. In G. L. Cohen (Ed.), *Women in sports: Issues and controversies* (pp. 95–103). New York: Sage.

Mace, R. D., & Carroll, D. (1985). The control of anxiety in sport: Stress inoculation training prior to abseiling. *International Journal of Sport Psychology, 16,* 165–175.

Mace, R. D., Carroll, D., & Eastman, C. (1986). Stress inoculation training to control anxiety and enhance performance in sport. In J. Watkins, T. Reilly, & L. Burwitz (Eds.), *'86 Glascow Confer-*

ence—*VIII Commonwealth and International Conference on Sport* (pp. 175–181). Cambridge, MA: Cambridge University Press.

MADDEN, C. C., KIRKBY, R. J., & McDONALD, D. (1989). Coping styles of competitive middle distance runners. *International Journal of Sport Psychology, 20,* 287–296.

MADDEN, C. C., SUMMERS, J. J., & BROWN, D. F. (1990). The influence of perceived stress on coping with competitive basketball. *International Journal of Sport Psychology, 21,* 21–35.

MADDI, S. R., & HESS, M. J. (1992). Personality hardiness and success in basketball. *International Journal of Sport Psychology, 23,* 360–368.

MAGILL, R. A. (1993). Augmented feedback in skill acquisition. In R. N. Singer, M. Murphey, & L. K. Tennant (Eds.), *Handbook of research on sport psychology* (pp. 193–212). New York: Macmillan.

MAGILL, R. A., & WOOD, C. A. (1986). Knowledge of results precision as a learning variable in motor skill acquisition. *Research Quarterly for Exercise and Sport, 57,* 170–173.

MAHEU, R. (1962). Sport and culture. *International Journal of Adult and Youth Education, 15,* 169–182.

MAHONEY, M. J. (1989). Psychological predictors of elite and non-elite performance in Olympic weightlifting. *International Journal of Sport Psychology, 20,* 1–12.

MAHONEY, M. J., & AVENER, M. (1977). Psychology of the elite athlete: An exploratory study. *Cognitive Therapy and Research, 1,* 135–141.

MAHONEY, M. J., GABRIEL, T. J., & PERKINS, T. S. (1987). Psychological skills and exceptional athletic performance. *The Sport Psychologist, 1,* 181–199.

MALEC, M. A. (1994). Gender (in)equity in the NCAA news? *Journal of Sport & Social Issues, 18,* 376–379.

MALEC, M. A. (1995). Sports discussion groups on the internet. *Journal of Sport & Social Issues, 19,* 108–114.

MANDLER, G. (1984). *Mind and body.* New York: Norton.

MANN, L. (1969). Queue culture: The waiting line as a social system. *American Journal of Sociology, 75,* 340–354.

MANN, L. (1974). On being a sore loser: How fans react to their team's failure. *Australian Journal of Psychology, 26,* 37–47.

MANN, L. (1989). Sports crowds and the collective behavior perspective. In J. H. Goldstein (Ed.), *Sports, games, and play: Social and psychological viewpoints* (2nd ed., pp. 299–331). Hillsdale, NJ: Erlbaum.

MARCUM, J. P., & GREENSTEIN, T. N. (1985). Factors affecting attendance of Major League baseball: II. A within-season analysis. *Sociology of Sport Journal, 2,* 314–322.

MARK, M. M., BRYANT, F. B., & LEHMAN, D. R. (1983). Perceived injustice and sports violence. In J. H. Goldstein (Ed.), *Sports violence* (pp. 83–109). New York: Springer-Verlag.

MARK, M. M., MUTRIE, N., BROOKS, D. R., & HARRIS, D. V. (1984). Causal attributions of winners and losers in individual competitive sports: Toward a reformulation of the self-serving bias. *Journal of Sport Psychology, 6,* 184–196.

MARKUS, H. (1978). The effect of mere presence on social facilitation: An unobtrusive test. *Journal of Experimental Social Psychology, 14,* 389–397.

MAROVELLI, E., & CRAWFORD, S. A. G. M. (1987). Mass media influence on female high school athletes' identification with professional athletes. *International Journal of Sport Psychology, 18,* 231–236.

MARQUES, J. M., YZERBYT, V. Y., & LEYENS, J. P. (1988). The 'black sheep effect': Extremity of judgments towards ingroup members as a function of identification. *European Journal of Social Psychology, 18,* 1–16.

MARSH, H. W., PERRY, C., HORSELY, C., & ROCHE, L. (1995). Multidimensional self-concepts of elite athletes: How do they differ from the general population? *Journal of Sport & Exercise Psychology, 17,* 70–83.

MARTENS, R. (1969). Effect of an audience on learning and performance of a complex motor skill. *Journal of Personality and Social Psychology, 12,* 252–260.

MARTENS, R. (1974). Arousal and motor performance. In J. Wilmore (Ed.), *Exercise and sport science review* (pp. 155–188). New York: Wiley.

MARTENS, R. (1975). *Social psychology and physical activity.* New York: Harper & Row.

MARTENS, R. (1980). From smocks to jocks: A new adventure for sport psychologists. In P. Klavora (Ed.), *Psychological and sociological factors in sport* (pp. 20–26). Toronto: University of Toronto Press.

MARTENS, R. (1981). Sport personology. In G. R. F. Luschen & G. H. Sage (Eds.), *Handbook of social science in sport* (pp. 492–508). Champaign, IL: Stipes.

MARTENS, R. (1987a). Science, knowledge, and sport psychology. *The Sport Psychologist, 1,* 29–55.

MARTENS, R. (1987b). *Coaches guide to sport psychology.* Champaign, IL: Human Kinetics.

MARTENS, R., & LANDERS, D. M. (1970). Motor performance under stress: A test of the inverted-U hypothesis. *Journal of Personality and Social Psychology, 16,* 29–37.

MARTENS, R., & LANDERS, D. M. (1972). Evaluation potential as a determinant of coaction effects. *Journal of Experimental Social Psychology, 8,* 347–359.

MARTENS, R., & PETERSON, J. A. (1971). Group cohesiveness as a determinant of success and member satisfaction in team performance. *International Review of Sport Sociology, 6,* 49–61.

MARTENS, R., VEALEY, R. S., & BURTON, D. (1990). *Competitive anxiety in sport.* Champaign, IL: Human Kinetics.

MARTIN, B. A., & MARTIN, J. H. (1995). Comparing perceived sex role orientations of the ideal male and female athlete to the ideal male and female person. *Journal of Sport Behavior, 18,* 286–301.

MARTIN, G. L., & HRYCAIKO, D. (1983). Effective behavioral coaching: What's it all about? *Journal of Sport Psychology, 5,* 8–20.

MARTIN, J. J., & GILL, D. L. (1991). The relationships among competitive orientation, sport-confidence, self-efficacy, anxiety, and performance. *Journal of Sport & Exercise Psychology, 13,* 149–159.

MARTIN, J. J., & GILL, D. L. (1995). The relationships between competitive orientations and self-efficacy to goal importance, thoughts, and performance in high school distance runners. *Journal of Applied Sport Psychology, 7,* 50–62.

MARTIN, K. A., & HALL, C. R. (1995). Using mental imagery to enhance intrinsic motivation. *Journal of Sport & Exercise Psychology, 17,* 54–69.

MARTIN, L. A. (1976). Effects of competition upon the aggressive responses of college basketball players and wrestlers. *Research Quarterly, 47,* 388–393.

MASHIACH, A. (1980). A study to determine the factors which influence American spectators to go see the olympics in Montreal, 1976. *Journal of Sport Behavior, 3,* 17–26.

MASTERS, K. S., & LAMBERT, M. J. (1989). The relations between cognitive coping strategies, reasons for running, injury, and performance of marathon runners. *Journal of Sport & Exercise Psychology, 11,* 161–170.

MASTERS, K. S., & OGLES, B. M. (1992, August). *Dissociation and injury revisited: There is still no relation.* Paper presented at the meeting of the American Psychological Association, Washington, D.C.

MAUSNER, B. (1953). Studies in social interaction: III. Effect of variation in one partner's prestige on the interaction of observer pairs. *The Journal of Applied Psychology, 37,* 391–393.

MAY, J. R., & SIEB, G. E. (1987). Athletic injuries: Psychosocial factors in the onset, sequelae, rehabilitation, and prevention. In J. R. May & M. J. Asken (Eds.), Sport psychology: The psychological health of the athlete (pp. 157–185). New York: PMA.

MAYNARD, I. W., HEMMINGS, B., & WARWICK-EVANS, L. (1995). The effects of a somatic intervention strategy on competitive state anxiety and performance in semiprofessional soccer players. *The Sport Psychologist, 9,* 51–64.

MAYNARD, I. W., SMITH, M. J., & WARWICK-EVANS, L. (1995). The effects of a cognitive intervention strategy on competitive state anxiety and performance in semiprofessional soccer players. *Journal of Sport & Exercise Psychology, 17,* 428–446.

MAZUR, J. E. (1994). *Learning and behavior* (3rd ed.). Englewood Cliffs, NJ: Prentice-Hall.

MCANDREW, F. T. (1993). *Environmental psychology.* Pacific Grove, CA: Brooks/Cole.

MCARTHUR, L. A. (1972). The how and what of why: Some determinants and consequences of causal attributions. *Journal of Personality and Social Psychology, 22,* 171–193.

MCAULEY, E. (1985). Success and causality in sport: The influence of perception. *Journal of Sport Psychology, 7,* 13–22.

MCAULEY, E. (1992). Self-referent thought in sport and physical activity. In T. S. Horn (Ed.), *Advances in sport psychology* (pp. 101–118). Champaign, IL: Human Kinetics.

MCAULEY, E., DUNCAN, T. E., & RUSSELL, D. (1992). Measuring causal attributions: The revised Causal Dimension Scale (CDSII). *Personality and Social Psychology Bulletin, 18,* 566–573.

MCAULEY, E., & GROSS, J. B. (1983). Perceptions of causality in sport: An application of the causal dimension scale. *Journal of Sport Psychology, 5,* 72–76.

McAuley, E., & Tammen, V. V. (1989). The effects of subjective and objective competitive outcomes on intrinsic motivation. *Journal of Sport & Exercise Psychology, 11,* 84–93.

McCallum, J. (1993, December 6). Scorecard. *Sports Illustrated,* pp. 13–14.

McCallum, J. (1994a, May 23). Way out of control. *Sports Illustrated,* pp. 26–31.

McCallum, J. (1994b, April 25). Final justice. *Sports Illustrated,* pp. 10.

McCarthy, J. F., & Kelly, B. R. (1978a). Aggressive behavior and its effect on performance over time in ice hockey athletes: An archival study. *International Journal of Sport Psychology, 9,* 90–96.

McCarthy, J. F., & Kelly, B. R. (1978b). Aggression, performance variables, and anger self-report in ice hockey players. *The Journal of Psychology, 99,* 97–101.

McClelland, D. C., Atkinson, J. W., Clark, R. A., & Lowell, E. L. (1953). *The achievement motive.* New York: Appleton-Century-Crofts.

McCullagh, P. (1986). Model status as a determinant of observational learning and performance. *Journal of Sport Psychology, 8,* 319–331.

McCullagh, P. (1987). Model similarity effects of motor performance. *Journal of Sport Psychology, 9,* 249–260.

McCullagh, P. (1993). Modeling: Learning, developmental, and social psychological considerations. In R. N. Singer, M. Murphey, & L. K. Tennant (Eds.), *Handbook of research on sport psychology* (pp. 106–126). New York: Macmillan.

McCutcheon, L. E. (1984). The home advantage in high school athletics. *Journal of Sport Behavior, 7,* 135–138.

McDonald, S. A., & Hardy, C. J. (1990). Affective response patterns of the injured athlete: An exploratory analysis. *The Sport Psychologist, 4,* 261–274.

McDougall, M. (1908). *An introduction to social psychology.* London: Methuen.

McElroy, J. C. (1982). A typology of attribution leadership research. *Academy of Management Review, 7,* 413–417.

McElroy, M. A., & Willis, J. D. (1979). Women and the achievement conflict in sport: A preliminary study. *Journal of Sport Psychology, 1,* 241–247.

McGuire, E. J., Courneya, K. S., Widmeyer, W. N., & Carron, A. V. (1992). Aggression as a potential mediator of the home advantage in professional ice hockey. *Journal of Sport & Exercise Psychology, 14,* 148–158.

McGuire, M. (1994, June). Baseball played a special role during World War II. *Baseball Digest,* pp. 66–70.

McGuire, R. T., & Cook, D. L. (1983). The influence of others and the decision to participate in youth sports. *Journal of Sport Behavior, 6,* 9–16.

McHugh, M. C., Duquin, M. E., & Frieze, I. H. (1978). Beliefs about success and failure: Attribution and the female athlete. In C. Oglesby (Ed.), *Women and sport: From myth to reality* (pp. 173–191). Philadelphia: Lea & Febiger.

McIntyre, N. (1992). Involvement in risk recreation: A comparison of objective and subjective measures of engagement. *Journal of Leisure Research, 24,* 64–71.

McKenzie, T. L. (1980). Behavioral engineering in elementary school physical education. In P. Klavora (Ed.), *Psychological and sociological factors in sport* (pp. 194–203). Toronto: University of Toronto Press.

McKenzie, T. L., & Rushall, B. S. (1974). Effects of self-recording on attendance and performance in a competitive swimming training environment. *Journal of Applied Behavioral Analysis, 7,* 199–206.

McNair, D., Lorr, M., & Droppleman, L. (1971). *Manual for the Profile of Mood States.* San Diego: Educational and Industrial Testing Service.

McPherson, B. (1975). Sport consumption and the economics of consumerism. In D. W. Ball & J. W. Loy (Eds.), *Sport and social order: Contributions to the sociology of sport* (pp. 243–275). Reading, MA: Addison-Wesley.

McPherson, B. (1976). Socialization into the role of sport consumer: A theory and causal model. *Canadian Review of Sociology and Anthropology, 13,* 165–177.

McTeer, W. G., White, P. G., & Persad, S. (1995). Manager/coach mid-season replacement and team performance in professional team sports. *Journal of Sport Behavior, 18,* 58–68.

Meacci, W. G., & Price, E. E. (1985). Acquisition and retention of gold putting skill through the relaxation, visualization, and body rehearsal intervention. *Research Quarterly for Exercise and Sport, 56,* 176–179.

MEAD, M. (1955). *Male and female.* New York: New American Library of World Literature.

MEIER, K. V. (1979). "We don't want to set the world on fire": We just want to finish ninth. *Journal of Popular Culture, 13,* 289–301.

MEIER, K. V. (1989). The ignoble sports fan. *Journal of Sport & Social Issues, 13,* 111–119.

MEINDL, J. R., & EHRLICH, S. B. (1987). The romance of leadership and the evaluation of organizational performance. *Academy of Management Journal, 30,* 91–109.

MELNICK, M. J. (1989). The sports fan: A teaching guide and bibliography. *Sociology of Sport Journal, 6,* 167–175.

MELNICK, M. J. (1993). Searching for sociability in the stands: A theory of sports spectating. *Journal of Sport Management, 7,* 44–60.

MEYERS, A. (1995, Winter). Ethical principles of AAASP. *Association for the Advancement of Applied Sport Psychology, 10*(1), 15, 21.

MEYERS, A. W., COOKE, C. J., CULLEN, J., & LILES, L. (1979). Psychological aspects of athletic competitors: A replication across sports. *Cognitive Therapy and Research, 3,* 361–366.

MEYERS, A. W., & SCHLESER, R. (1980). A cognitive behavioral intervention for improving basketball performance. *Journal of Sport Psychology, 2,* 69–73.

MEYERS, A. W., SCHLESER, R., & OKWUMABUA, T. M. (1982). A cognitive behavioral intervention for improving basketball performance. *Research Quarterly for Exercise and Sport, 53,* 344–347.

MEYERS, M. C., LEUNES, A. D., ELLEDGE, J. R., TOLSON, H., & STERLING, J. C. (1992). Injury incidence and psychological mood state patterns in collegiate rodeo athletes. *Journal of Sport Behavior, 15,* 297–305.

MIHOCES, G. (1995, May 23). Fans fight post-strike hangover. *USA Today,* pp. 1C, 2C.

MILLER, B. P., & MILLER, A. J. (1985). Psychological correlates of success in elite sportswomen. *International Journal of Sport Psychology, 16,* 289–295.

MILLER, D. T., & ROSS, M. (1975). Self-serving biases in the attribution of causality: Fact or fiction? *Psychological Bulletin, 82,* 213–225.

MILLER, G. A. (1956). The magical number seven, plus or minus two: Some limits on our capacity for information processing. *Psychological Review, 63,* 81–97.

MILLER, N. E. (1948). Theory and experiment relating psychoanalytic displacement to stimulus-response generalization. *Journal of Abnormal and Social Psychology, 43,* 155–178.

MILLER, N. E., SEARS, R. R., MOWRER, O. H., DOOB, L. W., & DOLLARD, J. (1941). The frustration-aggression hypothesis. *Psychological Review, 48,* 337–366.

MILLER, S. M. (1981). Predictability and human stress: Toward a clarification of evidence and theory. In L. Berkowitz (Ed.), *Advances in experimental social psychology* (Vol. 14, pp. 203–256). New York: Academic Press.

MIRACLE, A. W., & REES, C. R. (1994). *Lessons of the locker room: The myth of school sports.* Amherst, NJ: Prometheus.

MITCHELL, T. R., GREEN, S. G., & WOOD, R. E. (1982). An attributional model of leadership and the poor performing subordinate: Development and validation. In B. M. Staw & L. L. Cummings (Eds.), *Research in organizational behavior* (Vol. 3). Greenwich, CT: JAI Press.

MITCHELL, T. R., & WOOD, R. E. (1979). An empirical test of an attributional model of leaders' responses to poor performance. In R. C. Huseman (Ed.), *Academy of management preceedings, '79* (pp. 94–98). Atlanta: Academy of Management.

MIZRUCHI, M. S. (1985). Local sports teams and the celebration of community: A comparative analysis of the home advantage. *The Sociological Quarterly, 26,* 507–518.

MONETTE, D. R., SULLIVAN, T. J., & DEJONG, C. R. (1994). *Applied social research: Tool for the human services* (3rd ed.). Fort Worth: Harcourt Brace.

MONTELEONE, B. R., & WHITE, M. J. (1994, May). *Social facilitation in college baseball pitchers: Throwing the good stuff.* Paper presented at the annual meeting of the Midwestern Psychological Association, Chicago, IL.

MOORE, J. C., & BRYLINSKY, J. (1995). Facility familiarity and the home advantage. *Journal of Sport Behavior, 18,* 302–311.

MOORE, W. E., & STEVENSON, J. R. (1991). Understanding trust in the performance of complex automatic sport skills. *The Sport Psychologist, 5,* 281–289.

MOORE, W. E., & STEVENSON, J. R. (1994). Training for trust in sport skills. *The Sport Psychologist, 8,* 1–12.

MORAY, N. (1959). Attention in dichotic listening: Affective cues and the influence of instructions. *Quarterly Journal of Experimental Psychology, 11,* 56–60.

MORGAN, W. J., & MEIER, K. V. (Eds.). (1988). *Philosophic inquiry in sport.* Champaign, IL: Human Kinetics.

MORGAN, W. P. (1978, April). The mind of the marathoner. *Psychology Today,* pp. 38–49.

MORGAN, W. P. (1979). Prediction of performance in athletics. In P. Klavora & J. V. Daniel (Eds.), *Coach, athlete, and the sport psychologist* (pp. 172–186). Champaign, IL: Human Kinetics.

MORGAN, W. P. (1980a). The trait psychology controversy. *Research Quarterly for Exercise and Sport, 51,* 50–76.

MORGAN, W. P. (1980b). Personality dynamics and sport. In R. Suinn (Ed.), *Psychology in sport—methods and applications* (pp. 145–155). Minneapolis, MN: Burgess.

MORGAN, W. P. (1985). Selected psychological factors limiting performance: A mental health model. In D. H. Clarke & H. M. Eckert (Eds.), *Limits of human performance* (pp. 70–80). Champaign, IL: Human Kinetics.

MORGAN, W. P., HORSTMAN, D., CYMERMAN, A., & STOKES, J. (1983). Facilitation of physical performance by means of a cognitive strategy. *Cognitive Therapy and Research, 7,* 251–264.

MORGAN, W. P., & JOHNSON, R. W. (1977). Psychological characterization of the elite wrestler: A mental health model. *Medicine and Science in Sports, 9,* 55–56.

MORGAN, W. P., & JOHNSON, R. W. (1978). Personality characteristics of successful and unsuccessful oarsmen. *International Journal of Sport Psychology, 9,* 119–133.

MORGAN, W. P., O'CONNOR, P. J., ELLICKSON, K. A., & BRADLEY, P. W. (1988). Personality structure, mood states, and performance in elite male distance runners. *International Journal of Sport Psychology, 19,* 247–263.

MORGAN, W. P., O'CONNOR, P. J., SPARLING, P. B. & PATE, R. R. (1987). Psychological characterization of the elite female distance runner. *International Journal of Sports Medicine, 8,* 124–131.

MORGAN, W. P., & POLLOCK, M. L. (1977). Psychological characterization of the elite distance runner. *Annals of the New York Academy of Science, 301,* 382–403.

MOTOWILDO, S. J., PACKARD, J. S., & MANNING, M. R. (1986). Occupational stress: Its causes and consequences for job performance. *Journal of Applied Psychology, 71,* 618–629.

MUCZYK, J. P., & REIMANN, B. C. (1987). The case for directive leadership. *Academy of Management Executive, 1,* 301–311.

MULLEN, B., & RIORDAN, C. A. (1988). Self-serving attributions for performance in naturalistic settings: A meta-analytic review. *Journal of Applied Social Psychology, 18,* 3–22.

MUMFORD, B., & HALL, C. (1985). The effects of internal and external imagery on performing figures in figure skating. *Canadian Journal of Applied Sport Sciences, 10,* 171–177.

MURDOCK, G. P. (1949). *Social structure.* New York: Macmillan.

MURPHY, A. (1994, May 16). Toothsome. *Sports Illustrated,* p. 44–47.

MURPHY, S. M. (1994). Imagery interventions in sport. *Medicine and Science in Sports and Exercise, 26,* 486–494.

MURPHY, S. M., GREENSPAN, M., JOWDY, D., & TAMMEN, V. (1989, October). *Development of a brief rating instrument of competitive anxiety: Comparison with the CSAI-2.* Paper presented at the meeting of the Association for the Advancement of Applied Sport Psychology, Seattle, WA.

MURPHY, S. M., & JOWDY, D. P. (1992). Imagery and mental practice. In T. S. Horn (Ed.), *Advances in sport psychology* (pp. 221–250). Champaign, IL: Human Kinetics.

MURPHY, S. M., & WOOLFOLK, R. L. (1987). The effects of cognitive interventions on competitive anxiety and performance on a fine motor skill accuracy task. *International Journal of Sport Psychology, 18,* 152–166.

MURPHY, S. M., WOOLFOLK, R. L., & BUDNEY, A. J. (1988). The effects of emotive imagery on strength performance. *Journal of Sport & Exercise Psychology, 10,* 334–345.

MURRAY, H. A. (1971). *Thematic Apperception Test.* Cambridge, MA: Harvard University Press.

MURRAY, M., & MATHESON, H. (1993). Competition: Perceived barriers to success. G. L. Cohen (Ed.), *Women in sport: Issues and controversies* (pp. 217–229). Newbury Park, CA: Sage.

MURRELL, A. J., & CURTIS, E. M. (1994). Causal attributions of performance for black and white quarterbacks in the NFL: A look at the sports pages. *Journal of Sport & Social Issues, 18,* 224–233.

MURRELL, A. J., & DIETZ, B. (1992). Fan support of sport teams: The effect of a common group identity. *Journal of Sport & Exercise Psychology, 14,* 28–39.

MURRELL, A. J., & GAERTNER, S. L. (1992). Cohesion and team sport effectiveness: The benefit of a common group identity. *Journal of Sport & Social Issues, 16,* 1–14.

MYERS, D. G. (1989). *Psychology* (2nd ed.). New York: Worth.

MYERS, D. G. (1993). *Social psychology* (4th ed.). New York: McGraw-Hill.

NANCE, R. (1995, February 8). Maxwell faces fight fallout. *USA Today,* p. 4C.

The National Sports Review. (1992). Seattle, WA: Preview Publishing.

The National Sports Review. (1993). Seattle, WA: Preview Publishing.

NEIL, G. (1982). Demystifying sport superstition. *International Review of Sport Sociology, 17,* 99–124.

NEIL, G., ANDERSON, B., & SHEPPARD, W. (1981). Superstitions among male and female athletes of various levels of involvement. *Journal of Sport Behavior, 4,* 137–148.

NELSON, M. B. (1992, June 16). Disrobing not way to success. *USA Today,* p. 12C.

NEWTON, M., & DUDA, J. L. (1993). The relationship of task and ego orientation to performance: Cognitive content, affect, and attributions in bowling. *Journal of Sport Behavior, 16,* 209–220.

NIDEFFER, R. M. (1976a). Test of attentional and interpersonal style. *Journal of Personality and Social Psychology, 34,* 394–404.

NIDEFFER, R. M. (1976b). *The inner athlete: Mind plus muscle for winning.* New York: Crowell.

NIDEFFER, R. M. (1979). The role of attention in optimal athletic performance. In P. Klavora & J. V. Daniel (Eds.), *Coach, athlete, and the sport psychologist* (pp. 98–112). Champaign, IL: Human Kinetics.

NIDEFFER, R. M. (1980). Attentional focus—self-assessment. In R. Suinn (Ed.), *Psychology in sports—Methods and applications* (pp. 281–290). Minneapolis, MN: Burgess.

NIDEFFER, R. M. (1989). Psychological aspects of sports injuries: Issues in prevention and treatment.

International Journal of Sport Psychology, 20, 241–255.

NIDEFFER, R. M. (1990). Use of the Test of Attentional and Interpersonal Style (TAIS) in sport. *The Sport Psychologist, 4,* 285–300.

NIDEFFER, R. M. (1992). *Psyched to win.* Champaign, IL: Leisure Press.

NIDEFFER, R. M. (1993a). Attention control training. In R. N. Singer, M. Murphey, & L. K. Tennant (Eds.), *Handbook of research on sport psychology* (pp. 542–556). New York: Macmillan.

NIDEFFER, R. M. (1993b). Concentration and attention control training. In J. M. Williams (Ed.), *Applied sport psychology: Personal growth to peak performance* (2nd ed., pp. 243–261). Mountain View, CA: Mayfield.

NIDEFFER, R. M., & DECKNER, C. W. (1970). A case study of improved athletic performance following use of relaxation procedures. *Perceptual and Motor Skills, 30,* 821–822.

NIDEFFER, R. M., DUFRESNE, P., NESVIG, D., & SELDER, D. (1980). The future of applied sport psychology. *Journal of Sport Psychology, 2,* 170–174.

NIDEFFER, R. M., & SHARPE, R. C. (1978). *A.C.T. Attention Control Training: How to get control of your mind through total concentration.* New York: Wyden.

NISBETT, R. E. (1968). Birth order and participation in dangerous sports. *Journal of Personality and Social Psychology, 8,* 352–353.

NOBLE, C. E., SALAZAR, O. G., SKELLEY, C. S., & WILKERSON, H. K. (1979). Work and rest variables in the acquisition of psychomotor tracking skill. *Journal of Motor Behavior, 11,* 233–246.

NOEL, J. G., WANN, D. L., & BRANSCOMBE, N. R. (1995). Peripheral ingroup membership status and public negativity toward outgroups. *Journal of Personality and Social Psychology, 68,* 127–137.

NOEL, R. C. (1980). The effect of visuo-motor behavior rehearsal on tennis performance. *Journal of Sport Psychology, 2,* 221–226.

NOLL, R. G. (1974). Attendance and price setting. In R. G. Noll (Ed.), *Government and the sports business* (pp. 115–157). Washington DC: Brookings.

OAKES, P. J., & TURNER, J. C. (1980). Social categorization and intergroup behavior: Does minimal intergroup discrimination make social identity more positive? *European Journal of Social Psychology, 10,* 295–301.

O'BRIEN, R. (1994, April 4). Scorecard. *Sports Illustrated*, p. 22.

OGILVIE, B. C. (1976). Psychological consistencies with the personality of high-level competitors. In A. C. Fisher (Ed.), Psychology of sport (pp. 335–358). Palo Alto, CA: Mayfield.

OGILVIE, B. C. (1979). The sport phychologist and his professional credibility. In P. Klavora & J. V. Daniels (Eds.), *Coach, athlete, and the sport psychologist* (pp. 44–55). Champaign, IL: Human Kinetics.

OGILVIE, B. C., & TUTKO, T. A. (1966). *Problem athletes and how to handle them.* London: Pelham.

OGLES, B. M., MASTERS, K. S., & RICHARDSON, S. A. (1995). Obligatory running and gender: An analysis of participative motives and training habits. *International Journal of Sport Psychology, 26,* 233–248.

OGLESBY, C. A. (1989). Women and sport. In J. H. Goldstein (Ed.), *Sports, games, and play: Social and psychological viewpoints* (2nd ed., pp. 129–145). Hillsdale, NJ: Erlbaum.

OMMUNDSEN, Y., & VAGLUM, P. (1991). Soccer competition anxiety and enjoyment in young boy players. The influence of perceived competence and significant others' emotional involvement. *International Journal of Sport Psychology, 22,* 35–49.

O'NEAL, E., McDONALD, P., HORI, R., & McCLINTON, B. (1977). Arousal and imitation of aggression. *Motivation and Emotion, 1,* 95–102.

ONESTAK, D. M. (1991). The effects of progressive relaxation, mental practice, and hypnosis on athletic performance: A review. *Journal of Sport Behavior, 14,* 247–274.

ORDMAN, V. L., & ZILLMANN, D. (1994). Women sports reporters: Have they caught up? *Journal of Sport & Social Issues, 18,* 66–75.

ORLICK, T. (1993). *Free to feel great: Teaching children to excel at living.* Carp, Ontario, Canada: Creative Bound.

ORLICK, T., & McCAFFREY, N. (1991). Mental training with children for sport and life. *The Sport Psychologist, 5,* 322–334.

ORLICK, T., & PARTINGTON, J. (1987). The sport psychology consultant: Analysis of critical components as viewed by Canadian Olympic athletes. *The Sport Psychologist, 1,* 4–17.

ORNSTEIN, R. (1988). *Psychology: The study of human experience* (2nd ed.). New York: Harcourt Brace Jovanovich.

OSTROW, A. C. (Ed.). (1990). *Directory of psychological tests in the sport and exercise sciences.* Morgantown, WV: Fitness Information Technology.

OVERMAN, S. J., & RAO, V. V. P. (1981). Motivation for and extent of participation in organized sports by high school seniors. *Research Quarterly for Exercise and Sport, 52,* 228–237.

PARFITT, G., & HARDY, L. (1993). The effects of competitive anxiety on memory span and rebound shooting tasks in basketball players. *Journal of Sports Sciences, 11,* 517–524.

PARGMAN, D. (1993). Sport injuries: An overview of psychological perspectives. In D. Pargman (Ed.), *Psychological bases of sport injuries* (pp. 5–13). Morgantown, WV: Fitness Information Technology.

PARKER, K. B. (1994). "Has-beens" and "wannabes": Transition experiences of former major college football players. *The Sport Psychologist, 8,* 287–304.

PASTORE, D. L. (1994). Strategies for retaining female high school head coaches: A survey of administrators and coaches. *Journal of Sport & Social Issues, 18,* 169–182.

PATRICK, G. T. W. (1903). The psychology of football. *American Journal of Psychology, 14,* 104–117.

PATTERSON, A. H. (1974). Hostility catharsis: A naturalistic quasi-experiment. *Personality and Social Psychology Bulletin, 1,* 195–197.

PAVLOV, I. P. (1927). *Conditioned reflexes* (G. Anrep, Trans.). London: Oxford University Press.

PEDERSEN, D. M., & KONO, D. M. (1990). Perceived effects of femininity of the participation of women in sport. *Perceptual and Motor Skills, 71,* 783–792.

PEDHAZUR, E. J., & TETENBAUM, T. J. (1979). Bem sex role inventory: A theoretical and methodological critique. *Journal of Personality and Social Psychology, 37,* 996–1016.

PELHAM, B. W. (1993). On the highly positive thoughts of highly depressed people. In R. F. Baumeister (Ed.), *Self-esteem: The puzzle of low self-regard* (pp. 183–199). New York: Plenum.

PELLETIER, L. G., FORTIER, M. S., VALLERAND, R. J., TUSON, K. M., BRIÈRE, N. M., & BLAIS, M. R. (1995). Toward a new measure of intrinsic motivation, extrinsic motivation, and amotivation in sports: The Sport Motivation Scale (SMS). *Journal of Sport & Exercise Psychology, 17,* 35–53.

PENNEBAKER, J. W., & LIGHTNER, J. M. (1980). Competition of internal and external information in an exercise setting. *Journal of Personality and Social Psychology, 39,* 165–174.

PEPLAU, L. A. (1976). Impact of fear of success and sex-role attitudes on women's competitive achievement. *Journal of Personality and Social Psychology, 34,* 561–568.

PESSIN, J. (1933). The comparative effects of social and mechanical stimulation on memorizing. *American Journal of Psychology, 45,* 263–270.

PETERS, L. H., HARTKE, D. D., & POHLMANN, J. T. (1985). Fiedler's contingency theory of leadership: An application of the meta-analysis procedures of Schmidt and Hunter. *Psychological Bulletin, 97,* 274–285.

PETERSON, C. (1980). Attribution in the sports pages: An archival investigation of the covariation hypothesis. *Social Psychology Quarterly, 43,* 136–141.

PETERSON, L. R., & PETERSON, M. J. (1959). Short-term retention of individual verbal items. *Journal of Experimental Psychology, 58,* 193–198.

PETITPAS, A. J., BREWER, B. W., RIVERA, P. M., & VAN RAALTE, J. L. (1994). Ethical beliefs and behaviors in applied sport psychology: The AAASP ethics survey. *Journal of Applied Sport Psychology, 6,* 135–151.

PETRIE, G. (1993). Injury from the athlete's point of view. In J. Heil (Ed.), *Psychology of sport injury* (pp. 17–23). Champaign, IL: Human Kinetics.

PETRIE, T. A. (1993). Coping skills, competitive trait anxiety, and playing status: Moderating effects of the life stress-injury relationship. *Journal of Sport & Exercise Psychology, 15,* 261–274.

PETRIE, T. A., & WATKINS, C. E. (1994). A survey of counseling psychology programs and exercise/sport science departments: Sport psychology issues and training. *The Sport Psychologist, 8,* 28–36.

PETRUZZELLO, S. J., LANDERS, D. M., & SALAZAR, W. (1991). Biofeedback and sport/exercise performance: Applications and limitations. *Behavior Therapy, 22,* 379–392.

PHARES, E. J. (1991). *Introduction to personality* (3rd ed.). New York: HarperCollins.

PHILLIPS, D. P. (1983). The impact of mass media violence on U.S. homicides. *American Sociological Review, 48,* 560–568.

PINDER, C. C. (1991). Valence-Instrumentality-Expectancy theory. In R. M. Steers & L. W. Porter (Eds.), *Motivation and work behavior* (pp. 144–164). New York: McGraw-Hill.

POLLARD, R. (1986). Home advantage in soccer: A retrospective analysis. *Journal of Sport Sciences, 4,* 237–248.

PORTER, K., & FOSTER, J. (1986). *The mental athlete.* New York: Ballantine.

PORTER, L. W., & LAWLER, E. E. (1968). *Managerial attitudes and performance.* Homewood, IL: Irwin-Dorsey.

PORTER, P. K., & SCULLY, G. W. (1982). Measuring managerial efficiency: The case of baseball. *Southern Economic Journal, 48,* 642–650.

POWELL, G. E. (1973). Negative and positive mental practice in motor skill acquisition. *Perceptual and Motor Skills, 37,* 312.

PRAPAVESSIS, H., GROVE, J. R., MCNAIR, P. J., & CABLE, N. T. (1992). Self-regulation training, state anxiety, and sport performance: A psychophysiological case study. *The Sport Psychologist, 6,* 213–229.

PREDEBON, J., & DOCKER, S. B. (1992). Free-throw shooting performance as a function of preshot routines. *Perceptual and Motor Skills, 75,* 167–171.

PRISUTA, R. H. (1979). Televised sports and political values. *Journal of Communication, 29,* 94–102.

PROCTOR, R. C., & ECKERD, W. M. (1976). "Toot-toot" or spectator sports: Psychological and therapeutic implications. *The American Journal of Sports Medicine, 4,* 78–83.

PRUITT, D. J., & INSKO, C. A. (1980). Extension of the Kelley attribution model: The role of comparison-object consensus, target-object consensus, distinctiveness, and consistency. *Journal of Personality and Social Psychology, 39,* 39–58.

QUACKENBUSH, N., & CROSSMAN, J. E. (1994). Injured athletes: A study of emotional responses. *Journal of Sport Behavior, 17,* 178–187.

RAEDEKE, T. D., & STEIN, G. L. (1994). Felt arousal, thoughts/feelings, and ski performance. *The Sport Psychologist, 8,* 360–375.

RAGINS, B. R., & SUNDSTROM, E. (1989). Gender and power in organizations: A longitudinal perspective. *Psychological Bulletin, 105,* 51–88.

RAGLIN, J. S., & MORRIS, M. J. (1994). Precompetition anxiety in women volleyball players: A test of ZOF theory in a team sport. *British Journal of Sport Medicine, 28,* 47–51.

RAINEY, D. W. (1995a). Sources of stress among baseball and softball umpires. *Journal of Applied Sport Psychology, 7,* 1–10.

RAINEY, D. W. (1995b). Stress, burnout, and intention to terminate among umpires. *Journal of Sport Behavior, 18,* 312–323.

RAINEY, D. W., & CHERILLA, K. (1993). Conflict with baseball umpires: An observational study. *Journal of Sport Behavior, 16,* 49–59.

RAINEY, D. W., SANTILLI, N. R., & FALLON, K. (1992). Development of athletes' conceptions of sport officials authority. *Journal of Sport & Exercise Psychology, 14,* 392–404.

RANDALL, L. E., & MCKENZIE, T. L. (1988). Spectator verbal behavior in organized youth soccer: A descriptive analysis. *Journal of Sport Behavior, 11,* 200–211.

RATHUS, S. A., & NEVID, J. S. (1989). *Psychology and the challenges of life: Adjustment and growth* (4th ed.). New York: Holt, Rinehart and Winston.

RAVIZZA, K., & HANSON, T. (1995). *Heads-up baseball: Playing the game one pitch at a time.* Indianapolis, IN: Masters Press.

REAL, M. R., & MECHIKOFF, R. A. (1992). Deep fan: Mythic identification, technology, and advertising in spectator sports. *Sociology of Sport Journal, 9,* 323–339.

REDDY, M. K., BAI, A. J. L., & RAO, V. R. (1977). The effects of the transcendental meditation program on athletic performance. In D. J. Orne-Johnson & I. Farrow (Eds.), *Scientific research of the transcendental meditation program* (Vol. 1, pp. 346–358). Weggis, Switzerland: Meru Press.

REEVE, J. (1992). *Understanding motivation and emotion.* New York: Harcourt Brace Jovanovich.

REEVE, J., & DECI, E. L. (1996). Elements of the competitive situation that affect intrinsic motivation. *Personality and Social Psychology Bulletin, 22,* 24–33.

RÉGNIER, G., SALMELA, J., & RUSSELL, S. J. (1993). Talent detection and development in sport. In R. N. Singer, M. Murphey, & L. K. Tennant (Eds.), *Handbook of research on sport psychology* (pp. 290–313). New York: Macmillan.

REHBERG, R. A., & SCHAFER, W. E. (1968). Participation in interscholastic athletics and college expectations. *American Journal of Sociology, 73,* 732–740.

REIFMAN, A. S., LARRICK, R. P., & FEIN, S. (1991). Temper and temperature on the diamond: The heat-aggression relationship in Major League Baseball. *Personality and Social Psychology Bulletin, 17,* 580–585.

REIS, H. T., & JELSMA, B. (1980). A social psychology of sex differences in sport. In W. F. Straub (Ed.), *Sport psychology: An analysis of athlete behavior* (2nd ed., pp. 276–286). Mouvement Publications.

REJESKI, W. J. (1979). A model of attributional conflict in sport. *Journal of Sport Behavior, 3,* 156–166.

REJESKI, W. J., & BRAWLEY, L. R. (1983). Attribution theory in sport: Current status and new perspectives. *Journal of Sport Psychology, 5,* 77–99.

RENGER, R. (1993). A review of the Profile of Mood States (POMS) in the prediction of athletic success. *Journal of Applied Sport Psychology, 5,* 78–84.

RHODEWALT, F., SALTZMAN, A. T., & WITTMER, J. (1984). Self-handicapping among competitive athletes: The role of practice in self-esteem protection. *Basic and Applied Social Psychology, 5,* 197–209.

RICHARDSON, A. (1976a). Mental practice: A review and discussion. Part I. *Research Quarterly, 38,* 95–107.

RICHARDSON, A. (1976b). Mental practice: A review and discussion. Part II. *Research Quarterly, 38,* 263–273.

RICHARDSON, A. (1994). *Individual differences in imaging: Their measurement, origins, and consequences.* Amityville, NT: Baywood.

RIEMER, H. A., & CHELLADURAI, P. (1995). Leadership and satisfaction in athletics. *Journal of Sport & Exercise Psychology, 17,* 276–293.

RINTALA, J., & BIRRELL, S. (1984). Fair treatment for the active female: A content analysis of *Young Athlete* magazine. *Sociology of Sport Journal, 1,* 231–250.

RIORDAN, C. A., THOMAS, J. S., & JAMES, M. K. (1985). Attributions in a one-on-one sports competition: Evidence for self-serving biases and gender differences. *Journal of Sport Behavior, 8,* 42–53.

ROADBURG, A. (1980). Factors precipitating fan violence: A comparison of professional soccer in Britain and North America. *British Journal of Sociology, 31,* 265–276.

ROBERTS, G. C., KLEIBER, D. A., & DUDA, J. L. (1981). An analysis of motivation in children's sport: The role of perceived competence in participation. *Journal of Sport Psychology, 3,* 206–216.

ROBERTS, G. C., & TREASURE, D. C. (1992). Children in sport. *Sport Science Review, 1,* 46–64.

ROBINSON, D. W. (1992). A descriptive model of enduring risk recreation involvement. *Journal of Leisure Research, 24,* 52–63.

ROBINSON, T. T., & CARRON, A. V. (1982). Personal and situational factors associated with dropping out versus maintaining participation in competitive sport. *Journal of Sport Psychology, 4,* 364–378.

RODGERS, W., HALL, C., & BUCKOLZ, E. (1991). The effect of an imagery training program on imagery ability, imagery use, and figure skating performance. *Journal of Applied Sport Psychology, 3,* 109–125.

RODRIGO, G., LUSIARDO, M., & PEREIRA, G. (1990). Relationship between anxiety and performance in soccer players. *International Journal of Sport Psychology, 21,* 112–120.

RORSCHACH, H. (1942). *Psychodiagnostics: A diagnostic test based on perception* (P. Lemkau & B. Kronenberg, Trans.). Berne: Huber (1st German ed. published 1921; U. S. distributor, Grune & Stratton).

ROSE, J. M. C. (1986). Association and dissociation cognitive strategies in endurance performance—A brief review. In J. Watkins, T. Reilly, & L. Burwitz (Eds.), *'86 Glascow Conference—VIII Commonwealth and International Conference on Sport* (pp. 229–236). Cambridge, MA: Cambridge University Press.

ROSS, L. (1977). The intuitive psychologist and his shortcomings: Distortions in the attribution process. In L. Berkowitz (Ed.), *Advances in experimental social psychology* (Vol. 10, pp. 173–220). New York: Academic Press.

ROSS, M. (1975). Salience of reward and intrinsic motivation. *Journal of Personality and Social Psychology, 32,* 245–254.

ROTELLA, R. J., & HEYMAN, S. R. (1993). Stress, injury, and the psychological rehabilitation of athletes. In J. M. Williams (Ed.), *Applied sport psychology: Personal growth to peak performance* (2nd ed., pp. 338–355). Mountain View, CA: Mayfield.

ROTELLA, R. J., & LERNER, J. D. (1993). Responding to competitive pressure. In R. N. Singer, M. Murphey, & L. K. Tennant (Eds.), *Handbook of research on sport psychology* (pp. 528–541). New York: Macmillan.

ROTELLA, R. J., & NEWBURG, D. S. (1989). The social psychology of the benchwarmer. *The Sport Psychologist, 3,* 48–62.

ROWLAND, G. L., FRANKEN, R. E., & HARRISON, K. (1986). Sensation seeking and participation in sporting activities. *Journal of Sport Psychology, 8,* 212–220.

ROWLEY, A. J., LANDERS, D. M., KYLLO, L. B., & ETNIER, J. L. (1995). Does the iceberg profile discriminate between successful and less successful athletes? A meta-analysis. *Journal of Sport & Exercise Psychology, 17,* 185–199.

RULE, B. G., & NESDALE, A. R. (1976). Emotional arousal and aggressive behavior. *Psychological Bulletin, 83,* 851–863.

RUSHALL, B. S. (1973). The status of personality research and application in sports and physical education. *Journal of Sports Medicine, 13,* 281–290.

RUSHALL, B. S., HALL, M., ROUX, L., SASSEVILLE, J., & RUSHALL, A. C. (1988). Effects of three types of thought content on skiing performance. *The Sport Psychologist, 2,* 283–297.

RUSHALL, B. S., & SIEDENTOP, D. (1972). *The development and control of behavior in sport and physical education.* Philadelphia: Lea & Febiger.

RUSHALL, B. S., & SMITH, K. C. (1979). The modification of the quality and quantity of behavior categories in a swimming coach. *Journal of Sport Psychology, 1,* 138–150.

RUSSELL, D. (1982). The Causal Dimension Scale: A measure of how individuals perceive causes. *Journal of Personality and Social Psychology, 42,* 1137–1145.

RUSSELL, D., MCAULEY, E., & TARICO, V. (1987). Measuring causal attributions for success and failure: A comparison of methodologies for assessing causal dimensions. *Journal of Personality and Social Psychology, 52,* 1248–1257.

RUSSELL, G. W. (1974). Machiavellianism, locus of control, aggression, performance and precautionary behavior in ice hockey. *Human Relations, 27,* 825–837.

RUSSELL, G. W. (1979). Hero selection by Canadian ice hockey players: Skill or aggression? *Canadian Journal of Applied Sport Science, 4,* 309–313.

RUSSELL, G. W. (1981a). Aggression in sport. In P. F. Brain & D. Benton (Eds.), *Multidisciplinary approaches to aggression research* (pp. 431–446). New York: Elsevier/North Holland Biomedical Press.

RUSSELL, G. W. (1981b). Conservatism, birth order, leadership, and the aggression of Canadian ice hockey players. *Perceptual and Motor Skills, 53,* 3–7.

RUSSELL, G. W. (1981c). Spectator moods at an aggressive sports event. *Journal of Sport Psychology, 3,* 217–227.

RUSSELL, G. W. (1983). Psychological issues in sports aggression. In J. H. Goldstein (Ed.), *Sports violence* (pp. 157–181). New York: Springer-Verlag.

RUSSELL, G. W. (1992). Response of the macho male to viewing a combatant sport. *Journal of Social Behavior and Personality, 7,* 631–638.

RUSSELL, G. W. (1993a). *The social psychology of sport.* New York: Springer-Verlag.

RUSSELL, G. W. (1993b). Violent sports entertainment and the promise of catharsis. *Medienpsychologie, 5,* 101–105.

RUSSELL, G. W., ARMS, R. L., & BIBBY, R. W. (1995). Canadians' belief in catharsis. *Social Behavior and Personality, 23,* 223–228.

RUSSELL, G. W., DI LULLO, S. L., & DI LULLO, D. (1988–89). Effects of observing competitive and violent versions of a sport. *Current Psychology: Research & Reviews, 7,* 312–321.

RUSSELL, G. W., & DREWRY, B. R. (1976). Crowd size and competitive aspects of aggression in ice hockey: An archival study. *Human Relations, 29,* 723–735.

RUSSELL, G. W., & GOLDSTEIN, J. H. (1995). Personality differences between Dutch football fans and nonfans. *Social Behavior and Personality, 23,* 199–204.

RUSSELL, G. W., HORN, V. E., & HUDDLE, M. J. (1988). Male responses to female aggression. *Social Behavior and Personality, 16,* 51–57.

RYAN, E. D. (1962). Effects of stress on motor performance and learning. *Research Quarterly, 33,* 111–119.

RYAN, E. D. (1970). The cathartic effect of vigorous motor activity on aggressive behavior. *Research Quarterly, 41,* 542–551.

RYAN, E. D., & SIMONS, J. (1981). Cognitive demand, imagery, and frequency of mental rehearsal as factors influencing acquisition of motor skills. *Journal of Sport Psychology, 3,* 35–45.

RYAN, E. D., & SIMONS, J. (1983). What is learned in mental practice of motor skills: A test of the cognitive-motor hypothesis. *Journal of Sport Psychology, 5,* 419–426.

RYCKMAN, R. M., & HAMEL, J. (1992). Female adolescents' motives related to involvement in organized team sports. *International Journal of Sport Psychology, 23,* 147–260.

RYCKMAN, R. M., & HAMEL, J. (1993). Perceived physical ability differences in the sport participation motives of young athletes. *International Journal of Sport Psychology, 24,* 270–283.

SACHS, M. L., BURKE, K. L., & BUTCHER, L. A. (Eds.). (1995). *Directory of graduate programs in applied sport psychology* (4th ed.). Morgantown, WV: Fitness Information Technology.

SACHS, M. L., SITLER, M. R., & SCHWILLE, G. (1993). Assessing and monitoring injuries and psychological characteristics in intercollegiate athletes: A counseling/prediction model. In D. Pargman (Ed.), *Psychological bases of sport injuries* (pp. 71–84). Morgantown, WV: Fitness Information Technology.

SACKETT, R. S. (1934). The relationship between amount of symbolic rehearsal and retention of a maze habit. *Journal of General Psychology, 13,* 113–130.

SADALLA, E. K., LINDER, D. E., & JENKINS, B. A. (1988). Sport preference: A self-presentational analysis. *Journal of Sport & Exercise Psychology, 10,* 214–222.

SAGE, G. H. (1975). An occupational analysis of the college coach. In D. W. Ball & J. W. Loy (Eds.), *Sport and social order* (pp. 395–455). Reading, MA: Addison-Wesley.

SAGE, G. H. (1980). Parental influence and socialization into sport for male and female intercollegiate athletes. *Journal of Sport & Social Issues, 4,* 1–13.

SAGE, G. H. (1993). Introduction. In R. C. Althouse & D. D. Brooks (Eds.), *Racism in college athletics: The African-American athlete's experience* (pp. 1–17). Morgantown, WV: Fitness Information Technology.

SAGE, M., & FURST, D. M. (1994). Coverage of women's sports in selected newspapers. *Perceptual and Motor Skills, 78,* 295–296.

SALMELA, J. H. (1981). *The world sport psychology source book* (1st ed.). Ithaca, NY: Mouvement Publications.

SALMELA, J. H. (1992). *The world sport psychology source book* (2nd ed.). Champaign, IL: Human Kinetics.

SALMON, J., HALL, C., & HASLAM, I. (1994). The use of imagery by soccer players. *Journal of Applied Sport Psychology, 6,* 116–133.

SALWEN, M. B., & WOOD, N. (1994). Depictions of female athletes on *Sports Illustrated* covers, 1957–1989. *Journal of Sport Behavior, 17,* 98–107.

SANDERS, G. S., BARON, R. S., & MOORE, D. L. (1978). Distraction and social comparison as mediators of social facilitation effects. *Journal of Experimental Social Psychology, 14,* 291–303.

SANDERSON, F. H. (1983). Length and spacing of practice sessions in sport skills. *International Journal of Sport Psychology, 14,* 116–122.

SANTAMARIA, V. L., & FURST, D. M. (1994). Distance runners' causal attributions for most successful and least successful races. *Journal of Sport Behavior, 17,* 43–51.

SAPOLSKY, B. S. (1980). The effect of spectator disposition and suspense on the enjoyment of sport contests. *International Journal of Sport Psychology, 11,* 1–10.

SAPP, M., & HAUBENSTRICKER, J. (1978). *Motivations for joining and reasons for not continuing in youth sports programs in Michigan.* Paper presented at the American Alliance for Health, Physical Education, and Recreation (AAHPER) Convention, Kansas City, MO.

SASFY, J., & OKUN, M. (1974). Form of evaluation and audience expertness as joint determinants of audience effects. *Journal of Experimental Social Psychology, 10,* 461–467.

SAVIS, J. C. (1994). Sleep and athletic performance: Overview and implications for sport psychology. *The Sport Psychologist, 8,* 111–125.

SCANLAN, T. K. (1977). The effects of success-failure on the perception of threat in a competitive situation. *Research Quarterly, 48,* 144–153.

SCANLAN, T. K., & LEWTHWAITE, R. (1984). Social psychological aspects of competition for male youth sport participants: I. Predictors of competitive stress. *Journal of Sport Psychology, 6,* 208–226.

SCANLAN, T. K., & LEWTHWAITE, R. (1986). Social psychological aspects of competition for male youth sport participants: IV. Predictors of enjoyment. *Journal of Sport Psychology, 8,* 25–35.

SCANLAN, T. K., & PASSER, M. W. (1977). The effects of competition trait anxiety and game win-loss on perceived threat in a natural competitive setting. In D. M. Landers & R. W. Christina (Eds.), *Psychology of motor behavior and sport—1976* (pp. 157–160). Champaign, IL: Human Kinetics.

SCANLAN, T. K., & PASSER, M. W. (1978). Factors related to competitive stress among male youth sport participants. *Medicine and Science in Sport, 10,* 103–108.

SCANLAN, T. K., & PASSER, M. W. (1980). The attributional responses of young female athletes after winning, tying, and losing. *Research Quarterly for Exercise and Sport, 51,* 675–684.

SCANLAN, T. K., & SIMONS, J. P. (1992). The construct of sport enjoyment. In G. C. Roberts (Ed.), *Motivation in sport and exercise* (pp. 199–215). Champaign, IL: Human Kinetics.

SCARR, S. (1966). Genetic factors in activity motivation. *Child Development, 37,* 663–673.

SCHAFER, W. (1992). *Stress management for wellness* (2nd ed.). New York: Harcourt Brace Jovanovich.

SCHLENKER, B. R., PHILLIPS, S. T., BONIECKI, K. A., & SCHLENKER, D. R. (1995a). Championship pressures: Choking or triumphing in one's own territory? *Journal of Personality and Social Psychology, 68,* 632–643.

SCHLENKER, B. R., PHILLIPS, S. T., BONIECKI, K. A., & SCHLENKER, D. R. (1995b). Where is the home choke? *Journal of Personality and Social Psychology, 68,* 649–652.

SCHLIESMAN, E. S. (1987). Relationship between the congruence of preferred and actual leader behavior and subordinate satisfaction with leadership. *Journal of Sport Behavior, 10,* 157–166.

SCHMID, A., & PEPER, E. (1993). Training strategies for concentration. In J. M. Williams (Ed.), *Applied sport psychology: Personal growth to peak performance* (2nd ed., pp. 262–273). Mountain View, CA: Mayfield.

SCHMIDT, G. W., & STEIN, G. L. (1991). Sport commitment: A model integrating enjoyment, dropout, and burnout. *Journal of Sport & Exercise Psychology, 8,* 254–265.

SCHMIDT, R. A. (1975). A schema theory of discrete motor skill learning. *Psychological Review, 82,* 225–260.

SCHMIDT, R. A., & YOUNG, D. E. (1991). Methodology for motor learning: A paradigm for kinematic feedback. *Journal of Motor Behavior, 23,* 13–24.

SCHMITT, B. H., GILOVICH, T., GOORE, N., & JOSEPH, L. (1986). Mere presence and social facilitation: One more time. *Journal of Experimental Social Psychology, 22,* 242–248.

SCHOFIELD, J. A. (1983). Performance and attendance at professional team sports. *Journal of Sport Behavior, 6,* 196–206.

SCHRIESCHEIM, J. F. (1980). The social context of leader-subordinate relations: An investigation of the effects of group cohesiveness. *Journal of Applied Psychology, 65,* 183–194.

SCHULTZ, D. P. (1981). *A history of modern psychology* (3rd ed.). New York: Academic Press.

SCHULTZ, D. P., & SCHULTZ, S. E. (1994). *Psychology and work today: An introduction to industrial and organizational psychology* (6th ed.). New York: Macmillan.

SCHUNK, D. H. (1995). Self-efficacy, motivation, and performance. *Journal of Applied Sport Psychology, 7,* 112–137.

SCHURR, K. T., ASHLEY, M. A., & JOY, K. L. (1977). A multivariate analysis of male athlete personality characteristics: Sport type and success. *Multivariate Experimental Clinical Research, 3,* 53–68.

SCHURR, K. T., RUBLE, V. E., & ELLEN, A. S. (1985). Myers-Briggs Type Inventory and demographic characteristics of students attending and not attending a college basketball game. *Journal of Sport Behavior, 8,* 181–194.

SCHURR, K. T., WITTIG, A. F., RUBLE, V. E., & ELLEN, A. S. (1988). Demographic and personality characteristics associated with persistent, occasional, and non-attendance of university male basketball games by college students. *Journal of Sport Behavior, 11,* 3–17.

SCHURR, K. T., WITTIG, A. F., RUBLE, V. E., & HENRIKSEN, L. W. (1993). College graduation rates of student athletes and students attending college male basketball games: A case study. *Journal of Sport Behavior, 16,* 33–41.

SCHUTZ, R. W., & GESSAROLI, M. C. (1993). Use, misuse, and disuse of psychometrics on sport psychology research. In R. N. Singer, M. Murphey, & L. K. Tennant (Eds.), *Handbook of research on sport psychology* (pp. 901–917). New York: Macmillan.

SCHWARTZ, B. (1989). *Psychology of learning and behavior* (3rd ed.). New York: Norton.

SCHWARTZ, B., & BARSKY, S. F. (1977). The home advantage. *Social Forces, 55,* 641–661.

SCHWARTZ, B., & REISBERG, D. (1991). *Learning and memory.* New York: Norton.

SCHWARZ, N., STRACK, F., KOMMER, D., & WAGNER, D. (1987). Soccer, rooms, and the quality of your life: Mood effects on judgments of satisfaction with life in general and with specific domains. *European Journal of Social Psychology, 17,* 69–79.

SCHWEITZER, K., ZILLMANN, D., WEAVER, J. B., & LUTTRELL, E. S. (1992). Perception of threatening events in the emotional aftermath of a televised college football game. *Journal of Broadcasting & Electronic Media, 36,* 75–82.

SEABOURNE, T. G., WEINBERG, R., & JACKSON, A. (1984). Effect of individualized practice and training of visuo-motor behavior rehearsal in enhancing karate performance. *Journal of Sport Behavior, 7,* 58–67.

SEASHORE, S. E. (1954). *Group cohesiveness in the industrial work group.* Ann Arbor, MI: Institute for Social Research.

SEIDEL, R. W., & REPPUCCI, N. D. (1993). Organized youth sports and the psychological development of nine-year-old males. *Journal of Child and Family Studies, 2,* 229–248.

SEIFRIZ, J. J., DUDA, J. L., & CHI, L. (1992). The relationship of perceived motivational climate to intrinsic motivation and beliefs about success in basketball. *Journal of Sport & Exercise Psychology, 14,* 375–391.

SELYE, H. (1956). *The stress of life.* New York: McGraw-Hill.

SELYE, H. (1974). *Stress without distress.* Philadelphia: Lippincott.

SELYE, H. (1982). History and present status of the stress concept. In L. Goldberger & S. Breznetz (Eds.), *Handbook of stress: Theoretical and clinical aspects.* New York: Free Press.

SHAW, D. (1978, February). The roots of rooting. *Psychology Today,* p. 48–51.

SHAW, P. L. (1995). Achieving Title IX gender equity in college athletics in an era of fiscal austerity. *Journal of Sport & Social Issues, 19,* 6–27.

SHELTON, T. O., & MAHONEY, M. J. (1978). The content and effect of "psyching-up" strategies in weight lifters. *Cognitive Therapy and Research, 2,* 275–284.

SHERIF, M., HARVEY, O. J., WHITE, E. J., HOOD, W. R., & SHERIF, C. W. (1961). *Intergroup cooperation and competition: The Robber's Cave experiment.* Norman, OK: University Book Exchange.

SHICK, J. (1970). Effects of mental practice on selected volleyball skills for college women. *Research Quarterly, 41,* 88–94.

SHIELDS, D. L., & BREDEMEIER, B. J. (1995). *Character development and physical activity.* Champaign, IL: Human Kinetics.

SHIELDS, D. L., BREDEMEIER, B. J., GARDNER, D. E., & BOSTROM, A. (1995). Leadership, cohesion, and team norms regarding cheating and aggression. *Sociology of Sport Journal, 12,* 324–336.

SHIFFLETT, B., & REVELLE, R. (1994a). Gender equity in sports media coverage: A review of the *NCAA News. Journal of Sport & Social Issues, 18,* 144–150.

SHIFFLETT, B., & REVELLE, R. (1994b). Equity revisited. *Journal of Sport & Social Issues, 18,* 379–383.

SIEDENTOP, D. (1980). The management of practice behavior. In W. Straub (Ed.), *Sport psychology: An analysis of athlete behavior* (2nd ed., pp. 49–55). Ithaca NY: Mouvement Publications.

SIEGEL, B. S. (1986). *Love, medicine, and miracles: Lessons learned about self-healing from a surgeon's perspective.* New York: Harper Row.

SIEGEL, B. S. (1989). *Peace, love, and healing, bodymind communication and the path to self-healing: An exploration.* New York: Harper Row.

SIEGFRIED, J. J., & HINSHAW, C. E. (1977). Professional football and the anti-blackout law. *Journal of Communication, 27,* 169–174.

SILVA, J. M. III (1979). Behavioral and situational factors affecting concentration and skill performance. *Journal of Sport Psychology, 1,* 221–227.

SILVA, J. M. III (1980a). Assertive and aggressive behavior in sport: A definitional clarification. In C. H. Nadeau, W. R. Halliwell, K. M. Newell, & G. C. Roberts (Eds.), *Psychology of motor behavior and sport—1979* (pp. 199–208). Champaign, IL: Human Kinetics.

SILVA, J. M. III (1980b). Understanding aggressive behavior and its effects upon athletic performance. In W. Straub (Ed.), *Sport psychology: An analysis of athlete behavior* (2nd ed., pp. 177–186). Ithaca NY: Mouvement Publications.

SILVA, J. M. III (1984). Personality and sport performance: Controversy and challenge. In J. M. Silva & R. S. Weinberg (Eds.), *Psychological foundations of sport* (pp. 59–69). Champaign, IL: Human Kinetics.

SILVA, J. M. III, & ANDREW, J. A. (1987). An analysis of game location and basketball performance in the Atlantic Coast Conference. *International Journal of Sport Psychology, 18,* 188–204.

SIMONS, J. P., & ANDERSEN, M. B. (1995). The development of consulting practice in applied sport psychology: Some personal perspectives. *The Sport Psychologist, 9,* 449–468.

SIMONS, Y., & TAYLOR, J. (1992). A psychosocial model of fan violence in sports. *International Journal of Sport Psychology, 23,* 207–226.

SINGER, R. N. (1965). Effect of spectators on athletes and non-athletes performing a gross motor task. *Research Quarterly, 36,* 473–482.

SINGER, R. N. (1969). Personality differences between and within baseball and tennis players. *Research Quarterly, 40,* 582–588.

SINGER, R. N. (1980). Sports psychology: An overview. In W. F. Straub (Ed.), *Sport psychology: An analysis of athlete behavior* (2nd ed., pp. 1–14). Ithaca, NY: Mouvement Publications.

SINGER, R. N. (1984). What sport psychology can do for the athlete and coach. *International Journal of Sport Psychology, 15,* 52–61.

SINGER, R. N., MURPHEY, M., & TENNANT, L. K. (Eds.). (1993). *Handbook of research on sport psychology.* New York: Macmillan.

SIPES, R. G. (1973). War, sports, and aggression: An empirical test of two rival theories. *American Anthropologist, 75,* 64–86.

SKINNER, B. F. (1948). 'Superstition' in the pigeon. *Journal of Experimental Psychology, 38,* 168–172.

SKINNER, B. F. (1971). *Beyond freedom and dignity.* New York: Knopf.

SKUBIC, E. (1956). Studies of Little League and Middle League baseball. *Research Quarterly, 27,* 97–110.

SLATER, M. R., & SEWELL, D. F. (1994). An examination of the cohesion-performance relationship in university hockey teams. *Journal of Sport Sciences, 12,* 423–431.

SLOAN, L. R. (1979). The function and impact of sports for fans: A review of theory and contemporary research. In J. H. Goldstein (Ed.), *Sports, games, and play: Social and psychological viewpoints* (1st ed., pp. 219–264). Hillsdale, NJ: Erlbaum.

SLOAN, L. R. (1989). The motives of sports fans. In J. H. Goldstein (Ed.), *Sports, games, and play: Social and psychological viewpoints* (2nd ed., pp. 175–240). Hillsdale, NJ: Erlbaum.

SMITH, D. (1987). Conditions that facilitate the development of sport imagery training. *The Sport Psychologist, 1,* 237–247.

SMITH, D. (1993, May 3). Seles flies to USA; Security tightened at tournament site. *USA Today,* p. 2C.

SMITH, G. J. (1988). The noble sports fan. *Journal of Sport & Social Issues, 12,* 54–65.

SMITH, G. J. (1989). The noble sports fan redux. *Journal of Sport & Social Issues, 13,* 121–130.

SMITH, G. J., PATTERSON, B., WILLIAMS, T., & HOGG, J. (1981). A profile of the deeply committed male sports fan. *Arena Review, 5*(2), 26–44.

SMITH, J. C. (1993). *Understanding stress and coping.* New York: Macmillan.

SMITH, M. D. (1976). Precipitants of crowd violence. *Sociological Inquiry, 48,* 121–131.

SMITH, M. D. (1980). Interpersonal violence in sport: The influence of parents. In P. Klavora (Ed.), *Psychological and sociological factors in sport* (pp. 139–147). Toronto: University of Toronto Press.

SMITH, R. E. (1980). A cognitive-affective approach to stress management training for athletes. In C. H. Neadeau, W. R. Halliwell, K. M. Newell, & G. C. Roberts (Eds.), *Psychology of motor behavior and sport—1979* (pp. 54–72). Champaign, IL: Human Kinetics.

SMITH, R. E. (1989). Conceptual and statistical issues in research involving multidimensional anxiety scales. *Journal of Sport & Exercise Psychology, 11,* 452–457.

SMITH, R. E., & CHRISTENSEN, D. S. (1995). Psychological skills as predictors of performance and survival in professional baseball. *Journal of Sport & Exercise Psychology, 17,* 399–415.

SMITH, R. E., SCHUTZ, R. W., SMOLL, F. L., & PTACEK, J. T. (1995). Development and validation of a multidimensional measure of sport-specific psychological skills: The Athletic Coping Skills Inventory-28. *Journal of Sport & Exercise Psychology, 17,* 379–398.

SMITH, R. E., SMOLL, F. L., & BARNETT, N. P. (1995). Reduction of children's sport performance anxiety through social support and stress-reduction training for coaches. *Journal of Applied Developmental Psychology, 16,* 125–142.

SMITH, R. E., SMOLL, F. L., & CURTIS, B. (1978). Coaching behaviors in Little League baseball. In F. L. Smoll & R. E. Smith (Eds.), *Psychological perspectives in youth sports* (pp. 173–201). Washington, D.C.: Hemisphere.

SMITH, R. E., SMOLL, F. L., & SCHUTZ, R. W. (1990). Measurement and correlates of sport-specific cognitive and somatic trait anxiety: The Sport Anxiety Scale. *Anxiety Research, 2,* 263–280.

SMOLL, F. L., & SMITH, R. E. (1993). Educating youth sport coaches: An applied sport psychology perspective. In J. M. Williams (Ed.), *Applied sport psychology: Personal growth to peak performance* (2nd ed., pp. 36–57). Mountain View, CA: Mayfield.

SMOLL, F. L., SMITH, R. E., BARNETT, N. P., & EVERETT, J. J. (1993). Enhancement of children's self-esteem through social support training for youth sport coaches. *Journal of Applied Psychology, 78,* 602–610.

SNYDER, C. R., LASSEGARD, M., & FORD, C. E. (1986). Distancing after group success and failure: Basking in reflected glory and cutting off reflected failure. *Journal of Personality and Social Psychology, 51,* 382–388.

SNYDER, E. E., & KIVLIN, J. E. (1975). Women athletes and aspects of psychological well-being and body image. *Research Quarterly, 46,* 191–199.

SNYDER, E. E., & PURDY, D. A. (1985). The home advantage in collegiate basketball. *Sociology of Sport Journal, 2,* 352–356.

SNYDER, E. E., & SPREITZER, E. (1976). Correlates of sport participation among adolescent girls. *Research Quarterly, 47,* 804–809.

SNYDER, M. A. (1993). The new competition: Sports careers for women. In G. L. Cohen (Ed.), *Women in sport: Issues and controversies* (pp. 264–274). Newbury Park, CA: Sage.

SNYDER, M. L., & JONES, E. E. (1974). Attitude attribution when behavior is constrained. *Journal of Experimental Social Psychology, 10,* 585–600.

SNYDER, M. L., STEPHAN, W. G., & ROSENFIELD, D. (1976). Egotism and attribution. *Journal of Personality and Social Psychology, 33,* 435–441.

SOLMON, M. A., & BOONE, J. (1993). The impact of student goal orientation in physical education classes. *Research Quarterly for Exercise and Sport, 64,* 418–424.

SOLSO, R. L. (1991). *Cognitive psychology* (3rd ed.). Boston: Allyn and Bacon.

SONSTROEM, R. J., & BERNARDO, P. (1982). Individual pregame state anxiety and basketball performance: A re-examination of the inverted-U curve. *Journal of Sport Psychology, 4,* 235–245.

SPEARS, B., & SWANSON, R. (1983). *History of sport and physical activity in the United States* (2nd. ed.). Dubuque, IA: Brown.

SPENCE, J. T., HELMREICH, R., & STAPP, J. (1975). Ratings of self and peers on sex role attributes and their relation to self-esteem and conceptions of masculinity and femininity. *Journal of Personality and Social Psychology, 32,* 29–39.

SPENCE, K. W. (1956). *Behavior theory and conditioning.* New Haven, CT: Yale University Press.

SPENCE, K. W., FARBER, I. E., & McFANN, H. H. (1956). The relation of anxiety (drive) level to performance in competitional and noncompetitonal paired-associates learning. *Journal of Experimental Psychology, 52,* 296–305.

SPERLING, G. (1960). The information available in brief visual presentations. *Psychological Monographs: General and Applied, 74,* 1–29.

SPIELBERGER, C. D. (1983). *Manual for the state-trait anxiety inventory.* Palo Alto, CA: Consulting Psychologists Press.

SPIELBERGER, C. D., GORSUCH, R. L., & LUSHENE, R. F. (1970). *Manual for the state-trait anxiety inventory.* Palo Alto, CA: Consulting Psychologists Press.

SPINK, K. S. (1992). Group cohesion and starting status in successful and less successful elite volleyball teams. *Journal of Sport Sciences, 10,* 379–388.

SPINK, K. S. (1995). Cohesion and intention to participate of female sport team athletes. *Journal of Sport & Exercise Psychology, 17,* 416–427.

SPINK, K. S., & LONGHURST, K. (1990). Participation motives of Australian boys involved in traditional and modified cricket. *Australian Journal of Science and Medicine in Sport, 22,* 28–32.

SPINK, K. S., & ROBERTS, G. C. (1980). Ambiguity of outcome and causal attributions. *Journal of Sport Psychology, 2,* 237–244.

SPINRAD, W. (1981). The function of spectator sports. In G. Luschen & G. Sage (Eds.), *Handbook of social science of sport* (pp. 354–365). Champaign, IL: Stipes.

SPREITZER, E., & SNYDER, E. E. (1976). Socialization into sport: An exploratory path analysis. *Research Quarterly, 47,* 238–245.

STANGL, J. M., & KANE, M. J. (1991). Structural variables that offer explanatory power for the underrepresentation of women coaches since Title IX: The case of homologous reproduction. *Sociology of Sport Journal, 8,* 47–60.

STANKEY, G. H. (1972). A strategy for the definition and management of wilderness quality. In J. V. Krutilla (Ed.), *Natural environments: Studies in theoretical and applied analysis* (pp. 88–114). Baltimore: Johns Hopkins University Press.

STAUROWSKY, E. J. (1995). Examining the roots of a gendered division of labor in intercollegiate athletics: Insights into the gender equity debate. *Journal of Sport & Social Issues, 19,* 28–44.

STEADMAN, J. R. (1993). A physician's approach to the psychology of injury. In J. Heil (Ed.), *Psychology of sport injury* (pp. 25–31). Champaign, IL: Human Kinetics.

STEIN, M. (1977). Cult and sport: The case of Big Red. *Mid-American Review of Sociology, 2*(2), 29–42.

STENNETT, R. G. (1957). The relationship of performance level to level of arousal. *Journal of Experimental Psychology, 54,* 54–61.

STEVENSON, C. L. (1975). Socialization effects of participation in sport: A critical review of the research. *Research Quarterly, 46,* 287–301.

STOGDILL, R. M. (1948). Personal factors associated with leadership: A survey of the literature. *The Journal of Psychology, 25,* 35–71.

STONE, G. P. (1971). Wrestling—The great American passion play. In E. Dunning (Ed.), *Sport: Readings from a sociological perspective* (pp. 301–335). Toronto: University of Toronto Press.

STORMS, M. D. (1973). Videotape and the attribution process: Reversing actors' and observers' points of view. *Journal of Personality and Social Psychology, 27,* 165–175.

STRAUB, B. (1995). Die Messung der Identifikation mit einer Sportmannschaft: Eine deutsche adaptation der "Team Identification Scale" von Wann und Branscombe. *Psychologie und Sport, 4,* 132–145.

STREAN, W. B. (1995). Youth sport contexts: Coaches' perceptions and implications for intervention. *Journal of Applied Sport Psychology, 7,* 23–37.

STRUBE, M. J., & GARCIA, J. E. (1981). A meta-analytic investigation of Fiedler's contingency model of leadership effectiveness. *Psychological Bulletin, 90,* 307–321.

SUINN, R. (1972). Behavior rehearsal training for ski racers. *Behavior Therapy, 3,* 519–520.

SUINN, R. (1976, July). Body thinking: Psychology for Olympic champs. *Psychology Today,* p. 38–43.

SUINN, R. (1993). Imagery. In R. N. Singer, M. Murphey, & L. K. Tennant (Eds.), *Handbook of research on sport psychology* (pp. 492–510). New York: Macmillan.

SULLIVAN, D. B. (1991). Commentary and viewer perception of player hostility: Adding punch to televised sports. *Journal of Broadcasting and Electronic Media, 35,* 487–504.

SULS, J., & MULLEN, B. (1981). Life change and psychological distress: The role of perceived control and desirability. *Journal of Applied Social Psychology, 11,* 379–389.

SWAIN, A., & JONES, G. (1991). Gender role endorsement and competitive anxiety. *International Journal of Sport Psychology, 22,* 50–65.

SWAIN, A., & JONES, G. (1992). Relationships between sport achievement orientation and competitive state anxiety. *The Sport Psychologist, 6,* 42–54.

SYER, J., & CONNOLLY, C. (1987). *Sporting body sporting mind: An athlete's guide to mental training.* Englewood Cliffs, NJ: Prentice Hall.

TAJFEL, H. (1981). *Human groups and social categories.* Cambridge: Cambridge University Press.

TAJFEL, H., & TURNER, J. (1979). An integrative theory of intergroup conflict. In W. Austin & S. Worchel (Eds.), *The social psychology of intergroup relations* (pp. 33–47). Monterey, CA: Brooks/Cole.

TANNENBAUM, P. H., & GAER, E. P. (1965). Mood change as a function of stress of protagonist and degree of identification in a film-viewing situation. *Journal of Personality and Social Psychology, 2,* 612–616.

TANNENBAUM, P. H., & NOAH, J. E. (1959). Sportugese: A study of sports page communication. *Journalism Quarterly, 36,* 163–170.

TANNER, J., SEV'ER, A., & UNGAR, S. (1989). Explaining the steroid scandal: How Toronto students interpret the Ben Johnson case. *International Journal of Sport Psychology, 20,* 297–308.

TAYLOR, A. H. (1986). Sport specificity in attentional style testing (pp. 237–242). In J. Watkins, T. Reilly, & L. Burwitz (Eds.), *'86 Glascow Conference—VIII Commonwealth and International Conference on Sport.* Cambridge, MA: Cambridge University Press.

TAYLOR, A. H., & DANIEL, J. V. (1987). Sources of stress in soccer officiating: An empirical study. *First world congress of science and football* (pp. 538–544). Liverpool, England.

TAYLOR, J. (1991). Career direction, development, and opportunities in applied sport psychology. *The Sport Psychologist, 5,* 266–280.

TAYLOR, J. (1992). Coaches are people too: An applied model of stress management for sports coaches. *Journal of Applied Sport Psychology, 4,* 27–50.

TAYLOR, J. (1994). Examining the boundaries of sport science and psychology trained practitioners in applied sport psychology: Title usage and area of competence. *Journal of Applied Sport Psychology, 6,* 185–195.

TAYLOR, J. (1995). A conceptual model for integrating athletes' needs and sport demands in the development of competitive mental preparation strategies. *The Sport Psychologist, 9,* 339–357.

TAYLOR, J., & OGILVIE, B. C. (1994). A conceptual model of adaptation to retirement among athletes. *Journal of Applied Sport Psychology, 6,* 1–20.

TAYLOR, J. A. (1953). A personality scale of manifest anxiety. *The Journal of Abnormal and Social Psychology, 48,* 285–290.

TAYLOR, P. (1994, May 30). Flash and trash. *Sports Illustrated,* pp. 20–24.

TAYLOR, P. (1995, January 30). Bad actors. *Sports Illustrated,* pp. 18–23.

TAYLOR, S. E. (1991). *Health psychology* (2nd ed.). New York: McGraw-Hill.

TELANDER, R. (1994, February 21). Who's in charge here? *Sports Illustrated,* pp. 78, 80.

TEMPLIN, D. P., & VERNACCHIA, R. A. (1995). The effect of highlight music videotapes upon the game performance of intercollegiate basketball players. *The Sport Psychologist, 9,* 41–50.

TENENBAUM, G., & BAR-ELI, M. (1992). Methodological issues in sport psychology research. The *Australian Journal of Science and Medicine in Sport, 24,* 44–50.

TENENBAUM, G., & FURST, D. (1985). The relationship between sport achievement responsibility, attribution and related situational variables. *International Journal of Sport Psychology, 16,* 254–269.

TERRY, P. (1995). The efficacy of mood state profiling with elite performers: A review and synthesis. *The Sport Psychologist, 9,* 309–324.

THEBERGE, N. (1991). A content analysis of print media coverage of gender, women, and physical activity. *Journal of Applied Sport Psychology, 3,* 36–48.

THEEBOOM, M., DE KNOP, P., & WEISS, M. R. (1995). Motivational climate, psychological responses, and motor skill development in children's sport: A field-based intervention study. *Journal of Sport & Exercise Psychology, 17,* 294–311.

THELEN, M. H., DOLLINGER, S. J., & KIRKLAND, K. D. (1979). Imitation and response uncertainty. The *Journal of Genetic Psychology, 135,* 139–152.

THEODORAKIS, Y. (1995). Effects of self-efficacy, satisfaction, and personal goals on swimming performance. *The Sport Psychologist, 9,* 245–253.

THIRER, J., & RAMPEY, M. S. (1979). Effects of abusive spectators' behavior on performance of home and visiting intercollegiate basketball teams. *Perceptual and Motor Skills, 48,* 1047–1053.

THOITS, P. A. (1983). Multiple identities and psychological well-being: A reformulation and test of the social isolation hypothesis. *American Sociological Review, 48,* 174–187.

THOMAS, J. R., THOMAS, K. T., & GALLAGHER, J. D. (1993). Developmental considerations in skill acquisition. In R. N. Singer, M. Murphey, & L. K. Tennant (Eds.), *Handbook of research on sport psychology* (pp. 73–105). New York: Macmillan.

THOMAS, P. R., & OVER, R. (1994). Psychological and psychomotor skills associated with performance in golf. *The Sport Psychologist, 8,* 73–86.

THOMAS, R. M. (1986, June 4). 7 of 10 in survey say they're fans. *The New York Times,* p. 89.

THOMPSON, J. (1993). *Positive coaching: Building character and self-esteem through sports.* Dubuque, IA: Brown and Benchmark.

THORNDIKE, E. L. (1898). Animal intelligence: An experimental study of the associative processes in animals. *Psychological Monographs, 2* (Whole No. 8).

THORNDIKE, E. L. (1905). *The elements of psychology.* New York: Seiler.

THORNDIKE, E. L. (1931). *Human learning.* New York: Appleton.

THRILL, E., & VALLERAND, R. J. (Eds.). (1995). Motivation and emotion in the sport context. *International Journal of Sport Psychology, 26*(1).

TIGER, L. (1969). *Men in groups.* New York: Random House.

TITLEY, R. W. (1976, September). The loneliness of a long-distance kicker. *The Athletic Journal,* pp. 74–80.

TJOSVOLD, D. (1984). Effects of leader warmth and directiveness on subordinate performance on a subsequent task. *Journal of Applied Psychology, 69,* 422–427.

TOWLER, G. (1986). From zero to one hundred: Coaction in a natural setting. *Perceptual and Motor Skills, 62,* 377–378.

TRAVIS, C. A., & SACHS, M. L. (1991). Applied sport psychology and persons with mental retardation. *The Sport Psychologist, 5,* 382–391.

TREISMAN, A. M. (1964). Verbal cues, language, and meaning in selective attention. *American Journal of Psychology, 77,* 206–219.

TRIPLETT, N. (1898). The dynamogenic factors in pacemaking and competition. *American Journal of Psychology, 9,* 507–533.

TROPE, Y. (1986). Identification and inferential processes in dispositional attribution. *Psychological Review, 93,* 239–257.

TRUDEL, P., & GILBERT, W. (1995). Research on coaches' behaviours: Looking beyond the refereed journals. *Avante, 1,* 94–104.

TRUJILLO, C. M. (1983). The effect of weight training and running exercise intervention programs on the self-esteem of college women. *International Journal of Sport Psychology, 14,* 162–173.

TRUJILLO, N., & KRIZEK, B. (1994). Emotionality in the stands and in the field: Expressing self through baseball. *Journal of Sport & Social Issues, 18,* 303–325.

TRULSON, M. E. (1986). Martial arts training: A novel "cure" for juvenile delinquency. *Human Relations, 39,* 1131–1140.

TULVING, E. (1985). How many memory systems are there? *American Psychologist, 40,* 385–398.

TULVING, E. (1986). What kind of a hypothesis is the distinction between episodic and semantic memory? *Journal of Experimental Psychology: Learning, Memory, and Cognition, 12,* 307–311.

TURNER, C. W., & BERKOWITZ, L. (1972). Identification with film aggressor (covert role taking) and reactions to film violence. *Journal of Personality and Social Psychology, 21,* 256–264.

TURNER, E. T. (1970). The effects of viewing college football, basketball, and wrestling on the elicited aggressive responses of male spectators. In G. S. Kenyon (Ed.), *Contemporary psychology of sport: Proceedings of the Second International Congress of Sport Psychology* (pp. 325–328). Chicago: The Athletic Institute.

TUTKO, T. A. (1989). Personality change in the American sport scene. In J. H. Goldstein (Ed.), *Sports, games, and play: Social and psychological viewpoints* (2nd ed., pp. 111–127). Hillsdale, NJ: Erlbaum.

TUTKO, T. A., LYON, L., & OGILVIE, B. C. (1971). *Motivation in athletics: The Athletic Motivation Inven-*

tory. Paper presented at the meeting of AAHPER, Detroit.

TZINER, A., & VARDI, Y. (1982). Effects of command style and group cohesiveness on the performance effectiveness of self-selected tank crews. *Journal of Applied Psychology, 67,* 769–775.

UNGAR, S., & SEV'ER, A. (1989). "Say it ain't so, Ben": Attributions for a fallen hero. *Social Psychology Quarterly, 52,* 207–212.

UNGERLEIDER, S., & GOLDING, J. M. (1991). Mental practice among Olympic athletes. *Perceptual and Motor Skills, 72,* 1007–1017.

US Olympic Committee establishes guidelines for sport psychology services. (1983). *Journal of Sport Psychology, 5,* 4–7.

USA Today Baseball Weekly. (1993, December 30). Even at chapel, missing game a Cardinals sin, p. 31.

VALLERAND, R. J., GAUVIN, L. I., & HALLIWELL, W. R. (1986). Negative effects of competition on children's intrinsic motivation. *The Journal of Social Psychology, 126,* 649–657.

VALLERAND, R. J., & RICHER, F. (1988). On the use of the causal dimension scale in a field setting: A test with confirmatory factor analysis in success and failure situations. *Journal of Personality and Social Psychology, 54,* 704–712.

VAN RAALTE, J. L., BREWER, B. W., LEWIS, B. P., LINDER, D. E., WILDMAN, G., & KOZIMOR, J. (1995). Cork! The effects of positive and negative self-talk on dart throwing performance. *Journal of Sport Behavior, 18,* 50–57.

VAN RAALTE, J. L., BREWER, B. W., NEMEROFF, C. J., & LINDER, D. E. (1991). Chance orientation and superstitious behavior on the putting green. *Journal of Sport Behavior, 14,* 41–50.

VAN RAALTE, J. L., BREWER, B. W., RIVERA, P. M., & PETITPAS, A. J. (1994). The relationship between observable self-talk and competitive junior tennis players' match performances. *Journal of Sport & Exercise Psychology, 16,* 400–415.

VAN SCHOYCK, S. R., & GRASHA, A. F. (1981). Attentional style variations and athletic ability: The advantages of a sports-specific test. *Journal of Sport Psychology, 3,* 149–165.

VANDELL, R. A., DAVIS, R. A., & CLUGSTON, H. A. (1943). The function of mental practice in the acquisition of motor skills. *The Journal of General Psychology, 29,* 243–250.

VANDEN AUWEELE, Y., DE CUYPER, B., VAN MELE, V., & RZEWNICKI, R. (1993). Elite performance and personality: From description and prediction to diagnosis and intervention. In R. N. Singer, M. Murphey, & L. K. Tennant (Eds.), *Handbook of research on sport psychology* (pp. 257–289). New York: Macmillan.

VARCA, P. E. (1980). An analysis of home and away game performance of male college basketball teams. *Journal of Sport Psychology, 2,* 245–257.

VARE, R. (1974). *Buckeye: A study of coach Woody Hayes and the Ohio State football machine.* New York: Harper's Magazine Press.

VEALEY, R. S. (1986). Conceptualization of sport-confidence and competitive orientation: Preliminary investigation and instrument development. *Journal of Sport Psychology, 8,* 221–246.

VEALEY, R. S. (1992). Personality and sport: A comprehensive view. In T. S. Horn (Ed.), *Advances in sport psychology* (pp. 25–59). Champaign, IL: Human Kinetics.

VEALEY, R. S. (1994). Current status and prominent issues in sport psychology interventions. *Medicine and Science in Sports and Exercise, 26,* 495–502.

VERGINA, A. D., & DUGONI, B. L. (1993, May). *Performance of team members: The effects of cohesiveness feedback.* Paper presented at the meeting of the Midwestern Psychological Association, Chicago.

VOGLER, C. C., & SCHWARTZ, S. E. (1993). *The sociology of sport: An introduction.* Englewood Cliffs, NJ: Prentice Hall.

VOKEY, J. R., & RUSSELL, G. W. (1992). On penalties in sport as measures of aggression. *Social Behavior and Personality, 20,* 219–226.

VOLKAMER, N. (1971). Investigations into the aggressiveness in competitive social systems. *Sportwissenschaft, 1,* 33–64.

VON WRIGHT, J. M., ANDERSON, K., & STENMAN, U. (1975). Generalization of conditioned GSRs in dichotic listening. In P. M. A. Rabbitt & S. Dornic (Eds.), *Attention and performance* (Vol. 5, pp. 194–204). London: Academic Press.

VROOM, V. H. (1964). *Work and motivation.* New York: Wiley.

VROOM, V. H., & JAGO, A. G. (1978). On the validity of the Vroom-Yetton model. *Journal of Applied Psychology, 63,* 151–162.

VROOM, V. H., & JAGO, A. G. (1988). *The new leadership: Managing participation in organizations.* Englewood Cliffs, NJ: Prentice-Hall.

VROOM, V. H., & YETTON, P. W. (1973). *Leadership and decision making.* Pittsburgh: Pittsburgh University Press.

WACHTEL, P. L. (1967). Conceptions of broad and narrow attention. *Psychological Bulletin, 68,* 417–429.

WAKEFIELD, K. L. (1995). The pervasive effects of social influence on sporting event attendance. *Journal of Sport & Social Issues, 19,* 335–351.

WALDROP, J. (1989). Ball-park figures. *American Demographics, 11,* 6.

WALL, B. R., & GRUBER, J. J. (1986). Relevancy of athletic aggression inventory for use in women's intercollegiate basketball: A pilot investigation. *International Journal of Sport Psychology, 17,* 23–33.

WALLACE, R. K., & BENSON, H. (1972). The physiology of meditation. *Scientific American, 226,* 85–90.

WALLEY, P. B., GRAHAM, G. M., & FOREHAND, R. (1982). Assessment and treatment of adult observer verbalizations at youth league baseball games. *Journal of Sport Psychology, 4,* 254–266.

WALSTER, E., BERSCHEID, E., & WALSTER, G. W. (1973). New directions in equity research. *Journal of Personality and Social Psychology, 25,* 151–176.

WANG, Y., & MORGAN, W. P. (1992). The effect of imagery perspectives on the psychophysiological responses to imagined exercise. *Behavioural Brain Research, 52,* 154–167.

WANKEL, L. M. (1973). An examination of illegal aggression in intercollegiate hockey. In I. D. Williams & L. M. Wankel (Eds.), *Proceedings of the Fourth Canadian Psych-Motor Learning and Sport Psychology Symposium* (pp. 531–544). Ottawa, Canada: Fitness and Amateur Sport Directorate.

WANKEL, L. M., & BERGER, B. G. (1990). The psychological and social benefits of sport and physical activity. *Journal of Leisure Research, 22,* 167–182.

WANKEL, L. M., & KREISEL, P. S. J. (1985). Factors underlying enjoyment of youth sports: Sport and age group comparisons. *Journal of Sport Psychology, 7,* 51–64.

WANKEL, L. M., & SEFTON, J. M. (1989). A season-long investigation of fun in youth sports. *Journal of Sport & Exercise Psychology, 11,* 355–366.

WANN, D. L. (1993). Aggression among highly identified spectators as a function of their need to maintain positive social identity. *Journal of Sport & Social Issues, 17,* 134–143.

WANN, D. L. (1994a). The "noble" sports fan: The relationships between team identification, self-esteem, and aggression. *Perceptual and Motor Skills, 78,* 864–866.

WANN, D. L. (1994b). Biased evaluations of highly identified sport spectators: A response to Hirt and Ryalls. *Perceptual and Motor Skills, 79,* 105–106.

WANN, D. L. (1995). Preliminary validation of the Sport Fan Motivation Scale. *Journal of Sport & Social Issues, 19,* 377–396.

WANN, D. L. (1996). Seasonal changes in spectators' identification and involvement with and evaluations of college basketball and football teams. *The Psychological Record.*

WANN, D. L., & BRANSCOMBE, N. R. (1990a). Die-hard and fair-weather fans: Effects of identification on BIRGing and CORFing tendencies. *Journal of Sport & Social Issues, 14,* 103–117.

WANN, D. L., & BRANSCOMBE, N. R. (1990b). Person perception when aggressive and nonaggressive sports are primed. *Aggressive Behavior, 16,* 27–32.

WANN, D. L., & BRANSCOMBE, N. R. (1992). Emotional responses to the sports page. *Journal of Sport & Social Issues, 16,* 49–64.

WANN, D. L., & BRANSCOMBE, N. R. (1993). Sports fans: Measuring degree of identification with their team. *International Journal of Sport Psychology, 24,* 1–17.

WANN, D. L., & BRANSCOMBE, N. R. (1995a). Influence of level of identification with a group and physiological arousal on perceived intergroup complexity. *British Journal of Social Psychology, 34,* 223–235.

WANN, D. L., & BRANSCOMBE, N. R. (1995b). Influence of identification with a sports team on objective knowledge and subjective beliefs. *International Journal of Sport Psychology, 26,* 551–567.

WANN, D. L., & DOLAN, T. J. (1994a). Spectators' evaluations of rival and fellow fans. *The Psychological Record, 44,* 351–358.

WANN, D. L., & DOLAN, T. J. (1994b). Attributions of highly identified sport spectators. *The Journal of Social Psychology, 134,* 783–792.

WANN, D. L., & DOLAN, T. J. (1994c). Influence of spectators' identification on evaluation of the past present and future performance of a sports team. *Perceptual and Motor Skills, 78,* 547–552.

WANN, D. L., DOLAN, T. J., McGEORGE, K. K., & ALLISON, J. A. (1994). Relationships between spectator identification and spectators' perceptions of influence, spectators' emotions, and competition outcome. *Journal of Sport & Exercise Psychology, 16,* 347–364.

Wann, D. L., & Fortner, B. V. (1995). *The application of the equity theory of motivation to sport settings: The importance and impact of overpayment inequity.* Manuscript submitted for publication.

Wann, D. L., & Hamlet, M. A. (1994). The joiners' scale: Validation of a measure of social-complexity. *Psychological Reports, 74,* 1027–1034.

Wann, D. L., & Hamlet, M. A. (1995). Author and subject gender in sports research. *International Journal of Sport Psychology, 26,* 225–232.

Wann, D. L., Hamlet, M. A., Wilson, T. M., & Hodges, J. A. (1995). Basking in reflected glory, cutting off reflected failure, and cutting off future failure: The importance of group identification. *Social Behavior and Personality, 23,* 377–388.

Wann, D. L., & Lingle, S. E. (1994). Comparison of team and individual sports participants tendencies to join groups. *Perceptual and Motor Skills, 79,* 833–834.

Wann, D. L., & Schrader, M. P. (1996). An analysis of the stability of sport team identification. *Perceptual and Motor Skills, 82,* 322.

Wann, D. L., Tucker, K. B., & Schrader, M. P. (1996). An exploratory examination of the factors influencing the origination, continuation, and cessation of sports team identification. *Perceptual and Motor Skills, 82,* 995–1001.

Wann, D. L., & Weaver, K. A. (1993). The relationship between interaction levels and impression formation. *Bulletin of the Psychonomic Society, 31,* 548–550.

Wann, D. L., Weaver, K. A., & Davis, S. F. (1992). The effects of situation, disposition, and setting on in-group favoritism. *Bulletin of the Psychonomic Society, 30,* 268–270.

Warren, W. (1983). *Coaching and motivation.* Englewood Cliffs, NJ: Prentice-Hall.

Watkins, D. (1986). Attributions in the New Zealand sports pages. *The Journal of Social Psychology, 126,* 817–819.

Watkins, O. C., & Watkins, M. J. (1980). The modality effect and echoic persistence. *Journal of Experimental Psychology: General, 109,* 251–278.

Webb, D. (1986). Sport and the hooligan. In M. L. Krotee & E. M. Jaeger (Eds.), *Comparative physi-*

cal education and sport (vol. 3, pp. 305–316). Champaign, IL: Human Kinetics.

Webb, E. J., Campbell, D. T., Schwartz, R. C., Sechrest, L., & Grove, J. B. (1981). *Nonreactive measures in the social sciences* (2nd. ed.). Boston: Houghton Mifflin.

Webber, P. A. (1993, March 4). Racer fans let team down. *The Murray State News,* p. 4.

Weinberg, R. S. (1979). Intrinsic motivation in a competitive setting. *Medicine and Science in Sports, 11,* 146–149.

Weinberg, R. S. (1984). Mental preparation strategies. In J. M. Silva & R. S. Weinberg (Eds.), *Psychological foundations of sport* (pp. 145–156). Champaign, IL: Human Kinetics.

Weinberg, R. S. (1992). Goal setting and motor performance: A review and critique. In G. C. Roberts (Ed.), *Motivation in sport and exercise* (pp. 177–197). Champaign, IL: Human Kinetics.

Weinberg, R. S. (1994). Goal setting and performance in sport and exercise settings: A synthesis and critique. *Medicine and Science in Sports and Exercise, 26,* 469–477.

Weinberg, R. S., Bruya, L., & Jackson, A. (1985). The effects of goal proximity and goal specificity on endurance performance. *Journal of Sport Psychology, 7,* 296–305.

Weinberg, R. S., & Gould, D. (1995). *Foundations of sport and exercise psychology.* Champaign, IL: Human Kinetics.

Weinberg, R. S., Gould, D., & Jackson, A. (1980). Cognition and motor performance: Effect of psyching-up strategies on three motor tasks. *Cognitive Therapy and Research, 4,* 239–245.

Weinberg, R. S., Gould, D., Yukelson, D., & Jackson, A. (1981). The effect of preexisting and manipulated self-efficacy on a competitive muscular endurance task. *Journal of Sport Psychology, 4,* 345–354.

Weinberg, R. S., & Jackson, A. (1979). Competition and extrinsic rewards: Effect on intrinsic motivation and attribution. *Research Quarterly, 50,* 494–502.

Weinberg, R. S., Jackson, A., & Seabourne, T. G. (1985). The effects of specific and nonspecific mental preparation strategies on strength and endurance performance. *Journal of Sport Behavior, 8,* 175–180.

Weinberg, R. S., & Ragan, J. (1980). Effects of competition, success-failure and sex on intrinsic motivation. In P. Klavora (Ed.), *Psychological and sociological factors in sport* (pp. 289–297). Toronto: University of Toronto Press.

WEINBERG, R. S., & RICHARDSON, P. A. (1990). *Psychology of officiating*. Champaign, IL: Human Kinetics.

WEINBERG, R. S., SEABOURNE, T. G., & JACKSON, A. (1981). Effects of visuo-motor behavioral rehearsal, relaxation, and imagery on karate performance. *Journal of Sport Psychology, 3*, 228–238.

WEINBERG, R. S., SEABOURNE, T. G., & JACKSON, A. (1982). Effects of visuo-motor behavior rehearsal on state-trait anxiety and performance: Is practice important? *Journal of Sport Behavior, 5*, 209–219.

WEINBERG, R. S., STITCHER, T., & RICHARDSON, P. (1994). Effects of a seasonal goal-setting program on lacrosse performance. *The Sport Psychologist, 8*, 166–175.

WEINBERG, R. S., & WEIGAND, D. (1993). Goal setting in sport and exercise: A reaction to Locke. *Journal of Sport & Exercise Psychology, 15*, 88–96.

WEINER, B. (1979). A theory of motivation for some classroom experiences. *Journal of Educational Psychology, 71*, 3–25.

WEINER, B. (1980a). A cognitive (attribution)—emotion—action model of motivated behavior: An analysis of judgments of help-giving. *Journal of Personality and Social Psychology, 39*, 186–200.

WEINER, B. (1980b). *Human motivation*. New York: Holt, Rinehart and Winston.

WEINER, B. (1982). The emotional consequences of causal attributions. In M. S. Clark & S. T. Fiske (Eds.), *Affect and cognition: The 17th Annual Carnegie Symposium on Cognition* (pp. 185–209). Hillsdale, NJ: Erlbaum.

WEINER, B. (1985). "Spontaneous" causal thinking. *Psychological Bulletin, 97*, 74–84.

WEINER, B. (1989). *Human motivation*. Hillsdale, NJ Erlbaum.

WEIR, P. L., & LEAVITT, J. L. (1990). Effects of model's skill level and model's knowledge of results on the performance of a dart throwing task. *Human Movement Science, 9*, 369–383.

WEISMAN, L. (1994, February 17). Jurisprudence. *USA Today*, p. 7C.

WEISS, M. R. (1987). Self-esteem and achievement in children's sport and physical activity. In D. Gould & M. R. Weiss (Eds.), *Advances in pediatric sport sciences* (Vol. 2, pp. 87–119). Champaign, IL: Human Kinetics.

WEISS, M. R. (1991). Psychological skill development in children and adolescents. *The Sport Psychologist, 5*, 335–354.

WEISS, M. R., & CHAUMETON, N. (1992). Motivational orientations in sport. In T. S. Horn (Ed.), *Advances in sport psychology* (pp. 61–99). Champaign, IL: Human Kinetics.

WEISS, M. R., & DUNCAN, S. C. (1992). The relationship between physical competence and peer acceptance in the context of children's sports participation. *Journal of Sport & Exercise Psychology, 14*, 177–191.

WEISS, M. R., & FRIEDRICHS, W. D. (1986). The influence of leader behaviors, coach attributes, and institutional variables of performance and satisfaction of collegiate basketball teams. *Journal of Sport Psychology, 8*, 332–346.

WEISS, M. R., & KNOPPERS, A. (1982). The influence of socialization agents on female collegiate volleyball players. *Journal of Sport Psychology, 4*, 267–279.

WEISS, M. R., McAULEY, E., EBBECK, V., & WIESE, D. M. (1990). Self-esteem and causal attributions for children's physical and social competence in sport. *Journal of Sport & Exercise Psychology, 12*, 21–36.

WEISS, M. R., & TROXEL, R. K. (1986). Psychology of the injured athlete. *Athletic Training, 21*, 104–109, 154.

WENNER, L. A., & GANTZ, W. (1989). The audience experience with sports on television. In L. A. Wenner (Ed.), *Media, sports, and society* (pp. 241–268). Newbury Park, CA: Sage.

WERNER, A. C., & GOTTHEIL, E. (1966). Personality development and participation in college athletics. *Research Quarterly, 37*, 126–131,

WHELAN, J. P., MEYERS, A. W., & DONOVAN, C. (1995). Competitive recreational athletes: A multisystemic model. In S. M. Murphy (Ed.), *Sport psychology interventions* (pp. 71–116). Champaign, IL: Human Kinetics.

WHITE, G. F. (1989). Media and violence: The case of professional football championship games. *Aggressive Behavior, 15*, 423–433.

WHITE, S. A. (1993). The effect of gender and age on causal attribution in softball players. *International Journal of Sport Psychology, 24*, 49–58.

WHITNEY, J. D. (1988). Winning games versus winning championships: The economics of fan interest and team performance. *Economic Inquiry, 26*, 703–724.

WIDMEYER, W. N., & BIRCH, J. S. (1979). The relationship between aggression and performance outcome in ice hockey. *Canadian Journal of Applied Sport Sciences, 4,* 91–94.

WIDMEYER, W. N., & BIRCH, J. S. (1984). Aggression in professional ice hockey: A strategy for success or a reaction to failure? *The Journal of Psychology, 117,* 77–84.

WIDMEYER, W. N., BRAWLEY, L. R., & CARRON, A. V. (1985). *The measurement of cohesion in sport teams: The group environment questionnaire.* London, Ontario: Sports Dynamics.

WIDMEYER, W. N., BRAWLEY, L. R., & CARRON, A. V. (1990). The effects of group size in sport. *Journal of Sport & Exercise Psychology, 12,* 177–190.

WIDMEYER, W. N., CARRON, A. V., & BRAWLEY, L. R. (1993). Group cohesion in sport and exercise. In R. N. Singer, M. Murphey, & L. K. Tennant (Eds.), *Handbook of research on sport psychology* (pp. 672–692). New York: Macmillan.

WIDMEYER, W. N., & WILLIAMS, J. M. (1991). Predicting cohesion in a coacting sport. *Small Group Research, 22,* 548–570.

WIESE, D. M., & WEISS, M. R. (1987). Psychological rehabilitation and physical injury: Implications for the sportsmedicine team. *The Sport Psychologist, 1,* 318–330.

WIESE-BJORNSTAL, D. M., & SMITH, A. M. (1993). Counseling strategies for enhanced recovery of injured athletes within a team approach. In D. Pargman (Ed.), *Psychological bases of sport injuries* (pp. 149–182). Morgantown, WV: Fitness Information Technology.

WIGGINS, D. K. (1993). Critical events affecting racism in athletics. In R. C. Althouse & D. D. Brooks (Eds.), *Racism in college athletics: The African-American athlete's experience* (pp. 23–49). Morgantown, WV: Fitness Information Technology.

WIGGINS, M. (1995). Facilitative and debilitative anxiety: Preperformance symptoms, expectations, and temporal patterns in athletes. Unpublished Doctoral Dissertation, Northern Colorado University, Greeley, CO.

WILENSKY, H. L. (1964). The professionalization of everyone? *The American Journal of Sociology, 70,* 137–158.

WILLIAMS, J. M. (1980). Personality characteristics of the successful female athlete. In W. F. Straub (Ed.), *Sport psychology: An analysis of athlete behavior* (2nd ed., pp. 249–255). Ithaca, NY: Mouvement Publications.

WILLIAMS, J. M., & HACKER, C. M. (1982). Causal relationships among cohesion, satisfaction, and performance in women's intercollegiate field hockey teams. *Journal of Sport Psychology, 4,* 324–337.

WILLIAMS, J. M., & KRANE, V. (1989). Response distortion of self-report questionnaires with female collegiate golfers. *The Sport Psychologist, 3,* 212–218.

WILLIAMS, J. M., & PARKHOUSE, B. L. (1988). Social learning theory as a foundation for examining sex bias in evaluation of coaches. *Journal of Sport & Exercise Psychology, 10,* 322–333.

WILLIAMS, J. M., & ROEPKE, N. (1993). Psychology of injury and injury rehabilitation. In R. N. Singer, M. Murphey, & L. K. Tennant (Eds.), *Handbook of research on sport psychology* (pp. 815–839). New York: Macmillan.

WILLIAMS, J. M., & WIDMEYER, W. N. (1991). The cohesion-performance outcome relationship in a coacting sport. *Journal of Sport & Exercise Psychology, 13,* 364–371.

WILLIAMS, J. M., & WHITE, K. A. (1983). Adolescent status systems for males and females at three age levels. *Adolescence, 18,* 381–389.

WILLIAMS, K. D., HARKINS, S., & LATANÉ, B. (1981). Identifiability as a deterrent to social loafing: Two cheering experiments. *Journal of Personality and Social Psychology, 40,* 303–311.

WILLIAMS, K. D., NIDA, S. A., BACA, L. D., & LATANE, B. (1989). Social loafing and swimming: Effects of identifiability on individual and relay performance of intercollegiate swimmers. *Basic and Applied Social Psychology, 10,* 73–81.

WILLIAMS, L. (1994). Goal orientations and athletes' preferences for competence information sources. *Journal of Sport & Exercise Psychology, 16,* 416–430.

WILLIAMS, L., & GILL, D. L. (1995). The role of perceived competence in the motivation of physical activity. *Journal of Sport & Exercise Psychology, 17,* 363–378.

WILLIAMS, L. R. T. (1978). Transcendental meditation and mirror-tracing skill. *Perceptual and Motor Skills, 46,* 371–378.

WILLIAMS, L. R. T., & HERBERT, P. G. (1976). Transcendental meditation and fine perceptual-motor skill. *Perceptual and Motor Skills, 43,* 303–309.

WILLIAMS, L. R. T., LODGE, B., & REDDISH, P. S. (1977). Effects of transcendental meditation on rotary pursuit skill. *Research Quarterly, 48,* 196–201.

WILLIAMS, L. R. T., & VICKERMAN, B. L. (1976). Effects of transcendental meditation on fine motor skill. *Perceptual and Motor Skills, 43,* 607–613.

WILLIAMS, M., & DAVIDS, K. (1995). Declarative knowledge in sport: A by-product of experience or a characteristic of expertise? *Journal of Sport & Exercise Psychology, 17,* 259–275.

WILLS, T. A. (1981). Downward comparison principles in social psychology. *Psychological Bulletin, 90,* 245–271.

WINKLER, J. D., & TAYLOR, S. E. (1979). Preference, expectations, and attributional bias: Two field studies. *Journal of Applied Social Psychology, 9,* 183–197.

WITTIG, A. F., & SCHURR, K. T. (1994). Psychological characteristics of women volleyball players: Relationships with injuries, rehabilitation, and team success. *Personality and Social Psychology Bulletin, 20,* 322–330.

WOLFF, A. (1994, March 28). Giant killers. *Sports Illustrated,* pp. 14–22.

WOLFF, A., & O'BRIEN, R. (1995, January 30). Somber soccer. *Sports Illustrated,* p. 12.

WOLFF, A., & STONE, C. (1995a, May 22). Baseball . . . Anyone? *Sports Illustrated,* p. 18.

WOLFF, A., & STONE, C. (1995b, June 5). Hot pants night-mares and other horrors. *Sports Illustrated,* p. 20.

WOLFF, R. (1993). *Good sports.* New York: Dell.

WONG, P. T. P., & WEINER, B. (1981). When people ask "why" questions, and the heuristics of attributional search. *Journal of Personality and Social Psychology, 40,* 650–663.

WOOD, N., & COWAN, N. (in press). The cocktail party phenomenon revisited: How frequent are attention shifts to one's name in an irrelevant auditory channel? *Journal of Experimental Psychology: Learning, Memory, and Cognition.*

WOOLFOLK, R. L., MURPHY, S. M., GOTTESFELD, D., & AITKEN, D. (1985). Effects of mental rehearsal of task motor activity and mental depiction of task outcome on motor skill performance. *Journal of Sport Psychology, 7,* 191–197.

WOOLFOLK, R. L., PARRISH, M. W., & MURPHY, S. M. (1985). The effects of positive and negative imagery on motor skill performance. *Cognitive Therapy and Research, 9,* 335–341.

WORRELL, G. L., & HARRIS, D. V. (1986). The relationship of perceived and observed aggression of ice hockey players. *International Journal of Sport Psychology, 17,* 34–40.

WORRINGHAM, C. J., & MESSICK, D. M. (1983). Social facilitation of running: An unobtrusive study. *The Journal of Social Psychology, 121,* 23–29.

WRIGHT, E. F., JACKSON, W., CHRISTIE, S. D., McGUIRE, G. R., & WRIGHT, R. D. (1991). The home-course disadvantage in golf championships: Further evidence for the undermining effect of supportive audiences on performance under pressure. *Journal of Sport Behavior, 14,* 51–60.

WRIGHT, E. F., VOYER, D., WRIGHT, R. D., & RONEY, C. (1995). Supporting audiences and performance under pressure: The home-ice disadvantage in hockey championships. *Journal of Sport Behavior, 18,* 21–28.

WRIGHT, R. A., & BREHM, J. W. (1984). The impact of task difficulty upon perceptions of arousal and goal attractiveness in an avoidance paradigm. *Motivation and Emotion, 8,* 171–181.

WRIGHT, R. A., & BREHM, J. W. (1989). Energization and goal attractiveness. In L. A. Pervin (Ed.), *Goal concepts in personality and social psychology* (pp. 169–210). Hillsdale, NJ: Erlbaum.

YATES, W. R., PERRY, P., & MURRAY, S. (1992). Aggression and hostility in anabolic steroid users. *Biological Psychiatry, 31,* 1232–1234.

YERGIN, M. L. (1986). Who goes to the game? *American Demographics, 8,* 42–43.

YERKES, R. M., & DODSON, J. D. (1908). The relation of strength of stimulus to rapidity of habit-formation. *Journal of Comparative Neurology and Psychology, 18,* 459–482.

YIANNAKIS, A. (1976). Birth order and preference for dangerous sports among males. *Research Quarterly, 47,* 62–67.

YUKELSON, D., WEINBERG, R. S., & JACKSON, A. (1984). A multidimensional group cohesion instrument for intercollegiate basketball teams. *Journal of Sport Psychology, 6,* 103–117.

YUKL, G. A. (1989). *Leadership in organizations* (2nd ed.). Englewood Cliffs, NJ: Prentice–Hall.

ZAICHKOWSKY, L. D., & FUCHS, C. V. (1988). Biofeedback applications in exercise and athletic performance. *Exercise and Sport Science Review, 16,* 381–421.

ZAICHKOWSKY, L. D., & TAKENAKA, K. (1993). Optimizing arousal levels. In R. N. Singer, M. Murphey, & L. K. Tennant (Eds.), *Handbook of research* on sport psychology (pp. 511–527). New York: Macmillan.

ZAJONC, R. B. (1965). Social facilitation. *Science, 149,* 269–274.

ZAJONC, R. B. (1980). Compresence. In P. B. Paulus (ed.), *Psychology of group influence* (pp. 35–60). Hillsdale, NJ: Erlbaum.

ZAJONC, R. B., HEINGARTNER, A., & HERMAN, E. M. (1969). Social enhancement and impairment of performance in the cockroach. *Journal of Personality and Social Psychology, 13,* 83–92.

ZEBROWITZ, L. A. (1990). *Social perception.* Pacific Grove, CA: Brooks/Cole.

ZIEGLER, S. (1980a). Applied behavioral analysis: From assessment to behavioral programming. In P. Klavora (Ed.), *Psychological and sociological factors in sport* (pp. 204–214). Toronto: University of Toronto Press.

ZIEGLER, S. (1980b). An overview of anxiety management strategies in sport. In W. Straub (Ed.), *Sport psychology: An analysis of athlete behavior* (2nd ed., pp. 257–264). Ithaca, NY: Mouvement Publications.

ZIEGLER, S., KLINZING, J., & WILLIAMSON, K. (1982). The effects of two stress management training programs on cardiorespiratory efficiency. *Journal of Sport Psychology, 4,* 280–289.

ZILLMANN, D. (1971). Excitation transfer in communication-mediated aggressive behavior. *Journal of Experimental Social Psychology, 7,* 419–434.

ZILLMANN, D. (1988). Cognition-excitation interdependencies in aggressive behavior. *Aggressive Behavior, 14,* 51–64.

ZILLMANN, D., & BRYANT, J. (1974). Effect of residual excitation on the emotional response to provocation and delayed aggressive behavior. *Journal of Personality and Social Psychology, 30,* 782–791.

ZILLMANN, D., BRYANT, J., & SAPOLSKY, B. S. (1989). Enjoyment from sports spectatorship. In J. H. Goldstein (Ed.), *Sports, games, and play: Social and psychological viewpoints* (2nd ed., pp. 241–278). Hillsdale, NJ: Erlbaum.

ZILLMANN, D., & CANTOR J. R. (1976). Effect of timing of information about mitigating circumstances on emotional responses to provocation and retaliatory behavior. *Journal of Experimental Social Psychology, 12,* 38–55.

ZILLMANN, D., JOHNSON, R. C., & DAY, K. D. (1974a). Provoked and unprovoked aggressiveness in athletes. *Journal of Research in Personality, 8,* 139–152.

ZILLMANN, D., JOHNSON, R. C., & DAY, K. D. (1974b). Attribution of apparent arousal and proficiency of recovery from sympathetic activation affecting excitation transfer to aggressive behavior. *Journal of Experimental Social Psychology, 10,* 503–515.

ZILLMANN, D., KATCHER, A. H., & MILAVSKY, B. (1972). Excitation transfer from physical exercise to subsequent aggressive behavior. *Journal of Experimental Social Psychology, 8,* 247–259.

ZILLMANN, D., & PAULAS, P. B. (1993). Spectators: Reactions to sports events and effects on athletic performance. In R. N. Singer, M. Murphey, & L. K. Tennant (Eds.), *Handbook of research on sport psychology* (pp. 600–619). New York: Macmillan.

ZIMBARDO, P. G. (1970). The human choice: Individuation, reason, and order versus deindividuation, impulse, and chaos. In W. J. Arnold & D. Levine (Eds.), *Nebraska Symposium on Motivation, 1969* (pp. 237–307). Lincoln: University of Nebraska Press.

ZIMMER, J. (1984, July). Courting the gods of sport: Athletes use of superstitions to ward off the devils of injury and bad luck. *Psychology Today,* pp. 36–39.

ZIMMERMAN, B. J., & KOUSSA, R. (1979). Social influences on children's toy preferences: Effects of model rewardingness and affect. *Contemporary Educational Psychology, 4,* 55–66.

ZUCKERMAN, M. (1960). The development of an affect adjective checklist for the measurement of anxiety. *Journal of Consulting Psychology, 24,* 457–462.

ZUCKERMAN, M. (1984). Sensation seeking: A comparative approach to a human trait. *The Behavioral and Brain Sciences, 7,* 413–471.

AUTHOR INDEX

SUBJECT INDEX